ENCYCLOPEDIA OF SOVIET LAW

Documentation Office for East European Law
University of Leiden

ENCYCLOPEDIA OF SOVIET LAW

edited by

F. J. M. FELDBRUGGE

Professor of Law,
University of Leiden

Vol. I (A-L)

OCEANA PUBLICATIONS, INC., DOBBS FERRY, N.Y.

A. W. SIJTHOFF - LEIDEN

1973

ISBN 0 379 00481 x (Oceana)
ISBN 90 286 0293 3 (Sijthoff)

Library of Congress Catalog Card Number: 73-85236

Printed in the Netherlands

IN MEMORIAM Z. SZIRMAI
1903-1973

Professor Zsolt Szirmai, who founded "Law in Eastern Europe" in 1958 and has been its editor ever since, died on February 24 of this year. A commemorative volume of "Law in Eastern Europe" in his honour is being planned. At this moment the publisher and the editor of this volume would like to pay tribute to the memory of a serious scholar, an inspiring organizer and a good friend.

J. H. Landwehr
F. J. M. Feldbrugge

LIST OF CONTRIBUTORS

Dr. Andreas Ådahl
Slaviska Institutionen
Uppsala Universitet

Donald Barry
Department of Government
Lehigh University, Bethlehem, Pennsylvania

Dr. R. Beermann
Institute of Soviet and East European Studies
University of Glasgow

G. P. van den Berg
Documentation Office for East European Law
University of Leyden

Harold J. Berman
Law School of Harvard University
Cambridge, Massachusetts

S. H. Bloembergen
The Hague

Leon Boim
Faculty of Law
Tel-Aviv University

Dr. Albert Boiter
Director of Research, Radio Liberty
Munich

Georg Brunner
Institut für Politische Wissenschaft, Ostrecht und Vergleichendes Staatsrecht
Universität Würzburg

W. E. Butler
Faculty of Laws
University College London

Gabriele Crespi Reghizzi
Facoltà di Giurisprudenza
Università di Pavia

Dr. M. Csizmas
Schweizerisches Ost-Institut A.G.
Bern

Bernard Dutoit
Institut de Droit Comparé
Université de Lausanne

F. J. M. Feldbrugge
Faculty of Law
University of Leyden

Dr. Martin Fincke
Institut für Strafrecht
Universität München

George P. Fletcher
University of California, Los Angeles
School of Law

George Ginsburgs
New School for Social Research
New York, N.Y.

T. Grygier
Centre of Criminology
University of Ottawa

Dr. A. Hastrich
Opladen

John N. Hazard
Russian Institute
Columbia University
New York, N.Y.

Jeffrey M. Hertzfeld
Law Offices of Samuel Pisar
Paris, France

E. H. de Jong
Documentation Office for East European Law
University of Leyden

A. K. R. Kiralfy
University of London, King's College
Faculty of Laws

L. Kos-Rabcewicz-Zubkowski
Centre of Criminology
University of Ottawa

Samuel Kucherov †
Washington D.C.

Pierre Lavigne
Université de Paris I - Panthéon - Sorbonne

Serge L. Levitsky
New York, N.Y.

D. Richard Little
Northern Illinois University
De Kalb, Illinois

Dietrich A. Loeber
Institut für Recht, Politik und Gesellschaft der Sozialistischen Staaten
Christian-Albrechts-Universität Kiel

Peter B. Maggs
College of Law
University of Illinois
Champaign, Illinois

Chris Osakwe
Russian Research Centre
Harvard University
Cambridge, Massachusetts

John B. Quigley Jr.
College of Law
Ohio State University
Columbus, Ohio

Dr. Bernard A. Ramundo
The George Washington University
School of Law
Washington, D.C.

L. Révész
Schweizerisches Ost-Institut A.G.
Bern

Bernard Rudden
Oriel College
Oxford

Lothar Schultz
Universität Göttingen

Z. Szirmai †
Documentation Office for East European Law
University of Leyden

Alice Erh-Soon Tay
Australian National University
Canberra

Jan F. Triska
Institute of Political Studies
Stanford University, Stanford, California

Th. J. Vondracek
Documentation Office for East European Law
University of Leyden

Stephen M. Weiner
Boston, Massachusetts

David Winter
Solicitor, London
University of Surrey
University of London

Zigurds L. Zile
Law School
The University of Wisconsin, Madison.
Wisconsin

INDICATIONS FOR USE

How to use the Encyclopedia

The list of subject headings has been compiled on the basis of a corresponding list in the *Index to Foreign Legal Periodicals* and of the lists contained in Soviet legal encyclopedias (*Iuridicheskii Slovar'*, 1956, and *Entsiklopedicheskii Slovar' Pravovykh Znanii*, 1965). A small number of headings deriving from other sources have been added. It is believed that this method provides access to relevant articles both in the case of approach through a Western concept or term (e.g. insurance, appellate procedure) as well as through a Soviet concept or term (e.g. kolkhoz, Presidium of the Supreme Soviet). Gaps in this system have been closed as much as possible by a liberal use of references such as LARCENY, see THEFT).

Cross-references (references to other articles included in the Encyclopedia) are indicated by "(*q.v.*)" placed immediately behind the term to which a special article is devoted, or by "see" or "see also" followed by the term (in capitals).

Example: "The first group comprises such agencies as the Councils of Ministers of the USSR, of the Union and Autonomous Republics (see COUNCILS OF MINISTERS), the individual Ministries (*q.v.*), the State Committees (*q.v.*), ..."

Cross-references are used in the text of articles and at the end of articles. As a rule cross-references incorporated in the text have not been repeated at the end of articles. The Editor is responsible for cross-references placed at the end of articles (below the author's signature).

Another means of access to relevant articles is provided by the *Analytical Table of Contents*, inserted at the end of Volume II. This table is designed to offer an insight into the system and depth of coverage and the conceptual structure of the Encyclopedia.

Citation of legislative materials

The Soviet Union is a federal state in which one of the fifteen constituent republics, the RSFSR (Russian Soviet Federative Socialist Republic), occupies a predominant place in almost every respect. Although most of the fundamental enactments emanate from federal agencies, a large part of current legislation (in particular the codes covering the main branches of law) is of republican origin. Unless otherwise indicated legislative materials of republican origin are quoted in the RSFSR version (the same practice is followed in the Soviet Union). In most cases it can safely be assumed that the law of the other fourteen republics is not significantly different.

In the text of articles, legislative materials have been identified by date only.

For further particulars the reader is referred to the *Selected List of Statutory Materials* (pp. 743-774).

Dates

On February 14, 1918, the Soviet government introduced the Gregorian calendar. All old style dates have been changed into new style dates in this work by adding 13 days.

Indications for use

Legal history
The history of concepts and institutions has, as a rule, not been traced beyond the Revolution of 1917. The history of the pre-revolutionary law of the main constituent parts of the present Soviet Union is discussed in a small number of general articles (see LEGAL HISTORY).

Terminology
For a short discussion of the terminology employed in this work the reader is referred to the article on TERMINOLOGY.

Bibliography
A bibliography of books and articles on Soviet law would exceed the scope of this work. Short bibliographical notes may be found at the end of many articles. For a brief general discussion of the subject, see the article on BIBLIOGRAPHY.

Status iuris: December 31, 1972. The most important developments of the first seven months of 1973 are covered by the *Appendix* (pp. 737-741).

The Editor

ABDUCTION, see KIDNAPPING

ABORTION

Abortion as the intentional procurement of a miscarriage is an interesting topic for the study of changes in Soviet forensic policies.

Pre-revolutionary Russian law regarded abortion as a serious felony and punished the guilty by five or six years' imprisonment with hard labour in convicts' labour gangs (*arestantskie otdeleniia*), together with the loss of all special rights and privileges (partial attainder). Midwives, doctors, etc. had to suffer an even harsher penalty. Lenin in his famous letter to *Pravda* (June 6, 1913) against Malthusianism ("an evil invention of the capitalist to ease his conscience over the enslavement of the working population") demanded the abolition of all laws prohibiting abortions and the publication of medical books on birth control, etc. He argued that not only do such laws reflect a mere hypocrisy of the dominant classes, but they also infringe the elementary freedoms of the citizens (male and female) and the freedom of medical propaganda (Lenin, Works 23, p. 257, fifth edition). A slight change of emphasis can be discerned in the law of November 18, 1920, of the People's Commissariats of Health and Justice permitting clinically performed abortions on demand because "survivals of the past and economic hardships of the present sometimes force women to decide in favour of such operations". The gradual shift towards a more conservative forensic and moral attitude brought about a total reversal of the former policy: the law of June 27, 1936, prohibited abortions on demand and permitted only those properly performed by doctors in hospitals for health reasons. "The socialist October revolution has finally eliminated all forms of class exploitation, the abolition of classes themselves has laid the foundations of the total and final liberation of the woman . . ." Here again Lenin's anti-malthusian letter is quoted to back up the new law—"we are unconditional enemies of neomalthusianism—that cowardly movement, that warped and egoistic [teaching] for lower middle class couples who anxiously mumble: may God help us to survive in some way ourselves but without children please", *Sovetskoe ugolovnoe pravo, chast' osobennaia*, 1951, pp. 209-216.

The gradual liberalisation that took place after Stalin's death for a second time reversed the policies towards abortions on demand. The law of November 23, 1955, abolished the prohibition; the main reasons in favour of the law were given as: the measures taken by the Soviet state to encourage motherhood and to protect children; the constant growth of consciousness (*soznatel'nost'*) and the cultural level among women; the possibility in the future of reducing the numbers of abortions by means other than prohibition; the abolition of prohibitions which would help to reduce the great harm done to the health of women by abortions improperly performed by quacks and, lastly, the means of giving "the woman the freedom to decide the issue of motherhood for herself". Thus, the present law permits abortions to be performed on demand by doctors in hospital except in those instances when an abortion would be harmful to the health of the woman. Abortions performed elsewhere than in hospitals and by persons without a higher medical degree are prohibited. Art. 116 Criminal Code RSFSR punishes illegal abortions by deprivation of freedom for up to one year or correctional labour for the same term, with the prohibition on the person convicted from continuing in medical practice; people without a medical degree are imprisoned for up to two years, or are sentenced to correctional labour for up to one year. The maximum punishment is increased to eight years' deprivation of freedom in the case of a second offender and/or when the operation resulted in the death of the woman or in serious consequences to her health.

R. Beermann

ABSENTEES

The regulations on declaring a person an absentee and on declaring him dead are uniform in all the republics of the Soviet Union, art. 10 Principles of Civil Legislation of the Soviet Union, art. 4 Introductory decree of April 10, 1962.

A person may be declared an absentee by a court decision if a) he is absent from his domicile, b) no news of his whereabouts have been received for at least one year, and c) inquiries of his whereabouts by relatives and the court have failed, art. 18 Civil Code RSFSR, art. 254 Code of Civil Procedure RSFSR. The year begins on the day when the last news of him was received. If the day cannot be established, on the first day of the following month; and, if the month cannot be established, on the first day of the following year, art. 18 Civil Code.

On the basis of the court decision declaring a person an absentee, a trusteeship of his property is instituted by the guardianship authority. The maintenance of the persons to whom the absentee is legally liable to pay alimony and his debts to other persons are paid out of the property. Dependants on the absentee who would be entitled to a pension in the event of his death acquire the right to this pension from the moment the court's decision becomes legally valid, art. 60 of the Law on State Pensions. The spouse of the absentee gets the right to a simplified divorce procedure, see CIVIL STATUS REGISTRATION.

Even before the end of the year, interested persons may apply for the institution of a trusteeship over the absentee's property to secure its preservation, art. 19 Civil Code, art. 254 Code of Civil Procedure.

If the absentee reappears or his whereabouts are established, the court and the guardianship authority cancel their decisions, art. 20 Civil Code.

A person may be declared dead by a court decision if no news of his whereabouts have been received at his domicile for at least three years (the term of 3 years is fixed in the same way as explained above for the one year period). In the case of a person who has gone missing in circumstances involving danger to life or justifying the supposition of his death in a particular accident, the period is 6 months, art. 21 Civil Code.

A soldier or any other citizen who has got lost in connection with war operations can be declared dead by court decision not earlier than two years after the end of the war operations art. 21 Civil Code.

The day when the court decision becomes valid counts as the day of death but the court may fix the presumed day of death as the day of death in cases where the person was missed in circumstances involving danger to life or justifying the supposition of death in a particular accident, art. 21 Civil Code.

The declaration of death leads to the dissolution of marriage, the opening of succession and the end of rights and obligations of the person declared dead.

If the person declared dead reappears or his whereabouts are established, the court cancels the declaration of death. He can claim restitution of his property still in existence from other persons to whom it has gone gratuitously after the declaration of death. Property acquired by other persons against payment must be restored to him if it is proved that at the moment of acquisition the acquirer knew that the person declared dead was still alive. If the property was inherited and sold by the state, the proceeds are restored to him, art. 22 Civil Code. Other heirs who knew that the person declared dead was still alive and disposed of the estate are liable to indemnity on general terms, art. 444 Civil Code.

In the case of the reappearance of a person

declared dead and the cancellation of the corresponding court decision, his marriage is deemed to persist unless the other spouse has contracted a new marriage.
In the case of the reappearance of an absentee, cancellation of the corresponding court decision and of the dissolution of his marriage in accordance with the declaration of his being an absentee, his marriage may be reentered in the books of the registry office on the basis of a common declaration of both spouses unless the other spouse has contracted a new marriage, art. 42 Family Code of the RSFSR.

A. Hastrich

ACCIDENT INSURANCE,
see INSURANCE

ACCIDENTS, see TRAFFIC ACCIDENTS; EMPLOYEE PROTECTION

ACCOMPLICES
The questions arising when more than one person takes part in the commission of a crime are discussed in Soviet law under the heading "participation" (*souchastie*). Participation is defined by art. 17 of the RSFSR Criminal Code as the taking part, intentionally and jointly, by two or more persons in the commission of a crime. Art. 17 divides participants into organizers, instigators, accomplices and the perpetrators themselves. The intentional character of participation requires first of all that the participant contributed knowingly and willingly towards the commission of the crime; furthering through negligence the commission by somebody else of a crime does not constitute participation. Secondly it is argued that one can only be a participant in an intentional crime. However, there are cases which seem to indicate that one can also participate (intentionally) in the commission of a negligent offence.
The term "jointly" in connection with "intentionally" implies that the participant must have realized that this activities were promoting the commission of a crime by somebody else.
Participants in a crime are responsible for their activities. This is not expressly stated in the criminal law (as it should have been, because according to art. 3 only persons who have committed an act forbidden by the criminal law may be punished, and the essential feature of participation is that the participant does not fully commit such an act). In fact there is absolutely no doubt about the criminal responsibility of participants; such responsibility is also implied in the last paragraph of art. 17, which provides that the character and degree of the participation of each participant must be taken into consideration by the court in determining the penalty. Penalties for participants are not necessarily lower than for the actual perpetrators; indeed, in exceptional cases they may be higher.
Another question not answered in the Criminal Code, but extensively discussed in criminal law literature concerns the extent of the participant's responsibility. The general answer to this question is that it is determined by the participant's intention. There are no difficulties in the standard case of participation; e.g. A instigates B to organize the theft of a private car, which theft is then carried out by C while D acts as an accomplice. All four would be punishable under art. 144 par. 1 of the Criminal Code (simple theft of personal property). Problems arise in such cases as where B is an "especially dangerous recidivist", C uses violence against the owner of the car, and D is a minor. In such a case C will be punishable under art. 145 par. 2 ("open" theft, accompanied by violence against the victim); B's responsibility is determined by his knowledge of C's intention to use violence; if B knew about this beforehand he will be punishable under art. 145 par. 3 ("open" theft committed by an especially dangerous recidivist) otherwise under art.

144 par. 3 (secret theft committed by an especially dangerous recidivist). In the case of A the question is even more complicated, because his responsibility depends on his previous knowledge of the status of C and B (did A know C would use violence and that B was an exceptionally dangerous recidivist?). The fact that the accomplice D was a minor will, of course, only work to the advantage of D. The situation can be made even more puzzling if the stolen car turned out to be socialist property. All such questions are solved by reference to the principle that a participant will be held responsible, not automatically for the offence committed, but for the offence in which he thought he was participating. If necessary, he will be considered responsible for an attempt to participate in a crime (e.g. if an organizer believes he is organizing theft of socialist property, while in fact personal property is stolen). The entire treatment of participation in Soviet law in illustrative of the central function of the concept of guilt (see MENS REA).

Along with the intentional character of participation a second important aspect is the required causal link between participation and the commission of the offence. This aspect is implied in the definition of the various forms of participation. Only such cooperation with the actual perpetrator as promotes the commission of the offence can constitute participation. This is best illustrated by the treatment allotted to persons who hide the offender, traces of the crime, or goods acquired by means of a crime. A person who promises such help *beforehand* is considered an accomplice (art. 17 par. 6); but if such help has not been promised beforehand, it may constitute an offence *sui generis* in specific cases (art. 18).

A special form of participation is the commission of a crime by an organized group or a criminal organization. Commission of a crime by an organized group is a general aggravating circumstance (art. 39 point 2). Obviously, the presence of an organized group cannot be assumed in every case of participation; it has been argued that the group must have been organized in order to commit more than one crime. A criminal organization seems to require an even higher degree of permanence and organization; the principal examples are the anti-Soviet organization (art. 72) and the armed band of art. 77 (see BANDITRY).

The definition of participants also includes the perpetrator (*ispolnitel'*) himself, the person who commits the crime defined by the criminal law. By general consent "perpetrators" include persons who cause crimes to be committed by another person who is himself not responsible (a lunatic, a young child). Also persons who directly take part in the commission of a crime are all considered to be perpetrators, even if they did not each do everything required for that particular crime (e.g. the man who holds the victim so that another person may kill him is considered a perpetrator of the crime of intentional homicide and not an accomplice).

Organizers are persons who organize or direct the commission of a crime. Instigators are persons who persuade others to commit crimes. An accomplice is defined in art. 17 as a person who aids the commission of a crime by giving advice or instructions, by providing means or removing obstacles, or a person who has promised beforehand to hide the offender, the instruments or means for the commission of the crime, the traces of the crime, or goods acquired by means of the crime.

Two minor forms of complicity are mentioned by arts. 18 and 19 of the Criminal Code. Art. 18 has been touched upon already. Art. 189 of the Criminal Code lists the offences referred to in art. 18; the offence defined by art. 189 is committed by persons who provide help to persons who have committed any of the offences listed in art. 189, provided such help has not been promised beforehand (in that case the helper would be an accomplice). Art. 19 is devoted to failure to report crimes which are being prepared or which have been committed already. According to art. 190, only failure to report specific offences (as listed in art. 190) is an offence in itself. The duty to report arises only in cases where there is reliable information.

In addition to arts. 189 and 190, a number of crimes against the state receive special treatment in arts. 88-1 and 88-2 (introduced in 1962). Failure to report a number of specifically mentioned crimes against the state is covered by art. 88-1; and help not promised beforehand to the person who has committed a number of specifically mentioned crimes against the state is covered by art. 88-2 (see POLITICAL CRIMES).

F. J. M. Feldbrugge

ACCOUNTING

The accounting system in the Soviet Union has three main functions. First is that of providing data to planning agencies and ministries on which those bodies may base economic decisions. Second is that of providing a check on obedience to orders of superior organizations. Third is that of protecting against the theft, embezzlement or improper use of state property. The function of accounting in the United States or Western Europe which is taking on increasing importance, the provision of accurate information for managerial decision-making at the enterprise level is recognized as important by Soviet theorists and is beginning to be implemented in practice.

The role of accounting as an instrument of economic planning is enhanced by the legal enforcement of a uniform accounting system throughout the Soviet Union. Uniform accounting rules and model accounting forms are promulgated by the Ministry of Finances and the Central Statistical Administration. Where matters important to economic planning are involved the State Planning Committee (*Gosplan*) also participates in the approval of necessary regulations. Details are worked out by the central accounting office of each ministry.

The accounting system is designed to reflect all significant transactions in enterprise property. Since both the production of goods by enterprises and their delivery to other enterprises involve property transactions which are reflected in the enterprise accounts, the accounts form an effective means of checking on enterprise compliance with production and delivery plans.

Thus an enterprise which fails to fulfill its plans will be subject to swift action by superior authorities when this failure is discovered by examination of the accounting documents. The enterprise manager who would be tempted to falsify his accounts to hide such failures faces two legal barriers. First of all, as might be expected, alteration or distortion of such accounting documents is a criminal offense. It is punishable under article 152-1 of the Criminal Code of the Russian Republic and similar articles of the criminal codes of the other republics. Secondly, the legal position of the accountant in the Soviet enterprise is designed to insure against such improper management action. The accountant has a duty under administrative law to correctly reflect the operations of the enterprise in its books, and is under a specific duty to disobey orders of enterprise management involving violations of accounting rules. The position of the accountant is further strengthened by the provision that he may not be discharged or transferred without the approval of a superior organization. (See the Statute on the Basic Rights and Duties of Chief Accountants adopted by the Council of Ministers of the USSR on November 6, 1964.)

The standard Soviet textbook on accounting is M. V. Dmitriev and A. M. Dmitriev, *Bukhgal'terskij ucet i analiz khoziaistvennoi deia-*

tel'nosti promyshlennogo predpriiatiia (Accounting and Analysis of the Economic Activity of the Industrial Enterprise), 1968. The best work in English is Robert W. Campbell, Accounting in Soviet Planning and Management, 1963.

Peter Maggs

See also PLANNING; STATE ENTERPRISES

ACCOUNTS AND PAYMENTS, see NEGOTIABLE INSTRUMENTS; BANKING

ACT OF GOD, see FORCE MAJEURE

ACTIONS

Actions here refer to the remedies provided by Soviet law and form part of the substantive law (as to the procedure to be followed, which is fairly uniform in all cases, see CIVIL PROCEDURE).

Actions may be classified in several ways. In the first place, according to the legal basis on which they rest, e.g. proprietary and personal. Proprietary actions are based on the plaintiff having been owner of property of which he has been wrongfully dispossessed (see OWNERSHIP). Personal actions are based on violations of law of other kinds, such as torts or breaches of contract. However this distinction is not of great practical importance. Property cannot be recovered if it has ceased to exist or, in some cases, if it has come into the hands of an acquirer in good faith (see POSSESSION). On the other hand specific relief is usually obtainable in personal actions, e.g. delivery of goods sold *in specie* or return of property taken by means of a tort. A hire is part of the law of obligations, not property, but the owner can generally recover his property from the hirer.

Actions may also be classified according to the type of relief sought, e.g. into a. positive claims for payment of money or delivery of property; b. negative claims to prevent some act or correct its consequences, e.g. restrain the erection of a fence, or demolish it; c. actions for special steps to be taken, e.g. to partition property among co-owners, increase or reduce the amount of a judgment for periodic payments; d. actions for declarations, e.g. that a marriage is void, that a contract is ineffective, that a person is the true first author of a book or is the lawful tenant of a house.

Each branch of law has characteristic forms of action, e.g. in contract you may often sue for fines and penalties as alternatives to, or in addition to damages. In tort you may sue for recovery of property or damages. In family law you may proceed for divorce, for support, or to partition community property between spouses. In labour law you may sue for restoration to work or to have a misclassification of your job corrected, and so on. Judgments for maintenance of spouses or children and for damages payable to injured persons are for periodic payments, not lump sums, and may be adjusted from time to time as the plaintiff's circumstances change.

A. K. R. Kiralfy

ACTS OF LEGAL SIGNIFICANCE (JURIDICAL ACTS)

Soviet legal science uses the term "juridical act" (*iuridicheskii akt*) to denote an action (*deistvie*) of a person or organization consciously directed toward the establishment, change, or termination of "legal relations" (*pravootnosheniia*). A juridical act is a species of the genus "juridical fact" (*iuridicheskii fakt*); other species of the same genus are, in general, actions or events which establish, change, or terminate legal relations independently of the will of the actor (e.g., the birth or death of a person, the occurrence of a natural catastrophe, etc.). Juridical facts, in turn, are distinguished from "legislation" (*zakonodatel'stvo*), which is another means of affecting legal relations and to which juridical acts are subordinate. The term "legal relations" is used very broadly to refer to all kinds of social relations insofar as they are manifested in legal rights and duties; thus a treaty is said to establish "international legal relations" between two states, an indictment is said to establish "criminal legal relations" between the accused and the state, etc. The essential feature, then, of a juridical act is that it is a non-legislative action intended to affect the legal rights or duties of one or more persons or organizations.

The most important examples of juridical acts are "transactions" (*sdelki*) and administrative actions ("orders" (*prikazy*), "petitions" (*zaiavleniia*), "complaints" (*zhaloby*), etc.).

The term "transaction" is confined to civil law. It is defined in Soviet legislation as "an action of a citizen or organization directed to the establishment, change, or termination of civil rights or duties" (cf. RSFSR Civil Code, art. 41). Transactions may be unilateral (e.g., the making of a testament or the issuance of a cheque) or bilateral or multilateral (e.g., the making of a bilateral or multilateral contract). The civil codes of the various republics establish rules concerning the requirement of written or notarial form for certain types of transactions and the invalidity of transactions which do not conform to the requirements of law, or which are concluded for a purpose contrary to the interests of state and society, or which contradict the purposes of a legal entity, or which are concluded by a minor or by a person lacking legal capacity or by a person under the influence of alcohol or who is incapable of understanding the significance of his actions or who is under the influence of FRAUD, MISTAKE, DURESS, etc. (cf. RSFSR Civil Code, arts. 42-60). A sham transaction concluded only for appearances, without the intent to create legal consequences, is invalid; and if a transaction is concluded for the purpose of concealing another transaction, the rules relating to the transaction which the parties actually had in mind are applicable (*id.*, art. 53).

As stated in the Soviet civil codes, the law governing transactions is in general not essentially different from that of prerevolutionary Russia or of Western European countries, especially those under the influence of the German Civil Code. Perhaps the most distinctive feature of the Soviet law on this subject is the rule that where a transaction has been concluded for a purpose intended to be against the interests of the socialist state and society, anything received by any party to the transaction is forfeit to the state (*id.*, art. 49).

The second major form of juridical acts, administrative actions, include such actions as checking on fulfillment of plans by state enterprises, supervision of the acts of a subordinate organization or person, calling up of a particular citizen for military service, awarding of a prize to an outstanding worker, etc., as well as petitions or complaints of citizens presented to organizations or individual officials invoking the application of norms of administrative law. In general, Soviet legal science distinguishes administrative orders from decrees (*postanovleniia*) and resolutions (*rasporiazheniia*) of republican and All-Union councils of ministers. Orders are usually treated as juridical acts even when they are normative in character (e.g., work rules issued by a ministry, or traffic regulations issued by the executive committee of a city soviet), whereas decrees and resolutions of the executive branch of government above the regional level are usually treated as part of "legislation" (although they are not "laws", *zakony*) even when they are not normative in character (e.g., a decree of the Council of Ministers requiring a particular plant to be built in a particular location).

A petition is defined as a formal resort of one or more persons to an institution or an official for the purpose of realizing a right or legal interest or for the purpose of giving information concerning deficiencies and possibly proposing remedies for such deficiencies. A petition is distinguished from a complaint in that the latter is connected with the violation of a right or lawful interest of a citizen and with a demand for the elimination of such violation.

Petitions and complaints play a very important role in Soviet law. They represent an important form of popular participation in the system of administration and an important means of manifesting criticism and eliminating bureaucratism and red tape. They also constitute one of the principal legal methods for protecting the rights of citizens. Under Soviet administrative law an institution which has received a petition from any citizen is obliged to reply to it within a certain time. If a petition contains information concerning inadequacies in the work of an institution or enterprise or of individual officials, the reply must indicate measures taken, or to be taken, to eliminate such inadequacies, or else the reasons why such measures cannot be taken.

Similarly, complaints may be submitted by any citizen against the action of any official or any state agency. The 1965 "Encyclopedic Dictionary of Legal Knowledge", in a rather long article on Complaints, states: "Citizens whose complaints do not have a maliciously and knowingly slanderous character are guaranteed complete safety and, at the wish of the complainant, the secrecy of his name is preserved." The law prohibits the transfer of the complaint to the officials whose actions are being complained of. Complaints to central, territory, and provincial agencies must be answered in not more than one month from the day the complaint was submitted; complaints to *raion* and town agencies in not more than 20 days; complaints of servicemen in 15 or 7 days, depending on the type of complaint; complaints to a court concerning the imposition of an administrative fine in 10 days; etc. Also every state agency, organization, institution, and enterprise is required to allocate particular hours of particular days for the personal reception of citizens to hear their complaints. Officials guilty of a bureaucratic attitude towards the consideration of complaints are liable to disciplinary—and in some cases, criminal—punishment.

The procedure for dealing with complaints and petitions is regulated by a decree of the Presidium of the Supreme Soviet of the USSR of April 12, 1968.

Harold J. Berman

See also CONTRACTS; LEGISLATION; TESTAMENTS; PUBLIC ADMINISTRATION

ADMINISTRATION OF JUSTICE

Notwithstanding the rejection, in principle, of the doctrine of the separation of powers (*q.v.*), the administration of justice is mentioned as a distinct task of the state in art. 102 of the USSR Constitution. The basic rules concerning the administration of justice may be found in the "Principles of the Legislation on Judicial Organization of the USSR and the Union and Autonomous Republcs", enacted on December 25, 1958. The Principles serve as the basis of the somewhat more elaborate laws on judicial organization of the Union republics (law of October 27, 1960, in the RSFSR). The administration of justice is entrusted to the civil courts (see COURTS) and to military tribunals (*q.v.*)—art. 1 of the Principles. It embraces the trial of civil cases in disputes concerning the rights and interests of citizens, state enterprises, institutions, kolkhozes, and cooperative and other social organizations, and the trial of criminal cases (art. 4 of the Principles). However, there are some important exceptions to this rule. A large number of disputes between state enterprises are not tried by the ordinary courts, but by the State Arbitration (see ARBITRATION). On the other hand, as in many other countries, the civil court is competent in a number of cases which do not concern disputes (e.g. most of the proceedings described in chapters 26-33 of the RSFSR Code of Civil Procedure). Furthermore, penalties for administrative offences (*q.v.*), which include fines, detention, and exile in a number of cases, are not imposed by the criminal court, but by a variety of administrative agencies (in some cases the ordinary judge is designated as such; e.g. petty hooliganism may be punished by an administrative penalty imposed by the people's judge).

The Principles spell out a number of general guidelines for the administration of justice: the equality of citizens before the law and the court (art. 5); the courts must decide cases according to the laws of the USSR and the republics (art. 6); all judges are elected (art. 7); all cases are tried by a panel of judges: cases in first instance by a professional judge and two people's assessors (*q.v.*), and in appeal and supervision proceedings by a court of three professional judges (art. 8); judges are independent (art. 9); linguistic guarantees (art. 10; see LANGUAGE) trials are held in public, unless otherwise provided by law (art. 11). Most pervasive and most characteristic of all, however, is the principle mentioned in art. 3: the educational role of the Soviet court. "Through its entire activity the court educates the citizens of the USSR in a spirit of loyalty towards the Motherland and the cause of communism, in a spirit of exact and unswerving observance of Soviet law, of a careful attitude towards socialist property, of observance of labour discipline, of an honest attitude towards state and public duties and of respect for the rights, honour and dignity of citizens, and for the rules of socialist community life." An important practical elaboration of this principle is the institution of special decisions (*chastnye opredeleniia*), which the court may issue in civil and criminal proceedings (art. 225 of the RSFSR Code of Civil Procedure and art. 321 of the RSFSR Code of Criminal Procedure); through such decisions the courts draw the attention of specific citizens or organizations to undesirable or unlawful situations. The addressee of the decision is obliged to report within a month to the court about the measures taken.

The proper functioning of the machinery of the administration of justice receives extra protection through chapter 8 of the special part of the RSFSR Criminal Code: crimes against the administration of justice. These crimes include the prosecution of obviously innocent persons (art. 176) or a prosecution which is obviously unlawful (art. 178), a.o.

F. J. M. Feldbrugge

See also SUPREME COURT; PROKURATURA; RES IUDICATA; MINISTRY OF JUSTICE

ADMINISTRATIVE AGENCIES

Executive-administrative activities require agencies to exercise diverse functions, such as issuing general rules and specific commands, planning and organising, staffing, directing and coordinating, ordering, reporting, budgeting and controlling.

In the context of the Soviet Union as a country which is governed by the principles of democratic centralism (*q.v.*), the smooth and well-organised functioning of administrative agencies becomes of paramount importance. As the economy and the social life of the country are basically centrally planned and directed, the role and significance as well as the number of and the powers vested in administrative agencies are greater than in the countries of Western Europe and America.

Administrative agencies derive their power and status either directly from norms expressed in the Constitution or from subsidiary legislation (see CONSTITUTION). The first group comprises such agencies as the Councils of Ministers of the USSR, of the Union and Autonomous Republics (see COUNCILS OF MINISTERS), the individual Ministries (*q.v.*), the State Committees (*q.v.*), the State Departments (*vedomstva*) and the executive committees of the local soviets and their departments. To the second group belong such administrative agencies as the committees and chief administrations (*glavnye upravleniia*) of the Council of Ministers of the USSR for economic, cultural and defence development (*stroitel'stva*), analogous bodies in the Union republics, other agencies set up by ministries, departments, local soviets of workers' deputies and their executive committees, the administrations of industrial and other economic enterprises, and/or of groups of enterprises, and umbrella organisations (such as *kombinaty*, *ob''edineniia*, *trusts* and *firms*; see STATE ENTERPRISES), and scientific research, design, construction-, social-cultural, health, welfare and educational institutions and diverse commissions (the administrative-judicial administrative commissions of the executive committees of *raion* or town soviets, the commissions for delinquent youth and children in need of care and protection, local commissions for pensions and for the allocation to institutions and enterprises of graduates from higher and secondary colleges etc.). Administrative agencies are staffed either by election (e.g. of Ministers by the Supreme Soviets, or of members of executive committees by their corresponding Soviets—*oblast'*, *raion*, village), or by appointment by the leaders or the heads of their organisations. The appointment itself may be based on either the personal selection of the head of the organisation (usually based on *nomenklatura* indexes; see COMMUNIST PARTY), or on some kind of competitive selection (*konkurs*) (this happens mostly in the arts and sciences—actors, researchers, etc.) or on the "distribution" (*raspredelenie*), of university and college graduates for the first two to three years after graduation. Frequently the nominator has either to consult or to consider the wishes of some other organisation (e.g. T.U.'s, Party, Komsomol; or the Supreme Soviet in considering the suggestions of the Procurator General for his assistants.)

Administrative agencies may further be classified according to their specific functions: 1) Planning, accounting and finance; 2) administering economic life and the functions of the state; 3) administering social-cultural development (*stroitel'stva*); 4) administering political and administrative affairs; 5) administering foreign affairs.

1) We omit here the governing and legislative functions of the Supreme Soviets and their committees and commissions, and consider the direct leadership over planning, accounting and finance which belongs to the Council of Ministers of the USSR, whose duty it is to submit the plan for the national economy to the Supreme Soviet of the USSR and to direct and collate the planning activities of the state committees, ministries and departments of the USSR and the Union republics and to exercise overall guidance. The drafting of the plans is the function of the *Gosplan* of the USSR and the *Gosplany* of the Union and autonomous republics, down to the planning commissions of the executive of the local Soviets. These are all agencies of collated (*svodnye*) planning. Ministries, state committees, departments, institutions and enterprises (their organisations) have their own planning administrations, departments, groups or sectors. These are departmental (as distinct from collated) planning agencies (for details see PLANNING).

The centralised functions of accounting and statistics are exercised by the Central statistical bureau (*upravlenie*) (TsSU) of the Council of Ministers of the USSR; and by an analogous organisation in the Union republics which has a dual subordination to the Council of Ministers of the Union republic and to the TsSU. The autonomous republic, the *krai, oblast'*, some cities and *okruga* have statistical administrations (*upravleniia*), while the *raiony* and the towns have inspectors of state statistics. They finally are all accountable to the TsSU of the Union republics.

The management of finance and credit may be considered under four headings: the state budget; the financing of branches of the national economy and of socialist enterprises; the bank-credit system; insurance of state property and personal insurance. The authority in charge of finance is the Ministry of Finance of the USSR and corresponding ministries of the Union and autonomous republics. The Ministry of Finance works out and submits to the Council of Ministers of the USSR the state budget of the USSR. It is also the supervisory agency over the proper handling of the budgetary sums; it works out and implements rules and regulations for accounting, and checks on the activities of the state insurance agencies. It has the right to request data from enterprises and institutions and it may restrict or even suspend the financing out of the state budget of enterprises, organisations and institutions when illegal use of funds has taken place or in default of these bodies submitting proper accounts. The Ministry has the right of audit. Analogous arrangements exist in the subordinate political bodies down to the finance departments of local executive committees. See also BUDGET OF THE STATE.

Credit and banking functions are exercised by *Gosbank* and *Stroibank*, the State Bank and the Investment Bank, which are directly subordinated to the Council of Ministers. Closely linked to *Gosbank* is the *Vneshtorgbank*—the Bank for Foreign Trade. The state savings banks function as savings banks for workers' earnings (*gosudarstvennye trudovye sberegatel'nye kassy*); see also BANKING.

2) Administrative agencies for the national economy may be classified as agencies a) for general guidance, such as the Council of Ministers of the USSR or of the Union republics, etc.; b) agencies of an interdepartmental character, like *Gosplan* and *Gosstroi*, and c) departmental or branch agencies, like the industrial ministries and industrial departments (*vedomstva*), special departments (*upravleniia*) and departments of the executive committees of local soviets.

Industry and trade are managed either by All-Union ministries, such as the aviation-, automotive-, gas-, machine-building, etc. industries, or by Union republican ministries like light industry, the meat and dairy industry, the oil extraction industry, agriculture, non-ferrous metallurgy, ferrous metallurgy, power and electrification, etc., or by republican ministries such as automotive transport and highways, household services, local industries, construction, fuel, etc. The three different types of ministries were created in order to have democratic centralism applied to all the governments of the country. Local issues are handled by republican ministries, All-Union concerns by either All-Union or Union republican ministries. There are at present 58 All-Union and Union republican ministries, including ministries which are not directly concerned with industry or trade like the Union republican Ministries of Foreign Affairs and of Defence, etc., which will be considered below. The Union republics have about 18 Union republican and about 10 local ministries. The number and categorisation of ministries are frequently changed and their number may vary greatly in different Union republics (see MINISTRIES). Enterprises may be subordinate either directly to one of these ministries, their chief departments (*Glavki*) or other departments, or there may be intermediate agencies between the Ministry and the industrial enterprise,

such as *kombinaty*, *firmy* or *tresty*.
"Trusts" (*tresty*) may be of three different kinds: they may be either an intermediate unifying body of independent enterprises retaining their full legal status as juridical persons; or they may combine enterprises with internal cost-accounting (*khozraschet*) only, while the full legal rights are vested in the trust; or, lastly, they may comprise enterprises of the first and second type. Nowadays it is common for trusts to have enterprises of both types under their jurisdiction. A trust is run by a manager and his staff. Some trusts may have special councils consisting of the directors of the subordinate enterprises. The trusts function as fully independent enterprises, as juridical persons, and they are answerable only for their own liabilities. Together with the ministries, the trusts are frequently referred to as fund holders (*fondoderzhateli*). They function as the distributors of material and financial funds, in accordance with the state plan, to the individual, subordinate enterprises. A *kombinat* is a unifying umbrella organisation of industrial enterprises predominantly in the coal, metallurgy, timber and light industries. Here, as with trusts, the combined enterprises may or may not possess the rights of independent juridical persons. In the coal industry, *kombinaty* function as umbrella organisations for enterprises and trusts.
The *kombinaty*, as well as the trusts, have their statutes confirmed by the agency of state to which they are subordinated.
"Firms" have become a leading and fast developing organisational form since 1965. They have one principal enterprise and a number of satellite enterprises which all serve the production lines of the principal enterprise (e.g. a major footwear enterprise will have leather-tanning factories, factories producing component parts, etc. under its jurisdiction). The legal status of the subordinate enterprises may also vary to a considerable degree; some may retain full independence and the status of a juridical person, others may lose some of these rights and retain others, some may become branch enterprises, others may even be reduced to the status of workshops of the principal enterprise. The firms are managed by a director, his deputies and heads of departments. The administration of the firm has under its management all subsidiary services: planning and accounting, supply and sales departments, etc. See also STATE ENTERPRISES.
In 1970, in the chemical industry, the All-Union industrial independent (*khozraschetnye*) associations (*ob"edineniia*) came into existence. These combine and centralise on an even larger scale the administrative functions normally attributed either to the ministries or to the trusts: guidance, planning, development, the introduction of new processes for the subordinate enterprises, etc.
The single enterprises are managed by an appointed director and his deputy or deputies. These may be responsible for special departments, like sales, supplies, or production. The principle of *edinonachalie* (one man authority and responsibility) is always maintained and the director rules supreme over his deputies and staff. In all enterprises the chief accountant's department (*sluzhba glavnogo bukhgal'tera*) and the department of the technological inspectorate are directly subordinated to the director.
To enhance the participation of the workers and social organisations of the working population in the running of enterprises, permanent production conferences (*postoianno deistvuiushchie proizvodstvennye soveshchaniia*) are set up in enterprises with a staff of 100 or more workers. Engineering-technical staff, employees and workers, serve on these "conferences". They function as a body of the local T.U. committee. These in their turn exercise a number of vital administrative functions (see UNIONS and LABOUR LAW).
Capital construction (*kapital'noe stroitel'stvo*)

has, besides the usual administrative agencies of the Council of Ministers, etc., a special body—the State Committee of the Council of Ministers of the USSR for the Construction Industry—the *Gosstroi* of the USSR, with corresponding organisations in the Union republics. Furthermore, special ministries of Union republican subordination are created to further the construction of heavy industry (*Mintiazhstroi*), or industrial construction (*Minpromstroi*) and of construction in general (*Minstroi*). Issues of planning and building in built-up areas are taken care of by the State committee of civil engineering (*grazhdanskogo stroitel'stva*) and of architecture—a body of *Gosstroi*, USSR. Analogous bodies are set up in the Union republics. *Gosstroi* controls the quality of construction work through the Chief State Construction Inspectorate (*Glavgosstroi inspektsiia SSSR*).
Agriculture, as a particularly important and specific industry, has its own special administrative agencies. Besides the general activities of the Councils of Ministers there is the Union republican Ministry of Agriculture of the USSR with ministries in the Union republics and the autonomous republics. The two kinds of agricultural organisations, collective farms and state farms, have their separate management departments (*glavki*) at the Ministry. Since 1969 special *Raiispolkom* agricultural departments have exercised direct guidance over collective and state farms (up to 1969 they were separate offices not attached to the *raiispolkomy*). The collective farms (see kolkhoz), as cooperative organisations of collective farmers, have their own councils organised at all levels of the country's administrative structure. The state farms are normally organised in trusts according to the specialisation of the individual farms. In the RSFSR there were 217 such trusts in 1968. In the Ukraine all state farms are organised in trusts and a special ministry of state farms has been set up. The supply of machinery, tools and fertilizers to agriculture is the function of the All-Union Association of the Council of Ministers for the Supply of Agricultural Technology, Spares, etc. (*Soiuzsel'khoztekhnika*). The Ministry of Agricultural Procurements (*zagotovki*) was set up in 1969 by a decree of the Presidium of the USSR Supreme Soviet. This Ministry coordinates all agricultural procurement activities. In the Union republics there are republican Procurements Ministries; Inspectorates for the purchase and quality of agricultural produce operate in the autonomous republics, provinces, *oblasti*, *krai* etc.
The exploitation of natural resources and the preservation of nature is carried out by the Council of Ministers of the USSR, and down the administrative scale by the executive committees of the soviets. All land in the Soviet Union is managed by the Councils of Ministers (Union, Republic and autonomous republics) and by all soviets and their executive committees. The specific responsibility for land use is entrusted to the chief department for land use, land tenure and land preservation (*Glavnoe upravlenie zemplepol'zovaniia, zemleustroistva i okhrany prirody*) of the Union republican Ministry of Agriculture. Analogous arrangements exist in Union republics and autonomous republics (see also LAND TENURE).
The mining industry is managed by the USSR Union republican Ministry of Geology. A state committee for the supervision of safety precautions in industry and mining of the USSR Council of Ministers (*Gosgortekhnadzor*) is specifically entrusted with the function of allocating land for the mining of minerals. The *Gosgortekhnadzor* has a special management (*upravlenie*) for the preservation of mineral wealth (*po kontroliu za okhranoi nedr*), with special inspectors functioning in the 44 mining regions of the country.
The Ministry for Improvement and Water Resources (*M. melioratsii i vodnogo khoziaistva SSSR*) has a chief department for the

complex utilisation of water resources and a state inspectorate for the preservation of water sources (see also WATER & WATERCOURSES). The forestry of the country is taken care of by the State Committee for Forestry of the Council of Ministers of the USSR, but the economic use of timber is in the hands of the Ministry of Timber and the timber processing industry of the USSR. In Union republics forestry is in the care either of the Ministry or its departments. See also FORESTS & FORESTRY.

A special Ministry and its subordinate agencies are in charge of transport and communications (*MPS*); for sea-going vessels there is a Ministry for the Sea Fleet of the USSR with numerous subordinate bodies and agencies, the most important of which is the Sea Steamship Navigation Agency (*Morskoe Parokhodstvo*), which is a juridical person (with full *khozraschet* rights) under the charge of a head official (*nachal'nik*) appointed by the Ministry of the Sea Fleet of the USSR. Seaports have harbour masters.

Wholesale and retail trade (*q.v.*) has a rather complicated structure because it has to satisfy different groups of people living in different social and economic conditions. Most trading organisations come under the jurisdiction of the Ministry of Trade of the USSR, corresponding organisations in the Union and autonomous republics and the local departments for trade in the towns, *oblasti*, *krai* etc. Some retailers are under the direct management of the Ministries of Trade of Union republics, such as the *kurorttorgi* (shops in spas) and the trust for railway restaurants. Some Ministries have their own trading organisations such as the Ministry of Railways (*putei soobshcheniia*) of the USSR, the Ministry of the Sea Fleet and the Ministry for Coal Mining, etc. Such networks of retail organisations as *orsy* (workers' supply departments) or *prodsnaby* (produce supplies) are organised for the better and more efficient supply of goods to the employees and workers of these ministries in remote regions. The country is supplied with goods by a network of cooperatives—the *sel'po* at local village level, which are guided and organised by their central authority, the *Tsentrosoiuz* (Central Union of Cooperatives) of the USSR. In 1969 the trading cooperatives had a total membership of 56,000,000 shareholders. Pricefixing is the duty of the State Committee of Prices of the USSR (checking on the proper observance of the rules and regulations for trade and the sale of goods at the fixed prices is the duty of thc special inspectorate); (see also PRICES).

Municipal amenities and economics are under the jurisdiction of the republican ministries for communal economics (city transport, hotels, lighting, cleaning departments, etc.). The local executive committees each have their own administration or department of communal economics. Housing is managed by housing departments of the local executive committees. Single houses or groups of houses are administered by a special official, the *upravdom* (house-manager). Housing space is allocated to citizens by executive committees which issue them with special warrants (*order*) for a particular flat or living space according to a complicated rota system. The public participates in the management of houses by electing a house committee (*domkom*), whose duty it is to inspect the state of the building, check the sanitary conditions and enforce socially acceptable behaviour on the part of the people living in the house; see also HOUSING and PUBLIC UTILITIES.

A comparatively new A.A. (only since 1962-1963) is the consumer service organisation which is headed by the Union republican ministries for consumer services. In *oblasti*, *krai* and larger cities special administrations (*upravleniia*) are set up as offices of the executive committees. Industry itself is organised locally into *kombinaty*, each headed by a director who manages its affairs on the basis of special statutes. The director is appointed either by the local executive committee or by the administrative agency above it. *Kombinaty* comprise all sorts of local industries —bakeries, tailors', dressmakers', cobblers', joiners', plumbers', electricians' workshops, laundries, hairdressers, dry cleaners, etc. *Kombinaty* may even include factories of considerable size and turnover.

3) Agencies for socio-cultural development (*stroitel'stvo*) include the Union republican. Ministries for Education and Ministries for Higher and Secondary Professional Education. In some Union republics (Turkmenia, Kirgizia, Moldavia and Tadzhikistan) one single ministry of education rules over higher and secondary, primary and professional education (see EDUCATION). Special departments take care of education at *oblast'* and *raion* level, the *oblono* and *rono*. Scholarly research organisations are administered by the All-Union State Committee of the Council of Ministers of the USSR for Science and Technology. The Union republican Ministries for Culture are the principal agencies for culture and art. They are divided into chief departments (*glavki*); thus in the RSFSR there are *glavki* for the arts, for cultural-educational institutions, for educational establishments, personnel departments, etc. Certain cultural functions have been subordinated to special State Committees of the Council of Ministers of the USSR, such as the ones for radio and television (*q.v.*), and for cinematography. Since 1966 a chief administration (*Glavnoe Upravlenie*) at the Council of Ministers of the USSR for the safeguarding (*okhrana*) of state secrets in the press has been set up and therefore the former chief administration for the safeguarding of military and state secrets in the press, which until then was a department of the committee for the press, has been rearranged (see also PRESS). The public participates in the management of cultural issues by being organised into special Unions: for writers; for journalists; for composers; for architects; for artists; for cinematographists. These *creative unions* were set up by All-Union congresses and function on the basis of special statutes. See also ASSOCIATION. Union republics and autonomous republics have their corresponding unions; in *oblast'* and *krai*, departments are set up. The Unions have subsidiary organisations for the management of special funds such as thc *litfond* for writers.

The Union republican Ministries of Health and their departments are the administrative agencies for health (see HEALTH). A special committee for physical training and sport was set up as a Committee of the Council of Ministers of the Soviet Union and with corresponding bodies at the Union and autonomous republican levels. The public is organised in a Union of Sports Societies with its highest body, the conference, usually convened once every four years; the subdivisions are special *Federations* such as the ones for light athletics, for gymnastics, for ski-ing, etc., which are under the guidance of a bureau. Similar bureaux exist for water sports, games, chess, football, etc. At the local level, sporting activities are taken care of by voluntary sporting societies (*Dinamo, Kalev*). See also SPORTS.

Social security is managed by republican Ministries and the Ministries of Social Security of the Autonomous Republics and their subordinate bodies, the departments of the executive committees of the *oblast'*, *raion* and town Soviets. These Ministries do not deal with all questions of pensions and social security (see SOCIAL SECURITY). Special subdivisions of the Defence Ministry, the Ministry of Internal Affairs and the KGB (Committee for State Security) deal with questions of social security for their staffs and subordinate units. At the local level social security issues are taken care of by departments of the executive committees (the *raisobesy*, the *gorsobesy*).

4) Administrative agencies for political-

administrative issues are varied and of considerable complexity. Only the most important can be given here in outline.

The defence of the country, being one of the most important national and political issues, is in many respects directly subordinated to the Supreme Soviet, its Presidium and the Council of Ministers. The Union republican Ministries of Defence have under their guidance all three services, army, navy and airforce. Although defence is a Union republican Ministry, the Union Republics have abstained from setting up Ministries in order to preserve a unified, clear-cut management of defence issues. The strategic issues are taken care of by the General Staff and the political by the Chief Political Administration for the army and of the Central Committee of the CPSU. The rules of double subordination do not apply to the military agencies. The public participates in diverse voluntary organisations, the most important of which is the DOSAAF—the voluntary association for assistance to the Army, Air Force and Navy.

Securing the political integrity and security of the nation is the duty of the KGB (*komitet gosudarstvennoi besopasnosti*—committee for state security). It is a committee of the Council of Ministers of the USSR. Its duties are to wage a constant war against spies, saboteurs, traitors and agents of foreign intelligence services, the detection and investigation of political crimes, the guarding of the borders of the country and the protection of state secrets, i.e. of documents on a special index and other secret items. For the defence and integrity of the borders, the KGB has under its command the frontier-guard units, a powerful military organisation comprising several branches of the armed services, land, sea and air. The KGB works in close contact with the public, whose "holy duty" it is to assist the KGB in general and in particular in the defence of the borders. Here the *druzhinniki* (see PEOPLE'S GUARDS) in border regions are specially recruited and trained for special tasks and to assist the KGB troops; the local KGB commands the voluntary militia and may mobilise and arm them when necessary. There is no double subordination for organs of the KGB. See also SECURITY; SECRETS; BOUNDARIES.

The agencies for the medical-sanitary security of the borders is the Ministry of Health and its subordinate agencies, functioning on the basis of international conventions and the administrative law of the Soviet Union. See also HEALTH.

The crossing of borders is permitted only for persons in possession of specific documents authorizing them to do so (diplomatic passports; general foreign passports; or special documents replacing passports and visas for coming into or going out of the country). See also PASSPORTS; BORDER CROSSING.

Agencies for the maintenance of public order are headed by the Union republican Ministries for Internal Affairs (MVD, *ministerstvo vnutrennikh del*) of the USSR, of the Union and of the Autonomous Republics. In *krai* and *oblast'* the MVD administrations (*upravleniia*) are bodies of the executive committees; in the *raion* and cities the MVD has its own departments in the executive committees. The MVD force to maintain public order is the Militia, whose external (*naruzhnyi*) service—the uniformed police—consists of the C.I.D., the members of the BKhSS—for the safeguarding of the integrity of economic organisations and institutions and the detection of economic offences (embezzlements, frauds, larceny of state or cooperative property etc.) and the GAI (see TRAFFIC REGULATIONS)—the traffic police, for the maintenance of good order by all road-users and persons in charge of vehicles, in buses, garages, etc. See also POLICE.

Water and railway communications have

their own militia. The "departmental" militia is in charge (on the basis of special contracts) of objects belonging to departments (*vedomstva*) of other agencies or organisations; for that purpose the MVD has special departmental (*vedomstvennaia*) detachments for guards' duties. The militia is in charge of the internal passport system and proper observance of the internal passport (identity card) regulations—in-and-out registering when changes of domicile take place, etc. From time to time a general check of all internal passports is carried out (see PASSPORTS). In its struggle with criminality and delinquency, the militia has special organisations (children's rooms); see JUVENILE DELINQUENCY. It may carry out preliminary inquiries and, in respect of a number of offences, even the preliminary investigation, sharing this duty with the investigators of the KGB and the procuracy (see PROCURACY). It is in charge of the surveillance of 1) individuals declared by the courts to be particularly dangerous recidivists; 2) persons released from penitentiaries, but who did not manifest a change of heart while serving their punishment; 3) people who have served their punishment for the *most dangerous* offences and who after release continue systematically to offend against public order. Such persons [1)-3)] may be subjected to certain restrictions: 1) a curfew; 2) restraints on visiting certain places in the *raion* or town; 3) restraints on leaving one's *raion* or town on personal matters; 4) orders to report at the local militia office from one to four times a month.

The licensing (*razreshitel'naia sistema*) of firearms, explosives, printing and engraving machines and other duplicators (*rotatory*) is in the hands of the militia. One does not need a licence for a shotgun but must have a hunting ticket; rifles and side-arms (flick knives, Finnish knives) must be licensed (see WEAPONS). Certain licences are issued by other offices—thus the health authorities have the power to license the sale of dangerous drugs and proprietary medicines. The public participates with and aids the militia in the maintenance of public order and the prevention of offences as members of the voluntary militia (*druzhinniki*) and of comrades' courts (*q.v.*). The fire-fighting services, such as fire-brigades, are ruled by a chief department of the MVD for fire protection (*Glavnoe upravlenie pozharnoi okhrany*). The MVD is in charge of the corrective labour colonies (see also FIRES & FIRE PREVENTION; PENITENTIARY INSTITUTIONS).

The main agencies of justice are the Union republican Ministries of Justice which were re-established in 1970 (abolished as a Union republican ministry of the USSR in 1956, with the subsequent abolition of the ministries by the Union republics in the course of 1960-1963, when their duties were transferred to the Supreme Courts of the Union republics and the Legal Commissions). Its statutes have been passed by the Council of Ministers of the USSR on March 21, 1972.

There are republican and autonomous republic's Ministries of Justice and, at the local level, of *krai*, *oblast'* and town, departments of justice of the executive committees. The Ministry of Justice exercises a great number of special administrative duties, *inter alia*, it organizes the election of People's Judges. The Minister of Justice participates in the Plenary Sessions of the Supreme Courts and has the right to submit suggestions and requests to the Supreme Courts for explanations and directions on points of law to the subordinate institutions of justice. See also MINISTRY OF JUSTICE.

Foreign affairs are taken care of by the Union republican Ministries of Foreign Affairs. For foreign trade there is a USSR Ministry for Foreign Trade. Both institutions have representatives in foreign countries. Whenever political questions arise, the Ministry of Foreign Trade has to communicate the issue to the Foreign Ministry (see FOREIGN TRADE).

In order to control and enforce the law on separation of Church and State, a special Council for Religious Affairs (*Soviet po religioznym delam*) has been set up under the Council of Ministers of the USSR. It is the connecting link between the religious communities and the government of the USSR. It is an administrative agency which keeps a detailed register (*vedët uchët*) of all religious denominations and buildings in use for religious purposes and it deals with problems concerning religion in general. The Council has the right to request and obtain information and materials concerning religion; it has the right to decide about registering or cancelling the registration of dissolved communities, to decide on the opening or closure of buildings used for religious purposes, to keep an eye on the activities of such communities and to issue ordinances (*obiazatel'noe postanovlenie*) and directives (*predpisanie*) for them. It also has the right to give explanations and directives to other authorities and to demand the abolition of illegal instructions, orders, decisions, etc. by authorities. Any measures concerning religious communities which are intended by the governments of Union or autonomous republics, or of local soviets or their executive committees, must first be agreed by the Council. In localities the Council has its representatives, whose duty it is to act as supervisors of religious matters at local government level. See also CHURCH & STATE.

The public participates through Commissions for Assistance (*Komissii sodeistviia*). They are composed of deputies of the local soviet, of employees of administrative agencies and finance departments, departments of education and of representatives or organisations of the public (Party, Komsomol, T.U., etc.). One of the primary duties of the Commissions for Assistance and the local representatives is to keep a watch on the fostering or devising of "superstitious practices" or the compulsory collecting, etc., by members of religious communities or their clergy.

R. Beermann

ADMINISTRATIVE LAW

Administrative law is a less clearly defined part of a legal system than some other branches, such as the criminal and civil substantive and procedural laws. In the Soviet Union, with its planned economy, nationalised industry and agriculture, administrative law is even more difficult to circumscribe and define than for countries with a bourgeois-capitalist system of economics and government.

The Soviet Encyclopedic dictionary of legal terms defines administrative law as that branch of the Soviet legal system which regulates public relations concerning the state (*gosudarstvennyi*) administration, i.e. [such relations] as arise in the course of the administrative-executive activities of state agencies, which directly (*neposredstvenno*), and with the participation of the toiling masses, organise and bring about the practical implementation of tasks and functions of the Soviet all-people's (*obshchenarodnoe*) state (see STATE OF THE ENTIRE PEOPLE). The definition, although tautological, may serve as a nutshell description of administrative law. The functions of administrative law agencies are said to be administrative-executive (*rasporiaditel'naia-ispolnitel'naia*). The terms are usually used together, and a rigorous definition of their separate meanings seems to defy the semantic powers of legal scholars. Basically it means that administrative law agencies are usually involved in two activities—the passing of legal norms (such as by-laws) and the issuing of individual acts of administration based on some legal norm. In the Soviet Union administrative law also comprises the extraction, production and distribution processes which are regulated by such administrative agencies as *Gosplan*, the Council of Ministries, individual industrial ministries, etc. (see ADMINISTRATIVE AGENCIES).

The administration and its administrative-executive functions are based on principles of DEMOCRATIC CENTRALISM (a concept originally applied to the organisation of the Communist Party), involving on the one hand the strict subordination of lower organs to the hierarchically superior departments and, on the other hand, containing the principle of double subordination: "the departments of soviets are responsible both to the executive committee and to the soviet at the level at which they work, and also to the corresponding department in their own line of business at the next higher level up to the ministry" (D. J. R. Scott, *Russian Political Institutions*, fourth ed., 1969, p. 60). The same rule applies also to the executive committees who are likewise responsible to their local soviet and to the superior executive committee of the higher soviet. In reality democratic centralism means, on the one hand, central guidance and final determination of the administrative-executive issue by the higher authority and, on the other, that local issues are decided on the spot by the elected local bodies the soviets, their executive committees and departments. Some important state agencies, such as the Committee for State Security (KGB), the Military, the Procuracy, etc., are exempt from double subordination and are administered exclusively by the higher authority. The popular-democratic principle of administrative law can also be seen in the participation of various bodies of the public either independently or together with government agencies in administrative-executive functions (decrees issued by the Central Committee of the CPSU and the Government; the participation of the different bodies of trade unions in administrative functions, etc.). Whenever a special function has been specifically allocated to a particular state agency, then, as a rule, is must adhere strictly to its powers, while other agencies are not entitled, without special legal authorisation, to interfere with these functions. This general rule is frequently broken by higher authorities and by the lower standing agencies, often due to a misreading of the principle of democratic centralism.

Administrative law consists of administrative legal norms which govern administrative relations. These norms determine 1) the system, the setting up (*obrazovanie*) and the powers of state agencies, their interrelationship, the rights and duties of officers of state and of employees; 2) the participation of the toiling masses in the administration of public affairs; 3) the order and the ways in which administrative acts are issued; 4) the methods of enforcement and persuasion in the implementation of the acts; 5) specific administrative jurisdiction in the case of ADMINISTRATIVE OFFENCES; 6) the rights and duties of citizens in respect of administrative-executive functions of state; 7) the means and ways of safeguarding and enforcing legality.

We should regard the Constitutions of the USSR and of the Union and autonomous republics, their subordinate laws and decrees (*ukazy*), government decrees (*postanovleniia*), frequently issued jointly by the Central Committee of the CPSU and the Council of Ministers, orders (*rasporiazheniia*) of the Council of Ministers and those of single ministries and their departments and decisions of local soviets and their executive committees as sources of administrative law. Furthermore we must also regard the internal working orders (or regulations) of ministries and departments, of the state auditing committee and of the local agencies of the state power, and such special statutes as those issued for railways, other means of communication, passport and registration orders, etc., as part of administrative law.

The determining feature of legal relationships according to administrative law is that at least one party must always be a state agency, functioning in the name of the state and exercising state authority in some way. The breach of administrative norms and orders makes the offender answerable to the state.

R. Beermann

See also PUBLIC ADMINISTRATION; ADMINISTRATIVE PROCEDURE

ADMINISTRATIVE OFFENCES

Administrative Offence is a term not often used in common law countries; it implies the more familiar expression of "regulatory offences". Soviet legal scholars define administrative offences as culpable acts which do not constitute a criminal offence (i.e. are not included in the criminal codes and do not create a criminal record for the offender), or disciplinary transgressions (see DISCIPLINARY OFFENCES) or civil law torts. They contain the elements either of a public nuisance or of a potentially dangerous act or omission, or are breaches of statutory regulations. In order to educate and to chastise the citizen, administrative offences are punishable by 1) warning, 2) administrative fine, 3) deprivation of certain rights and privileges, including deportation and exile, 4) dismissal from employment, 5) confiscation of property, 6) administrative detention, 7) corrective labour, 8) dissolution of organisations and the prohibition of certain works, 9) increased liability to taxation, 10) a special credit restriction (see D. N. Bakhrakh, *Sovetskoe zakonodatel'stvo ob administrativnoi otvetstvennosti*, 1969, p. 197).

1. *Warning and* 2. *Administrative Fines*

Soviet law repudiates the notion of strict or absolute responsibility: it requires, at least in theory the presence of *dolus* or culpable negligence for criminal and administrative offences. The rather broad interpretation given in some statutes to the concept of negligence considerably narrows the gap between the notion of culpable behaviour and that of strict responsibility as the latter is used in common law countries. Some administrative punishments are provided neither for acts nor for culpable omissions but for conditions —e.g. parents and guardians of delinquent children—known in common law countries as status offences.

Administrative offences are not yet expressed in any "Principles" or administrative offences codes as is the case with criminal offences, although such a possibility has been envisaged. Administrative offences occur in diverse statutes. The readiness of authorities to adopt statutes and by-laws containing penal measures induced the Presidium of the Supreme Soviet of the USSR to pass a law (June 21, 1961). "On further restrictions on the use of fines in administrative procedures", which may be regarded as temporary principles delimiting to some extent the power of authorities to pass statutes containing punitive measures; the same law regulates the competence to pass such statutes of different authorities according to their hierarchical standing. On the basis of the USSR law, the Union republics passed their own decrees „On further restrictions . . ." (RSFSR: March 3, 1962). According to these laws the general rule obtains that decrees or orders providing fines for administrative offences may be passed only by the supreme authorities of the state, such as the Presidia of the Supreme Soviets or the Government—the Councils of Ministers of the USSR and the Union republics. Some special powers, though more restricted than those of the supreme organs, are delegated to autonomous republics, the provincial (*oblast'*), the *krai* and the national district soviets, down to the *raion* or town soviets, leaving to the executive committees of the *raion* or town soviets the right to pass emergency regulations containing fines exclusively in the case of natural disasters, epidemics and epizootics. The USSR Supreme Soviet, the Presidium and the Council of Ministers have retained the right to pass administrative penal legislation in matters which concern the country as a whole, such as safety regulations for rail, sea and air transport, breaches of the rules for registering (*uchet*) for military service, border regulations, violation of customs laws, and rules against smuggling. The USSR and Union republics may pass legislation for breaches of technical safety regulations (*tekhnika besopasnosti*) and the protection of labourers in industry, the building trade, transport and agriculture, for breaches of registration and licensing regulations for individual self-employed artisans, fines for the pursuit of prohibited business, for breaches of sanitary and epidemological regulations, quarantining of animals, ground, air and water pollution, violations of the passport (internal identity cards) regulations etc.

Only individuals (i.e. physical persons) may be punished for administrative offences (the former law permitted the punishment of organisations and institutions). This injunction, however, is by no means watertight in spite of the reasonable argument that culpable behaviour is possible only in human beings. The State Bank (*Gosbank*) and the Investment Bank (*Stroibank*) have the right to fine the enterprises they finance or which have current accounts with them for certain economic and financial irregularities. Collective and state farms and industrial and construction enterprises may be fined for avoidance of their duty to participate in the building and repair of roads. Juridical persons may also be fined for violation of regulations of the Customs Code. These exceptions to the rule are believed to be essential because of the difficulty of ascribing the violation of such laws to any particular person. (Bakhrakh, *op. cit.*, p. 216 even suggests that the number of such laws should be increased.) These are obvious deviations from the principle that only the culpable actions of individuals justify punishment. Responsibility for administrative offences starts at the age of 16. The maximum fines are limited for private individuals to 10 roubles and for officials to 50 roubles. The supreme soviets and their presidia have the right to increase these amounts for private individuals to 50 roubles and for officials to 100 roubles. Such an increase was granted by the decree of the Presidium of the USSR Supreme Soviet (27.3.64) for violation of the fishing and hunting regulations. A decree of the Presidium of the RSFSR Supreme Soviet (8.5.61) provided for a fine of up to 50 roubles for obtaining privately produced alcoholic drinks. Likewise individuals violating the regulations for registering and licensing as self-employed craftsmen may be fined up to 50 roubles. Generally it seems that the limitations are not taken too seriously. Thus (previous to the law of June 21, 1961) regulations were passed that the illicit manufacturing and use of radio transmitters were to be punished by a fine of 50 roubles for the first offence; the fine was then increased three times for recidivists.

Service personnel and the officers and men of the armed forces are granted exemption from fines for administrative offences (art. 9, Law of June 21, 1961), but instead they are liable to be dealt with in accordance with their disciplinary codes (see DISCIPLINARY OFFENCES).

Prosecutions are limited to one month from the day of the offence. An administrative penal order can not be executed after the lapse of more than three months from the date of the order.

The question of the administrative tribunals for administrative offences has been solved by adopting three different solutions: 1) by creating special tribunals, 2) by giving the power to fine (sometimes on the spot) to the law enforcement officers themselves,

3) by letting the people's judges or courts sit in *administrative* sessions (something similar to summary jurisdiction in Great Britain).
Basically administrative offences are disposed of by Administrative Commissions of the Executive Committees of the *raion* (or town) soviets. These bodies are composed of deputies of the *raion* or town soviet and representatives of public organisations (the Party, the Komsomol, the trade unions). They consist of a chairman, a deputy and at least four members. The Administrative Commissions are permitted to reconsider their own cases, i.e. they may themselves change a previous decision, but their decisions may also be changed by the Executive Committees of the *raion* or town soviets. Instead of taking up a case, the Administrative Commission may submit it for disposal to a comrades' court or to the public organisations set up "for the taking of measures of public influence" (i.e. by exerting moral pressure on the offender to mend his ways). As with the courts, the Administrative Commissions are encouraged to hold their sessions in the place where the offence was committed or to which the offender belongs (like clubs, factory premises, libraries, offices, apartment houses, etc.). Such arrangements are regarded as more effective for the exercise of the main task of the Commissions which is "to educate citizens to the spirit of unflinching observance of Soviet laws and care for socialist property, an honest attitude to their duties to the state and the public and consideration [*uvazhenie*] for the legal rights [*prava*], the honour and dignity of [*other*] citizens and for socialist community life". The employer and the public organisations of the place of employment or educational institution (school, university) and/or of the dwelling place of the offender (management of communal flats, etc.) ought as a rule to be informed of any administrative punishment (*vzyskanie*). Although punishments for administrative offences do not constitute a criminal record for the offender, they are recorded and thus a further administrative offence may involve graver consequences for the offender. But if within a year no new administrative offence has been committed, the record is expunged. Fines must be paid within 15 days after the administrative order has been handed over to the offender, refusal or inability to pay leading to attachment of his earnings. If offenders are not gainfully employed their property is attached and sold by auction (see also CORRECTIVE LABOUR). An offender disagreeing with an order by which he is fined may appeal to the people's courts within 10 days. The submission of an appeal stops the procedure for the collection of the fine.
Instead of imposing a fine, the authorities have the right to admonish the offender. The number of officials entitled to impose fines and other measures for administrative offences has steadily increased. Frequently these are for cases when "on the spot" fines are possible: traffic offences, violations of rail, water or air travel regulations, petty hooliganism, drunkenness in public places, petty speculation and the violation of numerous other regulations. Whenever these officials impose fines, appeals to the people's courts may be made, and generally most of the formal rules apply here as well, as in the case of commissions, with the exception that the appeal against measures not involving a fine is made to the official or authority immediately superior to the officer who handled the administrative offence. The bulk of all administrative offences is dealt with by officers of the Departments of Internal Affairs (mainly the militia). Other officials who do not have to approach the administrative commissions but are entitled themselves to take administrative measures and to fine the offenders are listed in art. 13 of the law of June 21, 1961. One of the latest of such offences was defined by the decree of March 25, 1970, of the Presidium of the

USSR Supreme Soviet. "On the responsibility of [persons] for the purchase, sale and exchange of small amounts of foreign currency and/or the purchase of objects from aliens", which is punishable by a fine of from 10-30 roubles and the confiscation of the currency and objects so obtained. A second offence within a year is punishable by a fine of up to 50 roubles. After two such punishments the next offence is punished by deprivation of freedom or corrective labour for up to one year. The offence is regarded as petty as long as the value of the currency (money, cheques, etc.) and/or objects does not exceed 25 roubles. The first offence is dealt with by the local chief of the department of internal affairs, the second by the administrative commissions and the third by the courts.

3. *Deprivation of certain rights and privileges, banishments and deportations*

The Militia or the local officers of the Ministry of Internal Affairs possess considerable administrative powers in cases where passport (internal identity card) laws are violated. There are rules which prohibit certain categories of people from residing in the cities or towns under so-called special orders (*rezhimnye goroda*). Here the militia may refuse to register passports (*propiska*) for a residence visa, or withdraw a visa already granted (see PASSPORTS) and thus force people to leave the city. In many instances these powers affect individuals released after serving a prison sentence, or others suspected of having harboured criminals. The difficult position created by these rules relating to former convicts has been referred to repeatedly in Soviet writings. Persons trying to reform are said to revert to crime because of the many obstacles blocking their way towards a new life. In regions where special conditions are proclaimed (e.g., war conditions—*voennoe polozhenie*) and extraordinary powers are conferred on the authorities, any person regarded as a danger to the public because of his criminal activities or because of his association with criminals may be exiled on administrative orders (see STATE OF WAR).

In Moscow city and province and in Tashkent it is within the militia's competence to fine people for violations of passport regulations, while elsewhere it is the business of the administrative commission. Likewise the militia is competent to deal with violations of passport, travel, residence and registry rules committed by aliens residing in the USSR—they may be fined or, in more serious cases, expelled from the Soviet Union. Deportation of parasites (work-shy people) has recently been abolished (see PARASITES).

Among other rights and privileges which may be withdrawn on administrative orders are driving licences. In the course of two years (1966-1967) the militia withdrew in Lithuania alone 14,000 licences, 12,322 of them from drivers found drunk in charge of a vehicle. (Bakhrakh, *op. cit.*, p. 219). Driving licences may be withdrawn for a year or, in the case of repeated traffic offences, for three years. In some republics the disqualification from driving for gross violation of traffic rules may last as long as five years (Belorussia, Ukraine, Turkmenia). The disqualifying procedures are dealt with by special commissions of the militia-departments of the *raion* or town executive committee; they are chaired either by the chief of the militia, his deputy or the chief of GAI (State Automobile Inspectorate). Drivers who refuse to submit for medical examination, or to stop their vehicle, or wilfully leave the scene of an accident lose their driving licences for up to one year in Estonia, and for up to three years in Lithuania (see TRAFFIC OFFENCES).

The administrative authorities may deprive citizens of the use of parcels of land if rules of land use are not observed, e.g. for violation of the rules for combatting weeds, or of the use of hunting grounds (for violations of hunting and wild-life preservation laws); they may withdraw from citizens the privileges of using pastures for grazing cattle, or grasslands for making hay. The right of a citizen to use land for a *dacha* (weekend cottage) may be administratively withdrawn if the *dacha* is used for mercenary purposes. This may force the owner to sell or demolish the *dacha*. The executive committees of *raion* (or town) soviets have the right to deprive able-bodied individuals who refuse to take up socially useful work of the privilege to own cattle, fowl or bees.

On the application (*predstavlenie*) of the Councils of Universities, the higher degree commissions (*Vysshie Attestatsionnye Komissii*) have the right to deprive the teaching staffs of universities and colleges of their degrees if they do not produce any scholarly work for a substantial period and are unable to provide high quality teaching at their place of work. The councils of ministers of autonomous republics, the *krai* executive committees and the executive committees of Moscow and Leningrad (in agreement with the trade union) have the right to deprive workers employed in communal services of the titles of "Master of the highest quality" or "First class Master" whenever their work ceases to be of the expected standard.

4. *Dismissal from employment*

Some administrative bodies have the right to *suggest* to employers the dismissal of employees or workers. Such a right is given to the labour safety inspectorate. Others, such as the committees of the people's control (the auditing authority), may even *demand* dismissals, and this is mandatory on the management of an enterprise. Instances of disobedience of such orders have been overruled by the Committee of the People's Control at the Council of Ministers of the USSR. The enterprise under such orders may either dismiss such a member of staff or give him another job. It is assumed, on analogy with the one year rule of expunging records of administrative offences, that after a year the staff member may be returned to his previous job. Ministers (*sluzhiteli*) of religious denominations must be registered with the provincial deputy (*upolnomochennyi*) of the council for religious denominations. For violations of laws on religious denominations their registration licence may be cancelled. (An interesting instance where the constitutionally expressed separation of State and Church is disregarded.)

5. *Administrative confiscation of property*

Administrative confiscation of property is possible in relation to 1) objects which may not be dispatched by post, 2) objects conveyed by any means of transport, conveyance of which is prohibited in the interests of public order and/or health and safety, 3) objects which were obtained by or used for the sake of petty speculation, 4) radio transmitters manufactured or used without a licence, 5) smuggled objects and the vehicles used to transport them, 6) firearms belonging to people violating regulations for the keeping and use of firearms, 7) guns used for the violation of hunting rules (see Bakhrakh, pp. 229-30).

6. *Administrative detention*

Administrative detention (arrest) is possible on the orders of the people's judges (sitting alone without assessors) 1) for petty speculation (arrest from 3 to 15 days), 2) for wilfully (*zlostno*) disobeying orders of a militia officer or a member of the people's volunteer brigades (*narodnyi druzhinnik)* (up to 15 days), 3) for petty hooliganism (10-15 days), 4) for malicious disobedience of the rules of conduct during detention for petty hooliganism—the term may be extended for a further 20 days but not exceeding a total of 30 days, 5) for malicious violations of prescribed behaviour (*rezhim*) in places of banishment for idleness (3-15 days—this has not applied since the new parasite law was passed—see PARASITES). Petty hooligans must pay for their board in prison—one rouble for 24 hours. The prison regulations for detainees of this category are rather harsh: bedding is not provided, smoking is forbidden, and it is not permitted to write letters, purchase food or to receive parcels (*peredachi*). The detainees are fed according to rules prescribed for prisoners on 'general' prison rules (see PRISONS) with hot meals only every second day and on other days, only bread, salt and hot water. They may be permitted improved conditions if they are given work (sweeping streets and other unskilled manual jobs, etc.). If they perform the work conscientiously they receive hot meals daily. They are not paid for the work. Board and lodging in gaols and fines must be paid by parents for their wayward children from 16 to 18 if the latter are unable to pay themselves (a further instance of the strict or status responsibility mentioned above). The detention for petty hooliganism may be interrupted to give the offender the chance to continue with his usual job, the Saturday and Sunday being used for the serving of the detention order. It is interesting to note that the Estonian law (*postanovlenie*) of 25.10.68 treats the driving of a vehicle without a licence and in a state of intoxication as an instance of hooliganism; such a person may be punished by administrative order with a fine of up to 50 roubles or 15 days detention, with the same conditions of detention as petty hooligans.

Likewise a fine or arrest is possible in Estonia for persons manufacturing, carrying or keeping stabbing or cutting weapons (*kholodnoe oruzhie*). (If the person is a minor under 16, the parents or guardians are fined.) In Lithuania the possession of privately distilled alcohol or apparatus for distilling is punishable by arrest. The same applies to petty larceny of state or public property (10 to 15 days). A special instance of detention is that of people found in a state of excessive drunkenness. They are picked up by the militia and taken to the medical sobering-up stations. For a night spent in such a place and for the treatment received the citizen has to pay 10-15 roubles. The inspectorate for the supervision of corrective labour may punish citizens with detention for up to 10 days for refusal to work (see CORRECTIVE LABOUR).

(The Children's Commissions with their considerable powers in respect of minors and their parents are discussed under JUVENILE DELINQUENCY.)

7. *Corrective labour*

Corrective labour as an administrative punishment can be imposed now only by the people's courts, and decrees and orders containing such punishments may be made only by the highest authorities of state. Formerly (before the law of June 21, 1961) the administrative commissions of *raion* (town) executive committees were competent to apply the measure against persons violating their bylaws. Corrective labour with a deduction of 5-20% from wages or salaries for one month can be applied as administrative measures against individuals maliciously disobeying lawful orders of militia officers or members of the people's brigades (*narodnye druzhinniki*); for petty hooliganism (besides the above-mentioned arrest and fines) corrective labour may be imposed for from one to two months with a deduction of 20% from wages and salaries (Bakhrakh, pp. 230-232, see also CORRECTIVE LABOUR).

8. *Dissolution of organisations*

The administrative authorities have the right to dissolve organisations which violate Soviet law, or act contrary to the general policies of Soviet power, or violate the aims stated in their statutes. Besides the right of dissolution, the authorities may merely remove some of the members or members of the board; they may dissolve the board, presidium or other body managing the organisation before the end of its term of office and prescribe new elections. The Executive Committee of the provincial (*oblast'*) soviet may, with the permission of the Council for Religious Affairs of the Council of Ministers of the USSR, deregister religious societies or smaller groups of believers, and close the places of worship of any religious faith. The executive committees of the district or town Soviets may dissolve housing cooperatives for violations of their statutory aims. Administrative authorities have the right to close radio transmitters permanently or temporarily for violation of the appropriate rules and regulations. The Ministry of Civil Aviation has the right to close airports for a stated period or indefinitely.

9. *Punitive increase in taxation*

A punitive increase in taxation, as in the law on "agricultural tax", has again the character of strict responsibility and that of a status offence. Furthermore it is not an individual but a collective which suffers the punishment. Collective farmers' households (see PRIVATE PLOTS) pay a tax increased by 50% if any member of the household without a valid excuse does not perform the minimum amount of work prescribed for an able-bodied collective farmer. But if members of a collective farmer's family are not members of the collective farm, or have left or been expelled from the collective farm membership and are not even working in the collective farm on a contractual basis, the tax is increased by 75%. A list of such households (with wayward members) is drawn up by the farm management, confirmed by the general meeting of the farm and submitted for increases of taxation to the Executive Committee of the *raion* soviet. The Finance Department then raises the taxes accordingly. Single farmers (*edinolichniki*) pay double agricultural tax. This, however, is regarded not as a punitive measure but as a normal attitude towards people continuing to persist in individual farming. In Kirgizia individuals who occupy plots of land in excess of the allocated area without permission (*samovol'no*) must pay a 100% higher income tax from their agricultural earnings. In the RSFSR individuals who occupy land without permission and erect buildings must pay double the building tax, the land rent (*zemel'naia renta*) and the income tax due from agricultural earnings.

10. *Credit and monetary restrictions*

The State bank of the USSR (*Gosbank*) has the right to penalise state enterprises by submitting them to special credit regulations. These are as follows: the normal percentage rate for credits is increased by 20%, new credits are given only with a special guarantee issued by a higher authority and all overdraft credits (*raschetnye kredity*) are stopped. These measures are applied against enterprises who do not fulfil their planned targets, and/or their sales targets (*realizatsii*), and who are unable to preserve their turnover capital (*oborotnye sredtsva*). If the situation of the enterprise does not improve within six months, the State Bank acquires the right to stop all further credit facilities (see BANKING and CREDIT).

Conclusions

The administrative offences have been discussed at considerable length because of their importance in the Soviet setting and the great powers accorded to the administrative authorities in exercising punitive functions. We may expect a further proliferation of such measures, if only because the ever-growing complexity of social life requires new solutions and new and different means of law enforcement. Furthermore some Soviet jurists regard the increase of instances of administrative penal regulations for diverse offences as a natural process in a socialist society with its ideology of the withering away of state and law. They feel that administrative offences replacing the criminal law are thus something of a half-way house on the road towards the purely social measures and technical rules predicted to be the only forms of discipline enforcement in the future communist society. Already it is up to the administrative authority, as stated above, to submit the case to the comrades' courts for disposal.

There is still another reason for the knowledge and study of the diverse administrative regulations containing measures for administrative offences. Frequently certain violations which were previously criminal offences are changed to administrative offences and thus it is possible that certain fluctuations (e.g. a drop in criminal activities) in the crime rate can sometimes be attributed to changes in forensic policy or simply to changes of definition. So far Soviet legal writing has lacked any detailed study on administrative justice and offences. It is only the recent book by D. N. Bakhrakh (*op. cit.*) which gives a detailed account of the subject and has been widely used in this article.

R. Beermann

See also ADMINISTRATIVE LAW; PUBLIC ADMINISTRATION

ADMINISTRATIVE PROCEDURE

Administrative procedure is a fairly new term in the Soviet legal system. It has enjoyed a far greater usage in Western Europe where it developed into a third branch of formal law alongside civil and criminal procedure. The Soviet Union does not have a codified law comprising all the rules concerning administrative procedure, but only diverse separate enactments and even procedural customs. Administrative procedure therefore appears less streamlined and sometimes ambiguous. Administrative procedure is closely linked to laws regulating the business of GOVERNMENT but, in spite of their close connections and frequent overlapping, the scope of administrative procedure is more restricted. It may be defined as the rules applicable to administrative agencies for the handling of individual cases in the exercise of their executive-administrative functions. Some scholars prefer the narrower definition of administrative procedure as applicable exclusively to instances of administrative litigation. Here, obviously, administrative procedure is construed by analogy with the civil and criminal procedural laws. There are many features common to the three forms of procedure: they are formal rules, they contain the procedural rights and duties of the parties and rules for initiating procedures, rules for deliberations and for the examination of evidence, for decision-making, for appeals and protests and the execution of decisions.

An important distinction between the civil and criminal procedural laws and administrative procedure is that the former must be laws passed by the legislative authority—the Presidia and the Soviets of the USSR and those of the Union republics—whereas administrative procedure rules may be contained in laws passed not only by the legislature, but also by orders of government, and/or contained in statutes issued for and by special ministries and State Committees, etc. At least one of the parties must be a state agency, while the claimant, or the second party involved, can be a citizen, some other organ of state, a state enterprise, an organisation of the public, an individual employee endowed with administrative procedural rights and duties, some other official *qua* official, or a representative of state powers (including even people's courts, judges, militia officers, etc.). Administrative liabilities for offenders are subject to special administrative procedural rules (see ADMINISTRATIVE OFFENCES).

The laws of administrative procedure frequently refer to proceedings (*proizvodstvo*) and procedure (*protsess*). The first implies activities of state agencies concerning an individual case, while the second refers to all rules and regulations governing the administrative activity of an agency.

Administrative proceedings may be subdivided as follows: 1) Legislative activities (e.g. central or local government by-laws and statutes); 2) Administrative procedural treatment of proposals, declarations, petitions and complaints by citizens; 3) Disputes between state enterprises and between these and co-operatives and institutions are subject to special rules or arbitration (see ARBITRATION); 4) Cases involving the state authorities and conflicts arising between them; 5) Claims and counterclaims between state authorities and state enterprises.

The courts, special tribunals for administrative litigation, such as the Administrative Commissions of the Executive Committees (see LOCAL AUTHORITIES) and government agencies of the executive-administrative authorities themselves, may act as agencies for administrative procedure. Principles governing administrative procedure include 1) the strict observance of the law of the Soviet Union; 2) the participation in administrative procedure of the toiling masses; 3) the speed and efficiency of proceedings; 4) the safeguarding of the interests of the state and of individual citizens; 5) the publicity (*glasnost'*) of proceedings; 6) the establishment of the material truth; 7) the equality of the parties; 8) the conducting of proceedings in the predominant language of the local resident population; 9) the independence of judgments; 10) the two stages of administrative procedure; 11) the responsibility of the authority and individuals for inappropriately conducting administrative proceedings. All the above principles are applicable whenever the ordinary courts or the special administrative commissions of the Executive Committees are involved. Only some of the principles may apply when the deciding authority is an administrative agency of the government or an official. Most of these principles are self-evident. Only 9) and 10) may require some explanation. 9) implies that the competent agencies and officials have to decide the case before them independently, while the superior authorities may not (without good reason) interfere with the proceedings of subordinates. 10) implies that parties ought to have the right of appeal, but that as a rule the decisions of the second instance are to be regarded as final (thus decisions of the people's courts on appeals by citizens against primary decisions of administrative agencies, such as the Administrative Commissions of Executive Committees, are final).

The most important law governing administrative procedure is the decree of the Presidium of the Supreme Soviet of the USSR of April 12, 1968, on the "Procedural order for dealing with the suggestions, declarations and complaints of citizens". Further laws containing administrative procedure rules include the Regulations on the Administrative Commissions of Executive Committees; Regulations of Town, *Raion* and Village Soviets; regulations of individual ministries and of state committees, the Labour Code, housing laws, etc.

R. Beermann

See also PUBLIC ADMINISTRATION; ADMINISTRATIVE LAW

ADMINISTRATIVE SUPERVISION

Administrative supervision exists for the sake of maintaining socialist legality. Textbooks on administrative law speak about control and supervision. The first concept implies a more direct and active interference in the affairs of the supervised body, the second a more indirect means of control. Both activities are directed towards prevention and elimination of illegalities.

All soviets (from the Supreme Soviets of the USSR and the Union republics down to the village or settlement soviets) exercise supervision and control over their executive bodies and their subordinate departments: Council of Ministers, Ministries and their departments, executive committees of lower soviets and their departments, etc. In addition to the plenary sessions of soviets, control and supervision is exercised by the standing or *ad hoc* appointed commissions of these soviets, and by individual deputies (see LOCAL AUTHORITIES).

The hierarchical structure of government and administration provides for supervision and control of the subordinate bodies by the higher agencies: the Council of Ministers over the State Committees and Ministries, and these in turn over their subordinate departments, industrial organisations and enterprises. In the economic life of the country the hierarchical levels of subordination may number as many as six or even more (Ministry, *Glavk*, Trust, *Ob"edinenie*, head enterprise of the *ob"edinenie* and a member enterprise of an *ob"edinenie* with independent accounting; in the case of Union republican Ministries the number of subordinates is even higher). It is the duty of any leaders to educate their employees and workers in a spirit of strict observance of socialist legality and to exercise a systematic control of bodies under their jurisdiction. The superior agency has the right to abrogate or change the decisions and acts of subordinates on account of illegality and/or inexpediency.

A special form of control is the right of all deputies of soviets to put questions (*zaprosy*) to the subordinate bodies of their soviets. The questions of deputies of the Supreme Soviets have to be answered within three days, either in writing or verbally. A growing importance has been attributed to *groups of deputies* comprising all the deputies of different Soviets residing in a particular district. In the course of time these groups are said to have acquired an increasing significance as supervisory and control bodies especially for the promotion of the interests and demands of the local population. See also DEPUTIES.

The People's Control has been dealt with elsewhere (see PEOPLE'S CONTROL). Here it suffices to state that its supreme task is to eliminate in all administrative agencies "bureaucracy" in the sense of red tape, and red tape mongering (*volokita*), and all types of other excesses and shortcomings.

The Committees of People's Control have the right to suspend officials for disruption (*sryv*) in the execution of decisions of Party and government, for gross violations of state discipline and for other shortcomings in their work. The subsequent final dismissal is then carried out by the agencies who appointed the defaultees. The Committees of People's Control have their official apparatus and also voluntary collaborators. An important role is played by groups and "posts" of people's control in enterprises, institutions and organisations. The members of these groups are elected for two years by the collective of workers or their representatives in enterprises, institutions and organisations.

Administrative supervision in a narrower sense is exercised by special state inspectorates. These inspectorates are created for the constant supervision of certain branches of public life, economics and the administration. There are a number of such inspectorates: the state inspection of mining (*gornogo nadzora*) and boilers; state inspectorates of forest preservation; commercial inspection (*torgovli*); inspection of fisheries, of automobiles (and traffic) (*Gosudarstvennaia avtomobil'naia inspektsiia*, or *GAI*); inspections for testing (*probirnogo nadzora*); game inspectorates (*okhotnichego nadzora*) and others. The inspectorates may be either interdepartmental or departmental. The first have the right to inspect different enterprises, organisations and institutions of the state and of the public, while the second may be concerned only with the business of their own departments. Thus the *GAI* embraces the inspection of motorised transport (*avtokhoziaistva*) of all ministries, departments, organisations of the public and individual citizens. The same interdepartmental character applies to the health inspectorate of the Ministry of Health. All inspectorates have the right to issue binding orders to the offender to eliminate breaches of law; some, like the *GAI*, even have the right to impose fines on the offender.

The General Supervision of the Procuracy, of the courts and of the *Arbitrazh* have been dealt with under the appropriate headings (see PROCURACY; COURTS; ARBITRATION).

Administrative supervision is exercised also by bodies of the public such as the Communist Party of the S.U., the Trade Unions and the Komsomol. The statutes of the C.P. grant the right of control to primary party organisations of industrial and commercial enterprises, state and collective farms, design organisations, construction bureaux, scientific-research institutions, educational establishments, cultural-educational organisations, health and other institutions and organisations, whenever their administrations are exclusively concerned with the business of their own collectives. Generally the Party, as the political body of the S.U., exercises leadership in safeguarding socialist legality throughout the state and the public life of the country. See also ADMINISTRATIVE AGENCIES.

R. Beermann

ADMIRALTY, see MARITIME LAW

ADOPTION

The 1968 Federal Principles of Marriage and Family Law, and the RSFSR Code which came into force on November 1969 make few serious alterations to the existing system (cf. RSFSR Marriage and Family Code, arts. 98-118).

Adoption is authorised by the local authority's executive committee which is also the Agency of Guardianship and Curatorship. The adoption and details must be registered at the Registry of Civil Status, and can be annulled only by judicial decision.

Any adult not deprived of parental rights and fully *sui juris* may adopt; but if he is not a Soviet citizen and the child is, special permission is required. A married adopter, where both spouses do not adopt, must have the other's consent. The adopter may be inserted in the register of births as the child's parent; and provision is made for changing names etc.

Only minor children may be adopted, and only in their own interests. Certain consents are required: that of the natural parents, though this may be waived (with limited powers to have the waiver set aside) in cases of serious neglect; that of the child if over 10, though this may be dispensed with if he has lived with the adopter and considered him his parent; and, in appropriate cases, that of the child's guardian or curator.

The adopter and his relatives and the child and his issue acquire the same legal relationships as if they were blood kin, while the child loses all legal connection with his natural family. If, however, the child is adopted by a man his natural mother may retain the link; and vice versa. Further, if one of the natural parents is dead, the natural grandparents may, with the adopter's consent, retain the link. In any event the adopted child does not lose an accrued right to a loss of breadwinner pension (see SOCIAL INSURANCE).

The secrecy of adoption is preserved.

Adoption may be set aside and the status quo ante restored if a court is satisfied that it was procured by false documents or by someone not entitled to adopt. The child is returned to his natural parents or, if this would be against his interests, to the Agency of Guardianship and Curatorship.

Children with Soviet citizenship living abroad may be adopted through a USSR embassy or consulate; if the adopter is not a Soviet citizen Ministerial permission is required.

B. Rudden

ADULTERY, see DIVORCE

ADVOCATES, see LAWYERS

AGENCY

In Soviet law, agency must be by contract, by a consensual agreement under which one party, the agent, binds himself to perform specified legal acts in the name and on the account of another, the principal. The contract may be for reward, at a fee fixed by regulations, scales of charges or agreements; it is gratuitous unless law or contract provides otherwise. Obligation to pay is taken to be implied by law if general scales of charges for such service exist (e.g. lawyers, transport enterprises).

The parties must be legally capable citizens and/or juridical persons acting within the limits of their legal power. Contracts of agency may therefore be entered into for the exercise of legal powers of representation in lawful, juridical acts such as representation by advocates in civil, criminal or administrative matters, contract-making, management of property, acceptance of inheritance, etc. A citizen may not enter into a contract of agency to act as a "commercial middleman", since Soviet law forbids "speculation" (*q.v.*). State, co-operative or public bodies may, within their power and state and planning directives, enter into such commissions (see COMMISSION AGENTS). Persons who do certain acts for others (even if they are legal acts) as part of a contract of service do not act as agents for the purpose of civil law; their conduct is governed by labour law and subjcct to administrative discipline.

The general principles of agency are to be found in the Civil Codes of the republics (arts. 396-403 of the RSFSR code), but specific statutes, regulations, decrees of the Council of Ministers, charters of organisations, etc. govern particular classes of agency. Between socialist organisations, agencies are frequently created for the purpose of enabling one organisation to market its surplus stock through the facilities of another or, as between internal trade organisations and All-Union associations, for the conduct of foreign trade.

The agent acting properly acts, "in the name and on the account of" the principal; he acquires no rights and incurs no obligations himself. The agent must carry out the charge strictly according to the principal's instructions if he is to escape liability for loss, damage or extra expenses. He may deviate only in cases of real necessity in the interest of the principal, if he is unable to ask for instructions or has asked for them but cannot wait for the reply. He must then inform the principal of the steps taken as soon as possible. The agent must always, on request from the principal, report on the progress of the entrusted tasks. On their fulfilment, he must without delay account to the principal, producing evidentiary documents where appropriate, and transfer all property interests, rights, etc. received under the charge. The principal must accept the consequences of proper performance by the agent, provide means for carrying out the charge, reimburse for expenses necessarily incurred and pay any agency fee, after the charge has been carried out.

Soviet writers see a contract of agency as a particularly personal transaction, founded on a relationship of trust that stands outside the contract. Either party may therefore withdraw from or renounce the contract at any time and any attempt to limit such power by contract is invalid. The contract is terminated on the actual or judicially declared death of either party (or the liquidation of an organisation), on the recognition of legal incapacity or presence of limitation of capacity. An agent who renounces in circumstances in which the principal is unable to protect his interests is liable for losses caused by the renunciation. If the contract is terminated before the fulfilment of the charge, the principal must pay all expenses incurred and the agent's fee *quantum meruit.* The principal is not liable for work carried out after the agent knew or ought to have known of the termination. Heirs of a deceased principal acquire rights and obligations arising from the execution of the agency, but heirs of deceased agents do not. The latter have only to inform the principal of the agent's death and to take measures necessary to protect any of the principal's property, documents and other interests to the extent of the assets of the deceased. Generally, the agent cannot appoint a deputy to replace him (as distinct from an assistant to help him) unless he is authorised to do so or if real necessity compels deputising in the interest of the principal. In such cases, the agent must notify the principal of the need and communicate concerning the character of the deputy; an agent exercising due care in his appointment and observing these requirements is not liable for wrongful acts by the deputy. The principal may challenge the appointment. Once accepted, the deputy carries out the principal's trust, not the agent's.

Contracts of agency between citizens need not be in writing unless the value of the contract exceeds 100 roubles. This value is arrived at by adding the fee to the value of the transaction to be executed with the third party. A contract of agency between organisations and between an organisation and a citizen must be in writing.

Some republican Civil Codes (Kazakh, Latvian, Tadzhik) recognise some degree of agency by necessity or implication as creating rights and obligations not based on specific contract. (In republics whose Civil Codes do not recognise such involuntary or implied agencies, these obligations may be enforced through provisions covering obligations arising from unjust enrichment or the rescue of property; see OBLIGATIONS). Such implied or involuntary agencies (or obligations) arise where the acts are directed to the avoidance of loss or property (repairing the roof of an absent neighbour to prevent damage to house and furniture through rain) or to the interest of another (buying medicine for sick children temporarily uncared-for). The acts must be necessary and expedient and the "agent" must be unable to communicate with the interested person to obtain instruction or agreement to act. The "agent" then has the right to be reimbursed for necessary expenses, even where the attempt to save property etc. was unsuccessful due to no fault of the agent. The agent has a duty to inform the interested person as soon as possible, to carry out all necessary acts to the end, to transfer property received, to give an account of his acts, and to compensate for damage or loss caused by him through his fault. Acceptance by the interested person of the acts has retrospective effect, enabling the adoption of all acts committed by the agent, whether known to be agent or not.

A. E.-S. Tay

AGRESSION,
see INTERNATIONAL CRIMES

AGRICULTURE, see LAND TENURE; KOLKHOZ; SOVKHOZ

AIR LAW (see also *Appendix*)

Introductory remarks

In the Soviet Union air law is subject to federal legislation as stated in art. 14, point 13 of the Constitution of 1936, at least as far as "the management of transport and communication of All-Union importance" is concerned. In fact no legislation of the republics

themselves has ever existed even for minor questions of air law.
The Air Code of December 26, 1961, entered into force on January 1, 1962 and superseded the federal Air Code of August 7, 1935, which substituted the Air Code adopted on April 27, 1932.
The Air Code of 1961 is a mixture of public and private air law. The importance of the former is underlined by the fact that, according to art. 2, the first duty of the code is "to protect State interests". Because of the substantial power of making detailed rules which is delegated to the Chief Administration for Civil Aviation, the Air Code by no means deals with all problems arising from civil air transport.
The Soviet Union ratified the Warsaw Convention of October 12, 1929 and The Hague Protocol of September 28, 1955. It adhered to the Chicago Convention on October 15, 1970, and became a member of the ICAO on November 14, 1970. Soviet air law is still based primarily on national regulations especially in the Air Code of 1961, and on bilateral agreements concluded with foreign countries.

Main features of the Air Code of 1961

a) *General principles*
The fundamental principle of Soviet air law is expressed in art. 1 which provides, similar to art. 1 of the Chicago Convention, that "the complete and exclusive sovereignty over the airspace of the USSR shall belong to the USSR". Soviet airspace is defined as "the airspace above the land and water territory of the USSR, including the space above the territorial waters as determined by the laws of the USSR and by international treaties concluded by the USSR" (art. 1, par. 2). The upper limits of airspace are not defined more precisely in Soviet legal theory than elsewhere.
The Air Code is aimed first at protecting state interests but also at securing "the safety of air flight and [at meeting] the needs of the national economy of the USSR and that of its citizens" (art. 2). The field of application of the Air Code covers all civil aircraft entered in the Government Register for Civil Aircraft of the USSR even during the time when they are outside the boundaries of the USSR, "unless the country they are stationed in otherwise provides" (art. 3, par. 2).
Civil aircraft, as well as airports, aerodromes and ground facilities are owned by the State, but, according to art. 5, par. 2, "cooperative and public organizations may have ownership of civil aircraft, the ground facilities necessary for carrying out their tasks and operate aerodromes", with the permission of the Council of Ministers of the USSR.

b) *Registration and nationality of aircraft*
Although private ownership of aircraft is not possible in the USSR (art. 3 of the Constitution of 1936), the Air Code retains the concept of "civil aircraft", which is defined functionally and negatively in art. 9 as "all flying devices, both lighter and heavier than air, with the exception of the flying devices of the armed forces".
As far as the registration and consequently the so-called nationality of aircraft is concerned, it is worth mentioning the discriminatory system provided for in art. 11 of the Air Code: on the one hand the registration of a Soviet aircraft in a foreign country will not be recognized by the USSR as long as its registration in the Soviet Union has not been cancelled, but on the other hand as soon as an aircraft is entered in the Soviet Register, "no previous registration concerning such aircraft in the register of aircrafts of foreign countries may be recognized by the USSR", no account being taken at all of a previous cancellation of the foreign registration.

c) *Flight crew*
Among the dispositions devoted to the flight

crew (arts. 18-26) one ought to mention the obligation imposed upon all members of the crew of an aircraft entered in the Register for Civil Aviation of the USSR to be Soviet citizens (art. 19).

The commanding officer "shall take all necessary measures for the safety of persons on board the aircraft, of the aircraft and of property" (art. 22, par. 2). This implies the right of the commanding officer "to use all necessary measures against persons who by their acts cause a threat to the safety of the flight or who disobey his orders" (art. 24), as well as the right to jettison any luggage, cargo or mail in case of necessity (art. 25, par. 2). In such circumstances even the passengers are obliged to participate in the rescue of an aircraft and of persons (art. 25, par. 3). This obligation is based on the idea that all persons inside the aircraft are forming a sort of community.

d) *Internal and international flights*

Two different chapters (5 and 6) deal in detail respectively with internal and international flights. The latter are those which cross the boundaries of the USSR and another state, but not those which cross for instance the boundaries of the USSR and the space over the high seas.

As far as internal flights are concerned, it suffices to remark that, according to art. 67, par. 2, which reflects the general duty of all citizens to protect state property, there is a general duty to inform the authorities about known cases of aircraft in distress. Art. 68, par. 2, introduces a new rule regarding liability in the case of aerial collision.

International flights are subject to the restrictive rule according to which an aircraft entered in the Soviet Register may undertake an international flight from the USSR only with the authorization of the Chief Administration for Civil Aviation, even in cases of non-commercial international flights (art. 71).

Flights of foreign aircraft in the airspace of the USSR, which can be undertaken on the basis of international agreements or by the authorization of the Chief Administration for Civil Aviation, may be carried out only along the established international air routes (arts. 72-73). Furthermore, "foreign aircraft shall have no right on the territory of the USSR to take on board passengers, luggage, cargo or mail for commercial transportation to another place in the territory of the USSR" (art. 75). Exceptions to that prohibition of cabotage, which is to be found also in art. 7 of the Chicago Convention, can be awarded by the special authorization of the Chief Administration for Civil Aviation.

The flight documents of a foreign aircraft are recognized as valid in the Soviet Union provided they meet the requirements of the laws of the state in whose register such an aircraft is entered (art. 79).

Infringement of the rules concerning international flights constitutes a criminal offence (cf. art. 84 Criminal Code).

e) *Internal and international carriage by air*

Chapter 7 (arts. 81-119) deals with the internal carriage by air, while a new chapter 8 (arts. 120-136) is devoted to international carriage. It seems that the provisions of chapter 7 have to be construed as being *ius generale* in comparison with the provisions of chapter 8 which must be understood as *ius speciale*. Both kinds of carriage are subject to the monopoly of the Soviet government (art. 81).

No obligation to carry passengers, luggage, cargo or mail is laid down in the Air Code. Moreover air carriage appears to be a sort of privilege in the light of art. 89 which provides that "*acceptance* of an application for reservation must be confirmed by the carrier indicating the period of time during which the reservations are effective" (italics added). According to art. 86 no granting of credit is allowed in principle in the field of carriage by air.

The most important question dealt with in chapter 7 relates to the consequences of breach of contract which is governed by the principle of strict liability. Nevertheless there are different situations in which the parties to the contract are released from liability:

a) In cases of failure to deliver cargo for air carriage or of delivery of only part of the cargo, the shipper is relieved from liability, "if it occurred as a result of an act of God, or of an accident on the premises of the shipper, which caused interruption of operations for a period of time of not less than three days and nights" (art. 93, par. 1).

b) In cases of failure to supply means of transport, the carrier is relieved from liability, "if it occurred as a result of an act of God or because of the impossibility of making flights due to meteorological conditions" (art. 93, par. 2).

c) The provisions laid down under a) and b) above have to be read with art. 92 which is devoted to the consequences of infringement of planned shipments, i.e. shipments which must be carried out on the basis of a "planned task", obliging given enterprises to offer for shipment definite quantities of goods to specific transport organizations. In the case of failure to supply the necessary means of transport or to submit the cargo provided for in the plan for air carriage, the carrier and the shipper respectively are mutually liable for liquidated damages in the amount of 25% of the cost of air carriage for the arrears, if the circumstances laid down in art. 93 did not occur.

d) In cases of death, impairment of bodily health or other injury to health caused to a passenger at take-off, during the flight or at the landing of the aircraft, or at the boarding and disembarking of a passenger, the carrier is liable in accordance with the laws of the USSR and the constituent republics, "unless he proves that the injury occurred as a result of an intentional act of the injured person" (art. 101, par. 1). By omitting *force majeure* (*nepreodolimaia sila*) as a circumstance excluding the carrier's liability, art. 101, par. 1, goes further than the rule laid down in art. 454 Civil Code of the RSFSR for liability for harm caused by sources of increased danger in general. Furthermore, if no relief of liability can be awarded, the carrier does not benefit from any limitation of liability.

e) In cases of loss or spoilage of, damage to luggage, cargo or mail, the carrier is relieved from liability when he proves that the damage occurred because of circumstances which he could not avert or elimination of which did not depend on him, in particular on account of a number of the circumstances enumerated in art. 102, par. 2.

f) In cases of loss or spoilage of, or damage to personal effects of the passenger that were not delivered as luggage, the carrier is liable only if it is proved that the damage to these objects was due to the fault of the carrier (art. 102, par. 3).

g) In cases of loss, decrease in weight or spoilage of, or damage to cargo accepted for air carriage which could have been caused by the circumstances listed in art. 103, the carrier is relieved from liability, in so far as "it shall be assumed that they occurred because of these reasons, until the person filing the claim or bringing the action proves otherwise" (art. 103, par. 2).

h) In cases of shortage of the cargo the packaging of which on arrival was in good condition and with the seals of the shipper unbroken, the carrier is relieved from liability, "unless the person filing the claim or bringing the action proves that the shortage of the cargo is the result of a loss of, or damage to the cargo on the part of the carrier" (art. 104).

It must be mentioned that in all cases of loss of, or damage to cargo, luggage or personal effects of the passengers, if the carrier cannot be relieved from liability under the conditions listed under e) to h) above, art. 105 provides for no limitation of liability within the meaning of art. 22 of the Warsaw Convention.

i) In cases of delay in delivery of the cargo, the carrier is relieved from liability "if he proves that the delay resulted from the impossibility of making the flight due to adverse weather conditions, or other causes which he could not avert" (art. 106, par. 2). Each day of delay obliges the carrier to pay the consignee a fine of 5% of the cost of air carriage, but the fine cannot exceed 50%.

If the cargo has not been delivered to the consignee within 10 days from the date scheduled for delivery, the shipper or the consignee are entitled to consider the cargo lost and to claim indemnity for it (art. 106, par. 3).

As mentioned before, a new chapter 8 of the Air Code deals with international carriage, i.e. any carriage by aircraft in which the place of departure and the place of destination, whether or not there has been a transshipment or a break in the carriage, are situated either within the territory of two states or within the territory of a single state if there is an agreed stopping place within the territory of another state (art. 121).

It must be recalled that the Soviet Union is party to the Warsaw Convention as amended in The Hague. Consequently carriage of passengers or goods will be subject to the rules of that Convention in the relations between the USSR and any other state party to the Convention. Chapter 8 of the Air Code is therefore intended to govern only the international carriages not covered by the Convention or carried out between the USSR and another state not a party to the Warsaw Convention.

With these restrictions, international carriages are regulated as follows in the Air Code: strict liability of the carrier is provided for as well for damages arising from the death of, or bodily injury to a passenger (art. 127), as for damages arising from the destruction, loss of, or damage to cargo or luggage registered by a passenger (art. 128). Relief of liability imposed in both articles is admitted "when (the carrier) proves that he or persons authorized by him have taken all necessary measures to avoid damage, or that it was impossible to take such measures" (art. 129, par. 1). According to art. 129, par. 2, "when the carrier proves that the fault of the person who suffered the damage was the cause of the damage or contributed thereto the court may relieve the carrier from liability or limit this liability".

Contrary to the solution adopted for internal carriage (art. 105), the Air Code limits the carrier's liability for international carriage to the amount established by international agreements concerning liability for air transportation to which the USSR is a party (arts. 130-132). The limits so provided for in these articles shall not apply "when it is proved that the damage occurred as a result of the intent or gross negligence of the carrier or persons authorized by him while performing their official duties" (art. 135).

International agreements

The aim of the following considerations is to summarize the most characteristic features of the bilateral conventions concluded by the USSR in the field of air transport.

The air transport conventions concluded by the USSR with other countries recognize generally the right for the contracting parties to enjoy the so-called "first freedom of the air", i.e. the freedom of transit flights through the territory of the USSR, but only on given air routes (see for instance the conventions passed with Ghana, of April 6, 1962, Denmark, of March 31, 1956, and Belgium, of June 5, 1958).

As far as the "second freedom of the air", i.e. the freedom of non-commercial (or technical) stops in the territory of the USSR, is concerned, it seems that the agreements concluded by the USSR do not mention such a freedom on its own without connecting it with the right to undertake transport (see for instance the agreement with Afghanistan, of March 24, 1956).

The "third freedom of the air", i.e. the freedom of disembarking passengers or discharging cargo, luggage or mail in the USSR taken on board in the state of registration of the plane, and the "fourth freedom of the air", i.e. the freedom of taking on board in the USSR passengers, cargo, luggage or mail for a transport to the state of registration of the plane, are of course provided for in the conventions concluded by the USSR, but they are not always mentioned expressly. They may be connected with the "fifth freedom of the air", i.e. the freedom of carrying into the USSR passengers, cargo, luggage or mail, irrespective of their state of origin, or taking them on board in the USSR to any other third country. That occurs when the convention contains a broad formula such as "the right of carrying passengers, cargo and luggage having international character" (see for instance the conventions concluded by the USSR with the Sudan, Burma, Indonesia, Denmark).

The heart of the air transport conventions consists in defining the content of the commercial freedoms of the air. It has to be decided first whether only a precise line (for instance Moscow—Prague) can be flown by the contracting parties or whether a given route will be provided for, being admitted that each party is entitled to choose which lines and which countries it wants to open to the traffic on the basis of the route agreed upon in the convention.

While the agreements concluded by the USSR up to 1958 were of the first type, a more liberal system of determining given routes has been admitted since, for instance in the conventions with the Netherlands (1958), Indonesia (1961), Ghana (1962), and the Sudan (1962).

The adoption of the "route system" raises the difficult question of fixing the points of the route where the commercial rights can be exercised.

The starting point must be located within the territory of the country to which those rights have been recognized. It can be done either by designating in the convention a city from which the route must start (see the agreements with Belgium, Great Britain, Denmark, Sweden, India, the Netherlands, France, Ghana, the Sudan, Indonesia), or by leaving to each contracting party the right to declare which will be the starting point of the route in its territory (see the agreements with Korea, Mongolia, United Arab Republic, Finland).

As far as the intermediate points of the route are concerned, two different situations may occur:

a) If these points are located within the territory of the contracting parties, they must be referred to expressly in the agreement, as for instance in the convention with India where an intermediate point is provided for in the USSR (Tashkent) and another in India (Amritsar).

b) If these points are located outside the territory of the contracting states, Soviet practice seems to be in favour of fixing these points, with the consequence that the possible direction of the route is determined in advance; but that does not mean at all that the actual lines to be flown will correspond with these points, because on the one hand the agreement of the third state concerned must be obtained and on the other each party remains free to pick up among these points those which are the most favourable for it (see for instance the convention with the Sudan which provides that the intermediate points of the Soviet lines between Moscow and Khartoum will be Belgrade and Cairo, while the Sudanese lines between Khartoum and Moscou can fly either through Cairo—Athens—Belgrade—Prague—Vienna—Warsaw or Cairo—Athens—Rome—London—Amsterdam—Frankfurt—Berlin). The point of arrival of the route can of course be situated in a country other than the contracting parties. In such a case the point of arrival will not be precisely determined. For instance the convention concluded with Ghana provides that Soviet lines can be continued beyond the territory of Ghana "into points situated within the territory of third states". In the convention concluded with Denmark (1956) the Soviet Union was given the right to fly lines through Danish territory up to points situated in Great Britain, France, the Netherlands and Belgium, while Denmark was allowed to fly through the USSR up to points situated in Roumania, Turkey, the Lebanon and the UAR.

Apart from the determination of the routes which can be flown, the volume of the traffic to be allowed to each party constitutes another important aspect of commercial air transport. Generally the conventions concluded by the USSR contain a broad formula according to which the airlines are obliged to solve all questions, including the volume of traffic, connected with the exploitation of the route (see agreements with Bulgaria, Hungary, Denmark). In other conventions the parties have agreed that the volume of the traffic will meet the requirements of transport (see agreements with Afghanistan, Belgium, Great Britain, India, the UAR). These vague formulas are sometimes made more precise by indicating that the volume of traffic shall be divided equally between the parties, as in the convention concluded with France (1958).

As far as the number of flights and the types of planes are concerned, the conventions concluded by the USSR with other states (especially East-European countries) generally do not mention these points expressly, but are satisfied again with the broad statement that agreement will be reached on all technical and commercial questions linked with flights and air transport.

Bernard Dutoit

AIR POLLUTION

Air pollution (*zagriaznenie atmosfernogo vozdukha*) has only recently become an object of Soviet legal regulation. The first USSR decree on control over the establishment and operation of factories and plants emitting ashes, coal particles, soot, dust or noxious fumes or vapors was issued in 1949. It was deemed a public health measure, specifically for the benefit of the inhabitants of cities and other urban-type settlements. The decree called upon various state agencies (industrial ministries, state committees on matters of technology, scientific institutions) to work out methods and devices for reducing or eliminating industrial air pollution. The responsibility for enforcing the decree and the contemplated, subsidiary technical standards was given to the USSR State Sanitary Inspectorate. The same decree, however, empowered the inspectorate to approve the opening of new and remodeled factories and plants that would continue to emit atmospheric pollutants. The Soviet record of industrial air pollution over the next decade suggests that this power was freely used; the air pollution problem was graver ten years later than at the issuance of the decree. As was the case with conservation (*q.v.*) in general, absent a genuine commitment to environmental quality, the available economic resources went into air pollution rather than the preservation of aerial purity.

The provisions regarding air pollution, contained in the republic laws on protection of nature of the late 1950's and the early 1960's did not go much beyond the prior law. As part of essentially exhortative statutes, the air pollution provisions matched the generalities which had proved ineffective in the years before. Subsequently, somewhat more detailed laws and regulations were adopted by republic and local governments. The health services were urged to intensify sanitary supervision over the protection of the air from pollution.

Managers of industrial enterprises which emit atmospheric pollutants may be subject to administrative sanctions in accordance with the general principles of administrative liability as well as to criminal sanctions. Enforcement, which has to be directed at individuals rather than legal entities, apparently continues to be lax. The direct effects of industrial air pollution are occasionally reduced by proper observance of urban planning and zoning (*q.v.*) rules in connection with plant siting. Such rules require that industrial districts be separated from residential neighborhoods by sanitary protection zones of varying widths.

Air pollution by exhaust fumes of motor vehicles (*q.v.*) is becoming a problem in some localities. But by reason of their relatively small number, motor vehicles are not among the principal contributors to the country's total air pollution. Remedial measures have included inspection of vehicles for mechanical defects, the upgrading of fuels, dispersion of traffic and attempts to develop anti-pollution equipment. However, the planned drastic increase in Soviet automobile production in the 1970's might be a countervailing factor.

Z. Zile

AIRSPACE

Airspace is defined in Soviet legislation as the expanse superjacent to the land and water territory of the USSR, including territorial waters, the boundaries of said territory being established in the laws of the USSR and in international agreements to which the Soviet Union is a party. The Union of Soviet Socialist Republics exercises complete and exclusive sovereignty over the airspace of the USSR (art. 1, 1961 Air Code of the USSR). These principles, generally recognized in international law, were also cited in the judgment of the Military Chamber of the USSR Supreme Court convicting Francis Gary Powers, the pilot of an American U-2 aircraft shot down over Soviet territory on May 1, 1960, of espionage. Although many Soviet jurists once contended that there was no upward limit to sovereignty over airspace, at present the majority view is that airspace does not extend in infinity to outer space even though a generally-recognized norm fixing the upward limit of airspace does not exist.

All aircraft and their crews, passengers, cargo, and mail are subject to the administrative, civil, criminal, and other jurisdiction of the USSR during their sojourn in Soviet airspace.

International flights are governed by both the General Provisions and by Ch. VI of the 1961 Air Code of the USSR, and by the Flight Rules for Foreign Civil Aircraft Within the Territory of the USSR. Flights by foreign aircraft in Soviet airspace are permitted on the basis of and in conformity with international air agreements contracted by the USSR or special permits for single flights issued by the Ministry of Civil Aviation of the USSR. Every flight across the Soviet frontier is considered to be an international flight. Foreign aircraft must follow prescribed air lanes and may land only at specially-designated airports. A violation of international flight rules is a criminal offense punishable by imprisonment or fine under article 21 of the USSR Law on Criminal Responsibility for Crimes Against the State. Foreign military aircraft may enter Soviet airspace only with the preliminary authorization of the Soviet government requested through diplomatic channels.

The Soviet Union has concluded an extensive network of bilateral air transport agreements with other states, including Bulgaria, Canada, the People's Republic of China, Cuba, Czechoslovakia, Denmark, France, the German Democratic Republic, Great

Britain, Hungary, India, Iran, Iraq, Japan, Norway, Pakistan, Poland, Roumania, Sweden, the United States, and others. The Soviet government ratified the 1929 Warsaw Convention for the Unification of Certain Rules Relating to International Transportation by Air in 1934 and signed, but has not ratified, the Hague Protocol of September 28, 1955, amending the Warsaw Convention. The Soviet Union joined the International Civil Aeronautics Organization in 1970, but remains outside the International Air Transport Association, although observers have been sent to meetings in recent years.

W. E. Butler

See also AIR LAW; TERRITORY; BOUNDARIES

ALCOHOLISM, see INTOXICATION

ALIEN PROPERTY

On the international plane, the Soviet Union subscribes here to the principle of formal reciprocal grant of the national regime to foreigners, whereby citizens of one state enjoy on the territory of another state an identical quantum of private rights as the citizens of the latter state and *vice versa,* without regard for the effective equivalence of the material rights thus guaranteed in each case. Domestically, Soviet law subsumes foreigners under the national regime, i.e., offers foreigners in the USSR the same quantum of civil (non-political) rights as are exercised by Soviet citizens. In that vein, Art. 122 of the 1961 Principles of Civil Legislation of the USSR and Union Republics directs that "aliens shall enjoy in the USSR legal capacity equally with Soviet citizens. Exemptions may be established by the law of the USSR. The Council of Ministers of the USSR may impose retaliatory restrictions on citizens of countries imposing special limitations to the civil legal capacity of Soviet citizens." Art. 123 applies the first two propositions to stateless persons residing in the USSR.

First, it follows from the above that, while foreigners in the USSR possess the same property rights as Soviet citizens, these do not exceed what is available to Soviet citizens themselves. Just as Soviet citizens, foreigners may not, for instance, purchase or sell land, or open commercial or industrial enterprises. Second, according to Soviet commentators, the aforementioned clauses establish for the foreigner an "unconditional national regime", meaning that neither a court or any other organ of the Soviet state may make a foreigner's claim to have his legitimate property right recognized contingent on the prior submission of proof by the *de cujus* that in his homeland Soviet citizens are likewise entitled to national regime treatment. Third, so far Soviet municipal legislation has not seen fit to circumscribe in any way the full range of civil rights afforded foreigners by the 1961 Principles of Civil Legislation, so the original status of foreigners in this respect has to date remained unimpaired. Fourth, the power entrusted to the federal Council of Ministers to curtail the civil legal capacity of citizens of particular countries guilty of discrimination against Soviet citizens constitutes an emergency measure of retortion which does not negate the basic concept that, in general, the civil status of foreigners in the USSR falls under the national regime rubric.

Questions of the legal position of alien property in the USSR usually arise in connection with inheritance. Again, Art. 127 of the 1961 Principles of Civil Legislation states on that count that "relations arising from succession shall be determined by the law of the country where the decedent had his last permanent domicile", except that "inheritance of structures located in the USSR shall in any case be determined by Soviet law." Hence, the process of inheritance of movable possessions left in the USSR by a deceased alien is now governed by the law of the country of his or her last domicile (and not by the criterion of territoriality (*lex situ*) or citizenship (*lex patriae*)), whereas Soviet law always defines the regime of inheritance of buildings situated on Soviet soil. Soviet administrative instructions sanction the free transmission to foreigners and persons residing abroad, on the basis of reciprocity, of all sums of money inherited or realized from the sale of inherited property within the confines of the USSR. An inheritance may also be received in kind by an heir resident outside the USSR, in which case the items in question may be taken out of the country in accordance with the customs regulations of the USSR.

The treaties on the granting of legal assistance in civil, family and criminal cases signed by the USSR with nine of its "socialist" allies, plus Yugoslavia, confirm that the citizens of one signatory have the same rights as regards acquisition of property by inheritance on the territory of the other as the latter's own citizens, that the right of inheritance of movable property is governed by the legislation of that Contracting Party whose citizen the deceased was at the time of death. (N.B.: as distinct from the 1961 Principles of Civil Legislation, the crucial yardstick here is the citizenship of the deceased, not the locus of his or her last permanent domicile) and that the right of inheritance of immovable property, in turn, is subject to the law of the Party on whose territory the property lies. They further add that escheated movable property accedes to the state whose citizen the deceased was at the time of death, whereas title to escheated immovable property vests in the state on whose territory it is located (the Soviet-Albanian text contains no comparable provision).

In the event a citizen of one Party dies on the territory of the other, the latter's competent agencies must without delay communicate the fact to the former's diplomatic or consular institutions, informing them, *inter alia*, of the size and value of the estate. The same procedure is observed when the citizen of one Party dies on the territory of a third state but leaves an estate on the territory of the other Party (a clause omitted from the Soviet-Hungarian edition which, instead, requires communication of any knowledge that the deceased has left property on the territory of a third state and notification of the opposite side even when the deceased died on home soil if the latter's citizens have an interest in the estate). If the diplomatic or consular institutions receive the news of the death earlier, they must get in touch with the institutions of justice competent to take steps to safeguard the estate. In all cases of inheritance arising on the territory of one Party the diplomatic or consular personnel of the other has the right *ex officio* to represent their own citizens before the appropriate institutions of justice if they are absent or have not entrusted the matter to another authorized person. If a citizen of one Party dies while travelling on the territory of the other Party where he had no permanent residence or domicile, the articles he had with him for personal use are forthwith delivered to the diplomatic or consular institution of the other Party whose citizen he was. A notarized copy of the will must be supplied to the institutions of justice of the country of the deceased if it is probated on the territory of the other Party.

The institutions of both signatories take all necessary measures to protect or administer estates left on their respective territory by citizens of the other Party. Such steps are immediately communicated to the diplomatic or consular agencies of the other Party, which may take part in their execution, suggest that they be revised, rescinded or suspended, or demand that the movable property and documents of the deceased be turned over to them right away. At the close of the proceedings, the movable property or the money realized from the sale of movable or immovable property forming the estate which is inherited by individuals residing or domiciled on the territory of the other Party is delivered to the latter's diplomatic or consular institutions for transmission to the heirs, subject to prior notification of local creditors to file claims against the estate, the payment of all taxes and levies and permission from the competent authorities for the export of inherited articles or the transfer of money obtained through the sale thereof.

The numerous consular conventions concluded by the USSR in recent years with foreign states, "socialist" as well as "bourgeois", feature analogous clauses stipulating the consul's right to initiate steps for the protection of the interests of heirs to an estate left by a citizen of the consul's country who died within the latter's district, to be notified by the local authorities when such a death occurs and the steps taken to settle the inheritance, to request the implementation of special measures to safeguard the estate, to participate in inventorying the estate, to guarantee it against harm and injury and, if need be, arrange for its sale, to take possession in certain circumstances of the property and documents of the deceased and transmit them to the heirs after satisfying all legitimate claims and encumbrances. In the Sino-Soviet consular convention (there is no treaty of legal assistance between the two countries) a somewhat different norm applies to personal property left on the territory of one Party by a citizen of the other: instead of being subject to the law of the state of which the deceased was a citizen at the time of death, the property is governed by the law of the country where it is located (escheated personal property, however, is surrendered to the consul of the country of which the deceased was a citizen—as per the standard formula).

George Ginsburgs

ALIENS

Aliens in the USSR fall under the so-called "national regime", i.e., in most essential respects they are equated with local citizens and enjoy a comparable juridical status. Thus, the 1961 Principles of Civil Legislation of the USSR and Union Republics stipulate (arts. 122-123) that aliens and stateless persons residing in the USSR shall enjoy civil legal capacity equally with Soviet citizens, with such exemptions as may be established by the law of the USSR. The Council of Ministers of the USSR may, however, impose retaliatory restrictions on citizens of countries imposing special limitations on the civil legal capacity of Soviet citizens. Identical provisions, *mutatis mutandis*, appear in the 1961 Principles of Civil Procedure of the USSR and Union Republics (arts. 59-60). In sum, *de lege* foreigners resident in the USSR can, just as Soviet citizens, own personal property, inherit and will property, and exercise other corporeal and incorporeal rights, attend schools free of charge and, if admitted to institutions of higher learning, receive the regular stipendium allocated to their Soviet colleagues.

Soviet legal doctrine has always denounced such concepts as minimum standards of treatment of aliens, extraterritoriality, capitulations, etc., as flagrant encroachments on the sovereignty of the weaker nations by the leading imperialist powers.

In contrast with earlier Soviet practice, today aliens in the USSR do not enjoy political rights and, as in most countries, are not subject to the draft. Moreover, a number of specific rules and prohibitions apply to the foreigner living in the USSR which distinguish his position from that of the Soviet citizen. For example, an alien who arrives to the USSR for a protracted sojourn must register in the visa or foreigner's registration bureau of the police department and receives a special document—a *permis de séjour*. Upon transferring domiciles, the *de cujus* must report the change of address to the organs of the civil police. A short-term visitor to the USSR from abroad is required to register, but does not get a *permis de séjour*. An alien may be expelled from the USSR by administrative order for conduct prejudicial to the interests of the Soviet Union, but if he has been granted political asylum (*q.v.*) he cannot be returned to the country from which he originally fled.

Further, certain professions are barred to aliens, e.g., foreigners may not be members of the crew of a Soviet vessel (however, exceptions to this rule may be allowed in the procedure established by the USSR Council of Ministers). They cannot be plane crew members. They cannot engage in industrial fishing and exploitation of animal and plant marine resources within the territorial and internal waters of the USSR.

In several areas, the range of the rights afforded to alien residents by virtue of domestic legislation has been expanded through the conclusion of appropriate international treaties. For instance, a battery of bilateral agreements signed by the USSR and most of its socialist allies guarantees the citizens of one contracting power permanently residing on the territory of the other full parity with local citizens in all matters of social security and labor relations. The grid of accords linking the USSR and most members of the "socialist Commonwealth" which define the terms of mutual extension of legal assistance between the interested parties envisage the waiver of judicial taxes and court costs in rendering such services. The consular conventions which the Soviet Union has negotiated with quite a few countries (the list is steadily growing) likewise contain various clauses affecting the rights of the citizens of the respective states on each other's territory.

In principle, the Soviet law's attitude on the treatment of aliens in the USSR compares favorably with that of most countries. In the past, however, due to the realities of Soviet political life, the record here has often fallen far short of promise. With the current move toward liberalization of the domestic scene, theory and practice now show greater congruence and, despite occasional setbacks, the trend may be expected to continue, albeit progress is apt to come slowly and painfully.

George Ginsburgs

ALIMONY

The position is now governed by the 1968 Federal Principles of Marriage and Family Law and republican Codes (see FAMILY LAW).

The word here means payment by one spouse for the support of the other whether during or after marriage. Mutual duties arise only within a registered union. A spouse who is unable to work or a wife during pregnancy or for a year after confinement is entitled to a judicial award of alimony if the other spouse is in a position to provide it (Family Code, art. 25). The amount is assessed at a monthly figure depending on the financial and family position (Family Code, art. 28). Further, the right survives the dissolution of marriage if the claimant becomes unable to work during or within a year of the marriage; and if a wife conceives during marriage (the Code does not say by whom) she is entitled to support during pregnancy and for a year after confinement (Family Code, art. 26, par. 1 and 3).

If spouses have long been married (the Code does not say how long) a divorced spouse who reaches pensionable age within five years of dissolution may claim alimony (art. 26, par. 2). Conversely the court may take into account the brevity of the period of cohabitation and the unworthy behaviour of the claimant and cut alimony (art. 27).

The right is lost on re-marriage or recovery of working capacity (art. 29).

Payment is generally made by the employer, whether on the debtor's instructions or by court order.

B. Rudden

See also SUPPORT OF DEPENDANTS

ALL-UNION CHAMBER OF COMMERCE (see also *Appendix*)

The All-Union Chamber of Commerce (*Vsesoiuznaia Torgovaia Palata*) was set up in 1932 and is governed by a Statute of March 24, 1967. It is a "social [*obshchestvennaia*] organization" (see ASSOCIATIONS) and as such has legal personality. Its ordinary members are Soviet economic, co-operative and social organizations and also individual enterprises. They may be admitted to membership by decision of the Presidium of the Chamber of Commerce. The Presidium may invite Soviet and foreign organizations and private persons to become corresponding members. The general assembly of members elects a Council, which in turn elects the Presidium.

The function of the All-Union Chamber of Commerce is to promote foreign and internal trade. The internal function of the Chamber is less important and manifests itself mainly in the organization of trade and industry fairs. The Chamber plays a central role in the Soviet foreign trade organization. It establishes contacts with foreign economic and trade organizations, organizes Soviet trade and industrial fairs abroad, co-ordinates Soviet participation in trade and industrial fairs abroad, serves as an intermediary in the registration of Soviet trademarks, patents, etc. abroad, and of foreign ones in the Soviet Union, issues statements of origin for goods exported from the Soviet Union, provides expert opinion concerning the quality of goods, etc.

The Foreign Trade Arbitration Commission (*q.v.*) and the Maritime Arbitration Commission (*q.v.*) are attached to the All-Union Chamber of Commerce.

F. J. M. Feldbrugge

AMBASSADORS,
see DIPLOMATIC OFFICERS

AMNESTY

Art. 14 of the 1936 Constitution of the USSR deals *inter alia* with the rights of the Union of Soviet Socialist Republics and under par. x notes the issue of federal acts of amnesty. Such prerogatives belong also to the Union republics in respect of convictions passed by their courts, but so far as one is aware have never been used by them. The act of amnesty means the premature release of certain categories of convicted persons, or mitigation of the sentence. The act of amnesty may extend to the cancellation (expunging) of records of conviction (arts. 56, 57 Criminal Code RSFSR). An act of amnesty can also exclude criminal proceedings from being started or continued against persons who had committed the offences previous to the act but had not been tried, unless the accused person objects to the cessation for some reasons of his own, e.g. to establish by trial his innocence (art. 5 of Principles of Criminal Procedure of the USSR). Acts of amnesty may extend to administrative and disciplinary offences. As a rule it will not free the offender from the duty of making restitution. It is necessary to differentiate between amnesty and rehabilitation: amnesty pre-supposes that a real offence has been committed, rehabilitation pertains to people who were innocently convicted or convicted for offences which a more enlightened subsequent sense of justice would not regard as criminal, or when the convictions were passed in conditions contrary to the rule of law.

It is perhaps somewhat surprising that the Constitution omits to designate the office of state entitled to issue amnesties. Art. 31 of the Constitution states that the Supreme Soviet exercises all rights vested in the Union of Soviet Socialist Republics insofar as these rights have not been delegated to the competence of the Presidium of the Supreme Soviet or the Council of Ministers. Art. 49 deals with the special functions of the Presidium: it contains under (k) the right of pardon (i.e. individual acts of mercy) but does not mention amnesty. This lack of precision has not impeded the Presidium from issuing acts of amnesty on a rather large scale. From 1938 up to 1968 there were 18 acts of amnesty. All of them were passed by the Presidium, and only one, issued on the occasion of the twenty years' jubilee of the Red Army (January 24, 1938), was later confirmed by the Supreme Soviet. All acts of amnesty have been passed as decrees (*ukazy*), with the exception of the act of September 25, 1956, which was merely designated as an order (*postanovlenie*), as it extended only the application of the decree of the Presidium of September 17, 1955, "On the amnesty to Soviet citizens who collaborated with the enemy during the Great Fatherland War 1941-1945" to "military personnel of the Soviet Army and Fleet, who had surrendered into captivity" (*sdavshimsia v plen*). Acts of amnesty have been issued either to commemorate some special occasions (jubilees, anniversaries), or to mitigate and release from punishment persons whose initial treatment seemed either too harsh, or whose offence was elicited only by the special circumstances of the time and was not a manifestation of some ingrained criminal mentality (e.g. military personnel taken prisoner during the war).

The Procuracy of the USSR, the Supreme Court and the Presidium have the task of preparing and working out acts of amnesty. The applications for such acts are made by Soviet Government. There have been instances when pardons (but not amnesties) were granted by the Presidium of the Supreme Soviet on the application of foreign Heads of State. Thus it is known that such successful appliations have been made by the President of Austria, the German Democratic Republic and the Government of the German Federal Republic.

Bibl.: Basic Laws on the Structure of the Soviet State, translated and edited by Harold J. Berman and John B. Quigley Jr., 1969; T. A. Sintsova *Amnistiia i pomilovanie v sovetskom gosudarstvennom prave, Pravovedenie* No. 6, 1969, pp. 118-121.

R. Beermann

See also PARDON

AMUSEMENTS, see ENTERTAINMENTS

ANALOGY

Art. 12 of the 1961 USSR Principles of Civil Procedure provides that "in the absence of a statute (*zakon*) regulating a disputed relationship the court shall apply a statute regulating a similar relationship, and that in the absence of such a statute it shall proceed from the general principles and the sense of Soviet legislation". Application of a statute regulating similar relationships is called "analogy of statute" (*analogiia zakona*), while application of the general principles and the sense of Soviet legislation is called "analogy of law" (*analogiia prava*).

Analogy of statute is distinguished from extensive interpretation on the ground that the statute applied by analogy does not directly govern the disputed relationship, even if extensively interpreted (see INTERPRETATION OF LAWS). The difference, as one Soviet writer has put it, is that in extensive interpretation the operation of the statute is extended to facts which the legislator foresaw or could foresee but which he did not include in the text of the statute, while in analogy the operation of the statute is extended to instances which the legislator did not foresee and could not foresee.

Some Soviet jurists point out that analogy of law, as contrasted with analogy of statute, is a misnomer, since it involves extension of general legal principles to cases to which they are logically applicable rather than application of them to situations that are merely analogous to those provided for.

A typical example of analogy of statute is found in the decree of the Plenum of the USSR Supreme Court of December 12, 1940, in which a 1937 law requiring that dwelling space be reserved for six months for a person who departs temporarily from his family was held to be applicable by analogy also to a tenant sentenced to deprivation of freedom up to six months. The Supreme Court apparently took the view that the 1937 law was not directly applicable, even by extensive interpretation, since it speaks of the (voluntary) departure of the tenant.

Application of a statute by analogy is said to be permissible only when a) no statute is directly applicable to the given case, b) a statute does exist which provides for analogous cases, c) the analogous cases are similar in essential respects, and d) the given case is one which under general principles of law is subject to legal, and not merely moral, regulation.

A typical example of analogy of law is found in several cases in the 1940's and 1950's in which the USSR Supreme Court required state and social organizations to compensate citizens for harm suffered by them in saving socialist property from destruction. At that time there was no provision in the civil codes specifically dealing with this situation, but the Supreme Court awarded damages on the basis of Art. 131 of the USSR Constitution, which obliges every Soviet citizen "to safeguard and strengthen social, socialist ownership". Other examples of gap-filling by the courts on the basis of analogy of law derive from the fact that the early civil codes made no provision for contracts of bailment, for compensation (or liability) of persons who conduct the affairs of others without authorization (a common situation during the war when persons took care of the property of evacuees or draftees, paid their rent, etc.), and for many other matters.

In the first four decades after the Revolution, Soviet law authorized the application of the doctrine of analogy not only in civil cases but also in criminal cases. Indeed, Soviet jurists denounced as "bourgeois" the doctrine of *nullum crimen, nulla poena sine lege*. Thus Article 16 of the 1926 RSFSR Criminal Code and corresponding articles of the criminal codes of the other Republics stated: "If a given socially dangerous act is not directly provided for in the present Code, the basis and limits of responsibility for it shall be determined by application of those articles of the Code which provide for crimes most similar in nature." Under this provision the Soviet courts created a variety of new crimes and sometimes increased penalties for crimes already provided for.

In the late 1930's the doctrine of analogy in criminal law came under attack from Soviet writers, and its scope was severely restricted. During the war years, however, it was given new vitality. Thus in 1942, for example, the USSR Supreme Court decreed that theft committed by a group, either repeatedly or by persons previously convicted of stealing, should be characterized by analogy as banditry (an especially dangerous crime against the state, punishable by deprivation of freedom from three to 25 years or by death).

The 1958 USSR Principles of Criminal Law finally eliminated the doctrine of analogy from Soviet criminal law. Art. 3 of the Principles and corresponding articles of the republican criminal codes provide that only a person who has intentionally or negligently committed a socially dangerous act provided for by a criminal statute shall be subject to criminal responsibility or criminal punishment. The doctrine of analogy in criminal law is now generally condemned by Soviet jurists as contradictory to the principle of socialist legality.

The elimination of the doctrine of analogy from criminal legislation does not, of course, guarantee that it will not recur in judicial decisions under the guise of interpretation, especially in the application of criminal statutes that are not defined with sufficient precision. Also it may recur outside the criminal law in the narrow sense, that is, in the punishment of administrative offenses. Thus the republican statutes on comrades' courts give to those tribunals jurisdiction to apply "measures of social pressure" short of criminal punishment to persons who commit a variety of non-criminal acts, including "other anti-social acts not involving criminal liability". This is an example of "analogy of law" in quasi-criminal proceedings.

Harold J. Berman

See also CIVIL LAW; CIVIL PROCEDURE; CRIMINAL LAW; INTERPRETATION OF LAWS; LAW

ANNEXATION

Annexation, as a means of acquiring territory, is rejected by Soviet international law as a typical instrument of capitalist imperialism. The addition of territory by a one-sided and often violent act of a sovereign state is said to be contrary to the supreme principle of allotting territory to states—the principle of the self-determination of peoples (see SELF-DETERMINATION).

Nevertheless, Soviet international legal doctrine recognizes other means of acquiring territory which have about the same effect as annexation, in particular the realization of historical rights and the deprivation of territory owned by an aggressive state. It is not clear whether in these cases the principle of self-determination is still applicable with regard to the population of the territories in question.

The realization of historical rights is advocated against the opposite principle of prescription as a means of acquiring territory (which is rejected in this case). An example is the incorporation of former Polish, Czech, Hungarian and Roumanian territory after the Second World War.

Depriving an aggressor of part of his territory is considered lawful, partly as reparation for damage inflicted, and partly as a means of preventing future aggression. An example is the incorporation of half of East Prussia into the RSFSR after the Second World War. Another method of avoiding the use of the term "annexation" in regularizing territorial acquisitions is to resort to "voluntary adherence" as a universally recognized procedure for changing sovereignty and territory. The time-honoured *modus operandi* in this case is the setting-up of a shadow government accompanied by the military occupation of the area in question; this is shortly followed by elections or a referendum in which until now the population of the respective territories have always voted overwhelmingly in favour of joining the Soviet Union.

F. J. M. Feldbrugge

See also LEGAL HISTORY, BALTIC STATES; id., AZERBAIDZHAN; id., ARMENIA; id., GEORGIA; TERRITORY

ANNULMENT,
see DISSOLUTION OF MARRIAGE

APPELLATE PROCEDURE, CIVIL PROCEDURE

There are three main types of appellate procedure in Soviet law. The most common is *cassationary procedure* (arts. 282-318 RSFSR Code of Civil Procedure) and this will be dealt with first. In this case parties and participants in the original trial may appeal (see PARTIES). The public procurator may also initiate an appeal of this type, whether or not a procurator appeared in the court of first instance (see PROCURACY). Appeal lies from most courts but not from the Supreme Court of the USSR or of the Union republics. The appellant wishing to set aside a judgment (or to have the findings of the court changed, even if the result is materially the same), files a cassationary complaint, corresponding to an appeal motion or petition, within ten days of the judgment, in the trial or appeal court, usually the former, so that arrangements can be made to fix a trial and notify all interested parties. The complaint refers to the case and the decision and deals specifically and successively with the points on which the judgment is faulty, in the view of the complainant, following the successive paragraphs of the judgment. It asks for a reversal of the judgment, wholly or partially, and annexes various relevant documents. Failure to state grounds of appeal may be cured by providing later particulars. In any case the appeal court, once seized of the case, is not limited to the grounds stated, but will study all parts of the judgment and look after the interests of all parties, whether or not they appeal. The respondent is notified and can give explanations and file answering documents. He often files a formal case for the respondent, with paragraphs meeting the various points raised in the complaint, concluding with a request for the judgment to be sustained. The appeal court may proceed with an appeal even if it is withdrawn, since part of its function is to educate courts and not only to correct injustices. Fresh evidence may be submitted on appeals, and the appeal court may itself require the same to be sought. Non-appearance of the parties is also no obstacle to a trial of the appeal.

The appeal is heard orally and in public, by a court of three professional judges (no lay assessors). The case is called and the presence or absence of the parties noted. One judge acts as *rapporteur*, in the Continental fashion, and summarises the case and the judgment appealed from, and points out the effect of the materials filed in connection with the appeal. The parties may then give oral explanations. Witnesses are not summoned, as it is the original judgment rather than the case itself which is being judged at this point. Representatives of the public may give their views (see REPRESENTATION). The procurator will also state his opinion. The court must retire to consider its judgment, which is drawn up by one judge and signed by all three. Soviet law provides for a private opinion to be filed by a dissenting member of a court, and this appears more usual in appeal courts, since lay assessors would not have the skill to do this in trial courts. However only the majority judgment is announced publicly.

The powers of the appeal court do not differ markedly from those of other Continental courts, such as the French. The judgment can be upheld, but insubstantial errors of the trial court pointed out; the judgment may be reversed wholly or in part and a new trial ordered by the trial court, with the same or different judges sitting; the case may be reversed without further trial if the errors were of law, so that no further facts have to be established, e.g. the wrong measure of damages was applied or the law totally excludes claims of the kind made. Court practice follows the rule that the appellant is not to be made worse off as a result of his appeal, corresponding to the specific provision in the law of criminal procedure.

The decision of the appeal court identifies the case on appeal, describes the course of proceedings and the result in the trial court, gives reasons for the appeal court's findings of fact and application of legal rules, and concludes with specific conclusions for the disposal of the case. Although the court of re-trial is bound by procedural directions given on the appeal, it is not strictly bound by the appeal court's view of the facts or law, as judicial precedent is not recognised, but it normally tends to respect these. For a general discussion of the character of Soviet cassationary procedure, see CASSATION.

The second type of *appeal* is *by way of review* (arts. 319-332 of the RSFSR Code of Civil Procedure). We have seen that the Procuracy may file ordinary cassationary appeals before the time to appeal has expired. However, unlike the litigants themselves, the Procuracy may also file protests against judgments after they have entered into effect. Legal stability leads to a single ordinary appeal in the USSR and within a short time limit. Exceptional cases, however, demand a different treatment, in the interest of uniformity of interpretation of the law and to prevent serious injustice. In practice most reviews begin with complaints to the Procuracy by litigants who have no ordinary right of appeal or have lost a cassationary appeal and cannot go higher. The Procuracy occasionally rely on other sources, e.g. press reports. It is not uncommon for litigants to retain a lawyer to draft a formal revisory complaint similar to a cassationary complaint, e.g. where permission to exchange dwellings has been refused, it may point out that the court relied on a ground for refusal which is not listed in the appropriate statute.

There is a complicated system of review initiation, with hierarchies of courts and of procurators able to act in various circumstances. It may suffice to say that high judicial and Procuracy members may initiate reviews and that they are heard in general in the *Presidia* of city and provincial courts and in the civil chambers of the supreme courts of republics. Three or four successive appeals may be possible, terminating in the Full Bench (Plenum) of the Supreme Court (*q.v.*) of the USSR in some cases. The procurator may refuse to act or he may be overruled by a higher procurator, but he must give reasons for any refusal. The protest which he files with the court of review is like a cassationary complaint, and summarises the case and the decision under review, stating the mistakes which he believes to have been committed. Important cases go up to supreme courts, and the resulting decisions are reported in their bulletins.

Civil chambers consist of three trained judges; the number of judges in *Presidia* varies. The procedure is much the same as in ordinary appeals and the powers of the court are the same. However a mistake of law must be serious for a reversal of a judgment here in view of the inconvenience of a re-trial after so long a delay. The court of re-trial is free to make its own findings of fact and law (see also RES JUDICATA).

A third form of "appeal" is possible where *new facts* (arts. 333-337 of the RSFSR Code of Civil Procedure) come to light after the time to appeal from a judgment has expired. This is not a matter of fresh evidence, e.g. discovering a lost receipt where receipt had been alleged. (Of course fresh evidence on new facts can be proved which could not have been dealt with at the original trial, e.g. where all sides assumed a house in dispute was due for demolition, but it was later discovered that its inclusion on the demolition list was a mistake and demolition had never been ordered. (Of course fresh evidence on known facts may be the subject of appeal by way of review, discussed above.) It must also appear that the facts, if true, would have led to a different decision. Re-trial will usually follow.

If witnesses are convicted of perjury or documents used in evidence are shown to have been forged, this type of procedure can similarly be used, if in the result the decision was wrong.

There is also such an "appeal" where the court has acted in a criminal fashion, in order to verify the situation.

The application for review on newly discovered facts is filed in the court which gave the judgment complained of and not in a higher court. The application is in the same general form as a cassationary complaint and the proceedings are like those in most appeals. However there is a special rule that the court under this third form of appeal must itself try the case, instead of ordering a re-trial by a different court. Participants in the litigation must apply not later than three months after discovering the true facts. The Procuracy is not bound by this time limit. This proceeding partakes of some of the features of an ordinary trial and some of an appeal; in a sense the court completes its unfinished business.

Reversal of a judgment by way of cassation usually entails the return of damages received under the judgment, but where it is reversed by way of review this does not apply to physical tort or labour dispute cases. However future periodic payments will not be made.

A. K. R. Kiraffy

APPELLATE PROCEDURE, CRIMINAL PROCEDURE

Appellate courts enjoy broad powers of review over the decisions of trial courts in criminal matters. Five different types of "appeals" must be distinguished: appeal from actions of the investigator (or person conducting the inquiry), cassational appeal, cassational protest, private appeal, and private protest. (In addition to the system of appeals, court decisions may be reviewed by higher courts by way of supervision. See RES JUDICATA.)

An appeal (*zhaloba*) from an action of the investigator (or person conducting the inquiry) is taken not to a court but to a procurator, either orally or in writing (cf. arts. 218-220 Code of Criminal Procedure). If the appeal is oral, it is recorded in a protocol, which is signed both by the person making the appeal and by the person receiving it. The individual (or his attorney) may make his appeal to a procurator either directly or through the investigator (or person conducting the inquiry). If the appeal is made to the investigator (or person conducting the inquiry), he must send it to a procurator within twenty-four hours along with his own explanations on the substance of the appeal. Such an appeal does not act to suspend execution of the action being appealed, unless so decided by the procurator or investigator (or person conducting the inquiry). The procurator must render a decision on the appeal within three days and must inform the person who made it of his decision. If he rejects the appeal, the procurator must state his reasons. The decision of a procurator with respect to an appeal may in turn be appealed to a higher procurator. Apart from any appeals, the procurator also has the power to transfer the case to a different investigator.

The procedure under which the remaining four types of appeals are made is called cassation (see also CASSATION). Cassation is the ordinary procedure for review of trial court decisions by higher courts. When the action is brought by a procurator, it is called a "protest". When brought by any other party, it is called an "appeal". When the action is brought against the final judgment of the trial court, it is called "cassational" (cassational appeal, cassational protest). When brought against any other decision of the trial court, it is called "private" (private appeal, private protest).

The cassation procedure may be resorted to only where the trial court decision in question has not yet entered into force. After that time, either of two extraordinary procedures may be used: supervision proceedings and reopening of the case on the basis of newly-discovered circumstances (see REMEDIES).

The procurator and parties may appeal the decisions of any trial court, with the exception of the Supreme Court of the USSR and the supreme courts of the Union republics. Decisions of the supreme courts as courts of first instance may, however, be reviewed in supervision proceedings. An appeal is always taken to the next higher court within the judicial hierarchy. Where the court of first instance is a people's court (as is normally the case), the appeal thus is taken, depending on the administrative unit in which the court is located, to a court at the level of an autonomous republic, territory (*krai*), province, city, autonomous province, or national area. Where one of the latter courts was the court of first instance, the appeal is taken to the supreme court of the Union republic.

A broad range of individuals is empowered to bring appeals. The procurator has the right (and the duty) to bring a cassational protest against any trial court judgment he deems illegal or unfounded. The judgment may also be appealed by the defendant, his attorney or legal representative, or by the victim or his representative. A defendant acquitted at trial may appeal the court's statement of the reasons for the acquittal. A civil plaintiff, civil defendant, and their representatives may appeal that part of the judgment relating to the civil suit. The social accuser and social defender, however, do not have the right to file an appeal (see TRIAL; DEFENDANT).

Cassational appeals and protests are ordinarily made through the court that rendered the judgment, though they may also be made directly to the appellate court. The time limit for bringing an appeal or protest is set by the republican criminal procedure codes. In most republics, this limit is seven days from the day trial court judgment is rendered; in all republics, the time period begins to run against a defendant in confinement from the day he receives a copy of the court judgment (which may be up to three days after it is rendered). The trial court must inform other interested parties of the filing of an appeal or protest, and these latter may familiarize themselves with the appeal or protest and may file written arguments.

If a person who has the right to appeal or protest misses the deadline for doing so, he may request an extension from the trial court. The court hears such a motion in an administrative session and may call in the person who made the motion to give explanations. If the court refuses the extension, the person who made the motion may appeal (or protest, in the case of the procurator) to the next higher court, which may decide to hear the case on the merits.

The trial court keeps the case until the deadline for filing appeals and protests expires, at which time it sends the case up to the appellate court. The filing of an appeal or protest automatically suspends execution of the challenged judgment or ruling.

Under the republican codes, the appellate court must hold its hearing on the case on a date set either by the trial court or by the appellate court itself, but in any event within a relatively short period of time (the maximum in most instances is ten days after receipt of the case by the appellate court). The panel hearing the case in an appellate court consists of three judges, with no people's assessors.

The hearing must ordinarily be public, unless state secrets might be revealed. The court may exclude observers, however, where the defendant is under sixteen years of age, where the offense is of a sexual nature, or where intimate aspects of the lives of the parties might be revealed. The procurator and defense counsel normally participate, though their failure to appear does not act as a bar to consideration of the case. The defendant may also appear, if the court so decides.

The codes require that one of the three judges, acting as reporter, explain the case and state the grounds for the appeal or protest. Then the procurator, defense counsel, and other participants make their arguments.

The appellate court may resolve the case in one of four ways: it may leave the judgment unchanged, annul the judgment and return the case for further investigation or re-trial, annul the judgment and terminate the case, or modify the judgment. If the appellate court sends the case back, it must specify the stage at which further work on the case is to commence. If the court returns the case because of errors made by the trial court, it returns the case to the same court (but to a new judge and assessors) or to a different court.

If the appellate court modifies the trial court's judgment, it may not do so by establishing new facts not proved at trial or by relying on evidence rejected by the trial court. (If the appellate court disagrees with the trial court's finding on the facts, it may return the case for a new trial.) In order to decide whether or not it agrees with facts established at trial, or whether facts not established at trial should have been investigated, the appellate court may receive new evidence not presented at trial.

The codes place limits on the appellate court's right to modify a trial court judgment. The appellate court may not increase the punishment or apply a criminal code provision concerning a more serious crime. It may, however, upon protest by the procurator or appeal by the victim, annul a judgment on the grounds that the punishment should have been more severe or that a harsher section of the criminal code should have been applied. An appellate court may annul a judgment of acquittal only upon protest of the procurator or upon appeal by the victim or the acquitted defendant himself.

The All-Union Principles of Criminal Procedure list those circumstances under which an appellate court may annul or modify a trial court's judgment. These are: one-sidedness or incompleteness of the inquiry or preliminary investigation or trial proceedings, nonconformity of the court's conclusions as stated in the judgment to the factual circumstances of the case, substantial violation of the criminal procedure law, improper application of the criminal law, and nonconformity of the punishment assigned by the court to the seriousness of the crime or to the personality of the defendant. A "substantial violation" of the criminal procedure law is defined by the codes as such a violation that, by depriving a participant of his rights as guaranteed by law or by any other means, prevented the court from uncovering all circumstances of the case or prevented (or might have prevented) the court from reaching a legal and well-founded judgment. Thus, in each instance the appellate court must determine the extent to which the procedural violation served to keep the court from establishing truth in the case.

The codes do, however, list certain violations that are considered so "substantial" as to require annulment of the conviction in every instance. While the violations so listed vary from republic to republic, they typically include the rendering of a judgment by an improperly composed panel; consideration of the case in the absence of the defendant, where the law requires his participation; consideration of the case without participation of defense counsel in those instances when his participation is obligatory; violation of secrecy during discussion by the court of the judgment; failure of one of the members of the court to sign the judgment. In addition, the appellate court must overturn a conviction if the trial court entered a conviction despite the presence of one of the following factors: the crime was not committed; the act does not contain the elements of a crime; the period of limitations had expired; an act of amnesty prevented prosecution for the given offense; the defendant had been pardoned; the defendant had not attained the age at which it is permissible to indict for the given offense; in the case of a crime prosecuted by private accusation, there has been a reconciliation between the victim and the defendant, or the victim failed to make a complaint; the defendant is dead (except where the purpose of the proceedings is to "rehabilitate" the person, or where the case is being re-opened with respect to other defendants on the basis of newly discovered circumstances); and *res judicata.*

Cf. also arts. 325-355 RSFSR Code of Criminal Procedure.

John B. Quigley, Jr.

APPEAL, see APPELLATE PROCEDURE; REMEDIES

APPRENTICES, see TRAINING; YOUNG EMPLOYEES

ARBITRATION

Three different types of arbitration operate in the USSR; State Arbitration, Third-Party Arbitration and Foreign Trade Arbitration.

State Arbitration. This machinery dates back to a decree of the Russian Republic of 21 September 1922 but its legal basis has been modified from time to time, most recently in 1960 (December 3). The main idea is that the economy is governed by state departments, but through the instrumentality of state businesses (economic enterprises) which enjoy juridical personality. Legal relations are entered into by the appropriate enterprises in accordance with the overall State Plan and in order to fulfil that Plan.

Disputes which arise between these enterprises are not triable by the ordinary courts or by higher administrative echelons but by state arbitration tribunals which partake of some of the characteristics of each. The ordinary courts proved inexpert in technical matters and too remote from the economic administrative machine to observe its changing requirements. On the other hand, administrative control of relations between enterprises was, it was feared, likely to lead to mutual excuses and a lack of reliability and responsibility by enterprises. Under the present system the enterprise is liable to suffer material loss, if found guilty by State Arbitration, as well as disciplinary sanctions from above.

The State Arbitration tribunal differs markedly from the regular judicial court. In a court there is a professional lawyer as permanent judge in most cases and two lay assessors. The chairman of an arbitration may be a chemist or engineer and he sits with two persons, each nominated by one of the parties to the dispute. A regular judge has only one of the three votes, but the arbitrator may decide a case by himself if he cannot persuade the two representatives to agree. Parties are also bound to try to reach a peaceful settlement before resorting to arbitration.

Just as the Supreme Court (*q.v.*) of the USSR issues directives binding on all other courts, and the Supreme Soviet passes basic laws binding in all the Soviet republics, so the Court of Arbitration of the Council of Ministers of the USSR gives directives to lower echelons of arbitration as to the interpretation of economic regulations and enacts rules of procedure (1963) for them, as well as drafting legislation in the economic field.

Like the Procuracy the arbitration tribunal has power to initiate proceedings *ex officio* and to take steps to bring to the attention of the appropriate government bodies any shortcomings discovered in the working of state enterprises and their higher organs.

There is considerable dispute as to whether the arbitrator is really a judicial officer or an administrative official, since his decision is based on economic planning as well as legal sources. The Chief Arbitrator of a tribunal is responsible for the awards made by his subordinates and has power to change them, like the presidium of a regular court (see RES JUDICATA). There is no other appeal, unlike the opportunities in court procedure.

The jurisdiction of state arbitrators is partly territorial, partly a matter of administrative subjection, in the sense that where two enterprises in the same district have a dispute it is dealt with locally, and if in different parts of the same republic by a republican arbitrator. The supreme tribunal deals with disputes between enterprises operating in different republics or under direct federal administration. If disputes arise within the same ministry they are dealt with in that ministry.

The former system of economic councils also had its own arbitration tribunals.

There are two main types of dispute submitted to arbitration: refusals by contract partners to sign contracts where required to do so by the Plan, and defaults in performance of contracts, such as delays in delivery and deliveries of poor quality goods. In the first type of case a note of the terms in dispute is submitted to the arbitrator, who resolves them and can then sign the contract on behalf of the unwilling party or parties. In the second type of case he applies the general rules of liability imposed by law for breach of contract, modified by special decrees on state industry. Procedure under the 1963 Rules is broadly similar to court procedure, e.g. statements of claim and defences are filed by the parties.

The materials used by the arbitrators are generally commercial documents like contracts, invoices, delivery notes and inspector's reports. The arbitrator may inspect the goods or premises involved and use his own expert knowledge, or may consult another expert. Various bodies connected with the production process may be asked to assist, and various links in the chain of production may be involved, even if not technically parties to the contract.

An actual oral hearing is provided, and decisions are not made merely by correspondence, unless the parties waive their attendance and the documents sufficiently prove the case.

Awards of the tribunals are enforced by warrant, which is generally served on the losing party's bank by judicial bailiffs (*q.v.*).

Third-Party Arbitration. The 1960 By-law on State Arbitration and the 1964 By-law for (Citizens') Arbitration (Appendix 3 to the RSFSR Code of Civil Procedure) allow litigants to submit disputes to a third party if both are willing to do so. This arbitrator may be selected *ad hoc* in each case or named in the original contract. An individual or a body may be chosen. Sometimes two representative arbitrators are chosen to select an impartial referee, or several arbitrators are appointed and may give a majority decision. No strict procedural rules are laid down, but each side must have a fair opportunity to put its case and reasons must be given for all decisions. Awards are enforced through judicial channels.

Foreign Trade Arbitration. The USSR trade monopoly is here exercised by special import and export enterprises. The USSR enters into bilateral trade treaties, and some multilateral treaties (e.g. the Comecon Convention). Provision is generally made for the submission of disputes to the national chamber of commerce of the defendant's country. Any system of law may be stipulated by the parties as applicable. See FOREIGN TRADE ARBITRATION.

A. K. R. Kiraffy

See also MARITIME ARBITRATION

ARCHIVES

Public archives in the USSR are under the control of the Chief Department of Archives, which is attached to the Council of Ministers of the USSR. The most important archives are: the Central Party Archives, the Central State Archives of the October Revolution and the Supreme Organs of State Power and State Administration of the USSR, the Central State Archives of the Economy of the USSR, the Central State Archives of the Soviet Army, the Central State Archives of the Soviet Navy, the Central State Archives of the Literature and Art of the USSR, the Central State Archives of Ancient Documents, the Central State Historical Archives of the USSR, the Central State Archives of Military History and the Central State Archives for Film, Photographic and Sound Documents of the USSR. There are other central archives in the Union republics and archives at province and *raion* (town) level. The material in these archives, together with the contents of departmental archives and specified material in libraries and museums makes up the State Archival Fund (*Gosudarstvennyi Arkhivnyi Fond*). The Chief Department of Archives is headed by a Chief (*nachal'nik*), who is appointed by the Council of Ministers of the USSR. The Chief of the Archives Department is chairman of the departmental board (*kollegiia*), which consists of the chiefs of some of the department's sections and of some of the central state archives, the chief of the Central Party Archives, the director of the Historical Institute of the Academy of Sciences, and some other high-ranking officials from the sphere of archives and history.

F. J. M. Feldbrugge

ARMY & NAVY, see MILITARY LAW; MILITARY SERVICE

ARRAIGNING & EXAMINING MAGISTRATES, see CRIMINAL INVESTIGATION

ARREST

Arrest is a compulsory measure of criminal procedure consisting of detention and/or custody. For arrest of property, see SEIZURE.

Habeas Corpus as formulated in the USSR Constitution ("No one may be subjected to arrest except by decree of a court or with the sanction of a procurator") does not apply to detention, although it may last up to three days and includes an interrogation. The power of the procurator to sanction custody decreed during preliminary proceedings is justified by his supposed status as supervisor, and by not being directly engaged in investigation and prosecution; however, the procurator is not only the future prosecutor, but may also order any investigative action or even conduct it personally at any time. Distinguished Soviet authors demand also the requirement of a court warrant for custody during preliminary proceedings based on a special session in which the defendant participates.

Immunity from criminal prosecution includes a prohibition of arrest. Foreign diplomats may be subjected to procedural action only with their consent which should be obtained through the (Republic or Union) Ministry of Foreign Affairs. Deputies of the Supreme Soviet of USSR, Union republics and autonomous republics may be arrested only with the consent of their soviet or its presidium, members of the USSR Supreme Court only with the consent of the USSR Supreme Soviet or its presidium, members of Union republic supreme courts only with the consent of the respective Supreme Soviet and other judges only with the consent of the presidium of the republic Supreme Soviet. Minors may be arrested only in exceptional circumstances (depending on the gravity of the crime).

Detention means temporary deprivation of liberty of the suspect without procuratorial sanction which leads either to custody (if sanctioned) or to speedy release and which is possible only in the period from before the initiation of the case until the charging of the suspect as accused (see DEFENDANT). It must be distinguished from the administrative detention of violators of the public order which is not a procedural measure. The agency of inquiry and the investigator, procurator, and judge are entitled to detain. It is doubtful whether all members of inquiry agencies (in practice: policemen) have the right to detain; legal doctrine assumes that apprehension by policemen who are not specifically entrusted with inquiry but with maintaining public order is not a procedural but an administrative detention, so that the detained person must be handed over to the competent agency of inquiry without any delay. There is no procedural right to detention by private people even in flagrant cases; but, in practice, such detention is treated like legitimate defence, i.e. as a privilege of substantive law. In case of hooli-

ganism (see HOOLIGANISM) the right of citizens to detain is codified by federal law. A detainee can only be a suspect because the accused (see DEFENDANT) is subject to custody or compulsory appearance.
Conditions: Suspicion of the commission of a crime punishable by imprisonment; administrative offences and non-criminal violations of order in judicial sessions cannot entail detention. Suspicion alone is sufficient a) in flagrant cases, b) if the suspect is identified immediately by an eye-witness, or c) if traces are found on or around the suspect. If suspicion is based on other circumstances, one of the following additional grounds must be given: a) attempt to escape, b) lack of fixed abode, or c) lack of identification. If these conditions are fulfilled, detention is permitted, but is mandatory only in cases of hooliganism.
The inviolability of the person, a constitutional principle requiring the order of a court or procurator for the legitimacy of arrest, is considered to be observed because of the provisional character of detention: within 24 hours the procurator has to be informed and within another 48 hours he must decide either to sanction custody or to release the suspect; before his decision he should, but need not necessarily, interrogate the suspect. An interrogation by the police, which must be conducted immediately, at the latest within 24 hours, is sufficient. The detainee may make a complaint against the agency of inquiry, investigator, or procurator (see REMEDIES; APPELLATE PROCEDURE), give an explanation or file a petition; before his interrogation, he must be informed of these rights. But the suspect has no right to counsel, nor to be informed precisely of the complete charge before answering questions. The detainee is held in a "cell of preliminary confinement", which is distinguished both from the "isolation for inquiry" (see below) and from prison. Detention which is known to be unlawful, i.e. lacking the aforementioned conditions, is a crime, the punishment of which differs among the Union republics, but is considerably lower than the punishment for unlawful custody; this provision is not applicable to judges who are punished more severely for delivering an unjust decision.
Custody is the strongest restraining measure (see RESTRAINING MEASURES) consisting in the confinement under guard of the accused or, exceptionnally, the suspect with the sanction of the procurator or upon court ruling. The execution of custody is regulated not only by the Code of Criminal Procedure (art. 96) but also by a special federal law of 1969. Custody is distinguishable from detention in that it is a restraining measure, applicable only after the institution of a case and as a rule only after charging (see DEFENDANT), its duration is different (maximum of nine months instead of three days) and although decreed by the police or investigator, it is executable only after sanction by the procurator if not based on court warrant.
The conditions of custody are a) the conditions of restraining measures (i.e. suspicion of escape or of obstruction of the investigation or of repetition; for details see RESTRAINING MEASURES); b) that the case involves a crime punishable by imprisonment (i.e. suspicion of such a degree as to enable the making of a formal charge; for details see DEFENDANT); c) that no other restraining measure suffices to prevent escape, obstruction or repetition. As an exception to a), the Union republic codes enumerate a fairly extensive list of serious crimes, among them political crimes, the suspicion of which permits custody without any other grounds; moreover, federal law lays down a rule that in cases of hooliganism the defendant is taken in custody.
The ordinary maximum term of custody is two months; in extraordinarily complex cases it can be extended up to three months by the

middle rank procurators of Union republic level and up to an absolute maximum of nine months by the USSR Procurator General. These terms are counted from the factual deprivation of liberty, i.e. in the case of preceding detention, from the day of detention. A suspect may be taken into custody only by way of exception: if there is sufficient ground to justify a charge, but a formal charge cannot yet be presented because specific circumstances have not yet been investigated. In this case, the formal charge must be presented within ten days; this term too begins with the first day of any preceding detention.

The warrant, if not decreed by court decision or direct resolution of the procurator, is formulated and reasoned by the agency of inquiry or investigator, but is effective only with the written—but usually not reasoned—sanction of the procurator. Not all republics require that relatives and workplace be informed; if a foreigner is taken into custody, a copy of the warrant has to be sent to the Ministry of Foreign Affairs.

The ordinary place of custody is the "investigative isolation cell". The prisoner may only be kept provisionally in a "cell of preliminary confinement" for up to three days or, if otherwise impossible, up to 30 days, or even in a prison. Prisoners are usually kept in community cells, though they may be kept in single cells with the sanction of the procurator. Money and other things are seized and mail is censored. They are kept separate from prisoners serving punishment; minors are separated from adults and from convicted minors. Labour is voluntary. If counsel is admitted to the case, he is entitled to unrestricted contact with the prisoner. The prisoner has the right to receive money transfers and parcels up to 5 kg a months, to buy food and articles of daily consumption and to wear his own clothes. Women may have their children up to two years of age with them; other minor children must be transferred to the care of relatives or institutions by the agency of inquiry, investigator, procurator, or court which has also to take measures to protect the property and dwelling space of the prisoner. As a rule, the prisoner may be visited not more than once a month for up to two hours with the permission of the investigating person. The prisoner is entitled to make a complaint and give an explanation to state agencies, social organizations, and functionaries; if it is adressed to the procuracy, it has to be mailed uncensored within 24 hours.

The term served in custody must be completely deducted from the term of punishment when the accused is sentenced to deprivation of freedom or assignment to a disciplinary battalion, and at the rate of one day for three days when sentenced to corrective labour, exile or banishment. Custody known to be unlawful is a crime punishable by imprisonment, the maximum term of which differs among the Union republics (e.g. RSFSR 1 year; Latvia 3 years). Unlawful custody is compensated for by money amounting to double the former wage and by privileges concerning dwelling space; the time spent in custody is put to the account of working time with respect to social security.

M. Fincke

ARSON

Arson is not mentioned as a separate offence in any of the criminal codes of the Union republics. It is usually included in the definition of offences of a more general nature.

A basic distinction with regard to arson is to be made between state and public property on the one hand, and personal property on the other.

Arson is named as a means of intentional destruction or damaging of state or public property in arts. 68 and 98 par. 2 Criminal Code of the RSFSR. Art. 68 is devoted to sabotage, for which offence the specific intent of weakening the Soviet state is required. The penalty in this case is from 8 to 15 years' deprivation of freedom combined with (mandatory) confiscation of property, and with (non-mandatory) exile (from 2 to 5 years), or the death-penalty combined with (mandatory) confiscation of property (see also SABOTAGE).

Where the specific intent to weaken the Soviet state is absent, the intentional destruction or damaging of state or public property by means of arson is governed by art. 98 par. 2, the maximum penalty in this case being 10 years' deprivation of freedom.

The same offence committed against the personal property of citizens is punished by a maximum of 8 years' deprivation of freedom.

Arts. 99 and 150 mention the destruction or damaging of property (state public, and personal, respectively) through careless behaviour with fire (maximum penalty in both cases: 3 years' deprivation of freedom, or 1 year corrective labour).

The intentional destruction or damaging, by military personnel, of military property is governed by art. 251. The unlawful destruction of property belonging to the local population, by military personnel, in an area of military actions is governed by art. 267 Criminal Code.

F. J. M. Feldbrugge

See also FIRES AND FIRE PREVENTION

ARTEL', see COOPERATIVES

ASSAULT

The Criminal Code of the RSFSR distinguishes various types of assault and infliction of bodily injury.

Art. 108 of this Code deals with an *intentional infliction of grave bodily injury*. This is defined as an intentional infliction of bodily injury dangerous to life or resulting in loss of sight, of hearing, or of any organ, or in loss by an organ of its functions, or in mental illness or any other impairment of health, in combination with persistent loss of at least one third of the capacity to work, or an interruption of pregnancy or permanent disfigurement of the face; it is punished by deprivation of freedom for a term not exceeding eight years.

The same actions, if they cause the victim's death or assume the character of torment or torture or are committed by an especially dangerous recidivist, are punishable by deprivation of freedom for a term of five to twelve years. (For the meaning of "intentional", see MENS REA).

Art. 109 of the Criminal Code of the RSFSR deals with an *intentional infliction of less grave bodily injury*. This is defined as an injury not dangerous to life and not causing the consequences provided for in art. 108 of the Code, but provoking a lengthy impairment of health or a significant persistent loss of at least one third of the capacity to work. This offence is punishable by deprivation of freedom for a term not exceeding three years or by corrective labour for a term not exceeding one year.

The same actions, if they assume the character of torment or torture or are committed by an especially dangerous recidivist, are punished by deprivation of freedom for a term not exceeding five years.

Art. 110 of the Criminal Code of the RSFSR deals with an *intentional infliction of grave or less grave bodily injury while in a state of strong mental agitation*. This is defined as an action provoked by force or grave insult on the part of the victim or provoked by any other unlawful actions of the victim or such actions as result or could result in grave consequences for the guilty person or his near ones. This offence is punished by deprivation of freedom for a term not exceeding five years or by corrective labour for a term not exceeding one year.

According to art. 111 of the RSFSR Cri-

minal Code the *infliction of grave or less grave bodily injury while exceeding the limits of necessary defence* is punishable by deprivation of freedom for a term not exceeding one year or by corrective labour for the same term (see NECESSARY DEFENCE).
Art. 112 of the RSFSR Criminal Code provides that an *intentional causing of light bodily injury or the infliction of a beating* resulting in an impairment to health of short duration or an insignificant persistent loss of capacity to work is punishable by deprivation of freedom for a term not exceeding one year or by corrective labour for the same term.
The same actions not resulting in the above mentioned consequences are punishable by deprivation of freedom for a term not exceeding six months or by corrective labour for the same term, or by a fine not exceeding fifty roubles, or entail the application of measures of social pressure.
Art. 113 of the RSFSR Criminal Code states that the systematic infliction of a beating or other action which assume the character of torture if they do not result in the consequences indicated in arts. 108 and 109 of this Code, are punishable by deprivation of freedom for a term not exceeding three years.
According to art. 114 of the RSFSR Criminal Code a *negligent infliction of grave or less grave bodily injury* is punishable by deprivation of freedom for a term not exceeding two years or by corrective labour for a term not exceeding one year or by social censure. (For the meaning of "negligent", see MENS REA).
Generally an assault may result from commission or omission, an example of the latter case being a systematic deprivation of food.
Assault may be committed either by physical or by psychological actions. The latter may cause mental illness.
As the RSFSR Criminal Code distinguishes between i) grave, ii) less grave, and iii) light bodily injury, forensic medical experts determine the degree of such injury.
Rules determining these degrees of injury were laid down for the RSFSR on April 4, 1961, by the Ministry of Protection of Health of the RSFSR.
An intentional infliction of grave bodily injury which causes the death of the victim is distinguished from homicide only by the intent of the offender.
An impairment of health exceeding four weeks is considered to be "lengthy" in the meaning of the Criminal Code.
An impairment of health during a period of between seven days and four weeks is considered to be of a "short" duration.
In the case of a light bodily injury the offender is accused only upon a complaint by the victim (art. 27 of the Code of Criminal Procedure of the RSFSR).
Criminal responsibility for assault is, in principle, confined to persons aged 16 years or more. However, in the case of an intentional causing of grave and less grave bodily injury, including the exceeding of the limits of necessary defence in these cases, and also in the cases of intentional causing of light bodily injury which causes impairment of health, those aged 14 years or more are held to be criminally responsible.

L. Kos-Rabcewicz-Zubkowski

ASSIGNMENTS
The transfer (assignment) of the rights and duties of contracting parties to third parties is governed by rules laid down in arts. 211-216 Civil Code. The rules relating to transfer have undergone only minor changes since the 1922 Code. When applied to an actual case both the set of rules concerning assignment of rights and those regulating assignment of duties may well come into play at the same time and are often thus interwoven. This is due to the above-mentioned fact that either party often performs the roles both of debtor and creditor at least to some extent (particu-

larly in bilateral contracts). Both sets of rules are then applied.

As the transfer of the rights and duties of one or both parties means a considerable change in the contractual situation (even if the legal content is unchanged), any kind of agreement to make an assignment requires the same formalities as the original contract (written form, notary's attestation, etc.) at the risk of invalidity.

The rules on transfer may, with a few exceptions, be excluded by agreement outside the important field of obligations based on planning norms, which always require specific performance by the individual addressees of the plan (creditor as well as debtor).

Transfer of the creditor's rights normally only requires an agreement between the assignor and the assignee (which may also regulate the handing over of documents relevant to the claim, etc.), for the personality of the creditor is generally of minor importance to the debtor so long as the content of the latter's obligation remains unchanged. In a few cases where the right to receive the debtor's performance is exclusively bound up with the personality or individuality of the creditor, assignment of rights cannot take place.

Damages for personal injuries, maintenance obligations, etc., may be mentioned on the one hand as examples and, on the other hand, obligations under a plan where the rule of specific performance by every organization prevails. The Civil Code also anticipates that the right of assignment can be limited by special legislative provisions; transport legislation, for instance, restricts the right to assign a claim against a carrier.

Furthermore, as these rules have the character of rules of construction, the debtor and creditor always have the right to exclude, by agreement, the power of the latter to transfer his rights without the consent of the former.

The new creditor's rights and duties towards the debtor will, in principle, be the same as his predecessor's—the legal position between the parties will not be altered by an assignment on the creditor's side. It follows that the assignor—and not the debtor—will be responsible for any shortcomings in the creditor's position, account of which has not been taken in the contract of assignment (this rule differs from that laid down by the 1922 legislation). The assignor will not be responsible for the debtor's failure to perform (unless he makes himself responsible by a separate guarantee). The debtor is entitled to perform his contractual obligations to the former creditor as long as he has not been given notice of the assignment.

The aim of the assignment rules is that the content of the mutual legal relations of the parties should remain unchanged not only in legal terms but also in terms of quantity and quality. That is the reason why the new party never acquires a better contractual position than his predecessor, unless the parties agree otherwise. And that also explains why substitution of the debtor—transfer of an obligation—cannot take place without the consent of the creditor, as the personal qualities of the debtor normally are of the greatest importance in considering the likelihood of proper performance. For the same reason any security (in the form of suretyship or a pledge or mortgage) provided by a third party for the original debtor will not remain valid if the third party does not agree to the assignment. The new debtor cannot claim any right of set-off to which his predecessor was entitled, but he may put up his own counter-claim, if any, for the same purpose.

As in the case of the assignment of a creditor's rights, the parties' freedom to modify the rules of assigment by agreement is limited by the planning norms which usually do not admit of any substitution of the parties originally designated.

A. Ådahl

ASSOCIATION

Societies

In a broad sense any voluntary association or society of citizens which aims at the development of the initiative of the popular masses in the area of socio-political organization and activities, in the interests of the building of communism, is regarded as a "social organization" (*obshchestvennaia organizatsiia*) by Soviet law.

The definition of social organization derives from art. 126 of the Constitution, which, while recognizing the right of citizens to unite in social organizations, contains a non-limitative list of such organizations.

First of all, because of its size, importance and the scope of its functions, the Communist Party of the Soviet Union (*q.v.*) is mentioned, the most elevated form of socio-political organization, the vanguard of the workers in the struggle for the achievement of a communist society, the leading core of any state or social organization, the voluntary association of the most conscious and active Soviet citizens. Furthermore, trade unions (see UNIONS), youth organizations (especially the Komsomol), co-operative organizations (collective farms, building and consumers' co-operatives, etc.), sports and defence organizations and other voluntary associations and groups of individuals, even if they are not expressly mentioned in the law (such as the commissions for the affairs of minors, the voluntary people's guards, the comrade's courts, the Foreign Trade Arbitration Commission). (See also CO-OPERATIVES; SPORTS; KOLKHOZ; PEOPLE'S GUARDS; COMRADES' COURTS; MINORS; FOREIGN TRADE ARBITRATION).

Social organizations, as a rule, own property and enjoy more or less full legal personality. Social organizations in a strict sense (i.e. as a civil law category) enjoy full legal personality (art. 11 Principles of Civil Legislation) and may pursue any aims which are not economic (socio-cultural, technical, educational, scientific). The non-economic purpose of its own activities distinguishes the social organizations *stricto sensu* from co-operative enterprises, which by virtue of the Constitution and, above all, of the Principles of Civil Legislation are not entered in the category of social organizations (although a voluntary association may be allowed to found and operate auxiliary enterprises, provided the enterprises directly serve the institutional objective of the organization).

Within the category of social organizations a further distinction can be made between trade unions, voluntary associations (*dobrovol'nye obshchestva i soiuzy*), professional unions and artists' societies (*soiuzy lits tvorcheskikh professii*).

The foundation, extinction and supervision of the activities of voluntary associations are generally regulated by republican law (in the RSFSR: Regulations of July 10, 1932).

Founder-members may be legal entities or natural persons (who have attained the age of eighteen). Federal, republican or local administrative agencies (according to the federal, republican or local character of the association to be founded) exercise original control covering the lawfulness and the expediency of the association on the basis of the draft by-laws submitted by the founders. They also have the power, as a rule, to dissolve the association if the activities of the association are not in accordance with its statutory aims, or harm the interests of the state. But, once approved, it is the by-laws which determine the aims of the association, the rights and duties of members, the admission requirements for new members, the grounds for discontinuation, the criteria for the appointment and the functioning of managing and supervising agencies (to which only members of the association may be appointed), the amount of membership fees (which contribute to the assets of the association), etc. DOSAAF (Voluntary Association for Assisting the Army, the Air Force and the Navy) and the Union of Red Cross and Red Crescent Associations are examples of associations active in the sphere of national defence. *Dinamo* and *Spartak* are famous sports societies (both are members of the Union of sports societies and organizations of the USSR; see SPORTS). As further examples one might add the Union of Soviet societies for friendship and cultural relations with foreign countries (USSR—Italy, USSR—Bulgaria, etc.), the All-Union Society of inventors and rationalizers, the Union of scientific-technical societies, etc.

Unlike the voluntary associations (*dobrovol'nye obshchestva*), professional societies and unions of writers, musicians, painters, actors, etc., require, according to their own by-laws, special governmental authorization, and not only approval of the by-laws. (Societies for the disabled, the blind and the deaf-mute belong to the same category). Another distinctive feature of these societies is their institutional duty to protect, aid and represent the economic and legal interests of their members. In this way these societies may be said to combine aspects of trade unions (protection of specific interests) and of voluntary associations (development of the cultural life and the creativeness of members).

All social organizations are subject to Party control (*rukovodstvo*) without regard to the category to which they belong or the characteristics and specific functions outlined in their respective by-laws. Some organizations are also subject to control by the state (professional societies, unions of artists) and consequently they may be dissolved by a decision of their own competent agencies (general assembly or assembly of delegates), or by a decision of the proper administrative authorities, or at least in agreement with the latter.

All organizations are in any case subject to supervision by the Procuracy (*q.v.*) with regard to the lawfulness of their activities.

One should also bear in mind that a new form of socialist ownership of a "non-productive" character has been introduced by the Principles of Civil Legislation in 1961: ownership of trade unions and other social or community organizations of enterprises, buildings, installations, sanatoriums, rest homes, cultural centres, clubs, stadiums and Young Pioneers' camps, together with all appurtenances, cultural and educational funds and any other assets serving the purposes of the activity of the organization in question (art. 24).

Similar to co-operative property, social property differs from state property by "the lesser degree of socialization" (*obobshchestvlenie)*; unlike state property, social property does not constitute "one single fund" and functions chiefly in the sphere of consumption, not production. The main source of social property, unlike co-operative property, is not income from economic activities but association contributions and membership fees. See also OWNERSHIP.

Trade union property, to limit ourselves to a conspicuous and important example, constitutes a unitary fund belonging to all Soviet trade unions together (i.e. to their All-Union organization); local trade union organizations (insofar as they are legal entities) only have a "right of operative management" with regard to the property entrusted to them. This offers a striking parallel to the right of operative management of the state enterprise with regard to the property entrusted to it by the state. The fixed capital of trade unions is not subject to compulsory execution and may be transferred without compensation between trade union organizations on the basis of a decision of a higher trade union organization.

According to the most recent Soviet doctrine, the role of social organizations in the management of society and the state steadily increases with the gradual approaching of communism. In the phase of the "state of the entire people" (*q.v.*) in particular, one would observe a constant transfer of state functions to social organizations, and a growing use of methods of coercion (characteristic of state agencies) by social organizations, which, insofar as they are voluntary, actually ought chiefly to employ methods of persuasion.

Companies in general (see also CORPORATIONS).

The Soviet Civil Code of 1922 devoted more than 90 articles (276-366) out of 436 to companies (*tovarishchestva*): simple (*prostoe*), with a collective name (*polnoe*), *Kommanditgesellschaft* (*na vere*), with limited liability (*s ogranichennoi otvetstvennost'iu*)—in which the liability of a partner is limited to a multiple of his share—and with shares (*aktsionernoe* or *paevoe obshchestvo*).

Any company with a commercial objective (*torgovli i promysla*) was considered to be a legal entity from the moment of registration in the commercial register (registration of the company contract) according to a rule already established in the 19th century by a judgment of the Senate; an exception was made for the simple company, which combined elements of the company and the association contract, was not subject to registration and did not constitute a legal entity.

This treatment of the matter in the 1922 Code can hardly be called original in view of the prerevolutionary rules of company law (which distinguished, however, between civil and commercial companies; see respectively arts. 2126-2198 of vol. 10 part 1 and arts. 63-104 of vol. 11 part 2 of the *Svod Zakonov*) or, more generally, of the models offered by many West-European legal systems.

Since the end of the NEP-period the provisions of the Code concerning companies have been considered obsolete by doctrine and by the courts as a consequence of the "liquidation of the capitalist elements" in the Soviet Union and (excepting those governing the simple company and perhaps the company with shares), it seems, as also formally repealed from the beginning of the fourth decade of the century, by virtue of arts. 4, 9 and 10 of the Stalin Constitution.

In the simple company "two or more persons are obliged reciprocally to unite their own contributions (*vklady*) and to act jointly for the promotion of a common economic goal". The expression "economic" (*khoziaistvennyi*) differs from "commercial" (*torgovyi*) in the exclusion of the profit motive. Nevertheless it was interpreted in a sufficiently broad way to include "the creation of the material basis necessary to satisfy the cultural needs of citizens, to improve their well-being, and to realize the citizens' right to relax". With regard to the simple company a decree of the Council of Labour and Defence of February 19, 1926, had allowed state institutions and enterprises to participate, resolving thereby a famous controversy concerning the possibility of a legal person (public or private) assuming the quality of a partner in a simple company.

Enterprises (*predpriiatiia*) and institutions (*uchrezhdeniia*) could unite in simple companies, in which co-operative organizations could also participate with the authorization of their own boards or, alternatively, of their own economic directors, and on condition that the aims of the company did not exceed the statutory objective of the enterprise, and, for the institution, that its entry in the company would be directed at the performance of "individual economic-organizational activities required by its own current needs" (e.g. the organization of a club or a canteen for its own personnel).

The participation of state enterprises and institutions in simple companies of which natural persons could also be partners required the permission of the Council of Labour and Defence or of the economic assemblies of the Union republic, provided the new partner did not join in the place of a deceased partner.

The contributions of the state enterprises and institutions were to be paid exclusively out of the circulating capital; this was also in accordance with art. 279 of the 1922 Civil Code, which provided that only money and goods to be used or consumed became the common property of the partners, while any other contributions (including therefore any parts of the fixed capital of a state enterprise) remained at the disposal of partners for "common utilization".

The participation of state agencies excluded the possibility of a joint and several liability of the partners for company debts and made obligatory the rule of the liability of each partner in proportion to his own contribution (art. 287).

Finally, the agencies which were competent in allowing state enterprises and institutions to found or join simple companies, were charged with supervising the activities of these enterprises and institutions as partners in companies; they were to see to it that the company did not pursue other aims than those approved when the state enterprises or institutions founded or joined the company.

All the same, the decree of 1926 quickly became obsolete. Only private persons resorted to the outdated contract of *prostoe tovaishchestvo* (simple company), mainly for the common construction of housing or summer cottages.

The Principles of Civil Law of 1961 do not mention any contract of association. This does not mean that associations of persons have become illicit, but rather that they have become, from typical contracts, atypical sources of obligations within the limits provided by art. 4 of the Principles.

The RSFSR Civil Code of 1964 regulates in arts. 434-438 the contract of common, collective, or "combined activities" (*sovmestnaia deiatel'nost'*), through which the parties bind themselves to act "unitedly in order to achieve a common economic goal", such as the construction, organization of exploitation of an inter-kolkhoz or state-kolkhoz enterprise or service, or the construction of waterworks, sports installations, roads, schools, maternity clinics, housing etc. Unlike socialist organizations, individuals may conclude this contract only in order to satisfy their personal needs, never for "productive" purposes. The parties bind themselves also to make the contributions necessary to achieve the common purpose (in money, in kind, or through labour). The property which is formed out of the contributions, or acquired by virtue of the common activities, becomes the common property of the parties, and may be disposed of only with the permission of them all. (Where all the parties to the contract are state organizations they have a right of "operative management", not of common ownership). The common property serves to cover the expenses and the eventual losses caused by the common activities, unless the contract provides otherwise. Expenses and losses which exceed the common assets are divided among, and borne by, the contracting parties in proportion to their respective contributions.

The contracting parties are together entitled to run the common affairs of the group, but one or more of them may also be appointed on the basis of a written authorization signed by all the others.

With regard to the contract in question, Soviet doctrine argues that it is not a matter of a simple change in terminology, effected in order to replace the term "company" by another which does not evoke private entrepreneurial activity; rather, it is argued, a new institution has been created for which the old rules are utilized only when "they serve to regulate the new social relations formed under present circumstances".

The contract of "combined activities" may not be concluded between private persons and public agencies (socialist organizations), owing to art. 116 of the Civil Code, which does not allow the forming of common property between socialist organizations and individual citizens.

The new institution embraces the "simplest forms of inter-kolkhoz collaboration" or of state-kolkhoz collaboration, which do not give rise to an independent legal entity or separate property. Indeed the activities of stable or permanent organizations of a mixed state-kolkhoz or inter-kolkhoz character (e.g. for building or for packing), endowed with legal personality, are not regulated by the contract in question, but by arts. 24 and 117 par. 2 of the Civil Code and by special statutes and regulations (decree of the USSR Council of Ministers of February 3, 1951, "Concerning the manner of construction and exploitation of inter-kolkhoz electrical power-stations and installations"; a model statute of 1955 "Concerning the inter-kolkhoz building organization for the production of local agricultural materials", etc.), in accordance with art. 438 of the Civil Code. As for limited liability companies; see CORPORATIONS.

G. Crespi Reghizzi

ASYLUM

Pursuant to Art. 129 of the USSR Constitution of 1936, the Soviet Union "affords the right of asylum to foreign citizens persecuted for defending the interests of the working people, or for scientific activities, or for struggling for liberation".

The right of asylum was already recognized by the decree of the RSFSR Central Executive Committee of March 28 (15), 1918, which directed that any foreigner persecuted in his homeland for an offence of a political or religious nature, upon making his way to Russia enjoyed the right of asylum there. The extradition of such individuals at the request of the states whose nationals they were was barred and, if a request for extradition was received from some foreign country, it was studied by the People's Commissariat for Foreign Affairs which then submitted it to a court to determine whether the offence charged was of a political or religious order or a common crime. Depending on the findings, a decision was reached on the possibility of sanctioning extradition. Comparable provisions on the right of asylum were featured in the RSFSR Constitution of 1918 and the constitutions of the other Soviet republics and in the constitutions of the Union republics adopted after the formation of the federation.

Prior to World War II, all questions of material assistance to political emigrés granted asylum were handled by the Soviet section of the International Organization for Aid to the Fighters of the Revolution (MOPR), founded in 1923, while the care of non-political emigrés was entrusted to the corresponding Soviet organs. Until 1924, the Executive Committee of MOPR alone could authorize admission into the USSR in the capacity of political emigré, but since 1924 that power has been vested in the competent Soviet state agencies. Today, the Union of Soviet Societies of Red Cross and Red Crescent looks after the physical welfare of individuals granted asylum in the USSR.

According to Soviet legal doctrine, the right to grant asylum belongs exclusively to the state, which may *a priori* define through its internal legislation the class of individuals to whom it pledges to offer a safe haven. In the case of the USSR Art. 129 of the current Constitution spells out the necessary qualifications. The enumeration does not include common criminals who, though they may find refuge in the USSR under some circumstances and be protected from subsequent rendition, will nevertheless not be formally granted asylum status. Soviet theory and policy only accept the principle of territorial asylum and reject the validity of the usage of harbouring fugitives in diplomatic or consular quarters, on board public ships, etc. Asylum is granted upon the express application of the interested person and, once confirmed, entails the corollary obligation not to surrender the *de cujus* (not always observed in past Soviet practice, incidentally) and to assure him a suitable livelihood in the host country. The USSR extends to persons enjoying asylum on its soil the so-called "national regime", i.e., concedes them most of the social and economic privileges guaranteed to its own citizens.

In general, Soviet legal sources maintain that, since the right of asylum is an institution of public international law, each state must exercise it in conformity with certain well-established standards and rules. Thus, it is claimed that at present all states are obliged to give asylum to "individuals engaged in the struggle for national independence" and "persons fighting for peace", and refusal to do so allegedly constitutes a breach of international law. Conversely, asylum must *ipso jure* be denied to individuals accused of having committed international crimes, e.g., crimes against peace, war crimes, crimes against humanity, acts of terrorism, propaganda of war, genocide, etc., and offering such elements immunity from criminal prosecution at the scene of the offence is likewise viewed as tantamount to a violation of international law. As yet, however, this thesis does not command widespread diplomatic support.

George Ginsburgs

ATOMIC ENERGY

The Soviet Union's cooperation with other states in the sphere of the peaceful uses of atomic energy develops along three lines: through the mechanism of the International Atomic Energy Agency (IAEA), the Joint Institute for Nuclear Research, and also through an intricate network of bilateral agreements.

The IAEA, a related agency of the UN, was established on the basis of an international agreement which came into force on March 1, 1958, and has since been amended on January 31, 1963. The primary objectives of the agency include the acceleration and enlargement of the contribution of atomic energy to peace, health and prosperity throughout the world. The agency has to ensure, as far as possible, that assistance provided by it or at its request or under its supervision or control is not used in such a way as to further any military purposes. The Soviet Union joined the Organization as an original member in 1958 and has since undertaken to cooperate with the other members of the Agency to encourage and assist research into, and the development and practical application of, atomic energy for peaceful uses throughout the world, to make provision, in accordance with the Agency's Statute, for materials, services, equipment and facilities to meet the needs of research into and the development and the practical application of, atomic energy for peaceful purposes and to foster the exchange of scientific and technical information on the peaceful uses of atomic energy, etc. Membership obligations also include the exchange of information under Art. VIII, the supply of materials under Art. IX, and the rendering of certain services and the provision of equipment and facilities to the Agency under Art. X. Art. XII provides for special agency safeguards with regard to Agency projects that may be set up under the terms of Art. XI. In order to establish a system of controls to enable the Agency to comply with Statutory Obligations with respect to the activities of member states in the field of the peaceful uses of nuclear energy as provided in the Statute, the 9th General Conference of the IAEA in 1965 adopted the Revised Safeguards System of the IAEA to which are annexed the Special Procedures for re-processing plants prepared by the Agency's Working Group as adopted by the Board of Governors on June 17, 1966. The 1965 Safeguards System requires members to submit to the Agency reports with regard

to the production, processing and use of safeguarded nuclear material in or outside any principal nuclear facilities. It also grants to the Agency the right to conduct initial, routine and special inspections of safeguarded nuclear materials and principal nuclear facilities in the member states.
The Soviet Union ratified the Statute of the Agency on February 9, 1957 thus becoming the first of the nuclear powers to do so. The Soviet Union was very active in shaping the general features of this Agency—she was the author of the sovereignty clauses of Art. IV (c) and Art. III (c).
In addition to her cooperation within the framework of the IAEA the Soviet Union also coordinates its atomic energy policies with its East European satellites. Within this framework the general tendency is to explore the uses of atomic energy for defence, as a source of energy and as a tool in industry, medicine and scientific research. Whereas the defence aspects of the uses of nuclear energy are turned over to the Warsaw Treaty Organization (*q.v.*), all other uses of the atom are referred to COMECON (*q.v.*), and this includes the rational deployment of nuclear energy in economic development and for industrial projects within the member states. At its 13th Session COMECON decided to establish a permanent commission on cooperation among the Council countries with regard to the peaceful uses of atomic energy.
In addition to asserting absolute control over the mining of uranium inside the Soviet Union itself, the Soviet government has used the platform of the WTO and COMECON to acquire some mining and prospecting rights for uranium in Czechoslovakia, the German Democratic Republic and to a lesser extent in Hungary, Poland and Bulgaria. On the basis of the Declaration of January 17, 1955, the Soviet Union entered into a series of bilateral agreements with its European allies on cooperation and assistance in the area of the peaceful uses of atomic energy. She entered into such agreement with Roumania on April 22, 1955, with Czechoslovakia and Poland on April 23, 1956, with China on April 27, with the German Democratic Republic on April 28, with Hungary on June 13, and with Yugoslavia on June 28, 1956.
By the terms of these agreements the Soviet Union is to furnish the other parties with an experimental pile of nuclear materials and to render technical and scientific assistance to them as well—all these forms of assistance are in exchange for the mining of uranium by the Soviet Union in each of these countries. The commitment to render scientific and technical assistance in the area of peaceful uses of atomic energy led to the setting up on March 6, 1956 of the Joint Institute for Nuclear Research (JINR). Originally conceived as a rival organization to the Center for Atomic Research for Western Europe (CERN) from which the Soviet Union was excluded, the JINR has grown into an international institution for nuclear research to which scholars from non-socialist countries have been granted access—notably scholars from France and Great Britain. The JINR has its seat at Dubna, USSR, and operates on the basis of a Statute which was adopted at the September 1956 Conference of representatives of the member countries of the Institute.
At this first session of the Institute (September 20-27, 1956) the Democratic Republic of Vietnam was admitted to regular membership of the JINR. The Institute is headed by a Director who is elected for a three-year term by the Conference of the Representatives-Plenipotentiary of the member states. It also has a Scientific Council to which each Institute member appoints three representatives.
While willing to cooperate with the other countries in the field of the peaceful uses of atomic energy through the institutional framework of the IAEA, the JINR, WTO and COMECON, and through a system of

bilateral cooperation agreements, the Soviet Union still strongly guards its domestic production and the processing of nuclear materials and throws a thick screen of secrecy over such activities—a fact which makes any meaningful Western study of the Soviet legislative activities in this area almost an impossibility. *C. Osakwe*

ATTACHMENT OF WAGES

If a citizen judgment-debtor has insufficient property to satisfy a debt, his wages may be attached for the deficiency (cf. arts. 380 ff. RSFSR Code of Civil Procedure). The maximum deduction is usually 20% but up to 50% may be deducted in cases of maintenance of the family and torts to the person. These continue until the debt is paid in full. The employer is served with a warrant of execution (see EXECUTION OF JUDGMENTS) and must take the deductions on pain of a ten rouble fine plus personal liability to the creditor for the omitted deductions. *A. K. R. Kiralfy*

ATTEMPT

Soviet criminal law distinguishes between two preparatory stages in the commission of crimes, both of which are punished: preparation and attempt. Preparation is defined by art. 15 par. 1 of the RSFSR Criminal Code as the procuring or adaptation of means or instruments, or, in any other way, intentionally creating the conditions for the commission of a crime. Procuring implies acquiring the possession of means and instruments, adaptation refers to objects already in the possession of the offender which are made suitable for the commission of a crime. Means are all objects which are necessary or helpful to commit the crime; instruments are those means by which the crime is committed (e.g. the weapon used in killing or wounding somebody). Instruments are subject to confiscation under art. 86 of the RSFSR Code of Criminal Procedure.

Since preparation is intentionally directed at the commission of a crime, one can only speak of the preparation of intentional crimes (and not of preparation to commit a crime by negligence).

The Criminal Code and legal literature do not offer much guidance in answering the question at what stage preparation becomes a crime. The least that can be said is that preparation—in order to be a crime—must be to some extent socially-dangerous. Consequently, a preparatory act which is still very remote from a complete crime, may be regarded as not socially-dangerous and thereby outside the scope of criminal law. The present tendency in Soviet criminal law seems to be to limit the application of the preparation concept to more serious cases—serious in two ways: preparation at an advanced stage of a serious offence.

At the other end of the line, preparation has to be distinguished from attempt. This is done by defining attempt; anything which falls short of coming within the definition of attempt may still constitute preparation. Attempt is defined in art. 15 par. 2 of the RSFSR Criminal Code as an intentional act immediately directed at the commission of a crime. The decisive term, in distinguishing between preparation and atempt, is obviously "immediately". Attempt is an act which, without the intervention of factors outside the offender's influence, will naturally lead to a complete crime; e.g. the purchase of a gun may constitute preparation, while aiming the gun and pulling the trigger may constitute attempted homicide, if it was the offender's intention to kill the victim.

The difference between attempt and a complete crime is in the result of the criminal action, which is missing in the case of attempt. There will be a complete crime when all the elements mentioned in the definition of a particular crime in an article of the Criminal Code are present. There may even be attempt where not only the result is lacking, but also the criminal action required of the offender is incomplete (e.g. in the above-mentioned example of *aiming* a gun). Such attempts are termed "incomplete" (a complete attempt being an attempt which does not require any further action by the offender). The border-line between attempt and a complete crime is drawn clearly by the words immediately following the Criminal's Code's definition of attempt; attempt obtains only "provided the crime is not completed owing to circumstances independent of the offender's will". This formula covers various typical cases: voluntary withdrawal, which is not punished, and receives special treatment in art. 16 of the Code; and two types of attempt which are punished: the general kind of attempt, where the offender's act is interrupted before he has completed the entire crime by outside circumstances (e.g. arrest), and the so-called faulty attempt (Russ. *negodnoe pokushenie*), where the crime could not be completed due to inherent causes (e.g. an attempt to poison somebody with sugar; an attempt to kill somebody who is already dead).

Art. 16 of the RSFSR Criminal Code provides that a person who of his own free will desists from the commission of a crime is not punishable, provided the actions he has committed do not already constitute another crime. The motive for desisting is irrelevant, as long as there is a voluntary decision.

The penalty for preparation and attempt is determined according to the provision in the special part of the Criminal Code which defines the complete crime (par. 3 of art. 15 of the RSFSR Criminal Code); the maximum penalty is not lowered in this case. However, according to the fourth paragraph of the same article, the court will consider the stage of realization (together with a number of other circumstances) in determining the penalty for preparation and attempt.

F. J. M. Feldbrugge

ATTORNEYS, see LAWYERS

AUTHORS, see COPYRIGHT

AUTOMOBILES, see MOTOR VEHICLES

AUTONOMOUS PROVINCE

The autonomous province is a manifestation of the federated nationality structure of the Soviet state system, along with the Union republic, autonomous republic, and national district, and reflects the principle of permitting to compact nationality groupings varying measures of autonomy in internal administration. In Soviet parlance, the autonomous province possesses administrative autonomy within a Union republic, but is not a state as is an autonomous republic. The province possesses autonomy in order to encourage the development of national economy and culture by a relatively homogeneous group.

There are presently eight autonomous provinces in the USSR: five in the RSFSR (Adyge, Mountain-Altai, Jewish, Karachai-Cherkes, Khakas), and one each in Azerbaidzhan (Nagorno-Karabakh), Georgia (South Ossetian), and Tadzhik (Mountain-Badakhshan).

The internal administrative structure of the province is similar to that of other administrative sub-divisions of the USSR: an elected soviet, which appoints an executive committee; a provincial court elected by the soviet; a procurator appointed by the Procurator of the USSR. Similarly, the higher republican organs of power exercise the same control over the institutions of the autonomous province as they do over the parallel organs of the administrative province or *krai's*. For example, the Council of Ministers of the Union republic may annul decisions of the executive committee of the soviet of an autonomous province.

The province's autonomy, though, is manifested in a number of ways:

First, within the administrative structure of the autonomous province established by the republican Constitution, the region's soviet is mandated to draw up a "Statute on the autonomous province" for confirmation by the republican Supreme Soviet. The Statute is intended to take into account the special nationality features of the province. Within the scope of this Statute, the province may determine its own boundaries and administrative sub-divisions, subject to confirmation at the republican level.

Further, while the official language of a Union republic is the language of the nationality forming the majority of that republic, the administrative organs of the autonomous province are constitutionally permitted to conduct their activities in the language of the nationality for whose benefit the province was established.

Further, again, the autonomous province has a legal relationship not only with the Union republic but with the federal level as well: each autonomous province is represented by five deputies in the Soviet of Nationalities of the USSR Supreme Soviet.

One of the peculiar problem issues relating to the autonomy of these provinces arises from the fact that the five autonomous provinces within the RSFSR are officially subdivisions of the administrative-territorial unit known as the *krai* (*q.v.*). The *krai* is not established on a nationality basis. The legal issue resulting from this structure is the appropriate extent to which the *krai* organs can regulate the institutions of the autonomous province.

It appears as if autonomous provinces were originally placed within *krai's* to assure the coordinated overall economic and political development of the territory, regardless of national composition. There have in the past been suggestions that the autonomous provinces should be separated entirely from the *krai* structure. Until 1962, the RSFSR did have a model for this arrangement, in that Tuva was an autonomous region not situated within a *krai*. However, in that year Tuva's status was elevated to that of an autonomous republic with no change made in the status of the remaining five autonomous provinces, suggesting a decision to maintain the pre-existing *krai*-autonomous province relationship.

Despite the fact that the five RSFSR autonomous provinces are located within *krai's*, as indicated above, the provinces have direct relations with the Republic and specific representation at the USSR level that provide it independence from the *krai*. Other specifics of the relationship were spelled out relatively early in the development of the RSFSR. In 1928 the RSFSR adopted a decree "On mutual relations between autonomous provinces as components of *krai* (provincial) entities, and the organs of *krai* (provincial) authority". The decree established the independence of the autonomous provinces from the *krai's* in the areas of organization and administration, popular education, health, social security, justice, land management, local economy, local budget, and archival matters. In such areas as labour, taxation, trade, statistics and other branches of state administration, the autonomous province has to be guided by the decisions of the *krai* soviet and its executive committee.

The decree grants the autonomous province's executive committee the right to protest to the RSFSR Council of Ministers decisions and directions of the *krai* executive committee that affect the province's budget or relate to the portion of the *krai's* budget affecting the province. Where the *krai* executive committee does not agree with a decision of the provincial committee, the former may request a reconsideration from the latter. When the provincial comittee reaffirms its previous decision, the *krai* committee may then appeal to the RSFSR Council of Ministers. Where the provincial committee disagrees with a decision or instruction of the *krai* committee, by a specific resolution in each instance the provincial committee may suspend the operation of the decision or instruction within the territory of the province and may appeal it to the RSFSR Council of Ministers.

Finally, the decree specifically authorizes the autonomous provinces to communicate directly with higher governmental organs of the Union republic, but requires copies of such communications to be provided to the *krai* authorities for information.

The decree recognizes the anomaly of a putatively autonomous unit placed within an administrative hierarchy while retaining, by virtue of its autonomy, certain rights to communicate with levels of the hierarchy higher than the immediate superior. The RSFSR still sees certain planning and coordination advantages to maintaining this arrangement, so that the 1928 decree continues to provide the basic principles for rationalizing a rather complex relationship.

Stephen M. Weiner

AUTONOMOUS REPUBLICS

Autonomous Soviet Socialist Republics (autonomous republics or ASSR's) along with Union republics, form a segment of the federal structure of the Soviet Union established along nationality lines. The autonomous republics represent autonomous groupings geographically located within the predominant national majority of Union republics (*q.v.*). The autonomous republics possess their own territory, national population, and organs of state power and administration. They have internal self-rule, subject to supervisory powers vested in the Union republics in which they are located; but, unlike the Union republics, do not possess any of the indicia of external independence (the right to secede, to maintain foreign relations, etc.). The structure and powers of the autonomous republics are established both by the USSR Constitution and by the Constitutions of the Union republics in which they are located. Since the majority of autonomous republics are located in the RSFSR, that republic's Constitution will be used as the model for the general description of the constitutional relations between Union republics and autonomous republics.

Relationship between USSR and autonomous republics: The Constitution of the USSR enumerates the autonomous republics, establishes the general principles of their state organization, and gives to the All-Union government the power to confirm the formation of new autonomous republics.

The autonomous republics, as they presently exist, are as follows: in the RSFSR: Bashkirian, Buriat, Dagestan, Kabardian-Balkarian, Kalmyk, Karelian, Komi, Mari, Mordovian, North Ossetian, Tatar, Tuva, Udmurt, Chechen-Ingush, Chuvash, and Yakut; in Azerbaidzhan: Nakhichevan; in Georgia: Abkhaz and Adzhar; in the Uzbek SSR: Kara-Kalpak.

The USSR Constitution gives to each autonomous republic the right to have its own constitution, which is to be drawn up in full conformity with the Constitution of the Union republic, but may take into account special features of the autonomous republic. Each autonomous republic is represented at the All-Union level by eleven deputies to the Soviet of Nationalities of the Supreme Soviet of the USSR.

Relationship between Union Republic and Autonomous Republic (*RSFSR as model*): The USSR Constitution gives to the Union republics the right to confirm the constitutions of constituent autonomous republics and to determine the boundaries of the territory of such republics.

The RSFSR Constitution enumerates the autonomous republics contained within the territory of the RSFSR, sets out the principles governing the relationship between the RSFSR and the autonomous republics, and establishes the autonomous republican state structure with greater specificity than does the USSR Constitution.

Generally, as indicated earlier, the Union republic has the power to confirm constitutions drawn up by autonomous republics. Laws of the Union republic are supreme within the republic, so that any divergence between a statute of the autonomous republic and a statute of the Union republic is resolved in favour of the latter.

The RSFSR Constitution also bestows on the Union republic the right to propose the formation of new autonomous republics within its territory to the Supreme Soviet of the USSR for confirmation, and to confirm boundaries and district divisions of autonomous republics.

The ASSR is represented at the Union republic level in that the Presidium of the RSFSR Supreme Soviet has at least one vice-president from each autonomous republic. The RSFSR Presidium has authority to annul decrees and regulations of the Council of Ministers of an autonomous republic that do not conform with law. The Council of Ministers of the RSFSR is empowered to give direction to and verify the work of Councils of Ministers of the autonomous republics, and may suspend decrees and regulations of the Councils of Ministers of autonomous republics.

State Structure: The state structure of an autonomous republic parallels that of the USSR itself and of the various Union republics. The highest agency of state power and the sole legislative agency of the ASSR is its Supreme Soviet. The Supreme Soviet is elected for a term of four years by the citizens of the ASSR, according to norms of representation contained in the ASSR constitution. The ASSR Supreme Soviet has the power to adopt the ASSR constitution and to submit it to the Union Republican Supreme Soviet for confirmation. The ASSR Supreme Soviet also is directed to establish the district (*raion*) divisions of the republic and the borders of its districts and cities, and to submit same to the Supreme Soviet of the Union republic for confirmation; to confirm the national-economic plan and the budget of the ASSR; and to confer titles of honour.

The ASSR Supreme Soviet, as with Supreme Soviets at higher levels of government, elects a Presidium which is accountable to it. The Supreme Soviet also appoints the ASSR Council of Ministers and the judges of the ASSR Supreme Court.

The highest executive and regulatory agency of the ASSR is its Council of Ministers. The Council is responsible to the ASSR Supreme Soviet and is accountable to that body or, between sessions, to its Presidium. The Council, in supervising the activities of the ASSR ministries, issues decrees and regulations on the basis of and in execution of USSR, RSFSR, and ASSR laws, and on the basis of decrees and regulations of USSR and RSFSR Council of Ministers, and verifies execution of same. The ASSR Council of Ministers has the right to annul orders and instructions of subordinate ministries of the ASSR, decisions and regulations of executive committees of area, city and *raion* Soviets of Working People's Deputies in the territory of the ASSR, and to suspend decisions and regulations of area, city and *raion* Soviets of Working People's Deputies.

The administration of justice is carried out by a Supreme Court and various inferior courts. The ASSR Supreme Soviet elects the judges of the ASSR Supreme Court to terms of five years, while the ASSR Supreme Court is under the supervision of the Supreme Court of the Union republic. ASSR Procurators, however, are appointed by the Procurator General of the USSR, and exercise their functions independently of all local agencies. Reflecting the nationality base of the state structure, judicial proceedings within an ASSR are conducted in the language of the ASSR (see also LANGUAGE).

Stephen M. Weiner

See also SUPREME SOVIET; PRESIDIUM OF THE SUPREME SOVIET; COUNCILS OF MINISTERS

AVERAGE, MARITIME

Average refers to a loss inflicted on carriage by sea, or on a vessel, cargo, or freight, as well as to expenses incurred in averting such loss. Maritime law distinguishes between general and particular average. In the USSR average is governed by Ch. 13 of the 1968 Merchant Shipping Code (MShC).

General average encompasses those losses borne as a result of expenses or sacrifices intentionally and reasonably incurred for the purpose of saving the vessel, freight, or cargo carried on the vessel from a peril common to them (art. 232, 1968 MShC). When used in this connection, the term "freight" also includes payment for the carriage of passengers and their baggage.

Three elements are essential to general average: 1) the deliberateness and reasonableness of the actions causing the losses; 2) the extraordinary nature of the losses, in that such actions exceed the limits of customary actions performed under normal sailing conditions; and 3) such actions were performed in order to save the vessel, freight, and cargo from their common peril.

The purpose of consciously inflicting losses classified as general average is to avert large-scale losses, such as the destruction of the entire vessel or cargo, by suffering smaller losses. Examples of general average losses under Soviet law are: losses resulting from jettison of cargo; losses inflicted upon the vessel or cargo by intentionally running aground; expenses incurred for the purpose of obtaining assistance; etc. (arts. 234-236, 1968 MShC).

General average losses are contributed to by the vessel, freight, and cargo in proportion to their value. The responsibility for determining the existence and the extent of general average lies with average adjusters (*dispashery*). In contrast to Anglo-American and continental practice, where the adjuster is either an insurance agent employed by the carrier's insurance company or an independent arbitrator selected by the parties, an average adjuster in the USSR is a quasi-official individual who operates under the aegis of the All-Union Chamber of Commerce on the basis of a statute adopted by that Chamber. The 1968 MShC outlines the procedure to be followed in drawing up an average statement (*dispasha*). In determining the type or the amounts of general average, and in drawing up the average statement, the Soviet average adjuster is to resort to international merchant shipping custom if the law is incomplete.

Although there are a few differences of form, the general average provisions of the 1968 MShC are in general conformity with the York-Antwerp Rules of 1950. Detailed rules for depreciation deductions on "new for old" are contained in a special administrative order established by the Registry of the USSR.

Any losses not falling within the terms of arts. 232, 234, and 235 of the 1968 MShC are treated as particular average. Such losses are not subject to contribution by the vessel, cargo, and freight, but are borne by the one who suffered them or by the one who is liable for causing them.

Bibl.: W. E. Butler and J. B. Quigley, Jr. (eds. & trans.), *The Merchant Shipping Code of the USSR (1968)*, 1970.

W. E. Butler

AVIATION, see AIR LAW

BAIL

In criminal procedure bail is a measure of restraint (see RESTRAINING MEASURES) consisting in the deposit of money or valuables with a court to secure the appearance of the defendant when summoned by the agency of inquiry, investigator, procurator or court (cf. art. 99 Code of Criminal Procedure).

Formerly ideologically taboo, bail today is known only to the codes of RSFSR and Tadzhikistan, and even there it is meant to be applicable only by way of exception. Ideology forbids the possibility that a man could "buy" his relief from custody. The peculiarity of Soviet bail therefore consists in not being a privilege accorded to an arrested person but a means of restraint existing independently of and as an alternative to custody in cases where custody is not necessary. Yet naturally it cannot be applied against the will of the person bailed, unlike the other restraining measures, and it therefore requires two constitutive documents: besides the decree of application, a record with the signature of the person bailed is necessary. The exceptional character of bail is underlined by the provision that it must be backed by a court ruling or sanction of the procurator, while most other restraining measures are applied by the agency of inquiry or the investigator on their own. Although bail can be applied against the mere suspect (like other restraining measures, only exceptionally), the person bailed, even if he himself is the suspect, must be informed of the "nature of the case", which partly anticipates the defence function of the presentation of the charge which has to follow within ten days. The amount of bail is determined by the applying agency. In the case of non-appearance later upon summons, the bail is converted to state revenue by a court ruling; the ruling is made at the trial of the case, if the summons to trial is disobeyed, otherwise in an "administrative" court session (see TRIAL).

In practice, bail nowadays is not applied at all.

M. Fincke

See also ARREST

BAILIFFS

Bailiffs are attached to people's courts; they are appointed by the justice departments of the provincial executive committees and work under the supervision of the people's judge (see COURTS). Their chief function is the execution of all judgments enumerated in art. 338 of the Code of Civil Procedure: court decisions in civil cases and in some criminal cases (fines, confiscation), arbitration awards confirmed by the court and a host of other decisions made by administrative and quasi-judicial agencies.

F. J. M. Feldbrugge

See also EXECUTION OF JUDGMENTS; MINISTRY OF JUSTICE

BAILMENT

Soviet law has no general concept of bailment as the situation in which legal duties arise simply as the result of a person's goods having entered the control, care or custody of another without change of title. Strictly, bailments are defined as contracts of deposit for safe-keeping, in which the agreement to accept possession, to care safely and to return safely is the sole or predominant term of the contract. Such bailments are regulated by specific articles of the Civil Codes of the Union republics (arts. 422-433 of the RSFSR Code). They are distinguished from other situations in which a duty to care for another's property is present, but arises from contracts where such duty is not the predominant term (contracts of sale, agency, work and carriage) or from the operation of law (duties of hotels, rest-homes, sanatoria, etc. *vis-à-vis* their clients and their property).

Contracts of bailment (deposit for safe-keeping) are gratuitous unless statute or contract provides for a fee. The fee may be regulated by law, by model contracts and charters governing the activities of socialist (state or public) organisations or by the terms of an agreement. Contracts of deposit for safe-keeping may be concluded between socialist organisations (where goods of a certain kind are usually involved, e.g., grain, meat, etc.), between citizens and between socialist organisations and citizens (where specific goods are usually involved, e.g., pledges, valuable documents, coats, suit-cases, etc.). Deposits with socialist organisations are normally governed by special regulations as well as being determined by administrative and planning acts. All contracts of deposit, whether arising solely from agreement between the parties or dictated from above, are governed by the norms of the Civil Code, but special rules affecting any particular deposit apply in so far as they do not agree with the provisions of the Civil Code.

Under the Civil Code, all contracts of deposit in which one of the parties at least is a citizen must be made in writing if the value of the goods exceeds 100 roubles unless it is a deposit for safe-keeping for a short period in cloakrooms, etc., where the depositor receives a numbered ticket or a token. All contracts between socialist organisations must be in writing. In practice, receipts, invoices, tickets, acknowledgements, warehouse slips, suffice. Where one of the parties is a socialist organisation, all deliveries must be receipted and the liability of a socialist organisation accepting goods arises only on issue of the receipt. Legal relations where goods are deposited in automatic safety-deposit cells or boxes (at railway stations, etc.) arise on the basis of concrete acts of the depositor and/or the custodian defined by relevant regulations, regardless of the value of the goods. The presentation of a numbered ticket or token issued by an organisation on accepting the goods 'legitimises' the claimant, even if he is not the depositor; (additional) fault is required to make his delivery actionable. Only deposits in exceptional circumstances, such as fires and floods, may be proved by oral testimony.

The depositor can demand the return of goods at any time, even in a deposit with a fixed term. The custodian may renounce the contract only if it is for an indeterminate term or for a term made determinable on demand; he must give the depositor reasonable time to resume possession. The Civil Codes also provide for reimbursement of expenses incurred in accepting or caring for a gratuitous deposit, regulate the basis and extent of the custodian's liability for loss or damage in general terms (which may be further regulated by specific legislation, model contracts, or administrative acts) and contemplate compensation to the custodian for any losses resulting from the condition of the deposited goods. The depositor has the right to defend the goods against interference. Where goods are deposited as of a generic characteristic by a number of persons and the custodian commingles, generally an ownership in common shares arises. In most republics the Civil Code does not presume the passing of ownership to the custodian, but permits such passing to be done by agreement—in which case the custodian is bound to return to the depositor an equal or contractually stipulated amount of things of the same kind and quality. There cannot be a deposit of things of which possession cannot be passed, e.g., a building, growing crops, a fruit garden, or other objects the protection of which is an economic function of the owner; in these cases, the owner can only conclude contracts of labour with watchmen for security.

Hotels, rest-homes, sanatoria, hostels and "similar organisations" are made responsible, under a separate and independent provision of the republican Civil Codes, for the property of persons staying in these premises even where such property has not been deposited for safe-keeping, except in the case of money and valuables.

A. E.-S. Tay

BANDITRY

In a vast and in many places thinly populated country like Russia which has known much political unrest, the appearance of armed bands has been a chronic phenomenon until recent times. This may explain why a special provision in the Criminal Code, in the chapter concerning crimes against the state, is devoted to banditry. Although examples of collective rural lawlessnes, which may be regarded as banditry, do still occur from time to time, the main thrust of the banditry provision has shifted now to the most serious cases of armed robbery in urban surroundings.

Banditry is defined in art. 77 as the organization of armed bands in order to attack state or public institutions or enterprises, or individual citizens or taking part in such bands, or in the raids carried out by them. It is closely related to armed robbery, one of the aggravated forms of robbery (*q.v.*). The main differences are: armed robbery may be committed by one person or by a group which does not have a sufficient degree of organization and permanence; armed robbery requires the *use* of weapons, while the fact that one member of the band *carries* a weapon is enough to make the band an armed band; robbery is a crime against property-rights, while banditry may have other purposes.

There can only be talk of a band where at least two persons have got together in order to commit more than one armed attack; the definition of banditry does not require that any actual attack is committed. Once the band has been organized, anybody who joins the "organization", or who even takes part in one of the attacks or raids of the band, becomes a bandit. The term "attack" or "raid" implies a great variety of violent acts; the result of this is that the crime of banditry absorbs most other crimes committed in the course of bandit activities, such as murder, assault, rape, theft, etc.

The penalty for banditry is deprivation of freedom for from three tot fifteen years accompanied by confiscation of property and possibly followed by exile (from two to five years), or the death penalty with confiscation of property.

F. J. M. Feldbrugge

See also WEAPONS; ORGANIZED CRIME

BANISHMENT, see EXILE

BANKING

In the USSR the banks are state institutions. Soviet law dealing with banking and credit relationships may be found in the Principles of Civil Legislation of 1962 and in more detail in the various Civil Codes of the Union republics.

In the USSR there are a number of types of banks. There is the bank known as the *Stroibank* (the construction bank). Among other fields of activity, this bank has as its primary object the provision of finance for capital investment in the public sector and provides for example long term credits. Regulations for the *Stroibank* were issued by the Council of Ministers of the USSR on October 1, 1964. The State Bank of the USSR (*Gosbank*) is the central bank of the USSR and *inter alia* issues bank notes and is charged with the banking application of the financial policy of the government of the USSR. Thus among its functions is the obligation to check that funds which it makes available are dealt with in accordance with the Plan. Regulations for the State Bank were issued by the USSR Council of Ministers on October 29, 1960. Another extremely important bank is the *Vneshtorgbank* (the Foreign Trade Bank) which deals with foreign trade finance. Thus, for example, the Foreign Trade Bank signs agreements with foreign banks relating to large scale financial transactions, it gives guarantees and generally acts in relation to all the spheres of operation which the title of the bank clearly indicates. It is with this bank that foreigners will primarily deal. Regulations for the *Vneshtorgbank* were issued by the USSR Council of Ministers on August 22, 1962.

There are also in the USSR savings banks which are the organisations through which personal savings in the USSR are arranged. They are part of the State Bank and apart from their purely personal savings function, they conduct other banking transactions such as the making of specialised payments and the holding of certain current accounts. See also SAVINGS ACCOUNTS.

The banking system, in particular the State Bank and the Construction Bank, is an important organ of financial control in the Soviet economic system.

Finally, reference has been made elsewhere to the International Bank for Economic Co-operation and the International Investment Bank in the article dealing with Foreign Exchange (*q.v.*).

David Winter

BANKRUPTCY, see INSOLVENCY

BARRISTERS, see LAWYERS

BARTER, see SALES

BASTARDS, see ILLEGITIMACY

BATTERY, see ASSAULT

BAYS, see TERRITORIAL WATERS

BIBLIOGRAPHY (OF SOVIET LAW)

By any standard, current and retrospective legal bibliography in the Soviet Union is in a highly unsatisfactory state.

Current legal materials are recorded in two types of publication: 1) universal bibliographic annuals which undertake to record all items issued within a given time span except for classified documents and administrative materials for internal use; 2) scholarly and professional legal journals.

The principal registration bibliographies are *Knizhnaia letopis'*, *Letopis' zhurnal'nykh statei*, *Letopis' gazetnykh statei*, and *Letopis' retsenzii*. Weekly issues of *Knizhnaia letopis'* are cumulated annually in *Ezhegodnik knig SSSR*. Despite their broad scope, however, these series are neither complete nor, from the lawyer's point of view, satisfactorily organized. Of the legal books listed in *Knizhnaia letopis'* for 1966, for example, nearly twenty-seven percent were placed arbitrarily under non-legal categories. The contents of official unclassified periodicals which publish the texts of normative acts are not broken down analytically in the *Letopis' zhurnal'nykh statei*. Nor is information about legislation in general and special journals or newspapers fully recorded; e.g., surveys or chronicles of legislation. Some legal serials have not been indexed at all in the *Letopis' zhurnal'nykh statei*; for example, *Morskoe pravo i praktika* and the *Trudy* of the Higher School of the Ministry for the Protection of the Social Order of the RSFSR. The occasional collection of essays usually is listed only by title.

Bibliographies and lists on the subject of state and law containing a minimum of thirty items and published in books, periodicals, and catalogs are indexed in *Bibliografiia sovetskoi bibliografii*, an annual compilation begun in 1939.

Sovetskoe gosudarstvo i pravo, published monthly by the Institute of State and Law of the USSR Academy of Sciences, contains the most extensive listings of new legal literature in the Soviet Union. It tends to include primarily scholarly publications and to omit popular legal materials and textbooks. Since

1965, the space devoted to bibliography has been much reduced; periodical articles are excluded, although the contents of occasional volumes are sometimes described. Only Russian language items are mentioned. Of 1598 legal books listed in *Knizhnaia letopis'* in 1966, only 367 were referred to in *Sovetskoe gosudarstvo i pravo*. Very selective bibliographies appear twice annually in *Sovety deputatov trudiashchikhsia* and in the Ukrainian journal *Rad'ians'ke pravo*. Russian and Belorussian publications are selectively listed in a Belorussian serial, *Literatura po voprosam sovetskogo stroitel'stva*. Some Estonian books are reviewed in *Sovetskoe pravo* (Tallin).

Foreign legal literature fares even worse. *Pravovedenie* contains a useful but selective bibliography of legal literature in other socialist countries. Since 1962, the Institute of State and Law has published a mimeographed bulletin of new accessions on foreign law received in the Institute's Library, the Lenin Library, the Fundamental Library of the Social Sciences, and the Library of Foreign Literature; the bulletin emphasizes socialist legal literature.

For all practical purposes, there is no current bibliography or information service for legislation. Research institutes have their own card files, but these are inaccessible to the overwhelming majority of jurists. Informational lists of new normative acts are compiled for internal use only and issued in a very limited number of copies.

As for retrospective bibliography, there are a number of important cumulative general and specialized publications; an extensive annotated bibliography of legal bibliography compiled by T. E. Ksenzova and embracing the period 1831-1970 was published during late 1972 in the USSR under the title: *Iuridicheskaia literatura*. Suffice it to point here to some of the most significant items.

Among general bibliographies, the most important is a volume published in 1960 by the Institute of State and Law in cooperation with UNESCO with parallel Russian and English text. Entitled *Literatura po sovetskomu pravu; bibliograficheskii ukazatel'*, it was issued in only 700 copies; a microfiche edition can be obtained from IDC.

Several extensive specialized bibliographies have appeared. Among the more noteworthy are:

I. I. Solodkin (ed.), *Sovetskoe ugolovnoe pravo; bibliografiia (1917-1960)*, M., 1961. (For the period of 1961-1968, see *Sovetskoe ugolovnoe pravo, sovetskoe ispravitel'noe-trudovoe pravo; sovetskaia kriminologiia, Bibliografiia (1961-1968 gg.)*, Vladivostok, 1969, 2 vols. Mimeo in 500 copies.)

V. F. Kotok (ed.), *Sovetskoe gosudarstvennoe pravo; bibliografiia 1917-1957*, M., 1958.

I. V. Pavlov and G. M. Sverdlov (eds.), *Sovetskoe grazhdanskoe pravo; sovetskoe semeinoe pravo. Bibliografiia 1917-1960*, M., 1962.

S. S. Karpinskii (ed.), *Sovetskoe trudovoe pravo; ukazatel' literatury 1917-1969*. Kazan, 1971.

M. N. Kulazhnikov (ed.), *Teoriia gosudarstva i prava, bibliografiia 1917-1968*, M., 1969. (Apparently superseding a publication from Rostov bearing an identical title for the period 1954-1964.)

An excellent classified index to judicial practice of the USSR and RSFSR Supreme Courts in criminal proceedings is S. V. Borodin (ed.), *Voprosy ugolovnogo prava i protessa v praktike verkhovnykh sudov SSSR i RSFSR (1938-1969 gg.)*, 2d ed. M., 1971.

The law of economic planning still has not received separate bibliographic treatment. Numerous references can be found in A. E. Probst (ed.), *Bibliografiia po voprosam razmeshcheniia i raionirovaniia promyshlennosti SSSR 1901-1957*. M., 1960; and in two bibliographies prepared by the Fundamental Library of Social Sciences: *Narodnoe khoziaistvo SSSR* v *1917-1920 gg*. M., 1967; and

Narodnoe khoziaistvo SSSR v *gody velikoi otechestvennoi voiny*. M., 1971. Both embrace books and periodical literature in the Russian language published respectively from 1917-1963 and 1941-1968.

International law has received better treatment from Soviet bibliographers than any branch of Soviet Law. In 1959 the Soviet Association of International Law published *Sovetskaia literatura po mezhdunarodnomu pravu; bibliografiia 1917-1957*, edited by V. N. Durdenevskii. This work was republished in Russian with a parallel German text in two volumes and updated through 1962 by B. Meissner and A. Uschakow (eds.), *Sowjetunion und Völkerrecht, 1917 bis 1962* (Köln, 1963); *Das sowjetische internationale Privatrecht 1917 bis 1962* (Köln, 1964). An extensive annual bibliography, somewhat tardy and confined to Russian language materials, appears in the *Sovetskii ezhegodnik mezhdunarodnogo prava*, published since 1958. International legal literature from other socialist countries has been selectively recorded in the *Sovetskii ezhegodnik mezhdunarodnogo prava* since 1960 and *Pravovedenie* since 1968. A new comprehensive bibliography of Soviet international legal literature is reportedly being prepared in the USSR.

Dissertations are another important source of Soviet legal writing. A classified bibliography of *kandidat* and doctoral dissertations in all fields of law defended from 1938-1962 was compiled by V. A. Rakhlevskii and K. G. Borisov, *Bibliograficheskii spravochnik dissertatsii na soiskanie uchenoi stepeni kandidata i doktora iuridicheskikh nauk* (Dushanbe, 1965). Published in only 500 copies, it is available on microfiche from IDC. For dissertations defended since 1962, no comprehensive specialized listing is available.

Western holdings of Soviet legal materials are recorded in a variety of forms. The Cyrillic Union Catalog, now available on microcard, and the *List of Russian Accessions*, regrettably defunct, both prepared by the Library of Congress, give a good indication of that institution's holdings in this field. Harvard Law School Library's holdings as of January 1, 1965, are classified and annotated in V. Mostecky and W. E. Butler (eds.), *Soviet Legal Bibliography* (Cambridge, 1965). Several institutions issue lists of new accessions in Soviet Law; especially noteworthy are those of the Documentation Office for East European Law in Leiden and the University of Illinois.

Massive subject and author central catalogues of monographs, periodical literature, and legislation are maintained by the Central Information Office for Legal Literature from Socialist Countries housed at the Institut für Ostrechtsforschung of the University of Hamburg. Created in 1967, the Central Information Office is undertaking to record the holdings of all western collections.

There are several publications which record the titles and issue data of Soviet legal journals and gazettes. The most useful is R. Smits, *Half a Century of Soviet Serials 1917-1968* (Washington D.C., 1968.) A classified and annotated bibliographic catalogue of Russian and Soviet legal material available on microfiche is issued at irregular intervals by the Inter Documentation Company (Zug, Switzerland).

An extensive classified compendium of books and articles published from 1917 to mid-1966 in languages other than East European is the present author's *Writings on Soviet Law and Soviet International Law* (Cambridge, 1966). Excellent coverage of English language books and articles on Russian and Soviet law is given by C. Szladits, *A Bibliography on Foreign and Comparative Law* (New York, 1955). Three volumes have appeared for the period up to 1965, and bound supplements issued through 1969. *The American Journal of Comparative Law* prints annual installments as well. Extended reading lists also are to be found in J. Hazard,

I. Shapiro, and P. Maggs, *The Soviet Legal System* (2nd ed.; New York, 1969; also see the first edition, 1962).

American doctoral dissertations on Russian and Soviet law through 1959 are recorded in J. Dossick, *Doctoral Research on Russia and the Soviet Union* (New York, 1960) and supplemented annually in the *Slavic Review*.

British doctoral dissertations, and other writings on Soviet law published in British journals, are listed in ABSEES.

German writings on Soviet and East European law from 1945-1964 are gathered in a classified bibliography by C. Bussman and W. Durchlaub, *Bibliographie des deutschsprachigen Schrifttums zum Ostrecht* (Trittau/Holst., 1969). *Osteuropa-Recht* has published bibliographies of Soviet and western writings in the field from time to time since 1955. German, French, Spanish, and Italian books and articles up to 1954 are cited in R. David and J. Hazard, *Le Droit soviétique* (Paris, 1954), II, pp. 329-377; partially revised in a Spanish edition, *El derecho soviético* (Buenos Aires, 1964), II, pp. 378-430.

Japanese scholarship of the late 1950's in this field is discussed by H. Uchida, "Japanisches Schrifttum zum Recht der Ostblockstaaten", *Osteuropa-Recht*, IV (1960), 295.

For additional references, see Butler, "A Survey of Bibliography on Soviet Law", in *Soviet Legal Bibliography*, pp. 1-4.

W. E. Butler

BIGAMY

Bigamy and polygamy are defined in Soviet law as the cohabitation and the running of a common household by a man with more than one woman (irrespective of the existence of a formal registration of marriage). The offence can be committed only by the male partner and in the RSFSR (art. 235 and 236 Criminal Code RSFSR) only in areas where bigamy and/or polygamy (*dvoe- i mnogozhenstvo*) still exist as a survival of former tribal customs. Thus the elements constituting the offence require it to be committed in such regions as the Tatar, Bashkir, Dagestan etc. autonomous republics, or the Mountain-Altai autonomous province or the Komi-Permiak national district. The law does not apply in parts of the country where such survivals of tribal customs have not been common (e.g., in Moscow, Leningrad, Orel, Smolensk etc., cohabitation and common households with any number of women would not constitute an offence). The Ukrainian, Belorussian, Lithuanian, Moldavian, Latvian and Estonian codes do not contain a corresponding offence. But the republics with considerable Moslem populations all have such a law. The punishments vary: In Turkmenia the offence is punished with up to five years' deprivation of freedom (art. 131 Criminal Code); in Tadzhikistan and Armenia with up to three years' deprivation of freedom or up to one year of corrective labour; in Kirgizia with up to two years' deprivation of freedom or up to one year of corrective labour; in the RSFSR and Georgia the punishment is up to one years' deprivation of freedom or up to one year of corrective labour; in Uzbekistan it is either up to one years' deprivation of freedom, or up to one year of corrective labour or a fine not exceeding 100 roubles. The most lenient code is the Kazakh Criminal Code punishing the offender with only up to one years' corrective labour.

However, in all republics the concealment from the Registrar of circumstances which would bar the registration of a marriage, and the making of false statements are punishable offences. The offence carries, depending on the republican codes, corrective labour of up to one year, or a fine of up to 50 roubles, or merely a public censure (thus the codes of the RSFSR, Armenia, Kazakhstan, Kirgizia, Tadzhikistan, Turkmenia, the Ukraine, BSSR). The Uzbek code provides only for up to 6 months corrective labour, or 30 roubles fine or a censure. Azerbaidzhan, Lithuania and Latvia punish the offence with corrective labour for up to one year or a fine of up to 100 roubles. The Estonian adds to this the alternative of a censure.

The law is regarded as an important measure for the liberation of women and their protection from exploitation and the enforcement of their equal rights with the male population in areas where under the old dispensations the woman occupied an inferior position. *R. Beermann*

See also TRADITIONAL CRIME

BILLS OF EXCHANGE,
see NEGOTIABLE INSTRUMENTS

BILLS OF LADING,
see NEGOTIABLE INSTRUMENTS; CARRIERS

BLACKMAIL, see EXTORTION

BONDS,
see NEGOTIABLE INSTRUMENTS

BORDER CROSSING

Unlawful border crossing is the subject of art. 83 of the Criminal Code. According to this provision, any exit from, or entry into, the Soviet Union without an approved passport or without permission from the authorities is regarded as unlawful border crossing. The manner in which the border is crossed (on foot, by boat, train, aeroplane, etc.) is not relevant.

The provision is directed only against intentional border crossing, and does not cover accidental or careless crossings. Neither does it apply to foreign citizens entering the USSR in order to avail themselves of the right of asylum (*q.v.*) as defined in the Soviet Constitution.

The penalty is deprivation of freedom for from one to three years.

A special case of border crossing, together with some related activities, is described in art. 84: crossing the USSR state frontiers by aeroplane, without proper permission, and other violations of international flight rules (non-observance of the routes, landing places, air gateways, or flight altitude indicated in the permission, etc.). The penalty in this case is deprivation of freedom for from one to ten years, or a fine of up to ten thousand roubles, possibly accompanied by confiscation of the aeroplane. The offence can only be committed by the pilot of the plane.

F. J. M. Feldbrugge

See also BOUNDARIES; AIR LAW; TREASON

BOUNDARIES

The regime of the Soviet frontier is currently governed by the Regulation on the Protection of the State Border of the USSR, promulgated on August 5, 1960 (as subsequently amended), which defines the state frontier of the USSR as the line marking the limits of the land and water territory of the USSR. The vertical plane coinciding with this line forms the frontier of the airspace and sub-surface of the USSR. The Soviet state frontier is determined in accordance with the decisions of the supreme organs of state authority of the USSR and operative agreements of the USSR with foreign states. The location of the state frontier *in situ* is established by survey-protocols and other demarcation documents. Coastal sea waters with a width of 12 marine miles (22.25 kms), measured from the line of maximum ebb-tide on the continental shore as well as around islands or from the line of outer periphery of the internal sea waters of the USSR, and in those localities where the coastline is deeply indented and cut or if there is a fringe of islands along the coast in its immediate vicinity—from straight base lines joining appropriate points, constitute the territorial waters of the USSR. In individual instances, pursuant to agreements concluded between the USSR and foreign states, the width of the territorial waters may vary. The outer perimeter of the territorial waters represents the state frontier of the USSR at sea. The Soviet maritime frontier in sectors where the territorial waters of the USSR abut on the territorial waters of adjacent states is fixed in conformity with agreements signed between the USSR and the respective states and, absent such agreements, in accordance with the principles accepted in the international practice of states or in a direct line joining the exit points of the land frontier to the sea (several exceptions to the 12-mile rule now exist, e.g., vis-à-vis Finland stemming from various treaties and in the Bering Strait and in the straits between Hokkaido and the Soviet Kuriles where a median line serves as the boundary). The total length of Soviet land frontiers runs to 20,285 kms and of Soviet sea frontiers to 46,705 kms.

The internal sea waters of the USSR comprise: the waters of the USSR's ports, separated seaward by a line traversing the coordinates of the hydrotechnical and other port constructions situated furthest from land; the waters of the gulfs, bays, bights and estuaries the shores of which belong entirely to the USSR up to a straight line drawn from shore to shore where from the direction of the sea is first formed one or several passages, if the width of each of them does not exceed 24 marine miles; the waters of gulfs, bays, bights and estuaries, seas and straits which historically belong to the USSR.

The state frontier of the USSR on navigable border rivers follows the middle of the main navigable channel or thalweg of the river, and on non-navigable rivers—the middle of the river or the middle of the main branch. (Treaty-made exceptions to this rule also exist. Thus, prior to 1946, the line of the Soviet-Afghan frontier on the Amu-Daria ran along the Afghan bank of the river, leaving the stream wholly in Russian possession; the agreement of June 13, 1946, set the boundary on the Amu-Daria and the navigable portion of the Piandzh in the thalweg or, given the impossibility of identifying the thalweg, in the middle of the main channel and in the non-navigable portion of the Piandzh—in the middle of the river. The current border dispute between the USSR and China on the Amur and Ussuri Rivers centers around the location of the boundary-line which, according to the Chinese should follow the middle of the thalweg and which now generally runs on or close to the Chinese bank of both waterways). On border lakes, the state frontier traces the middle of the lake or forms a straight line joining the exit points of the land frontier to the shores of the lake. The state frontier following a river or a lake does not fluctuate in pace with changes in the topography of the banks or the water level or shifts in the course of the river in either direction, unless otherwise provided for by the USSR's agreements with the interested foreign states. The state frontiers of the USSR are indicated by clearly visible frontier signs (posts, pyramids, barrows, buoys, etc.). The outer perimeter of the territorial waters of the USSR may for purposes of orientation be designated in particular places by buoys and beacons.

The regime of the state frontier (the procedure for crossing the border, the format of the border signs, the execution of works along the border, etc.) is governed by the legislation of the USSR and the agreements entered into by the USSR with foreign states. In the interests of protecting the state frontier on the land and water territory of the USSR, the federal Council of Ministers or on its instructions the Councils of Ministers of the Union and autonomous republics establish where necessary border zones and border cordons. Border zones are established, as a rule, within the territorial limits of a *raion*, town, village or hamlet soviet contiguous with the state frontier. Such border zones also include the territorial and internal sea waters of the USSR and the Soviet portion of the border rivers and lakes. Border zones fall under a special regime. The width of the border cordons cannot exceed 2 kms from the line of the state frontier on land or from the banks of border rivers (lakes): the practice on the USSR's frontiers with different states is not uniform and the width in fact ranges from 100 to 2,000 m. Within the boundaries of the border cordons, the frontier troops introduce a supplementary set of restrictions. The Soviet portion of the waters of border rivers and lakes, as well as the islands located in these rivers and lakes belonging to the USSR are subject to the exclusive control of the frontier units.

In individual sectors of the internal sea and territorial waters of the USSR zones may be established by decision of the competent organs in which is permanently or temporarily prohibited the sailing or anchoring of vessels, as well as the exploitation of marine resources. Announcements of the creation of such zones appear in the "Notices to Mariners", published by the federal Ministry of the Maritime Fleet. Entry within the bounds of a border zone by a person not a permanent resident of that zone is forbidden without permission of the organs of the civilian police, if no other procedure has been prescribed. Entry into the border cordon and residence there occurs only on the authorization of the border troops. Persons may cross the state frontier of the USSR solely upon the presentation of requisite and duly certified documents attesting to the right of entry into or exit from the USSR and must proceed through the check-points manned by the frontier troops.

The transit of freight, other property and valuables across the state frontier of the USSR, as well as of diplomatic mail, is monitored by the customs offices in accordance with the Customs Code of the USSR and special instructions. Agricultural and forest products, plants, animals and fowl, as well as products of animal origin, are subject, in addition to customs inspection, to medical-sanitary, veterinary and phyto-sanitary control. Railroad, water, air, automobile and other traffic across the Soviet state frontier is governed by current domestic legislation and agreements concluded with foreign states. Means of transportation, other than by air, are admitted across the frontier at the border check-points and aircraft of all types traverse the frontier at designated locations (air-gates). All aircraft must depart from or land on the territory of the USSR only at those airports where function such check-points, except by special permission of the competent organs. Violations of the foregoing rules are punishable by law.

Foreign non-military vessels have the right of peaceful passage through the territorial waters of the USSR. Foreign military vessels may cross the territorial and enter the internal sea waters of the USSR solely by prior permission of the Soviet Government obtained in accordance with existing regulations. Foreign submarines authorized to enter the territorial and internal waters of the USSR must stay on the surface at all times. Foreign vessels may not engage in the exploitation of marine resources within the territorial and internal sea waters of the USSR, except where an agreement between the USSR and a foreign state provides otherwise (at present Finnish and Japanese nationals alone enjoy certain treaty exemptions in this regard). Hydrographic work and research are also prohibited. Violations entail arrest of the vessel and proceedings against the culprits in accordance with Soviet legislation. Navigation, fishing, lumber floating, water use and the construction of various hydrographic installations on the border rivers and lakes are conducted and regulated by corresponding agreements between the USSR and adjoining states and, lacking these, are governed in the Soviet portion of the border rivers and lakes by regulations issued by the competent authorities (e.g., the executive committees of the local soviets in the case of measures ensuring the observance of the border regime by the population in traveling in the border zone, in carrying out agricultural work and in utilizing the waters of the seas, rivers and lakes).

Customs, medical-sanitary, veterinary and phyto-sanitary control at the state frontier is performed respectively by the organs of the Ministry of Foreign Trade, Public Health, Agriculture, and at border railroad-stations medical-sanitary control is enforced by the Ministry of Means of Communications (the USSR is a signatory of the International Sanitary Convention of June 21, 1926). These Ministries, in consultation with the frontier troops, the Ministry of Foreign Affairs and other interested departments issue binding rules pertaining to the exercise of these controls. In the event of peril of spread of especially dangerous infections on the territory of the USSR or a neighboring state, the frontier may be temporarily sealed by decision of the Main Administration of Frontier Troops of the Committee of State Security of the USSR Council of Ministers in consultation with the USSR Ministry of Public Health and other interested departments. Violation of the medical-sanitary and administrative-sanitary rules is punishable by a fine of up to 10 roubles.

In order to ensure the implementation of agreements on questions of the regime of the state frontier, other agreements on frontier matters, and the settlement of border disputes, a number of officers of the frontier troops are appointed border representatives of the USSR (border commissars, border plenipotentiaries, their deputies and assistants); on sectors of the frontier where there are no specially assigned border representatives, their functions are performed by commanders of units of frontier troops acting on special instructions.

In the sundry agreements concluded by the USSR with adjacent countries dealing with the status of their common frontier many of these issues are resolved in similar fashion, with, on occasion, partial accommodation to suit the circumstances. For example, the USSR's treaties with Hungary, Roumania, Poland, Czechoslovakia and Finland on the regime of the frontier establish a mobile boundary on border rivers, streams and canals. However, a shift in the course of the border waterway as a result of cataclysmic natural phenomena does not alter the line of the frontier—unless the two sides agree otherwise—and the parties jointly and on a basis of equality undertake to correct the position of the water-course. The USSR's treaties with the "socialist" states likewise feature a proviso to the effect that bridges over border rivers are divided by the line of the frontier in the middle, regardless of where the boundary-line runs in the water. The Soviet Union's treaties with adjacent states usually contain a rule that the characteristics of every border sign and its location with reference to the boundary-line are determined by corresponding demarcation documents. Identification of the frontier by other means not adopted at the time of demarcation or the replacement of existing border signs with border signs of a different type is permitted only by special agreement of the states concerned. In the event of loss, destruction or damage of a border sign, its restoration or repair is effected at once, with particular care not to disturb its site. Moving border signs even without modifying the line of the frontier is allowed solely in exceptional cases due to natural causes and by agreement of the parties. Border posts are then installed in spots where their physical safety is guaranteed without affecting the alignment of the frontier.

The parties must take steps to make certain that border waters are maintained in proper condition and initiate measures to prevent the deliberate destruction of the banks. The position and course of running border waters must insofar as possible be kept immutable even where a mobile frontier is established. There is no right unilaterally and without prior clearance to do anything that might change the water level which in turn could lead to local changes in the territorial configuration of the adjoining state. For that reason, all the corresponding Soviet treaties specify that in the event of a need to rebuild or raze bridges, dams, locks, embankments and other similar erections on running border waters, if such actions may ensue in alterations in the level of the water on the territory of the other state, such works may be undertaken only with the advance consent of the opposite party. This also applies to the construction and exploitation of new installations of this type.

The Soviet Union's treaties with Poland, Roumania and Hungary sanction (with certain minor variations) navigation by ships on the respective border rivers in the entire width of the main channel regardless of where in it the boundary-line is situated. Boats may sail only up to the frontier-line. Ships and boats of one side may pull up to the river or lake banks, gulf coast or sea shore of the other side only in those instances where they are in distress (storm, accident, etc.). As a rule, shipping is not permitted to anchor in the middle of the main channel or on the boundary-line. Fishing in border waterways is ordinarily permitted to residents of either side up to the line of the frontier, but just during daytime and without employment of explosive, poisonous and other means of mass extermination of fish. Hunting in the border areas is allowed as long as the rules are strictly observed. Shooting and pursuing animals or birds across the frontier is forbidden. Special rules apply to mining operations in the vicinity of the frontier. They must be conducted in a manner calculated not to impair the territory of the other side, usually may not get closer than 20 m. to the border, except by joint agreement of the competent authorities.

The matter of preventing illegal crossings of the frontier in either direction is entrusted to appointed border representatives. Especially grave violations of the frontier are generally handled through diplomatic channels, with the border personnel investigating and drawing up a protocol of their conclusions. Otherwise, decisions rendered by the border representatives on items within their official jurisdiction are binding and final and enter into force from the moment of signature of the corresponding protocol. In the performance of their functions, border representatives may cross the frontier, and enjoy in that connection inviolability of the person and the official papers in their possession. Other persons crossing the frontier to elucidate a question or carry out a task assigned by the border representative as well as persons engaged on the basis of agreements between the proper authorities in work on the construction or maintenance of communication and water installations, the regulation of the water flow, measurements, etc., commonly are assured inviolability too and may not be detained during their sojourn on the territory of the other side.

George Ginsburgs

See also PASSPORTS; TERRITORY; INTERNATIONAL WATERS; BORDER CROSSING; AIR LAW; SMUGGLING

BRIBERY

Three separate crimes connected with bribery are included in the Criminal Code in the chapter concerning "official crimes" (*q.v.*). In fact only one of them (the taking of a bribe, art. 173) is an official crime in a strict sense, i.e. a crime committed by somebody who answers the definition of an official (cf. art. 170).

The taking of a bribe in any form by an

official, either in person or through an intermediary, for the performance or non-performance, in the interests of the person who gives the bribe, of any kind of action which the official has a duty to perform or may perform by using his official position, is the first type of bribery offence, defined in art. 173. It entails a penalty of deprivation of freedom for a term of from three to ten years. In more serious cases the penalty may be extended to a term of from eight to fifteen years, or to the death penalty (second paragraph of art. 173). The words "bribe in any form" imply any form of financial or material advantage derived by the official. The definition is interpreted to include actions in the interest of persons close to the person giving the bribe, or of organizations to which that person belongs. Furthermore it is clear that actions which are in themselves legal are covered as well as illegal actions.

Art. 173 is reflected in art. 174, which states simply that the giving of a bribe entails a penalty of deprivation of freedom for from three to eight years (seven to fifteen years in a number of serious cases, spelled out in the second paragraph). However, the various circumstances described in art. 173 (the bribe must be given to an official, in order to make him do certain things in the interest of the person giving the bribe) must be considered as implied in the term "giving a bribe". A note attached to art. 174 lays down that persons who have given a bribe shall be relieved of criminal responsibility if the bribe was extorted from them or if they voluntarily reported what happened (to the authorities). The offering of a bribe (which is not accepted) constitutes an attempt to commit the offence defined in art. 174.

Acting as an intermediary in bribery is made a separate offence in art. 174-1. It entails a penalty of from two to eight years, and in serious cases of from seven to fifteen years. The precise contents of the term "intermediary" are defined in an instruction by the Plenum of the Supreme Court of the USSR of July 31, 1962.

F. J. M. Feldbrugge

BUDGET OF THE STATE

The word "budget" has several meanings in Soviet terminology depending on whether it is taken in its material sense, as an economic, or as a legal concept.

In its material sense the state budget of the USSR represents the state's centralized funds of monetary means.

As an economic concept the budget is a system of economic relations, through which the centralized funds of the state are collected and utilized on the basis of a planned distribution of the revenue. The state budget of the USSR represents slightly more than 50% of the national income (52% in 1964, 50.8% in 1973), whereas in most Western countries the state budget normally does not exceed one third of the national income. This is in no way surprising, in view of the fact that through the plan the Soviet state intervenes directly in the economic life of the country. During the last years more than 40% of budgetary expenditure has been devoted to financing the economy. The economy in its turn is the prime source of budgetary revenue: more than 90%. Since the economic reforms started in 1965, which included an extension of the financing of the economy from its own resources, a sharper distinction between state funds and the funds of enterprises should be developing.

As a legal concept the state budget of the USSR may be regarded as the financial basis-plan for the collection and utilization of the state funds. Budgetary and economic planning are closely connected: the economic plan and the budget are discussed together at the same session of the Supreme Soviet. All other financial plans are realized in accordance with the budget, which must be seen as the moving and coordinating force behind them.

The budgets of enterprises working on a *khozraschet* (*q.v.*) basis contain an item "relations with the state budget" which lists the amounts of obligatory payments to the budget (turnover tax, contributions from funds, etc.) and of sums allocated to the enterprise by the state budget. The financial means necessary for the activity of state institutions (hospitals, schools, etc.) are provided by the state budget. The financial plans of banking institutions are connected with the state budget, because the financial resources originating from the state budget are one of the principal sources of credit and because a part of the profits are returned to the budget. Finally, since 1938, the state budget of the USSR includes the budget of the state social insurance system; the social insurance administrations at the Union republic level, which work on a *khozraschet* basis, turn over a part of their profits to the republican budgets.

A particular feature of budget law is that it supplies the basis for activities which may not last for more than one year; on the other hand, these activities are of a systematic and continuous nature and are renewed therefore almost every new budgetary year.

Art. 14 of the 1946 Constitution of the USSR lays down the tripartite budgetary system (budget of the Union, republican budgets, local budgets) and the manner of imposing taxes and indicating resources which contribute to the formation of these budgets. Art. 68 defines the competence of the Council of Ministers of the USSR. Art. 60 enunciates the right of every Union republic to adopt its own budget. Art. 97 grants the same right to local soviets.

The constitutions of the Union republics devote a special chapter to the budget (e.g. chapter IX (arts. 103-106) of the Constitution of the RSFSR, chapter VI (arts. 80-83) of the Constitution of the Ukraine, etc.).

The procedure for the elaboration, execution and control of the budget is laid down by a law on the budgetary rights of the Soviet Union and the Union republics of October 30, 1959; this law also defines the nature of the receipts and expenditure to be included in these budgets.

At this moment, the state budget of the USSR comprises about 50,000 separate budgets, among which are the budget of the Union, 15 budgets of the Union republics, 2 budgets of autonomous republics, 8 budgets of autonomous provinces (*oblasti*), more than 120 budgets of provinces and territories, and the budgets of towns, *raion*'s and villages. The state social insurance budget, which is also included, is prepared by the Central Federal Council of the Trade Unions and is executed by trade union organs; the financial resources of the state social insurance are used for the payment of pensions, disability and maternity benefits, and for all expenses connected with the safety of the workers.

The tripartite structure of the budget (budget of the Union, republican budgets, local budgets) does not affect the basic unity of the budget, because the various budgets consecutively include each other. Thus, the budget of the Union comprises the federal budget and the budgets of the Union republics. In its turn the budget of a Union republic comprises the republican budget, the budgets of autonomous republics (if present in the Union republic), and the local budgets, i.e. the budgets of provinces, territories, and towns with *oblast'* standing, and, in republics not subdivided into provinces, the budgets of *raion*'s and towns with *raion* standing. The province (*oblast'*) budget itself contains the budgets of towns with *raion* standing and the budgets of *raion*'s. The *raion* budget contains the budget of the *raion* proper, and the budgets of subordinate towns, settlements and villages.

The Minister of Finance of the USSR is charged with the preparation of the state budget of the USSR, after he has examined the draft budgets of the Union republics (together with representatives from the Union republics), the draft budget of the state social insurance (together with representatives from the Central Council of Trade Unions), and the projects for the financial plans and estimates of the ministries and services of the USSR (together with their respective representatives).

After examining these drafts, the Minister of Finance of the USSR draws up a draft federal budget; subsequently, on the basis of the draft for the federal budget, the budgets of the Union republics, and the budget of the state social insurance, he prepares a draft state budget of the USSR and submits this to the Council of Ministers of the USSR.

After examining this draft, the Council of Ministers of the USSR submits to the Supreme Soviet of the USSR; the state budget of the USSR (sum total of receipts, indicating the principal sources of income; sum total of expenses, indicating the allocations for financing the national economy, social and cultural activities, defence, running costs of governmental, administrative and judicial agencies, and of the *prokuratura*), the federal budget (divided into payments into the budget and allocations for ministries and services of the USSR), the budgets of Union republics and of the state social insurance and, finally, the proposals as to the distribution of tax returns and other federal revenue among the budgets of the Union republics.

At the Supreme Soviet of the USSR all these proposals are examined by the budgetary commissions of the Soviet of the Union and the Soviet of Nationalities. The commissions hear the reports from the agencies concerned and amending proposals, after which they present their findings to the Supreme Soviet. The proposed state budget, with eventual amendments, is voted on by the Supreme Soviet during its December session.

The state budget consists of two parts, receipts and expenditure. The 1973 budget provides for total receipts of 181.8 billion roubles, of which 8.6% is derived from direct taxation of the population, and 90.7% from the national economy (various payments from profits 35.2%, turnover tax 31.8% and other receipts, among which the social insurance payments of enterprises, tax on kolkhoz income, etc., are included 23.7%).

The expenditure, worked out on the basis of the receipts of the state, is defined by the four functions served by the Soviet state. Economic expenditure represents 47.6% of the total, 37.0% is allotted to social and cultural needs, defence takes up 9.8%, and the administration 1.0%; public debts account for 0.2%. The sum total of these five items never adds up to 100% in Soviet budgetary documents (either at the voting on the budget, or during the reporting of the performance of previous budgets).

The state budget always shows a surplus, which is directed towards the forming of a reserve fund of the Council of Ministers at the State Bank, and which guarantees the issue of money without danger of inflation.

Receipts and expenditure are distributed between the three levels of budgets: federal, republican, and local.

Receipts are divided into two groups: direct payments into the budget, and regulatory payments. The first group consists of regular payments of sums which are handed over in full, and of regular payments made according to fixed percentages. This system simplifies the budgetary technique and favours local initiative; but it creates inevitably a disproportion in the distribution of resources between the different budgets. Therefore regulatory payments are aimed at a redistribution; they consist of: a. percentage payments originating from regular income, fixed every year by higher soviets for the budgets of lower soviets, and b. subsidies, i.e. sums of money necessary to balance a budget and allocated by the higher soviet. Turnover tax occupies a special place among regulatory payments; the difference between expected expenditure and fixed and other income determines which part of this tax is payed into the budget of Union republics. Hereby the balance of these budgets is always assured.

The distribution of receipts between the budget of the Union and the budgets of the Union republics is worked out according to the principles expressed in the Law of October 30 1959.

The following resources feed the Union budget: a) turnover tax (except the percentage allotted to the budgets of the Union republics); b) profit from enterprises under federal control; c) income tax (except the percentage allotted to the budgets of the Union republics); d) customs duties and various other payments.

The budgets of the Union republics receive: a) profit from enterprises under republican control; b) taxes on the income of kolkhozes, cooperatives, social organizations and on the income from forestry; c) agricultural tax; d) part of the income tax and the turnover tax; e) state insurance deductions for the payment of pensions.

Local budgets receive; a) profits from enterprises under local control; b) local taxes and duties; c) state taxes which are directly paid into local budgets; d) state taxes allocated to local budgets as regulatory payments; e) other sources of income (credit balance from the previous year, subsidies, etc.).

Budgetary expenditure is dominated by the rule that an institution or an activity may be financed by one budget only. The importance of the activity is reflected by the level of the budget which is financing it.

Union expenditure comprises the cost of national defence, of the functioning of federal state agencies, the Supreme Court of the USSR, and the *Prokuratura*. For economic, social and cultural expenditure the level of control (federal, republican, local) of services, enterprises and activities, determines which level of budget is charged. The financing of services, enterprises and activities is not invariably within the province of the same budget, if the control of these services, enterprises and activities is changed. Activities which affect several territorial units of the same level are financed from the budget of the next territorial unit which embraces them.

In accordance with art. 68 of the Constitution of 1936 and art. 22 of the law of 30 October 1959 the Council of Ministers of the USSR organises the execution of the state budget by the Minister of Finance of the USSR. The Minister of Finance of the USSR executes the federal budget and directs the execution of republican and local budgets. Within the Soviet financial and economic system this execution implies primarily accountancy and financial control of all enterprises at all levels, because economic expenses account for almost 50% of budgetary expenditure, and income from the economy for 90% of budgetary receipts.

Until 1947 the federal budget and republican and local budgets were executed in the course of one year according to plans which were laid down every three months. At present a three-monthly division of receipts and expenditure is included in yearly budgets, but the plans for carrying budgets out are no longer laid down every three months.

The basic principle of the cash execution of budgets is the principle of cash unity, according to which the receipts from a budget are concentrated completely in one purse which is entrusted with the execution of the budget. This purse grants the monetary means to all services and enterprises which depend on the budget. Services and enterprises do not have the right to retain sums which they receive and to spend them again; they have to turn them over completely to the exchequer.

The principal cashier charged with the execution of the state budget of the USSR is *Gosbank*, which keeps accounts at the disposal of the Minister of Finance of the USSR for the federal budget, of the republican ministers of finance for the republican budgets, and of local financial departments for local budgets. All expenditure must in principle be paid out of these accounts.

The cash execution of receipts is facilitated by auxiliary agencies which are closer to the citizen: savings banks (which receive taxes from the population and may pay out various pensions), local soviets, services of the ministry of communications, special cashiers (attached to various services by executive decision, for the receiving of particular kinds of payments: customs duties, registration fees, etc.). These cashiers do not correspond with budgetary execution accounts, but simply represent a network at the disposal of *Gosbank*. The state budget of the USSR is characterized in its procedures by rigourous centralization of execution, and by a close centralized interdependence in the elaboration of the system of budgets.

P. Lavigne

See also BANKING; BUDGETS OF ENTERPRISES ETC.; PLANNING

BUDGETS OF ENTERPRISES, ETC.

In addition to the state enterprises which operate on the basis of economic accountability (see KHOZRASCHET) and in general cover their operating expenses with income received for sales and services, there are many institutions and organizations in Soviet society which are financed through the general state appropriations budget (see BUDGET OF THE STATE). These institutions include social welfare and cultural institutions, administrative organizations, and national defense organizations.

Each such organization has an appropriation budget (*smet*). Such a budget is a legal act, which establishes the volume, purpose and allowed quarterly disbursement, of state funds allotted to the enterprise. A typical budget might make allowances for such matters as wages, office expenses, travel on official business, purchase of vehicles, purchase of machinery, purchase of non-durable items, construction of new facilities, repair of existing facilities. Uniformity is achieved through norms of expenditures, which attempt to provide that organizations performing similar services will be allotted similar appropriations for equivalent purposes. Such norms are divided into three types "material", financial, and budgetary. The material norms establish how much of various types of items may be used, for instance food for one hospital patient per day, within a given time period. The financial and budgetary norms are similar to the material norms but are expressed in financial terms rather than material terms.

The appropriations budget of an enterprise (see STATE ENTERPRISE) is made up for the calendar year corresponding with the period of the effectiveness of the current law on the State Budget on the USSR, since the amounts included in the budget of each organization eventually find their way into the state budget's aggregate figures.

Such "budget" institutions and organizations also in certain instances have certain "nonbudgetary funds". These are funds arising from various types of income received by such organizations through user service fees and other, generally minor sources of income.

Bibl.: V. Bescherevnykh, S. D. Tsypkina (eds.), *Finansovoe pravo* (Finance law), 1967, pp. 310-331.

Peter B. Maggs

BURIALS

The basic rules concerning burials are contained in a decree "On graveyards and funerals" of December 7, 1918. Graveyards and funeral parlours are operated by the local soviet. The graveyard administration may allow burials (or cremations) only after receiving a document affirming the registration of a person's death in the civil status register. The expenses of the funeral are borne by the relatives; there is no charge for the grave. A death must be registered within three days of its occurrence, or after the discovery of a corpse. Registration may be effected by relatives, neighbours, the housing administration, the police and "other persons" (art. 159 of the Marriage and Family Code of the RSFSR). Religious ceremonies preceding the interment are allowed. As a rule, interment is not allowed within 48 hours after death has occurred. Detailed rules about graveyards and burials are found in republican enactments.

F. J. M. Feldbrugge

BURGLARY, see THEFT

BUSINESS LAW,
see COMMERCIAL LAW

CAMPS,
see PENITENTIARY INSTITUTIONS

CAPACITY

Following Continental European legal science, Soviet law distinguishes between the capacity to have rights and duties (*pravosposobnost'*) and the capacity to perform legal acts (*deesposobnost'*). According to the civil codes of the various republics, the capacity to have rights and duties is accorded equally to all citizens of the USSR from their birth to their death (cf. RSFSR Civil Code, art. 9), and includes the right to own and use property, to inherit property and dispose of it by will, and to choose any type of employment and place of residence (*id.*, art. 10), as well as the right to vote, the right to marry, the right to work, and other rights. Aliens and stateless persons have the capacity to have civil rights and duties to the same extent as Soviet citizens, but individual exceptions to this rule may be established by laws of the USSR and in the case of aliens the Council of Ministers of the USSR may impose retaliatory restrictions upon citizens of those states in which special restrictions exist on the capacity of Soviet citizens to have civil rights and duties (cf. *id.*, arts. 562, 563). Juristic persons have the capacity to have civil rights and duties only in accordance with the purposes of their activities as established by their charters and by-laws.

The capacity of a citizen to perform legal acts, that is, to acquire civil rights and to create civil duties for himself through his own acts, arises when he reaches 18 years of age, except that a citizen who lawfully marries before 18 acquires such capacity upon marriage (cf. *id.*, art. 11). No citizen may be restricted in his capacity to perform legal acts except by express provision of a law (*id.*, art. 12). Such restrictions are expressly provided with respect to minors, mentally ill or feeble-minded persons, and persons who place their families in a difficult financial situation through the misuse of alcoholic beverages or narcotics (*id.*, arts. 13, 14, 15, 16, 51, 52, 54). Nothing is expressly said in the Soviet civil codes about the capacity of aliens to perform legal acts, except that foreign enterprises and organizations may, without special permission, conclude transactions in the USSR in connection with foreign trade and related payment, insurance, and other operations with Soviet foreign trade organizations and with other Soviet organizations which have been given the right to conclude such transactions (cf. *id.*, art. 564). Presumably aliens are capable of performing at least those legal acts that are inherent in their capacity to have civil rights and duties.

The procedure for declaring a citizen to be incapable of performing legal acts, or to have a limited capacity to perform legal acts, is set forth in the various republican codes of civil procedure (cf. RSFSR Code of Civil Procedure, Chapter 29). A suit to declare a person to have limited capacity to perform legal acts because of misuse of alcohol or narcotics, or to be incapable of performing legal acts because of mental illness or feeble-mindedness, may be commenced on petition of members of his family, trade unions or other social organizations, the procurator, agencies of guardianship and curatorship, or a psychiatric institution. If there is evidence of mental illness or feeble-mindedness, the court is required to appoint a psychiatric expert to determine such mental condition. In a suit to declare a citizen to have a limited capacity to perform legal acts, the participation of the citizen himself as well as of the procurator and a representative of an agency of guardianship or curatorship is required at the trial of the case. In a suit to declare a citizen to be (entirely) incapable of performing legal acts, the citizen himself need not be summoned if his health does not permit.

Harold J. Berman

See also ALIENS; CIVIL RIGHTS; INSANITY; INTOXICATION; GUARDIANSHIP AND CURATORSHIP; NARCOTICS; MINORS; PERSONS; FOREIGN TRADE; FORENSIC PSYCHIATRY

CAPITAL PUNISHMENT

Capital punishment has been known in Russia since time immemorial. Thus Arab writers of the early middle ages mention the use of capital punishment in Ancient Russia for larceny. The Grand Duke of Kiev, St. Vladimir, (10th century), ordered capital punishment to be applied to robbers. Analogous laws existed in the cities of Novgorod and Pskov. But in comparison with the West-European laws of that time historians note the milder character of the Russian provisions. The Tatar invasion and the centralising tendencies of the Moscow Grand Dukes increased the use of capital punishment. Its application became rather widespread. But many capital sentences were not executed due to the right of the Orthodox clergy to claim the prisoner (*pechalovanie*) for the church and instead of an execution to imprison him for life in a monastery. Capital punishment, maiming and torture reached their apogee in the early years of the empire under Peter the Great and his immediate successors. Disgusted with the bloody reign of Anna Ioannovna, and influenced by Western humanitarian philosophy, the Empress Elisabeth (the daughter of Peter the Great) abolished capital punishment in 1753/4 altogether. The attitude to capital punishment of her successor, Catherine II, proved important for subsequent developments in Russia. In her directives of policy—the *Nakaz* (1770) she stated as follows (art. 210): "L'experiénce montre que la profusion des supplices n'a jamais rendu les hommes meilleurs. Si donc je démontre que, dans *l'etat ordinaire* (emphasis supplied) de la société, la mort d'un Citoyen n'est ni utile ni nécessaire, j'aurai gagné la cause de l'humanité." But she admitted two exceptions 1) when a prisoner is able to stir up unrest even beyond the walls of his prison and 2) when in times of trouble and anarchy "... lors que les desordres mêmes tiennent lieu des Loix."

In 1832 under Nicholas I the principles of the *Nakaz* became law. Capital punishment was, henceforth, to be applied exclusively to the most serious political offences, or for breaches of quarantine rules in the case of plague epidemics and for grave military offences. The forensic policies of the Western powers and those of Russia went in opposite directions. West and East alike tried to limit the use of capital punishment. Whereas in the West the tendency was to restrict its use exclusively to the most serious common offences (murder), in Russia the policy was to restrict it to political offences only. However, these expressly stated policies did not work properly. The retention of some cruel and dangerous modes of corporal punishment, such as running the gauntlet and whipping with the *knout*, which were frequently administered in a way which assured a fatal outcome (*zasechenie)*, made the restrictions rather hypocritical. Corporal punishment of that type was abolished in 1871. But there remained another loophole, the right of the Minister of the Interior and the Governors General to transfer the trial of any case under emergency regulations to the jurisdiction of the Military Tribunals, which had the right to sentence offenders to capital punishment for serious common and political offences.

Russian liberal circles and the great Russian novelists Turgenev, Dostoevsky, Tolstoi and the best Russian criminalists Foinitsky, Kistiakovsky, Tagantsev, waged a constant struggle for the abolition of capital punishment. The Criminal Code (the Tagantsev code) of 1903 retained capital punishment for political offences only. All types of corporal punishment were abolished in 1904. The revolutions of 1917 abolished capital punishment, but in 1918 it was introduced for counter-revolutionary offences, sabotage and 'diversion'. In September 1918 the "Red Terror" was proclaimed; it permitted "the shooting of all persons having links with White Guard organisations, or involved in conspiracies and revolts . . ." After the end of the civil war and a certain lull in internal unrest the Government abolished capital punishment for a second time in 1920, but it was soon re-introduced because of new insurrections and unrest. The Basic Principles (*Osnovnye Nachala*) and the Code of 1922 retained capital punishment as the most extreme (*vyshka*) penal measure and prescribed death before a firing squad for the most serious offences "which threaten the very foundations of Soviet power and authority". The Criminal Code of the RSFSR of 1926 retained capital punishment for political offences. In amendments of the Codes in 1927 and 1934 (art. 58^{1}, 58^{1a-d}, 58^{2-14}) such offences were extensively defined, embracing all conceivable activities against the state, and with the use of the analogy clause (see ANALOGY) they were frequently interpreted to include common offences as well. The use of these articles in the purge trials and in the sentencing policies of the GPU (OGPU, NKVD, MVD and MGB) is widely known. After the Second World War, capital punishment was abolished in 1947. A decree of January 12, 1950, reinstated capital punishment for cases of treason, espionage, sabotage and 'diversion'. In 1954 the application of capital punishment was permitted in cases of aggravated murder. Thus the policies initiated by Catherine II, though never pursued wholeheartedly, came to an end. This extension of capital punishment to common offences was continued in the law reforms of 1958-61. The new Principles and the new Criminal Codes of 1960/61, particularly an amendment of May 1961, greatly extended the catalogue of offences for which capital punishment as the severest (*vyshka*) (but never mandatory—always only as an alternative) measure was provided. They asserted again that capital punishment is kept on the statute books as a temporary measure only. Now a number of common crimes besides the usual political offences of betrayal of the fatherland, espionage, terrorism, the killing of a representative of another state, sabotage and 'diversion' (see SABOTAGE), may incur capital punishment. So may common crimes such as murder with aggravating circumstances, the killing of an official, while refusing to submit to his orders or when forcing him to contravene regulations, an attempt on the life of an officer of the militia (police) or of a member of the people's guards (*druzhinnik*) in connection with the exercise of their duties for the preservation of public order, the misappropriation of state or public property on a large scale, the receipt of bribes with aggravating circumstances, and rape with aggravating circumstances (such as by a group of people, or by a recidivist, or rape of a minor, or rape with serious consequences to the victim). The death penalty is also incurred by banditry, by insurrection of recidivists in penal institutions, and by a number of the most serious military offences. Capital punishment may not be applied to pregnant women or to persons under 18 years old. The statute of limitation does not apply automatically (by force of law) but only at the discretion of the courts whenever an offence has been committed for which capital punishment may be incurred. But in such instances the court may not sentence the offender to capital punishment, but must apply some term of imprisonment. Capital punishment is carried out by shooting before a firing squad. Hanging is reserved and has been applied to war criminals.

R. Beermann

CARRIAGE AND TRANSPORT

Rights and obligations arising from the carriage of goods, persons and baggage are governed, in a general way, by the Principles of the Civil Legislation of the USSR (arts. 72-77) and the Civil Codes of the Union republics, which incorporate these articles (see e.g. the RSFSR Civil Code, arts. 372-385). In the Soviet Union, as in free enterprise economies, however, the particular provisions surrounding a specific contract of carriage are usually far more important to the carrier, the passenger and/or the consignor/consignee than those general provisions of the civil law that relate to transport and carriage. In the USSR, these particular provisions do not primarily derive from contracts in principle freely negotiated between the parties: they derive, rather, from economic-administrative planning acts and directives and from legislation that deals specifically with the various modes of transport and carriage, viz., sea, air, rail, road, inland waterways and, most recently, carriage by pipe-line. All these modes except road transport fall within the All-Union jurisdiction; the principal legislation is the USSR Statute on Railways (*Ustav zheleznykh dorog SSSR*—UZhD), approved by resolution of the USSR Council of Ministers on April 6, 1964, as amended by the decree of the Council of Ministers of July 22, 1969; the USSR Statute on Inland Water Transport (*Ustav vnutrennogo vodnogo transporta*—UVVT), approved by resolution of the USSR Council of Ministers on October 15, 1955, as amended by decrees of the USSR Council of Ministers; the USSR Merchant Shipping Code (*Kodeks torgovogo moreplavaniia*—KTM), approved by the USSR Presidium of the Supreme Soviet on September 17, 1968; the USSR Air Code (*Vozdushnyi kodeks*—VK) approved by decree of the USSR Presidium of the Supreme Soviet of December 26, 1961; and the RSFSR Statute on Motor Transport (*Ustav avtomobil'nogo transporta RSFSR*—UAT), approved by resolution of the RSFSR Council of Ministers on January 8, 1969, paralleled by similar statutes in other republics. Further special decrees and regulations govern still more specific forms and aspects of carriage and set out scales of charges; they are supplemented by orders, instructions and rules emanating from *Gosplan* (see PLANNING) and the appropriate ministries and departments. Thus, the VK is supplemented by Rules Governing the Carriage of Passengers, Baggage and Goods on Airlines of the USSR, affirmed by decree of the USSR Ministry of Civil Aviation No. 750 of November 24, 1967; the RSFSR Statute on Motor Transport is supplemented by Uniform Tariffs on Carriage of Goods by Motor Transport, approved by resolution of the RSFSR Council of Ministers on May 5, 1961 and by Rules and Model Agreements for Carriage of Goods by Motor Transport approved by the RSFSR Ministry of Motor Transport and Highways. All carriage and transport statutes etc. must be consistent with the general principles contained in the Principles. Pipeline transport, expected to play an increasing role in Soviet economy, is yet to be regulated by statute. Soviet writers have been discussing the peculiar features of this form of carriage in anticipation of problems that will arise in legislating for it.

All transport and carriage of goods belonging to state, public and co-operative organisations and enterprises is subject to planning acts and directives which place on particular transport organisations and carriers the obligation to carry goods as specified by planning authorities, and make planning directives binding on both consignor and consignee. Such directives are formulated to cover and take into account plans for production, capital construction, material-technical supply, trading, inter-republican deliveries, deliveries of necessaries, etc. Failure to carry out this obligation is actionable as such under the Civil Code. Within the pre-contractual planning requirements, enterprises enter into contracts relating to carriage, and the obligations that arise independently from these are also provided for by Civil Codes and special legislation and are actionable as breaches of contract. If both parties are state economic enterprises (and not kolkhozes, co-operatives, etc.), the dispute is heard by *Arbitrazh* (see ARBITRATION). The Principles of Civil Legislation and the Civil Codes provide that contracts of carriage are real, bilateral agreements for fixed charges to carry goods, passengers and registered baggage (being excess baggage in air transport) to appointed destinations and, in the case of goods, to deliver them there to an authorised recipient. In air transport, however, contracts of carriage of goods, except for perishable goods, are at present interpreted as unilateral, the state plan being binding only on the carrier (art. 92 of the VK, which treats the contracts as bilateral, is taken to foreshadow a development still in the future). Charter-parties and long-term contracts of carriage are consensual agreements. Contracts for carriage of goods not subject to transport plans (which include carriage of citizens' goods, carriage of goods not provided for by plan, i.e. *extra*-plan, and carriage of goods produced in excess of plan requirements, i.e. *ultra*-plan) are permitted. They must be made in the manner provided for by specific transport legislation. Here the carrier may refuse to carry on such grounds as the unsuitability of the form of transport or his organisation's lack of resources for *extra* or *ultra*-plan carriage. While plans of carriage are worked out on an annual or quarterly basis, the parties must work out details for the execution of the plan on a quarterly or monthly basis. Failure to fulfil planned carriage in part of a period may be adjusted by carrying over such carriage into the remaining periods in a manner agreed upon between the parties.

Administratively, for the purpose of making or investigating claims, Soviet procedures throw great emphasis on the transport documents that must be drawn up in connection with each contract of carriage. The principal types are:

a) *Goods Order* (*gruzovaia nakladnaia*)—the most fundamental document of transport, used for rail, inland water and air transport. It must name a definite consignee, determine the journey involved, appoint a destination, describe the goods, state the period of the journey, etc. A copy must be given to the consignor on delivery of goods into carriage; the original is handed to the consignee when the goods are delivered.

b) *Goods Receipt* (*gruzovaia kvitantsiia*)—used for carriage by rail and inland water transport. It is made in the name of the consignee and given to the consignor in confirmation of receipt of goods for transport. It must be presented in any claim for damages for loss of goods.

c) *Road Record* (*dorozhnaia vedomost'*)—used in rail and inland transport as a supplementary document providing evidence of delivery of goods into carriage, but in itself neither a transport nor a contractual document.

d) *Bill of Lading* (*konosament*)—used to confirm a contract of sea carriage of goods and, together with charter-parties, the fundamental shipping document which sets out the conditions of carriage. It names the parties to the contract and the consignee, the ship and the cargo, place of landing, etc. The KTM lists exhaustively all the terms of contract which must appear in the bill of lading if the document is not to fail to have effect as a bill of lading (see also MARITIME LAW).

e) *Goods-Transport Order* (*tovaro-transportnaia nakladnaia*)—the fundamental transport document for carriage by motor transport, without which the motor transport enterprise may not accept goods.

Obligations under Plan

Under civil law, the carrier and the consignor are liable for damages for unlawful acts or omissions leading to improper fulfilment or non-fulfilment of transport plans, e.g. non-supply, supplying in short quantity or supply of unsuitable transport, failure to present goods for carriage, breach in making an application for transport in proper time, delay in loading, refusal to load, etc. The limits of such liability are established by the various statutes and codes (see UAT, UZhD, UVVT, VK, KTM) as well as the resolution of the USSR Council of Ministers on October 27, 1967, "Concerning material responsibility of enterprises and organisations for non-fulfilment of duties and obligations", and by the decree of the USSR Presidium of the Supreme Soviet on November 24, 1967, "Concerning the strengthening of material responsibility for organisations of air and sea transport". The carrier's and the consignor's liability for loss resulting from breaches of duty under the transport plan is strict and not based on fault, but various transport statutes etc. (VK, UAT, UZhD, UVVT) provide exhaustive lists of events excusing the parties from liability, the most common being natural calamities, accident in the enterprise that interrupts work for more than three days, temporary prohibition or restriction of transport of goods, etc. The VK, UAT and UZhD have further exhaustive lists freeing the consignor from liability in specified circumstances. Absence of fault, where breach is due to a change of plan effected by the party's superior agency, or to fault of a third party does not free from liability. For breach of carriage plan obligations (delay in delivery, damage, loss, etc.), a liquidated sum (a fine or penalty) fixed by law, or by agreement before the breach, becomes payable to the injured party, who may be the consignee to whom the duty is owed. Actual losses over and above the fine, even if they exceed the liquidated damages, cannot be recovered. The liquidated sum is usually fixed at a percentage of the transport fee chargeable, e.g., 25% in air transport. In recent years, there has been a trend toward increasing the amount recoverable in liquidated damages in rail, sea, inland water and motor carriage: see e.g., the decree enacted by the RSFSR Council of Ministers on November 23, 1967, "Concerning the strengthening of material liability for non-fulfilment of transport plan and delay in delivery of goods by motor transport", in which increases were effected.

Obligations under Contract

Unhampered by any doctrine of privity of contract, Soviet legislation treats the contract of carriage as conferring rights and imposing obligations on the carrier, the consignor and the consignee. The Principles and the Civil Codes establish the basic obligations in carriage: the carrier's duty to carry to an appointed destination and to deliver to an authorised recipient; the consignor's duty to pay for the carriage; and the consignee's duty to take delivery. Specific legislation imposes additional and/or particularised duties. The UVVT states conditions for presentation of tonnage for loading, loading according to the schedules of dates, terms of loading and unloading, conditions of packaging, etc. which must meet state standards of adequacy (see also UZhD, VK and KTM on packaging). The VK imposes on air transport enterprises the duty to carry goods to an appointed place within an established period, to protect the goods en route from the moment of acceptance to that of delivery, to deliver to the consignee at the appointed place, to notify all proper territorial authorities of the transit of goods, to secure the passage of goods through airport and other authorities within the period of carriage, to inform the consignee of the arrival of the goods, to verify the correctness of the data in the transport order. They have the right to demand the opening of the consigned goods for inspection and verification that the declared value of goods does not exceed the actual value and to reject carriage of perishable goods if unable to secure suitable transport promptly. The consignor must deliver for transport the exact quantity and quality of goods indicated in the transport order, provide in the order an exact description of the goods, and pay transport charges. The consignor has the right to demand delivery at the appointed time and in a proper condition, to demand the return of goods not yet put en route, to change the address of the destination of goods and the name of the consignee in good time. The terms of a contract of carriage can be changed and the contract itself can be terminated only in circumstances permitted by law (set out in detail in the various transport codes) or by an agreement not contrary to law.

In all the legislation relevant to transport activities, the carrier is made liable for loss of, shortage in and damage to, goods accepted for carriage. In the Principles and the Civil Codes, he is presumed at fault and liable unless he proves otherwise. Various transport codes list circumstances in which the carrier is not presumed at fault—where the harm could not have been avoided by any action on the part of the carrier, where it was caused by fault of the consignor or consignee, where it was due to inherent characteristics of the goods, inadequate packaging not obvious on a superficial examination, absence of indication in the transport order of peculiarities of the goods, etc. In these cases, the burden of proof shifts to the consignor/consignee making a claim. Civil legislation specifically permits special transport legislation to provide for instances in which the carrier will be liable only on proof of fault. Such instances have been specified and provided for in the UZhD, VK, and UAT: they are largely concerned with situations where the natural or prepared condition of goods sent for transport normally makes them unsuitable for handling. Under the KTM carriers are liable for loss resulting from *force majeure* (*q.v.*), dangers and risks at sea, fire, acts of war and rebellion, acts or omissions of the consignor or the consignee, the nature of goods and hidden defects, unnoticeable breaches in packaging, the saving of human lives, ships and goods, acts of state, inadequate marking, etc. This liability begins on acceptance of goods for carriage and continues until delivery to the consignee. It may not be altered by agreement, except to start at loading and to end on unloading.

The measure of liability is usually the declared value of the lost or damaged goods or portion thereof or, if no value has been declared, the actual value or portion thereof (VK, UZhD, UVVT and UAT). In some forms of transport, the transport fee is recoverable if its value does not, as a result of the loss or damage, enter into the goods: Decree of the USSR Presidium of the Supreme Soviet of November 24, 1967, and Regulation of the USSR Council of Ministers of October 27, 1967. The UZhD and UVVT impose upon carriers who convert to their own use goods accepted for transport liability for twice the value of the goods.

The date of due delivery may be specified in transport legislation; if not, it is fixed by agreement. The carrier is not liable if delay is not his fault. A carrier who is liable for delay is fined at a sum fixed by law not subject to alteration by agreement; it varies according to the form of transport and the length of delay, being tied to a percentage of the transport fee payable. In recent years, the measure of liability has been increased by decree of the USSR Council of Ministers on October 27, 1967, for rail, sea and river carriage and by decree of the RSFSR Council of Ministers on November 28, 1967, for inter-city motor transport.

The carrier's liability to a fine for delay is independent of damage suffered by the consignee. The consignee cannot demand compensation for losses over and above the fine imposed. The RSFSR Civil Code, however, provides that motor transport enterprises paying a fine for delay are not discharged from liability for loss, shortage and damage caused by such delay. Soviet writers vary in their understanding of the relations between fine and damages and between damages and the transport fee. Some writers believe that a consignee who has suffered provable damages can bring a claim on these instead of accepting the fine imposed. Others go on to argue that the measure of such damages may not exceed the transport fee, even if the actual loss suffered does. The value of goods transported appears not to be a basis for the calculation of the measure of damage. The various transport codes and regulations establish scales of fines for breaches of duty by the consignor (improper indication in the transport order of the nature of the goods, failure to present goods for transport, etc.).

Claims and suits in carriage are subject to a number of special conditions. The RSFSR Code of Civil Procedure provides that actions against carriers arising out of a contract of carriage must be brought at the place where the administration of the transport organisation that acts as carrier is situated and that this requirement cannot be altered by agreement of the parties. The Principles and the Civil Codes also require a claim to be presented to a carrier before action may be taken on a suit, usually within 6 months. Claims for payment of fines should be made within 45 days. Carriers must examine claims and notify the claimant of the response, after which the claimant may file a suit if necessary. The obligation to present a claim to the carrier applies in the arbitrational as well as in the judicial jurisdiction.

Contract of Dispatch

A contract of dispatch (*dogovor ekspeditsii*) is an agreement for carrying out acts normally ancillary to the activities of carriage—e.g., delivery of goods to sea or air ports and stations, receipt of goods at points of unloading or disembarkation, etc. Specialist organisations as well as some ordinary transport organisations enter into such contracts. They undertake to direct or accept goods belonging to the client on his behalf or to carry out other acts of a dispatching nature, and the client undertakes to pay a reward for the service rendered. Such a contract is consensual, bilateral and for reward. It must generally be in writing, except in the case of the dispatch of letters, postcards and parcels through organs of communications, which are under no liability for non-delivery or delayed delivery.

Neither the Principles nor most of the Civil Codes contain any specific provisions referring to the contract of dispatch, which is governed by general norms of civil obligations, special transport statutes, etc. and the decrees of the RSFSR Council of Ministers of July 7, 1962, "Concerning the improvement of transport-dispatch services of the population" and of July 6, 1964, "Concerning tariffs for transport-dispatch services rendered to the population by organisations of the Ministry of Motor Transport and Highways of the RSFSR" and several others. Dispatch services rendered by postal agencies are governed by the USSR Statute on Communications approved by decree of the USSR Council of Ministers on May 27, 1971, together with the order of the USSR Ministry of Communications of August 31, 1960, No. 558 and Postal Regulations approved by order of the USSR Ministry of Communications of June 4, 1957, No. 333.

The nature of the contract of dispatch is seen as a complicated one. It has features in common with a number of other contracts—such as contracts of carriage, of work and of agency—but its peculiarity lies in the fact that the dispatcher has no interest in the goods he handles, or in the carriage he is facilitating. Citizens and state or public organisations may be clients, but only a state or public organisation (usually a motor transport enterprise) may be a dispatcher.

A. E.-S. Tay

CASSATION AND APPEAL

There were two kinds of remedy for an adverse judgment in Tsarist Russia: appeal and cassation. The appeal was the right to ask a court higher than that of original jurisdiction to review a decision or sentence of the court of first instance according to its merits. Cassation was the right to petition a court of second or third instance to re-examine the sentence or decision of the court of first or second instance in respect of its formal and procedural validity. Thus, the appellate court re-examined the case on its merits, whereas the cassation court, only on its formal and procedural correctness.

The Soviet Decree No. 1 on Courts which abrogated all the Tsarists institutions and proceedings in the administration of justice discarded the appeal in criminal and civil procedure but retained cassation (see COURTS). Since what was to be understood by cassation was not defined in the Decree, it must be assumed that the Soviet legislator used the term "cassation" in the same sense as it was applied in the Tsarist codes of criminal and civil procedure of 1864. With regard to the scope of Soviet legislation in eliminating a second examination of the case on its merits, N. V. Krylenko, one of the leading jurists at the beginning of Soviet power, wrote that one of the reasons for a complete abrogation of appeal was the necessity that the court, as a state organ, should enjoy full confidence in the eyes of the population.

The formal abrogation of appeal was steadfastly maintained in all subsequent legislation, but cassation, as will be shown below, developed into a fully-fledged appeal.

Indeed, Decree No. 2 on Courts already provided that the cassation court had the right to reverse the sentence not only because of formal violation which were deemed to be substantial, but also if it found that the sentence subject to the complaint was evidently unjust.

It is clear that the finding of an "evident injustice" by the cassation court is a judgment on the merits of the case.

The People's Commissariat of Justice issued an instruction defining the activities of the cassation court on July 23, 1918. The right to reverse the sentence in the case of evident injustice was repeated in this instruction, and the right of the cassation court to mitigate the punishment and, in exceptional cases, to dispense with punishment completely, was added.

Although the Statutes on the People's Courts of November 25, 1918, upheld the principle of excluding a second examination of the case on its merits, the cassation court received the right to reverse sentences and decisions, along with cases of procedural violations or erroneous applications of the law, on the ground that the sentence or decision was evidently unjust, or that the preliminary investigation was incomplete. Furthermore, not only did an imperfect preliminary investigation become a new cassation ground, requiring the examination of the case according to its merits, but the cassation court was also charged with the *ex officio* consideration both of the cassation grounds brought forward in the complaint (the stating of a cassation ground was in general not necessary in the petition for cassation) and of any cassation ground appearing in the procedure. Clearly, this duty of the cassation court could not be fulfilled without the examination of the case on its merits.

The first Code of Criminal Procedure of 1922 retained the double-tongued language of the legislator, forbidding the touching upon the merits of the case on the one hand and including in the cassation grounds imperfect preliminary investigation and evident injustice, on the other.

The Basic Principles of Criminal Procedure

of 1924 established the "cassation-revisional" character of the Soviet cassation. Whereas in France and Tsarist Russia the "pure" cassation procedure was applied, the German *Reichsgericht* (Supreme Court) used the "revision procedure". The German *Revision*, in contradistinction with "pure cassation", empowered the *Reichsgericht* to change the decision or sentence under revision if the evidence gathered by the court of original jurisdiction was sufficient for a judgment on the merits of the case.

The revisional character of Soviet cassation brought it a step nearer to the appeal, since the cassation court could change the sentence "if this [were] possible without a review of the evidence". The basic grounds for cassation were: a) violation of procedural forms which hindered the court in examining all the aspects of the case and had, or could have had, an influence on the pronouncing of the right sentence; b) violation or incorrect application of USSR or Union republic laws, if the error committed by the court caused a different measure of social defence to be used than that which would have had to be prescribed by the court had the law been correctly applied. However, parallel with these grounds, the insufficiency and irregularity of the preliminary investigation and the evident injustice of the sentence remained on the books as cassation grounds.

The provision that the cassation court was not limited to the cassation grounds indicated in the complaint was retained. It must be emphasized that the Union republics were also empowered to lay down other grounds for cassation within the limits of their own individual republics, or to exclude cassation in some cases completely.

The Basic Principles of Court Structure of the USSR and the Union Republics of 1938 required the cassation court to examine the motivation as well as the legality of the sentence or decision on the basis of evidence filed in the case or presented by the parties to the cassation court.

The New RSFSR Code of Criminal Procedure of 1961, passed in conformity with the Principles of Criminal Procedure of the USSR and the Union Republics of 1958, upholds the duty of the cassation court *ex officio* to examine the legality and motivation of the sentence or decision according to the evidence produced in the court of original jurisdiction and the additional material submitted to the cassation court. The cassation court is still not limited to the cassation grounds listed in the complaint, but has to examine the entire procedure in all its aspects, also with regard to others convicted in the trial or involved in the trial or civil suit and to other persons, even if they are not covered by the complaint.

Although the examination of the legality of the sentence is the purpose of every cassation procedure, the review of the motivation of the sentence, i.e., as to whether the conclusions of the court of original jurisdiction correspond to the facts and the evidence gathered by that court, is a clear evaluation of the case on its merits.

An element of the cassation procedure contributing to the transformation of the work of the cassation court into the activities of a court of appeal, is the provision of art. 337 of the new Code of Criminal Procedure, namely the right of the parties involved in the cassation procedure to present "new material" to the cassation court in support of or against the complaint. "New material" means new evidence not known to the court of original jurisdiction. Since the law does not define the kind of material which may be presented, it must be concluded that any material capable of functioning as new evidence, supporting or refuting evidence produced in the court of original jurisdiction, can be submitted to the cassation court.

Although the question of whether the cassation court has the right to hear witnesses is denied by some Soviet writers, cases have, however, been known where the witnesses were interrogated by the cassation court. It seems to the present writer that since it is not disputed that written testimony of witnesses or experts can be submitted as "new material", the cassation court must have the power to check the written testimony by oral interrogation. It must be assumed that if the legislator had wished to exclude oral testimony as a new material he would provide for it in the law.

According to the new Code, the cassation court is empowered a) to reject the complaint or the protest and leave the sentence unchanged; b) to review the sentence and remand the case for a new preliminary investigation, or for retrial; c) to reverse the sentence and quash the procedure; and d) to change the sentence.

The cassation court acts as an appellate court in some cases: it has the duty to examine the entire procedure at the preliminary investigation, and at trial, as well as the legality and motivation of the sentence or decision, and it has the right to reject the complaint, to remand the case, to quash the procedure, or to change the sentence on the basis of the original or of new evidence.

G. Z. Anashkin, in the commentary on the RSFSR Code of Criminal Procedure (*Nauchno-prakticheskii kommentarii k ugolovno-protsessual'nomu kodeksu RSFSR*, 1963, p. 604), enumerates the questions to be resolved by the cassation court: a) have the inquest, the prelimary and the court investigations been carried out completely and thoroughly? b) do the court's conclusions described in the sentence correspond to the actual circumstances of the case? c) did an essential violation of the law of criminal procedure take place? d) is the penal law correctly applied? e) does the punishment prescribed by the court correspond to the importance of the crime committed and the person of the convict? f) is the kind of penal colony in which the convict has to serve his punishment correctly chosen? g) are the reasons for and the conditions which contributed to the commission of the crime clarified and are measures taken for their liquidation? Indeed, how can all these questions be answered without a judgment on the merits of the case?

The basic rules governing cassation in criminal cases are applied to cassation in civil suits. The civil cassation court also has to examine the legality and motivation of the decision of the court of original jurisdiction according to the evidence gathered at the first instance hearing or presented additionally to the cassation court. The civil court also is not limited to the cassation grounds enumerated in the complaint, but has to examine the entire procedure.

It is obvious that the examination of the cassation grounds requires the review of the decision on its merits in civil suits also.

Thus, the appeal eliminated in the Soviet legislation was artificially restored in practice by enlarging the activities of the cassation court, bringing it *de facto* to the reviewing of criminal and civil cases on their merits. The reasons for such a procedure were, on the one hand, the desire to uphold the principle of the examination of a case on its merits in one instance only and, on the other, the feeling of possible injustice if there is no opportunity also to review a case on its merits.

The review of cases already in force is discussed by the same author under RES JUDICATA.

Samuel Kucherov

See also APPELLATE PROCEDURE; REMEDIES

CAUSALITY, CIVIL

The 1964 RSFSR Civil Code (following the 1961 USSR Principles) requires a causal connection between the conduct of defendant and the plaintiff's loss mainly in the law of obligations: in contract by articles 219, 221,

224, 225; and in delict by articles 444, 454, 455, and 458.

Soviet jurists agree on the following propositions about the nature of causality: 1) it is not an *a priori* category of thought but an objective connection existing regardless of consciousness; 2) strictly, therefore, questions of foreseeability are irrelevant (but see CAUSALITY, CRIMINAL); 3) although a material category it is knowable by the human mind; 4) causality in law does not differ from causality in fact; 5) the lawyer, however, is especially interested in those facts which infringe normal social conditions; 6) since the principles of causality are objectively true, the concept cannot differ from one branch of law to the other; 7) there is no special difficulty in analysing the consequences of an omission.

Apart from the above Soviet jurists differ *inter se*. Wth one major exception (see CAUSALITY, CRIMINAL) they reject the theory of conditions; and the adequacy theory. The majority favour a distinction (based on Engels, Dialectics of Nature, Eng. ed. 1954, p. 219) between necessary and accidental causality. One approach (which to an outsider is difficult to distinguish from a theory of conditions) regards a necessary cause as one "so essential to the given result that otherwise it would not have occurred" and an accidental cause as one "so inessential . . . that the result would nonethless have happened" (Matveev). Other views look rather like an adequacy theory: "One fact is in causally-necessary connection with another if in practice—in experience—it is shown that facts of the first type produce results of the second" (Novitskii & Lunts). Similarly Ioffe offers the test of whether or not the circumstances were "objectively repetitious".

The courts (as reported) never cite doctrine. Their decisions establish the following: 1) defendant's conduct must be at least a condition of plaintiff's loss; 2) this, without more, is insufficient; 3) in finding a condition not 'the' or 'the immediate' cause the courts look to see whether, between defendant's conduct and plaintiff's loss there occurred any unusual act of a third party, of the plaintiff, or of nature; 4) in actions based on art. 444 or against plaintiff's employer (see DELICT) defendant is frequently exonerated for lack of fault with specific reference to causality.

Where defendant's obligation is backed by a penalty (*q.v.*) or where delayed payment is sanctioned by interest, plaintiff need show no causal connection between his loss and the sum due.

CAUSALITY, CRIMINAL

The 1960 RSFSR Criminal Code defines crime in relation to consequences, a topic which Soviet jurists discuss separately from causality. In fact the two issues seem to be one; but the question of causality is not so acute in Soviet criminal law since the mental element for guilt specifies foresight of, or negligent failure to foresee, consequences (see MENS REA).

In theory (see CAUSALITY, CIVIL) there is no difference in the concept between various branches of law. The leading writer (Tsereteli) on this topic in criminal law, however, admits that the theory of conditions is irrefutable, and that to find whether given conduct is a condition, methods of notional elimination and substitution must be applied. But the court, having ascertained that defendant's conduct is a condition must, before a finding of guilt, ask if it had a socially dangerous character by considering three variables: the purpose of his conduct; the social significance of his aim; and the degree whereby his conduct facilitated the attainment of that aim. Further, the court must consider whether the purpose of the rule which was broken was to prevent the type of consequence which occurred: thus a worker's own carelessness might not break the causal connection between his injury and his employer's

breach of safety regulations.
The cases establish that defendant's conduct must be at least a condition: thus a bank clerk who failed to check signatures was exonerated when it was shown that his only carelessness occurred after the fraudulent withdrawal. Even though a condition, causal connection may be broken by the victim's act, careless medical treatment etc. And, in several cases, the courts fuse causality and foreseeability: defendant chases the victim who falls, breaks his leg, and dies of blood poisoning. "There is no causal connection between defandant's behaviour and victim's death, because [defendant] could not foresee this course of events."

Bibl.: Feldbrugge, F. J. M., Soviet Criminal Law (Law in Eastern Europe No. 9, 1964), pp. 102-110.

B. Rudden

CENSORSHIP, see FREEDOM OF THE PRESS; PRESS; RADIO & TV

CERTIFICATES OF AUTHORSHIP
Certificates of Authorship are obtainable by qualified authors of inventions, technological innovations and rationalization proposals (art. 520 Civil Code). In the area of inventions, the certificate may be elected as an alternative to a patent. For factory inventions, *i.e.*, inventions made in the course of state employment or subsidization, only a certificate is available. Similarly, only certification is possible for certain products, such as pharmaceuticals, medical processes and food products manufactured in a non-chemical manner.
Technological innovations and rationalization proposals are, in all cases, eligible solely for certification. "Technological innovations" encompass constructions or technological processes which are new for a given industry or enterprise, although lacking the absolute novelty required for an invention. "Rationalization proposals" are ideas of an industrial-technical character which improve the efficiency of labour, use of materials, and so forth, but do not essentially alter the construction or technological processes of production. In brief, taken together, these two forms of industrial property comprise what is commonly known as "industrial know-how".
The Certificate of Authorship is awarded by the State Committee for Inventions and Discoveries upon consideration of a properly filed application. The application form and procedure are rather simple and no fees are imposed. The application may be made by the inventor, his heirs or an assignee institution. A certificate may be challenged only within one year of issuance. Thereafter, it is valid in perpetuity in consideration of the author's social contribution.
Upon issuance of a Certificate of Authorship all rights to use and ownership of the particular invention or know-how vest in the state. The certificate holder is entitled to a monetary reward in an amount calculated upon a percentage of the annual saving resulting from use of his discovery, subject to legal ceilings. His first 1000 roubles compensation is tax exempt. In addition, he is afforded preferential treatment in assignment of living quarters and appointment to scientific research posts at better salaries. Finally, he derives social recognition and prestige from the award of the certificate and from his right to have his invention bear his name.
As in the case of patents, disputes over registrability are determined by administrative procedures, but all other controversies are within the general competence of the people's courts.
As a theoretical matter, foreigners should be entitled to obtain local Certificates of Authorship on a national treatment basis, either on the condition of formal reciprocity, or under the Paris Treaty on Iudustrial Property to which the USSR adheres. In practice,

the Certificate of Authorship would appear to have little value to foreigners, who can better exploit their private know-how in the form of licensing agreements.
Certificates of Authorship are regulated by arts. 520-526 of the Civil Code, and in more detail by the Regulations concerning inventions, innovations, and rationalization proposals of April 24, 1959, the Instruction of the Committee for Inventions and Innovations of September 2, 1959, and the Instruction concerning Awards for Inventions, Innovations, and Rationalization Proposals of April 24, 1959.

Jeffrey Hertzfeld

See also INDUSTRIAL PROPERTY; PATENTS

CHEQUES,
see NEGOTIABLE INSTRUMENTS

CHILDREN, see MINORS

CHURCH AND STATE
Among the sources of law determining the legal position of the church in the Soviet Union is a decree of the RSFSR, signed by Lenin in 1918 and still in force. More detailed regulations are contained in a decree of the RSFSR issued in 1929 and in an Instruction made under it, released in the same year (and re-issued in 1931). The other 14 Republics enacted similar provisions. An unpublished All-Union decree of 1945 brought a change in the legal position of the Church (a summary of the 1945 decree was published outside the USSR).

I. CONTENT AND LIMITS OF THE RIGHT TO FREEDOM OF CONSCIENCE

The Constitution of the USSR proclaims the separation of the Church from the State (Art. 124).
The situation of religious communities is further based on the principle that the "freedom to indulge in cult-like practices" does not include the right to spread "religious propaganda". Such a right was, in fact, provided for by the RSFSR Constitutions of 1918 and 1925, but is was revoked in 1929. Since then, only its opposite number has enjoyed the protection of the Constitution, namely the "freedom of anti-religious propaganda". In a state whose "leading core" raises the demand "to systematically conduct scientific atheistic propaganda on a wide scale" (Programme of the CPSU in 1961), every utterance of a religious nature easily leads to a conflict with the secular authorities.
A third characteristic feature of the legal situation of the church under the Constitution results from the nationalization of church property.

1. *Inferences from the Separation of the Church from the State*
The church enjoys no public legal status; it is regarded as a private society. It possesses, therefore, no extra privileges over other private bodies. Religious ceremonies may not be held in state institutions and religious objects may not be displayed there. The religious oath is abolished. Religious instruction in the schools is forbidden, all the more so because the schools are separated from the church.
The individual citizen may not refuse to fulfil his civil obligations on religious grounds, in particular the refusal to undergo military service because of religious convictions is not recognised and is punishable. A citizen's rights may not be prejudiced because of his attitude to religion. Non-observance of this prohibition is punishable under the regulations governing the separation of Church and State.

2. *Inferences from the Ban on Religious Propaganda*

Religious bodies are restricted to the holding of religious ceremonies. They are allowed nothing further, therefore, than the "satisfaction of the religious needs" of their members. Any activity going beyond this is considered to be religious propaganda and is forbidden.

A wide range of activities are classified as religious propaganda. Religious bodies are forbidden to give religious instruction, for example, including any form of biblical or (in the Protestant Church) of Confirmation instruction. Only within the family is a religious upbringing for the rising generation legally possible. But even in the family, religious upbringing of the children is not guaranteed. The organs responsible for supervising family affairs are entitled to regard it as an abuse of parental authority. In such a case a court may order the taking away (*otobranie*) of a child and may place it in the charge of the guardianship agencies. The court can also revoke parental rights.

The church is further deprived of the possibility of being active in the cultural and social fields, and may not, therefore, form children's or women's circles, arrange literary or handicraft meetings, organize excursions, lay out children's playgrounds or maintain libraries. The church is also forbidden to conduct any form of charitable work and may not render any material aid to its members.

3. *Inferences from the Nationalization of Property*

After the October Revolution in 1917 church property was nationalized. The acquisition of new property is forbidden. For this reason it is not possible for wealth or property to be left to the Church in a will. The ban of the acquisition of wealth applies not only to real property, but also to movable goods.

An All-Union Decree of 1945 provides for an exception to this rule, allowing church organizations to purchase means of transportation and houses for ecclesiastical needs. Such a purchase is only possible, however, with the approval of the state supervisory board for church affairs.

Church communities wishing to use church buildings and religious objects belonging to the state must apply to the state. If the relevant state agency approves the application, it concludes an appropriate contract with the religious community. The use of the buildings set aside for religious services (and of the land) is free of charge, but there are other financial obligations, the most burdensome of which is frequently the need to pay house and ground rates.

The church is not authorized to establish "mutual-aid funds, provident or production associations". The congregations may not sign any contracts that involve "trade and industrial purposes".

These restrictions make the church heavily dependent on the state—the owner of the property and objects necessary for the performance of religious ceremonies.

4. *Positive Content of the Right to Freedom of Conscience*

What the church still possesses after all this is the right to "practise its cult". The freedom to hold religious services embraces the right to hold "gatherings" of the faithful, i.e. divine services, and to perform religious rites. "Gatherings for prayer" (*molitvennye sobraniia*) may freely take place (i.e. without interference from the state authorities) only "in the buildings of a religious cult". If the assembly is held outside a church building (e.g. in private rooms), the state authorities must be notified in advance. Open-air meetings, processions and religious congresses require the approval of the state controlling body (in addition to any permission required from the traffic police). The scope of the clergy's activity is restricted to its own locality.

Religious rites which are not performed in

"gatherings" are generally permissible, as far as the written and published law is concerned. In practice, however, the state supervising bodies require a prior sanction. They insist that applications are made for permission to practice, for example, a home christening or a requiem mass within a family.

The right to join together in religious associations applies only to believers who have reached the age of 18. The smallest number of people forming a "religious society" is 20; associations consisting of less than 20 members comprise a "religious group".

CPSU members cannot avail themselves of the freedom to choose a creed because they are obliged to "combat religious prejudices and other relics of the past with determination" (CPSU Rules of 1961, Art. 2).

5. *Protection under Criminal Law*

Violation of the laws on the separation of Church and State constitutes a criminal act. A religious ceremony involving damage to health or any other attack on the person or rights of the citizen is punishable.

On the other hand, freedom of worship also enjoys the protection of criminal law. The hindrance of religious rites is punishable and can lead to a sentence of up to six months' corrective labour.

II. DEPENDENCE OF THE CHURCH ON THE STATE UNDER ADMINISTRATIVE LAW

The dependence of the church upon the state is expressed in the necessity of state "co-operation" when and where the practice of religion coincides with the secular aspect of church life. Practice conveys an impression of how the church is hampered in its activities by this dependence upon the state. Documents from the Soviet Union published in the West contain abundant material on the situation of the church in the Soviet Union in this respect.

The pressure to which the communities and their clergy are subjected is applied primarily by the central state supervisory organ (the Council for Religious Affairs at the USSR Council of Ministers) and its local agents. At the lower administrative level the executive committees (*ispolkom*) of the *raion* Soviets exercise the functions of a supervisory body. Furthermore, since about 1963 "Social commissions for the control of the observance of religious legislation" exist at raion level. Their primary task is (in accordance with an Instruction unpublished in the Soviet Union) to keep an eye on the activity of religious associations in their own district, to report any infringements of the law and to submit suggestions for the restriction and weakening of the church's work within the framework of the law. They should note, among other things, which people participate in religious rites (e.g. baptisms, weddings, funerals), who are the active members of religious associations, and whether the clergy practise tax evasion and fulfil their duties with regard to registration.

III. RESTRICTIONS ON THE LEGAL CAPACITY OF THE CHURCH UNDER CIVIL LAW

Religious associations possess to a certain extent "legal rights", such as the acquisition of means of transport and houses for church requirements and also for the manufacture and sale of religious objects. The rights of church organizations are, however, limited in substance and according to their purpose. In this sense one can speak only of a "special legal capacity".

The limitations are illustrated by court practice. In 1925 the Supreme Court of the RSFSR dismissed an action against a church parish council on the grounds that religious organizations are not legal entities and, therefore, cannot be either plaintiff or defendant. After World War II, on the other hand, some courts regarded congregations as proper defendants. Court decisions in cases where a church organization appears as plaintiff have not become known.

IV. LEGAL ASPECTS OF THE "PUBLIC TRUCE" BETWEEN CHURCH AND STATE

The *modus vivendi* which began to come about in the 1920's as a result of the subordination of the church leadership to the demands of the state, and which during World War II developed into a state of "truce", bears a predominantly political character. Legal security, as provided by an agreement in the way of a concordate, is lacking. This became clear during the anti-church measures of the Khrushchev era during the years 1959-1964.

The present legal situation is vague and unsatisfactory in many respects. This is also acknowledged in the Soviet Union. The church obviously cannot rely throughout and with confidence on positive legal statutes in support of its activities. Moreover, an effective use by the church of the rights envisaged by religious legislation is not adequately guaranteed. The use which the church can make of these rights is heavily dependent upon the intensity of the anti-religious policy of the Soviet leaders at a given time. The supervisory authorities are in a position to apply the law in force in a more oppressive or a more liberal manner according to circumstances. Reliable legal protection is lacking (on the limited scope of judicial control over administrative acts see JUDICIAL REVIEW OF ADMINISTRATIVE ACTS, see also PROKURATURA).

A further characteristic feature is the peculiar shaping which the principle of the separation of Church and State has undergone in legal reality. It has been undermined and practically riddled. The Soviet leaders use all means at their disposal to interfere in church life. The supervisory bodies see as their task the control of religious associations, the influencing of their autonomy and the forging of these associations into an instrument in harmony with the state's aims. This they do, among other things, by referring to the ban on religious propaganda and by exploiting the prevailing regulations on the ownership of property. The principle of the separation of Church and State has thus practically been transformed into its opposite, to the unilateral disadvantage of the church. The Soviet authorities would indignantly reject such an assertion, however. They take great pains to preserve an appearance of non-interference in church affairs by the state. For this reason the supervisory bodies prefer to give their instructions via the church leaders rather than directly, using the latter as their tool. This is the reason for the non-publication of relevant regulations and the secrecy which surrounds church-state relations in the Soviet Union. But none of this can disguise the fact that in a legal system of the Soviet type there is no room for a sphere of activity that is free of state interference. The state arrogates to itself the right to control entirely the material and spiritual life of its citizens. It can grant the church no exceptional position.

For a *Table of Statutory Materials* with references to published translations and for a *Bibliography* of pertinent legal literature published in the USSR and outside it (about 95 titles), covering the period 1917-1969, see: Loeber, D. A., The Legal Position of the Church in the Soviet Union, Appendix II and III, in: Studies on the Soviet Union, Vol. 9 (1969), pp. 42-50.

D. A. Loeber

CITIES, see TOWNS

CITIZENSHIP

The basic norms governing the definition, acquisition and loss of Soviet citizenship are set forth in the federal Law of August 19, 1938. The statute reaffirms the principle of a single Union citizenship and provides that every citizen of a Union republic *eo ipso* counts as a citizen of the USSR. The reverse is not necessarily true, and a person may be accepted into Soviet citizenship without ever being identified as a citizen of one of the fifteen republics that today comprise the federation.

De lege are recognized as citizens of the USSR: 1) all those who on November 7, 1917, were subjects of the former Russian empire and who have not lost their Soviet citizenship; and, 2) persons who have acquired Soviet citizenship in a manner prescribed by law. The directive does not spell out the mechanics of acquisition of Soviet citizenship at birth: until not long ago, it was assumed that Soviet practice here continued to abide by the rule whereby an individual was deemed a citizen of the USSR by virtue of descent if at the moment of birth either both parents were citizens of the USSR or just one parent was. More recently, however, administrative policy seems to have shifted to the previous formula according to which a person was vested with Soviet citizenship at birth if at the time both of the parents were Soviet citizens; if only one of the parents was then a citizen of the USSR, Soviet citizenship did not automatically devolve unless the birth occurred on the territory of the USSR or, in case the event took place abroad, the father at that juncture was located on Soviet soil. The above procedure has since been officially ratified by the Principles of Marriage and Family Legislation of the USSR and the Union Republics of 1968.

Foreigners, irrespective of nationality and race, are admitted to the citizenship of the USSR upon their request by the Presidium of the USSR Supreme Soviet or the Presidium of the Supreme Soviet of the Union Republic in which they reside: thus, applications for naturalization filed by individuals living abroad fall within the exclusive competence of the central authorities, while federal and republican organs share concurrent powers in the matter of petitions emanating from aliens already domiciled in the USSR. The statute does not list any special prerequisities in connection with naturalization, but in fact the latter is granted only after the most careful and exhaustive scrutiny of the candidate's antecedents and qualifications.

Release from Soviet citizenship calls for the express permission of the Presidium of the USSR Supreme Soviet. Marriage between a citizen of the USSR and a foreign national does not affect the citizenship of the parties in the eyes of Soviet law. Upon change of citizenship by both parents, when both of them become citizens of the USSR, or when both of them cease to be such, the citizenship of children under 14 years of age changes correspondingly. The change of citizenship of children over 14 but under 18 may take place only with their consent. In all other situations, the change of citizenship of children under 18 follows the standard modus operandi, which means that a special petition must be submitted on their behalf by joint agreement of the parents or by the sole surviving parent and, in regard to the minor members of the family who fit the 14 to 18 age bracket, meet in each instance with the approval of the *de cujus*.

Forfeiture of Soviet citizenship may today ensue only as a result of a special decree of the Presidium of the USSR Supreme Soviet. Prior to the adoption of the new Principles of Criminal Legislation of the USSR and the Union Republics, Soviet citizenship could likewise be cancelled in certain circumstances by court order, but that penalty was abandoned in 1958. Finally, the 1938 measure officially introduced the concept of statelessness into Soviet jurisprudence by stipulating that individuals residing on the territory of the USSR who pursuant to the language of the present act are not citizens of the USSR and who possess no proof of foreign citizenship, shall be considered as persons without a citizenship.

In the intervening years, the statute's general provisions have been supplemented by a large body of *ad hoc* legislation as well as a wide sample of pertinent international treaties. For example, various decrees issued in 1939-1941 extended Soviet citizenship to the inhabitants of Eastern Poland, the Baltic states, Bessarabia and Northern Bukovina after the incorporation of these lands into the USSR, subject to the exercise of the right of option and free departure by the *Volksdeutsche* component in their midst guaranteed by appropriate conventions. In exchange, sundry Russian, Ukrainian, Belorussian and Lithuanian elements located in areas under German jurisdiction could transfer to the USSR and thereby acquire Soviet citizenship. Next, a series of decrees promulgated in 1945-1947 sanctioned the restoration of Soviet citizenship by summary methods to persons now residing in Manchuria, Sinkiang, the cities of Shanghai and Tientsin, France, Yugoslavia, Bulgaria, Japan, Czechoslovakia and Belgium who on November 7, 1917, had been nationals of the former Russian empire as well as persons who had once held Soviet citizenship and later had lost it, and their children.

Soviet citizenship was also conferred upon the indigenous inhabitants of Memel and the Memel region upon its reversion to (Soviet) Lithuania and a 1948 directive put it within easy reach of the citizens of the Baltic states and natives of Bessarabia living in Latin America through the medium of simple registration with local Soviet diplomatic and consular missions. Extensive option-cum-resettlement programs were carried out after the war in cooperation with Poland and Czechoslovakia which sparked mass organized movements of population between the Soviet Union and these two countries accompanied by the corresponding loss of Soviet citizenship by those involved in the exodus and the concurrent acquisition of Soviet citizenship by the corps of "repatriants". A steady influx of Armenians from abroad since the end of the war led to the grant of Soviet citizenship to each "returnee" upon arrival on Soviet territory. Conversely, the step taken in 1956 whereby persons of Spanish origin domiciled in the USSR could choose to emigrate to Spain *pro tanto* entailed loss of Soviet citizenship by the principal parties to the experiment.

Thus far, the Soviet regime has been opposed to international efforts aimed at abating the incidence of statelessness, except for adhering to the Convention on the Citizenship of the Married Woman which is designed to prevent loss of citizenship incurred through marriage to a foreigner. However, the Soviet Union has not yet instituted any remedial measures to facilitate the acquisition of Soviet citizenship by an alien woman so penalized through contracting matrimony with a Soviet man. On the other hand, a 1954 resolution which consummated the conversion into Soviet citizenship of a class of individuals long resident on the territory of the USSR who had been born abroad and who arrived in the USSR at various periods and did not produce documents to show possession of a foreign nationality, as well as their children, is reported to have virtually liquidated the phenomenon of statelessness within the confines of the USSR. By contrast, the issue of dual citizenship has inspired the conclusion during 1956-1958 of a set of bilateral agreements between the USSR and the majority of its "socialist" allies, plus Yugoslavia, intended to eliminate the problem by offering the individuals concerned a choice of citizenship. Subsequent accords between the USSR and Hungary, Poland and Bulgaria have sought to prevent the further development of dual citizenship conflicts between the signatories by devising permanent procedures for their consequent resolution in favour of one or the other side either upon inception or shortly thence.

George Ginsburgs

See also NATIONALITY

CIVIL LAW

Apart from a first and soon abandoned attempt in 1918, the question of drafting a civil code arose for the first time in 1920. At that time it was purely a question concerning the Russian republic because the individual Soviet republics possessed full sovereignty. The term "All-Russian", current at that period, refers to the supreme agencies of the Russian Federation (RSFSR).

The first federal Constitution of January 31, 1924, authorized the federal legislature to enact only the general principles (*osnovy*) of civil law and civil procedure; the Union republics retained their competence to enact codes of civil law and civil procedure (see CONSTITUTIONAL HISTORY).

In 1921 a commission had already been instituted with the task of working out "a code of laws concerning obligations arising out of contract". In his famous letter to Kurskii, Lenin remarked with regard to this project that it would be necessary not to copy the old bourgeois conception of civil law, but to create a new civil law, "a new attitude towards private contracts", and also to incorporate in the future code "the absolute guarantee of the rights of our state, not only to revise and to supervise, but also to rescind for serious reasons of state".

Complaining that the project did not follow his directives, Lenin ordered the creation of a committee of three lawyers to draw up a list of modifications and amendments. In any case the draft code was to be approved "politically", not only by the Council of People's Commissars, but also by the *Politbiuro*, and to be submitted for inspection by Lenin himself.

In his letter of February 28, 1922, to the People's Commissar of Justice ("On the Civil Code"), Lenin supplied further directives for the compilation of the code, which was not to be "a servile imitation of Western civil law", but "a series of limitations of the same, in the spirit of our laws, without restricting economic or commercial activities". In particular, one was to utilize everything which could be found in Western doctrine or practice in order to protect the interests of the workers, and not to "please Europe, but continue to strengthen state intervention in private law relationships".

After inspecting the new draft in March 1922, Lenin decided to postpone its promulgation for a while, and considered it wiser not to go further than the publication of a "declaration of basic property rights" of the citizens of the RSFSR, protected by law and by the courts of the RSFSR; the declaration was to indicate the basic line "outside which we do not intend to make concessions in the sphere of property relations". The Declaration (one provision of which ensured the possibility of submitting to a court of justice any asserted violation of individual rights) was accepted on May 22, 1922.

On the same day a commission of experts was appointed to draft a civil code under the chairmanship of professor Krasnokutskii within the department of legislative proposals of the People's Commissariat of Justice. A draft Code, later on described as "bourgeois", was ready in the month of August. This draft was considered unsatisfactory, and the author of a popular work on Russian economic law, and possibly the best known lawyer of the era, Goikhbarg, was called upon to introduce amendments and write the final text on the basis of the commission's first draft. Goikhbarg was a person who sympathized with the solidarist and socializing currents in Western Europe, inspired by the writings of Hedemann, Renner and Duguit (which were to be attacked later on in the Soviet legal literature under the general title of *Goikhbargizm*).

Goikhbarg completed the work in two months, with the aid of only a younger assistant (Bernshtein), taking his inpiration largely from the German *BGB*, the Swiss Civil Code and the Russian draft of 1905 (1913), but eliminating anything which did not seem suitable to the new type of society, and introducing a number of norms which appeared to be more in harmony with the directives of communism—"those communist principles which constitute the characteristic traits of our code in the period of transition". It seems that Stuchka must be credited with the drafting of the general part.

The All-Russian Central Executive Committee met on October 10 and 25 to discuss Goikhbarg's draft, which had already been approved by the Commissariat of Justice and had been presented to the Council of People's Commissars (*sovnarkom*). On October 31, before the final approbation of the code, Lenin closed the session with the words which were to remain famous in the history of Soviet civil law:

"Here [in the Civil Code] also we have tried to maintain a distinction between what constitutes the legitimate satisfaction of the individual citizen, with regard to the present economic circulation, and what represents an abuse of the NEP, which is legitimate in all [other] states and which we will not legitimize . . . We do not want to tie our hands in any case. If everyday life shows up abuses which we have not succeeded in seeing beforehand, we shall bring about immediately the necessary corrections".

The Russian Code of 1922 is a document of the NEP period, the legal superstructure of the economic policies of the Soviet state. It is, in the words of Stuchka, the milestone of a temporary retreat, which fixes the ultimate perimeter of the concessions to bourgeois law. The Soviet legislator had limited himself, according to Stuchka, to a partial return to Western law:

"When it was also our turn to draft our code we rightly rejected the idea of restoring our prerevolutionary civil law, which was backward and semi-feudal. We took over therefore the civil law of the West, but only within certain limits and without any special system; we only introduced a few articles with a class character . . ."

Undoubtedly the Code was put together in great haste and in an unsatisfactory and defective manner due to the excessive abbreviation and the lack of co-ordination and system. One critic remarked that it was nothing but "a collection of fragments of obsolete bourgeois legal relations", and that 60% of this was only a "dead zone" of the law. The best answer to such attacks was provided by the intention, abandoned later on, of keeping the Code only for a period of two or three years by way of experiment. Another objection was that the Code was written only in favour of the enemies of socialism (foreigners and capitalists), but that these showed themselves extremely dissatisfied. It should be noted, however, that present-day interpretation of the Code is essentially positive: it is not only a "temporary retreat", but also a necessary stage in the transition to socialism.

The Civil Code of the RSFSR of 1922 was divided into three parts: general part, rights *in rem*, and rights *in personam* (obligations), and into 436 articles, each part subdivided into a number of chapters.

The Code represents a compromise between collectivist ideas and the traditional conceptions of Western law. The prevalence of the former is ensured by a number of purely "Soviet" rules, which are regarded as the safeguards of the socialist economy and the predominance of the public over the private sector, and by their flexible application through politically reliable courts.

These "commanding heights" of private law are: art. 1, which prohibits the exercise of rights in a manner contrary to their economic and social purpose (one is reminded of art. 2 of the Swiss Civil Code); art. 4, which attributes legal capacity to any citizen with the sole aim "of developing the productive forces of the country"; art. 4 of the Code of Civil Procedure, which allows the judge, in the case of a legislative hiatus, to be guided by the general principles of the system and by the "general policies of the Workers' and Peasants' Government"; art. 30 (of the Civil Code), which spells out the nullity of transactions which are meant to violate or circumvent the law and, in particular, of transactions which are "patently detrimental to the state"; art. 59 note 1, which bars the revindication by owners whose goods have been expropriated "on the basis of revolutionary law", or, generally, which "came into the possession of the workers prior to the Declaration on basic property rights"; art. 53, which declares that the land, the subsoil, the forests, the waters, the railways in general use and the means of transport belonging thereto, are *res extra commercium* and exclusive property of the state; and finally art. 22, which excludes ownership by private physical or legal persons of industrial and transport enterprises and nationalized or municipalized buildings (see NATIONALIZATION).

Furthermore one should mention the presumption (*juris tantum*) that the state is the owner of any goods the ownership of which is contested on the territory of the RSFSR (based by the courts on art. 68), and the non-applicability of extinctive prescription against the state; also art. 147, which attributes to the state whatever is to be restituted in a case of unjustified enrichment (*q.v.*) resulting from illegal or anti-state transactions.

Above all, however, the Civil Code of 1922 was characterized by two fundamental elements: the declaration that its own foundation was the principle of socialist planning "which will be victorious in the struggle against the anarchy of freedom of competition and profit", and, thereby, the inclusion of norms of public law in a typically private law compilation (see PUBLIC AND PRIVATE LAW). The presence of these two elements represented in the eyes of Soviet lawyers the essential difference from, and the supreme guarantee against, any possible bourgeois degeneration of the Civil Code (see also PLANNING).

Civil codes based on the Russian model were promulgated in the Ukraine (December 16, 1922), Belorussia (February 2, 1923), Armenia (February 13, 1923), Azerbaidzhan (April 16, 1923 and November 14, 1927), and Georgia (August 18, 1923). In the Turkmen, Uzbek, Kazakh, Kirghiz and Karelo-Finnish republics the Russian Civil Code was made applicable. The Uzbek Code (i.e. the Russian Code with subsequent Uzbek amendments) was applied in Tadzhikistan. The three Baltic republics, at the moment of their annexation in 1940, "found it necessary to ask the Supreme Soviet of the USSR to apply temporarily" (until the promulgation of a federal code then still under discussion) the codes of the RSFSR, while in the Moldavian republic the Ukrainian code was to be applied.

Initially, the differences between the codes were insignificant. They all conformed to the Russian model (either in the organization, the divisions and numbering, or in the contents of the code) in honour of the "special position" of the same. Only the Ukrainian Code diverged to some extent, especially during the years of the so-called ukrainianization (1923-1927) until the law of July 8, 1927, concerning the equality between the Russian and Ukrainian languages.

With the passing of time and the accumulation of new republican legislation (until 1936), however, new provisions were introduced in the republican codes, even in those Asiatic republics which had taken over the Russian Code, while at the same time the amendments of the Russian Code based on RSFSR enactments were not necessarily incorporated in the codes inspired by it.

Some differences also arose because of lack of co-ordination of the codes (or parts of the codes), when civil law innovations were introduced by a federal enactment. The federal provisions were sometimes reproduced literally, and sometimes with distorting modifications, arbitrary selections or defective adaptations.

For these anomalies a radical remedy was introduced in 1936: art. 20 of the new Stalin Constitution, which provided that in cases of divergence between federal law and republican law (including the republican constitution), federal law would prevail. If the republican legislature had failed to introduce the amendments necessitated by a federal enactment, or had introduced such amendments with too many distortions or too late, the federal law had to be applied on the entire territory of the USSR.

The further one gets away from the 1924 Constitution, the more civil law tends to become federal (enactments concerning state enterprises, co-operatives and kolkhozes, industrial and banking law, cheques and bills of exchange).

In the Stalin Constitution of December 5, 1936, codification was henceforth concentrated in the hands of the federal legislature. The long list of art. 14 (which also prescribes the promulgation of a federal civil code) leaves little to the competence of the republics.

For almost twenty years one therefore discussed the elaboration of a federal civil code, according to the principle laid down in art. 14h of the Constitution. A draft produced by the federal Institute of Legal Sciences, on the order of the People's Commissariat of Justice, was examined during the first few months of 1939.

The law of February 11, 1957, however, put an end to the centralizing tendency in legislation. The republics again became "sources of codes", albeit only within the limits established by guiding principles emanating from the federal government. The competence of the Union, exercised by its Supreme Soviet (arts. 14 and 30 of the Constitution), is extended in particular to the enactment of basic principles governing the use of land (1968), of the subsoil, of the forests and waters (1970), of basic principles of labour law (1970), of civil law, and of marriage and family law (1968). (See also CODES & CODIFICATION.)

Within a few years the difficult question of whether to retain general civil codes, or to separate economic codes from civil codes, as was done later on in Czechoslovakia, was resolved, after much controversy. The Basic Principles of the Civil Legislation of the USSR and the Union Republics (*Osnovy grazhdanskogo zakonodatel'stva Soiuza SSR i soiuznykh respublik*, hereafter: Principles), enacted on December 8, 1961, and in force since May 1, 1962, have opted for the unitary conception of civil law, which regulates equally property relations and connected personal, non-property relations, independently of their subjects—private persons or socialist organizations (art. 2 Principles). Still, the unity of substantive civil law does not prevent a certain differentiation between the regulation of two types of relationships within the principles and the civil codes, nor the adoption of a vast body of special economic legislation, nor the independent teaching of economic law and the emergence of a separate legal discipline of the same name (see also ECONOMIC LAW). One should bear in mind at this point that, if the civil law for many years has been one of the most unstable branches of Soviet law, this is probably due, to a large extent, to the insecurity of its relations with the set of norms which govern economic relations *sensu lato*, affecting the identity, the co-existence and the internal hierarchy of these relations.

The Principles are divided into eight parts (*razdely*), thirteen chapters (*glavy*), and 129 articles (*stat'i*). They consist of an introduction (defining the political, economic and social objectives of civil legislation) and a general part (which tacitly amends or at least updates chapter 1 of the federal Constitution); they also provide general rules concerning property, obligations, rights of authors, inventors and discoverers, succession and private international law.

The relations between federal and republican legislation in the field of civil law is regulated by art. 3 of the Principles, which covers three positions:

1. As a rule, the codes and other republican enactments will incorporate, add to, and elaborate the rules contained in the Principles (e.g. with regard to ownerless property, leases, author's contracts: arts. 33, 55 and 98 of the Principles), with the possibility of introducing provisions for those property and personal relationships on which the Principles are silent (art. 3 Principles). This possibility has been utilized in the RSFSR Code for loans (*zaem*, arts. 269-274), "free use of goods" (*bezvozmednoe pol'zovanie imushchestva*, regulated by arts. 342-349), agency (*poruchenie*, arts. 396-403), commission contract (*komissiia*, arts 404-421), barter (*mena*, art. 225), gifts (*darenie*, arts. 256-257), deposit (*khranenie*, arts. 422-433), "combined activities" (*sovmestnaia deiatel'nost'*, a terminological metamorphosis of the simple company of the NEP, arts. 434-438), and competition (*konkurs*) for the best execution of public works (arts. 439-443). See also LOANS; USUFRUCT; AGENCY; COMMISSION AGENTS; GIFTS; CONTRACTS; CORPORATIONS; OBLIGATIONS.

2. The relationships defined in art. 3 par. 2 of the Principles or in other articles of the Principles (arts. 17, 22, 23, 24, 83, 84, 85, 86: no prescription for certain actions; forced execution of the monetary means of state farms, kolkhozes or trade unions; credit and account relations in the public sector) and other relationships indicated in the Constitution belong to the exclusive competence of the Union.

3. The foreign trade sector is governed by federal law by virtue of the state monopoly in this field (Regulations on foreign trade delegations and agencies of 1933; Rules concerning the form and the manner of signing foreign trade contracts of 1930; laws and regulations concerning the organization of foreign trade; statute of the Foreign Trade Bank of the USSR of August 22, 1962; Customs Code of the USSR of May 5, 1964). Republican law is also applicable (and applied in foreign trade arbitration), where it is not excluded by special federal laws. (See also FOREIGN TRADE).

Apart from art. 3, a sphere of mixed federal and republican competence is created by arts. 8, 22-4, 98, 100-1 and 105, governing respectively limitations on legal capacity, forced execution of the property of state and co-operative organizations, and copyright. According to some authors mixed competence implies that a matter may not be regulated by republican law until first a federal norm has been created. Others allow the republics to create their own rules in the absence of federal law.

Art. 18 of the Principles (art. 8 of the RSFSR Civil Code) regulates the "application of the civil legislation of one Union republic on the territory of another Union republic"; the criteria used differ from those employed for solving conflicts between Soviet and foreign law (see PRIVATE INTERNATIONAL LAW).

On the basis of, and in accordance with, art. 3 of the Principles the supreme soviets of the 15 republics adopted their own new civil codes in the years 1964-1965. The RSFSR Civil Code was enacted on June 11, 1964, and entered into force on October 1 of the same year.

After having been discussed in the entire Union, corrected after consultation with the legal department of the Presidium of the

USSR Supreme Soviet, and often drafted by mixed interrepublican commissions, the codes do not offer much diversity. If one studies the Russian and Ukrainian codes and, if scrupulous, a code of one of the Central Asian republics, one acquires an adequate picture of the civil codes of the USSR. They elaborate, extend and add to the provisions of the Principles, which are reproduced integrally (although scattered) in the republican codes. They synthesize "the latest achievements" of recent civil and arbitration practice and of legal scholarship, and the reforms introduced by recent decrees and other enactments. The technical drafting has considerably improved. In some of the republics (Moldavia, the Baltic republics) the codes represent the first civil codification under the Soviet regime.

All codes consist of a preamble and eight parts of which only the first three are subdivided into chapters. The Russian Civil Code is divided into 42 chapters and 569 articles (the law of obligations is divided into "general principles" and "individual types of obligations").

Apart from insignificant differences in the place and subdivision of some chapters and articles, an inventory of the more important differences is soon made.

The Uzbek, Kazakh, Azerbaidzhan, Ukrainian and Moldavian codes, in their original versions, regulate the dispatch contract, which is not mentioned in the other codes (see CARRIAGE & TRANSPORT). *Negotiorum gestio* (*vedenie chuzhikh del bez porucheniia*) is mentioned only in the codes of Azerbaidzhan, Tadzhikistan, the Ukraine, Moldavia and Latvia. Some of the differences result from the different dates of promulgation of the codes.

The largest number of differences are attributed by Soviet writers to the desire of each republican legislator to find the best solution to a series of practical problems. This may explain the republican variations in the maximum limit of dwelling space which private citizens may own: 60 sq. meters in the RSFSR, 100 in Lithuania, 110 in Estonia (where, however, the space required for auxiliary buildings, such as garages or verandahs, is included). See also HOUSING.

According to the Ukrainian, Uzbek, Latvian, Turkmen and Tadzhik codes, the executive committee of the local soviet may order the confiscation of unlawfully constructed private houses, but not the eviction of the citizen out of the same house, as is provided by the other codes (see EVICTION).

The Kazakh, Azerbaidzhan, Latvian and Armenian codes regulate in detail the manner of confiscation of buildings, cars and other goods acquired through non-labour income, while the Russian courts and those of the other republics are inclined towards a restrictive construction of the rules regarding confiscation (see FORFEITURE).

In the Ukraine, but not in Russia, a testament made in favour of an unborn child which is not the child of the testator is invalid.

Some of the codes make a third category of heirs out of the deceased's brothers and sisters who are able to work; in the Ukraine (though not in Russia) the adopted child inherits from his own parents as well as from his adopted parents. See also SUCCESSION; ADOPTION.

There are also some differences in the rules concerning *indignitas* and incapacity to succeed, claims against a deceased person and the accepting of the estate.

The Lithuanian Code alone regulates the problem of the *commorientes* (art. 569) and denies the validity of a partial acceptance of the inheritance (art. 530).

The Uzbek Code protects, among personal non-property rights, the right to correspondence, diaries and one's own picture; it allows in some cases the legitimate succession by representation of nieces and nephews of the *de cujus*.

The limitations on civil capacity on account

of intoxication or the use of drugs vary among the different codes. See also CAPACITY.

With the exception of the Russian Code (art. 253), the retention of a life interest accompanying the sale of immovable property constitutes an independent contract and is not considered to be a part of the contract of sale. Some of the differences between the codes derive from national or local traditions and from the different historical development of the various republics (*e.g.* the absence in the Kazakh Code of rules concerning the common property of an individual peasant household). These are small in number, however, because the affinity of the codes "manifests itself also in the unity of their contents, which is determined in particular by the unity of the political and economic basis of all the Union republics, by the identity of the duties concerned with the advancement of socialism which stand before them and which are contained in the preambles of the codes".

G. Crespi Reghizzi

See also ABSENTEES; AIR LAW; ALIMONY; ASSIGNMENTS; ASSOCIATION; AVERAGE; BAILMENTS; CARRIAGE AND TRANSPORTATION; CAUSALITY; CERTIFICATES OF AUTHORSHIP; CHAMBERS OF COMMERCE; CIVIL STATUS REGISTRATION; COMMERCE; COMMERCIAL LAW; CONTRACTORS; COPYRIGHT; DEBTOR AND CREDITOR; DEFAMATION; DEPENDANTS; DIVORCE; DOMICILE AND RESIDENCE; DURESS; ESCHEAT; FAMILY LAW; FAULT; FINES; FORCE MAJEURE; FRAUD; GUARDIANSHIP AND CURATORSHIP; HIRE PURCHASE AGREEMENTS; INDUSTRIAL PROPERTY; INTEREST; ILLEGITIMACY; LOST GOODS; MARINE INSURANCE; MARITIME LAW; MARRIAGE; MATRIMONIAL PROPERTY; MINORS; MISTAKE; MARITIME ARBITRATION COMMISSION; MORTGAGES; MOTOR VEHICLES; NAMES; NEGLIGENCE; NOVATION; PARENTS; PERSONAL PROPERTY; PERSONS; PLEDGES; POSSESSION; PATENTS; PROPERTY; RESTITUTION; RETAIL TRADE; SALES; SALVAGE; SAVINGS ACCOUNTS; SET-OFF; STATE ENTERPRISES; SUPPLY CONTRACT; SUPPORT OF DEPENDANTS; STRAY CATTLE; TESTAMENTS; TRADE MARKS AND TRADE NAMES; UNJUST ENRICHMENT; WARRANTY

CIVIL PROCEDURE

We are here concerned with the general characteristics of Soviet civil procedure (for details of various features of this procedure see separate headings, e.g. APPELLATE PROCEDURE, TRIAL).

The Soviet system falls half-way between the accusatory and inquisitorial extremes. In procedure by pure inquisition all the materials and testimony are collected by various examiners, on the initiative of the public, and the decision may be taken on these documents by another person. In the extreme accusatory procedure the conduct of the trial is in the hands of the parties, and the judge acts as a rather passive referee of the procedure. In the Soviet system the parties have the option to begin proceedings, bear the initial burden of proof, file or make statements, retain advocates, ask for witnesses, decide whether or not to appeal, and may cross-examine one another and each other's witnesses. Hence there are many accusatory features. On the other hand there are many officious features as well, reflecting the Leninist idea of all procedures affecting the public. Thus a case may be started by a public procurator if the party does not, and cases may be undertaken by various public bodies (see PARTIES). The court may insist on further evidence, appoint an expert on its own initiative, and go beyond the facts made out by the parties and the amount of the claim, though it may not decide a separate cause of action not referred to by the parties. The court need not allow the plaintiff to abandon his claim, or the defendant to concede it, and may refuse leave to settle the claim on terms acceptable to both parties (see SETTLEMENTS). On appeal the higher court is not restricted to the stated grounds of appeal or to the parties appealing (see APPELLATE PROCEDURE). Thus the parties are responsible for conducting the case but do not enjoy any exclusive authority over it. Of course the judge takes an active part in the trial and may question witnesses, as happens in many European countries.

The Soviet system also has oral and written elements. The case cannot begin without a fairly comprehensive written statement of claim by the plaintiff, but from then on most matters are orally discussed, e.g. applications for adjournments or for expert reports, even though these eventually end in written court orders, and the trial itself is oral (except for documents, which all legal systems admit) although it terminates in a written judgment and is recorded for future reference in court records, (see TRIAL; EVIDENCE; COURT RECORDS).

The Soviet lawyers ascribe eight elements to their system of civil procedure, one of which, the accusatory has been discussed. The other seven are: 1) Publicity of trial, unless state secrets are involved. The court may also decide to sit *in camera* where intimate personal details are involved, but reasons must be given for such an order. All decisions are announced in open court, though they are arrived at by the court in its retiring room. Publicity is important for public confidence and to educate the general public. 2) Equality of litigants without discrimination between plaintiffs and defendants or generally on grounds of race, creed or colour. Such matters are also not noted in court records. 3) Objective truth—this means that if the judge is not satisfied with the parties' proofs he can order better proofs to be sought, and he can give parties more than they ask, if they are entitled to it. This principle reflects the idea of legality, that all wrongs are to be put right, and the philosophic idea that it is possible to discover objective truth and not merely weigh up rival bodies of evidence. 4) Freedom of choice, e.g. whether to sue and for how much, but this is considerably limited by the officious elements already referred to when considering the adversary principle. 5) Orality. Witnesses testify orally and relevant documents are read out at the trial. Applications for various interlocutory orders are heard orally. Exceptionally, depositions may be used (see EVIDENCE). 6) Directness, i.e. the best sources of information must be used—hearsay is admitted but the original speaker should be produced if possible etc. 7) Uninterruptedness. A case must be tried without interpolating other cases, unless necessary adjournments are required, to prevent the court and persons involved losing the thread of the proceedings.

The republics have very detailed civil procedure codes which govern all situations (RSFSR Code of Civil Procedure of 1964). Obvious characteristics of the system in general are the wide range of persons and bodies entitled to take part in a case and the low level of costs and lawyers' fees.

A. K. R. Kiralfy

CIVIL RIGHTS

History

After the victory of the October Revolution the door was open to introducing the civil rights that had been elaborated in the first Party Programme of 1903. Instead, the Declaration of the Rights of the Working and Exploited People of January 25 (12), 1918, which is praised by Soviet writers as the beginning of a new, glorious epoch in the history of civil rights, was merely a political programme concerning the question of how to abolish exploitation and did not mention civil rights at all. These were listed in the RSFSR Constitution of July 10, 1918, for the first time, but referred to toilers only. In contrast to the demands of the 1903 Party Programme the non-working population was not included among the subjects of civil rights. The division of people into two groups according to their occupation or social origin was maintained until the adoption of the still valid Stalin Constitution of 1936. In order to camouflage the true nature of the Soviet system and to deceive the outside world, Stalin inserted a separate chapter on civil rights in the Constitution. Since then civil rights have been granted to all Soviet citizens regardless of their class position.

Doctrine

According to Marxism-Leninism civil rights are a product of class struggle. They appeared with the development of capitalist society, when they were used by the emerging bourgeoisie as a weapon in the fight for political power in addition to the economic power already obtained. After both powers had become a monopoly of the ruling bourgeoisie, civil rights were transformed into an instrument for defending and stabilizing the existing order. Consequently, in capitalist society the working masses are deprived of all liberties constitutionally granted to them, because they do not control the necessary political and economic prerequisites. Real freedom and equality become possible only in a classless society where there is neither an exploiting few nor an exploited many. In socalist and communist society where the working people exercise political power, are the owners of the means of production, and where an identity of social and personal interests prevails, civil rights are enjoyed by every individual of the collective.

Starting from these premises Soviet ideologists have developed some basic teachings on socialist civil rights. First of all, the great importance given to economic conditions leads to a new interpretation of civil rights from a material point of view. There is a strong emphasis on the material guarantees of each civil right in general and on the group of the so-called "social-economic" rights in particular. On the other hand, the traditional personal freedoms are rather neglected. Secondly, it is claimed that fundamental rights and duties constitute an inseparable unity, because "he who does not work, neither shall he eat". The material guarantees of civil rights can be created only when every citizen participates in building socialism. Therefore, the citizen must be interested in carrying out his duties thoroughly as he is assuring his rights at the same time. It is in the practical outcome of this concept that there is no distinction whatsoever between rights and duties: exercising rights is a duty, and performing duties is a right. Thirdly, natural law doctrine is rejected. There are no civil rights derived from sources other than positive law. As positive law is created by the State, all civil rights are to be granted by the State. There does not exist anything like innate human rights. On the other hand, positive law constitutes a part of the superstructure determined by the economic basis. Finally, from the assumed identity of social and personal interests it is concluded that exercising fundamental rights by the individual cannot and must not encroach upon social interests. If the use of civil rights were to infringe social interests, it would be a wrong use and, therefore, inadmissible. A possible conflict is to be resolved in favour of social interests. In any case, the interests of the working people—as it is expressed in several articles of the Constitution—are the inherent limits of every civil right. Who is to tell what the interests of the working people are at a given moment? At this point the Leninist teachings on the Communist Party enter the scene, according to which the Party is the most advanced and politically the most conscious section of the working people. In this capacity the Party always knows what is to be done and what is due to political leadership. The conclusion reached by lengthy ideological reasoning is simple: The interests of the working people and thus the inherent limits of civil rights are what the Party says they are. It is not easy to develop a legal doctrine of civil rights on ideological conditions like this. So, it was not by chance that Soviet legal science dit not take much care of civil rights until Stalin's death. But then, in the mid-1950's destalinization had some repercussions on civil rights doctrine, too. Some scholars (e.g. A. A. Piontkovskii, S. F. Kechekian, B. V. Sheidlin) took pains to elaborate a legal doctrine of civil rights more precisely and to strengthen the individual's legal position. They attempted to forge stronger links between subjective rights, objective law, and the material basis of society. In so doing they compressed the stages of the law-creating process to the effect that the subjective rights and the material basis have come closer together, weakening thereby the almighty position of State-created positive law. On these grounds it could be claimed that the State was to create norms in accordance with the exigencies of the developments taking place in the material basis of society. Of course, the crucial question has never been asked: What should happen when the material basis requires that a certain civil right should exist, but where there is no norm on which the existence of this right could be based or, what is more, where valid objective norms explicitly exclude its existence? Nevertheless, more liberally minded legal scientists holding such views were sharply attacked by their conservative colleagues (I. E. Farber, N. G. Aleksandrov). At the beginning of the 1960's the liberals reached a deadlock because developing their ideas further would have meant hurting ideological taboos.

As far as the legal nature of civil rights is concerned, a conformity of views prevails to the effect that civil rights are to be considered as subjective rights. A more thorough study of the relevant statements reveals, however, that there is remarkable difference between simple subjective rights and fundamental rights. Only the former are real rights in the sense that they come into being immediately by virtue of a legislative act. The latter are provided for by the constitution itself and are general in nature. It is concluded from this that an unfolding and break-up in sub-constitutional norms are necessary to transform fundamental rights in real claims. This means that fundamental rights are in themselves hardly more than declarations without any direct binding force. They are useful at best as an aid to law-application in the several branches of legal life.

Classification

Soviet legal science usually distinguishes between four groups of civil rights:

a) Social-economic rights, such as the right to work, the right to rest and leisure, the right to material support, the right to education, and the right of personal property. Communist doctrine lays the utmost stress on this group as it starts from the materialistic concept according to which the socio-economic conditions of man determine the extent and contents of his freedom. The proclamation of these rights at the beginning of the constitutional enumeration of specific civil rights is, indeed, a clearly distinctive feature compared with the corresponding chapters in Western constitutions. Most of these rights are directed at services and are, therefore, exclusively dependent on the willingness and ability of the government to abolish unemployment, to develop social insurance, to establish educational institutions, etc. As to personal property, it is assured only within narrow limits (see Section 2 of Article 7 and Article 10 of the Constitution).

b) Equality. This embraces equality before the law and uniformity of fundamental rights and duties of all citizens in economic, social-political, and cultural life, irrespective of their sex, nationality, or race. Notwithstanding the fact that the Constitution of 1936, unlike its predecessors, grants civil rights to all Soviet citizens, regardless of their class position, unlimited equality does not conform to the teachings on the dictatorship of the prole-rariat. The concept of a dictatorship necessarily involves the idea that there is a group of people to be suppressed and this group cannot be equal to the suppressors. In the Party Programme of 1961, however, it was declared that the dictatorship of the proletariat had fulfilled its historic mission and did not exist any more, but since Khrushchev's ouster this postulate has been de-emphasized and the connection between the present Soviet system and the dictatorship of the proletariat is stressed again.

c) Political liberties, such as the freedom of speech, the freedom of the press, the freedom of assembly, the freedom of conscience, the freedom of association, and the right to vote. All these liberties are severely limited by what is called "the interests of the working people". Every political activity that would encroach upon the objectives of the political leadership, which alone knows what the interests of the working people are, is inadmissible. The Marxist conception of freedom as insight into necessity is the starting point for theoretically transforming individual liberties into an instrument for submitting people to State discipline. The consequences of this attitude are clearly indicated by the constitutional provisions on the electoral system. According to Article 141 the right to nominate candidates is secured to the Communist Party and the various Party-led mass organizations only, so that the ordinary citizen has no other choice than to vote for a single candidate offered to him, directly or indirectly, by the Party.

d) Personal rights, such as the inviolability of the person, the inviolability of the home, the privacy of correspondence, the right to defence, and the right of asylum. Apart from the latter, which is afforded to foreigners persecuted for defending the interests of the working people, the extent of and limitations on these rights are mainly to be found in the Codes of Criminal Procedure. In considering the limitations on personal rights in the course of criminal procedure it is noticeable that the supervising agency of the investigation organs which conduct the examinations in the pre-trial phase is the procuracy. Appeals from abuses of pre-trial procedure may be taken only to the procuracy, not to the courts. This means that the final decision on the most significant measures, such as arrest, detention, search, attachment, etc., is in the hands of a prejudiced agency. Furthermore, the position of the accused is aggravated by the fact that legal aid by a defence counsel is normally not allowed during pre-trial investigation (but see DEFENCE).

Guarantees

The realization of civil rights can be ensured by ideological, material, legal, and political guarantees. The question of ideological guarantees has already been dealt with while analyzing the Soviet doctrine of civil rights, and we have seen that Soviet ideology, despite some progress achieved since Stalin's death, is not particularly qualified for developing standards of behaviour claiming much respect for the individual.

The material guarantees primarily concern the social-economic rights, because they can be realized only if the government provides for the necessary material prerequisites. In this respect the Soviet Union ranks, by and large, with the more developed capitalist countries. In 1962 the ratios of public expenditures for welfare, health, and education to the gross national product in the Soviet Union were 8.1, 2.5, and 3.8 as compared to 15.0, 3.2, 2.4 in West Germany and 6.7, 1.2, 3.0 in the United States. On the other hand, the standard of living is considerably lower than in most of the Western countries, e.g. about one third in comparison with West Germany. It follows from this that in the Soviet Union a greater effort by the government is needed in order to reach a certain level of social security and educational standards than is the case in countries where private wealth is greater.

The protection of civil rights by legal means is quite underdeveloped. There are no constitutional courts or other institutions specialized for this task. Civil rights are protected only within the general framework of administrative legality. An administrative procedure up to the legal standards of the rule of law does not exist. The citizen whose subjective rights have been infringed by the administration is granted formal legal remedies by way of exception only. According to a USSR decree of April 12, 1968, every citizen is allowed to make petitions to any government organ, which is obliged to settle the matter within the appointed time. However, there is no possibility of enforcement and the decision is up to the superior organ of the agency that issued the allegedly illegal act. As the whole procedure rests within the same organizational unit an unbiased handling of the matter is hard to imagine. More independent judicial controls are rare. In articles 233-244 of the 1964 RSFSR Code of Civil Procedure and in other legislative acts there are some cases listed where an appeal to the ordinary courts is possible. The most important agency for controlling administrative legality is the *Prokuratura*, which is empowered to lodge protests against illegal administrative acts. Although the *Prokuratura* is not allowed to take any final decision, its protests exert considerable influence. Nevertheless, the value of this institution for protecting civil rights should not be overestimated because the *Prokuratura* is a hierarchically structured apparatus directed from a centre whose major task consists in the defence of Party and State interests.

Finally, as regards the political guarantees, the political system of the Soviet Union is a one-party dictatorship. Such a system is, by its very nature, opposed to civil rights, as the existence of real freedom is incompatible with the idea of dictatorship. Undoubtedly, since Stalin's death there has been a loosening of the screws, a sort of liberalization, which has strengthened the position of the individual vis-à-vis the representatives of political power. The development cannot be considered, however, as a continuous one. It has been interrupted by several set-backs and, recently, there has been a plain turn for the worse. In any case, supremacy of party power has remained fundamentally unchanged and the activity of all law-applying agencies depends on Party consent as ever before. As a consequence, the actual significance of civil rights is determined by the Party will, which is the ever changing yardstick for measuring their realization.

Bibl.: Dmitri-Georges Lavroff, *Les libertés publiques en Union Soviétique*, 2nd ed., 1963; Georg Brunner, *Die Grundrechte im Sowjetsystem*, 1963; Lothar Roth, *Staatsauffassung und Grundrechte in der Union der Sozialistischen Sowjetrepubliken*, 1965; Socialist Concept of Human Rights, Budapest 1966.

G. Brunner

See also FREEDOM OF ASSEMBLY; FREEDOM OF ASSOCIATION; FREEDOM OF SPEECH; FREEDOM OF THE PRESS; PROCURACY; JUDICIAL REVIEW; SOCIALIST LEGALITY

CIVIL SERVICE

The activity performed in the fulfilment of state functions by persons appointed or elected to positions in state institutions and receiving compensation from the state for their labor. The term *gosudarstvennaia sluzhba* is also said by Soviet sources to refer to the body of legal norms establishing the legal position of civil servants, the conditions and procedures for the performance of their functions, their compensation and their liability. But this would be rendered more accurately in English as "civil service law". Norms controlling and defining the functions of the civil service are derived mainly from administrative law and labor law.

There are said to be several basic principles of the Soviet civil service. First, civil service positions are to be open to all Soviet citizens regardless of race, sex, nationality or property considerations. Civil service status is to be determined by political considerations and ability only. Second, a significant proportion of civil servants, especially leading workers in local executive organs, are elected rather than appointed. The Program of the CPSU envisages the gradual extension of the principle of election to all of the top officials of state agencies. Third, a civil servant has no permanent tenure in office. He may be relieved of his functions for improperly fulfilling duties, breaching state or labor discipline or having a bureaucratic attitude toward his duties. Finally, in comparison with other Soviet citizens civil servants are to have no special social or political privileges.

Soviet writers generally note that, as Lenin indicated, under communism the administrative functions of the state will cease to be the responsibility of a specific category of citizens, the civil service. Rather, they will be carried out by all members of society and there will be no special state apparatus. In accordance with this, the 1961 CPSU Program provides for a gradual reduction of the state apparatus with the aim of its eventual elimination. The Program puts it as follows: "As the socialist state system develops, it will gradually become public *communist self-government*... The agencies for planning, accounting, economic management and cultural development, now state bodies, will lose their political character and will become agencies of public self-government."

Civil servants (*gosudarstvennye sluzhashchie*) constitute the total body of the Soviet civil service. They fall into three basic categories: "auxiliary personnel" (*vspomogatel'nyi personal*), "officials" (*dolzhnostnye litsa*), and "representatives of authority" (*predstaviteli vlasti*). The work of auxiliary personnel is limited to routine or technical operations. Examples would be office clerks, typists in a typing pool, laboratory assistants, etc. Such employees do not issue legal acts or possess administrative authority. Their acts cannot have legal consequences of a kind that can create, change or terminate administrative relationships. Their activity involves the keeping of records, the preparing of documents, certificates and other materials which, of themselves, without the authorization of competent civil servants, have no legal force. Some Soviet writers limit the concept of civil servants to those who have the authority to perform actual administrative functions, and thus exclude auxiliary personnel from the category.

"Officials" are civil servants whose activity is connected with authoritative state functions in political-administrative and social-cultural matters, as well as in the administration of the economy. The basic trait that characterizes the official is his right to make decisions having the force of law. Under the law, his powers and duties may include hiring, discharging, transferring, rewarding and disciplining the employees under his jurisdiction, as well as managing credit and entering into contracts and other transactions. Thus, in contrast to auxiliary personnel, officials can, by their activity, initiate, change or terminate legal relationships. "Leading workers" (*rukovodiashchie rabotniki*) among the officials, such as ministers, chairmen of local executive committees, managers of enterprises or administrators of social-cultural institutions, may have broader powers of planning, control, and accounting with regard to the organs under their jurisdiction than do ordinary officials.

A sub-category of officials is known as functional workers and specialists, i.e., persons who occupy positions in the state apparatus and possess higher or intermediate education. These include, among others, teachers, physicians and architects. Although they are not granted the above mentioned administrative powers (e.g., hiring, discharging, rewarding and disciplining employees), they do perform other acts having legal significance and constituting the basis for the creation, alteration or termination of legal relationships. For instance, a statement by a physician that an individual is unable to work may serve as the basis for the awarding of compensation by the administration of an institution, enterprise or organization. Similarly, the grading of students taking state examinations constitutes the basis for the awarding of diplomas.

Art. 170 of the RSFSR Criminal Code of 1960 ("Abuse of Authority or of One's Official Position") defines "officials" as "persons who permanently or temporarily carry out the functions of the representatives of authority and also those who permanently or temporarily occupy positions in state or public [*obshchestvennye*] institutions, organizations or enterprises connected with fulfilling organizational-management or administrative-economic duties, or who fulfil such duties in these institutions, organizations or enterprises by special authority". Two things should be said about this definition. First, included within it is a specific reference to "representatives of authority", the third category of civil servants mentioned above. Their status as a sub-group of the category of officials will be discussed below. Second, the term "official" (*dolzhnostnoe litso*), as used in this definition, may refer not only to a functionary or a state organization but also to an official of a non-governmental (*obshchestvennyi*) organization such as a trade union.

"Representatives of authority", the narrowest category of civil servants, can, for most intents and purposes, be regarded as a subgroup within the category of officials. The distinctive characteristic of "representatives of authority" is their ability to issue orders to persons other than those who are their subordinates in an employment relationship. In contrast, "officials" can legally exercise their powers only within the institution or organization in which they serve or within lower-level organs directly subordinate thereto. The orders issued by representatives of authority must be obeyed and may be enforced by the police power of the state if necessary. Such powers are possessed by, among others, members of the police, the state security organs, the state sanitary inspection agencies and the procuracy, as well as local soviet executive committee chairmen.

In addition to compensation in money, civil servants are eligible for a variety of awards based on outstanding service. These include honorary titles (*zvaniia*), orders and medals as well as awards, gifts and honorable mention. The "highest degree of distinction" which a civil servant can receive is the title "Hero of Socialist Labor", which is awarded to persons who "by their particularly outstanding innovative activity in the field of industry, agriculture, transportation, trade, scientific discovery or technical invention have performed exceptional services to the state and have contributed to the development of the economy, culture, science or the strength and glory of the USSR". Recipients of this honor, which is awarded by the Presidium of the USSR Supreme Soviet, also receive the Order of Lenin and the gold medal "Sickle and Hammer". Lesser awards, which may be given at other levels of state administration, include: the Lenin Prize; a variety of "merited worker" awards, such as "merited worker of science", "merited teacher", "merited jurist", etc.; mention on an honor roll or in an honor book, etc.

For shortcomings in the performance of their functions, civil servants may be subject to four kinds of liability: criminal, administrative, material and disciplinary. Chapter Seven (arts. 170-176) of the RSFSR Criminal Code of 1960 provides criminal penalties for a variety of "service crimes" (*dolzhnostnye prestupleniia*), including abuse of authority or official position, exceeding authority, failure to exercise authority, misappropriation or embezzlement of state funds, bribery and forgery. Penalties for such offenses may range to the death penalty in the case of acceptance of bribes in particularly aggravated circumstances (art. 173 of the RSFSR Criminal Code).

Administrative liability ensues for an administrative fault or error. Such liability is imposed not by the organization in which the civil servant is employed, but by the organization having jurisdiction over the sphere of activity in which the error or fault was committed. For example, for violations of fire regulations, sanitary rules or traffic rules, liability is imposed on civil servants by state agencies responsible for enforcing the fire, sanitary or traffic rules, respectively, regardless of the agencies in which the civil servants are employed. Sanctions ensuing from administrative liability are limited to warnings and fines.

Material liability is based on an error or fault which results in damages to the state, public organizations or citizens. Material liability falls within the spheres of civil and labor law, rather than administrative law. Three types of material liability may be distinguished: limited, full and increased. Limited liability, under which a civil servant may be required to compensate an amount which, as a rule, will not exceed one-third of his average monthly wages, ensues for damages resulting from simple fault on the part of the civil servant. Full liability, in which the complete amount of the damages must be compensated, may be found in cases where damages have resulted from a criminal act of a civil servant. Increased liability is considered an exceptional measure designed to preserve certain types of state property used in economic activities. For the negligent loss or damage of certain tools or work clothes, a civil servant may be required to compensate up to five times the value of the articles in question. For stealing or intentional destruction of such articles, compensation will be exactly five times their value.

Disciplinary liability ensues for disciplinary violations, i.e., violations of the rules of internal operation of the state agency in which the civil servant is employed. A disciplinary violation may be based on either an act or a failure to act. The act or omission may be intentional or negligent. Penalties for disciplinary violations range from informal reproof to discharge from one's positions.

In recent years some Soviet writers have begun investigating the social and educational make-up of the civil service. So far, however, only a limited amount of detailed data have been published. A sample survey of civil servants in the city of Kazan—the results of which were described as "typical" for the country as a whole—showed that about 45% of civil servants came from working-class families, 21% from peasant families, and 34% from families of civil servants. The 1959 Census showed that 63.5% of white-collar workers (*sluzhashchie*) had higher or intermediate education. This category is made up mostly of civil servants, but also includes non-production employees of such non-governmental organizations as collective farms and other cooperatives. Most Soviet civil servants are said to work at the lower levels of state administration: only 6.2% are employed at the USSR level and another 15.4% at the Union republic level (Lunev, Piskotin, Iampol'skaia (eds.), *Nauchnye osnovy gosudarstvennogo upravleniia v SSSR*, 1968, pp. 205 and 301).

Donald Barry

See also PROCURACY; COURTS; POLICE; PUBLIC ADMINISTRATION; HONOURS; OFFICIAL CRIMES; DISCIPLINARY OFFENCES

CIVIL STATUS REGISTRATION

The registration of civil status comprises the registration of births, deaths, marriages, divorces, adoptions, ascertainments of paternity and changes of names, art. 27 Principles of the Legislation of the Soviet Union on Marriage and the Family. It is incumbent on the registry offices organized as departments of the executive committee of the *raion* or town soviet or on the executive committee of the village council, art. 141 Family Code RSFSR. The registration gives full proof of the act or fact certified; it can be annulled only on the basis of a court decision, art. 146 Family Code. Because of the great importance of the civil status registration for both the state (demographic statistics) and the citizens (proof of their legal relations to other persons) its correct functioning is secured by penal provisions, e.g. false declarations to the registry office or dissimulation of impediments to marriage are punishable by forced labour of up to one year or a fine of up to 50 roubles or social censure, art. 201 Criminal Code RSFSR.

Births are registered at the registry office of the place of birth of the child, or the domicile of the parents or of one of them. The registry office has to make provisions for a solemn form for the act of registration (thought of as an alternative to baptism). Parents or one of them or, in case of their disability (illness, death or other reasons), relatives, neighbours, the administration of the maternity hospital where the mother stayed at the birth, or other persons have to give notice of the birth orally or in writing. The notice must be given within one month of the birthday or, in case of a still-born child, within 3 days, art. 148 Family Code. The names of the child and of the parents are entered in the birthregister. If the parents are not married to each other, the name of the father is entered in accordance with a common indication of both parents, or in default of such common indication, on the basis of a court decision ascertaining the paternity or, in default of both conditions, according to the wishes of the mother alone. If the child is born to a widow within ten months of the death of her husband, the name of the deceased husband may be entered as the father's name. If the child is born within ten months of the annulment or the dissolution of the marriage of the mother, the child is entered as the legitimate child of the annulled or dissolved marriage, arts. 149, 49 Family Code.

Marriages are registered at the domicile of the bride or bridegroom or their parents in the presence of the couple. In their petition for the banns each must confirm that there are no impediments to marriage and indicate whether he or she was married previously and whether either has children. The registry office ascertains that the couple knows of each other's family status and state of health, instructs them on their rights as husband and wife and parent and on the penal responsibility for dissimulation of impediments to marriage. The marriage is entered in the passports of the couple with an indication of the date and place of the marriage and the name of the other spouse, art. 150 Family Code.

The registry office has to provide for a solemn form for the act of registration.

The divorce is registered at the registry office of the domicile of the couple or of one of them, art. 151 Family Code.

Divorces can be registered: a. on the basis of a court decision, presented by the couple or one of them, art. 152 Family Code; b. on the basis of a common petition of both spouses of their consent to divorce, if they have no minor children. In this case the divorce is registered and a certificate of divorce is issued after three months from the receipt of the petition. For this divorce procedure a fee of 50 roubles is charged, arts. 153, 38 Family Code; c. on the basis of the petition of one spouse, if the other spouse aa) is declared an absentee by a court decision, bb) is declared legally incapacitated by a court decision in consequence of mental illness or feeble-mindedness, or cc) is sentenced by a criminal court to not less than three years of deprivation of freedom. In these cases the petitioner has to present the relevant court documents. The registry office hears the other spouse whether there is a dispute concerning the children, the common matrimonial property, or the obligation to pay alimony to the incapacitated. In the absence of such a dispute the divorce is registered and a fee of 50 roubles is charged. In the case of a dispute the divorce must be decided by the court, arts. 154, 39 Family Code.

Deaths are registered on the basis of a medical certificate at the registry office of the place where the dead person lived or where he died. If there is a court decision ascertaining the fact of death or declaring a person dead, the registry office of the residence of the court is competent for the registration.

Notice of the death must be given within three days from the moment of death or discovery of the corpse by the relatives, neighbours, housing administration, hospital, or other persons, art. 159 Family Code.

Adoptions are registered on the basis of the decision of the guardianship authority (the executive committee of the *raion* or town soviet) by the registry office of that executive committee; paternity is registered on the basis ot a common declaration of both parents, or of a court decision ascertaining the paternity, by the registry office of the domicile of a parent or of the residence of the court; changes of names are registered at the registry office of the domicile of the person changing his name. For the procedure for changing names, see NAMES, arts. 156-158 Family Code.

The registration of births, adoptions, paternity, and death, and the first certificate of these registrations is free of charge; for the registration of marriage, change of name, divorce and further certificates (duplicates) of all registrations a fee, fixed by the Council of Ministers of the USSR, is charged, art. 147 Family Code.

More detailed rules concerning civil status registration may be found in the federal principles of June 2, 1969, laid down by the Council of Ministers of the USSR and in an RSFSR Instruction concerning the manner of civil status registration of October 17, 1969.

A. Hastrich

CIVIL SUIT

Action for criminally caused damages may be brought within the framework of criminal procedure (cf. arts. 54-56 Code of Criminal Procedure).

Known to the pre-revolutionary as well as to Continental European criminal procedure, civil suit was temporarily reduced in importance after the Revolution, then it was gradually re-established, since 1958 even in the military tribunal procedure, and finally it was considered as extremely desirable, almost obligatory. Given state economy and the immense annual damage caused by crimes against public property, the law does not confine itself to relying upon the initiative of the injured organization to sue for damages (the competent representatives are not always personally interested in recovery), but seeks to guarantee recovery procedures in many ways: it makes a civil suit mandatory for managers of state and public enterprises; if the injured party fails to bring action, the procurator can bring it for him in the public interest; even if a civil suit has not been brought at all, the court can—and is often called upon to—decide the compensation question on its own initiative. Nevertheless the agency of inquiry, procurator and court at every stage of the proceedings are obliged to inform the injured party of his right to take civil action. Finally, civil suit is free of costs and fees.

Civil action can be brought at every stage of first instance procedure up to the beginning of the taking of evidence in the trial. A person who is injured directly, but who is not identical with the victim (see VICTIM) in that he has to be materially (not only morally) injured on the one hand, but may be (and usually is) a legal person on the other is qualified to be plaintiff. Civil suit is not permissible if a civil action has been dismissed. Naturally (but this is not discussed by Soviet doctrine), the plaintiff need not be proved to be injured but alleged injury is sufficient. The claimant becomes plaintiff only upon declaration by a decree supported by reasons of the agency of inquiry, the investigator or by court ruling—according to the particular stage of procedure. By this declaration the plaintiff obtains the status of a party: the right to present evidence, submit petitions and challenges, participate at trial, request measures to secure his claim, become acquainted with the materials of the case after completion of the preliminary investigation, appeal from actions of the agency of inquiry, investigator, procurator and court, and appeal from judgment and from any court ruling concerning the civil suit.

Strange to say, the establishment of the status of civil defendant is independent of the existence or nonexistence of a civil action. As to the accused, no special act of prosecution as civil defendant is necessary; his rights as accused comprise those of a civil defendant anyway. But besides him, third persons who by law are liable for the damages (parents, guardians, curators, organizations) can be prosecuted as civil defendants by decree of the police, the investigator, the judge or by court ruling, no matter whether or not a civil action has been brought. This civil defendant has the same rights as the plaintiff.

Proof in the civil suit is not made in accordance with the rules of evidence of the civil procedure law (except the burden of proof), but according to the rules of the Code of Criminal Procedure. When giving judgment, the court decides simultaneously whether the civil suit is subject to satisfaction, in whose favour, and to what extent, and also, if a civil suit has not been brought, whether the material loss is subject to compensation. The resolutory part of the judgment must contain a decision concerning the civil suit presented or concerning compensation for loss: a) in the case of conviction: complete or partial satisfaction, or denial; in exceptional instances acknowledgment of the right to satisfaction while transferring the question of its amount to civil proceedings; b) in the case of acquittal for want of proof: denial; c) in the case of acquittal for want of the elements of a crime, the civil suit remains undecided and is thereby left to civil proceedings as if the action had not been brought.

M. Fincke

CLERKS OF COURT

The secretary of the court, as this functionary is called in Soviet law, is found at every level of the judicature (see COURTS). His chief duty is to make the court record (*q.v.*) of every civil and criminal trial. He signs the trial record together with the chairman of the court and, in case of disagreement, he has the right to attach remarks to the record.

The court then has to decide about the ultimate version of the record.
The secretary of the court may be challenged by the same persons and on the same grounds, or must excuse himself for the same reasons, as a member of the court with one exception: his participation as court secretary during an earlier phase of the same case does not prevent his repeated participation in that same capacity.
The secretary of the court, or one of them if there are several secretaries, heads the administrative apparatus of the court under the general direction and responsibility of the president of the court.

F. J. M. Feldbrugge

CODES AND CODIFICATION

The codification of law, in the sense of the enacting of legislation which purports to state basic rules of law in a comprehensive, systematic, and concise manner, has a long history in Russia, going back to the *Russkaia Pravda* of the 11th century, the *Sudebniki* (Court Manuals) of 1497 and 1550, the *Stoglav* ("One Hundred Articles", an ecclesiastical code) of 1551, and the much more comprehensive *Sobornoe Ulozhenie* (Code) of 1649. From 1700 on there were many unsuccessful attempts at further codification. Finally in 1830 Michael Speransky published a Complete Collection (*Polnoe Sobranie*) of the Laws of the Russian Empire, consisting of a 42-volume reproduction, in chronological order, of the more than 30,000 legislative enactments which had been promulgated since 1649. This was followed in 1832 by the 16-volume *Svod Zakonov* (Code of Laws), which was a systematic codification of the whole of Russian law, branch by branch. New editions appeared in 1842 and 1857. A new Criminal Code was enacted in 1845. Following the great law reforms of the early 1860's, other codes were promulgated. The Criminal Code of 1903 and the draft Civil Code of 1913 were considered to be outstanding achievements of European legal science.
Although the Bolshevik regime at first abolished all prerevolutionary law, and anticipated the early arrival of a time when even revolutionary law would die out, it nevertheless soon felt the need for the codification of two branches of law—family law and labour law. A Family Code was adopted in October 1918, and a Labour Code in December 1918. Thereafter, with the adoption of the New Economic Policy (1921-1928), the RSFSR enacted a Civil Code (1922), Code of Civil Procedure (1923), Criminal Code (1922), Code of Criminal Procedure (1923), Land Code (1922), a new Labour Code (1922), a new Family Code (1926), and a second Criminal Code (1926). Other Republics adopted similar codes. The Ukrainian SSR was alone in adopting an Administrative Code (1927). In addition, with the formation of the USSR in 1924, a few basic instruments of all-union legislation were adopted to govern the republican codes, namely, the Fundamental Principles (*Osnovy*) of Criminal Legislation, the Fundamental Principles of Criminal Procedure, and the Fundamental Principles of Court Organization. (The republics also adopted their own Statutes on Court Organization, which were similar to codes.) Subsequently the USSR adopted a Merchant Shipping Code (1929) and an Air Code (1935).
The 1936 Constitution of the USSR empowered the All-Union authority to adopt codes of civil and criminal law (and not merely fundamental principles). However, despite many efforts to draft such codes before and after World War II, none were adopted, and in 1957 the Constitution was amended to provide, once again (as in the 1924 Constitution), that the USSR had the power to adopt fundamental principles of civil and criminal law (leaving it to the republics to adopt codes in those areas). In December 1958 there were enacted the All-

Union Principles of Criminal Law and Principles of Criminal Procedure, as well as Principles of Court Organization. In December 1961 there were enacted the All-Union Principles of Civil Law and Principles of Civil Procedure. In 1968 there were enacted the All-Union Principles of Family Legislation and the Principles of Land Legislation, in 1969 the All-Union Fundamental Principles of Health Legislation and the Principles of Corrective Labour Legislation, and in 1970 the Principles of Labour Legislation and the Principles of Water Legislation.

On the basis of the Principles, the RSFSR has enacted (as of April 1973) a Criminal Code (1960), a Code of Criminal Procedure (1960), a Civil Code (1964), a Code of Civil Procedure (1964), a Family Code (1969), a Land Code (1970), a Corrective Labour Code (1970), and a Labour Code (1971). Other republics have followed suit. The USSR replaced the earlier Air Code in 1961 and the earlier Merchant Shipping Code in 1968.

The drafting of the fundamental principles and of the corresponding codes in the 1950's and 1960's was preceded by widespread public discussion and enlisted the active participation of many thousands of legal scholars, legal officials, and legal practitioners of various kinds as well as of non-legal personnel. The Commissions on Legislative Proposals of the USSR and republican supreme soviets met frequently to debate the new legislation, consulted experts, and in general showed a very high degree of activity.

The All-Union fundamental principles consist of basic concepts and general provisions, which are reproduced in the codes together with more detailed rules. In criminal law, the fundamental principles serve as the General Part of the code, followed by a Special Part containing definitions of specific crimes and statements of the specific penalties attached to each. Even apart from being governed by the fundamental principles, the republican codes are subordinate to specific all-union legislation. In the case of the criminal codes, for example, the sections on crimes against the state and military crimes reproduce the All-Union Statute on Crimes Against the State and the All-Union Statute on Military Crimes.

The differences among the republican codes are, on the whole, not very significant from a policy point of view, although they may be significant in individual cases. In the criminal codes, for example, one finds that although all contain provisions making it a criminal offense to make alcoholic beverages at home, the Georgian SSR permits the making of wine. In almost all the civil codes, heirs who may take by intestate succession are limited to direct ascendants and descendants, but Uzbekistan extends intestate succession to nieces and nephews as well. Statutes of limitation are also not uniform among all the republics. Some of the differences seem to reflect differences in social and economic conditions among the republics, but most of the other differences seem to reflect differences of opinion among the various republican branches of the Soviet legal profession.

Since the re-introduction of ministries of justice (*q.v.*) in 1970-71, the preparation of codification is one of the specific tasks of such ministries. *Harold J. Berman*

See also LEGISLATION; LAW; CONSTITUTION; LEGAL PROFESSION; FEDERATION; SUPREME SOVIET

COLLECTIVE FARMS, see KOLKHOZ

COLLEGES, see UNIVERSITIES

COMECON

The Council for Mutual Economic Assistance, sometimes popularly referred to as the

Eastern Common Market, is an international economic organization founded in January 1949 at the initiative of the Soviet Union, as a response, in part, to the West European Marshall Plan. Its current membership consists of the USSR, the German Democratic Republic, Poland, Czechoslovakia, Hungary, Bulgaria, Roumania, Mongolia, and most recently Cuba. Albania, a former member, no longer participates. Yugoslavia, Communist China, North Vietnam and North Korea have on various occasions participated in an observer capacity.

The role of the Organization is defined in the founding Communique and is elaborated in its 1959 Charter and in the Fundamental Principles of International Socialist Division of Labor which it adopted in 1961. Its purpose has been to promote broad economic cooperation and strong economic ties between the USSR and the other member states. Over the past two decades, Comecon has facilitated a considerable and on-going exchange of expertise and scientific-technical information among its members. It has also provided a framework for economic consultation between the participating socialist states, out of which have come recommendations designed to stimulate and improve the conditions of commercial relations *inter se* and to guide development of intra-Comecon trade and production specialization. It has furnished a central forum for the negotiation of bilateral trade and payment treaties between the member states and the coordination of various aspects of their national economic plans.

Comecon functions through five principal bodies. At the top of the hierarchy, although technically not within the organization, is the *Conference of First Secretaries of Communist Parties and Heads of Government* of the member states. The Conference determines broad policy matters and transmits recommendations thereon to Comecon for practical elaboration. According to the 1959 Charter, the supreme organ of Comecon is the *Session of the Council.* As a rule, it meets only semi-annually and rotates among the capitals of the member countries. It is empowered to make recommendations on measures regarding intra-Comecon economic cooperation. In practice, the role of the Session of the Council has become largely a symbolic one since the establishment in 1962 of an *Executive Committee* composed of Vice-Premiers of the governments of the member countries. This body also has preempted the role formerly played by the so-called Conference of Representatives to the Council which is apparently now defunct. The Executive Committee meets at frequent intervals and supervises and manages the actual work of the organization, examining the proposals put before the Council and directing the activities of the various organs toward the preparation of concrete measures. It has the power to make recommendations to the member states.

Permanent Working Commissions composed of high level delegates from interested member states exist within Comecon. Their general function is to analyze economic conditions, to collect and distribute technical information, and to make recommendations relative to their respective economic sectors. The activities of these commissions have led, *inter alia*, to the creation of new multilateral organizations such as *Interkhim* in the chemical industry, *Intermetal* in metallurgy, and two international banks for Comecon investment and commercial clearing. They are also entitled to credit for assisting the coordination of multilateral projects such as the Mir Power Grid in the field of electric power, the Druzhba Pipeline in the oil and gas industry, and the common Wagon Pool in the area of transportation. The Standing Foreign Trade Commission has accomplished a significant multilateral unification of Conditions relative to the Delivery of Goods and the Supply and Installation of Plants and Equipment in intra-Comecon trade.

The *Secretariat*, composed of the Secretary, a deputy from each member state and a large staff, performing economic, executive and administrative functions, prepares agendas for all Council organs, makes economic projections, elaborates study proposals, provides facilities for the negotiation of economic, scientific and technical cooperation treaties between member countries, represents the Council vis-à-vis official persons, foreign nations and other international organizations, and publishes a quarterly Bulletin of Economic Information and Collection of Translations. The Secretariat is permanently installed in Moscow and is the headquarters of the Organization. Its officials are deemed to be "international officials" under the Comecon Charter and are entitled to diplomatic privileges and immunities as provided in the Comecon Convention on Legal Capacity, Privileges and Immunities (April 13, 1960).

The legal power of Comecon is basically limited to the authority to make "recommendations" to the member states. Recommendations may be made only upon unanimous agreement of all interested members. Each member has, in effect, an absolute veto power.

A recommendation, once passed, although possessing great moral and political force, does not have binding legal effect on a member state until it is submitted to and adopted by its government according to national law, and this action is communicated to the Council.

There was a determined Soviet effort in the early nineteen-sixties to extend the powers of Comecon and to convert it into a supranational planning agency which would not merely facilitate the coordination of national plans of member states but would integrate these plans into a single program for the economic development of the entire Comecon region on the basis of international specialization and division of labor. This initiative was opposed by Roumania with equal determination on the grounds that an integrated Comecon would be Soviet controlled and would violate the national economic and political sovereignty of the smaller East European states. Roumania, as one of the less developed countries of the organization, was particularly concerned that centralized international specialization would relegate it to remain a supplier of agricultural produce for the more advanced member states and would prevent its own planned industrialization. Preoccupied with other problems, not the least of which was the growing rift with Communist China, the Soviet Union has, at least temporarily, abandoned its initiative. Comecon remains today an essentially international, rather than supranational, organization.

Jeffrey Hertzfeld

COMMERCE AND COMMERCIAL LAW

In the USSR, to the external observer, commercial activity differs little from that in other countries. However, its economic and legal bases are quite different from many countries outside of the member countries of the Council for Mutual Economic Assistance (COMECON or CMEA) and indeed in some respects differ from some of those countries.

Commercial activity in the USSR takes place within the framework of the socialist ownership of the instruments and means of production and the land, industrial enterprises and commercial institutions belong to the State. (This list is not exhaustive; cf. art. 6 of the USSR Constitution and art. 95 of the RSFSR Civil Code.) State enterprises and organisations have a "right of operative management" over property under their control, that is to say the right of possession, use and disposition of such property subject to the limits of the law, and its use *intra vires* their objects (art. 94 Civil Code). It must be against this background that even a brief exposition of commercial law in the USSR must be examined. Of course there is not necessarily a clear dividing line between the non-Comecon countries such as, by way of example only, the United Kingdom, and the member countries of Comecon, for example, the USSR. Thus in the United Kingdom there is government control of many forms of commercial enterprise and also the government exercizes a certain measure of financial control and this type of activity in economic affairs is of course carried out in the USSR but a conclusion drawn from these premises, though perhaps valid would be misleading. It is not the function of this article to deal with the aims of the socialist state but it is sufficient to say that a facile comparison between certain aspects of governmental intervention in the economic affairs in the non-Comecon countries with such intervention in the economic affairs of the Comecon countries completely ignores the underlying reason for the economic organisation of the socialist state which fulfils a very different role from government intervention in the non-Comecon countries.

This economic organisation goes to the very root of the socialist state, permeates its entire social, legal and political structure and encompasses the whole social life of the community in the socialist states and all that follows from this, for example not only the economic implications but questions of the education and cultural upbringing of the population of the socialist states.

It follows from the above that the type of relationships stemming from commercial activities in non-Comecon countries will not necessarily be found in member countries of Comecon and one is drawn, although a measure of generalisation must be admitted, to the following classification. There will be those commercial activities in the non-Comecon countries which are simply not found at all in the commercial life of the Comecon countries and there will be those commercial activities which can be found in the commercial life both of the non-Comecon countries and the Comecon countries that is to say are similar in both even though in the case of the Comecon countries the underlying reason (for example social and political) for these activities may be quite different from such activities carried out in the non-Comecon countries. There will also be commercial activities carried out in the Comecon countries which do not correspond to any found in the non-Comecon countries.

Even where the activities in the non-Comecon countries and the Comecon countries exhibit a degree of parallelism, this may well only be a question of external characteristics not only for the reasons previously mentioned and although the type of activity may be the same, the amount of such activity within each classified type in either the non-Comecon countries or the Comecon countries may differ. It follows from this that certain legal provisions found in the non-Comecon countries will simply not be found in the Comecon countries and vice versa but where there is the kind of parallelism mentioned, there will be a similarity of institutes whose content and importance will vary depending on whether such institutes are to be found in the law of the non-Comecon countries or the law of the Comecon countries.

In summary therefore, the commercial law of the USSR is quite clearly affected by its commercial life and in some cases there will be no institute of law in the commercial law of the USSR corresponding to such an institute of the law of a non-Comecon country and equally there will be institutes of law found in the law of the USSR which find no correspondence in the law of the non-Comecon countries and there will be the third category of institutes which are parallel both in the non-Comecon countries and the law of the USSR but which may well differ in their detailed provisions but at least furnish a comparative basis and are understandable and can be approached by someone not trained in Soviet law because of the parallelism previously mentioned.

The introductory part of this section referred to certain specific points which affect the commercial activity of the USSR and as an introduction to the part of this article dealing with commercial law it will be useful to expand the general points made by adding some more specific detail.

STATE ENTERPRISES and organisations are juridical PERSONS. Those operating on the basis of *khozraschet* (financial economic accountability) have assets allocated to them (cf. art. 24 Civil Code and KHOZRASCHET). They are liable to the extent of their property (with certain exceptions); cf. art. 32 and also arts. 98, 101 and 104. The state is not answerable for their obligations nor are they responsible for the obligations of the state (art. 33). However, certain of their assets are not subject to levying by EXECUTION, for example capital assets (art. 98). State enterprises and organisations have civil legal capacity with regard to the objects of their activity (a special legal CAPACITY); cf. art. 26. An important role in the overall management of the economy is played by the supreme organs of state power and the organs of state administration. Thus in accordance with art. 14 of the Constitution they have jurisdiction over:

The determination of the National Economic Plans;

The approval of the consolidated state budget of the USSR and of the reports on its fulfilment and the levying and allocation of taxes and revenues among federal, republican and local budgets;

The administration of the banks, industrial and agricultural enterprises and institutions and trading enterprises of All-Union subordination, the general guidance of industry and construction of Union republican subordination;

Foreign trade on the basis of the state's monopoly and other important industrial and commercial matters.

Commercial life in the USSR is guided by State Economic Plans. The long term Plan usually runs for a five year period (at the time of writing this article 1971 to 1975). There are Plans of shorter periods such as annual or quarterly Plans. Enterprises enter into economic contracts which CONTRACTS in themselves are instruments of PLANNING. A fundamental principle of the planned management of the Soviet economy is DEMOCRATIC CENTRALISM, the balance between central regulation and independence of local organs and enterprises in their commercial activities.

In the USSR, the economic system is being restructured for example by a fuller development of such factors as the principle of *khozraschet* in the fullest meaning of the word.

It will be appreciated from what has been said above that commercial law, as it might be used in the non-Comecon countries does not exist as such and indeed commercial law does not exist as an independent branch of law in the system of Soviet law unlike the position under certain civil law systems. Those parts of its rules which govern the corporate structure of state enterprises and organisations engaged in (for example) production and distribution and their relations *inter se* are governed by civil law or administrative law, or both. (It is of the very greatest interest that some eminent Soviet scholars consider that the law governing management and economic activities in fact forms a coherent branch of the law, self-sufficient and meriting the designation of Economic Law. If this is in fact so, then the totality of norms under such Economic Law could be considered as a "Commercial Law". See also ECONOMIC LAW.)

Those relationships which in some Civil Law and Common Law systems are loosely designated as commercial law are also covered by Soviet civil law. Therefore in this article there is meant by "Commercial Law", those relationships which could be classified under a specially formulated Soviet Economic Law and also relationships understood in other systems as commercial law relationships.

One should start a study of commercial law with the Constitution Articles 4 to 11, which contain certain basic premises for commercial law. Other principal provisions of commercial law can be found in the Principles of Civil Legislation of the USSR of December 8, 1961, for example, the provisions with regard to PROPERTY and OBLIGATIONS (SALE, delivery, work and labour).

Article 3 of the Principles provides that relationships between socialist organisations concerning the delivery of goods and capital construction, relations involving purchases of agricultural produce by the state, relations between organisations in transport (except motor transport and communication and credit institutions) (*inter alia*) are to be within the jurisdiction of the Union.

Various civil codes of the Union republics enacted on the basis of the Principles spell out in more detail many cases of and cover a wide range of relationships which one would expect to find encompassed by a study of commercial law. By way of example, in the Code, the "Law of Obligations", (arts. 158 ff.) one finds articles dealing with the creation and performance of obligations, the securing of the performance (such as by way of example, provisions as to liquidated damages, pledge and guarantee), liability for breach of obligations, discharge of obligations and a large number of sections dealing with specific types of obligations such as the contract of sale, barter, GIFT, SUPPLY, LOAN, the hire of property and other similar matters falling within the realm of Commercial Law.

With regard to very important questions relative to economic management, there are adopted joint resolutions of the Central Committee of the Communist Party of the Soviet Union and of the Council of Ministers of the USSR. Other norms of commercial law may be found in normative acts of the Council of Ministers of the USSR such as rules relating to the delivery of consumer goods (of April 9, 1969) and the Railway Charter (of April 6, 1964).

Ministries in charge of branches of industry or commerce can be of All-Union, Union republican or republican subordination depending on the degree of centralisation and guidance, thus for example there is only one Ministry of Foreign Trade.

Disputes arising out of economic contracts are heard by a special system of tribunals known as *Gosarbitrazh* (State ARBITRATION) operating at various levels throughout the Soviet Union (for example at the level of the Council of Ministers of the USSR). The kind of disputes heard by State Arbitration relate not only to the type of disputes one would expect to arise out of a contract (for example disputes arising during the course of the performance of the contract) but also disputes of a so-called pre-contractual type. If for example enterprises cannot agree on the provisions to be incorporated in a contract in order to give effect to a planning directive which binds them, then the dispute can be referred to State Arbitration. Disputes in such cases are very much planning disputes. It is worth pointing out that not only does State Arbitration of the Council of Ministers of the USSR hear economic disputes but it also issues normative acts. These, bearing in mind the economic basis upon which the USSR operates, are of the very greatest importance and certainly fall within the realm of commercial law. An example would be the promulgation of "Special Conditions of Delivery" relating to various kinds of products.

Falling within the realm of commercial law are undoubtedly the General Conditions for the Delivery of Goods adopted by Comecon. The latest General Conditions are those of the January 1, 1969, and these General Conditions are a normative act which has the force of law in relation to every contract in Comecon FOREIGN TRADE and *ipso facto* affect the contractual relationships of Soviet foreign trade corporations. Thus the General Conditions enter into the commercial law of the USSR by way of regulating civil law relationships in certain areas of activity.

No discussion of commercial law should ignore the two permanently functioning arbitration tribunals in the field of foreign trade in the USSR that is to say the FOREIGN TRADE ARBITRATION COMMISSION and the MARITIME ARBITRATION COMMISSION both in Moscow. The Foreign Trade Arbitration Commission was established "for the settlement by way of arbitration of disputes arising out of foreign trade transactions, in particular disputes between foreign firms and Soviet economic organisations". The Maritime Arbitration Commission hears disputes (to summarize) arising out of maritime law.

Why these two commissions have been mentioned in an article dealing with commercial law is that decisions, for example, of the Foreign Trade Arbitration Commission constitute a source of commercial law, albeit rising out of foreign trade transactions.

David Winter

COMMERCIAL LAW, see COMMERCE AND COMMERCIAL LAW

COMMISSION AGENTS

The contract of commission is a contract for services which must be distinguished from the contract of agency (cf. chapters 35 and 36 of the RSFSR Civil Code). A very precise definition can be found in the Code (art. 404), whereby it is stated that in accordance with the contract of commission one party (called the *komissioner* or in translation the Commission Agent) for payment undertakes to carry out in his own name one or more transactions for another party (called the *Komitent* and in translation the Principal) who instructs him.

This contract is widely applied in the USSR both in the sphere of the internal commerce of the country and it is also used in foreign trade in that Soviet foreign trade corporations effect the import of goods from abroad on the basis of this type of contract for Soviet socialist organisations.

The contract of commission is thus non-gratuitous. It is similar in some ways to a contract of agency but, as the Code specifies, the commission agent acts in his own name even though it is in the interest of another party.

The contract of commission must be made in writing.

The rights and obligations affect the commission agent directly even though his principal was named in the transaction or indeed entered into direct relations with a third party. Any property transferred by the principal to the commission agent or indeed acquired by the commission agent for the principal belongs to the principal.

An interesting feature of the contract of commission is the requirement under the Code that the commission agent must carry out the obligation he has accepted on the most favourable terms for his principal. Furthermore if the commission agent is successful in carrying out a transaction on more advantageous terms than those stipulated by his principal, his principal acquires the entire benefit. This rule, however, is a dispositive rule.

The commission agent has to perform his

duties personally.

The commission agent can only depart from his principal's instructions if in the particular circumstances of the matter it was necessary so to do in the interests of the principal and the commission agent was not in a position to obtain a prior consent of his principal or if in relation to an application for such consent, he did not receive such consent in time. In these circumstances however, the commission agent is under a duty to notify the principal as soon as he is able of his departure from his principal's instructions.

As might be expected, a commission agent who sells property at a price below that given to him by his principal is under a duty to repay his principal the difference between the price at which he sold the property and the price at which he was instructed to sell. He is however relieved of the duty to "make up" this difference if he can prove that he was unable to sell the property at the price given to him by his principal and that the sale by him at such lower price in fact prevented worse loss to his principal. In addition the commission agent must be able to show that he was not able to make prior enquiry of his principal or that he was not able to receive in time an answer to his enquiry. If a case occurs where a commission agent acquires property at a price higher than that within the authority given to him by his principal, the latter, if he does not wish to take the property, must so inform the commission agent without any delay once he has received notice of the conclusion of the transaction. If he fails to do this, then the acquisition will be regarded as having been accepted by the principal. Interestingly, in the event of the commission agent informing his principal that he will make up the difference in price at his (the commission agent's) own expense, then the principal, as might be expected, has no right to withdraw from the transaction concluded on his behalf by the commission agent.

Among widespread types of commissions are contracts of commission between citizens and commission shops specialising in the retail sale of consumer goods. The sale price of articles which commission shops sell is fixed by the agreement of the parties but must not exceed the state retail prices for the goods in question. The price of antiques and unique articles and works of art is determined by the commission shop taking into account the quality and value of the thing in question in each particular case (see also RETAIL TRADE).

As clearly would follow from the nature of the contract, the commission agent is under an obligation to carry out his duties and to take steps to enforce his rights arising out of the relationships ensuing from a transaction carried out by him with a third party. On the other hand the commission agent is not himself liable to his principal for the performance by such third party of the transaction entered into by the commission agent for his principal with the exception of those cases where the commission agent himself undertakes to guarantee performance of a contract by the third party. Where, however, the commission agent has so guaranteed such performance, then he is entitled to receive a special fee from his principal for having given such a guarantee. This is called *del credere*. A *del credere* agreement normally is to be found only in commission transactions in the field of foreign trade.

If the third party breaches the contract entered into between him and the commission agent, the commission agent is under a duty to notify his principal immediately and to take the necessary steps to collect and to ensure the safe keeping of the necessary evidence. The principal upon being notified of such breach by a third party can require the transfer to him of all the claims of his commission agent against such third party in relation to the transaction in question.

The commission agent is liable to his principal for any losses to or shortages in or damage caused to his principal's property unless he can show that the loss, shortage or damage in question was caused through no fault of his. In this case the quantum of damage is compensation of the principal for losses caused (art. 219). When a commission agent receives property sent to him by his principal or in the case of property coming into the commission agent's hands on behalf of his principal, external inspection would show damage or shortage, the commission agent must take the necessary steps to preserve his principal's rights, collect the necessary evidence and notify his principal of all details and without any delay. The same rule applies in the case of damage occurring to the principal's property caused by any person while such property is in the possession of the commission agent. The failure to insure a principal's property results in a commission agent being liable only if the principal required him to insure the property and he has not done so or if such insurance was compulsory by law.

Upon fulfilment of the commission entrusted to him, the commission agent has to supply his principal with an account. Moreover, he must hand over to his principal everything he received during the course of the commission and transfer to his principal, if his principal so requests, all rights in relation to the third party arising out of the transaction entered into by the commission agent with the third party. If the principal wishes to object to the account, he has three months to put forward his objections from the date of receiving the same from the commission agent. If he fails to do so, (unless agreed otherwise) the account is deemed accepted. The law does not lay down the form nor content of the account but clearly sufficient information must be given supported where necessary by written evidence.

The law relating to contracts of commission in many cases deals with problems arising out of the sale of agricultural products but only the general rules are given here and further details can be found in the Code (see also KOLKHOZ; SALES).

The primary obligations of the principal are to accept what has properly been carried out for him by his commission agent, pay the appropriate fee and reimburse the commission agent for expenses incurred by him in carrying out his principal's directions. More specifically, the position is as follows: the principal has to accept from the commission agent everything carried out in the transaction by the commission agent with the third party, for example, money. Should the principal fail to carry out this obligation then he is liable as provided by the Code (art. 227). The principal also is under a duty to examine property which has been acquired for him by his commission agent and to let the commission agent know at once about any defects discovered in such property. The principal is also under a duty to relieve his commission agent from obligations accepted by the commission agent in relation to the third party.

It was stated at the beginning of this article that the commission agent performs his duties for payment and consequently upon completion of his duties, the commission agent is entitled to obtain a fee from his principal. Mention has already been made of the fact that if a commission agent actually guarantees the performance by the third party of the transaction in question, then the commission agent is entitled to a special fee from his principal (the *del credere* fee). The amount of fee to be paid (including of course the *del credere* fee) may be arranged by agreement between the parties unless otherwise provided by law. It is of great interest that in relation to all contracts of commission (with the exception of those in the field of foreign trade) it is not permissible to pay the commission agent by way of the difference (or part of the same) between the price given by the principal and the more favourable price at which a commission agent might conclude a transaction. The normal case where a price is fixed by agreement takes place in agreements between citizens and in relation to foreign trade transactions.

Among a principal's duties, there was mentioned above the duty to reimburse the commission agent for expenses. Such reimbursement (unless by agreement or law otherwise stipulated) does not extend to the cost of looking after the property of the principal while it is in the possession of the commission agent.

A commission agent has a right of set-off (*q.v.*) in that he is entitled to keep back any sums properly due to him by reason of the commission contract by setting off the same from any monies coming into his hands on behalf of his principal. This right in particular extends to remuneration due to the commission agent in a normal case and to the *del credere* fee. It also covers the ordinary case of expenses properly incurred (cf. art. 229 of the Civil Code).

If prior to completion of the contract of commission, the principal should die, be declared incapable or have his dispositive capacity (*q.v.*) limited, or should the principal be declared missing and if the principal is a juridical person and is dissolved, the commission agent is under a duty to postpone the performance of the contract of commission until he receives instructions from the appropriate person.

This deals with the postponement of the performance of the contract but turning finally to questions of the renunciation or revocation by the commission agent or the principal as the case may be of the contract of commission, the following rules apply.

A commission agent has no right to renouncc thc contract. He acquires the rights however to do this in any one of the following three events, that is to say,

1) if so provided by the contract;
2) due to impossibility of performance;
3) breach by the principal of the contract of commission.

Where the commission agent has this right of renunciation, he must give written notice to his principal and the contract of commission continues to remain binding for two weeks from the date of receipt of such notice by the principal. Where the commission agent renounces performance by reason of breach by the principal (see above), in addition to payment, the commission agent is entitled to be reimbursed his expenses.

Upon notification of the fact that the commission agent has renounced the contract, the principal is bound to arrange for the disposal of his property (if the same be in the hands of the commission agent) within one month from the date of receipt of the refusal by him. He may either take the property back from the commission agent or state where he wants it delivered. The same rule applies where the principal revokes the contract (see below). Failing such disposal, the commission agent can store the property at the principal's expense or alternatively sell the same at the best price possible if he wishes to be put in funds sufficient to reimburse him in respect of his claims against his principal. As a general rule if the commission agent's claims can be satisfied by selling part of the property, he has no right to sell the whole of it.

The possibility of the revocation of the contract by the principal was mentioned above. If the principal does this prior to the commission agent concluding the corresponding transactions with third parties, then the principal must pay the commission agent his fee for those transactions already performed prior to such revocation and in addition reimburse the commission agent for all the expenses incurred prior to such revocation. This right of revocation is to be distinguished from the rule mentioned earlier that, as a general rule, a commission agent is not entitled to renounce the contract that he has undertaken (detailed provisions in arts. 404-421 Civil Code).

David Winter

See also AGENCY; FOREIGN TRADE CONTRACTS

COMMUNICATIONS

The supply of means of communication is the main responsibility of the Ministry of Communications of the USSR. The internal organization of the ministry itself is based on a statute of March 22, 1968, confirmed by the Council of Ministers of the USSR. The principal source defining the duties of the ministry and its subordinate bodies is the Communications Statute of the USSR (*Ustav Sviazi*), confirmed by the Council of Ministers of the USSR on May 27, 1971.

The ministry is in charge of post, telephone, telegraph, radio, television, distribution of printed works and transport communications. It should be stressed that the ministry is concerned only with supplying the means of communication, and not with the contents of it.

The Ministry of Defence, the State Security Committee and the ministries of internal affairs possess their own communications networks and are outside the scope of the Communication Statute.

Immediately subordinate to the Ministry of Communications are the republican ministries of communications and a small number of very large communications enterprises, such as the Central Telegraph Office of the USSR, the Central Long-Distance Telephone Exchange, the organization for the construction of radio stations (*Radiostroi*), a.o.

The USSR Ministry of Communications contains (chief) departments for long-distance telephone and telegraph, radio, local telephone service, postal service, a.o. There is no ministry of a communications in the RSFSR; its place is taken by the USSR ministry. The other republics have their own ministries of communications, which head the network of republican communications enterprises and the communications departments (*upravleniia*) at *oblast* level (provided the republic is divided into *oblasts*). At the lowest level the communications department coincides with the communications enterprise which offers its services to the consumer (post offices, telegraph offices). Communications enterprises work on a *khozraschet* (*q.v.*) basis and are governed by the Statute on Socialist State Production Enterprises (see STATE ENTERPRISES).

The conditions for making use of the means of communication are regulated in detail in the Communications Statute. More detailed rules are issued by the Ministry of Communications; such rules may be backed up by administrative fines and other sanctions.

The privacy of correspondence is guaranteed by art. 128 of the Constitution of the USSR. The conditions under which correspondence may be seized by the authorities are spelled out in the codes of criminal procedure.

Intentional or negligent damage to or destruction of means of communication may constitute a criminal offence (cf. arts. 68, 205 and 205-1 of the RSFSR Criminal Code).

The Soviet Union takes part in international cooperation in the field of communications. It is a member of the Universal Postal Union and the International Telecommunication Union.

F. J. M. Feldbrugge

See also RADIO & TELEVISION; PRESS

COMMUNIST PARTY OF THE SOVIET UNION

According to the introduction to the Party Rules currently in force (approved in 1961 by the 22nd Congress of the CPSU, altered in 1966 and 1971 by the 23rd and 24th Congresses), "the Communist Party of the Soviet Union is the battle-tested vanguard of the Soviet people... The Communist Party, the Party of the working class, has today become the Party of the whole Soviet People."

The CPSU is a *vanguard and not a mass organization*. At the time of the 24th Party Congress (March 30 till April 9, 1971), there were 14,455, 321 Party members and candidates, i.e. 5.9% of the entire population of the Soviet Union, and 9% of Soviet adults (over 18 years old). The following table shows the development:

Years	Full members and candidates	Population	%
1917 (February)	40,000	161,000,000	0.02
1917 (October)	240,000	161,000,000	0.14
1940	3,999,975	194,100,000	2.06
1950	6,340,183	178,500,000	3.62
1955	6,957,105	194,400,000	3.57
1960	8,708,667	212,400,000	4.10
1965	11,758,169	229,600,000	5.12
1967	12,684,133	234,800,000	5.40
1968	13,180,000	237,200,000	5.55
1971	14,455,321	245,000,000	5.90

Although, according to the introduction to the Rules the Party is the vanguard of the whole people, it *theoretically remained an organization of the working class*; but the greatest group in the party-membership is that of the civil servants and the clerks (white-collar workers) (44,0%), since many workers admitted to the party are rapidly promoted to the civil servant level.

An "irrevocable law of life" in the Party is expressed in the Rules and affirmed in actuality, namely *the ideological and organisational unity* which excludes any kind of federation within the Party. It is the most important difference between the organization of the Soviet state and the Party and, at the same time, is the most characteristic feature of the concept of the multinational socialist state. The state can be (must be, in a multinational society) federative. The Party however, which leads and controls the state, must always remain centralized (decision of the 8th Congress, in 1919).

The organizational principle of the CPSU is *the productive and territorial system* (art. 20 of the Rules): primary party organizations are set up in factories, plants, sovkhozes, kolkhozes, and other units of production, in schools, offices, and other places of work; the 1961 Rules also provided for primary organizations in housing complexes. There are 370,000 primary organizations (in 1971), 18 to 20% of them being territorial organizations.

The primary organizations are united in territorial ones, which correspond to the territorial units of the state administration (an exception is the Russian Socialist Federative Soviet Republic, which has no corresponding Republican Party). In 1971, there were the following territorial organizations: 14 Republican Parties ("national" parties until 1952), 6 organizations in territories (*krai's*), 142 organizations in the provinces (*oblast'*), 10 national area organizations, 760 town and 2810 ward (*raion*) organizations.

The "guiding principle" of the organization of the Party is that of *democratic centralism* (Rules, art. 19), which includes: a) the election of all leading organs from the lowest to the highest; b) systematic activity reports of all Party organs to their own Party organization and to higher organs; c. rigorous Party discipline and the subordination of the minority of the majority; d) the binding nature of the decisions taken by higher organs on those of a lower level.

Points a) and b) contain the democratic elements, the last two display the centralization characteristics (see also DEMOCRATIC CENTRALISM).

The *Party electoral system* operates at many levels and is indirect, small- and medium-sized primary organizations excepted. Party members have an "unlimited" right to reject candidates and to subject them to criticism (art. 24); a modification *contra constitutionem* of the Rules by decision of the Central Committee (CC) of March 24, 1962, allowed party members to suggest other candidates rather than the official ones.

The election of leading organs can be divided into three different parts: 1) nomination by the higher organs, 2) approval of the candidates by the constituent body (general meetings in the small- and medium-sized primary organizations, electoral conferences in the larger ones, as well as conferences and congresses) by public discussion, and 3) election by secret ballot. Officials are elected in the plenary sessions of the several committees by public vote and are approved by the higher organs (art. 49).

Further elements of the Party democracy which must be mentioned are: 1. the right to criticism before passing a resolution (art. 3c); 2. discussion especially at Union level, in the whole Party, but fraction groups (or opposition) within the Party are banned (art. 26). Criteria and limits of such discussions are the following: a. "Objective laws of development" recognized by the Party, cannot be criticized, b. the discussion must strengthen the unity of the Party; collective management (leadership), "the highest principle of Party management" (art. 27). According to the statute, collective leadership must always be related to individual responsibility. This restriction and the increasing role of the apparatus seem to weaken the value of the collectivist principle. Collective leadership means, that the "most important problems" must be solved only collectively, while "operative solutions" can be reached by minor officials, without distinction between principal and operative questions.

The *centralization of the Party* is most obvious in its hierarchical command structure (art. 19d), in the controlling of lower organs by the higher ones (art. 47), in the comprehensiveness of the hierarchy of the executive Party organs in which the lower organs must account for their activities to the higher ones (art.47) which systematically inform them (art. 29), in the approval of the managing officials (art. 49), etc.

Democratic centralism thus implies the double subordination of the leading organs and of the whole apparatus: a. they are subordinate to the constituent body (horizontal subordination) and b. to the higher organs (vertical subordination). This and the control of lower organs by the higher ones (art. 54) practically exclude any autonomy of Party organizations, an autonomy granted to them since 1961 by the Rules to deal with local problems, but only within the framework of Party policy (art. 21).

Within the Party, power is delegated in many ways from large organs to small collective bodies, and even to executive organs. The powers of the Congress (which met every four years until 1971, and will, from now on, be held every five years) have been taken over by the CC (art. 55), with some exceptions listed in art. 31 of the Rules (enactment or changes of Rules and Programme, approval of the general trend in internal and foreign policies, election of CC and Central Commission for Revision); the CC accordingly leads (art. 34) and controls (art. 40) the entire Party and thus the state. The committees of the territorial organizations have similar powers (arts. 43, 50, 56) limited to their own territory.

The committees of each level delegate their own powers to the offices which they have elected themselves, the Politburo of the CC always being on top. Certainly, there is often a certain amount of rivalry between the various offices, the highest collective leading organs and the secretariats which are composed of full-time Party officials and direct the entire apparatus of the corresponding committee. Sometimes far-reaching bonds link the two organs. In 1971, after the Republican party congresses, a total personal union took place in 13 of the 14 republican parties: the entire secretariat was incorporated into the politburo. As a consequence of this measure the secretariats in six republican organizations acquired the majority in the highest policy-making bodies of the republic. The only exception was the CP of the Ukraine, where three members of the secretariat became full members of the politburo while three other secretariat members acquired candidate member status in the politburo. At the central level, there is remarkably little personal union; from this it may be inferred that it was necessary to strengthen the apparatus in the border regions, while Party constitutionalism was observed more closely in the centre. Among the 10 members of the Party Secretariat, only four are full members and two have candidate member status in the Politburo.

	Politburo		Secretariat		Central committee	
	full members	candidates	full members	candidates	full members	candidates
1919	5	3	1		19	8
1920	5	3	3		25	15
1923	7	3	3		40	17
1925	9	5	5	2	63	43
1927	9	8	5	3	71	50
1931	10	5	5	2	71	67
1934	10	5	4		71	68
1939	9	2	4		71	68
1952	25	11	10		125	111
1956	11	6	8		135	122
1961	11	5	9		175	155
1966	10	9	10		195	165
1971	15	6	10		240	155

The most important attribute of the ruling Communist Party is its leading role in state, society and economics. The rejection of this principle or the restriction of the Party leadership to the field of ideology is considered to be revisionism.

The leading role of the CP is a constitutional principle: the CPSU is "the leading core of the organizations of the working people" (Constitution, art. 126). This provision was not included, however, in the first Soviet constitutions (1918, 1924). Lenin felt that Party leadership did not need to be anchored in laws, decrees, and constitutions (Works, 31, p. 342); it only had to be stated in Party statutes.

Party leadership is expressly mentioned in the Rules: the CPSU is the "leading and directing force of Soviet society. The Party leads the great constructive activity of the Soviet people" (introduction to the Rules). It is the Party congress, not the Supreme Soviet, which deliberates and "decides on the most important problems of the building of communism" (art. 32c) and supplies general directions for the Supreme Soviet. The "operative leadership" of the Supreme Soviet and the government is the duty of the CC, which "directs the work of the central organs of state and society" (art. 34). Each organ of state and society is led and controlled by the parallel Party organ: "The organizations of the Party in republics, *Krai's*, provinces, national areas, towns and wards (*raion's*) and their committees... direct all activities" in the relevant territorial units of state administration: "for the realisation of the policy of the Party" (art. 41), they lead and control the soviets, the trade unions and the Komsomol by party-groups inside them (art. 42c). Plants, factories, kolkhozes, sovkhozes, offices, etc. are led and controlled by their own primary organizations (art. 60). In this context, it should be pointed out, that the right—and the duty—to control was gradually increased between 1961 and 1971. Since 1971, all primary organizations possess a right of direct control. This implies a right to issue binding instructions to the administration in order to prevent failures and a duty to report to the Party any shortcomings of the administration or of individual employees. The primary organizations have a network of control commissions for the several branches and divisions of the plant.

Legal literature defines the leadership of the Party as follows: 1. the most important problems of state, society and economics must be solved by Party directives and instructions, 2. the Party appoints the most qualified individuals, wholly devoted to the communist cause, to key positions, 3. the Party points out the defects in the activity of corresponding organs and decides how to eliminate them.

An important guarantee of Party leadership is the monopoly of the Party on personnel policy (Rules, art. 2h). There are departments for organizational work in the lower Party committees with full-time instructors, as well as departments for personnel in the higher committees, which carry out the personnel policy, provide for the education of members and check on them, mostly in cooperation with special commissions.

Each Party committee has a "nomenclature-list", indicating the positions which can only be filled on the basis of a Party recommendation. The competent committee recommends one of the so-called nomenclature-reserves. The distribution of the positions among committees of various levels is not constant; when the Party strengthens its leadership and control over a particular economic or cultural branch, the nomenclature-lists of higher organs are enlarged at the expense of the nomenclature-lists of lower committees.

E.g. in February, 1971, the Congress of the CP of Moldavia transferred all kolkhoz chairmen, sovkhoz directors and many factory directors from the nomenclature-list of the ward (*raion*) and town committees to the Central Committee list (*Sovetskaia Moldaviia*, February 25, 1971). The Party must be consulted not only in the case of appointments but also when it comes to the dismissal of holders of nomenclature positions. Personnel policy orders issued by the Party must be obeyed, even with regard to positions which are filled by elections. This aspect of the personnel policy is reflected in the Constitution: art. 141 empowers social organizations and associations of the working people to nominate candidates; the leading role of the Party (art. 126 of the Constitution, arts. 68-69 of the Party Rules) serves as a guarantee that these organizations will only nominate individuals prescribed by the Party, mostly on the basis of the nomenclature-lists. The Party has its own candidates nominated by other social organizations. In the theoretically possible case that a number of voters does not accept the nominated person, the delegates of the social organizations concerned must meet and the matter will be decided by open ballot. Even the elections in the different representative organs must take place on the basis of Party recommendations submitted directly, or by a social organization (mostly trade unions). Elections to the Supreme Soviet take place on the CC's proposal, which is backed by the group of Communist deputies and the councils of seniors of both chambers. Party rules in the past banned any information about Party directives in personnel policy. This ban no longer exists, but Party secrecy is still prescribed by arts. 2-7 of the Rules. As to the question whether the director of a plant or factory should

justify the nomination or dismissal by referring to Party orders, the editor of *Partiinaia Zhizn'* (Party life No. 9, 1968, p. 32) replied that such a reference was not required.
Another guarantee of Party leadership is the parallelism between state, economic and Party agencies: each economic or state agency has a Party counterpart which directs and controls its activities. The departments in the CC of the CPSU and those of the republican parties are really Party ministries in which all of the important problems are studied and solved. The state ministry is to a certain extent the executive organ of the respective Party ministry.
The list of the Party ministries at central level is at present kept secret. From the fourteen republican parties twelve published such lists. Generally, there are ten to twelve Party ministries (for organizational activity of the Party, for propaganda and agitation, for industry and transport, for science and education, for agriculture, for construction and communal economy, for light industry, for state administrative organs—state administration, justice, police, public prosecutor's office—, for finance, for commerce, etc.). The committees in the *Krai's* and provinces have in general nine departments (for organisational activity of the party, for propaganda and agitation, for industry and transport, for agriculture, for construction, for administration, finance and commerce, for schools, a Party commission, etc.); in the town committee there are in general three departments (for organisation, propaganda/agitation and industry/transport), in the big towns seven; in the ward (*raion*) committees, there are usually two departments (for organization and propaganda/agitation).
Due to the position of the Party in the state, Party members enjoy some privileges in the sphere of the state. Along with their monopoly on personnel policy, which allows them to fill the highest positions, they benefit from a sort of penal immunity: if a Party member has committed a misdemeanor, he must be excluded from the Party before he can be tried (art. 12 of the Rules).

L. Révész

See also CONSTITUTIONAL LAW; DICTATORSHIP OF THE PROLETARIAT; ELECTIONS

COMMUNITY PROPERTY,
see MATRIMONIAL PROPERTY

COMPANIES,
see CORPORATIONS; ASSOCIATION

COMPLAINTS, see ACTS OF LEGAL SIGNIFICANCE; PUBLIC ADMINISTRATION; ADMINISTRATIVE PROCEDURE; REMEDIES; APPELLATE PROCEDURE

COMRADES' COURTS

The term *tovarishcheskii sud* (comrades' court) has been applied from the beginning of the Soviet state to a simplified judicial-like public hearing at which the accused person is judged before a tribunal of his fellow-workers, colleagues or neighbours. Although the basic idea of the comrades' court as an informal, in-group trial procedure has remained unchanged over the years, comrades' courts have varied considerably in their form, functions and punitive prerogatives. At times the institution has been in official favour and in widespread use, while at others it has sunk into oblivion. At present more than 300,000 formally constituted comrades' courts exist in the USSR, according to Soviet official sources, about 5,000 of them in Moscow alone.
After the October Revolution, military and civilian comrades' courts appeared because of official concern about problems of discipline during the period of civil war and War Communism. With the advance of the period

of the New Economic Policy comrades' courts gradually ceased to function and were completely dormant by the end of 1922.

A vigorous revival of the comrades' courts took place from 1927 to 1933 in connection with the Soviet government's effort to consolidate lower levels of the judicial system. Priority attention was given initially to rural areas of the USSR where judicial institutions of any sort were more deficient than elsewhere. After the collectivization of agriculture had begun, kolkhoz and sovkhoz comrades' courts began to appear in the countryside to replace the so-called conciliation chambers. A revival of factory comrades' courts also took place at this time. The result was a diversified network of amateur judicial forums constituting a social echelon below the state courts. They continued to exist throughout the 1930's but with declining effectiveness and all had ceased to function by the outbreak of World War II. Reasons for the decline were numerous, including the rise of secret-police terror and the discouragement by officials of the use of citizenry voluntary groups alongside state organs of justice.

The third period of widespread use of comrades' courts began dramatically with the report delivered by Khrushchev on January 27, 1959, to the 21st Party Congress in which he called for the reactivation of the comrades' court as one of several community agencies of "prophylaxis and educative work" which might assist in preventing certain kinds of violation of the law. He also attributed ideological significance to the comrades' court, classifying it as a "social organization" to which, as to similar institutions in this category, "many functions carried out by state organs should be gradually transferred." A draft model statute on comrades' courts was published on October 24, 1959, by the Legislative Proposals Commission of the USSR Supreme Soviet. Although the draft was never enacted as an All-Union law, it stimulated the creation of comrades' courts and set a general pattern for the eventual republican comrades' court statutes.

The comrades' courts are regulated legally by special statutes of the Union republics promulgated in 1961 (in the RSFSR on July 3, 1961). The typical comrades' court is designed to serve several hundred (or even thousand) adults in a given area who constitute an identifiably homogeneous group because of their common place of employment, study or residence. But a comrades' court may also be based on a group numbering as few as 50 adults, or even fewer with special permission. A comrades' court may be organized in any enterprise, in individual shops (or shifts) within a plant, in mines, building projects or transport lines, institutions of higher education, kolkhozes, sovkhozes, rural settlements, urban housing offices, single apartment houses, etc.

Official theory holds that a comrades' court is a voluntary creation of the entire group at any of these locations and is accordingly a public or social organization rather than a part of the state apparatus. Nonetheless, a comrades' court has at least semi-official status by virtue of the fact that its institutional attributes are defined by the law and that its activities overlap and bring it unavoidably into contact with the work of various administrative and judicial agencies.

The initial establishment of a given comrades' court takes place at a specially convoked mass electoral meeting which selects by open ballot a panel of comrades' court "judges" (numbering from five to twenty or more) for a two-year term.

The hearing in a comrades' court is scheduled on an ad hoc basis by summons of the comrades' court chairman at such times as cases involving members of the group arise. The right to prefer charges against an individual in his comrades' court is virtually unrestricted; any organization, official, individual citizen or the comrades' court itself may initiate a charge. The chairman of the comrades' court has limited powers of pre-trial investigation, but he may not conduct sessions in camera and must give advance public notice of each hearing conducted by a comrades' court. Procedural rules are kept deliberately to a minimum in a comrades' court hearing, in order to encourage an air of informality and maximum audience participation in the proceedings.

However, a written summary (protocol) is required; the comrades' court decision in each case must be put in writing and publicly read. The right to challenge the composition of the court on grounds of personal interest in the outcome is granted to the accused, who may also demand the summoning of additional witnesses and documents in his own defence and enjoys a traditional right to the last word. Any person present at the hearing is entitled to speak, to pose questions or to put forward motions. Lawyers and prosecutors are not used in the comrades' court. The three-man court, consisting of the comrades' court chairman and any two others from the elective panel, reaches its decision in each case by majority vote.

Soviet comrades' courts today are legally entitled to hear a broad range of cases. These fall into three general categories: (1) cases in which the comrades' court has exclusive jurisdiction because the charge preferred concerns moral standards or communal rules rather than a formal violation of law; (2) cases of crimes committed for the first time, which by their nature meet the classification of "alternative jurisdiction", by which is meant that the law-enforcement agency or official is granted powers of discretion to decide whether to hold the delinquent liable for prosecution by the normal judicial or administrative channels or, alternatively, to refer the whole matter to the individual's comrades' court (art. 7 of the RSFSR Code of Criminal Procedure); (3) cases already begun in a people's court which the presiding judge may elect to "transfer" for hearing in a comrades' court, thus terminating completely the state judicial proceeding at whatever stage it may be (art. 259 of the RSFSR Code of Criminal Procedure).

Rural citizens of the USSR are normally subject to only one comrades' court (i.e. that of their kolkhoz or village), but an urban resident may be answerable before two—one where he works and one where he resides. Possible conflicts of jurisdiction between the two are not specifically covered by current law, but in practice only the production-based comrades' court handles violations of labour discipline (e.g. absence from work without good cause, unpunctuality, breach of shop rules, etc.) and other on-the-job infractions, especially the unauthorized use of tools, equipment or vehicles and theft of private property belonging to fellow-workers. The housing-area comrades' court, on the other hand, is the normal setting for hearings concerning violations of dwelling regulations, damage to buildings and premises or petty quarrels between tenants. Other types of cases in addition to the above which fall within the competence of a comrades' court under current legislation include the following: insult; false or slanderous allegations; assault; home distilling without profit motive; petty theft of state or public property; petty speculation; petty hooliganism; poaching; trampling crops or causing damage to forests; failure to provide for aged parents; use of foul language; rearing children improperly; and disrespect toward women. Trial of "parasitic elements" (persons who refuse employment though able-bodied) does not take place in the comrades' court; this was suggested in the 1959 draft model statute, but the idea was later dropped in favour of an alternative (see PARASITES).

A vast array of civil law and property matters also may find their way into the comrades' courts. The original jurisdiction of comrades' courts in this field is limited by statute to disputes about reapportionment of peasant households, the division of marital property and to small-claim property disputes provided the parties belong to the same collective and both agree to the case being heard in the comrades' court. But many further civil suits may be aired in a comrades' court when a judge of the people's court specifically requests it to play an advisory or conciliatory role, jurisdiction being retained in the people's court in such cases until final disposition.

Penalties imposed by a comrades' court include not only those expressing social disapproval (warnings, demands for an apology, reprimand or censure), but also monetary fines of amounts up to 10 roubles (30 to 50 roubles in one type of case), a formal obligation to pay for damages caused, or the request to an appropriate state agency to inflict punishment or penalties more severe than those which a comrades' court is authorized to impose. Compliance on the part of the individual with the comrades' court decision is theoretically voluntary (and is frequently self-executing), but in case of a malicious refusal to comply the comrades' court may turn to the appropriate state agency with a request for compulsory execution of their decision.

Right of appeal against the verdict of a comrades' court does not formally exist. An appeal mechanism of sorts exists in places where local soviets appoint special legal councils to supervise the quality of trials in the comrades' courts of the area. The procuracy provides another possible channel for curbing flagrant abuses.

The practical utility of the comrades' court as a means of inculcating law-abiding attitudes and habits among Soviet citizens cannot be precisely assessed for want of definitive evidence. Even the permanence of the comrades' court in the USSR is open to doubt. A de-emphasis of the role of "social organizations" generally, including that of the comrades' courts, became apparent in Soviet official writings soon after the departure of Khrushchev from the leadership and this trend has persisted to the present. In the period 1965-1972 this de-emphasis on the comrades' courts coincided with numerous developments which, in their basic nature, tended in a contrary direction: greater reliance upon the professional law-enforcement agencies (particularly on the militia forces organized under the newly re-centralized Ministry of Internal Affairs), expanded use of administrative fines, reinforced authority for local magistrates to deal summarily with misdemeanor cases, introduction into the criminal codes of several loosely-defined amendments (e.g., on "hooliganism", "false fabrications, oral or written, damaging to the Soviet state", etc.) which in effect widened the parameters of criminal liability and in consequence the field of jurisdiction of the regular people's court, adoption of new labour law codes, new family law codes, etc. The net result is that comrades' courts and similar institutions have been pushed into the background. Nonetheless, the topic continues to be discussed in some legal journals as a matter of theoretical and practical concern to Soviet jurists and even the daily press occasionally makes reference to the practical existence and activity of comrades' courts at widely scattered localities.

Albert Boiter

CONDITIONAL SALES,
see HIRE-PURCHASE AGREEMENTS

CONFISCATION, see FORFEITURE

CONFLICT OF LAWS, see PRIVATE INTERNATIONAL LAW

CONFLICTS, see PRIVATE INTERNATIONAL LAW

CONSERVATION (see also *Appendix*)

Conservation or protection of nature (*okhrana prirody*) is emerging as a serious concern of the Soviet legal system. While protective provisions have traditionally been part of Soviet laws regulating the use and exploitation of particular natural resources (see LAND; SOIL PROTECTION & LAND RECLAMATION; MINES, MINERALS & MINING; FOREST & FORESTRY; HUNTING; WATER & WATERCOURSES; FISHING; AIR POLLUTION), until recently, they perceived nature mainly in economic terms. In other words, the purpose of the protective provisions was to reduce economic waste rather than safeguard the quality of the country's natural environment. The awareness of ecological interrelations did not find expression in law much beyond the establishment of isolated nature preserves (*zapovedniki*).

The damaging impact of industrialization and other forms of development on the natural environment as a whole began to be recognized in the Soviet scientific and popular literature, public policy statements and law only in the late 1950's. During the period from 1957 to 1963, all fifteen Union republics adopted legislation on protection of nature. (E.g., RSFSR Law of October 27, 1960, "On Protection of Nature"). But even this progressive step has been criticized by Soviet experts as inadequate. Conservation, they insist, should be coordinated at the All-Union level. First of all, they demand All-Union principles for legislation that would seek to conserve favorable conditions in the total natural environment, including the earth's subsurface, surface and atmosphere and all organic forces of nature taken in their unity and interconnection. Secondly, they urge the Soviet government to pursue international solutions to problems which cannot be satisfactorily dealt with by the Soviet Union alone (the penetrated outer space, earth's atmosphere, boundary waters, migratory birds, etc.). Finally, the critics propose redefinition and reallocation of the administrative responsibilities over conservation. The common practice of vesting the functions of protecting and exploiting a given resource in the same governmental agency is cited as especially unfortunate. For example, the Chief Administration for Land Use and Land Management is a department within the USSR Ministry of Agriculture; the State Inspectorate for Protection of Water Sources belongs to the USSR Ministry of Land Reclamation and Water Management. Each of these ministries is obliged to fulfill the production plans for the economic sector under its management. Thus, however well-intentioned the ministerial officials may subjectively be, objectively their first duty is concern for the volume of harvested crops or the acreage of improved lands, as the case may be, and not for protection of soil or water resources. Where a ministerial subdivision is responsible for protection of natural resources which are not entirely managed by it (as, e.g., the Chief Administration for Nature Protection, Nature Preserves and Hunting, another department within the USSR Ministry of Agriculture), the inner conflict is, of course, reduced. However, such a subdivision has to contend with external agencies of roughly equal rank, advancing conflicting interests. The critics of the present structure of conservation administration maintain that only a single centralized conservation agency of All-Union status would possess the proper perspective and the requisite authority to ensure effective protection of the natural environment.

Agencies charged with conservation responsibilities may impose administrative sanctions on violators of certain health measures, quarantine regime for plants and animals, regulations protecting the atmosphere, soil, resources of the earth's subsurface, forests, waters and fisheries, fire-safety rules, hunting and fishing regulations, and of measures protecting landmarks, natural monuments and urban greenery. The list of sanctions includes a warning, revocation of license, confiscation of the instruments and fruits of the unlawful act and, most frequently, a monetary fine. Since 1961, however, administrative fines can be collected only from individuals and not from enterprises, institutions and organizations. This means that the enforcement agencies must do more than show a violation by an entity; they must, as in a criminal case, identify the official responsible for the particular infringement. In those instances in which it is feasible to calculate the loss to the state in pecuniary terms, damages are collectible in conformity with the ordinary rules of civil liability. Unfortunately, in some cases, the civil sanction by itself may amount to little more than a payment for misappropriated resources at a state price. The more serious violations of conservation laws are criminally punishable. It seems, however, that prosecution of plant directors, engineers, and the like for violations committed in their managerial or technical capacity is virtually unknown. Instead, criminal law reaches people whose actions have no official connection (fish and wildlife poachers, timber thieves, suburban residents who graze their goats on river banks).

To sum it up, as in the case of NATURAL RESOURCES, there is no integrated body of Soviet law of conservation either at the All-Union level or within any of the republics. Each of the recently enacted sets of relevant All-Union principles (Principles of Land Law of 1968; Principles of Public Health Law of 1969; and Principles of Water Law of 1970) has provisions on conservation; so do the corresponding new republic codes. Other conservation laws and regulations addressed to problems of particular resources continue to be issued by all levels of government. Conservation concerns have been tangentially expressed in recent legislation on government organization (e.g., USSR and republic laws on the basic rights and duties of LOCAL AUTHORITIES), and one would expect the proposed reforms in ADMINISTRATIVE LAW and ADMINISTRATIVE PROCEDURE to have an eventual operational impact on conservation law.

Until now, Soviet top decision-makers have implicitly preferred massive and rapid technological development to the preservation of environmental qualities. They have, by and large, tended to overlook their own protective laws and regulations or treated them as a minor inconvenience. It seems that the effectiveness of Soviet conservation law and, ultimately, the fate of Soviet Union's natural environment will be determined by a frank redefinition of priorities rather than by mere tinkering with government organization charts, the contents of proscriptive clauses and the structure of sanctions.

Z. Zile

CONSPIRACY,
see ACCOMPLICES; ATTEMPT

CONSTITUTION

A second federal Constitution of the USSR was adopted on December 5, 1936, introducing several innovations: a) political monopoly for the Communist Party, previously exercising monopoly powers by custom only (art. 126); b) elimination of class restrictions on the right to vote and to hold office (art. 135); c) introduction of a federal bill of rights (Ch. X); d) centralization of the process of codification of civil, criminal and procedural law in the federal authority (art. 14-u); e) abolition of the Congress of Soviets and its Central Executive Committee with substitution of a bicameral Supreme Soviet (art. 30); f) seating in the chamber of nationalities of deputies not only from Union and autonomous republics but also from "autonomous provinces" and "national districts", created to recognize the cultural

identity of small and little developed ethnic groups (art. 35); g) confirming at the constitutional level various existing laws, notably prohibition of private employment for profit (art. 9), the right personally to own dwellings, bank accounts, artisans tools and articles of personal use and to inherit them (art. 10), and h) stipulation of a procedure for constitutional amendment (art. 146).
Some principles enunciated by previous constitutions were re-enacted, notably monopoly of ownership of productive resources by the state, limitation on enjoyment of civil rights to use in strengthening the socialist system, and prescription of the Soviet form for the state apparatus. Notably omitted was the preamble of the earlier constitutions capsulizing Marxist political doctrine and justifying adoption of the Soviet system of government.
Promulgation of a new constitution was justified in the press as necessary to reflect achievement of socialism, symbolized by complete abolition of private employment for profit and the disappearance of antagonistic classes, leaving only workers, peasants and intellectuals as differing strata of the "toilers". The dictatorship of the proletariat continued, but in a new phase, wherein "guilt" of class opposition was to be determined by an individual's acts rather than his membership in a hostile class.
The state's administrative structure was defined in detail, later requiring constitutional amendment as reorganizations occurred. The amending procedure was not onerous, however, requiring only a two thirds vote of the Supreme Soviet.
Substantial amendment occurred during and after World War II: notably transfer to Union republics of the right to conduct foreign relations (subject, however, to the federal authority's establishment of general procedures) and to create republic military formations (1944); grant to army units stationed abroad of the right to elect deputies to both chambers of the Supreme Soviet (1945); increase in the age required of Supreme Soviet deputies from 18 to 23 (1945); restoration to Union republics of their pre-1936 right to draft law codes (1957); and increase in the number of deputies representing each Union republic from 25 to 32 (1966).
Dissatisfaction with the constitution emerged after Stalin's death in 1953. Critics argued for clearer emphasis upon the rights of individuals and more prominence for the statement of the communist party's guiding role. A constitutional drafting commission was formed to propose changes (see CONSTITUTIONAL HISTORY).

J. N. Hazard

CONSTITUTIONAL HISTORY

Constitutional drafting began in committee in revolutionary Russia in April 1918, four months after the overthrow of the provisional government. The committee's draft was sent to the Central Committee of the Bolshevik wing of the Social Democratic Party for approval and was thereafter submitted to the Fifth Congress of Soviets where it was adopted on 10 July 1918. It was a novel document, drafted by men with no predetermined idea of state structure or desirable fundamentals.
Russians had no strong constitutional tradition, having received their first constitution only after the riots of 1905. Sharp differences over policy issues had emerged during the period of coalition government between Bolshevik centralizers and the left Socialist Revolutionary partisans of local autonomy. Only after withdrawal of the Socialist Revolutionaries from the coalition over the issue of the Brest Litovsk peace in the spring of 1918 was V. I. Lenin able to dominate drafting through his committee chairman Ia. M. Sverdlov and his uncompromising colleague J. V. Stalin.
The first Constitution of the "Russian Soviet

Federated Socialist Republic" incorporated two policy declarations: 1) Declaration of the Rights of the Toiling and Exploited Peoples and 2) a Declaration on State Structure, both adopted on 24 January 1918 by the Third Congress of Soviets plus the details of the Soviet hierarchical system through which the revolutionary victory had been won. The Third Congress had assumed state authority after forcible dispersal of the delegates to a constituent assembly, who on gathering in Petrograd in January 1918 had demonstrated their majority's desire to adopt a parliamentary system on the English model and a program of social democracy.

The Constitution opened with the January policy declarations placing all power in the "soviets of workers', peasants' and soldiers' deputies", prescribing a federal form of state structure, depriving bourgeois elements of the right to hold state office, establishing socialism as the national goal, abolishing private ownership of land, forests, mineral deposits, waters, livestock and banks, and instituting workers' control in industry and transport. Efforts made by moderates to introduce other principles and other forms were defeated, although the Socialist Revolutionaries' strong challenge to the Bolsheviks' centralist aspirations required compromise language on local soviet authority.

The second chapter created a Marxist-oriented bill of rights: establishing freedom of speech, press and assembly, but denying these freedoms to those "who use their right to the detriment of the interests of the communist revolution". In reflection of Marxist belief in world-wide working class solidarity, the franchise was extended to foreign workmen resident in Russia. In implementation of Marxist concepts of the "dictatorship of the working class" enemies could not vote or hold office, these being categorized as persons employing labour for profit, persons living on income not derived from their own labour, merchants, monks, priests, policemen of the former regime and members of the royal family. No monopoly of political party life was established for the Bolshevik party, as monopoly power was then only in process of evolution.

The provisions on state organization created no single elected head of state, for all power was placed in the Congress of Soviets, composed of one representative for every 25,000 electors in urban areas and one for every 125,000 inhabitants in rural areas so as to favour workmen over peasants. Deputies were not to be elected directly by the public but were named by provincial (*guberniia*) and large city soviets. To provide leadership during the intervals between the brief biannual sessions of the Congress a Central Executive Committee, named by it to establish policy lines, and a Council of People's Commissars to perform ministerial functions were prescribed. Local government was placed in the hands of village and town soviets, which named deputies to county (*uezd*) soviets, and these in turn named deputies to the provincial soviets. Each soviet, as an assembly, named its executive committee for routine administration of its area. Lenin devised a three month term for assembly deputies in local soviets so as to familiarize the masses with the governmental process. Not until 1921 was the term lengthened to two years.

The Russian Republic model was followed in creating state structures under communist party guidance as other areas of the collapsed Russian Empire were brought under Bolshevik rule; these structures being established by the constitutions of the Belorussian Soviet Socialist Republic (4 February 1919), Ukrainian SSR (10 March 1919), Azerbaidzhan SSR (19 May 1921), Armenian SSR (2 February 1922) and Georgian SSR (10 February 1922). A variation on the pattern was established in Central Asia for the ancient principalities of Bokhara and Khorezm, which had previously enjoyed nominal independence under treaties with the Tsar of the Russian Empire. Each adopted constitutions in 1922, differing from their neighbours in refraining from stating socialist goals and nationalizing property.

Independence was found difficult to maintain in the small republics during their early months because of the military threat from abroad and dislocation of long-established economic ties within the provinces of the former Empire. The reaction, stimulated by communists in each republic bent upon restoring centralized administration as soon as ancient animosities created by Great Russian predominance might fade, was a series of steps taken toward union. Thus, the Ukrainian SSR sought to exchange materials with the RSFSR in January 1919 and decreed joint military action with other republics in May 1919. RSFSR laws on transport, postal service, telegraph, military organization, production, labour and social insurance were extended to the Ukrainian SSR in January 1920. The Belorussian SSR and the Azerbaidzhan SSR sent delegates to sessions of the RSFSR Congress of Soviets in 1920. Late in 1920 and early 1921 the RSFSR concluded various treaties with other republics to concert economic and military administration by merging commissariats of finance, foreign trade, railways, posts and telegraph, labour, industrial planning and administration (the Supreme Council of National Economy), and military and naval affairs. Foreign policy was brought into concert to form a united delegation to meet with western European governments in the All European Economic Congress called by Great Britain's Lloyd George in 1922.

These mergers led to formal federation on 30 December 1922 in a Union of Soviet Socialist Republics and the ultimate adoption of a federal constitution. Final steps toward federation were initiated by the communist parties of the various republics during the summer of 1922, leading to a constitutional congress in December. In preparation for federation and to reduce historically oriented animosities in the Transcaucasian region, a federation subordinate to the prospective USSR was created by the joining of Armenian, Azerbaidzhan and Georgian SSR's in a Transcaucasian Socialist Federated Soviet Republic on 13 December 1922 to have a federal congress of soviets, a Central Executive Committee and a Council of People's Commissars. Each participating republic maintained, however, its own governmental structure under its original constitution. Consequently, it was the TSFSR that sent delegates to join those of the RSFSR, the Ukrainian and Belorussian SSR's to form a federation of the USSR by executing a treaty of union and approving a draft constitution. This draft was submitted to the four constituting members for review prior to formal provisional promulgation by the USSR's new Central Executive Committee and ultimate ratification by the new federal Congress of Soviets. In fulfillment of this plan the Constitution became effective on 6 July 1923 and was ratified on 31 January 1924.

The first federal Constitution followed the 1918 RSFSR model by opening with a statement of Marxist inspired aims and the reasons for federation. The federal compact of 30 December 1922 was the second chapter. Thereafter followed definition of the powers of federal and republic authority. The federal authority was granted not only powers familiar to students of other federations: conduct of foreign and military affairs, creation of a common citizenship, settlement of inter-republic disputes, coinage of money and establishment of a postal service, standard weights and measures, but also socialist features. These included development of a national economic plan, prescribing of fundamental principles for use of the soil, waters, mineral deposits, forests, and of law generally, the enactment of a state budget for the entire national economy, and the centralized direction of transport, telegraph services and foreign trade. It was a federal authority of delegated powers, the republics retaining the right to secede. This principle had to be read in consideration of communist doctrine expressing determination to oppose secession if exercised to return to capitalism.

The state structure was a transposition to the federal level of the system previously established in each republic, with one innovation. The Central Executive Committee became bi-cameral; one chamber composed of deputies representing each major ethnic group ranged according to categories of Union republics and autonomous republics. No bill of rights was included, the bills in the republic constitutions remaining in force. The Russian, Belorussian and Ukrainian republics conformed their constitutions to the new situation during 1924 and 1925. The Bokhara and Khorezm republics under communist party guidance were restructured as socialist republics and joined the federation as the Turkmen and Uzbek SSR's by decision of the federation's Central Executive Committee on 27 October 1924, an act ratified by the Congress of Soviets on 13 May 1925. In 1929 the Uzbek republic was divided so that its Tadzhik autonomous republic became a constituent republic of the federation. No more members entered the federation until 1936 when the second federal Constitution was promulgated, avowedly to reflect the national growth of industrialization and the expansion of the state-owned economy.

Steps toward a second federal Constitution were taken by the Communist Party's Central Committee in February 1935, and a drafting committee was named by the Congress of Soviets. Under Stalin's chairmanship it presented a draft accepted by the Central Executive Committee on 11 June 1936, and this was published immediately for discussion. Mass meetings followed and suggestions were screened. Stalin announced acceptance of some. The Congress of Soviets adopted his revised draft on 5 December 1936. (See CONSTITUTION for its provisions).

The number of constituent republics (now called "Union republics") was increased to eleven with dissolution of the Transcaucasian Federation and entrance of its three components directly into the USSR and with admission of two former autonomous republics of Central Asia as the Kazakh and Kirghiz SSR's. All Union republics conformed their constitutions to the new federal structure.

During the period of Soviet-Nazi concerted action in 1940 the sovietized Baltic states of Esthonia, Latvia and Lithuania were joined to the USSR and new republics were created in the north and south as the Karelo-Finnish and Moldavian SSR's, bringing the total to 16. The number remained constant to 1956 when the Karelo-Finnish SSR was dis-established and returned to autonomous republic status within the RSFSR.

A drafting commission was created in 1962 with Nikita S. Khrushchev as chairman to prepare a third federal Constitution. On his ouster in 1964 Leonid I. Brezhnev assumed its chairmanship.

Bibl.: Richard Pipes, The Formation of the Soviet Union: Communism and Nationalism, 1917-1922. Rev. ed., 1964. Merle Fainsod, How Russia is Ruled. Rev. ed., 1963. James H. Meisel and Edward S. Kozera (eds.), Materials for the Study of the Soviet System: State and Party Constitutions, Laws, Decrees, Decisions and Official Statements of the Leaders in Transition. 2d ed., 1953.

J. N. Hazard

See also CONSTITUTION

CONSTITUTIONAL LAW

The branch of law concerned with the definition of fundamental principles and state structure by the federal, Union republic and autonomous republic constitutions. Under Soviet doctrine it is implemented not only by the *prokuror*, the courts and administrative agencies (including the police) but also by the entire social and political structure established by the Constitution, notably the state ownership of productive property and guidance by the Communist Party. Union republics in joining the federation in 1922 were held by Soviet authors not to have reduced their sovereignty but to have enhanced it by expanding their international potential and their possibilities for creating economic abundance. The sovereignty of the federation and of each republic were held to be in organic unity and to be protected from the threat of disagreement by the overseeing unitary Communist Party.

Constitutional law concerns the procedure for the enactment of laws, the relationship between laws enacted at various levels of the state structure, the legal status of autonomous republics, autonomous provinces and national districts, the administrative agencies of the federation and of the republics, the state seals, flags and capital cities of the federation and of the republics, and the rights and duties of citizens.

Within the system of constitutional law, the supreme authority is the Constitution of the USSR (see CONSTITUTION). All legislative and administrative acts within the federation or the republics must conform to it, but no constitutional court or constitutional committee protects this supreme status. The Supreme Soviet of the USSR is the sole judge of constitutionality as the repository of all state power. Its own legislative acts cannot, therefore, be unconstitutional, and in practice legislation is frequently adopted requiring constitutional amendment, which is obtained subsequently. Legislative acts of republics and administrative acts of federal or republic agencies are made to conform to the constitution of the USSR through a procedure initiated by the Procurator-General of the USSR or his subordinates (see PROCURACY). His protest is directed to the offending agency, and if satisfaction is not given, to the Supreme Soviet of the USSR. No cases indicating the necessity of decision by the Supreme Soviet have been reported, but various protests to inferior agencies have resulted in publication of retractions of the offending act.

Two fundamental principles have been declared the foundation of constitutional law: democratic centralism (*q.v.*) and socialist humanism. Under the first category the authority of superior organs of power extends to the lowest levels, for there is no local autonomy, and under the second the maximum realization of the individual's identity is to be sought. This search conforms to the principle propounded by Karl Marx, "Personal freedom is possible only in the collective." (*The German Ideology*). A balance is required between individual and community, the balance varying in each historical period as the threat to the community varies.

After Stalin's 1953 death the 1961 program of the Communist Party proclaimed that the state, which arose as the dictatorship of the proletariat, had now become "a state of the entire people". Later writings clarified the new period as not the end but a final stage of the dictatorship and emphasized the fundamental change that was to occur in the relationship between state and individual in a society where no class enemies remained. Law was expected still to be severe in the exaction of penalties to preserve socialist legality, but the framework within which the severity was to be exercised had changed. Proposals were heard to evidence the change by offering a choice of candidates, but not of political parties, in elections (see ELECTIONS), and by showing greater vigilance in the protection of civil rights (see CIVIL RIGHTS). Authors called for a search for new forms of democracy consonant with Marxist fundamentals, emphasizing that the masses were best suited to performance of a "control" function in the governmental process, while the "leadership" function had to remain with the Communist Party, and the legislative function with the various soviets.

J. N. Hazard

CONSULS

A consul is an official appointed by one country as its permanent representative in another country to perform consular duties in conformity with the rules and formalities of the receiving country. The body of legal norms governing relations among states with respect to consular questions is called consular law. The major sources of Soviet consular law are international custom, the 1963 Vienna Convention on Consular Relations (not yet ratified by the USSR), bilateral consular conventions, and domestic legislation.

The basic legislative act regulating the Soviet consular service is the Consular Statute of 1926, as amended to 1929. There are four ranks in the Soviet consular service: consul general; consul; vice consul; consular agent. Soviet diplomats may hold consular assignments, and *vice versa*. Only Soviet nationals may be appointed as consuls of the USSR (in the opinion of some Soviet jurists, the appointment of honorary consuls to represent the interests of foreign states in the USSR is not proscribed by Soviet law). Soviet consuls are subordinate to the USSR Ministry of Foreign Affairs.

The general duties of Soviet consuls include: general supervision over activities of Soviet nationals, organizations, and institutions within the consular district; ensuring that Soviet nationals enjoy their full rights as guaranteed by local law, international treaties, and custom; taking measures to restore rights of Soviet nationals which have been transgressed; rendering administrative, notarial, and other services as provided for by law or treaty; observing the economic, legal, social, and political life in the consular district and reporting thereon to the Ministry of Foreign Affairs; and others. Unlike consuls of Western states, Soviet consuls are not charged with commercial functions (which are the responsibility of specially-appointed trade representatives); however, a sharp distinction between commercial and consular functions is difficult to draw in practice, and Soviet consuls often perform trade-related functions.

Except for socialist countries, which have agreed by treaty to recognize officially sealed documents reciprocally without further authentication, Soviet state agencies as a rule require that a Soviet consul have legalized a foreign document before it can be accepted for examination in the USSR.

Consular privileges and immunities in the USSR are defined by the 1966 Statute on Diplomatic and Consular Missions of Foreign States on the Territory of the USSR and in consular agreements. Under the 1966 Statute, consular archives, documents, and official correspondence are inviolable. The inviolability of consular premises and of the residence of the head of a consulate is accorded on the basis of reciprocity. A foreign consulate is guaranteed the right to communicate with its own government, diplomatic mission, or other consular representation of the same country situated on Soviet territory or in third states by ordinary means of communication, coded telegram, or diplomatic mail. Consular officers enjoy personal inviolability and may not be subjected to detention or arrest except for commission of a grave crime. A terrorist act committed against a representative of a foreign state is a criminal offense under art. 67 of the RSFSR Criminal Code. Official activity of consuls, excepting motor vehicle accidents, is exempt from Soviet civil, criminal, or administrative jurisdiction. Consular officers, certain consular employees and family members, and the consulate are exempted from general state and local taxes on the basis of reciprocity.

Consular duties, privileges, and immunities are also defined in consular agreements concluded by the USSR with other states. Since 1957, the Soviet Union has signed consular agreements with all the socialist countries and with Yugoslavia, the Federal Republic of Germany, Austria, Japan, Finland, Sweden, United States, France, Great Britain, Italy and others. Although Soviet consular agreements with socialist countries are basically similar to those with Western states, those contracted within the bloc emphasize the political function of consuls to protect the rights and interests of the sending state, require prior consent from the receiving state for appointment of a consul, eliminate use of honorary consuls, grant absolute immunity to consular premises, and make consular functions with regard to shipping coextensive for aircraft.

A new series of consular agreements among socialist countries, far more detailed than those of 1957-59, is being concluded to supersede the earlier model. Mongolia, Poland, and Bulgaria are among the states which already have ratified such arrangements.

As a general rule, Soviet consular agreements with Western states are drafted in greater detail and contain more minor variations. Nearly all incorporate special provisions to ensure that consular officers of the sending state are promptly notified in the event a national of the sending state is arrested or otherwise detained by Soviet authorities.

Since 1938, the Soviet Government has often imposed the requirement of parity in deciding whether to allow the establishment of additional foreign consulates in the USSR. The parity principle, however, has not been extended to the size of consular staffs.

Bibl.: For the texts of Soviet consular legislation and agreements, see *Soviet Statutes and Decisions*, Vol. III no. 2-3 (1967), pp. 55-148. The Consular Statute of 1926 has been superseded in part by subsequent administrative regulations whose texts are not available.

W. E. Butler

See also DIPLOMACY; DIPLOMATIC OFFICERS

CONTINENTAL SHELF,
see TERRITORY; TERRITORIAL WATERS

CONTRABAND, see SMUGGLING

CONTRACTORS (WORK CONTRACT)

The work contract is governed by arts. 64-66 of the Principles of Civil Legislation of the USSR and the Union republics (in the following: Principles), the corresponding provisions of the Civil Codes of the Union republics (RSFSR: arts. 350-367) and a large number of statutory instruments (see below). In a work contract "the contractor binds himself to perform at his own risk defined work on the instructions of the customer with either the customer's or his own materials; and the customer binds himself to accept the finished work and to pay for it".

This somewhat vague legal definition is supposed to include production of an *opus* (the building of a shed, the opening-out of a window) as well as the rendering of a service (e.g. the cleaning of a house). In some cases the vagueness of the definition will make it difficult to distinguish the work contract from a purchase, as e.g. in the case of a suit made on order; the distinguishing line seems to be the obligation of the supplier to produce the *opus* himself. It is even more difficult to distinguish the work contract from a labour contract in cases where the contractor is a private person and the work done necessarily implies a result (A. undertakes to irrigate B.'s garden, or do nightwatchman's duties in B.'s house, for say a week).

Use of the contractor's materials is the general rule; use of the customer's materials must be stipulated. As regards volume, the larger share of work under work contracts will be done by state organisations. Private persons, whether professionals ("one-man craftsman", e.g. shoemakers or tailors) or non-professionals, may undertake the performance of certain work under work contracts only if they perform all the work personally.

Customers can be state, or co-operative or other public organisations ("socialist organisations") or private persons. However, work ordered by the first two groups will come, again as regards the volume of the work done, overwhelmingly under the category of the capital construction contract, as to which see below.

A specific type of work contract is the "orders for domestic needs" (house-hold orders). They are governed by several statutory instruments, among others, by a decree of the Council of Ministers of the USSR of 1962 concerning orders for tailored clothing which provides credit facilities for the customers; and a decree of the same body of 1965 providing Standard conditions concerning the repair of dwelling houses.

The price of the work under a work contract will be agreed by the parties. If the contractor is a social organisation officially prescribed rates and prices will prevail. Small excesses over the estimates (the sum agreed), if they are based on "adequate grounds", must be borne by the customer. If the excess, though substantiated by "adequate grounds", is considerable and the contractor in due time warns the customer that such excess is to arise, the latter may terminate the contract paying the contractor the expenses the latter has incurred. If no warning is given the contractor must carry out the contract for the sum agreed.

A separate category of contracts of work is the work contract concerning capital construction (Capital Construction Contract, CCC; simplified translation: Building Contract). It is an economic contract, the planned version of the work contract, which can be entered into only by social organizations. Such a contract will provide for the building (*lato sensu*) of a block of flats, an office building, of a silo, a factory or an industrial building, an agricultural building or construction, a pipeline or bridge, and also a road, railroad or waterworks, or for "installations" (*montazh*; i.e. stable equipment such as e.g. electrical equipment, pipes, etc.).

As the history of the Soviet economy is substantially a history or large-scale industrialization at a forced pace the building contract is one of the most important legal transactions which, especially in recent years, has been dealt with thoroughly by the Soviet lawmaker. It is governed by arts. 67-71 of the Principles and the corresponding provisions of the Civil Codes of the Union republics (RSFSR: arts. 368-372) and a number of statutory instruments, among others a decree of the Central Committee of the CPSU and the Council of Ministers of the USSR concerning the Planning of building contracts, and Regulations of the Council of Ministers of the USSR on Building Contracts, both of 1969.

Building in general is (in addition to such state organs which are concerned with any kind of planning) under the care of a federal state commission (*Gosstroi*), the *Gosstroi*'s of the Union republics, and a number of building ministries and other departments. Building activities are financed to a large extent from centralized state funds, some from the specific funds of enterprises and some, as it is expressed, "from bank credits"; the latter *in ultima analysi* also means "from the means of the enterprise". Any "capital construction" (buildings and installations) must be planned. In relation to "capital constructions" of industrial enterprises the reform laws of 1965 provided that higher planning organs would establish only the general volume of the centralized capital investment. It seems that at least for the period from 1971-1975 this provision has been suspended and capital investment will be itemised in the 5-year plans of the ministries and departments, with an indication of the volume of work to be carried out in each of the 5 years. Obviously, though this is not mentioned in so many words in the respective provisions, corresponding data will be included in the plans of the would-be customers. Whether in fact the would-be customers do take the initiative concerning the authorization of new projects of capital construction or whether building plans are in fact imposed on them is a question to which we do not know the answer. Probably the situation varies according to branches and personalities.

Obviously, no building project can be included in a plan unless estimates of it have been agreed and, in so far as more substantial buildings or installations are concerned, no estimates can be made without at least general technical building plans. Though the respective provisions do not say so, it seems that such technical plans, blueprints and estimates are the first steps to capital construction, preceding the confirmation of plans.

After the confirmation of the capital investment plan several steps follow on the way leading to the conclusion of the capital construction contract. We prefer therefore to state in quite general terms the following: Before the 1st day of September of the year preceding the planning period the would-be customer must deliver to the would-be contractor, whose identity is already settled in the capital investment plan, "working drawings" which probably means rough, preliminary sketches; and within 15 days of the confirmation of the capital investment plan the would-be customer must give the would-be contractor among other things "technical documentation", i.e. blueprints, estimates and other documents necessary for the carrying out of the work, confirmed by the higher authorities, proof of the allocation of the land needed for the building and a so-called *titul'nyi spisok* ("letter of allocation"). The technical documentation is produced on the order of the customer and in the framework of a *sui generis* contractual relationship by state projecting organisations as "project makers" (*proektant*). Whether in practice there are or are not exceptions to this rule, e.g. for minor constructions, is not known to us. The letters of allocation are issued according to the type and volume of the work by different agencies ranking from the Council of Ministers of the USSR down to the director of the enterprise of the would-be customer. The letters of allocation contain another, more detailed description of the building work to be done: they are a permit and at the same time an order to start with the work. If the work is to last longer than one year, then on the basis of the letters of allocation there will be issued additionally "yearly letters of allocation" which specify the work to be done in the next planning year. The latter document, with several others, is needed for the opening of the building account with *Stroibank*, where the financing of the building branch has been centralized. One month after he has obtained the documents listed in the respective provisions, the contractor sends the customer the project of the capital construction contract.

Within 10 days of obtaining the project and not later than 2 months of the confirmation of the 5-year plan the would-be customer must sign the contract with or without adding a letter of dissent. Within further 10 days the contractor must accept the points of dissent or put the dispute, according to its character, before the superior administrative organ or to the state arbitration.

As a rule *one* capital construction contract will be made concerning the entire work with one contractor called the general contractor. The latter then may farm out particular parts of the work to sub-contractors who will be responsible only to the general contractor.

The customer may however, enter into a direct contract with contractors for the installation of equipment, and with the consent of the general contractor (it is not quite clear whether this consent is or is not needed also for a contract for the installation of equipment), also concerning another work of specialized character, with organizations specializing as contractors for such work. If the general contract is to run for a period less than a year or if it concerns only the building reparation of specified workshops of a plant, it will be called a capital construction contract made for one year.

If the capital construction contract runs over several years the "agenda" of the second and every consecutive year will be spelled out in a "supplementary contract".

In the cadre of the capital construction contract the customer must supply to the contractor technological, power producing, electro-technical and general industrial equipment. This implies without any doubt the supply of water and the electrical current. What "technological and general industrial equipment" exactly means we could not ascertain, the commentaries are satisfied by repeating the somewhat cryptic terms of the statute. (Is it the customer's task to provide drills, bulldozers and cranes as technological equipment?)

The contractor must produce the "building or installation" using his own materials unless special regulations provide for the customer to supply for the materials. The customer is entitled to exercise control and technical supervision over the carrying out of the work.

Similarly to the provisions on supply contracts the Regulations of 1969 provide penalties for delays and other breaches and violations of the capital construction contract.

The acceptance of the building by the customer is effected on the basis of the findings of a commission in which, in addition to representatives of the directly interested parties, also representatives of higher authorities have a seat.

The transactions and other measures of the building branch are to a large extent standardized.

Specific provisions govern the building contract of the kolkhozes.

Z. Szirmai

See also PLANNING

CONTRACTS

1. General considerations

As in all other legal systems of the world, contracts represent in Soviet law one of the most important means of giving rise to obligations (see OBLIGATIONS).

Contracts are understood as an agreement by which one person called the debtor is bound to perform a given action for the benefit of another person, called the creditor, or on the contrary to refrain from some defined action, the creditor being entitled to require the debtor to perform his duty.

A contract is *bilateral* where each party has to perform a given obligation in favour of the other (for instance the contract of sale). When one party is obliged and the other is only a creditor (for instance in a contract of gift), the contract is said to be *unilateral.* Furthermore a contract is *for value* where the performance by one of the parties is "paid" by the other in some way (for instance the contract of loan with interest), while a contract is *gratuitous* where such a payment does not occur, as in the contract of loan without interest.

Contracts can also be classified as *consensual* where the mere agreement of the parties is sufficient to give rise to the obligation; on the other hand *real* contracts are deemed to be concluded only at the moment of delivery of the object of the obligation to the creditor (for instance the contract of gift).

Contracts are concluded not only between socialist organizations, but also between socialist organizations and citizens, and between citizens themselves. Nevertheless, the role of contracts in the Soviet economy cannot be compared with the situation in capitalist countries because of the clear distinction which has to be made between the *planned contracts* (which are concluded only between socialist organizations on the basis of a planned duty) on one side, and the *ordinary contracts* (which are concluded either by socialist organizations outside the realm of their planned duties or by citizens) on the other.

II. Creation of contractual obligations

Concerning the *conclusion* of contracts, art. 160 Civil Code RSFSR contains the well-known rule according to which the contract shall be deemed to be concluded only when agreement is reached between the parties on all essential terms and is embodied in the special form, if any, provided for by the law.

It may be noted that contrary to the old 1922 Civil Code RSFSR a *new means of conclusion of contracts* has now been expressly admitted, as far as they "may be concluded by way of acceptance and performance of an order and, between socialist organizations where so provided by law, by way of acceptance and performance of an order or a warrant for goods" (art. 160).

As far as the juridical consequences of an offer to contract are concerned, the Civil Code RSFSR makes a difference between two situations: when the offer to conclude contains a time-limit for an answer, the contract is deemed to be concluded if the person making the offer receives an answer from the other party accepting the offer within the time set (art. 162). On the other hand, when the offer to conclude is made without a time-limit for acceptance, two cases must be distinguished: if the offer is made *orally* without fixing a time for an answer, the contract is deemed to be concluded if the other party immediately declares his acceptance (art. 163, par. 1); if the offer is made *in writing* the contract is deemed to be concluded if an acceptance is received within the time normally necessary for such receipt (art. 163, par. 2).

Although not expressly stated in the code, the *general rule* can be inferred from these provisions that a contract is deemed to be concluded at the time of reception of the answer by the person who proposed its conclusion.

In the case of the *belated arrival of an acceptance of an offer*, the answer having been sent off in due time, this answer shall be treated as too late only where the offeror immediately informs the other party that it was received after a delay. In this case the belated answer is considered to be a new offer to contract (art. 164).

If an *answer agreeing to contract varies the terms of the offer*, it is treated as a refusal of the latter and as constituting a counter-offer (art. 165). Nevertheless this rule does not apply if, in the course of concluding an economic contract, a dispute arises which has to be settled by an arbitration court. *Contracts in favour of third parties* are expressly provided for in article 167.

III. Plan and Contract

While the *ordinary contracts* concluded between citizens or more generally outside the realm of planning are governed, as in non-socialist countries, by the principle of freedom of will, the so-called *economic contract* may be regarded as the most interesting feature of the Soviet law of obligations.

These contracts are entirely devoted to the realisation of the planning goals in which their real "cause" is to be found, as well as the explanation of their particularities. The origin of these contracts lies in a given autonomy of management left to Soviet enterprises which are in a position to choose a contracting party and to discuss with him, for instance, the price, quality and time for delivery of the goods. Both parties will be personally liable out of their management fund for the correct performance of the contract. In so doing the authorities are intended to individualize production and consequently to set up some competition and initiative between enterprises.

The impact of planning on economic contracts is to be found at the three levels of their *conclusion, performance* and *dissolution.*

As far as the *conclusion* of economic contracts is concerned, it is stated that "the content of a contract concluded on the basis of a planned task must correspond with that task" (art. 159 Civil Code RSFSR). Furthermore "disagreements arising in the course of concluding a contract based on a planned task binding on both parties, between State, cooperative and other public organisations (other than collective farms) are resolved by the appropriate or a chosen arbitration court unless otherwise provided by law" (art. 166 Civil Code RSFSR).

In the case of *improper performance* (or *non-performance*) of an economic contract because of the inaction of planning agencies which for instance do not allocate the necessary planned products, this circumstance cannot be invoked as a valid defence, unless the organisation proves that it has done its best and has utilized all its economic capacities in order to avoid the breach of obligation.

This rule appears to be an exception in the Soviet law of obligations which generally makes the fault a condition of liability for breach of obligations "except in cases laid down by law or contract" (art. 222 Civil Code RSFSR).

During the performance of their agreement, the parties can change the contract terms only if it does not contradict the confirmed plan. Their freedom is restricted also insofar as no agreement between socialist organisations to limit their responsibility shall be permitted if the measure of responsibility for the given type of obligation is precisely determined by law (art. 220 Civil Code RSFSR). When *planning acts are edicted in violation of the law*, they are usually corrected before contracts are concluded. If *new planning acts* appear after the conclusion of economic contracts, these have to be adapted to the new acts because of the overriding force of planning (art. 234 Civil Code RSFSR).

Finally the *rescission of an economic contract by mutual agreement* is not left to the free will of the parties. Article 233 Civil Code RSFSR provides that "it is permitted in so far as this does not contradict the acts of planning of the national economy".

Furthermore *no economic contract can be terminated against payment* according to the cardinal principle of specific performance which is laid down in art. 191 Civil Code RSFSR: "The payment of liquidated damages (fine, penalty) stipulated in the event of delay or other defect in the performance of an obligation does not discharge the debtor from his duty to perform specifically except in cases where a planned task on which an obligation between socialist organisations was based has ceased to be required."

It is only in the light of the above-mentioned rules governing economic contracts that the general principles of obligations laid down in chapters XV-XX (arts. 158-236 Civil Code RSFSR) can be correctly understood. One has to bear in mind that these principles are really general, i.e. applicable to both ordinary and economic contracts only in so far as their scope is not limited by the requirements of planning tasks.

IV. Performance of contractual obligations

Obligations have to be performed properly and within the time fixed, and in conformity with the requirements of statute, act of planning, contract or, in the absence of such requirements, in accordance with the usual requirements in such cases (art. 168).

This broad principle has to be understood in the light of *two requirements expressly* stated in the same article: first, the performance of contractual obligations must occur "in the way most economical for the socialist national economy" and secondly, each party must "assist the other in every possible way to perform his own duties". Both requirements appear to be a way of introducing a kind of "equity" into the law of contracts. The *contractual performance in the way most economical for the socialist economy* relates primarily to contracts between socialist organisations. It means for instance that when the buyer eliminates the defects in the delivered products by his own means at the expense of the supplier, as provided for in art. 216 Civil Code RSFSR, he can rely upon this provision only if he is doing so at the lowest possible expense. According to the same principle, if the supplier delivers raw material at a higher price than that agreed upon in the contract, but if the buyer does not take advantage of the curtailment of manufacturing expenses due to the better quality of the delivered raw material, the buyer shall not be entitled to refuse the payment of the whole price difference.

Soviet doctrine underlines that the principle of the contractual performance in the most economical way can find application also in agreements between citizens. For instance, if in a work contract the performance of the contemplated work is subject to an approximate estimate (art. 352 Civil Code RSFSR) and if the real cost appears to be lower than this estimate, the customer can ask for a corresponding reduction of the final price.

As far as the *requirement for the mutual assistance of the parties to perform their contractual duties* is concerned, it also applies to socialist organisations, which, as a matter of fact, are in a situation of economic cooperation, but it can be relied upon also in agreements between citizens.

Another fundamental principle of Soviet law is the *specific performance of obligations*. This principle means that the *debtor* cannot refuse to perform the contract and the *creditor* cannot decline its performance (cf. art. 169 Civil Code). In the event of delay or other defective performance of the obligation, the debtor is still obliged to perform specifically, despite the payment of liquidated damages (art. 191) or the reimbursement of losses caused by the non-performance or improper performance (art. 221). As far as the creditor is concerned, he cannot in principle put an end to an *economic contract* because of the defective performance of the debtor, except in cases where a planned task, on which an obligation between socialist organisations is based, has ceased to be required. This circumstance is the only one also discharging the debtor from specific performance. On the other hand, in *ordinary contracts* concluded between citizens or outside the realm of planning, the creditor is entitled to depart from the contract in case of defective performance by the debtor (art. 225, par. 2).

Article 171 Civil Code RSFSR provides that the performance may be imposed on a third party wholly or partially, the creditor being

bound in principle to accept performance by a third party on behalf of the debtor, when the debtor is a *citizen*. If the debtor is a *socialist organisation*, no legal provision exists, so the question has to be solved in the light of all the circumstances of the case.
Soviet legislation also contains precise provisions concerning *joint and several obligations* (art. 179-184 Civil Code RSFSR). They can arise not only where the object of the obligation is indivisible, but more generally where so provided by the contract or laid down by statute (art. 180). The obligation in which several debtors or creditors are involved has to be performed in such a way that "each creditor is entitled to demand performance and each debtor is bound to perform the obligation in equal shares with the others unless statute or the contract otherwise requires" (art. 179).
In the case of the *joint and several liabilities of debtors*, the creditor is free to require performance either from all the debtors jointly or from any one of them in particular, in full or for part of the debt (art. 181). If one of the debtors has performed a joint and several duty in full, he discharges the remaining debtors from performance as regards the creditor (art. 183). The same article specifies that "a debtor who has performed such a duty is entitled to reclaim from the other debtors in equal shares, taking into account his own share, unless statute or the contract otherwise provides". Furthermore a debtor who is jointly and severally liable cannot "raise defences to a creditor's demands based on any relations of the other debtors to the creditor with which the said debtor is not concerned" (art. 182).
In the case of *joint and several claims*, art. 184 provides that any one of the creditors is entitled to call upon the debtor to perform in full. If the obligation has been performed in full in favour of any one of the joint and several creditors, the debtor is discharged from performing in favour of the remaining creditors. But the joint and several creditor who has so received full performance from the debtor "must reimburse the other creditors for the share due to them unless a different rule governs their relations among themselves" (art. 184).
Another important question raised by the law of contract is that of the *time of performance*. If it is not specified in the statute, act of planning or contract, "the creditor is entitled to demand performance and the debtor is entitled to perform, *at any time*" (art. 172). In such a case, the debtor must perform within seven days of the day when the creditor makes his demand, unless an immediate duty to perform arises from statute, the contract or the nature of the obligation. It is understood that *reciprocal duties* under a contract must in principle be performed simultaneously (art. 177).
Premature performance of an obligation is allowed, unless the contrary appears from statute, the contract or the nature of the obligation or, in the case of an obligation between state, cooperative and public organisations, where it is provided by statute or contract, or with the consent of the creditor (art. 173).
If the *place of performance* is not fixed by statute, the contract or the act of planning and does not appear from the nature of the obligation, art. 174 provides that the performance may be effected:
a) in the case of an obligation to transfer a building, in the place where the building is situated;
b) in the case of a debt (other than a debt of a state, cooperative or public organisation), at the place where the creditor was living when the obligation was incurred or, if the creditor has moved away before the time of performance of the obligation and has informed the debtor accordingly, then at the creditor's new place of residence;
c) in other cases, at the place where the debtor lives, or, if it is a juridical person, at

the place where it is situated.
The Soviet law of obligations contains some provisions related to the *manners of performance*. Whereas the *unilateral refusal* to perform an obligation or a unilateral alteration of the terms of a contract are not allowed except in cases laid down by law (art. 169), the *partial performance* of obligations is permitted "unless the contrary is provided by statute, act of planning or contract or results from the nature of the obligation" (art. 170). Concerning the *performance of an obligation in the alternative*, article 178 provides that the debtor has in principle the option of which obligation to perform.
Finally it must be noted that according to art. 176 "no interest is chargeable on debts or other obligations except within the field of operation of the credit institutions in the case of foreign trade obligations and in other cases provided by statute".

V. Securing performance of contractual obligations

For the first time in the history of the Soviet law of obligations, a general system of 5 means of securing performance of obligations is provided for in art. 186-210 Civil Code RSFSR; the first three can be used as well between socialist organisations as between citizens, while the fourth is meant only for citizens and the fifth, only for socialist organisations.
1) *Liquidated damages* (fine, penalty) are understood as "a sum of money fixed by statute or contract which the debtor must pay the creditor in the event of failure to perform or of imperfect performance of the obligation, in particular, in the event of delay in performance" (art. 187 Civil Code RSFSR). According to art. 187, al. 3, liquidated damages do not have to be paid "unless the debtor bears the liability for nonperformance or imperfect performance of the obligation". Exceptions to this rule can nevertheless be prescribed by statute.
The principle of *specific performance* of contract leads to the consequence that even the payment of liquidated damages "does not discharge the debtor from his duty to perform specifically except in cases where a planned task on which an obligation between socialist organisations was based has ceased to be required" (art. 191).
In cases where the liquidated damages are extraordinarily large in comparison with the creditor's actual losses, the court is entitled to *reduce the damages* (art. 190). Such a reduction is possible only in exceptional cases if socialist organisations are concerned.
2) *Pledge*, see PLEDGE
3) *Suretyship* is a written contract by which "the surety binds himself to the creditor of another person to answer for the performance of an obligation by the latter person in full or in part" (art. 203). This means that in the case of failure to perform the said obligation the debtor and the surety are in principle jointly and severally liable to the creditor (art. 204), the surety being liable to the same extent as the debtor. Where an obligation is secured by pledge and surety, it is left to the creditor to choose whether he wants to be paid first on the pledge or by the surety.
When the *surety performs the obligation himself*, he acquires all the rights of the creditor based on such obligation and has consequently a claim to a refund against the debtor (art. 206). As far as the *debtor* is concerned, he must immediately inform the surety once he has performed the obligation secured by the suretyship (art. 207) if he does not want the surety who performed the obligation to require it in turn from him.
4) *Earnest* is a written contract by which a sum of money is handed over by one contracting party to the other party (both parties necessarily being citizens) on account of a payment due from him by contract, as proof of the making of the contract and as security for its performance (art. 209).

It is also possible to give the earnest the form of a penalty. In such a case, if the earnest has been given by the party liable for non-performance of the contract, it is retained by the other party, while if it has been given to a party liable for non-performance that party is obliged to pay the other party double the amount of the earnest. Unless the contract otherwise provides, the party responsible for non-performance of the contract must in addition recompense the other party for his losses, deducting the amount of the earnest.

5) *Guarantee* is a particular kind of suretyship given by a superior socialist organisation to another inferior one in order to secure the payment of the debts of the latter specially against *Gosbank* or *Stroibank* (art. 210).

(As to assignment of claims and transfer of debts, see ASSIGNMENTS).

VI. Liability for breach of contractual obligations

In the realm of the general principle of specific performance the new Civil Code RSFSR provides expressly for two kinds of compulsory execution of obligations. On the one hand, "in the event of failure to perform an obligation to deliver an *individually defined article* into ownership, operational management or use of a creditor, the latter is entitled to demand that such thing be taken from the debtor and delivered to him" (art. 217). On the other hand, "in the event of non-performance by a debtor of an *obligation to perform defined work*, the creditor is entitled to have the work done at the debtor's expense, unless statute or the contract otherwise provide, or to demand reimbursement of his losses" (art. 218).

The broad principle of specific performance and its two particular applications laid down in arts. 217 and 218 do not exclude the *duty of the debtor to compensate for losses* (arts. 219-221). The measure of liability can be summarized in the following propositions:

a) Losses must be compensated in full, i.e. the expenses incurred by the creditor, loss of or damage to his property, and profits which he would have obtained if the obligations had been performed by the debtor.

b) The legislation of the USSR and the RSFSR may establish limited liability for the non-performance or improper performance of specified classes of obligation.

c) Limitation of liability can be provided for also by agreement between the parties, with the important exception that "where the measure of liability on a given class of obligation is precisely defined by law, socialist organisations may not limit such liability by agreement" (art. 220).

d) The reimbursement of losses caused by non-performance or improper performance of an obligation does not discharge the debtor from his duty to perform the obligation specifically except in those cases where the planned task on which an obligation between socialist organisations was based has lost its force (art. 221).

The legal consequences of a breach of obligation are governed by the *principle of fault as a condition of material liability.* According to art. 222, "a person who has failed to perform an obligation or has performed it improperly is materially liable only where he has been at fault (intention or negligence) except in cases laid down by law or contract. The burden of proof that he was not at fault rests on the person who violated his obligation". However, in practice the principle of fault has been turned into the principle of strict liability in relationships between socialist organisations.

In cases where the performance of an obligation has been imposed on *third parties*, the debtor is responsible in principle for the non-performance or improper performance of the obligation by them, it being understood that the debtor has a recourse action against the actual performer (art. 223).

If non-performance or improper performance of an obligation was due to the *fault of the debtor as well as of the creditor*, then the court or the arbitration reduces the measure of the debtor's liability accordingly (art. 224). The same solution is also provided where the creditor intentionally or by negligence contributed to the aggravation of losses caused by non-performance or improper performance.

The *delay by the debtor* in performing his obligation has two consequences (art. 225):

a) liability for losses caused by his delay and for accidentally supervening impossibility of performance during the delay;

b) the right of the creditor to reject the performance and to demand compensation for his losses, if performance of the obligation has lost its purpose for him in consequence of the debtor's delay. In a relationship between socialist organisations such a rejection of an overdue performance is permitted only in the cases and on the conditions laid down by statute or contract.

As far as *money obligations* are concerned, delay in their performance gives rise to three percent interest per annum for the period of the delay on the sum overdue unless some other rate is laid down by statute or by the contract. In the case of a money obligation between socialist organisations, the debtor must pay the creditor interest or a penalty for each day of the delay in the amount laid down by the legislation of the USSR (art. 226).

The *delay by the creditor* who has refused to accept a proper performance rendered by the debtor or who has failed to take those steps which must be taken before the debtor can perform his obligation, entitles the debtor to reimbursement for losses caused by the delay, unless the creditor can prove that the delay was not intentional or negligent (art. 227). As long as the creditor is in default, the debtor is not bound to pay interest on a money obligation.

VII. Discharge of obligations

Discharge of obligations can occur first by "performance carried out in the appropriate form" (art. 228) or by "setting-off a similar counterclaim which is already due or where no time is fixed for it or it can be claimed on demand" (art. 229). Nevertheless no set-off of claims on which the period of limitation of actions has expired nor of claims for compensation for damages resulting from harm to health or for causing death, nor for lifelong maintenance is permitted.

Furthermore an obligation can also be discharged by *coincidence* of the persons of the debtor and creditor or by *mutual agreement*. This method of discharge of an obligation is only permitted between socialist organisations "in so far as this does not contradict the acts of planning of the national economy" (art. 233). Logically "an obligation between socialist organisations is subject to discharge or alteration by the parties in the prescribed way in cases in which the *act of planning* on which the obligation was based has been altered by a ruling binding on both parties" (art. 234).

Finally, the *impossibility of performance* due to circumstances for which the debtor is not responsible (art. 235), the *death of the debtor* (if the obligation could be performed only with his personal participation) or of the *creditor* (if performance was intended only for the creditor personally) and the *dissolution of a juridical person* (whether debtor or creditor) are also listed as causes for the discharge of obligations.

As far as the *payment of obligations between state organizations*, collective farms and other cooperative and public organizations is concerned, art. 391 Civil Code RSFSR provides that they are made by the use of payment orders through the credit institutions in which, in accordance with statute, such organizations keep their funds. Settlements in money are allowed only within the limits laid down by the legislation of the USSR.

The above-mentioned organizations are *provided with credit* in accordance with approved plans by means of the issue of ear-marked fixed term loans by the State Bank of the USSR and other banks of the USSR (art. 393). One organisation cannot provide another with credit in the form of money or kind or by making advances except in cases laid down by the legislation of the USSR. *Bernard Dutoit*

See also AGENCY; AIR LAW; BAILMENTS; CARRIAGE AND TRANSPORT; COMMISSION AGENTS; FOREIGN TRADE CONTRACTS; GIFTS; HIRE PURCHASE AGREEMENTS; HOUSING LAW; INSURANCE; LEASES; LOANS; MARINE INSURANCE; SALES; SUPPLY CONTRACT; WARRANTY; WORK CONTRACT

CONTRIBUTORY NEGLIGENCE,
see TORTS

CONVEYANCING,
see LAND REGISTRATION

CONVICTS, see PENITENTIARY INSTITUTIONS

COOPERATIVES

In a number of areas of the Soviet economy, particularly in agriculture, productive and operative organizations take the legal form of cooperatives rather than that of state enterprises (*q.v.*) or budgetary institutions. At present the major types of cooperatives are agricultural (kolkhoz), fishing, consumer, construction (for housing, summer homes, and garages), gardening and livestock raising. Characteristic legal features of cooperatives include provision for the election of the governing bodies by the membership and for collective decision of questions of cooperative activity, typically by general meetings of the members. Cooperative organizations have legal personality. Unlike state enterprises, which receive orders from state administrative and planning agencies, cooperatives typically receive recommendations or advice. However, many of these differences between cooperatives and state enterprises both in internal organization and external relationships with state agencies have minimal effects in practice because both are under the leadership of officials who are subject to Communist Party discipline.

The agricultural cooperative (kolkhoz) is economically by far the most important type of cooperative; see further KOLKHOZ. The fishing cooperative has a form of organization similar to that of the collective farms. Fishing cooperatives also often engage in agriculture. Collective farms or fishing cooperatives may join together or form new cooperative organizations for major projects.

The consumer cooperative is the basic rural retail sales organization. Consumer cooperatives operate stores, cafeterias, bakeries, consumer service organizations, organizations for purchasing and resale of consumer goods and agricultural products, and enterprises for the processing of agricultural products. In theory the consumer cooperatives are governed by the general meeting of their member-shareholders, though in fact most administrative control is exercised by an extensive network of regional, republican and All-Union cooperative **unions.**

Cooperatives also exist in the area of construction, joining together groups of persons for the building of housing, summer homes, and garages. Such housing must be built in accordance with approved plans of urban development and is provided with financing, building materials, and with arrangement for contracting with construction organizations by the state planning agencies. The model charter of the housing construction cooperative provides that the cooperative shall be administered by a general meeting of the members, a meeting of delegates, and by an administration selected by the members. Similar rules apply to summer home and garage construction cooperatives.

Gardening and livestock raising cooperatives exist in order to provide an appropriate form or organization for residents of urban areas who wish to engage in small scale farming to supply their own food needs.

Citations to relevant legislation and fuller discussion may be found in O. A. Krasavchikova (ed.), *Sovetskoe grazhdanskoe pravo* (Soviet Civil Law), 1968, pp. 169-175, and in P. E. Orlovskii and S. M. Korneev (eds.), *Grazhdanskoe pravo* (Civil Law), 1969, pp. 168-176. See also the model charters regulating various types of cooperatives, of September 24, 1958 (*dacha*-building), July 8, 1959 (individual home-building), November 28, 1960 (fishing), October 2, 1965 (home-building).

P. Maggs

See also FISHING; BUILDING; HORTICULTURE; PERSONS

COPYRIGHT (see also *Appendix*)

System of norms governing legal relationships which arise in connection with the creation and use of original works of science, literature, music and the arts. Main body of applicable norms is found in the Principles of Civil Legislation, 1961 (arts. 96-109), and the civil codes of Union republics (arts. 475-516 in RSFSR Civil Code), but many relevant or related topics (incl. schedules of royalties and manner of payment; texts of standard authors' contracts, etc.) are dealt with in numerous administrative decrees and ordinances. A special Decree of the USSR Supreme Court, of December 19, 1967, provided authoritative interpretations of various norms of substantive and procedural law.

1) *Objects of copyright.* Copyright protection is accorded, without formal registration, to all original creative works of literature, science, music and the arts, whether published or unpublished, provided the work is extant in a concrete form capable of reproduction or imitation by others. The work is protected regardless of its purpose, form, merit, or method of presentation or reproduction. The product of the author's creative imagination may acquire concrete form through fixation on paper or canvas, public reading, performing in public, engraving, mechanical or magnetic recording, etc. It may be embodied in a manuscript, sketch, painting, scenario, motion picture, map, photograph, gramophone record, drama, sculpture, architect's blueprint, musical composition, etc. Protection does not extend to ideas tentatively expressed (theme of a book, plot for a play, spontaneous pantomime, melody without harmony and rhythm, etc.). The twin requirement of "originality" and "creativeness" excludes from protection non-literary works of predominantly "technical nature" (telephone directories, texts of decrees and court judgments, business correspondence, etc.), but it does include musical arrangements, adaptations, applied art, and use of another person's published works to create a new, substantially different work (e.g. anthologies, musical medleys, etc.).

Soviet law treats translations as original creative works and grants an independent copyright to the translator in his translations.

2) *Subjects of copyright.* Copyright is vested in the actual author of the work, regardless of his age. The author retains copyright title even in works created in the line of duty or under employment contract, although he is restricted by law in the *exercise* of certain subjective rights inherent in copyright (incl. right of publication and dissemination, and in most cases right to remuneration). Joint

copyright is conferred upon *co-authors* of works created in common, and it is exercised as a rule on the basis of mutual agreement. Each co-author, in addition to the joint copyright in the work as a whole, retains copyright in his own part, if it constitutes an identifiable separate entity. Copyright in the collective work as a whole does not belong to *contributors* of encyclopedias, periodical publications (incl. scholarly or scientific series), or to creators of individual parts of a motion picture, or a radio or television programme. Copyright in the finished work belongs in such cases to *juristic persons* under whose responsibility the collective work was created (scientific institute, university, news media, television or motion picture studio, etc.). Contributors retain copyright title only to their respective parts. Technical *collaborators* (research assistants, statisticians, manuscript editors, editors of memoirs, etc.) are not eligible as subjects of copyright in such works. Co-authorship may be sometimes unintentional, but the use of compulsion to create legal bonds of co-authorship is a criminal offence (art. 141, RSFSR Criminal Code).

Copyright title passes to *heirs* and legal *successors* for limited periods of time (in the RSFSR, as a rule 15 years), but the exercise of copyright *post mortem auctoris* is narrowly circumscribed by law.

The *state* may be subject of copyright in cases defined by law (compulsory purchase, decree to perpetuate copyright in state's title after expiration of the copyright term; liquidation of juristic person which possessed copyright title), and certain other cases.

3) *Contents of copyright.* Copyright confers upon the author a series of personal and of property rights. *Personal rights* include: a) Right of authorship (right to be recognised as the author; protection of author's name or pseudonym); b) right to publish, reproduce and disseminate the work; c) right to inviolability (integrity) of the work. The law restricts the author's freedom of publishing by a) reserving the state's right to intervene in the author's decision whether and when to publish; b) stipulating that publishing (*lato sensu*) may be effected, as a rule, only on the basis of authors' contracts concluded with appropriate socialist organisations (publishing house, television studio, concert organisation, exhibition hall, etc.); c) requiring (except in Kazakh SSR) that authors of works of pictorial fine arts obtain prior consent of the person whose likeness is reproduced in their work.

The right to reproduce and disseminate the published work, as a rule, is assigned under the standard author's contract, but, in cases provided by law, an author's work may be reproduced and circulated by others without his authorisation, either with or without payment of royalties. Such cases include: a) Without payment of royalties: Reproducing public speeches in news media; transmitting via radio or television live public concerts, recitals, etc.; copying public outdoor exhibits of sculpture; reprinting in scholarly, critical or pedagogical works extracts or passages from published works; reproducing published works for personal use; etc. b) With payment of royalties: Public performing, or sound recording for public use, of previously published works; use of published works of pictorial and fine arts on manufactured goods; etc.

The right to inviolability (integrity) of the work means that without consent of the author or his heirs, no one may alter or shorten it, make additions to it, provide it with illustrations, commentaries, postscripts, etc. The integrity of the work is not violated when the work is used by others a) to make translations; b) to create a new, independent work; c) when a literary work is used by a composer to create a musical composition with text. The author's consent is not required, but the original author is entitled to royalties in this last case.

The author's *property* rights consist in the right to collect remuneration or royalties when his work is *used* by others (with or without contract), and to claim compensation when such use infringed his copyright and resulted in losses of revenue.

4) *Duration of copyright.* Copyright originates with the creation of the work in a concrete form. No formalities are necessary, except for photographic works. Protection extends over the author's entire lifetime, but an abridged term is provided for in several republican civil codes (not RSFSR) for photographic works. Copyright devolves upon heirs and legal sucessors for 15 years *post mortem auctoris* but the right of authorship is not passed on, and a ceiling of 50% or below is imposed upon the amounts which may be collected in royalties or remuneration. Upon expiration of the statutory term of protection, copyright ceases to exist.

5) *Authors' contracts.* The author's contract is the principal legal instrument enabling an author to exercise his right to publish, reproduce and disseminate the work, and to derive pecuniary benefits therefrom. The author does not alienate or assign the copyright title under the author's contract. Contracts are concluded as a rule in writing, with appropriate socialist organisations, on the basis of obligatory standard (model) contracts approved by the council of ministers or individual ministries of the USSR and the Union republics. Separate model contracts have been approved for the principal categories of works, in accordance with a) the nature of the work (literary, artistic, musical, etc.); b) the method of reproduction or dissemination (printing, performing, filming, exhibiting, etc.); c) whether the work is extant in finished form or is to be created (contracts of commission). Author's contracts include the publishing contract, stage and screen production contracts, literary and artistic commission contracts, contracts for the utilisation in industry of an unpublished work of decorative-applied art, contracts for adaptation of a work into a different type of work, etc.

Under the author's contract, the author undertakes to deliver, or to create and deliver within a set period of time, a closely defined and described work to the contracting socialist organisation. As a rule, only such works are contracted for, which correspond to the thematic plan of the organisation. The latter undertakes to utilise the work in a specific manner (publish, produce, record, perform, exhibit, etc.) within a set period of time, and to pay the author the sums stipulated in the contract. The contract defines the size of the edition, responsibilities and liabilities of the parties, amount of the advance paid to the author, etc. For the distribution of motion pictures, the film studio (subject of copyright) signs an appropriate author's contract with the distributing organisation.

6) *Schedules of remuneration.* Amounts payable to the author for the use of his work are determined on the basis of official tariffs, enacted by the councils of ministers of the USSR or Union republics, individual ministries, and subordinate agencies. Such tariffs are binding upon the parties under authors' contracts. Separate tariffs exist for all major categories of author's works. Rates vary in accordance with type of the work, length, quality, degree of difficulty, social significance, size of the edition (i.e. number of copies), etc. The size of the first edition is pre-determined by norms for each relevant type of work, and overstepping of the limit constitutes a new edition. Payment is effected on the basis of such units as an "author's sheet" (40,000 printed characters); lines (poetry); minutes (music); number of acts (drama), etc. For each type of work, the schedules usually provide several possible rates, or a maximum-minimum range. Authors of works to be publicly performed receive, in addition to lump sum payments

(flat fee), also a percentage of gate receipts for each performance, up to a maximum limit. Such percentages (3%, 5%, etc.) vary according to the type of the work, and are payable even in the absence of a contract. Special rules apply to remuneration for textbooks and educational aids. Reduced rates are provided for translations, adaptations, new editions (sliding scale), etc. For works not listed in official schedules, remuneration may be determined by agreement of the parties based on analogy, but such cases are relatively rare.

7) *Infringements and remedies.* Plagiarism, i.e., using someone's copyrighted work under one's own name; and illegal reproduction or dissemination of someone's copyrighted work (e.g. despite the author's specific prohibition), are criminal offences punishable (art. 141, RSFSR Criminal Code) by a fine or deprivation of freedom for up to one year. Under civil law, the author may sue for restoration of his personal rights, and for compensation in case of violation of his property rights.

a) *Infringements of personal rights* include reproducing or circulating an author's work without mention of his chosen name; altering the author's text or providing it with illustrations, comments, etc., without his consent; reproducing an author's work without his consent where such consent is required by law; failure to observe conditions under which an author's work may be utilised without his consent, etc. Remedy consists in restoration of the author's personal rights by removing unauthorised additions or inserting appropriate rectifications; withdrawing the work from circulation; publishing a notice in the press, etc. The defendant's fault need not be established, and actions are *not* subject to any statute of limitations.

b) *Infringements of property rights* include failure to pay royalties to the author for utilisation of his work, where such work may be reproduced without his consent but with payment of royalties; material losses resulting from plagiarism; failure to pay the author the full amount according to official tariffs, etc. Remedy consists in compensation for loss of royalties within the limites established under regular schedules, and compensation for other material losses and related expenses, if they can be substantiated by the author. No punitive damages may be awarded. Actions are subject to the usual statute of limitations.

Protection of the author's personal and property rights may take on the form of actions in contract when the stipulations of the author's contract have not been carried out. Protection is also available under administrative law (settlement out of court), on the basis of author's complaint addressed to the appropriate socialist organisation, or to the authors professional association (Union of Soviet Writers, etc.), or to the Administration for Protection of Authors' Rights (VUOAP). The latter may act as the author's attorney in court actions, or bring suit in its own name on the author's behalf.

8) *International law.* Works created by Soviet citizens are protected even if they were first published or reproduced abroad, or are located there as a manuscript or unpublished original. Works by non-citizens are protected a) if they were first published on Soviet territory, or are located there as a manuscript or unpublished original; b) in all other cases, only on the basis of a treaty with the foreign country.

Serge L. Levitsky

CORPORATIONS

The history of the limited liability company in Tsarist Russia goes back to February 5, 1555, when Philip and Mary of England approved the charter of a Muscovy or Russian Company, which obtained a trading monopoly "with Muscovy and the other countries which may be discovered to the north, north-east and north-west of England". During the following centuries the number of foreign companies operating on Russian territory grew, and an imperial *ukaz* of June 15, 1758, defined the Russian companies as "places of refuge of bankrupt merchants" and forbade their founding. On January 1, 1807, the prohibition was repealed, but the emperor's (government's) permission was required henceforward for the founding of limited companies.

Section 6, Book 4, of Vol. 10 part 1 (the Civil Code) of the *Svod Zakonov* dealt at length (arts. 2139-2198) with shareholding companies (*tovarishchestva po uchastkam ili kompanii na aktsiiakh*). The Commercial Code (Vol. 11 part 2 of the *Svod Zakonov*) referred the regulation of the founding of companies to civil law and to local credit regulations (art. 87 of the 1887 edition; see also, with regard to banks, the Credit Code in the same volume of the *Svod*).

More detailed rules could be found in the charters of the fifteen limited companies existing in Russia in 1850; even art. 87 referred to these special charters, in particular with regard to the typology, the duration and the privileges of limited companies.

The number of limited companies grew impressively in the second half of the century, thanks to the pioneering activities of public and private banks, to reach the number of 1700 in the year 1900, of which 1450 were engaged in industry and 250 in commerce, insurance and transport. On December 21, 1901, a decision of the Council of Ministers, approved by the Emperor, completed and amended the legal regime of the limited company. From 1901 until 1918 the newly regulated companies (in which, as in the preceding century, state participation was not absent) grew in number and in importance, while participation of foreign capital fell in proportion.

During the revolution, companies of all shapes practically ceased to function: associations of persons—through the fading away of their objectives by virtue of nationalizations or confiscations, although they were never suppressed as legal institutions and limited companies—by the express intention of the legislator to abolish these also on a formal legal level, by annulling the shares of nationalized or confiscated enterprises, as legal relationships contrary to public order.

The limited company, supreme incarnation of capitalism, re-appeared, however, in the RSFSR with the decree of July 29, 1921, in connection with the Soviet attempt to attract foreign capital through a system of concessions.

The charters of the new Russian companies were based on pre-revolutionary models, but the legislator regarded this form of association with suspicion and hostility; in his eyes it was a most dangerous legal institution, in the service of abuse, speculation and fraud. This suspicion and prejudice were never again to leave him, and they would give rise, as already under the tsarist regime, to the requirement of special governmental permission for the founding of companies, and to a system of intensive supervision.

The Russian Civil Code of 1922 (which did not know the *Kommanditgesellschaft* with shares) regulated the *aktsionernoe obshchestvo* (limited company with shares) in 44 articles (322-366) in a way not dissimilar to the commercial legislation of the West. Its provisions were almost fully copied in the civil codes of the other republics, apart from some changes subsequently introduced in the Ukrainian Civil Code.

Starting from 1925, the intervention of the federal legislator became more and more noticeable, and on August 17, 1927, a decree of the Central Executive Committee and the Council of People's Commissars of the USSR unified the regulation of Soviet limited companies definitively and with great richness of detail.

A model charter was approved by the Peo-

ple's Commissariat of Trade by order of October 19, 1928.
In eight chapters, partially with retroactive force, the new decree forbade the creation of bearer shares and annulled bearer shares which were not transformed into nominal shares in 1927; it forbade the founding of companies which pursued non-economic objectives (a debated question in pre-1927 legal doctrine); it strongly facilitated companies in which the shares belonged fully or in part to the state.
It is very obvious that the legislator envisaged the limited company as a combination of state capital and private capital, rather than as an accumulation of private capital. This is confirmed by contemporary statistics. Of the 187 companies existing in 1926, only 36 were private, representing only 2.6% of the total capital in shares; in 1924 this percentage was still as high as 12%.
The conditions in which the state and its agencies participate in limited companies vary: sometimes there is purely a combination of state agencies and enterprises, while at other times there is private participation as well (but in that case the charter usually reserves 51% of the shares for the state).
The decree of 1927 provides that institutions (*uchrezhdeniia*), unlike enterprises working on a basis of *khozraschet* (*q.v.*), may participate in limited companies only where such a right has been granted to them by the law. For enterprises as well as bodies which are basically financed by the state, the following conditions must be fulfilled: a) that the funds necessary to found the company or acquire shares are included in the financial plan of the enterprise or in the current budget of the body in question; b) that the objective of the company is not contrary to the aims of the state agencies concerned; c) that the competent federal or republican economic authority has given the necessary permission.
A limited company is a state company when the charter provides that all its shares will belong exclusively to state enterprises or services; it is a "mixed" (*smeshannoe*) company when according to the charter at least 50% of the shares must be owned by state agencies, or when these have the right to appoint at least one half of the elected bodies of the company, or when at least one half of the dividends is guaranteed to be paid out to them.
Two founders are sufficient to set up a state company (three were required for a private company). The capital of the state company may also be formed by contributions of goods *extra commercium* which are valued according to the rules of administrative law. The soil, the sub-soil, forests and waters of course can not be contributed as property, but only the use of them.
The organs of the company are the administration (*pravlenie*), the supervisory board (*sovet*)—the institution of which is not obligatory—the revision commission (*revizionnaia komissiia*) and the general meeting of shareholders (*obshchee sobranie aktsionerov*).
Broad powers of control and supervision are reserved for the state element in the administration of companies. State-held shares may be transferred only to state enterprises and institutions (other transfers are null and void).
Losses and gains are distributed according to special rules; likewise the winding-up is governed by special rules (applicable also to state enterprises which are not structured as limited companies).
Mixed companies were still under the regime of private legal entities, apart from a number of special provisions concerning the transferability of shares, the withdrawal of absent or dissident private partners, the convening of meetings, winding-up and supervision.
The law of 1927 also solved the question, controversial in literature and case law,

concerning the legal nature of the limited company in public hands, i.e. whether state companies and mixed companies should be equated in law to state enterprises on a *khozraschet* basis, with all the privileges connected with the position of the latter. Previous case law and administrative practice had been favourable to equation in cases where the charter excluded participation by co-operatives or private persons; otherwise such companies were treated as private companies, even where all shares were in the hands of state agencies. The law of 1927, however (and likewise some statutes which immediately preceded or followed it), described the state limited company explicitly as a state enterprise on the basis of *khozraschet*, and extended to it the general norms concerning enterprises working on a *khozraschet* basis "regardless of its organizational form, and provided the law does not rule otherwise".

Consequently, legal literature emphasized the institutional aspect of the state limited company as the organizational form of the personified enterprise (*Unternehmen an sich*), while the associational or contractual element was moved noticeably into the background.

As for the rules concerning mixed companies they were made more similar to those concerning state enterprises, especially with regard to taxation and winding-up.

Private companies disappeared in the years following the NEP, chiefly through the unavailability of bank loans. The mixed and state limited companies also fell into disfavour.

With the 1936 Constitution, the category of private law legal entities disappeared, and from then on the limited company was seldom used domestically. After the Second World War the form of the mixed limited company was employed in areas which had recently become socialist, and where Soviet contributions consisted chiefly of local capital formerly in German hands. Any participation of private capital was excluded, however, unlike the system followed in the era of the concessions for mixed Soviet-foreign companies.

But also any form of joint-stock companies with Hungary, Roumania, Bulgaria, Poland, Yugoslavia and China seems to have disappeared since 1956. At present the joint venture type relationships with these countries may assume various forms within the Comecon (*q.v.*) framework, or on the basis of *ad hoc* agreement with the countries in question.

Although never formally repealed, the rules governing mixed and state limited companies are said not to be in force any longer. All-Union limited companies (*vsesoiuznye aktsionernye obshchestva*)—the large companies of federal importance (see STATE ENTERPRISES)—are all regulated by special *ad hoc* statutes or charters. While the foreign branches are usually incorporated according to the national law of the country where they are meant to operate (e.g. the Amtorg Trading Company in New York, the *Banque Commerciale pour l'Europe du Nord* in Paris, the Moscow Narodny Bank in London, the Wozchod Commercial Bank in Zurich), the mother organizations in the Soviet Union, such as *Inturist*, *Mezhdunarodnaia Kniga* and the *Vneshtorgbank*, are still based on the participation in shares by federal ministries, committees, institutions, enterprises and also co-operative organisations. According to its 1962 charter, the *Vneshtorgbank* is a corporation with a capital of 300 mill. Roubles, divided into 6,000 nominal shares.

Bibl.: Krimmer, *Sociétés de capitaux en Russie Impériale et en Russie Soviétique*, 1934; Feitelberg, *Staatliche and gemischte Aktiengesellschaften im Sowjetrecht (in rechtsvergleichender Darstellung)*, 1929; Lack, *Das Aktienrecht Sowjet-Russlands,*

1929; Landt, *Das Sowjetrussische Aktienrecht*, 1929; Crespi Reghizzi, *La sociedad como forma empresarial en la experiencia soviética*, in *La empresa pública*, 1970, p. 1771 ff.

G. Crespi Reghizzi

See also ASSOCIATION

CORRECTIVE LABOUR

Corrective labour without deprivation of freedom (for corrective labour with deprivation of freedom see PENITENTIARY INSTITUTIONS) has developed from the initially *ad hoc* orders (some of them by Lenin himself) to apply it against class enemies like "millionaire-saboteurs" and speculators (see Lenin's telegram in Works, 50, pp. 21-22). However, more regular legal enactments as early as December 19, 1917, and the third decree on Courts (July 20, 1918) were also conducive towards its development.

Something new and constructive was brought into the stale and unimaginative air of correctional and penal practice and, since its first formulation in the "Guiding principles of criminal law" of 1919 corrective labour (without deprivation of freedom) has retained its place in the catalogue of Soviet penal measures up to the present, its principles having been reaffirmed by inclusion in the latest Principles of Corrective Labour Legislation of the USSR and the Union Republics of July 11, 1969. It has been used mainly as a substitute for short-term imprisonment and ranges from one month to one year. The offender may either continue his usual work or may be given work elsewhere, but still in the district of his domicile; the main effect of the sentence nowadays is the deduction of up to 20% from the wages of the offender for the benefit of the state (the harsh measure of the early period, prescribing work in mines or other hard labour, with rigorous deductions from pay of from 25% to 75% have long ago been replaced by this milder punishment). The offender may be punished by corrective labour either as a basic punishment or it may be used instead of some more severe measure (imprisonment) in the case of mitigating circumstances or of partial remission of the term of imprisonment (or deprivation of freedom) for good behaviour. But it may also be used in place of a fine, when payment of the latter cannot be enforced. This has induced many Soviet scholars to regard corrective labour as a special type of monetary fine and not as a separate type of punishment. This conclusion seems particularly justified if it is considered that according to Soviet criminal law the non-payment of fines cannot be replaced by imprisonment, but the non-payment of deductions from earnings in the course of corrective labour can and, by order of the people's court, is converted into one day of imprisonment for three days of corrective labour.

The records, supervision and control of cases of corrective labour is the task of Corrective Labour Inspectorates (special officers of the local departments for internal affairs). The inspectors allocate to the offender the place of his corrective work, if the offender is unemployed, or the sentence prescribes work elsewhere than at his normal place of employment. They communicate with the employers and see to it that the public organisations and collectives at the offender's corrective employment endeavour to reform him. They have the power of reprimand, warning or even arrest for up to 10 days for absenteeism and other breaches of discipline by the offender. These rights are said to be more formal than actual, since it is the duty of the inspectors to plead in court for the substitution of corrective labour by imprisonment in the case of the offender's default.

Some corrective labour codes (the RSFSR, BSSR and others) provide that the time served in corrective labour is not counted for the purpose of seniority, pension rights or the right to annual leave. But good behaviour may, on the plea of public organisations or of the offender's work-mates, retain for him his rights of seniority. Some codes, such as the Estonian, Latvian and Moldavian, do not include this possibility of exemption from the seniority count. Others, like the Ukrainian Code, are even more rigorous and do not contain the possibility of restoring seniority. The new Principles of June 11, 1969, have taken a most rigorous and vindictive line: corrective labour not only brings about a loss of seniority, but such periods must be entered in the offender's labour book. As the latter has to be submitted to any new prospective or actual employer the practice of such entries had in most Union republics been discarded in order not to prejudice the future career of the offender. This was a reasonable practice because of the mild punitive measure itself, and because the criminal record of corrective labour is extinguished automatically after one year. For corrective labour and probation, see PROBATION.

Corrective labour may occur also as a penalty for administrative offences (*q.v.*).

R. Beermann

COSTS, CIVIL PROCEDURE

The Soviet law of costs (cf. arts. 79-96 Code of Civil Procedure) is similar to that of Germany. It is not based on a general survey of the difficulty of a case but on a fixed percentage relationship to the value of the matter in dispute. Hence it is fairly predictable and costs are comparatively small.

Witness fees are only payable if the witness is not regularly employed, since, in the latter case, he retains his wages as if he had been at work. In any case these fees are low.

Court fees (state tax) are payable on the original statement of claim and on certain other applications. If the case is dismissed without trial the fee is repaid to the plaintiff. If the case concerns a material thing or a sum of money, the initial fee is based on the valuation of the thing or on the sum stated. If a larger value or sum is eventually recovered, as can happen under the Soviet system by the intervention of the procurator or action of the court, a further fee becomes payable. There is no refund if less is recovered, and this may deter inflated claims, as may the rule that a plaintiff may be fined a small percentage of his claim if it was clearly not brought in good faith. In some cases there is no financial equivalent, e.g. divorce: here there is a general uniform fee on the statement of claim but the court may also charge a varying amount to either party, when giving judgment, which may deter some frivolous cases or defences. Costs of appeals are fixed at one-half the costs of the original proceeding.

An important rule exempts the plaintiff from court fees in cases of labour disputes, maintenance, torts to the person and patent and copyright cases. A plaintiff may also be exempted by the court in any other case where hardship would otherwise be caused. Alternatively his liability to pay costs may be deferred if he is in temporary difficulties.

Court fees are recoverable by a successful plaintiff from the defendant, in full or in proportion to his success. The court also incurs costs in certain cases and throws these ultimately onto the losing party, e.g. where the court has summoned an expert.

If the defendant voluntarily satisfied a claim before judgment, the court may make an order for payment of costs, calculated in the usual way to-date, e.g. including court fees but not witness fees.

Advocates' fees are recoverable from the unsuccessful party by the party who has gained a sum or been relieved of liability to pay it at percentages not exceeding 5%. In cases of a personal nature where no financial valuation is possible, the law on advocates' fees fixes the amounts recoverable. Where a party has had free legal aid from a lawyers' office that office recovers the amount of fees, which would have been payable, from the unsuccessful opponent, e.g. where a worker sues for wrongful dismissal and loss of mesne wages.

Soviet lawyers consider, in this connection, the topic of court fines, e.g. fines on witnesses who fail to appear, or for disturbing good order in court, or for failing to perform certain types of judgment. These cases, however, do not appear to fall properly within this subject.

The court deals with the question of awarding costs on its own initiative and the successful party does not have to apply specially for such an order. The order for costs is included in the rest of the judgment unless the action was limited to deciding the question of costs.

A. K. R. Kiralfy

COSTS, CRIMINAL PROCEDURE

In criminal procedure, costs comprise the reimbursement of the compensation of witnesses, victims, experts, specialists, interpreters and witnesses at investigative proceedings; remuneration of experts, specialists, and interpreters; expenses for preserving, transmitting and investigating real evidence, and the other expenses incurred in the conduct of a given case. Cf. arts. 105-107 Code of Criminal Procedure.

Costs are borne by the state in the case of acquittal, termination of the case, or insolvency of the person liable for them; in the case of an acquittal from a private accusation (see VICTIM), costs can be awarded totally or in part against the victim. If the accused is found guilty, costs can be imposed on him even if he is relieved of punishment; if several accused are found guilty, costs are apportioned among them according to guilt, responsibility and property status. The distribution of costs is decided upon in the judgment.

The court's costs and advocate's fees are not part of the costs. Even the payment for the legal aid of an assigned counsel whose participation in the preliminary investigation is obligatory (in cases of minors and persons with physical or mental defects) has been exempted from costs since 1963. In all cases of counsel assigned to the defence, the court has to fix the amount of remuneration payable by the defendant (not only the convict) simultaneously with the judgment. If he is insolvent, a special fund at the advocate's law office has to bear these costs.

M. Fincke

COUNCILS OF MINISTERS

In accordance with the variety of the federal system prevailing in the Soviet Union, councils of ministers are met at three levels: Union (federal), Union republic and autonomous republic. The council of ministers of the autonomous republic shares the comparative unimportance assigned to the autonomous republic itself within the framework of the Soviet federal system.

The Council of Ministers of the USSR

Arts. 64-71 of the USSR Constitution are devoted to the USSR Council of Ministers It is defined as "the highest executive and administrative organ of state power in the USSR". For the meaning of the terms "executive" and "administrative" in this context, see ADMINISTRATIVE LAW.

The Council of Ministers of the USSR is also called the government (*pravitel'stvo*) of the USSR, although the usual supreme governmental functions are divided between the Council and the Presidium of the USSR Supreme Soviet (see PRESIDIUM OF THE SUPREME SOVIET). The USSR Supreme Soviet Presidium exercizes a number of functions which in other states are usually vested in the head of state. Both the Presidium and the Council of Ministers possess legislative and executive powers. As a rule legislation addressed to the population at large (typically: criminal law enactments) is enacted by the Presidium (or by the Supreme Soviet itself), while legislation addressed to specific groups of persons or organizations will often assume the form of a decree of the Council of Ministers.

Otherwise the relation between the Council of Ministers and the Presidium is by no means unclear. The Council of Ministers is appointed by the Supreme Soviet or, in the intervals between sessions of the Supreme Soviet, individual ministers are appointed by the Presidium on the recommendation of the Chairman of the Council of Ministers and subject to subsequent approval by the Supreme Soviet (art. 49g of the Constitution). The Council of Ministers is responsible and accountable to the Supreme Soviet and, in the intervals between sessions, to the Presidium. The Presidium is entitled to annul decrees and orders of the Council of Ministers if they do not conform to the law (no such right is expressly granted to the Supreme Soviet because its power is paramount). Finally, "the Council of Ministers issues decrees and orders on the basis and in pursuance of the laws in operation" (art. 66 of the USSR Constitution), which includes decrees (*ukazy*) of the Presidium. The one thing these rules do not allow the Presidium to do is to instruct the Council of Ministers directly on policy decisions.

The functions of the Council of Ministers of the USSR embrace the overall control of the economy of the USSR, of public order in its widest sense, of foreign relations and of defence. The Council of Ministers co-ordinates and directs the work of the ministries and state committees of the USSR (see MINISTRIES and STATE COMMITTEES) and may set up state committees and similar agencies (cf. art. 68 of the USSR Constitution). In the exercise of its functions the Council of Ministers may issue decrees (*postanovleniia*) and decisions (*rasporiazheniia*); decrees are of a general (normative) character and decisions concern individual cases (such as appointments). (It is also held that the distinction is purely formal.) Decrees and decisions of the USSR Council of Ministers are binding throughout the territory of the USSR (art. 67). See also LEGISLATION.

The Council of Ministers of the USSR is appointed by the USSR Supreme Soviet at a joint session of its two chambers (see SUPREME SOVIETS). It consists of a Chairman, one or more First Vice-Chairmen, several Vice-Chairmen, the ministers of the USSR, the Chairmen of the Councils of Ministers of the Union republic and the Chairmen of the State Committees mentioned in art. 70 of the Constitution (for a list of these—see STATE COMMITTEES). A full meeting of the USSR Council of Ministers, because of its size and composition, is not a very frequent event. Therefore most of its powers are in fact exercized by a presidium, although the Constitution is ignorant of such a body. The presidium apparently consists of the Chairman, the First Vice-Chairmen, the Vice-Chairmen and others members appointed by the Council of Ministers.

The councils of ministers of Union republics

The Council of Ministers of a Union republic occupies the same position vis-à-vis the Presidium of the Supreme Soviet of the Union republic and the Supreme Soviet of the Union republic, as the USSR Council of Ministers vis-à-vis the USSR Presidium and the USSR Supreme Soviet. Additionally, there are three constitutional links between the Council of Ministers of a Union republic and federal agencies: the Council of Ministers of the Union republic, in exercizing its functions, is bound also by USSR (federal) law and by decrees and decisions of the USSR Council of Ministers (art. 82 of the

USSR Constitution); the Council of Ministers of the USSR is entitled to suspend decrees and decisions of councils of ministers of Union republics (but only "in respect of those branches of the administration and economy which come within the jurisdiction of the USSR—art. 69); the USSR Supreme Soviet Presidium is entitled to annul decrees and decisions of councils of ministers of Union republics if they do not conform to the law (art. 49f.).

The catalogues of duties of the councils of ministers of the Union republics (as provided by the constitutions of the Union republics) reflect the enumeration of functions of the USSR Council of Ministers in art. 68 of the Constitution: overall control of the economy, public order, foreign relations and defence in the Union republic concerned (the defence and foreign relations duties amount to very little; they were introduced at the end of the second world war in order to bolster the case for UN membership for the Ukraine and Belorussia). One significant addition is that the councils of ministers of Union republics "direct and verify" the work of the councils of ministers of autonomous republics and of the executive committees of *krai*'s and provinces (*oblasti*); see also KRAI and OBLAST'. The verb used with regard to the autonomous republics (*napravliat'*—to give direction) may connote a less stringent sort of leadership than "*rukovodit'* " (to direct), used in connection with the executive commissions. (N.B. the USSR Council of Ministers does not have the right to direct the work of the councils of ministers of the Union republics or to verify its execution.)

The councils of ministers of Union republics have the power to annul orders and instructions of ministers of the Union republic, to annul decisions of *krai* and provincial executive committees, and to suspend decrees and decisions of councils of ministers of autonomous republics and decisions of *krai* and provincial executive committees (cf. art. 46 of the RSFSR Constitution).

Councils of ministers of Union republics are appointed and constituted in a similar manner to the USSR Council of Ministers (by the corresponding agencies of the Union republic), but the chairmen of the councils of ministers of autonomous republics are not *ex officio* members.

Councils of ministers of autonomous republics

The organization, duties and powers of the councils of ministers of autonomous republics are an exact replica, at the lower level of the autonomous republic, of those of the council of ministers of the Union republic. See further AUTONOMOUS REPUBLICS.

F. J. M. Feldbrugge

See also UNION REPUBLICS; FEDERATION

COUNTERCLAIMS AND CROSS ACTIONS

Soviet law on this subject has much in common with other legal systems. Whereas set-off is a defence to an action and must be a smaller sum than that claimed, a counterclaim is a substantive independent action in which the defendant is in effect the plaintiff and the plaintiff the defendant. The defendant files a formal counterclaim which has the same requirements as the usual statement of claim beginning an action.

There must be some internal relation between the claim and counterclaim before a counterclaim can be used as of right, e.g. if the defendant has a claim to repayment of expenses exceeding the sums in his hands which the plaintiff seeks to recover, or if the defendant wishes to have a contract declared void which the plaintiff is seeking to enforce against him.

In all other cases it is in the discretion of the court whether or not to allow a counterclaim in effect consolidating two different actions.

The test is whether it would be clearly more convenient and less time-consuming to try the two actions together. It is too late if one is being tried already.
The court may ultimately give judgment on the claim or counterclaim or on one as reduced by the other.
Occasionally the defendant may elect whether to introduce matter by way of a defence to an action or by launching a counterclaim, e.g. if sued for maintenance of a child he may deny paternity simply, or may counterclaim for a declaration that he is not the father.

A. K. R. Kiralfy

COUNTERFEITING
The principal provision dealing with counterfeiting is art. 87 of the Criminal Code. The making (for the purpose of passing) or the passing of counterfeit state treasury notes, notes, notes of the State Bank of the USSR, coins, state securities, or foreign currency, entails a penalty of from three to fifteen years' deprivation of freedom. If the counterfeiting has not been committed on an isolated occasion, but regularly as a business or profession, the minimum penalty is increased to ten years, and the court may also apply the death penalty.
The essential characteristic of counterfeiting is the erosion of the value of state-issued money (in any form); therefore the production of false antique coins is not considered to be counterfeiting, but as fraud (or the preparation of fraud). The Soviet Union is a signatory of the International Convention for the Suppression of Counterfeit Currency of April 20, 1929.
Also, counterfeiting requires some act of producing (although not necessarily by the offender himself). Therefore the passing of pictures of rouble notes, published in a magazine, was not considered to be counterfeiting, but fraud. The act of production may consist in making new (counterfeit) money or notes, or in changing real money or notes (e.g. by adding a zero).
Art. 159 deals with the counterfeiting of postage stamps, international reply coupons, or other means of postal payment (including the passing of such valuables). The maximum penalty is two years' deprivation of freedom. The second paragraph of the same article is devoted to the counterfeiting or passing of tickets or documents for the transportation of passengers or freight. The maximum penalty is three years.
All crimes of counterfeiting require criminal intent; this requirement should be kept in mind especially in the case of passing counterfeit money.
The making of counterfeit rubber stamps and seals is considered to be a form of forgery in the Soviet Union.

F. J. M. Feldbrugge

See also FORGERY; FRAUD; MONEY

COUNTERREVOLUTION,
see POLITICAL CRIMES

COUNTIES,
see TERRITORIAL DIVISIONS

COURT RECORDS, CIVIL PROCEDURE
As in the Continental European system, Soviet civil courts build up a written file or dossier (*delo*) of each case, which forms a fairly detailed account of the entire proceedings. This record consists of several parts, with different sources. The first component consists of the plaintiff's statement of claim, which must contain a number of elements laid down by civil procedure codes. If a lawyer is consulted in its preparation, it constitutes a substantial document (up to 1,000 words in some cases). It identifies the court, parties etc., summarises the circumstances of the case, fixes the amount of money claimed or other relief required. Where drawn up by a lawyer it also refers

to the statutory sections on which the claim is based, and discusses the breaches of those sections which have occurred. The statement of claim is accompanied by various annexed papers, e.g. safety inspectors' reports in a tort case, medical reports on loss of earning capacity, certificates of amounts of wages earned before and after an accident. In a dismissal case the dismissal notice will be annexed, and the decision of the local labour disputes committee. In succession cases birth and death certificates will be appended. The defendant is not required by law to file a written defence but in practice he makes his "objection" or "explanation" in some cases in an equally formal document. In this the plaintiff's points are refuted and legal arguments based on statutes advanced. It is obviously useful to the court to have such a document in its hands.

The second component of the court record consists of the court minutes (*protokol*), compiled by the court secretary (see CLERK OF COURT), which is more specifically the court's own record of what it has done (cf. arts. 226-230 Code of Civil Procedure). It may run from 1,000 to 1,500 words in a typical case. It describes the court and its members, identifies the case by reference number and parties and follows the course of the trial: the appearance of the parties, the calling of the case and retirement of witnesses, the representatives appearing for parties, and applications for the examination of witnesses. The plaintiff's case is presented by him in person and recorded in the first person but not necessarily word for word. Questions put to him are recorded and the answers. The defendant's explanations, personally or by a representative, may then be recorded, and questions put to him, with answers. Next come the statements of the witnesses, and their answers to questions. All these questions are put by the court, the procurator and the opposing party in that order. The parties' closing statements, asking for judgment in their favour are made. The conclusions of the procurator and his recommendations to the court follow. The record then refers to the passing of judgment and the closing of the court hearing. The judge and secretary sign the minutes. The parties may raise objections to them and have them tried.

It will be noticed that the terms of the judgment are not part of the court minutes. This is because a whole range of judicial rulings exist, such as final and interlocutory orders, and these are not regarded as part of the minutes of the session, although the minutes must refer to the fact that orders have been made and the final judgment given. In the result there is a certain duplication in the record, since the third component, usually the judgment, covers much of the same ground. It identifies the court and the case in question, summarises the findings of fact, as made out in the explanations of the parties and the testimony of the witnesses, as these strike the court as true or not, and gives legal conclusions. The damages, if any, are then assessed and judgment given, obliging the parties therein named to make payments or perform acts, and informing them of their rights to appeal to higher courts. The judgment is signed by the judge and assessors. It may be from 500 to 1,000 words in length (see JUDGMENTS).

If an appeal is brought, this record is extended by the appeal complaint of the appellant. This refers to the original file and makes specific numbered objections to the findings in the judgment, generally on points of law, and concludes with a prayer for reversal of the judgment. The respondent may put in a formal reply in numbered paragraphs, asking for the judgment to be left unchanged. The judgment of the appeal court follows, with the usual reasoning. No minute of the hearing in the appeal court, however, is kept, as no evidence is taken, a re-trial being ordered if that is necessary (see APPELLATE PROCEDURE).

A. K. R. Kiralfy

COURT RECORDS, CRIMINAL PROCEDURE

These are documents in criminal proceedings, drawn up in a legally prescribed form by the agency of inquiry, investigator, or court clerk, which register the contents and the result of an investigative act or the course of a judicial session respectively, and perform in part an evidentiary function. Cf. art. 102 Code of Criminal Procedure.

There is an extensive duty to keep records, legally prescribed in detail, of all official procedural acts without exception, even at the stage of police inquiry. This duty is laid down in particular:

1) During preliminary proceedings: a) for all investigative actions, such as the interrogation of the defendant, witnesses, victim, and experts, the declarations of third persons, confrontation and identification parades, search, seizure and the impounding of property, inspection, bodily examination, investigative experiments, and comparative tests; b) for all prescribed formalities, such as the receiving of oral information about crimes, especially self-incrimination (*iavka s povinnoi*), the instruction of the interpreter, the informing of participants of their rights, esp. the victim of his right to civil suit and the civil action itself, the receipt of the declarations or petitions of participants and experts, announcing the termination of the preliminary investigation and the acquainting of participants (accused, defence counsel, victim, civil plaintiff, civil defendant) with the materials of the case; c) for detention (restraining measures (*q.v.*), however, are recorded in the respective decree).

2) During the judicial stage at first instance: a) for all administrative court sessions including those at the stage of execution; b) for trial.

3) The record is not provided for in cassational or supervision proceedings.

Contents: All records must indicate the place, date, time of commencement and completion of the action or session. Furthermore, they must mention: a) in preliminary proceedings: the recorder, all participants, the content of the recorded action and its result (and the circumstances to be disclosed); b) in court sessions: the name and composition of the court, clerk, participants and persons summoned, the case under consideration, the actions of the court in chronological order, the statements and petitions of participants, any court rulings given in the court room and the fact that a ruling was made in the conference room; c) at trial, in addition: the personal data of the accused and measures of restraint, legal information concerning the participants, the testimony, any questions put to the expert and his answers, the results of the taking of "real" evidence, facts the recording of which the participants request, violations of order with an indication of the violator, a summary of the oral argument and of the accused's last word, the fact of the disclosure of judgment and the fact that appeal procedures and time limits have been explained. Appendices: since 1966, interrogations may be tape recorded; the recording and any photographs, films, slides, plans, diagrams, molds and track impressions, taken during investigative action, must be appended to the record, in which appropriate reference must be made. In an appendix to the trial record, witnesses attest by signature that they have been informed and warned.

Procedure of recording: 1. *In preliminary proceedings*: The record is drafted during or immediately after the act to be recorded by the person conducting it (investigator, etc.). It must be read to the participants who are informed of their right to have their own remarks entered in the record. It is signed by the investigator and by the participants in the recorded action; if a participant refuses to sign, the investigator signs a note to that effect in the record, while the refuser is entitled to have his explanation entered. In the case of physical inability to sign, a note to that effect in the record must be signed by the investigator and the witnesses of the investigative action. 2. *In court sessions* the record is drafted by the court clerk (*q.v.*). In the case of trial, it must be prepared and signed within three days after the court sitting. It is signed by the secretary (court clerk) and the presiding judge. Whereas the latter is responsible for the completeness, exactitude and technical quality of the record, the secretary, if he disagrees with the presiding judge about the contents of the record, may append his remarks which are then subject to consideration by the court. The presiding judge must secure to the participants the opportunity to be acquainted with the record. They are entitled to submit their remarks within three days after signing it. If the presiding judge agrees with the remarks, he certifies their correctness and attaches them to the record; otherwise, they must be considered by an administrative court session at which the presiding member and at least one of the assessors must have participated in the trial. The ruling supported by reasons, must be attached to the record together with the remarks.

Effect: 1) The records constitute the most important part of the "materials of the case"; where persons are granted the opportunity to be acquainted with them (e.g. the accused, defence counsel, victim, civil plaintiff and civil defendant after completion of the preliminary investigation), the appended films or recordings must be shown to them. 2) The "records of investigative and judicial actions" are declared by federal law to be independent means of evidence alongside documents, testimony, expert opinions and real evidence. However, some of the Union republic codes confine this effect to the records of only some investigative actions (e.g. RSFSR: records of inspection, bodily examination, investigative experiments, identification parades, search, seizure, detention), because the principle of the directness and oral nature of the trial substantially restricts the usage of prior depositions by reading interrogation records (see below) and because the remaining recorded actions have no significance for the substance of the case but only for its form. Unlike other jurisdictions, the particular evidentiary value of records does not concern the observation of formalities, but the results of the investigation (with the exception of the trial record, see below). On the other hand, the expressly enumerated records do not enjoy any evidentiary privilege, because every written thought may serve as "documentary" evidence and the court is free in its evaluation of the means of evidence (inner conviction, see EVIDENCE); if there is any presumption in favour of the record's correctness, it is rebuttable by any means. 3) The depositions of the defendant or a witness as recorded during the preliminary proceedings can by no means be read in trial as "record", but only as a part of or a substitute for their direct interrogation; as such, they may be read, or the respective recordings be reproduced, only in the case of a contradiction, the complete silence of the defendant, or his absence (in the case of a witness, only if his appearance is impossible). 3) The procedural consequence of the violation of obligatory record rules is not quite clear. If the records of investigative actions are incomplete or incorrect, they are supposed not to constitute evidence. If the trial record or its signature is missing, the judgment is absolutely subject to being struck out. Moreover, the trial record proves that the recorded actions have taken place and that actions which must be recorded have not taken place if they are not mentioned in the record.

M. Fincke

COURTS

History

After the 1917 Revolution, the destruction of the former judicial system and the foundation of a new system were carried through by the three "decrees on the courts" (November 22, 1917; January 30, 1918; July 20, 1918). The first decree abolished all pre-revolutionary courts, with the exception of the local court, which was allowed to continue, the local judge being supplemented with two "people's assessors" (*q.v.*). There were limited possibilities of appeal to the district meeting of local judges. The local courts applied pre-revolutionary law, insofar as it had not been repealed or was opposed to "the socialist legal conscience". Alongside the local courts there were revolutionary tribunals of various hues (against counterrevolution, press tribunals, military tribunals) entrusted with the trial of offences which were considered of special danger for the revolution. The investigation of cases within the jurisdiction of revolutionary tribunals was carried out by the *Cheka* (secret police). The second decree provided a more elaborate system of appellate courts and retained the applicability of pre-revolutionary law. The third decree forbade all reference to pre-revolutionary legislation and introduced a court of cassation residing in Moscow, the forerunner of the Supreme Court. Generally speaking, the period of war communism and civil war is characterized by rapid and drastic organizational changes, bordering at times on complete chaos.

Order was restored in 1922 by the Statute on the Judicial Organization of the RSFSR, of October 31, 1922, and, with the foundation of the Soviet Union in 1924, the Principles of the Judicial Organization of the USSR of October 29, 1924. These enactments introduced the still-existing system of people's courts, *guberniia* courts (now *oblast'* or provincial courts), and the Supreme Court of the RSFSR. For the entire Union, in order to promote a uniform judicial policy, a Supreme Court of the USSR was created. The introduction of a new Constitution in 1936 led to the enactment (August 16, 1938) of a uniform Law on the Judicial Organization of the USSR. This law did not introduce very substantial changes although it replaced the 1924 Principles as well as all republican statutes on judicial organization. The four-level system of courts was retained but new special courts were established on the basis of the 1938 Law, such as railway courts and waterway courts. After the Second World War these courts were first merged into transport courts and then altogether abolished.

The wholesale revision of Soviet law after the death of Stalin brought new Principles on Judicial Organization (December 25, 1958). These Principles formed the basis and skeleton for republican laws on judicial organization (in the RSFSR: October 27, 1960).

Duties of the court

Although art. 2 (of the USSR Principles, and also of the RSFSR law) is devoted to the "objectives of the administration of justice", article 3 (of both enactments) offers the most pertinent information by providing that the administration of justice is realized by a. the trial of civil disputes, involving the rights and interests of citizens, state enterprises, institutions, kolkhozes, cooperative and other social organizations, and b. the trial of criminal cases and the application of lawful penalties to persons who have been found guilty of crimes and the acquittal of persons found not guilty. The trial of ordinary civil and criminal cases is the most important, but by no means the only function of Soviet courts. As in most countries declaratory statements may be elicited from the courts through non-contentious procedures (e.g. in order to have a person declared to be missing or dead; see ABSENTEES). The area of non-contentious procedure, however, is rather restricted in the Soviet Union, because many matters which in most countries are entrusted to courts are assigned to other agencies in the Soviet Union (e.g. the appointment of a guardian, the deprivation of parental rights).

Furthermore, a number of minor administrative infractions are tried by the people's judge (the chairman of the lowest court), but this is not regarded as criminal jurisdiction. Although there is a strong similarity to ordinary criminal trials (offences, such as breaches of the peace and small-scale speculation, are tried by a judge), the rules of criminal procedure do not apply and the fact that the offence is tried by a judge and not by some other civil servant is more or less a legislative accident (see further ADMINISTRATIVE OFFENCES).

An important ancillary function, which is only mentioned in passing in the RSFSR Law, is "judicial organization"—all those measures necessary to maintain a degree of organizedness and unity in the hierarchical organization of the courts. At the lowest level these function are fairly simple: the chairman of a people's court coordinates the study of the trial practice of the court, appoints bailiffs (*q.v.*) and directs their activities and provides general organizational guidance for the court's work (art. 32); at the intermediate level (the provincial court), the organizational functions are somewhat more extensive, but at the level of the republican supreme courts and the USSR Supreme Court, these functions include the issuing of general instructions to all lower courts and the right to make legislative proposals (see SUPREME COURT). After the reintroduction of the Ministry of Justice (*q.v.*) in 1970 the co-ordination and supervision of "judicial organization" has been entrusted again to this ministry without encroaching, however, on the independence of the judiciary in deciding individual cases.

A special aspect of this function is the disciplinary responsibility of judges regulated by a Statute on the disciplinary responsibility of the judges of the courts of the RSFSR, of June 12, 1965. Judges may be punished for various infractions, including omissions in their work, caused by carelessness or undisciplined behaviour. The penalties are imposed by the presidium of the court and consist of a warning or censure. In very serious cases the presidium can ask for the recall of a judge.

After the additions to the basic functions of the court (as spelled out in art. 3), the restrictions should be explained. Of the various special courts of earlier years, only the military tribunals have been retained (see MILITARY TRIBUNALS).

Military tribunals, together with the Supreme Court of the USSR, are the only federal courts in the USSR. Apart from these, however, there are several other state agencies performing judicial functions. The state arbitration (see ARBITRATION), which has exclusive jurisdiction in disputes between state enterprises, must be named as the foremost among these. In this way a very large and economically important area of litigation is removed from the ordinary courts. Similarly, most of the litigation connected with foreign trade is handled by special arbitration boards (see FOREIGN TRADE ARBITRATION; MARITIME ARBITRATION). Nor do most labour disputes reach the courts, but are settled in factory commissions for labour disputes (see LABOUR DISPUTES). In the field of criminal law, minor infractions of the criminal law may be referred to comrades' courts (*q.v.*).

Organization of the courts

The outcome of the historical developments outlined above has been the emergence of a four-level court system, not unlike the systems prevailing in many European countries. At the top of the pyramid stands the Supreme Court of the USSR, underneath this the fifteen supreme courts of the Union republics; then the courts of the provinces (*oblast'*) and at the lowest level, the people's court. The people's court is the general court of first instance. Specific types of important criminal cases (cf. art. 36 of the Code of Criminal Procedure) are tried at first instance by provincial courts. In provincial courts and all higher courts there are separate divisions for civil and criminal cases. In individual cases of exceptional importance a republican supreme court may assume first instance jurisdiction, either on its own initiative or on the initiative of the republican procurator (see PROCURACY). In civil cases provincial courts and republican supreme courts may assume jurisdiction where they see fit to do so (arts. 113-115 Code of Civil Procedure). There is only one appeal: to the provincial court from a judgment of a people's court, and to the republican supreme court from a judgment of a provincial court (there is no appeal from a judgment at first instance of a republican supreme court). In the smaller republics (such as the three Baltic republics), which are not divided into provinces, the supreme court is the appellate court for judgments of people's courts. The same rank as provincial courts is taken by courts of territories (*krai*'s), autonomous provinces, national districts and some cities (such as Moscow and Leningrad), and also by the supreme courts of autonomous republics, which retain a few extra prerogatives (see TERRITORIAL DIVISIONS; KRAI; AUTONOMOUS REPUBLICS; AUTONOMOUS PROVINCES; SUPREME COURT). In most of the national districts, however, the national district court has been disbanded, with a transfer of its power to the court of the province of which the national district is a part.

The organization of the courts in the Soviet Union is complicated by the existence of so-called supervision proceedings (*proizvodstvo v poriadke nadzora*, see RES JUDICATA). The essence of these proceedings is that presidents of courts and certain representatives of the *prokuratura* may file protests against final judgments of their own courts and lower courts. These protests are tried by the presidium of the court. The result of this is, for instance, that a case which has been tried on appeal in the civil or criminal division of a provincial court can still traverse a long path through the presidium of the provincial court, the civil division of the republican supreme court, the presidium of the republican supreme court, and finally the Plenum of the USSR Supreme Court until there is a genuinely final judgment. Also, the competence patterns which determine the routing of protests in the individual republics are not identical.

Principles governing the activities of courts

The USSR Principles and, in their wake, the RSFSR Law enumerate a number of principles which are considered to be basic to the activities of the courts. Some of these do not call for any comment, such as the principle of equality before the law of all citizens (art. 5), the principle of legality (art. 6: "the administration of justice is performed in strict accordance with the law"), the principle of public trial.

Other principles, such as the right of using one's own language and the right to be defended in criminal cases, are discussed elsewhere (see LANGUAGE and DEFENCE). Three remaining principles must be mentioned here: all members of courts are elected, all courts sit with three (or more) members, and the courts are independent.

Any Soviet court sitting as a court of first instance consists of a judge-chairman and two people's assessors (*q.v.*). An appellate court consists of three judges. A court presidium consists of the president of the court and his deputies and other members as prescribed by law. All judges and people's assessors are elected. Judges and people's assessors in provincial courts and all higher courts are elected by the (supreme) soviet of the corresponding level. Judges and people's assessors in the people's court are elected through general elections. The right to propose candidates is given to "social organizations and societies of the working people", primarily and practically the Communist Party. A district system of elections is in force with regard to people's assessors in people's courts, whereby every collective (factory, kolkhoz, housing-unit, etc.) numbering more than 100 voters elects one people's assessor, for a term of two years. Judges hold office for five years. Any Soviet citizen over 25 years of age is eligible. There are no formal requirements concerning the professional qualifications of judges (unlike members of the *Prokuratura*, the Bar, and notaries, who must possess an academic degree in law). In recent years, however, the overwhelming majority of judges consists of qualified lawyers. The details of elections of judges and people's assessors in people's courts are regulated by a Statute on the elections of *raion* (city) people's courts of the RSFSR, of October 28, 1960. The training of judges and the making of proposals concerning elections for the judiciary are among the functions of the USSR Ministry of Justice (*q.v.*) and the subordinate ministries of justice of the Union republics, after the re-introduction of such ministries in 1970-71.

The elective character of the judiciary is enhanced by the possibility of recalling judges and people's assessors before their term of office has elapsed. The procedure for recalling is regulated by a Statute on recalling judges and people's assessors of the courts of the RSFSR of October 5, 1961. The body which elects a member of a court has the right to recall him. The exercise of this right is not restricted in any way although the decision to recall must state the reasons for doing so.

The second principle (all courts sit with three or more members) implies that the court's decision is always a collective decision. In accordance with general continental practice, Soviet law does not admit dissent or minority opinions, with one exception: a minority opinion may be attached to the file although it is not published. In such a case it may influence the deliberations of other courts during appellate or supervision proceedings. Otherwise the deliberations of the court are secret and may not be divulged by the members of the court. No other persons are allowed to be present during the deliberations leading to the court's decision. A few preparatory procedural decisions, in civil as well as criminal procedure, are taken by a single judge.

Within the Soviet legal context, independence of the judiciary means that other state agencies, as a rule, do not interfere in the handling of individual trials. Soviet doctrine has always rejected the separation of powers (*q.v.*) in the traditional sense of Montesquieu's theory.

The dependence of the Soviet judiciary is also stressed (along with the possibility of premature recall, mentioned above) by their duty, imposed by law, to report on their activities to the agencies which elected or appointed them (i.e. the electorate of a people's court and various levels of soviets). The multiplicity of controls, which is so characteristic of Soviet public life, operates within the courts also through Party channels and through the hierarchical organization of the courts. Within a court there will normally be a Party cell whose typical task will be the implementation of Party policy in the work of the court. Furthermore all courts, under the direction of their presidents, engage in the study and evaluation of their own court practice and the practice of subordinate courts. Also, disciplinary powers of the presidia of courts may represent a potential threat to the independence of judges; on the other hand, judges may not be arrested or prosecuted without a special permission of the RSFSR Supreme Soviet Presidium (art. 63 of the RSFSR Law on Judicial Organization). It is difficult to estimate how far Party and internal control will affect the outcome of individual cases.

A judge who has a personal interest in the outcome of a case must excuse himself, or may be challenged by anybody who is a party in the case. In certain instances (if the judge is a relative of one of the parties, or if he is a party himself, or if he has participated in a previous stage of the trial) the judge is altogether precluded from participation as a judge; in other cases where there is reason to believe that he has a personal interest, the remaining members of the court decide on the challenge which has been made (cf. arts. 17-19, 22-24 of the Code of Civil Procedure, and arts. 59-62 of the Code of Criminal Procedure). *F. J. M. Feldbrugge*

CREDIT

In view of the economic-legal system prevailing in the USSR, credit relations occupy a central place in the entire field of industry, agriculture and commerce, involving almost anyone except the individual consumer. Because of this, credit relations occur in some way in all legal transactions of an economic or commercial nature, except those of a strictly private and personal nature (typically: family law relations). This article will limit itself to providing cross-references to the most important related subjects.

Payments of obligations between STATE ENTERPRISES and other state or PUBLIC ORGANIZATIONS are rarely made in cash, but almost invariably through accounts with the State Bank (see BANKING; MONEY). Various forms of LOANS are made available by the State Bank or the *Stroibank* (see BANKING); on most loans INTEREST will be charged. The expenditure of state enterprises, KOLKHOZES, SOVKHOZES, CO-OPERATIVES and other economic organizations (see also CORPORATIONS), including all payments made by them, is part of the overall system of PLANNING. The various types of bank accounts are discussed in the article on NEGOTIABLE INSTRUMENTS.

There are also close links between the credit system and TAXATION.

F. J. M. Feldbrugge

See also SUPPLY CONTRACT; SAVINGS ACCOUNTS; STATE LOANS: KHOZRASCHET; SALES; PUBLIC AND PRIVATE LAW; COMMERCE AND COMMERCIAL LAW

CREMATIONS, see BURIALS

CRIME PREVENTION

According to the Marxist doctrine of the USSR, the mere dynamic development of a socialist society towards communism is by itself conducive to a reduction and final disappearance of crime. Poverty, deprivation and social injustice are regarded as the most important crime-germinating factors. When they have been overcome—crime will start to disappear. However, most Soviet textbooks stress that a mere change in material conditions will not by itself make crime disappear: a simultaneous moral growth and greater moral insight amongst people is needed to bring about a harmonious society in the future. There is a dialectical interrelationship between actual material conditions and the ethical moral attitudes of man. At present there are still many shortcomings: 1) society is still unable, even under socialism, to satisfy all personal needs,

2) social organisation is still imperfect in such aspects as labour, social security, distribution, 3) there are still profound contradictions between personal strivings and demands on the one hand and the requirements of society as a whole on the other (see Glezerman, *Obshchestvo, kollektiv, lichnost'*, *Pravda*, October 31, 1966). In respect of 1) and 2) it is the duty of the authorities, proper planning and industry to act with a view to their elimination; in respect of 3) it is mainly the individual who must change through proper processes of learning and training.

All three aspects of an imperfect society concern us here, because the personal, according to Soviet dogma, must be seen in its relationship to the general; nevertheless 3) appears to be the most important in our present context.

More specifically, it is possible to divide measures of crime prevention into compensatory (such as deterrents by the threat of punishment, by effected punishment or by elimination of the offender from society) and/or measures eliminating causes of crime—re-education, improved living conditions, greater material wealth, reduced social stresses, improved social ecology, provision of better goods and services (including here more and better educational facilities). It is the task of forensic policy to combine the compensatory measures with measures against the causes of crime. At present the most important measures are thought to be the creation of conditions required for happy and harmonious families with enlightened and intelligent parents and the construction of schools and better and well-run youth organisations, such as the Pioneers and the Komsomol. The agencies more specifically concerned with crime prevention are the Procuracy (*q.v.*), the courts (*q.v.*), the militia (see POLICE) and other offices of the Ministry of Internal Affairs, the corrective labour institutions (colonies, prisons, corrective labour; *q.v.*), the state security police (see SECURITY), the comrades' courts (*q.v.*), the voluntary militia (*druzhinniki*), the special organisations of the public for auditing and checking offices, commercial and industrial enterprises and institutions (see PEOPLE'S CONTROL), the investigation officers and their voluntary assistants from amongst the public, the children's rooms of the militia and their voluntary councils consisting of members of the public, apartment house committees, children's committees, etc. Furthermore, diverse administrative measures such as passport (internal identity card) laws (see PASSPORTS), registration requirements, the demand for official approval for certain activities or the possession of certain goods (weapons, printing presses, machinery etc.), the prohibition on certain persons (former offenders) from exercising particular jobs, or from moving freely about the country, the requirement of certain categories of discharged prisoners to present themselves from time to time to the police or making certain entries in the passports or labour books of individuals, etc.

The centre for academic studies concerning crime prevention is the All-Union Institute for the Study of Causes of Crime and for the Elaboration of Measures of Crime Prevention (see also CRIMINOLOGY).

R. Beermann

CRIMINAL INVESTIGATION

Two forms of criminal investigation are employed in the Soviet Union. The first, used for most offenses, is called the preliminary investigation (see PRELIMINARY INVESTIGATION). A preliminary investigation is conducted by an official called an investigator, who is subordinate either to the Procuracy, the Military Procuracy, Ministry of Internal Affairs, or Committee for State Security. These investigators normally have received a legal education. Criminal-procedure codes list those offenses which must be investigated by preliminary investigation. The codes require a preliminary investigation, in general, for those offenses that are complex to investigate, or that carry heavy penalties, or that have particular political significance. However, even where the law does not require a preliminary investigation, a court or procurator may order that one be conducted in a particular case if they consider it appropriate. Cf. art. 126 RSFSR Code of Criminal Procedure.

For many minor offenses the codes do not require that a preliminary investigation be conducted. In such instances, the criminal investigation is called an "inquiry" and is carried out by the police or by some other administrative agency or official in charge of a given territory or responsible for administration of a given activity (commanders of military units, agencies of state security, heads of corrective-labor institutions, fire inspection agencies, border guard agencies, masters of oceangoing vessels on long journeys, and heads of winter encampments that have no transportation to the outside world, cf. art. 117 RSFSR Code of Criminal Procedure).

An inquiry is subject to the same procedural rules as a preliminary investigation, with the following exceptions: (1) a defense attorney may not take part in the case until it is given over by the procurator to the court; (2) the victim, civil plaintiff, and civil defendant are informed of the conclusion of the inquiry but are not permitted to inspect the dossier; (3) if the person conducting the inquiry disagrees with a procurator's directive to bring an accusation, to categorize the offense in a certain way, to send him the case for subsequent transfer to a court, or to terminate the case, that person may (like an investigator) appeal to a superior procurator, but such an appeal does not suspend the lower procurator's decision; (4) the ordinary maximum time period for conduct of an inquiry is one month (rather than two months in the case of a preliminary investigation).

Even in instances in which a preliminary investigation is to be conducted, the police normally perform certain initial investigatory actions before transferring the case to an investigator (e.g., formal commencement of a criminal case, search and seizure, detention and interrogation of a suspect, and interrogation of witnesses). This is also called an inquiry. The person conducting this initial inquiry must refer the case to an investigator not later than ten days after he commences the case.

John B. Quigley, Jr.

CRIMINAL LAW

The first comprehensive, although incomplete, item of criminal legislation after the October Revolution was the Leading Principles of the Criminal Law of the RSFSR of December 12, 1919. The Leading Principles were preceded by a number of enactments of a more or less ephemeral character on such subjects as counter-revolution, speculation, bribery, etc. The Leading Principles of 1919 dealt with general subjects, such as the purpose of criminal law, age limits, insanity, attempt, participation, etc. They did not contain a catalogue of crimes in accordance with the leading line of thought in early Soviet law: that law was a temporary phenomenon which would gradually disappear with the transition to socialism and communism. This line of thought was ultimately abandoned when the school of Vyshinsky acquired complete control in all areas of Soviet law as a corollary of Stalin's complete supremacy in the Soviet Union from the beginning of the 'thirties. Long before this it had already become obvious that the Soviet regime could not do without a criminal code. The first Criminal Code of the RSFSR was elaborated in great haste when the regime embarked on the New Economic Policy and was enacted on June 1, 1922. Soon afterwards the foundation of the USSR called for a new general law on the principles of criminal law. Such a law came into being on October 31, 1924: the Fundamental Principles of 1924 follow the example of the Leading Principles of 1919 in containing only provisions on general questions of criminal law (the general part), but not on individual types of crime (the special part). The enactment of complete criminal codes was left, as it still is, to the Union republics. The RSFSR enacted a new criminal code on November 22, 1926. Other Union republics enacted their own, very similar, criminal codes, or took over the Criminal Code of the RSFSR.

The 1926 Code remained in force until 1960. After the death of Stalin in 1953 the Soviet regime initiated an ambitious legislative programme aimed at a complete overhaul and a systematic re-codification of almost the entire legal system. It is certainly no co-incidence that the first attempts were made in the field of criminal law and procedure, since it was in this field that the abuses of the Stalin era had been felt most bitterly. On December 25, 1958, the Principles of Criminal Legislation of the USSR and the Union Republics were enacted and in the following years the Union republics drafted their own criminal codes on the basis of these Principles. In the RSFSR the new criminal code was enacted on October 27, 1960.

Considering that during the more than fifty years of Soviet rule, the country had to go through the cataclysms of civil war, forced industrialization and collectivization, the great political purges and the Second World War, it is not surprising that Soviet criminal law has undergone great changes since 1917. It is perhaps more cause for wonder that so many basic features of the criminal law system have proved to be lasting. As such one might mention the central notion of SOCIAL DANGER as the principal factor in determining whether behaviour is to be considered criminal; the division of offenders into "sinners", to be corrected and re-integrated, and "enemies", to be destroyed or isolated; the stress on the attitude of the offender, rather than the material harm done by the offence; the uninhibited incorporation of criminal law in the armoury of a totalitarian state by providing vague and sweeping definitions of offences which are in any way considered as especially harmful to the state. The Soviet version of the *nulla poena* maxim is formulated in art. 3 of the RSFSR Criminal Code, which provides that only a person guilty of committing a crime, that is, who intentionally or negligently commits a socially dangerous act provided for by criminal law, shall be subject to criminal liability and punishment. The second paragraph of the same article adds that criminal punishment shall be applied only by judgment of the court (see also ADMINISTRATIVE OFFENCES; DISCIPLINARY LAW).

Crime is defined by art. 7 of the Code as a socially dangerous act, provided for by the special part of the Code, which infringes the social or political system of the country, the socialist system of economy, socialist property, the person or the political, labour, property or other rights of citizens, and any other socially dangerous act, provided for by the special part of the Code, which infringes the socialist legal order.

On the basis of these definitions Soviet legal theory distinguishes between four different elements of a crime: an object, an objective side, a subject and a subjective side. These concepts are not mentioned in the Criminal Code, but the various provisions of the general part of the Code can be subsumed under these four headings.

The interest which is harmed or threatened by the crime is regarded as the object of the crime. Basically, a general list of possible objects is given in art. 7 ("the social and political system of the country, the socialist system of economy, . . ." etc.). The division of the special part of the Code into chapters is based on the different objects of the crimes defined there; otherwise there is little to say about it.

The essential part of the objective side of a crime is the criminal act, in many cases accompanied by a particular result and sometimes by other circumstances. The definitions of crimes as found in the special part of the Code describe the objective sides of various types of crimes.

Several of the most important topics of the general part of criminal law are connected with the objective side of crime according to Soviet legal theory. A criminal act includes not only positive actions but also OMISSIONS. The required result of a crime (e.g. the death of the victim must be the result of the criminal act of homicide) raises the question of CAUSALITY. If the criminal act is itself incomplete or the result has failed to occur, there may be criminal preparation or ATTEMPT. A criminal act may be committed by several persons, ACCOMPLICES, who do not each commit the entire act.

The subject of the crime is the person who commits it. Certain qualities, such as INSANITY, or age (see JUVENILE DELINQUENCY and MINORS), may make a person unfit to be a subject of a crime. INTOXICATION does not normally take away criminal responsibility.

Questions relating to the offender's attitude towards his crime are discussed in Soviet law under the subjective side of the crime. The principal element of the subjective side is the offender's guilt or MENS REA, which may find expression in criminal intent or in negligence. Other elements of the subjective side are the offender's motive or his purpose. Criminal guilt may be lacking (which means that the subjective side of the crime is absent and consequently that there is no criminal responsibility) where an offender acts in ERROR.

The presence of the four elements of a crime will normally lead to criminal responsibility and punishment, unless there are circumstances which take away the social danger of the forbidden act. The most important of these circumstances are SELF-DEFENCE, FORCE MAJEURE and NECESSITY. Some other circumstances are not mentioned in the Criminal Code, but are acknowledged in theory, such as the permission of the victim, execution of lawful orders, etc. Under certain conditions these circumstances may also take away criminal responsibility. When all the elements of a crime are present and circumstances which would take away the social danger are absent the court will impose PUNISHMENT. The purpose of punishment, according to art. 20 of the Code, is not only retribution (*kara*), but also correction and re-education of the offender, and general and special prevention. The RSFSR Criminal Code provides the following kinds of penalties: CAPITAL PUNISHMENT, deprivation of freedom (see PENITENTIARY INSTITUTIONS), CORRECTIVE LABOUR, EXILE and banishment, deprivation of the right to occupy certain offices or to engage in certain activities, FINES, dismissal from office, imposition to make amends for the harm caused, social censure, confiscation of property (see FORFEITURE) and deprivation of a military or special rank. The general part of the Code indicates general maximum and minimum limits for the various kinds of penalties. The provisions of the special part indicate the maximum penalty for each individual type of crime; in the case of serious crimes the special part often adds a mandatory minimum penalty.

Arts. 37-57 contain principles and rules governing the imposition of punishment. The court will consider mitigating circumstances (some of which are enumerated in art. 38) and aggravating circumstances (listed limitatively by art. 39). Furthermore there are rules concerning MULTIPLE OFFENCES, PAROLE, PROBATION, PRESCRIPTION, PATRONAGE, SENTENCING, a.o.

The special part of the RSFSR Criminal Code is divided into twelve chapters. The first chapter, "Crimes against the state", is subdivided into "especially dangerous crimes against the state" and "other crimes against the state". The first group might be termed POLITICAL CRIMES, and includes TREASON, ESPIONAGE and SABOTAGE; counterrevolution as such is not mentioned any more (see PROPAGANDA, ANTI-SOVIET). The second group contains a number of offences which are harmful to the Soviet regime, but which appear not to be directed immediately against it, such as BANDITRY, illegal BORDER CROSSING, divulgence of state SECRETS and COUNTERFEITING.

Crimes against property (see PROPERTY, CRIMES AGAINST) are dealt with in chapters 2 and 4; Chapter 2 enumerates the crimes against socialist property, chapter 4, those against personal property. Crimes against property include various forms of THEFT, and FRAUD, ROBBERY, EXTORTION, a.o.

The 3rd chapter is devoted to crimes against life, health, freedom and the dignity of citizens. The sequence of the chapters of the special part provides an indication of the relative seriousness of the crimes involved and this explains the position of this chapter between crimes against socialist property and crimes against personal property. The 3rd chapter deals with such crimes as HOMICIDE, ASSAULT, inducing a person to commit SUICIDE, KIDNAPPING, RAPE, SEDUCTION and other SEX CRIMES, illegal ABORTION, THREATS, INSULTS, a.o.

Crimes against the political and labour rights of citizens form the subject of the 4th chapter of the special part. This chapter offers criminal law protection to most of the civil rights mentioned in the Soviet Constitution.

The 6th chapter deals with ECONOMIC CRIMES, the most important of which is SPECULATION. Otherwise the chapter contains a great variety of offences, ranging from poaching to various kinds of FORGERY and administrative malfeasance.

The 7th chapter is devoted to "OFFICIAL CRIMES" (*dolzhnostnye prestupleniia*), a term denoting criminal acts committed by public officials in the execution of their duty, such as abuse of power, neglect of duty, or BRIBERY.

Chapters 8 and 9 deal with crimes against the administration of justice and against the administrative system respectively. Chapter 10 is entitled crimes against public safety, public order and the health of the population. Its first article defines HOOLIGANISM. Other crimes included in this chapter are RECEIVING STOLEN GOODS; VAGRANCY; various TRAFFIC OFFENCES; illegal possession of WEAPONS; the production of, and commerce in, forbidden drugs (see NARCOTICS); the organization of PROSTITUTION; and others.

The 11th chapter is devoted to TRADITIONAL CRIME, the 12th chapter to military criminal law (see MILITARY LAW).

F. J. M. Feldbrugge

See also FORENSIC MEDICINE; FORENSIC PSYCHIATRY; AMNESTY; CRIME PREVENTION; CRIMINALISTICS; CRIMINOLOGY; ORGANIZED CRIME; PARDON; RECIDIVISM; BIGAMY; ARSON

CRIMINAL PROCEDURE

Criminal procedure is that branch of law regulating the activities of the courts, Procuracy, and investigative agencies in the handling of criminal cases. The activities of penal institutions are regulated by a separate body of law—corrective labour law (see PENITENTIARY INSTITUTIONS). As with many other areas of law, legislative competence over criminal procedure is divided between the All-Union (or federal) level and the republican level. (No authority below the republican level may adopt laws or regulations on criminal procedure.)

At the All-Union level, a number of fundamental propositions about criminal procedure, as well as certain procedural safeguards, are stated in the Constitution of the USSR. These include: participation in court of people's assessors; inviolability of the person and dwelling; secrecy of correspondence; equal treatment for all citizens regardless of sex, nationality, or race; independence of judges; right of defense; supervision of legality by the Procuracy; and conduct of judicial proceedings in the local language, with provision of an interpreter for those not knowing that language. The Supreme Soviet of the USSR, under powers granted it by the Constitution (Article 14), has enacted the Principles of Criminal Procedure of the USSR and Union Republics (December 25, 1958). These Principles create a uniform system of handling criminal cases for the entire Soviet Union. The Principles require each of the fifteen Union republics to enact a more comprehensive code of criminal procedure on the basis of the Principles. This was done by the republics during the period 1959-1962 (RSFSR: 1960). That the Union republics possess considerable discretion in developing their own criminal-procedure legislation is evidenced by the fact that while the Principles contain only fifty-four articles, the codes each contain about four hundred articles. Should a norm contained in a republican code be found to be at variance with a norm contained in the Principles, the latter norm prevails.

The Principles consist of six chapters. The first contains certain general provisions, while the remaining five regulate, respectively, the rights and duties of participants in the criminal process, pre-trial investigation, trial procedure, appellate procedure, and execution of judgments.

The first chapter ("General Provisions") sets forth basic propositions about criminal procedure. In many instances these propositions elaborate principles stated in the Constitution. The chapter states the task of the criminal process as the swift and full detection of crimes, exposure of the guilty, and proper application of the law so that every person who has committed a crime shall be subjected to just punishment and so that no innocent person should be brought to trial or convicted. The criminal process is to strengthen socialist legality (*q.v.*), to deter and eradicate crime, and to educate citizens in a spirit of fulfilment of Soviet laws and respect for the rules of socialist communal living (see RULES OF SOCIALIST COMMUNITY LIFE).

The court, procurator, investigator, and agency of inquiry (see CRIMINAL INVESTIGATION) are obliged to commence a criminal case whenever they discover the indicia of a crime. No discretion is granted to these agencies as to whether or not to bring charges. No person may be presented with an accusation other than on the grounds and through the procedure established by law. The Principles list certain instances in which a criminal case may not be commenced (or where, if already commenced, it must be terminated): where no crime has been committed; where the act in question does not contain the indicia of a crime; where the period of limitations has run; where an amnesty (*q.v.*) has been declared for the crime in question or where the person has been pardoned (see PARDON); where the person had not reached the minimum age for criminal responsibility established by law at the time of commission of the crime; where the victim and accused reconcile their differences (for certain offenses only); where the victim has not made a complaint (for certain offenses only); where the person has died (except where the procedure is one to rehabilitate him, or where the case has been re-opened with respect to another person); where the person has already been tried for the crime in question.

No person, according to the Principles, may be arrested other than pursuant to a court decree or by sanction of a procurator. A procurator is obliged to release any person who is illegally in custody or who is kept in custody beyond the time provided by law or by the relevant court judgment.

Justice may be administered only by a court. No person may be found guilty of a crime or punished other than by judgment of a court. Equal justice must be meted out to all persons, regardless of their social, financial, or occupational status, and regardless of their ethnic background, race, or religion.

Cases in all courts of first instance are to be tried by a panel consisting of one professional judge and two people's assessors (*q.v.*). People's assessors enjoy equal rights with the professional judge during the trial in deciding all questions that arise. Appeals and protests are heard by a panel of three professional judges, while cases considered by way of supervision proceedings are heard by a panel of not fewer than three professional judges (see APPELLATE PROCEDURE; RES JUDICATA).

The Principles state that, in administering justice in criminal cases, judges and assessors are independent and subordinate only to law. They are to decide cases on the basis of the law, in accordance with "socialist legal consciousness", and are not to be influenced by outside sources.

Court proceedings are to be conducted in the local language. Participants in the case who do not know that language have the right to make motions, give testimony, and make statements in their native language. Such persons must also be afforded the services of an interpreter. Investigative and court documents must be given to the accused in a language he knows. (See also LANGUAGE.)

All court sessions must be open to the public, except where state secrets (*q.v.*) might be revealed. In addition, a court may exclude the public where the accused is under sixteen years of age, where the offense is a sex crime, and where intimate aspects of the lives of participants might be revealed. In any event, the court's judgment must be pronounced publicly.

The accused has the right to defend himself. The investigator, procurator, and court must afford him the opportunity to defend himself by all means provided by law and ensure protection of his personal and property rights. The court, procurator, and investigator are obliged to take all measures provided by law to investigate the circumstances of the case fully and objectively. They must seek exculpating as well as incriminating evidence and must look for circumstances mitigating as well as aggravating the suspect's degree of responsibility.

The Principles state that the court, procurator, and investigator do not have the right to place the burden of proof on the accused. They may not extract testimony from the accused through force, threats, or other illegal means.

The first chapter of the Principles also contains certain basic provisions on evidence (*q.v.*). During the investigation and trial the following acts must be proved: the occurrence of the crime, the guilt of the accused in commission of the crime, circumstances affecting the degree and character of the accused's responsibility, the character and extent of the damage caused by the crime. Any facts may be considered as evidence. Evidence may come from several different sources: the testimony of witnesses, the testimony of the victim, the testimony of the suspect, the conclusion of an expert witness, material evidence, records of investigative and court actions, and other documents. The court, procurator, investigator, and person conducting the inquiry are to evaluate evidence based on their internal conviction and are to be guided by the law and by socialist legal consciousness. No particular type of evidence has predetermined value.

A judge, people's assessor, procurator, investigator, person conducting the inquiry, court secretary, expert witness, or translator may not participate in a case if he has any personal interest in the matter. Higher courts exercise supervision over the activities of lower courts. This means, among other things, that higher courts may review lower court decisions even after the time for appeal has elapsed.

Supervision over execution of the laws is exercised by the Procurator General of the USSR and by procurators subordinate to him. A procurator is obliged at all stages of the criminal process to take measures to eliminate any violation of law. A procurator is to exercise his powers of supervision independently of any outside agencies or officials, being subordinate only to the law and being governed by directives of the Procurator General of the USSR. Decrees of a procurator rendered in accordance with law must be carried out by all institutions, enterprises, organizations, officials, and citizens.

The second chapter of the Principles ("Participants in the Criminal Process, Their Rights and Duties") states the rights and duties of the accused, defense counsel, victim, civil plaintiff, and civil defendant, and provides that the court, procurator, investigator, and person conducting the inquiry must explain to these persons their rights and must afford them the opportunity to take advantage of them. The accused is granted the right to know the charges against him, to give explanations in his own behalf, to present evidence, to make motions, to acquaint himself with all the materials of the case upon termination of the investigation, to have defense counsel, to take part in the trial, to make challenges at trial, to appeal the actions and decisions of the investigator, procurator, and court, and to say the "last word" at trial.

Defense counsel is allowed to participate in the case from the time the accused is informed of the termination of the investigation. In instances in which the legislator has determined that the accused is incapable of adequately looking after his own interests (where the accused is a minor or a person who, because of physical or psychological deficiencies, is unable to defend his own interests), defense counsel is permitted to participate somewhat earlier—at the time the accusation is presented to the accused. While an accused is normally represented by a member of a college of advocates, he may be represented instead by a representative of his trade union or a representative of some other social organization (see also DEFENDANT and DEFENCE).

The Principles grant the Union republics the power to establish instances in which an accused must be represented by counsel. The Criminal Procedure Code of the Russian Republic, for example, makes participation of counsel compulsory where a state or social prosecutor participates, where the accused is deaf, dumb, or blind, or is otherwise incapable of defending himself due to physical or psychological deficiencies, where the accused is a minor, where the accused does not know the language in which the proceedings are being conducted, where the interests of one accused conflict with those of another accused who is represented by counsel, and where the accused is charged with a capital offense. If in these instances the accused (or a relative or friend) does not contact counsel, the investigator or court is required to see that counsel is provided.

From the time he is allowed to participate,

counsel has the right to meet with the accused, to acquaint himself with all the materials of the case, to present evidence, to make motions, to take part in the trial, and to appeal the actions and decisions of the investigator, procurator, and court. With permission of the investigator, counsel may also attend the interrogation of the accused and take part in other investigative actions undertaken at the request of counsel or of the accused.

The third chapter of the Principles ("Inquiry and Preliminary Investigation") regulates pre-trial proceedings. It requires that a preliminary investigation (conducted by an investigator of the Procuracy, of an agency of state security, or of the Ministry of Internal Affairs) be held for the more serious cases—crimes against the state, military crimes, and any other crimes specified by republican legislation. An inquiry, normally conducted by the police, is held for those less serious crimes for which the law does not require a preliminary investigation (*q.v.*). An investigator or policeman may detain (see ARREST) a suspect in any of four enumerated instances: 1) when a person is caught in the act of committing a crime or immediately thereafter; 2) when witnesses indicate the person as having committed a crime; 3) when traces of a crime are found on the suspect's person or in his abode; 4) when other circumstances indicate that the suspect has committed a crime and when, in addition, he attempts to escape or has no permanent residence, or when his identity cannot be determined. A procurator must be informed of the detention within twenty-four hours, and within forty-eight hours from the time he is informed of the detention the procurator must either give it his sanction or set the person free. Pending trial, the suspect may be kept in custody or may be set free. He may normally not be kept in custody before trial for a period longer than two months, though this period may be extended, if the case is complex, to three months by a procurator at the provincial level, to six months by the procurator of a Union republic, and to nine months by the Procurator General of the USSR. A search may be performed only pursuant to a decree of an agency of inquiry or an investigator and with, in addition, the sanction of a procurator. By way of exception, in "instances not permitting delay", a search may be conducted by an agency of inquiry or by an investigator without prior sanction of a procurator. In these instances, a procurator must be informed of the search within twenty-four hours. Search and seizure (*q.v.*) must be conducted in the presence of lay witnesses. See also RESTRAINING MEASURES.

The fourth chapter of the Principles ("Handling of Cases in a Court of First Instance") regulates, though briefly, proceedings at trial. The decision to commit a case for trial is made by a judge, though if the judge disagrees with the procurator's decision to indict he must submit the case to an "administrative session" of the court. There the decision to commit the case for trial or to terminate it is made by a judge and two people's assessors.

The fifth chapter of the Principles ("Handling of Cases in Cassational and Supervisory Instances") regulates appellate proceedings. Such proceedings are of two types. Cassational appeals by the defendant and cassational protests by the procurator are the normal type of appellate proceeding. See APPELLATE PROCEDURE. After the time for such appeals and protests has expired, however, a case may nonetheless be reviewed by a higher court by way of supervision proceedings on the protest of certain high-ranking judges and procurators. See RES JUDICATA; REMEDIES.

The sixth and final chapter of the Principles ("Execution of a Judgment") concerns the entry of a judgment into force and its execution. It provides that a judgment enters into force only after the time for a cassational appeal or protest has expired or, if an appeal or protest is taken, following consideration of the case by the appellate court.

John B. Quigley, Jr.

CRIMINAL RECORD, see RECIDIVISM

CRIMINAL STATISTICS,
see CRIMINOLOGY

CRIMINALISTICS

Criminalistics is a concept not used in English, but is applied in the USSR and in many of the Roman law countries to designate a science about technical and tactical means of crime detection and of gathering, accumulating and analysing evidence in criminal investigation. It divides into a general part concerned with such technical matters like forensic medicine and chemistry, forensic photography, dactyloscopy (fingerprint identification), graphology, trace studies and ballistics, identifications, the keeping of criminal records and the best ways of applying them, the use of computers, etc.; and into a special part which deals with the problems of detection and proof of special crimes: killing, rape, crimes of violence, embezzlement of state and public property, speculation, larceny, the activities of criminal gangs, crimes against the state, criminal tribal customs, etc.

While studying methods of crime detection, criminalistics is at the same time concerned with the problems of crime prevention. Frequently the one follows the other: while studying forgeries the question is raised of better ways of preventing them; safeblowing shows the need for better security and storage facilities; public violence points towards the need for better policing and patrol services.

Unlike criminology, which was for a long time in disfavour in the Soviet Union (see CRIMINOLOGY), criminalistics continued to be developed and studied throughout the history of the USSR. Some of its scholars were accused of following too closely bourgeois theories and methods but, due to its more favoured position than criminology, many criminal lawyers and criminologists switched during the criminological freeze to writing books on and devoting their energies to criminalistics.

The history of criminalistics in the USSR dates back to 1922 when the Central Administration of Criminal Investigations in Russia was created (later reorganised into a special department). In 1923 a number of forensic laboratories (Kharkov, Kiev, Odessa) and an Institute of Criminalistics in Belorussia were set up. After the Second World War several research centres were established and they continue to function, e.g. the All-Union Scientific Research Institute of Criminalistics of the Procuracy of the USSR and the Scientific Research Institute of Criminalistics of the Head Administration of the Militia at the Ministry of Internal Affairs USSR. A number of laboratories for forensic expertise and a number of criminalistical laboratories were set up in the capital cities of the Union republics and in provincial capitals. Criminalistics is taught at law schools, and laboratories and departments (*kabinety*) function in many of the bigger universities. For a time the Institute of Criminalistics of the USSR Provuracy has been publishing occasional papers on criminalistic research entitled Problems of Criminalistics (*Voprosy Kriminalistiki*).

R. Beermann

CRIMINOLOGY

Textbooks published in the USSR speak of Soviet Criminology as the study of the extent, dynamics and causes of crime in a socialist society; it is said to be the function of the criminologist to work on methodological problems and to conduct research on the ways and means of crime prevention. Taken at its face value the Soviet definition is similar to those in the West where Criminology is also defined as a body of the scientific knowledge of crime, its causes and its prevention, and of the handling of offenders, and as a didactic discipline which assembles, analyses and integrates the findings of criminological research. The stress in the Soviet definition on a *socialist* society distinguishes Soviet work from similar studies in Western countries. It implies a special ideology, such as the doctrine of the withering away of state and law and the final disappearance of crime on the advent of a communist society. Soviet Criminology can be said to have an ideological and teleological bias. This immanent optimism may have caused difficulties for Criminology in the Soviet Union. There were times, beginning in the 30's, when it became a non-science and was altogether suppressed. This attitude reversed the vigorous and intensive development which the study of crime and the criminal took in Russia as early as the middle of the 19th century. The *svody*, statistical tables of judicial functions and crime, were by no means inferior to, and in many respects even surpassed, similar publications at that time in the West. In the early Soviet period and during the *NEP* (period of the New Economic Policy, 1921-1930) many forensic institutions with laboratories (*kabinety*) for the study of crime in Moscow, Leningrad, Saratov, Odessa and other cities pursued systematic research assisted by professional lawyers and academicians. The State Institute for the Study of Crime and the Criminal of the People's Commissariat for Internal Affairs of the RSFSR, and similar institutions in other Union republics, were set up as the chief organisations for criminological studies. There were still other bodies conducting criminological studies—the section of State and Law of the Communist Academy, the Institute of Soviet Law and the law schools of many universities. It was the law section of the Communist Academy which initiated the gradual decline of criminological studies with its accusations that the other bodies were following the lead of bourgeois-capitalist science and pursuing studies with methods used by biological sciences. In 1931 the State Institute for the Study of Crime and the Criminal was closed. Some research continued for a while but came to a complete standstill in the middle of the thirties. The ensuing sterile period forced criminologists either to turn their energies towards criminalistics (*q.v.*), the history of criminal law, or to positivist legal studies. The liberalising tendencies of the Second World War induced some criminologists to make a new, albeit timid start. However, until after Stalin's death and the 20th Party Congress, criminology remained in cold storage.

Criminology was resurrected only in the later half of the 50's by the All-Union Scientific Research Institute of Criminalistics of the USSR Procuracy, the Supreme Court of the USSR, the Scientific Research Institute of the Militia (now the All-Union Scientific Research Institute for the Protection of Public Order of the Ministry of the Interior) and by the sector for the study and prevention of crime of the Institute for State and Law of the USSR Academy of Sciences. In 1963 the above bodies set up the All-Union Institute for the Study of Causes of Crime and for the Elaboration of Measures for Crime Prevention. The Institute began regularly to publish collections of papers, "Problems of the Struggle against Crime" (*Voprosy bor'by s prestupnost'iu*). The Institute is the head organisation for all other researchers in the field; besides doing independent research it is supposed to collate and to coordinate the work of all other institutions. An ever increasing number of universities have been taking up criminological studies and research (Moscow, Leningrad, Odessa, Kiev, Kharkov, Riga, Tartu, etc.) and are publishing their findings in monographs and university annals. Criminology has become a syllabus subject for law students.

Statistical reporting, once the strength of Russian criminology, is still extremely poor and a serious obstacle to Soviet criminologists. There appears to be a general ban on publishing statistical data, with the exception of a few percentage figures, mainly of only local significance, and usually given without their bases or corresponding data for control groups and thus almost worthless. Criminological conferences have been held and their summary reports and resolutions have been published.

The dissatisfaction with the present state of affairs is a frequent topic in various writings by criminologists. *Inter alia* demands have been voiced to recreate republican criminological central research institutes which, it is believed, would be better able to cope with local crime problems.

The basic differences between Soviet and Western-type criminologies is the greater share of dogmatic *a priori* premises in the case of the former, and the greater pragmatism and positivism of the latter. Soviet textbooks still (1968) mention as the two most general causes of crime 1) the existence of two basically different and hostile political socio-economic systems in the world—the socialist and the capitalist—and their continuing mutual struggle, and 2) the objective law of the lag of consciousness behind existence. However, dissenting voices can be heard on the part of scholars who think that such dogmatic statements are harmful and obscure the real issues or imply only general attributive statements without any immediate explanatory value. Many of their reasonings are now similar to theories developed by West European or USA scholars such as the theory of differential association of E. H. Sutherland and D. R. Cressey, or the anomy principle of Robert K. Merton, which found its further development in the researches and proposed theories of R. A. Cloward and L. E. Ohlin on diverse opportunities creating different types of delinquents.

The Soviet encyclopedic dictionary of legal knowledge still rejects all bio-psychological factors as bourgeois-capitalist in essence and unimportant for the study of crime and the criminal. But this rejection is now disputed by a number of scholars and is slowly dying out. B. D. Ovchinnikov and V. N. Kudriavtsev point out the interdependence of social and biological factors and regard such statements as "the essence of man is the totality of his social relationships . . ." as rather academic; they note that Marx used this and similar expressions to attack the one-sided biological views of some of his contemporaries, but never meant to deny the psychosomatic character of man. Other scholars ask for more attention to be paid to psychological factors and to the importance of some neurological disorders which are frequently associated with delinquency (L. M. Zybin). In his original treatise on Causality in Criminology (1968), V. N. Kudriavtsev widely applies graphical annotations in expressing the interdependence of environmental-social and biological factors. But all Soviet scholars put the main stress in the study of crime on finding ways and means of crime prevention. This brings them into close contact with the law enforcement agencies and educational institutions (see CRIME PREVENTION).

Statistical shortcomings of Soviet crime reporting may be only a temporary fault due to the bashfulness of Soviet authorities before the capitalist world. This statistical timidity is rather surprising if one considers the great importance statistics were accorded by Lenin, who regarded them as "the most powerful tool of the social sciences". At present Soviet textbooks on criminology make good the deficiences by quoting Western or pre-revolutionary Russian statistics, those of the early Soviet period or of the years before the Second World War in the case of the later socialist countries. Better and more informative than the central reports are sample surveys and studies on a local basis, or local investigations of particular offences. Considering the meagre statistical data available it is worth paying special attention to those areas least neglected (in print) by Soviet criminologists in order to obtain some picture of how Soviet crime statistics deal with specific topics and of the reasonings of Soviet criminologists.

As in the West, a great deal of research in the Soviet Union is devoted to the study of recidivism. A sample survey of the most dangerous recidivists revealed the following relative gravity of crimes committed by them: 4.3% premeditated murder, 18% banditry, 4.3% rape, 21.9% robbery and open larceny (*grabezh*), 14% secret theft of personal property, 8.1% theft of state property, 7.9% hooliganism (rowdyism), 4.8% bodily injuries and 16.7% other offences. The data were published in 1968, so the survey refers to a time before that year. The more vicious character of crimes committed by recidivists is revealed if set against similar data of a survey regarding the general criminal population (1967): here crimes against the person are given as 15%, hooliganism and other crimes against public order 34%, larceny of state property 18%, that of personal property 16%, crimes by officials in respect of their public function (*dolzhnostnye*) 2.3%, economic crimes 5%, offences against the personal rights of citizens 0.5%, offences against the course of justice 1.5% and crimes derived from the survivals of local customs 0.4%. More recent statistics show an increase in the extent of larceny (*khishcheniia*) of state and public property to 23%, and of personal property to 34%, premeditated killing and bodily injuries 4.5%, rape 2.4% and hooliganism 28%.

Much attention is devoted in the press and other media to political crimes against the state. Here a hiatus exists between public opinion (as expressed in the press) and the learned and informed statements by criminologists; while the first incessantly stresses and warns the public of the great danger and ubiquity of potential offenders and the need for extreme vigilance, the latter speak of the insignificantly small and constantly dwindling numbers of such offences (particularly if compared with the 30's, 40's and early 50's).

Special interest is accorded in the Soviet Union to larceny (*khishcheniia*) of state and public property. It is obvious that, due to the Soviet economic and political structure, the frequency of such offences must be considerable and their character more harmful to the general welfare than theft of personal property. Although larceny of public and/or state property is generally referred to in criminological writing as *khishcheniia*, it is obvious that a division ought to be made between crimes of white and of blue-collar workers: the first will merge or overlap in many instances with professional (*dolzhnostnye*) offences, while the second will overlap with or border on petty pilfering, which is treated not as a criminal but only as a disciplinary offence (up to the sum of 50 roubles or even more) and in that case is not recorded in the crime statistics. An interesting comparison, revealing considerable differences in the sociological pattern between blue-collar pilfering and that of general property offences, is possible thanks to a survey conducted among worker-offenders at textile factories in Ivanovo (an industrial city near Moscow) and general property crime rate statistics given in the criminological textbook. The latter include theft, open theft and robbery. The main age groups of thieves are made up of younger people: 38% of persons convicted for theft, 74% for open theft and 80% for robberies were under the age of 25; 15% of them were minors (under 18 years). Generally it was found that 79% of all such offenders were under 30 years of age. Similar figures for robbery are noted: 85% under 30. Blue-collar pilfering showed a surprising difference: 80% in the age group 26-45 years, although the share of their age group in the working population of the factories was only 49-56% (workers aged 31-40 committed 46.5% of offences although constituting only 27% of the sample). Only very few crimes were committed by the young. The working experience of the offenders was considerable, 40% of them having worked more than 20 years. The educational and intellectual level of the offenders was found to be low: 48% had not completed 7 years of schooling, while 37% had only 7-8 years schooling. The number of male and female offenders in the factories was equal (obviously due to the character of the produce).

On crimes of violence there have been a few investigations dealing mainly with offences by minors; they show that the crime rate is increasing more quickly for minors than for adults.

In conclusion one could say that Soviet Criminology now displays a tendency towards more rational and pragmatic thinking and that local surveys show some similarity with developments in the West. The decline in property crimes in some parts of the Soviet Union seems to be due a) to the greater affluence and b) to purely legal measures such as delegating a number of smaller offences to administrative and extra-judicial procedures. The growth in alcohol consumption and crimes of violence in the younger age groups of offenders justifies the suspicion that feelings of frustration and alienation among some sections of the population are increasing.

Bibl.: Feifer, George, Justice in Moscow, 1964; Gertsenzon, A. A., An Attempt at a Concrete Sociological Study of the Elements of a Crime, Soviet Law and Government, 1968, Vol. VII, No. 2, pp. 10-18; Justice and the Legal system in the USSR, edited by Robert Conquest, 1968.

R. Beermann

CURRENCY, see MONEY

CURRENCY SPECULATION

Currency speculation is one of the forbidden operations with regard to financial valuables, to which art. 88 of the Criminal Code is devoted. Along with currency speculation the following are mentioned: violation of the rules on currency operations, and any speculation in financial valuables or documents of value. The main purpose of art. 88 is the protection of the Soviet financial system against foreign currency and equivalent influences.

Financial valuables in the sense of art. 88 are: foreign currency, foreign documents of value (bonds, shares, obligations, etc.), documents of payment made out in foreign currency (cheques, letters of credit, bills of exchange, etc.), precious metals in any form, and also objects made out of such metals, precious stones and objects containing such stones, Soviet currency, Soviet state bonds, and documents of payment made out in roubles. The rules on currency operations (to be found in particular in the Statute on the State Bank) forbid any purchase or sale or barter of foreign financial valuables or of precious metals, except through the State Bank; payment in foreign currency, except in the cases specifically allowed by law; the transfer of financial valuables to or from abroad, except in the cases specifically allowed by law.

The second element mentioned in art. 88, speculation in financial valuables or documents of value is narrower, because speculation requires purchase and sale, with the intention to make profit (see SPECULATION). Speculation in financial values, of course, implies currency speculation, which is the most typical and frequent offence covered by art. 88—in other words, the buying and selling of foreign currency, for which there is an eager market in all countries of Eastern Europe. It should be noted that this second element of art. 88 constitutes an independent offence, which in one sense is more embracing than the first element (the violation of rules on currency operations), because the violation of rules on currency operations is almost totally limited to foreign currency transactions. A result of the wording of art. 88, which lumps together two related offences under one definition, is that some offences are covered twice by this provision (e.g. speculation in foreign currency).

Where a person only purchases financial valuables, with the intention of selling them with a profit later on, he may be punished for attempted speculation. Private purchase and sale of some financial valuables (such as objects made of precious metals or containing precious stones) is allowed, provided there is no intention of making profit.

The documents of value mentioned in the second element of art. 88 embrace cheques, promissory notes, bills of lading, and in general all documents which have to be presented in order to receive the material benefit expressed in the document (see also NEGOTIABLE INSTRUMENTS and DOCUMENTS).

The penalty in the case of art. 88 is deprivation of freedom for from three to eight years with compulsory confiscation of the financial valuables or documents of value, with possible confiscation of other property and possibly followed by exile (two to five years). In serious cases (professional or large-scale speculation, or if there is a previous conviction under art. 88) the penalties are increased (five to fifteen years' deprivation of freedom, or capital punishment).

F. J. M. Feldbrugge

See also POLITICAL CRIMES; MONEY; BANKING; COUNTERFEITING

CUSTODY, see PARENTS; GUARDIAN & WARD

CUSTOMARY LAW

Almost from its very beginning Soviet law showed itself strongly in favour of written law emanating from a central authority. Under its predecessor, the imperial *Svod Zakonov* (see LEGAL HISTORY, RUSSIA), codes and statutes had indeed been the chief source of law, although considerable latitude was displayed towards rural custom, and the traditional laws and customs of the tribal population of Siberia and Central Asia, and also the precepts of Islam, were tolerated and allowed to function to some extent within the framework of Russian law.

Shortly after the Revolution the bolsheviks insisted on the necessity of wholesale abolition of customary law (*obychnoe pravo*) (with a temporary exception for a large part of rural customs), because "legal custom, as a rule, plays a counterrevolutionary and reactionary role", and in particular because in the USSR it was supposed to incorporate the customs of the bourgeoisie and of backward oriental tribes.

As Stuchka wrote in 1927: "While we won easily against the written law of the old regime, this same law, in the form of custom, retained its force—although it is losing ground all the time—among the peasants; we have even recognized it insofar as it is not inimical to our revolution and insofar as the peasants are not willing to abandon it spontaneously".

The general demise of rural custom coincided with the collectivization of agriculture. For purely practical purposes custom was tolerated "in commercial traffic" and also in civil law "insofar it appears advantageous for the masses of the workers and for the state"; as a source of civil law it lost in stature at the closing of the NEP-period.

At the moment *obychai* (custom) is said to have "a most insignificant role in Soviet civil law as a source of law, and then only when authorized by the legislator". Custom is not mentioned in the Constitution, nor in the

1961 Principles of Civil Legislation (and subsequent civil codes) and several recent textbooks of civil law simply ignore it. Many customs are described as "a degenerate relict of the bourgeois, colonial and feudal past", which the Soviet state should punish and eliminate. Chapter 10 of the first Russian Criminal Code and Chapter 11 of the present Criminal Code are devoted to "acts which constitute remnants of local customs" (see TRADITIONAL CRIME).

Nevertheless, the Soviet approach to custom is of a diversified nature, "according to the content of each individual custom". Practices which reflect the observance of socially dangerous and anti-socialist ways of life and traditions ("feudal or *bey* attitudes of moslem origin, islamic customs utilized by feudal elements in exploiting the workers, such as polygamy, parental control of marriages, payment of a bride-price or *kalym*, etc.") are suppressed, proscribed or restricted (e.g. the islamic institution of *waqf*), according to the general limits set to custom by Soviet legal principles. In other cases only moral persuasion is applied (a comparable situation occurs with regard to betting debts; they cannot be claimed in law but, once paid, are not subject to restitution).

In the rare cases, finally, where a custom is not contrary to the "interests of the people", it may be invoked "for the solution of legal questions" and the state will supply the "appropriate sanction and legal efficacy". However, no such cases are mentioned in present-day civil law. Reference to custom is found only in arts. 134 and 135 of the Merchant Shipping Code (which allow resorting to port usages in determining the duration of lay days and provide for the amounts of demurrage and dispatch money due to carriers and shippers respectively).

In foreign trade custom is recognized as a source of law (see also FOREIGN TRADE).

The abolition of custom as a source of law may appear as a radical departure from the situation existing before 1917 and the fundamental ideas of Marxist legal philosophy. However, the decline of custom is of a temporary nature. In a socialist society, customs of an entirely new nature emerge and take the place of old customs which have lost their meaning; this is witnessed, for instance, by the phenomenon of socialist competition (see OBLIGATIONS) or by the relationships between workers in the factory (*novye trudovye traditsii*) or in the family. These new customs may be summarized as the "rules of socialist community life" (*q.v.*); their legal content develops and grows richer as communism is gradually realized, when they will be the only source of law as the spontaneous product of social organization. Until that moment every Soviet citizen is at least "obliged to respect the rules of socialist community life" (art. 130 Constitution) and also to observe, in exercizing rights and executing obligations, "the rules of socialist community life and the moral principles of a society which is building communism (art. 5 of the Principles of Civil Legislation); they are not so much an alternative formula for *boni mores* or *ordre public*, nor are they new customs *praeter legem*, but rather norms which govern any activities through which the citizen participates in the administration of the country and which must be regarded as "a necessary supplement to our laws". The 1961 Party Programme directs the Party to encourage "all forms of conscious self-discipline of citizens which assert and promote the fundamental rules of socialist community life", and obliges every communist to cultivate and propagate the moral principles contained in the programme and the "Moral Code of the Builder of Communism", of which the rules of socialist community life constitute the essential nucleus. Party resolutions and decisions of an ideological nature "play a basic role in the formation and confirmation of new traditions and customs".

According to prevailing doctrine, however, the rules of socialist community life are not a source of law, unless backed up by a legal sanction (and thereby transformed into legal norms). They only serve as criteria in evaluating the conduct of parties in a civil law dispute.

Legal custom in the established sense (*vekovoe obychai*, *traditsii i obychai*) should be distinguished from business practice or usages (*delovye obyknoveniia*) among economic organizations or citizens. The latter may be of an auxiliary or subsidiary legal nature, as stated by art. 168 par. 1 of the Civil Code: "Obligations must be performed properly and within the time fixed for performance, and in conformity with the requirements of statute, act of planning, contract, or, in the absence of such requirements, in accordance with the usual requirements in such cases (*obychno pred"iavliaemye trebovaniia*)."

The term *obychai* (custom) is occasionally employed in an improper and pejorative sense in referring to frequent bureaucratic and administrative practices in the administration of the economy, which result in undermining the authority of the law.

G. Crespi Reghizzi

CUSTOMS DUTIES

The basic source of customs law in the Soviet Union is the Customs Code (*Tamozhennyi Kodeks*) enacted by the USSR Supreme Soviet Presidium on May 5, 1964, replacing the Customs Code of 1928. The chief function of customs law is the protection of the state monopoly in foreign trade (*q.v.*). Any goods passing the frontiers of the USSR (see BOUNDARIES), whether exports, imports or goods in transit (see EXPORTS AND IMPORTS) and including the mail and luggage of travellers (Soviet citizens as well as foreigners), are inspected by customs. Soviet customs are organized under a chief directorate for customs of the USSR Ministry of Foreign Trade; under the directorate there are a number of customs offices which in turn are subdivided into customs posts.

The great majority of customs duties are import duties. Export duties are levied in very few cases. Import duties have been fixed in the Customs Tariffs approved by the USSR Council of Ministers on July 28, 1961. Tariffs for mail parcels and passenger luggage are fixed on the basis of the Customs Tariffs by the Ministry of Foreign Trade in agreement with the Ministers of Finance and of Foreign Affairs.

Most customs tariffs are calculated as a percentage of the wholesale price augmented by the costs of packing, insurance and transport, export duties and other expenses necessary to buy the goods and bring them to the USSR border (i.e. c.i.f. port or *franco* border). Fixed amounts are levied only on the contents of certain mail parcels and on passenger luggage. The Customs Tariffs provide maximum and minimum tariffs for each category of goods. The minimum tariff is applied to imports from countries which do not levy import duties on goods from the USSR or apply the most favoured nation's regime. In other cases the maximum tariff is applied. For instance, in the category of fresh and dried fruit the minimum tariff is 1% and the maximum 15%.

Customs duties are paid by organizations and in some cases also by individual persons. The organizations paying customs duties are usually the specialized state organizations for foreign trade (e.g. *Promsyreimport, Soiuzplodoimport*). The amounts due are paid monthly into the budget. Natural persons (addressees of mail parcels and travellers) pay directly to the customs officials.

E. H. de Jong

See also SMUGGLING; BORDER CROSSING; TAXATION

DAMAGES, see CONTRACTS; TORTS

DANUBE

Of the rivers of Europe the Danube with its length of 2850 km (of which only 134 km is on Soviet territory) comes second after the Volga river. Navigation on the Danube is governed by the Convention concerning the regime of navigation on the Danube concluded at Belgrado on August 18, 1948, between the USSR, Bulgaria, Hungary, Roumania, the Ukrainian SSR, Czechoslovakia and Yugoslavia. Austria became a party to the Convention on January 7, 1960. Navigation on the Danube, according to the Convention, shall be free and open for the nationals, commercial vessels and goods of all states, on a footing of equality with regard to port and navigation charges and conditions for merchant shipping. The foregoing does not apply to cabotage. The regime established by the Convention applies to the navigable part of the Danube between Ulm and the Black Sea, through the Sulina arm, with an outlet to the sea through the Sulina channel. In contrast to the pre-war Danube regime, the present one does not apply to the tributaries of this river.

As provided for in the Convention of 1948, a Danube Commission was set up in 1949. Members of the Commission are all riparian states except the Federal Republic of Germany, the latter having only observer status. Nor is the Ukrainian SSR a member of the Commission. However there are always a number of Ukrainians on the Soviet delegation. The Commission meets once a year. Delegations attending this annual meeting are generally composed of river transport officials and experts. The Soviet delegation does not form an exception in this respect. Since 1954 the Commission has its seat in Budapest. Until 1954 it had its headquarters in Galatz in Rumania. The scope of territorial jurisdiction of the Commission coincides with the geographical field of application of the Convention.

The Commission has, in short, been charged with supervising the implementation of the provisions of the Convention, with establishing a uniform system of traffic regulations and rules concerning river inspection and with rendering all possible services to those who use the Danube as a waterway. Such services include the provision of hydrological and statistical data, sailing directions, navigational charts, etc. Decisions of the Commission are taken by majority vote. However, members cannot be outvoted in matters regarding the budget, the construction of water works in the territory of the member or members concerned, the drawing-up of uniform traffic rules and, finally, in the matter of a change of the Commission's seat.

The uniform regulations mentioned in the preceding paragraph are adopted in the form of recommendations to the member governments. Although technically non-binding in character, these recommendations have always been implemented by all states concerned since they are based on a careful study of the national regulations in force in the various riparian countries. The authorities in the Soviet Union charged with the supervision of these regulations are the harbour captains, each being responsible for that section of the river assigned to him. In the case of an infringement, the harbour captain, depending on the gravity of the infringement, is empowered to warn, to rebuke or to fine those responsible and also to take appropriate measures to prevent fresh infringements.

The Commission, in the field of river navigation, maintains contacts with various international organisations, in particular with the Inland Waterway Transport Committee of the Economic Commission for Europe, which, in turn, is a regional body subordinate to the United Nations' Economic and Social Council. In order to carry out its task the

Commission has a secretariat at its disposal staffed with nationals from the member countries. The official languages of the Commission are Russian and French.

S. H. Bloembergen

DEATH PENALTIES,
see CAPITAL PUNISHMENT

DEBTOR AND CREDITOR

The concepts of debtor and creditor in Soviet civil law (Civil Code art. 158)—as in many other legal systems—are regarded rather as roles which may alternately be played by both parties to a contract, for the party who, for practical reasons, is normally described as "the debtor" is usually also entitled to act as creditor in some respects at least (viz. when he receives the other party's performance). The distribution of creditor's and debtor's functions between the parties often gives reason to nominate one "creditor" and the other "debtor" for practical purposes, but it is obvious that this distribution will correspond to a point on a continuous scale. The bilateral contracts (*dvustoronnie dogovory*) are to be found on or in the neighbourhood of the equilibrium of such a scale. The debtor's duty can be either to act or to abstain from acting. The role as debtor or creditor can be the result of a contract concluded between the parties—with or without an underlying order from a regulating or planning authority—or it may result from a non-contractual obligation (e.g. the commission of a tort).

The rights and duties concerned may arise out of the performance of the primary obligation of a contract, or they may be secondary claims and liabilities brought into existence by improper performance.

A. Ådahl

See also ASSIGNMENTS; CONTRACTS; OBLIGATIONS

DECEIT, see FRAUD

DECREE, see LEGISLATION

DEEDS, see LAND REGISTRATION

DEFAMATION, CIVIL

Since 1961, citizens and organisations may sue at civil law for retraction of defamatory statements. Action will succeed if 1) there was *circulation* of statements by defendant; 2) the statements were *defamatory* to plaintiff's honour and dignity; 3) they were untrue.

1) Circulation consists in publication by defendant to person or persons other than plaintiff, regardless of the manner of publication (verbally, in print, at public meetings, in letters, on television, etc.). Statements uttered within the circle of family constitute actionable circulation. No publication is deemed privileged, although a) a *de facto* absolute privilege attaches to official communications of the Communist Party (but not to articles in Party-sponsored press); b) no action in defamation lies where the law has established separate procedure for contesting the contents of official documents; c) there is no actionable circulation if it falls within defendant's public duty.

2) Defamatory are those statements which impute to plaintiff behaviour or characteristics inconsistent with Soviet laws, rules of socialist community life (*q.v.*) or communist morality. Insults (*q.v.*) are not actionable under civil law. There is disagreement among the courts whether civil action covers only "facts" (deeds, events, actions), or likewise "evaluations of facts" (comments), and general characterisations of the plaintiff (*otsenki oblika istsa*) in the absence of any specific "facts". The *form* of the statement alone, however, is not actionable, no matter how derogatory or degrading. Injury must be to plaintiff's reputation in society, not to his self-esteem. Neither "moral prejudice"

(*dommage moral*), nor special damage are recognised, and there is no action for slander of title or slander of goods.

3) Untruthful statements are those in which a) the "facts" are invented; or b) accurate facts are tendentiously distorted (according to the courts). If defendant's statements are true only in part, there is no defamation if the fabrications did not materially affect plaintiff's reputation in society. Publication of plaintiff's natural defects or his medical history does not constitute defamation if defendant succeeds in his plea of justification. "Absence of cause" for the publication will not defeat this plea.

Malice or fault on defendant's part are not relevant in civil defamation and actions are not subject to any statute of limitations. The statutes appear to have saddled the defendant with the burden of justification, but the practice of the courts remains unsettled on many issues involving *onus probandi.*

In the absence of specific statutory language, the courts have formulated rules applicable to anonymous and pseudonymous libel; to suits involving minors and the mentally incompetent; to defamation blackening the memory of the dead, and to suits brought without personal interest on behalf of others. After initial uncertainty, the courts now require that in civil libel suits, both the editor (publisher) and the author, be sued as joint defendants. In case of libel in press media not endowed with legal personality, suits must be brought against supervisory juristic persons; this rule, however, is frequently disregarded by the courts.

Remedy consists in *retraction* of the defamatory statement. No monetary awards are made for general or special damage, nor may punitive damages be applied for. In case of libel by the press, retraction must also take place in the press. In all other cases, the court determines the manner of retraction (public apology; notice in local press; posting of the court decision at defendant's place of employment; etc.). In certain cases, an *injunction* may be ordered instead of the retraction.

If the court decision has not been carried out, the court may impose a fine on the offender which will be collected as state revenue. Payment of the fine does not relieve the offender of the duty to perform the acts prescribed in the original court decision. The time-limits for execution of *facere* obligations, and scales of fines, are provided for in the codes of civil procedure.

Suits brought in bad faith expose plaintiff to the obligation of paying courts costs; of reimbursing defendant's counsel fees; of compensating defendant for loss of working time; and in case of malice may lead to criminal prosecution.

In certain cases, comrades' courts (*q.v.*) have jurisdiction to hear cases involving civil defamation.

Serge L. Levitsky

See also DEFAMATION, CRIMINAL; INSULT

DEFAMATION, CRIMINAL

Offence against the honour and dignity of a person, consisting in the circulating of malicious falsehoods injurious to plaintiff's reputation in society (art. 130 Criminal Code of the RSFSR).

1) *Circulation* means communication ("publication") to person or persons other than the victim, regardless of whether plaintiff was present or not, and irrespective of the method of the communication (by word of mouth, in writing, in print or in works reproduced or duplicated in any form or manner). Action is also possible for defamation in songs, poems, drawings, or works publicly exhibited. It is irrelevant whether defendant was the actual author of the falsehoods or he merely repeated, duplicated or reproduced them, provided circulation was intentional and defendant was aware that the

statements were untrue. It is likewise without importance to whom the statements were circulated (friends, colleagues, strangers, even members of the family), but defamatory falsehoods addressed to agencies or authorities empowered to initiate criminal prosecution on the basis of the facts alleged, constitute malicious prosecution, a crime against the administration of justice.

2) *Malicious falsehoods.* Malice presupposes that defendant was aware that the statements were false and he nevertheless circulated them, or he knowingly allowed them to be circulated. The motives for the fabrication and circulation of the falsehoods (vindictiveness, personal gain, desire to create sensation, etc.) are not relevant for the *corpus delicti* of the offence, but they will have a bearing upon the severity of the punishment. Falsehoods are invented facts (deeds, events, actions, circumstances) as well as maliciously distorted facts or knowingly false characterisations, provided that they contained concrete or specific accusations, imputations, aspersions or innuendoes relating to plaintiff's past or present. The form in which the statements were presented (indecent, derogatory, insulting) is not by and of itself actionable as defamation, if the statements related to true facts. Defence consists in justification as to the facts, or absence of malice as to circulation, e.g. if defendant was unaware that the facts were untrue. It is not a defence to show that the falsehoods were not believed by those to whom they were circulated.

3) *Injury.* In contrast to insult, injury to plaintiff's personal dignity is not sufficient. Defendant's statements must have injured plaintiff's honour and dignity by lowering the esteem in which he is held in society. Partial falsehoods are not defamatory if the invented portion had no material effect on plaintiff's actual reputation. Actionable falsehoods must allege or imply that plaintiff's behaviour or attitudes were inconsistent with Soviet laws, norms of communist morality, or rules of socialist community life (*q.v.*). The courts do not rely on the plaintiff's own assessment of the injury to his reputation, nor do they take into consideration special damage, except in determining the severity of the punishment. No monetary damages are awarded to the plaintiff.

4) Actions for defamation may be brought even where injury was to the reputation of minors, the mentally incompetent, or to the memory of the dead. Juristic persons, as a rule, may not sue or be sued for criminal defamation, unless injury was also to the reputation of physical persons and suit is brought in their name. Defamation of the Soviet state and social system is prosecuted as a separate offence, either as a crime against the system of administration, or, in certain cases, as one of "especially dangerous" crimes against the state. If defamation occurred in a false testimony given in court by a plaintiff, witness, expert or interpreter, the offender is guilty of a crime against the administration of justice. Defamation by a public official who abused his authority is classified as an official crime (*q.v.*). Injury to the honour and dignity of individual citizens is not the principal object of the crime in such cases.

5) *"Simple" and "aggravated" defamation.* "Simple" defamation (by word; in writing) is actionable only upon victim's complaint, and action is subject to termination in case of reconciliation of the parties. Under certain circumstances, comrades' courts have jurisdiction over simple defamation and, indeed, several republican codes specifically restrict criminal prosecution to second offences. Punishments in the RSFSR range from social censure to deprivation of freedom for up to one year.

The RSFSR Code recognises three varieties of "aggravated" defamation with correspondingly increased penalties: a) in print or works duplicated or reproduced in any manner; b) by persons previously convicted for a similar offence; c) false accusations of political or other serious crimes. Deprivation of freedom in this latter case may be ordered for up to 5 years. In criminal codes of other Union republics, "aggravated" defamation is recognised if it had entailed "grave consequences"; if it was inflicted "publicly"; if it was contained in letters of complaint addressed to administrative agencies; etc.

Serge L. Levitsky

See also DEFAMATION, CIVIL; INSULT; PROPAGANDA, ANTI-SOVIET

DEFENCE (CRIMINAL PROCEDURE)

The right to be defended in a criminal trial is guaranteed by art. 111 of the Soviet Constitution (this guarantee is repeated in art. 19 of the RSFSR Code of Criminal Procedure). The principal provisions are arts. 47-51 of the RSFSR Code of Criminal Procedure. As a rule defence counsel is admitted at the end of the preliminary investigation (*q.v.*), before the beginning of the trial. If the defendant is a minor or if he suffers from physical or mental defects which would prevent him from exercizing his right to defend himself defence counsel will be admitted from the moment the defendant has been charged (*moment pred"iavleniia obvineniia*). This is the moment during the preliminary investigation where sufficient evidence seems to have been accumulated not to regard him any longer as *a suspect* but as *the accused* (cf. arts. 143 and 148 of the Code of Criminal Procedure). The procurator is entitled to admit defence counsel also in other cases from the moment the defendant has been charged. Participation of defence counsel *in the trial* is obligatory in a wide range of cases (specified in art. 49). Defence counsel is selected by the defendant; where the participation of counsel is obligatory and the defendant has failed to appoint counsel, the investigator or the court must do so. Defence counsel may be dismissed by the defendant at any moment, except in the case of the defendant being a minor or suffering from physical or mental defects, where the decision to retain counsel is left to the investigator, procurator or court. The absence of counsel in a case where his participation is required by law leads in appeal to mandatory reversal of the judgment.

The chief duty of defence counsel is to utilize all legal means to bring to light circumstances which may prove the innocence or mitigate the responsibility of the defendant. His rights include: to have meetings with the defendant, to see all the materials in the case and make notes from them, to present evidence, to file requests, to take part in the trial, to challenge judges, prosecutors, witnesses, etc., to file complaints against acts and decisions of the investigator, the procurator and the court. Where defence counsel has been admitted already during the preliminary investigation he may be present during interrogation. He may not be called as a witness concerning knowledge acquired in the performance of his duties as counsel.

As defence counsel may appear: lawyers (advocates) and representatives of trade unions and other social organizations. Also other persons (in particular relatives and legal representatives of the defendant) may be admitted as defence counsel by the court or the presiding judge. An advocate who has accepted to appear as defence counsel may not withdraw.

Defence counsel has the right to appear in appellate proceedings but not in supervision proceedings (where he can be invited by the court).

F. J. M. Feldbrugge

See also LAWYERS; DEFENDANT; CRIMINAL INVESTIGATION

DEFENDANT

In criminal procedure, this is the prosecuted person at all stages. From the initiation of the case until his detention or subjection to restraining measures (*q.v.*), the factual suspect has no particular procedural status. The defendant is called the "suspect" (*podozrevaemyi*) from the moment of his detention or subjection to restraining measures until his inculpation (formal charge), then he is called the "accused" (*obviniaemyi*) until the judgment has taken legal effect. In a more narrow sense, the term "accused" is restricted to the defendant from his inculpation until his committal for trial, after which he is called the "subject of the court" (*podsudimyi*) until judgment and then the "adjudged person" (*osuzhdennyi*), i.e. either the "convicted" or the "acquitted" person. In cassational and—more so—in supervision proceedings, the "convicted or acquitted" person is not considered to be a defendant in the sense of Art. 111 of the USSR Constitution.

There is a purely theoretical controversy among Soviet jurists as to whether the defendant has any procedural duties. In all cases he may be subject to coercion, but this distinguishes him from non-defendants less than in other jurisdictions. Thus, in the case of search and seizure, there is no difference between suspected and non-suspected possessors and bodily examination may be applied against witnesses in the same conditions as against the defendant. There is a difference concerning the obtaining of samples (e.g. of handwriting) which may be taken from the defendant without restriction but from witnesses only to verify whether they have left traces. The defendant as well as witnesses may be enlisted to participate in the conduct of a view. Like a witness, the defendant is principally obliged to appear when summoned and, if he does not appear without valid reason, may be subject to compulsory measures for compelling appearance (but not usually at night) by the police upon the investigator's decree which must be announced to the defendant. Only the defendant, however, may be subject further to restraining measures and, as a mere suspect, to detention; also, only the defendant may be committed to a medical institution for expert examination, which is considered to be closely enough related to custody that is must be deducted from the term of punishment.

The defendant (suspect and accused) has the "right to defence". The law expressly reserves it to the "accused"; but since it has no specific content except that the agency of inquiry, investigator, procurator and court shall "guarantee" the possibility of defending himself by the legally provided means, doctrine rightly extends it to the suspect, for almost all of the provided means are granted to him as well as to the accused, including the right to have his personal and property rights protected, which is also mentioned as part of the "right to defence" but is actually granted to the person subjected to restraining measures, no matter whether he is the suspect or the accused. The "right to defence" neither includes the right to have a defence counsel nor the right to silence or a privilege against self-incrimination, which as such is not discussed in Soviet law.

But it does require the objective investigation of all circumstances including those tending to acquit or to mitigate guilt, and that the burden of proof is not shifted to the accused and that his testimony is not solicited by threat or force.

In particular, the following are mentioned as "rights" of the defendant: to give explanations and testimony (in the case of the accused: concerning the present accusation); to give them in his mother tongue and to make use of an interpreter; to present evidence, which is a right in so far as the denial of taking it must be supported by reasons and communicated to the defendant; to submit petitions; to appeal from actions and decisions of the agency of inquiry and procurator (see APPELLATE PROCEDURE; REMEDIES) and to challenge them and the interpreter, expert and specialist. The defendant has no right to participate in investigative actions: where such participation is provided for (e.g. in conducting an inspection or investigative experiment), it is in the discretion of the investigator, while in the case of search, seizure and the impounding of property, the person concerned may be present (yet must not be notified), no matter whether or not he is a defendant; in the case of an identification parade, the defendant naturally must be present to identify or be identified, and only in these functions is his participation provided for. More important in this connection is his right to refuse participation in identification and investigative experiments which would emanate from a right not to incriminate himself, but which is mentioned only in doctrine, not in the codes.

The defendant's interrogation is recorded; the record must be given to him to read or read out to the defendant before signing; additions and corrections must be inserted upon his demand. Subsequently the defendant may write down a statement in his own hand. Refusal to give or the giving of false testimony is not punishable; yet a positive right to remain silent is not acknowledged, nor is the defendant to be warned of the fact that his statement may be used in evidence.

Substantial rights are conferred on the defendant (suspect and accused) if committed to a medical institution for expert examination: he must be acquainted with the decree assigning him to expert examination which indicates the questions put to the expert and the materials made available to him; he may challenge the expert, request the assignment of an expert from among persons indicated by him, present additional questions to the expert, become acquainted with the expert's opinion and give explanations to him. But these rights may be subject to reduction: the "right" to be present at the examination is subject to the permission of the investigator; in the case of psychiatric examination, neither the assigning decree nor the expert's opinion need be presented if the defendant's mental state makes this impossible, a provision which might be open to abuses in the prosecution of political opponents; the "right" to present additional questions to the expert boils down to the submission of a petition to that effect to the investigator, the denial of which—not necessarily supported by reasons—must be handed to the defendant. In cases of expert examination not connected with committal to a medical institution, the afore-mentioned rights are reserved to the accused.

The particular shape of the important right to know what the defendant is suspected or accused of depends on whether he is suspected or accused and above all constitutes the practical distinction between these procedural figures.

1) The technical term "suspect", taken from Tsarist law, is reserved to persons detained (see ARREST) or to whom restraining measures (see RESTRAINING MEASURES) have been applied, as long as they have not been formally charged (cf. art. 52 Code of Criminal Procedure). Hence, the rights of the suspect are not granted to the person actually suspected by the inquiring agency as long as it is not necessary to detain him or subject him to restraining measures and as long as there is not enough evidence gathered to present a complete formal charge. As a result of the relatively long postponed and formalized inculpation, as well as of the restrictive definition of the suspect, there are more chances to evade the defendant's privileges by interrogating or otherwise treating actual suspects at witnesses than in other jurisdictions.

Formerly, inculpation was reserved to the investigator or procurator so that the police could only interrogate persons as witnesses or suspects; moreover, the suspect was not formally interrogated, but simply questioned. Because of the undefined status of the suspect, practice tended even during investigation to postpone inculpation until its completion. In 1937, the General Procurator prohibited the use of the term "suspect" and the questioning of suspects in order to stop abuses which, on the other hand, led to interrogation as witnesses and to unfounded inculpations before every coercive measure. In the mid-1950's it was proposed to define more precisely the suspect as an independent figure beside the accused, as well as to remove this term altogether.

The new law extends the power to inculpate to the agencies of inquiry in cases, where preliminary investigation (*q.v.*) is not obligatory; in other cases, the police are confined to the preliminary interrogation of a suspect. The suspect's statements are admitted as evidence (without warning); his detention is permissible in strictly defined circumstances (see ARREST) and even restraining measures (including custody) may be applied against him by way of exception, but in the latter case inculpation must follow within 10 days. At the same time, detention and restraining measures now constitute the status of a suspect.

The suspect must be interrogated within 24 hours after his detention and he is then entitled to learn which crime he is suspected of. However—and this is the main difference from the interrogation of the accused—the charge need not be disclosed at the beginning as a coherent whole but may be revealed piecemeal in the course of questioning; moreover, it need not include any legal definition, but may be restricted to an individualization of the incriminating act to the extent that it is feasible for tactical considerations. Before interrogation, the suspect must be informed of his rights to give explanations, submit petitions and appeal, but not of the fact that he does not incur punishment by refusing to give testimony or by giving false testimony (a positive right of silence does not exist anyway). The suspect is not entitled to have a defence counsel, nor to see the materials of the case. The express prohibition in the Code of Criminal Procedure to solicit testimony by force, threats or other illegal means is reserved to the accused, while it constitutes a crime to apply these means to any person being questioned, including witnesses.

The suspect's position in the case of an identification parade, inspection, non-expert bodily examination, obtaining of samples and committal to a medical institution is the same as that of the accused. In the case of other expert examination, the suspect has no specific rights, but after his inculpation, i.e. if and when he has become the accused, the expert opinion and the record of his interrogation must be shown to him and he obtains the right to give his own explanation, submit objections and request additional questions to be put to the expert.

The status of a suspect lasts at most 72 hours in the case of detention, and 10 days in the case of other restraining measures; it ends either with inculpation or with the termination of the case or with release from detention or restraining measure. In the latter case he loses his position as "participant in the case", although he may still be actually suspect and awaiting possible inculpation.

2) The "accused" denotes the prosecuted person during preliminary and committal proceedings from the rendering of the decree of the formal charge until his committal for trial (cf. art. 46 Code of Criminal Procedure).

The inculpation, i.e. the transforming of a suspect into an accused, requires "sufficient" evidence. For that purpose, the investigator (or, if preliminary investigation is not mandatory, the person conducting the inquiry) issues a decree with reasons indicating the imputed actions as established by the material gathered so far and the criminal law providing for the alleged crime. Theoretically, the time for making this decree is not subject to discretion: it is to be rendered not before, but also not later than the moment when the evidence is "sufficient". In practice, "sufficiency" is interpreted as near completeness since restraining measures are also allowed against the suspect.

Within two days (or after discovery of a hidden accused) and *before* his interrogation, the accused must be formally charged by being acquainted with the decree. Simultaneously, he must be informed of his general rights as accused. In this way, his right to know from the very beginning what he is accused of is secured. It is even controversial—and a different wording of the various Union republic codes gives rise to the controversy—whether or not this presenting of the accusation is a constituent part of the inculpation so that nobody could become accused without being informed of it. Yet, if his abode is not known, it naturally must be permissible to conduct a search for him, while the law expressly permits search only for an "accused". He may be sought upon the decree of the investigator (during preliminary investigation) or of the court or judge (during committal proceedings).

The presented accusation limits the scope of the further proceedings; charges that have not been presented are no legitimate subject of investigation. If, on the basis of new disclosures, the accusation has to be changed, esp. if new charges have to be added, the altered accusation must be presented to the accused in due form including the interrogation; if part of the charges are not confirmed, they are subject to elimination from the accusation by formally terminating the case with respect to that part.

The accused must be interrogated immediately—but usually not at night—after the formal charge. The form of interrogation, its recording and the position of the interrogated is valid for both types of defendant (see above). The accused's statement is considered to be evidence; but, although at the beginning of the interrogation he is asked whether he acknowledges himself to be guilty, a confession may be taken as a basis for charging only if corroborated by other evidence.

The "right to defence" actually belonging to the defendant (including the suspect), is extended in respect of the accused by two important individual rights: to see the file and to have counsel. The general right to know the charges is made perfect by the right to become acquainted with all the materials of the case; however this right is not actually granted to the accused as such, but becomes effective only after completion of the preliminary procedure. Only then does the defendant's right to submit petitions obtain a more real value in respect of supplementary investigation; petitions to conduct specific investigative actions may be denied only exceptionally by a decree supported by reasons. Further, his right to have defence counsel, usually of his own choice, does not belong to the accused as such, but is available only after completion of the preliminary proceedings (see DEFENCE) in exceptional cases after inculpation, and in cases without preliminary investigation only after committal; counsel may be refused at any time, but only upon the accused's own initiative. The defendant's right to appeal especially applies to his committal to a comrades' court, to a commission for minors' affairs, or to a collective for patronage (*q.v.*).

In respect of investigative actions, the defendant does not gain new rights by his accusation, except in the case of expert examination not combined with committal to a clinic. In this case, the accused has all the rights in respect of every kind of expert examination which are granted to the defendant committed to a medical institution (see above, before 1). If at the time of the expert examination the accused was still a suspect, he must be acquainted with the opinion after his inculpation.

After the accusation, the defendant is not subject to any more coercive measures than before except search; however, inculpation as a rule should precede the application of restraining measures. The status of an accused ends either with the termination of the case, possibly combined with committal to a comrades' court, a minor's commission or a collective, or by committal for trial.

3) During the trial the accused is called *podsudimyi* (the "subject of the court proceedings") (see TRIAL). At this stage, the general constitutional right to defence is reflected first of all in the defendant's right to participate actively in the trial; yet this right is effective only during the first instance trial. Thereby the adversary principle (equal status with all participants, esp. with the accuser; see CRIMINAL PROCEDURE) is valid only in relation to the right to submit petitions, present evidence and participate in the taking of evidence.

The right to participate actively presupposes the presence of the defendant, which is required only at the trial of first instance, and even then the trial in his absence is possible in exceptional cases (see TRIAL). For the rest, his presence is not only a right but a duty: if the defendant does not appear, he may be compelled or subjected to a restraining measure, or a search for him may be conducted. A minor witness may be interrogated in the absence of the accused, who must then be acquainted with the statement and given an opportunity to submit questions to the witness. The illegal conduct of a trial in the absence of the defendant constitutes an absolute ground for striking out the judgment.

Furthermore, the right to participate actively presupposes knowledge of the charge and of the evidentiary material.

Therefore, the defendant is entitled to see the materials of the case, to receive a copy of indictment or the victim's complaint (in the case of a private accusation; see VICTIM) at least three days before the trial, to see the record (see COURT RECORD) and to have his own remarks inserted, and to be informed of statements made in his absence; any supplementary accusation or change in the charges violating the right to defence are prohibited.

Specifically, the right to participate actively consists of the right to offer and produce evidence: to submit petitions, esp. concerning the reading of documents as evidence, to present evidence or to petition for the taking of specific evidence, to give testimony at any moment during the taking of evidence, to direct the attention of the court to certain circumstances during an inspection, to be heard on the evidentiary petitions of other participants, to take an active part in the taking of evidence, personally putting questions to witnesses, experts and co-defendants, by presenting written questions to be examined by experts and putting oral supplementary questions to them and by viewing "real" evidence. The court must hear the defendant before ruling on the continuation or postponement of a trial because of non-appearance of a participant, witness or expert.

As to the right to defence counsel, see DEFENCE. If counsel does not appear at the trial, he may be replaced only with the consent of the defendant. The defendant has the right to challenge judges, the procurator, the secretary, the interpreter and the expert. He has in any case the right to have the last word, even after a reopening of the evidence. He has a right to propose questions to be considered by the court when deliberating judgment. He has a right to appeal against decrees of the presiding judge and against court rulings, esp. to file a cassational appeal even against acquittal (in relation to its grounds). He has a right to object to the procedural directions of the presiding judge and to have the objection inserted in the record, and the right immediately to be released after pronunciation of an acquittal. At the very beginning of the trial, the defendant must be informed by the presiding judge of his general rights as accused.

The presumption of innocence as a principle is expressly prescribed by law; its concrete contents, however, are still controversial among Soviet jurists. The often observed inclination to regard the accused as guilty is due to the large amount of evidence required for inculpation and to the Soviet inclination to consider the prosecution of innocents to be almost illegal.

The trial interrogation of the defendant is part of the taking of the evidence. It is preceded by the establishment of his identity and by the question of whether or not he acknowledges his guilt, both items having no evidentiary character. The interrogation begins with the invitation to give free (i.e. uninterrupted) testimony, which is followed by questioning by the judges and other participants, including co-defendants. Judges may question the defendant at any moment during the taking of evidence. Refusal to give and the giving of false testimony is not punishable. Interrogation in the absence of co-defendants is permissible only by way of exception and obliges the court to inform the co-defendant subsequently of the statements made and to grant an opportunity to ask questions. The reading out of the accused's statements made in preliminary proceedings is permissible in the case of a contradiction, of silence, or of the absence of the defendant.

During trial the court may apply, cancel, or alter restraining measures against the defendant, esp. in the case of non-appearance. The only measure of order applicable to the defendant is removal from the courtroom by court ruling after an unheeded warning.

For costs, see COSTS.

In cassational and supervision proceedings the defendant has virtually no right to defence. All rights mentioned are granted only to the defendant during the first instance trial, not during later stages. This situation is justified dogmatically: appellate proceedings are considered to be *ex officio* proceedings not subject to the adversary principle: hence there are no parties, neither accuser nor defendant.

M. Fincke

DELEGATION OF POWERS, see LEGISLATION

DELICTS, see TORTS

DELINQUENCY

Many statements of Soviet criminologists point to the existence of delinquent sub- or contra-cultures. A number of Soviet sources refer to the frequency of offences committed by groups of young people, and the comparative rarity of individuals acting on their own. Many scholars stress the frequency of the anti-utilitarian character of offences, which corresponds to findings in Britain and the USA. It is obvious from all reports that Soviet youths, like their counterparts in the West, resort to crime when frustrated in their aspirations and unable to achieve desired goals, acting in small and frequently casual groups of similarly disillusioned people and in some cases with the participation of adults. A Ukrainian survey reports that $\frac{3}{4}$ of minors charged for serious offences in 1964-1965 were acting in groups of 2-4 people. A corresponding Estonian survey reports that 82% in 1962, 78% in 1963 and 75.5% in 1964 of delinquents committed their offences as members of a group. The following reasons are given for the formation of such gangs: the natural desire of the young for company and concerted activities, desire for an accepted role and social prestige and fear that abstention from common activities would be interpreted either as cowardice or disloyalty. Most of the young offenders in all the reported surveys had a very limited education and poor scholarly achievements. The statistics of the Ukrainian survey gave 38.5% of the offenders as working and 36.5% as studying (mainly in technical training colleges); 25% were neither working nor learning. The Estonian survey reports that 77.6% of convicted youths in 1962 had less than a seven year education; in 1963 the figure was 78.2% and in 1964 81.2%. Most of the delinquents in the Ukrainian survey (58.4%) were negatively assessed by their employers or teachers. 60.7% lacked proper supervision and had a poor family background with inferior family training. Interesting in this respect are Grabovskaia's findings regarding delinquents in Leningrad. Although most of her figures refer back to 1961 they point to the exceptionally grave conditions in a city that has in recent history perhaps suffered more than any other great city. Thus 40% of convicted delinquents were brought up only by their mothers. In 1961 61% of all dischargees from children's educational colonies (borstals) had only a mother. The same applies to 58% of the children who appeared before a Children's Commission of a Leningrad district in 1961, while 7% had no parents, 10% a mother and a step-father and only 25% had both parents. Grabovskaia also states that 60% of the convicted delinquents were young workers with inadequate work training and poor professional skills.

Some further Estonian surveys may be regarded as of particular interest due to their scholarly and detailed analyses and unbiased observations. Thus they report the fluctuation of the crime figures from year to year and not, as usual, some spectacular reduction. (If 1964 is taken as the base year (100%) for delinquency, then in 1965 the figure was 82%, in 1966 112% and in 1967 97.9%.) Most of the crimes were committed in cities and towns (83.5% in 1965 and 76.3% in 1967). Property offences (state and personal property) have fluctuated in a manner similar to the general fluctuations, but an increase in crimes of violence and a spectacularly rapid increase in sexual crimes, particularly rape, have occurred. If 1964 is taken as the base year (100) the incidence of rape increased to 244.4 by 1965 and jumped to 411.1 by 1967. These figures, although significant and important, should not be accorded too great a weight in view of the overall small numbers of such serious crimes as killing and rape. However, similar complaints come from other parts of the USSR in the Kazakh republic 8% of all inmates in correctional institutions in 1965, and 4% in 1964, were sexual offenders (*Voprosy bor'by s prestupnost'iu nesovershennoletnikh*, 1968, p. 11). Estonian, Kazakh and Latvian reports speak of increases of hooliganism and crimes of violence.

The following picture may be drawn of existing contra- or sub-cultures amongst the working population of the USSR: they flourish among frustrated groups where members are poorly educated, with a worse than average family background and family structure, frequently with signs of mental retardation, occupying less favoured jobs with inferior social prestige and often unemployed. We could hypothesize that they belong mostly to the first and/or second generation of immigrants from the villages to the cities and towns. The considerable number of unemployed amongst the delinquents seems to be corroborated by the complaints of frequent job changes. The share of unemployed youth in delinquency is in some reports as high as 25%-33%. Many surveys have indicated that persons changing jobs are averaging 25 days of idleness between employment. Researches in Kaluga and Elets indicate that the percentage of "hereditary" workers (at least second generation in industry), with established working traditions, is greater in heavy industry. Thus in Kaluga in such industries 59% were of worker's origin and only 27% of peasant background. The proportion was reversed regarding employees in the city transport and the building trade—here 65% of the workers were of peasant origin and only 27% of employees were termed "hereditary workers" (L. A. Anokhina, M. N. Shmeleva, *K voprosu o klassifikatsii gorodskogo naseleniia pri etnograficheskom izuchenii goroda, Sovetskaia Etnografiia* No. 2, 1970, p. 121/9). This research indicates the inferior work usually given to peasant immigrants, which is obviously the reason for a sense of frustration which leads to delinquent behaviour.

Writing on circumstances facilitating sexual offences among juveniles and their prevention, L. A. Andreeva (*Voprosy bor'by s prestupnost'iu,* No. 10, 1969, p. 108-113) says that 90% of such offenders were 16-17 years old, 62% were employed at diverse enterprises, 10% were not working or being educated, only 6% were in secondary school, 18% in trade schools and 4% in technical colleges. She further concludes that in most instances the young were driven by a desire to flout social standards (*khuligānskie pobuzhdeniia*); this, she thinks, is proved by the fact that 70% of offences were committed by groups of young people. It is interesting that precisely these crimes were committed mostly by adolescents without the participation of adults. She blames also the uncouth, brutal and violent attitudes towards women (mothers and sisters) in the families of the young rapists. Andreeva's survey for Leningrad reports that 70% of the adolescent rapists committed their crime in a state of drunkenness. 60% of them had taken to drink at the age of 14 to 15 years. According to all these surveys it seems justifiable to speak of contra-cultures to which some of the young belong. Their employment in inferior jobs, frequent job changes with the inevitable periods of unemployment, low scholarly achievements, their insecurity and desire for the company of similar people and for manly, prestigious roles (sexual violence), the frustrating realisation of one's inferiority and inability to improve—all seems to apply in particular to the disenchanted first or second generation of peasant immigrants. That these people are mostly young is likewise more characteristic of immigrants from the villages, where there is a constant complaint that the young leave the village and only the old remain for the most unskilled and poorly paid jobs.

Conclusions

A better understanding of social changes and stratifications, their significance and the influences on different groups and strata may be possible by researches conducted, so to speak, from the negative sub-cultural end of the social structure. The incidence of delinquency, the character of deviant behaviour, the delinquent ratio between different groups and the character of offences may all be important indicators of the structure and dynamic trends existing in a society.

One example may be useful. If we postulate the hypothesis that the greater the social equality of sexes the greater will be their equality in all other aspects of life, the greater will be the mutual respect and regard for their integrity. Let us assume that Great Britain, the USA and the USSR all strive towards an equality of sexes, not merely as expressions of legal statutes, but as an expression of overall mores and folkways. Then, *ceteris paribus*, we may assume that the delinquency rate between male and female aberrations will tend towards a ratio of 1/1. A greater or lesser discrepancy would indicate the degree of still existing differences in attitudes and mores. It may be significant that the overall ratio of male to female delinquency in the USA is 5/1, in

Great Britain 6/1 and in the USSR 10/1. It seems to be a pointer towards greater equalising tendencies in the capitalist countries than in the Soviet Union. The spectacular increase of crimes of violence and of sexual crimes and similar phenomena seem to provide conclusive proofs of a society where in subcultures, or contra-cultures, the woman is still regarded as inferior to the male partner. The worsening of the situation in the cities may be explained by the influx of young peasant immigrants or the adolescents of a second generation feeling déclassés and disillusioned in their urban surroundings.

We have concentrated mainly our study on showing the applicability of A. Cohen's theory of sub- or contra-cultures to the delinquency problem in the USSR. It is one of the aspects where Western "bourgeois" countries and the Soviet Union show striking similarities. Hollander, in his admirable article on juvenile delinquency in the Soviet Union and the United States, finds that in both countries societies create expectations faster than opportunities for their satisfaction and that "the distribution of expectations is far more equitable than the possibilities for their fulfilment. In this realm, as in others, we are ahead of the Soviet Union. We not only inculcate more intense aspirations than Soviet society, but do a poorer job in controlling the expression of frustration—utilitarian or destructive—when they are met."

Bibl.: Paul Hollander, A Converging Social Problem: Juvenile Delinquency in the Soviet Union and the United States, *the British Journal of Criminology*, vol. 9 No. 2, pp. 148-166;
Russia—A new look at crime, an I.S.T.D. Report, 1966;
Sophia M. Robinson, *Juvenile Delinquency, Its Nature and Control*, 1960, pp. 38-44;
Cultural Factors in Delinquency, edited by T. C. N. Gibbens and R. H. Ahrenfeld, 1966;
Soviet criminology, Bibliographical series no. 4 (University of Cambridge, Institute of Criminology), compiled by Peter H. Solomon, jr.

R. Beermann

DEMOCRACY

In Soviet political theory, the establishment of democracy is a historically inevitable process, which develops through a series of stages. The sources of this theory are threefold: the writings of Karl Marx; the adumbrations to Marxism of Lenin during the revolutionary period; and the evaluations of recent Soviet development by contemporary Soviet theorists. Each of these sources has produced a theoretical description of a major form of democracy, and Soviet general theory embraces them all in historical succession.

Marx's analysis of the emergence of feudalism into capitalism led him to identify "bourgeois democracy" as the characteristic form of rule during the capitalistic stage of history. As capitalism flourishes as an economic system, the forms of democratic rule—election of officials by universal franchise, law-making by parliamentary process, the application of the laws to all citizens—come into existence, but actual political power remains in the hands of those members of the capitalist class who control the economic system. The further expansion of formal democratic rights merely serves to delude the propertyless classes by concealing the exercise of real political power by the bourgeoisie.

The Leninist concept of democracy, implemented in the immediate post-revolutionary period, was a development of Marx's idea of the "dictatorship of the proletariat" (*q.v.*) fused to the principle of "democratic centralism" (*q.v.*). Soviet leaders purported to find no contradiction between proletarian democracy and dictatorship in this formula, since both terms depended upon an understanding of class relationships for their meanings.

Proletarian democracy was held to be democratic with relation to the working and peasant classes, but dictatorial toward capitalist and petty bourgeois classes, just as the bourgeois system had been democratic for the capitalist class and dictatorial for the masses. The essense of democracy after the revolution, it was argued, lay in the fact that political power was henceforth to be used to serve the interests of the proletariat and peasantry and to eliminate all political and economic power of the former ruling classes. At the time of the revolution, it was assumed that this would be completed within a few years, and that simultaneously the Soviet masses would be re-educated for life in a truly democratic society.

By the 1930's, when communist party rule was stabilized under the leadership of Joseph Stalin, the social conditions which necessitated a dictatorship in the name of the proletariat were declared to have been eliminated. The former exploiting classes had been abolished, along with antagonisms among the remaining classes, inequalities in the social structure, and differential access to political and economic power. However, the conditions necessary for the transition to full communism were not yet established. Thus emerged, over the next two decades, a stage of development unforeseen by either Marx or Lenin: socialist democracy.

The new stage, which continues to the present time, is characterized by the presence of two non-antagonistic social classes: workers and peasants. The franchise is extended to all Soviet people, and participation in social and political processes is expected of all citizens. The pattern of governance involves the gradual transfer of state responsibilities from government agencies to public organizations, and the replacement of administrative coercion by popular persuasion. During this stage, the state remains in existence, however, to deal with lingering problems of social development, such as the uneven distribution of economic goods, manifestations of private-ownership psychology, and social distinctions between occupational groupings. Since socialism has not yet triumphed on a world-wide basis, the state is also required for the defense of the Soviet Union from external aggression and from internal anti-Soviet individuals.

Although the power of the Communist Party leadership in the Soviet system is far greater than the concept of socialist democracy reveals, the level of popular study and comment on pending legislative proposals, both national and local, is very high. Voting in elections is mandatory, though only one candidate is nominated for each office, and campaigning before each election is extremely intensive. On the local level, virtually everyone is involved in some aspect of governance. In general, however, the Soviet political system continues to adhere to the basic distinction, inherent in democratic centralism, between the power to decide, which belongs to the party leadership, and the duty to discuss, to approve, and, ultimately, to obey, the Party's decisions.

The final, theoretical stage in the development of Soviet democracy is communism, in which the state apparatus will no longer exist (although the party machinery may continue) and all authority will be exercised by the people. While Nikita Khrushchev was in power, Soviet theoreticians paid considerable attention to the nature of the future communist society. In the past few years, however, the concept has faded significantly as the more immediate problems of managing and developing the Soviet system have come to absorb the present generation of leaders.

D. Richard Little

DEMOCRATIC CENTRALISM

The principle of d.c. is the original and basic technique of the organization of the Communist Party and the Soviet state.

From the very beginning of the social-democratic movement in Russia, d.c. has been the basis of the bolshevik organisation plan for the party (at the 4th Congress of the Social-Democrat Workers' Party of Russia, in Stockholm 1906). It is now found in art. 19 of the Rules of the Communist Party of the USSR, adopted at the 22nd Congress in 1961:

"The guiding principle of the organizational structure of the Party is democratic centralism, which signifies:

a) Election of all leading Party bodies, from the lowest to the highest;

b) Periodic reports of Party bodies to their Party organizations and to higher bodies;

c) Strict Party discipline and subordination of the minority to the majority;

d) That the decisions of higher bodies are binding on lower bodies."

Since the October Revolution this principle has been extended to political organization as an essential element of governmental and administrative technique. "It is our task to implement d.c. in the domain of the economy, to guarantee complete coordination and unification in the functioning of economic enterprises, such as railways, post and telegraph, and other means of communication; at the same time, centralism, understood in a truly democratic sense, implies the heretofore unknown possibility of a full and unimpeded development of local peculiarities, as well as of local initiative and a variety of ways, means, and methods of achieving common goals" (Lenin, Works, Vol. 27, pp. 180-181).

The essence of d.c. according to Lenin's theory resides in the dialectical interaction between two antinomous concepts: decision-making power reserved for the centre, freedom and initiative granted to the periphery. A disruption of the interaction between these two concepts carries the risk of a tendency, on the one hand towards bureaucratic tyranny where the power to decide does not rest on the participation of the workers in reaching decisions, or, on the other hand, towards anarchy where subordinate bodies are not forced to execute the decisions of higher organs.

The principles of d.c. are not mentioned in the USSR Constitution of 1936, although they are basic to the particular technique of organization of power known as "unity of state power"; they find expression especially in the system of "double subordination" of the executive agencies of the state. During the period of Stalin's personality cult the essential deformation in the exercise of power was the insistence on socialist centralism (rigorous discipline and vertical subordination), rather than on socialist democracy (participation, eligibility, accountability).

P. Lavigne

See also COMMUNIST PARTY

DEPARTMENTS, see MINISTRIES; STATE COMMITTEES

DEPENDANTS

Dependants, according to Soviet law, are persons who are entirely living on the support of another, or whose main base of existence is such support. Dependants may be divided into persons supported by a breadwinner on the basis of a legal duty to support, and other persons supported in fact, but without any duty on the part of the breadwinner. The former category is defined, for purposes of support (alimony) in the Family Code of the RSFSR (arts. 67 ff. and 80 ff.; cf. also art. 108); see SUPPORT OF DEFENDANTS; and for purposes of establishing a claim for "a pension . . . owing to the loss of a breadwinner", in art. 28 of the Law on State Pensions of 1956. The members of the latter category (persons supported without a legal duty on the part of the breadwinner), if they are unable to work, are the so-called *izhdiventsy*. There are three main rights attached to the position of an *izhdivenets*: the right to inherit from the breadwinner (provided one has been supported for at least one year at the moment of death of the breadwinner), see further SUCCESSION; the right to claim damages in the case of the death of the breadwinner if caused by a tort (see further TORTS), and the right of the *izhdivenets* who lives with the tenant, to be considered a co-tenant.

With regard to the first mentioned right are considered to be unable to work: persons under 16 (or under 18 if they are students), women over 55, men over 60, and disabled persons. With regard to the other rights mentioned, inability to work has not been substantiated in a similar way, and it seems that in practice, at least in respect of successions, the criteria applied are less rigid.

F. J. M. Feldbrugge

DEPORTATION, see ASYLUM; ALIENS; EXTRADITION

DEPUTIES

Deputies are elected members of the USSR Supreme Soviet, the supreme soviets of Union and autonomous republics, and regional and local soviets. Constitutionally, they exercise the supreme legislative authority on each administrative level. Deputies are elected to office by popular, secret ballot for terms of four years on the national and republic levels and for two years on the local level. Minimum ages for eligibility are 23 years for the USSR Supreme Soviet, 21 years for soviets of Union and autonomous republics, and 18 years for local soviets.

While deputies may be nominated for office by any of a number of public organizations, including the Communist Party, labour unions, cooperative organizations, and cultural societies, they are not considered to represent the interests of the organization that nominated them. They do not, in fact, represent interests at all, even the collective interests of their constituents. Their responsibilities as deputies lie in two directions: toward individual constituents in their respective electoral districts, for whom they perform a wide range of services; and toward the governmental organ of which they are a part and the Communist Party organization on each level. The latter responsibility consists mainly in publicizing and helping to implement legislative enactments and policy pronouncements of the Party leadership.

The Soviet Constitution sets forth a very significant legislative role for deputies, including the initiation of new legislation, voting on legislative proposals, electing the executive officers of the legislature and appointing administrative officers of the government, and overseeing the operations of government. In practice, however, that role has been highly circumscribed by the dominance of the Communist Party apparatus in the political system. In recent years, deputies have become more actively involved in analyzing legislative proposals and investigating the operations of governmental ministries through membership on standing and ad hoc committees of the soviets. In this capacity, some deputies have undertaken extensive investigations of specific legislative proposals, especially in the areas of public health, education, and welfare. When legislative proposals are returned from the standing committees to the chambers for action, individual deputies who disagree with committee recommendations have the constitutional right to present their views to the legislature, but in fact this has never happened, and all votes in the soviets are unanimous.

Traditionally, deputies have faced numerous obstacles in the performance of their official duties, especially on the national level, but legislation in recent years has attempted to eliminate some of them. Deputies to the USSR Supreme Soviet have been granted free transportation by any public carrier throughout the country, whether for official business or not. Continuation of their wages or salary while they are engaged in legislative business has been guaranteed, and they are protected from dismissal from their jobs except with the concurrence of the legislature. New laws have made attendance at legislative and committee sessions mandatory for all members, and have provided that they be released from work not only for official sessions but for any additional duties arising out of these sessions as well.

The normal tenure in office of elected deputies is very short, especially on the national level. In the USSR Supreme Soviet, nearly two/thirds of the deputies serve only one term, and are not nominated for re-election. This occurs not because of incompetence, malfeasance in office, or loss of favour with the voters (except in rare cases), but because of a long-standing national policy which decrees a continual renewal of the membership of the Supreme Soviet. Nevertheless, election to the national legislature is regarded as a high honour in the Soviet Union and generally falls to those who are held in esteem in their local communities and who have achieved some prominence in their professions.

D. Richard Little

See also SUPREME SOVIET; LEGISLATION; ELECTIONS; COMMUNIST PARTY

Editor's Note

On September 20, 1972 (after this article was written), the USSR Supreme Soviet enacted a Law on the Status of Deputies to the Soviets of Workers' Deputies of the USSR. This Law contains the usual provisions concerning the rights of members of representative bodies (a degree of inviolability, guaranteed wages, free travel, etc.), but also emphasizes the function of a Soviet deputy as a link between the individual and the state. The deputy is entitled: to receive necessary information from state agencies, to file complaints with the proper agencies against violations of the law, to be received without delay by government officials and to be provided with legal advice.

DESERTION, see MILITARY LAW

DICTATORSHIP OF THE PROLETARIAT

The concept of "dictatorship of the proletariat" originated with Marx and Engels and appeared in the Communist Manifesto and later in their Critique of the Gotha Program. "Between capitalist and communist society", they wrote in the latter document, "lies a period of revolutionary transformation from the former to the latter. Corresponding to this period is also a transitional political period, and the government of this period cannot be anything but a revolutionary dictatorship of the proletariat".

In the midst of the 1917 Soviet revolution, the concept received more precise definition. Its primary functions were twofold: 1) to eliminate completely the economic and political power of the former ruling classes, and to establish the power of the working masses under the leadership of the Bolshevik party; and 2) to create within Soviet society the understanding and experience necessary to establish a true democratic society and to manage the affairs of the country, in particular the economic system.

Against the vehement opposition of Karl Kautsky and other leaders of the radical socialist movement in Europe, Lenin insisted that the proletariat would have to establish a dictatorship after the revolution, in order to protect its gains, but that such a dictatorship would actually be a higher form of democracy than had existed under bourgeois rule. Whereas the former provided a democratic mechanism through which members of the bourgeoisie could participate in government, the dictatorship of the proletariat would extend that participation to the vast majority of working people, even while it eliminated the bourgeoisie as a class.

Kautsky rejected this argument partly on the grounds that the industrial proletariat in Russia at the turn of the century was a small, though growing, minority of the working force, and that a dictatorship of that minority would be no more democratic than rule by the bourgeoisie. During the period of the 1905 revolution, Lenin had conceived of the masses of peasants as partners of the proletariat and had written of a "dictatorship of the proletariat and peasantry". By 1917, he had been persuaded, by Trotsky and others, that the peasantry could not be mobilized to support radical political activity, though they clearly were one of the oppressed classes. The proletariat, therefore, would rule, in alliance with and representing the interests of all oppressed classes. As Lenin defined it in *State and Revolution* (1917), the dictatorship of the proletariat meant "the domination of the proletariat over the bourgeoisie, untrammelled by law and based on violence and enjoying the sympathy and support of the toiling and exploited masses".

In 1936, Stalin presented a Soviet constitution which signified the victory of socialism in the Soviet Union. Stalin declared that the means of economic production were firmly controlled by the people, class antagonisms (though not classes themselves) had been eradicated, and the people had developed a democratic consciousness and a capacity to adjust to modern economic and social conditions. It would seem, therefore, that the purposes of the dictatorship of the proletariat had been fulfilled, yet Stalin described the new Constitution as preserving the "regime of the dictatorship of the working class". Indeed, the phrase endured for another twenty-five years as the official description of the Soviet political system.

It was finally superseded by a new concept at the 22nd Communist Party Congress in 1961. Khrushchev announced that the dictatorship of the proletariat as a state had evolved into a "state of the whole people", and that proletarian democracy had evolved into socialist democracy. This seemed, finally, to recognize officially the changes in Soviet society announced by Stalin in 1936. At the same time, it raised other theoretical questions concerning the role of classes and the nature of the state. In Marxist theory, "state" has always been defined as the political mechanism through which one economic class dominated other classes, and the dictatorship of the proletariat is a state in which the proletariat exercises political power over other classes, even where relations among those classes are friendly rather than antagonistic. In a "state of the whole people", the concept of class seems irrelevant, and thus the primary function of a "state" would seem to have disappeared.

In recent years, Chinese leaders have charged that this renders the notion of a "state of the whole people" self-contradictory and meaningless. They also argue that it is contrary to Marxism, which they say, defined "dictatorship of the proletariat" as the historical stage between capitalism and communism. Soviet leaders insist that Marx used the term in reference to the transition from capitalism to socialism, not to communism, and that the "state of the whole people" is the correct political form for the period of socialism. The polemics of the argument notwithstanding, Soviet leaders view their society as having progressed beyond the dictatorship of the proletariat into the period of socialist democracy.

D. Richard Little

See also COMMUNIST PARTY; STATE

DIPLOMACY

Diplomacy has been defined by Soviet scholars as the official activity of heads of states, of governments, and of special agencies for foreign relations concerned with the realization, through negotiations, correspondence, and other peaceful means, of the goals and tasks of a state's foreign policy, which are defined by the interests of the ruling class, as well as concerned with the protection of a state's rights and interests abroad. The basic forms of diplomatic activity include: 1) diplomatic conferences and meetings; 2) diplomatic correspondence in the form of declarations, letters, notes, memoranda, etc.; 3) preparation and conclusion of bilateral or multilateral international treaties or agreements; 4) day-to-day representation of a state abroad in embassies or missions; 5) participation in international organizations; 6) official publication of government documents and views regarding foreign policy. The general direction of Soviet diplomatic activity is the responsibility of the USSR Ministry of Foreign Affairs (*q.v.*), whose basic duties and authority are defined in a 1923 Statute, as amended. In relations among socialist countries, the Communist Party performs negotiating and other functions that are the exclusive prerogative of diplomats in non-socialist states. The major sources of Soviet diplomatic law are international custom, the 1961 Vienna Convention on Diplomatic Relations (not yet ratified by the USSR), bilateral international agreements, and domestic legislation.

The establishment of diplomatic relations is usually followed by the creation of a permanent embassy or mission of the accrediting state on the territory of the receiving state. The functions of the embassy or mission include the protection of the interests of the accrediting state and its nationals in the receiving state, the conduct of negotiations with the government of the receiving state, the collection by all lawful means of information concerning life and events in the receiving state, the promotion of friendly relations, and the development of economic, cultural, and scientific ties between the accrediting and receiving states. Under Art. 18(a) of the USSR Constitution, Union republics of the Soviet Union have the right to enter into direct relations with foreign states and to exchange diplomatic and consular representation. However, in practice such exchanges rarely occur.

Trade representations of the USSR are a constituent part of the local Soviet diplomatic representation and, in the Soviet view, are entitled to full diplomatic privileges and immunities. The activities of trade representations are governed by the 1933 Statute on Trade Representations and Trade Agencies of the USSR Abroad. The extension of full diplomatic status to Soviet trade representations has been strongly opposed by many Western governments, and the precise status of such representations is commonly determined by special provisions in trade and navigation agreements contracted with the USSR.

The privileges and immunities of diplomatic representations are set forth in the 1966 Statute of Diplomatic and Consular Representations of Foreign States on the Territory of the USSR. In contrast to an earlier 1927 Statute, which stressed reciprocity as the sole basis for according privileges and immunities, the 1966 Statute grants privileges and immunities for the performance of "functions defined in accordance with the norms of international law" and provides for the granting of subsidiary privileges and immunities on the basis of reciprocity.

Under the 1966 Statute, the premises of a diplomatic representation (including the residences of diplomatic staff and the means of transport of the representation) are inviolable. Access is permissible only by consent of the head of the diplomatic representation or the person replacing him. The representation is guaranteed the right of unobstructed communication with its own government and with consular or diplomatic representations via ordinary means of communication, enciphered telegrams, or diplomatic mail. However, radio transmitters may be installed and used only with the permission of the Soviet Government. The archives, documents, and official correspondence of the representation are inviolable. The flag of the accrediting state may be flown and its emblem displayed on the premises of the representation or the residence or transport of the head thereof. The diplomatic representation is exempted from all general state and local taxes on condition of reciprocity, and items imported for official use of the representation are duty-free.

Privileges and immunities granted to intergovernmental international organizations located on Soviet territory are defined in special treaties with the USSR.

The existence of a state of war (*q.v.*) between the accrediting and receiving states, a break in diplomatic relations, recall of diplomatic personnel, or the closing of an embassy or mission terminate the existence of a diplomatic representation. Nonetheless, the receiving state is obliged to respect and protect the property, premises, and archives of the former representation and to ensure the safe departure of diplomatic personnel with their families and possessions. Rupture of diplomatic relations frequently has been used as a means of political pressure or a sanction for improper actions. During the interwar period in particular, the USSR experienced breaks in diplomatic relations and has itself employed the same technique on several occasions.

Pursuant to an edict of December 16, 1947, Soviet state agencies and officials may communicate with foreign diplomatic representations located on Soviet territory only through, or with the express consent of, the USSR Ministry of Foreign Affairs.

Bibl.: Texts of relevant Soviet legislation are translated in *Soviet Statutes and Decisions*, III, no. 2-3 (1967), pp. 7-54.

W. E. Butler

See also CONSULS; DIPLOMATIC OFFICERS

DIPLOMATIC OFFICERS

Although in the aftermath of the Bolshevik revolution the Soviet regime emphasized the introduction of a new proletarian style to traditional forms of diplomacy, Soviet diplomats today observe the protocol, social amenities, and etiquette of diplomacy in essentially the same manner as other states. Foreign diplomats with the rank of ambassador or minister are accredited to the Presidium of the USSR Supreme Soviet; those with the status of chargé d'affaires are accredited to the USSR Ministry of Foreign Affairs. An accrediting state must obtain the *agrément* of the USSR to the appointment of a given person as the head of a diplomatic representation or as an army, naval, or air attaché.

Diplomatic ranks. On June 4, 1918, the Soviet Republic abolished the Imperial system of diplomatic ranks dating from the Congress of Vienna and substituted the single rank of Representative Plenipotentiary of the RSFSR. All foreign diplomatic officers, irrespective of rank, were likewise considered to be equal representatives plenipotentiary. Foreign governments promptly responded by treating Soviet representatives as lowest in rank of the diplomatic corps. The USSR thereupon resorted to specifying the ranks in credentials of their representatives or concluded special agreements with the receiving country concerning the ranks of their respective diplomatic representatives. Generally-accepted diplomatic ranks were restored in an edict of May 9, 1941, as supplemented on May 28, 1943. At present, Soviet diplomatic ranks are: ambassador extraordinary and plenipotentiary; minister extraordinary and plenipotentiary (first or second class); counsellor (first or second class); first secretary (first or second class); second secretary (first or second class); third secretary; attaché. The ranks of ambassador and minister are conferred by the Presidium of the USSR Supreme Soviet; all others are conferred by the USSR Ministry of Foreign Affairs.

In certain large cities or ports of the USSR frequented by foreigners (Odessa, Batumi, etc.), diplomatic agents are appointed by the Ministry of Foreign Affairs to facilitate the entry and departure of foreign diplomats or to assist aliens who need to communicate with their consulates.

Privileges and immunities. The privileges and immunities of foreign diplomats in the USSR, presumably representing the minimum standard acceptable for Soviet diplomats abroad, are set forth in the 1966 Statute on Diplomatic and Consular Representations of Foreign States on the Territory of the USSR. The head of a diplomatic mission and members of the diplomatic staff (counsellors; trade representatives; army, naval, and air attachés; first, second, and third secretaries; attachés; assistants to army, naval, or air attachés and deputies of trade representatives; secretary-archivists) enjoy personal inviolability and may not be subjected to detention or arrest. These persons are also immune from criminal, civil, and administrative jurisdiction unless the accrediting state expressly waives immunity. Civil immunity does not extend to civil-law relations entered into by diplomats in their capacity as private persons or concerning activity beyond the limits of their official duties. Exemption from general state and local taxes is accorded on condition of reciprocity. Family members of the head of the representation or of the diplomatic staff enjoy the same immunities provided they reside in common households and are not Soviet nationals.

Administrative and technical personnel who are not Soviet nationals enjoy privileges and immunities on the basis of reciprocity, except that civil and administrative immunity extends only to actions performed in the course of official duties. However, full privileges and immunities may be granted to such personnel on the basis of a special agreement. The USSR has concluded such agreements with the United States, Great Britain, and other countries. Service personnel are granted certain privileges and immunities on condition of reciprocity.

Diplomatic couriers, whether sent to or in transit across the USSR, enjoy personal inviolability in the performance of their duties and may not be subjected to arrest or detention. *Ad hoc* couriers enjoy inviolability until delivery of diplomatic mail is completed.

Foreign diplomats and their families accredited in a third state and in transit through Soviet territory enjoy personal inviolability and other immunities necessary for completion of their trip.

Full diplomatic privileges and immunities are also accorded to representatives of foreign states, members of parliamentary and government delegations, and, on the basis of reciprocity, employees of foreign delegations which come to the USSR to participate in official international talks, conferences, and meetings. Members of their families who are not Soviet nationals qualify as well.

The 1966 Statute requires that all persons enjoying diplomatic privileges and immunities must "respect the laws, decrees, and regulations in force in the USSR and the Union republics". Persons who have behaved in an unfriendly manner toward the Soviet Union may either be denied *agrément* for appointment to a foreign representation in the USSR or, having been appointed, be declared *non grata* and requested to leave.

A celebrated case occurred in 1952 when George Kennan was declared *non grata* for allegedly making anti-Soviet statements to press correspondents while in Berlin.
Restrictions on travel by foreign diplomatic personnel in the Soviet Union imposed May 16, 1941, as a wartime measure have been retained to the present in a somewhat revised form.

W. E. Butler

See also DIPLOMACY; CONSULS

DISCIPLINARY LAW
Disciplinary law may be defined as a body of binding rules, regulations and conflict solutions deemed necessary to ensure and promote the joint efforts of staffs towards the efficient working of enterprises and institutions. Soviet writers state that labour discipline in capitalist countries is something external and alien to the worker; in socialist countries, however, labour discipline is the expression of mutual trust, friendship, cooperation and mutual assistance. In spite of such statements, there are powerful controls in the hands of management and of the authorities in the USSR to enforce obedience among their staffs.
In the USSR two different ways of regulating labour discipline in enterprises and institutions have been adopted—either special disciplinary codes for a particular industry are issued (such as the disciplinary code for railway workers passed by the Council of Ministers of the USSR on July 31, 1964; the disciplinary code for the merchant navy (*rabotniki morskogo transporta*) of June 18, 1949, the disciplinary code for workers of the fishing fleet of June 30, 1966 and others, or general Model Rules (MR) on internal working order (*tipovye pravila vnutrennego trudovogo rasporiadka*) for workers and employees in state, cooperative and public enterprises and institutions, based on the Labour Code of 1922. The present Model Rules were passed on January 12, 1957, by an order (*postanovlenie*) of the State Committee on labour and wages of the Council of Ministers of the USSR and the All-Union Central Council of Trade Unions (*VTsSPS*). It consists of six sections: 1) General rules, 2) rules for the hire and discharge of workers and employees, 3) basic duties of management, workers and employees, 4) working hours and their utilisation, 5) incentives, 6) measures against breaches of discipline. Besides the Model Rules, Ministries or departments issue technical rules and regulations and staff instructions.
The Labour Code of 1971 reiterates many rules of the MR, but until now no new MR have been issued. On the basis of the MR, rules on internal working order are elaborated in individual enterprises and institutions.
Incentives. There are moral and material incentives. Both are frequently applied together, or the moral incentives issued as rewards give to the worker some rights and privileges of a material character. Thus to be nominated by a Government decree a "Hero of Socialist Labour" will give the holder the right to a house of 25 m^2 above the stated normal maximum of 60 m^2, to a personal pension (*personal'naia pensiia*) which is higher than ordinary pensions, and to other emoluments, as well as to the receipt of money rewards. There are a number of orders such as the Order of Lenin, Order of the Red Banner, the Badge of Merit, etc., which carry with them similar emoluments. Recipients of a Lenin Prize, beside its monetary value, enjoy several other material benefits. (See also HONOURS.)
In a more specific way the MR speak of a number of incentives of an internal character: expression of thanks (*blagodarnost'*), rewards with a writ of honour (*pochetnaia gramota*), entering of the worker's name in a Book of Honour, or on a notice board of honour, bestowing on the worker the title of

the best worker of the profession, rewarding the worker with a premium or with a valuable gift, etc. The mentioned separate codes for some industries include other incentives such as the titles of honorary miner, honorary railwayworker, etc.

Some codes provide for special badges to be issued to meritorious workers. Since the 23rd Party Congress, with its stress on efficient economy working, special attention has been paid to rewarding good team work and individual workers who have been instrumental in raising production per unit of capital (machinery) or worker. Titles of "teams of communist labour" are granted to well disciplined and good working teams. It is not only the enterprise which is expected to work according to the new principles of economic management, but departments and shops as well (*vnutrennii khozraschet*). Several experimental measures have been introduced to stimulate more rational and efficient production, such as the Shchekino experiment: money saved in wages funds (by reducing numbers of staff) is divided as rewards among remaining workers at the enterprise.

Disciplinary punishments. The MR provide the following measures against breaches of discipline: a) censure, b) reprimand, c) severe reprimand, d) transfer to some lower paid work in one's profession for up to three months, or direct demotion for three months, e) dismissal. For absenteeism a worker may be punished by one of the above measures, or he may be left for up to three months without increments for long service, or "one time" rewards for long services may be reduced by 25%; he may be deprived of his premium, wholly or partly; and lastly he may be dismissed. Measures for absenteeism may be taken only by the managers of the enterprises or the heads of institutions. Other disciplinary measures (if so stated in the working order of the enterprise) can be imposed by departmental chiefs or by foremen. Dismissals for absenteeism are entered in the work-book of the offender. Most common of the disciplinary measures are reprimands (*vygovor*) and severe reprimands (*strogii vygovor*).

Censure is rarely used, managers and foremen prefer to discuss minor breaches with the workers in a less formal way. The transfer and demotion to lower paid jobs have proved in many instances to be ineffective. Persons so punished left their jobs and were able to find alternative employment. In enterprises working according to "new rules of planning and economic stimulation", reprimands and severe reprimands are coupled with the loss of premiums. Drunkenness at work is treated as absenteeism (art. 33, Labour Code). A peculiar disciplinary measure for workers handling cash or merchandise is that of dismissal "for the loss of confidence", applicable in cases of carelessness and/or suspected dishonesty, such as unaccounted for losses of money or goods. Workers in schools and cultural institutions, and workers responsible for personnel policy may be dismissed for immoral behaviour, displayed in their jobs or outside.

Besides the above-stated measures, management has other means to enforce obedience: workers with a bad disciplinary record may be left without travel vouchers to holiday resorts, holidays may be granted at the most unpropitious times of the year, the worker may lose his place in the queue for a flat, or he may be refused membership in a building cooperative. Some enterprises resort to semi-legal means by entering in the work-book of the offender such disparaging notes as "dismissed for repeated absenteeism" or "dismissed as a malicious drunkard". Such entries have prevented the holders from finding alternative employment.

Procedures. Ne bis in idem is applicable to disciplinary offences—only one punishment may be imposed, but the loss of premiums and other advantages is not deemed to be a punishment. A disciplinary measure may be taken only within a month of the day the breach of discipline is discovered, and no later than six months after the date when it was committed. Good behaviour over a year leads to the expunging of the offence from the disciplinary record; this may take place even earlier on the decision of the manager. The worker must be heard before a disciplinary measure is imposed on him. The measure must be stated in writing. It is normal for such measures to be made public to the other members of staff either by public announcement on the factory notice board or by the newspaper of the enterprise (*mnogotirazhka*).

A worker aggrieved by a disciplinary measure may appeal to the Commission of Labour Disputes (KTS) at shop and or enterprise level. Dismissals can only take place with the agreement of the Trade Union Committee. Besides the MR and the special codes, there is still a third way of disciplining members of staff, but it is applicable exclusively to the more important people in the employment of the enterprise. It is called the "Disciplinary responsibility in the course of subordination" (*Disciplinarnaia otvetstvennost' v poriadke podchinennosti*). This applies to persons who have the right to hire and fire workers and are themselves appointed by higher authority, to persons publicly elected and to such responsible employees as chief engineers, chief accountants and specially listed other employees (the latest addition to this extensive list being various categories of employees of the Intourist Co. Ltd., such as directors, interpreters, translators, etc.). Such people may be punished by the superiors who have the right to appoint them, or even by a still higher authority. Punishments here are censure, reprimand, demotion to a lesser job for not more than a year, and dismissal. The aggrieved person may appeal within two weeks to the authority immediately above him, but he has no recourse to the KTS, to the Trade Union Committee or to the courts (Labour Code, art. 220). The employment or dismissal of these (usually higher) officials cannot be the subject of litigation.

Bibl.: Mary McAuley, Labour Disputes in Soviet Russia, 1969.

R. Beermann

See also LABOUR ARBITRATION; ADMINISTRATIVE OFFENCES; COURTS; CIVIL SERVICE

DISPLACED PERSONS

A term technically reserved for members of the civilian population of Allied countries forcibly removed from their lieu of domicile in areas occupied by the Axis powers in the course of World War II and transported to enemy-administered territory.

In 1945, the USSR concluded agreements with Great Britain, the United States, and France which provided for the organization of special camps to shelter Allied personnel liberated by their forces in expectation of their prompt repatriation. Representatives of the state whose citizens the inmates were enjoyed free access to these facilities and had "the right to appoint the internal management and establish the internal order and administration pursuant to the military regulations and legislation of their country". At the same time, a treaty was signed with Belgium in which the parties undertook to facilitate and hasten the mutual return of their respective citizens displaced as a consequence of the war and subsequently found within the other nation's jurisdiction. Clauses prescribing the concentration of displaced nationals of the Allied powers in separate centers and their maintenance at local expense while awaiting repatriation were likewise included in the armistice accords with Nazi Germany's European associates. Similar arrangements were later worked out between the USSR and Switzerland and Norway.

The bulk of displaced persons of Soviet origin (according to the pre-1939 definition) was repatriated *en masse* in the immediate post-war period, in principle on a voluntary basis, although cases of resort to coercion were occasionally reported then. The advent of the Cold War slowed down the movement, after 1948 Soviet repatriation missions were no longer allowed to operate in the Western occupation zones, and the core residue of camp inhabitants resisted the call to come home, so that other ways had to be devised to solve the problem as repatriation practically came to a stand-still. Nevertheless, the Soviet government has always insisted that repatriation offers the only acceptable answer to the whole DP question. It has continued to claim as its own citizens those among them who had been Soviet citizens on the eve of the German invasion of the USSR, rejecting the contention that they are now stateless persons by choice, and has formally protested the resettlement of these individuals in foreign lands without its prior consent. While the Soviet Union participated in the preparatory work which led to the creation of the International Refugee Organization, it refused to join that body or to cooperate either with it or the successor agencies on grounds that these institutions favored resettlement over repatriation and actively hindered the return of displaced persons to their home country.

In a nutshell, the Soviet position here has been that: the leaders of the various Russian emigré groups functioning in the West recruited from among DP elements are traitors, collaborators and war criminals who must be surrendered to the Soviet authorities for prosecution in connection with their wartime activities; the overwhelming majority of the ordinary DP's wish to go home, but are either deluded or pressured into applying for overseas emigration and the climate of oppression and misinformation to which they are subjected deprives them of all real freedom of choice; the Western powers rely on this contingent for a ready supply of cheap, virtually indentured, labour.

Since 1953, the Soviet authorities have waged a vigorous campaign to promote the repatriation of ex-Soviet citizens living abroad, most of them former displaced persons resettled by the I.R.O. or diverse national immigration programs. An amnesty was issued in 1955 which promised immunity from prosecution for lesser offences of an anti-Soviet nature committed during and after the war to enhance the appeal of the current "come home" drive and a worldwide effort has since been made to get increasing numbers of Russian emigrés to "return to the Motherland". These exertions have in recent years been crowned with moderate success.

George Ginsburgs

DISSOLUTION OF MARRIAGE

For history and sources see FAMILY LAW.
Divorce may be obtained at the Registry Office in the following cases: where spouses with no minor children both consent to divorce; or on the application of one of them if the other has been declared mentally incapable, imprisoned for at least three years, or declared missing without trace (Family Code, arts. 38-39). In this last case if he turns up the marriage revives unless the other has re-married (art. 42). In all these instances if there is any dispute over property, custody, alimony etc., divorce must take place in court.

Apart from the two exceptions above, the normal forum for dissolution of marriage is the people's court. It must first attempt to reconcile the couple. A husband may not petition for divorce in his wife is pregnant (the law does not say by whom) or within a year from the birth of a child, unless she consents (Family Code, art. 31).

To grant a decree the court must be satisfied that future life together would be impossible (art. 33). Decrees have been refused where the complaint was as to the wife's cooking; where marital lapses have been condoned; and where the petitioner pleaded his own adultery and rejected his wife's forgiveness. On the other hand, infertility, desertion and violence are widely accepted as a reason for ending a marriage.

At the hearing the court, if asked, makes orders dividing the matrimonial property and dealing with questions of custody; young children will usually be given to the mother. The state fee varies from 50 to 200 roubles and may be exacted from either party or, in any proportions, from both (arts. 34-37).

Either may retain the common surname or ask the divorcing agency to restore the former name (art. 41).

Nullity must be established in court at the suit of a spouse, the Procurator, or the Guardianship and Curatorship Agency. A decree does not affect the rights of children of the union. The grounds are: failure to fulfil the conditions for marriage, or intent to establish a sham marriage. Inability to consummate would be a ground for divorce, not nullity. The decree is retroactive and property acquired during the union is dealt with under the rules affecting civil co-ownership, not matrimonial property. If, however, one of the parties deceived the other into entering the union he may be ordered to pay alimony, and the matrimonial property regime prevails. An innocent party may keep the married name.

If, before the hearing, the grounds for nullity have disappeared the marriage may be held valid; such relations are not those of the civil law. See arts. 43-46 Family Code.

B. Rudden

DISTRICTS, see TERRITORIAL DIVISIONS; OBLAST'; RAION

DIVORCE, see DISSOLUTION OF MARRIAGE

DOCUMENTS

In a country where a predominance of the public sector is combined with a strong bureaucratic tradition, documents will of necessity occupy an important position. Soviet law has accordingly developed something like a theory of legal documents. Any piece of writing which is meant to affirm a fact, assert a right, or, in general, communicate information, may be regarded as a document. The definition is nowadays enlarged, so as to include photographs, films, various forms of sound registration, magnetic tapes, punchcards, etc.

Documents can conveniently be classified into official documents, issued by public officials or agencies, and private documents. In order to be admissible as legal evidence, private documents will often have to be drawn up in a special form; e.g. wills and various contracts must be drawn up by a notary (see NOTARIES).

There are a few general requirements which all documents have to satisfy; a document must bear the signature of the person who issues it, or who is entitled to sign for the agency issuing the document. A signature may be replaced by the imprint of a signature stamp, provided the person using the stamp has been duly authorized. Furthermore, official documents must bear a letterhead (*shtamp*) and a seal or stamp (*pechat'*), to be placed on the left of the signature. The letterhead will normally be printed, but may also be written. It is placed on the top left corner, or at the top of the document; it must indicate the ministry, department, sub-division, etc., to which the agency which issues the document is subordinate, and provides the necessary identification of the agency. Letterheads, seals, and stamps are produced in special enterprises; the foundation of such enterprises requires police permission. The production of special kinds of seals and stamps (such as those bearing the arms of the USSR or of Union republics) requires police permission in each separate instance.

The great number of official documents bearing various names is best divided into documents for more or less permanent and repeated use, and documents issued in order to achieve one specific result. The basic form for the first category is the testimonial (*udostoverenie*), an official document which confirms a factual or legal status (e.g. official position, job, marital status, military service). A testimonial cannot replace a passport (*q.v.*) or a document for which the notarial form is required. A document confirming a fact with legal consequences (e.g. a birth certificate, a certificate of copyright) is called a certificate (*svidetel'stvo*). Diplomas (*diplom*, issued to the bearer of an academic degree) and attestations (*attestat*, issued to persons who have completed general secondary education, and to holders of certain academic ranks) are special forms of certificates. The power of attorney (*doverennost'*) should also be mentioned as belonging to this class of documents. It is regulated by the Civil Code (arts. 64 ff.) and may also be issued by a private person.

Among the documents issued to achieve a specific result, the most important are the various documents providing the basis for executions (*q.v.*), such as the warrant of execution (*ispolnitel'nyi list*). Another example is the administrative "order" (*id.*), e.g. the "living quarters order", issued by local authorities, and entitling the receiver to be provided with housing. The general term employed for a (usually short) official document containing a specific bit of information about certain facts is *spravka* (information, declaration). A *spravka* will often be an excerpt from another document. Its issue must be registered by the agency issuing it; a copy should be kept by the agency.

Documents may be offered in evidence in civil and criminal proceedings (cf. art. 63 of the Code of Civil Procedure and arts. 87 and 88 of the Code of Criminal Procedure). Art. 177 of the Code of Civil Procedure provides a special procedure to be followed in case a document is contested.

A number of provisions of the Criminal Code deal with documents. Forgery of a testimonial (*udostoverenie*), or of seals, stamps, and letterheads, is the subject of art. 196; art. 175 deals with "official forgery": any kind of tampering by an official with official documents.

A duplicate of a document may be issued where the original is lost (and in some other cases) and must be marked accordingly (cf. arts. 274-281 of the Code of Civil Procedure). A duplicate has the same force as the original. Copies of documents, in order to have the same force as the original, must be certified by the agency which issues the original. Personal documents in such cases must be copied by a notary.

F. J. M. Feldbrugge

See also NEGOTIABLE INSTRUMENTS; EVIDENCE; FORGERY

DOMICILE AND RESIDENCE

The domicile of a person is defined as the place where he lives permanently or most of the time, art. 17 Civil Code RSFSR. This implies that the law recognises only one place as the domicile of a person. The citizen may freely choose his domicile, art. 10 Civil Code; husband and wife are independent in freely choosing various domiciles, art. 19 Family Code RSFSR. This, however, does not apply to certain urban centres e.g. Moscow, where settlement is only allowed with a special licence of the administrative housing authority. Moreover, by the sentence of a criminal court a person may be expelled from his domicile, or have assigned to him a special domicile or a special region within the boundaries of which he is forced to choose a domicile, art. 21 Criminal Code RSFSR.

Minors under the age of fifteen and persons under guardianship share the domicile of their parents, adoptive parents or guardians, irrespective of the fact that they actually live constantly at another place (compulsory domicile), art. 17 Civil Code.

The domicile of a juristic person is the place where the "permanently acting agency" of its administration is located, art. 30 Civil Code.

The domicile of a person is relevant to his legal relations in many respects. Thus the domicile of a debtor is the place of performance of his obligation unless provided otherwise by law or contract, art. 174 Civil Code. The domicile of the *de cuius* is the place of the opening of succession, art. 529 Civil Code. The local competence of a court for law suits against a person is usually determined by the domicile of the defendant, arts. 117, 118, 121 Code of Civil Procedure RSFSR. For the court proceedings on declaring a person an absentee or declaring him dead the court which has jurisdiction over the domicile of the petitioner initiating the proceedings is competent, art. 252 Code of Civil Procedure. The same is true for court proceedings aimed at establishing certain legal facts e.g. the fact of parental relations between persons, the fact of acceptance of an estate, arts. 247, 249 Code of Civil Procedure. For proceedings to deprive a person of legal capacity the court of the domicile of the person to be incapacitated is competent unless he lives in a psychiatric hospital; in the latter case the court of the location of the hospital is competent, art. 258 Code of Civil Procedure.

A. Hastrich

DOUBLE SUBORDINATION, see PUBLIC ADMINISTRATION

DRUGS, see NARCOTICS

DRUNKENNESS, see INTOXICATION

DRUZHINA, see PEOPLE'S GUARDS

DURESS

The Soviet legislation on duress in the field of civil law must be considered in the light of the fact that pressure on legal entities to influence their actions normally seems to be exerted not by contracting parties, but from above by the state organs entrusted with directive or planning power. Due to the difference in outlook and legal treatment, however, these latter phenomena form part of the administrative system and are, in case of excess of powers, subject to administrative sanctions. The more rigorous rules on duress laid down in art. 58 Civil Code therefore normally apply only between citizens.

Duress is defined as the infliction or threatened infliction of physical or mental pain by a contracting party (or potential party) or person taking a benefit under a legal transaction, in order to influence the outcome of the transaction in his favour; duress never includes acts, however painful they may be to the victim, which the threatening party is legally entitled to do (e.g. to claim the execution of a judgment). The victim of the act may be the party himself or somebody close to him (e.g. a relative). The act by means of which duress is exercised is often of such a nature that it gives rise to criminal sanctions apart from the civil law consequences.

In the instances mentioned so far, the other party provokes the transaction and intends to profit from it as well. Related are transactions dictated by need (e.g. the conclusion of a sale at a price well below the market level) where, however, the other party is not, or is only distantly, responsible for the facts giving rise to the transaction, but profits from his superior position in the circumstances.

This form of constraint is often referred to as *kabal'naia sdelka* or "serf's contract". It belongs to the rather few concepts of civil law which are really charged with strong ideological and political associations. On this point, a slight but important change in wording can be noted between the new Civil Code and the Code of 1922: the reference to the "utter need" of the acting party has been exchanged for "concurrence of adverse circumstances".

The former situation might possibly have existed during the NEP-period, according to present-day Soviet commentators, but by definition cannot occur in a developed socialist community, free, as it is, from exploitation and exploited classes. The concept has thus been "modernized" to fulfil somewhat different functions and the term "serf's contract" is no longer used in the statutory texts although it still appears in literature. Yet a certain reluctance can be detected—mainly for political and ideological reasons—even of admitting that cases of the kind suggested by the new formula can occur in to-day's society.

These various types of duress are treated in art. 58 Civil Code, together with fraud, abuse of confidence and severe distress. On proof of such circumstances, the legal transaction can be declared void by the court, provided there is sufficient causation between the exertion of the duress and the transaction in question; either the injured party or a socialist organization can bring the action.

When a legal transaction is declared void on account of duress, whatever has been transferred to the party at fault must be returned in kind, or, if that is no longer possible, compensation in money must be paid. What has been received in exchange (or its value) by the injured party is surrendered to the state (this is known as one-sided restitution). Furthermore, the injured party has the right to recover damages from the party responsible for the duress.

A. Ådahl

ECONOMIC LAW

In the wake of the decisions of the 21st Party Congress in 1959 with regard to economic problems, a number of lawyers (practising lawyers from the State Arbitration as well as scholars) have put forward the theory of the independence of economic law as a legal discipline. The task of economic law, according to them, is the regulation of relations arising from economic activities. The independence of e.l. is based on historical, theoretical and practical grounds. The history of Soviet civil law shows that the task of the Civil Code of 1922 was the regulation of relations between citizens, and between citizens and economic organizations; it does not deal with questions concerning the relations between socialist economic organizations.

From a theoretical point of view economic law can easily be distinguished both from civil law and from administrative law. E.l. concerns both "horizontal" relations between enterprises (which are essentially different from the property relations between citizens arising from civil law) and "vertical" relations between enterprises and economic organizations, and the economic administration. It regulates the organization and structure of the economic administration and of socialist economic activities (planning, economic contracts, financial supervision, credit, accounting, State Arbitration). The similarity between particular institutions of civil law and e.l. (e.g. contracts) is not more than an outward analogy. It is considered necessary to codify e.l.

From a practical point of view lawyers from the State Arbitration and legal advisers from the economic administration are well disposed towards the theory of e.l. The arbitration lawyers complain about the difficulties in solving disputes referred to them; traditional civil law does not offer solutions to the problems raised by the present development of the economy (growing autonomy of enterprises, efforts to improve the assortment and quality of products). The second group of lawyers stress that the works of reference published for the benefit of practising lawyers cannot fill the gap caused by the absence of a real codification; at any rate, from their point of view, e.l. has existed unofficially for a long time.

The principal spokesman in recent times for the theory of e.l. has been V.V. Laptev (of the Institute of State and Law of the Academy of Sciences). From its beginning this theory has been under attack by civil law theoreticians, in particular S. N. Bratus (director of the All-Union Institute of Legal Science attached to the Council of Ministers). The latter deny the unity of horizontal and vertical economic relations and thereby the entire basis of e.l.; the contract, which forms the foundation of horizontal relations, may be entirely regulated by civil law, whether it relates to relations between enterprises or relations between citizens. From a practical point of view they propose to publish complete works covering all the legal elements of economic activities, including those originating not only in civil law, but also in labour law, financial law, land law etc.

This discussion assumed wide proportions during the elaboration of the Principles of Civil Legislation of the USSR and the Union Republics, promulgated on December 8, 1961. It had been proposed by some to give a special place in these Principles to provisions which applied to economic organizations. However, the final solution was entirely hostile to the whole concept of e.l. The triumphant point of view of the All-Union Institute of Legal Sciences reduced the views of the partisans of the independence of e.l. for several years to a purely academic discussion.

Only the economic reforms of 1965 have made a reopening of the debate possible. The same arguments that were used several years ago were again put forward; the position of e.l. was strengthened by the elaboration of a special code of e.l. in Czechoslovakia; numerous Soviet civil law specialists insisted on the necessity of adapting the civil law to new economic conditions. V. V. Laptev (appointed chief of the e.l. sector in the Institute of State and Law) heads a team which is striving for the legislative implementation of the independence of e.l. after it has been recognized on the level of legal doctrine.

P. Lavigne

ECONOMIC OFFENCES

The twenty-odd economic offences defined in the sixth chapter of the special part of the Criminal Code present a great variety of actions infringing the economic interests of the Soviet state; some of the more important economic offences will be discussed separately under special headings (e.g. SPECULATION). The remainder may conveniently be divided into three categories: the professional (i.e. more or less full-time) exercise of forbidden economic activities, forbidden activities in regard to agriculture and natural resources, and other forbidden economic activities.

The first group consists of the offences covered by arts. 153, 154 and 162. Art. 153 embraces the activities of private entrepreneurs and commercial middlemen. Private entrepreneurial activity involving the use of state, cooperative, or other social forms, entails deprivation of freedom for a term not exceeding five years. It is essential in this case that the offender operated under the pretence of being or representing a socialist (state, cooperative, or social), and therefore legal, organization. One and the same action may be covered by art. 153 and one of the provisions concerning theft (*q.v.*) in cases where the offender misappropriated socialist property in the course of his entrepreneurial activities; also, the offence of art. 153, committed by an official in the exercise of his duties, will additionally constitute an official crime (*q.v.*); see also MULTIPLE OFFENCES. The provision itself does not indicate what should be understood by private entrepreneurial activities; elsewhere it is described as the execution of any work or the supplying of any service against a material compensation (see also PRIVATE ENTERPRISE).

Activities of commercial middlemen, the subject of the second paragraph of art. 153, are likewise not defined. According to textbooks, the scope of this provision is enormous; it covers, for instance, helping somebody for a reward to acquire goods (e.g. by selling a place in a queue, or by selling information of a commercial nature). It also covers similar activities by private individuals for the benefit of socialist organizations (e.g. the activities of operators whose task it is to buy materials or spare parts, or to sell the finished product outside the regular channels). The activities of commercial middlemen will be punished under art. 153 par. 2 if they have been committed regularly ("as a business") or for private gain. The maximum penalty is three years.

The simple provision of art. 162 (exercise of a forbidden profession) deeply affects the entire social and economic life of the Soviet Union. The chief list of forbidden professions is contained in the Rules for the Registration of Individual Trades- and Craftsmen (decree of the USSR Council of Ministers of June 30, 1949). These rules mention a great variety of businesses and professions (such as the production of chemicals, any kind of polygraphical activity); they also include any business in which hired labour or apprentices are employed. Other, and more detailed, rules draw very fine lines between what is and what is not a forbidden profession; e.g. the production and sale of lampshades by individual craftsmen is allowed except in the cities of Moscow and Leningrad, while repairing TV-sets by individual craftsmen is allowed only in rural areas, and the professional production of foodstuffs is forbidden altogether.

The exercise of a forbidden profession entails an administrative penalty, in more serious cases corrective labour not exceeding one year, and in the most serious cases (in the case of employment of hired labour, or of recidivism, or in view of the large scale of the offence) deprivation of freedom not exceeding four years (see PRIVATE ENTERPRISE).

Buying and selling for a profit, as the basic business of commerce, is made into a separate offence in the USSR (see SPECULATION).

Professional activities connected with agriculture and natural resources are mentioned in arts. 154-1 (buying of grain products for feeding animals), 160 (violation of veterinary rules), 161 (violation of rules for fighting plant diseases and pests), 163 and 164 (illicit fishing, see FISHING), 165 (violation of certain rules for the protection of fishes), 166 (illicit hunting, see HUNTING), 167 (violation of mining rules, see MINES, MINERALS, & MINING), 168 (damaging crops or plantations) and 169 (illicit felling of timber).

Other forbidden activities include the issuing or selling of low-quality, non-standard or incomplete products (art. 152 and art. 157), distortions of accounts concerning plan fulfilment (art. 152-1, see FRAUD), small-scale selling, buying or changing of foreign currency (art. 154-2, see CURRENCY SPECULATION), illicit use of trade marks (art. 155, see TRADEMARKS), defrauding customers (art. 156, see FRAUD), the illicit making, suplying, or storing of alcoholic beverages (art. 158, see INTOXICATION) and counterfeiting postal valuables or transportation tickets (art. 159, see COUNTERFEITING).

F. J. M. Feldbrugge

EDUCATION (see also *Appendix*)

Most forms of education in the Soviet Union are within the competence of the USSR Ministry of Education, with the exception of universities and some other special schools which are entrusted to the USSR Ministry of Higher and secondary Special Education, and professional-technical schools which are entrusted to the State Committee for Professional-Technical Education attached to the Council of Ministers of the USSR.

Until 1966, when the USSR Ministry of Education was formed (Regulations enacted by the USSR Council of Ministers on January 7, 1969), education was considered an affair of the individual Union republic, in the care of the Union republican ministries of education. At present the accent is still on the Union republic; most enactments in the sphere of education originate from various bodies at the level of the Union republic. The tasks and competence of the RSFSR Ministry of Education are defined in its regulations enacted by the RSFSR Council of Ministers of December 11, 1959. At the provincial (*oblast'*) and lower levels there are educational departments within the executive committees, subordinate (according to the general principle of double subordination) to local authorities and to the ministry of education.

Educational research with regard to general education is entrusted to the Academy of Pedagogical Sciences of the RSFSR which is attached to the RSFSR Ministry of Education.

The first form or organized education a Soviet citizen comes in contact with is the creche/kindergarten. Basic rules concerning these institutions are contained in the Temporary Regulations on Pre-School Children's Institutions-Creches/Kindergartens, enacted by decree of the RSFSR Council of Ministers on March 8, 1960. These institutions cater for children of from two months up to seven years. Parents of children attending creches/

kindergartens have to pay a fixed fee, depending on the length of the daily stay of the child in the institution.

From the age of seven until they are fifteen or sixteen, children attend the primary school, called "eight years' school" in the Soviet Union. In small places there may be only a "beginners' school" (*nachal'naia shkola*), covering the first four years of the primary school. Regulations on the Eight Years' School were enacted by the RSFSR Council of Ministers on December 29, 1959. Primary schools are designated to a certain district, and all children within the district must attend the district school. In areas with a linguistically mixed population there may be several schools (since teaching is in the child's mother tongue) and consequently the parents will have a choice of schools in such cases.

Local authorities provide hot meals at school, and, if necessary, transportation to and from school.

The curriculum and programme of the primary school are determined by the RSFSR Ministry of Education; the day-to-day running of the school is the task of the director of the school. Important questions are discussed and decided by the school council, consisting of the director, some of the teachers, and some other officials (such as the school doctor). Each school has a parents' council with advisory capacities.

Upon completion of the eight years' school, children start work in agriculture or industry, which may be combined with further schooling in the evening or through correspondence courses, or continue their education in various other types of schools. There are two main types of school offering further general (secondary) education: the evening (seasonal) secondary general school, and the secondary general polytechnical school.

A decree of the RSFSR Council of Ministers of December 29, 1959, contains the Regulations on the Evening or Seasonal Secondary General Schools. This school provides continued general education during three years for children who have completed the eight years' school and who have started to work (the seasonal school is designed for pupils who, because of the nature of their work, are able to attend a day school for a part of the year). Along with general subjects, special professional and technical subjects are optional in this type of school. Completion of the evening general school course gives the right to seek admittance to institutions of higher education. Tuition in evening and seasonal general schools is free.

Regulations on Secondary General Polytechnical Schools were enacted on the same day. The purpose of these schools is also to provide further general education, but along with this they offer programmes preparing pupils for a number of specific technical jobs. A full course in a general polytechnical school takes a minimum of two years, depending on the specialty chosen by the pupil. The final part of the course usually involves practical work; for this purpose many of these schools have permanent connections with local enterprises. General polytechnical schools are day schools; tuition is free. Completion of a general polytechnical school course gives the pupil the right to seek admittance to institutions of higher education; general polytechnical schools may be attached to primary schools.

A more marked attempt to create something like a comprehensive school is the promotion of boarding schools, which has taken place since the RSFSR Council of Ministers enacted the Regulations on Boarding Schools (April 13, 1957). These schools offer a ten-year course which incorporates primary and secondary education. The parents pay a fee, depending on their income. Some categories of children (orphans, etc.) are admitted free.

The above-mentioned schools, notwithstanding a certain orientation towards professional training, are considered to be institutions of general education in the Soviet Union. Professional training in the strict sense is not the responsibility of the ministries of education, but of the State Committee for Professional-Technical Education and the corresponding committees at the level of the Union republics. There are two main types of professional schools: professional-technical schools and technical schools. The former category (governed by regulations enacted by the RSFSR Council of Ministers on May 31, 1961) is open to pupils who have completed the primary school course. The professional-technical schools have a permanent connection with one or more local enterprises, and offer courses of from one to three years, leading to the necessary qualifications for jobs in agriculture and industry. A large part of the training consists of practical work. Tuition is free, but admittance is restricted. The local agencies for professional-technical education determine the number of students to be admitted to the various departments of the professional-technical schools. There are also professional-technical schools with evening or seasonal courses (regulations of March 20, 1962).

Technical education at a higher level is offered by the technical schools (regulations of December 27, 1966) which are open to students who have completed general secondary education. Otherwise the organization of technical schools is similar to that of the professional-technical schools.

Other forms of professional education are provided by a host of other schools, called secondary special schools, governed by regulations of March 1, 1961. These schools (organized as day schools or as evening courses) provide education and training for a great number of professions of middle echelon specialists. The management of enterprises must enable workers and employees following courses in professional schools to combine work and study (art. 187 Labour Code).

In the RSFSR and a few other republics, the secondary special schools are subordinate to the ministry of higher and secondary special education of the Union republic. In other republics again there is no such ministry, and the ministry of education is competent.

For higher education, see UNIVERSITIES.

On December 24, 1958 the USSR Supreme Soviet passed the Law on Strengthening the Ties between the School and Life; to some extent this law may be considered the basic law of Soviet education. Its professed aim was to check the growth of day schools for young people, redirecting thereby a stream of young workers to the national economy. On the basis of this law the Union republics enacted their own "school and life" laws (April 16, 1959, in the RSFSR) and a host of other regulations and decrees. The act inaugurated a campaign of glorification of manual labour which did not altogether yield the expected results. Industry was flooded in some cases with totally inexperienced and uninterested young workers and the training of badly needed specialists was delayed by the number of years they had to spend in factories.

F. J. M. Feldbrugge

ELECTIONS

The Constitution of the RSFSR of 1918 and the first USSR Constitution of 1924 adopted a form of unequal and indirect representation which was advantageous to the working proletariat. The designation of supreme deliberating bodies rested with the hierarchical, pyramidal organization of the soviets. Only town and village soviets were directly elected by the electorate. All higher soviets, up to the Congress of Soviets of the USSR, were elected indirectly. The right to vote and to be elected were regulated by the constitution of the RSFSR of July 10, 1918; citizens of both sexes were able to vote and to be elected at the age of eighteen, but several categories of persons were excluded: merchants, employers and clergymen, among others.

The Constitution of December 5, 1936, has both extended the right to vote, and to some extent restricted the right to be elected. The right to take part in elections has been granted very largely according to art. 135 of the Constitution. All citizens of the USSR who have reached the age of eighteen years, independent of their ethnic or national origin, their sex, religion, education, residence, social origin, material situation, or past activities, have the right to take part in the election of deputies, with the exception of persons who have been deprived of this right through a procedure established by law. Although the Constitution makes no mention of it, it is taken for granted and generally practised that those serving prison sentences and, generally speaking, all those who have been deprived of their freedom cannot exercise the right to vote. All persons entitled to vote are eligible for membership of the Supreme Soviet, with the additional condition that they have reached the age of twenty-three years.

The details of the electoral system have been worked out by a Law of January 9, 1950, on the elections for the Supreme Soviet of the USSR (most recently amended December 27, 1961).

Art. 1 of the Law repeats the provision of art. 136 of the Constitution which provides that the right to vote shall be universal and equal, and that elections shall be direct and secret. Art. 9 adds that resident aliens of the USSR may not vote and may not be elected. The equal right to vote (art. 4 of the Law of 1950) means that each citizen has one vote. In order to vote it is necessary to be registered in the electoral register. It is forbidden to be registered more than once. The register is kept by the executive committees of the *raion* soviets (urban or rural) for each electoral section. The register contains in alphabetical order the names of all voters. The list is posted in a public place, or otherwise made available for general inspection at least thirty days before the election day. In case of disagreement complaints are heard by the people's court. A person who changes his address receives a certification which must be produced at his new place of residence in order to be registered as a voter.

In all elections, for local soviets as well as for the Supreme Soviet, the rule is voting according to electoral district, as provided by art. 141 of the Constitution and art. 10 of the Law of 1950: "Candidates are nominated by electoral districts". As a rule (and in the case of elections for the Supreme Soviet, without any exception) the list contains a single name.

The territory of oblasts and towns which are part of electoral districts, are divided into electoral sections. Usually a section contains from about 500 to 3000 inhabitants, but in remote and inaccessible parts of the country a section may contain no more than 50 persons. Everything is done to facilitate voting; sections may be set up in hospitals, hostels, maternity hospitals, sanatoriums, ships, passenger trains, railway stations, airports; for the military, sections may correspond to military units.

On the election day (always a Sunday) the voting bureau consists of three members of the electoral commission of the section. The voter presents some identification document, a member of the bureau checks his name on the list and gives him the ballot paper (or papers). The voter passes through a room or a box where he will find a table and pencils, enabling him to fill in the ballot paper. The paper is filled in by deleting the names of candidates for whom the voter does not want to vote. Since there is in fact only one name on the paper (in the case of elections for the Supreme Soviet), the voter has only the choice between voting for or against the only candidate. The ballot paper is folded once and dropped into the ballot box by the voter.

In effect the most important phase of the Soviet electoral system is the designation of candidates. According to art. 135 paragraph 2 of the Constitution, every Soviet citizen who has the right to vote and has reached the age of 23 years may legally be a candidate for the Supreme Soviet. However, the existence of only one party in fact results in single candidacies in every district. The candidate need not necessarily be a member of the Communist Party and is as a rule not proposed by the Party, but has at least the Party's approval which is implied in the procedure by which the candidates are selected. According to art. 141 of the Constitution the names of candidates are proposed by electoral district. The right to propose candidates is given to social organizations and associations of workers: organizations of the Communist Party, trade unions, cooperatives, youth organizations, cultural societies. The unity of all these organizations is evident; a resolution of the Communist Party of January 22, 1957, concerning the strengthening of the ties between the soviets and the masses, stresses the inadmissibility of any kind of haste in the proposing of candidates, and recommends preparatory discussions during meetings of workers and kolkhoz-farmers, in order to bring out a general consensus and, consequently, to propose a single candidate to the general meeting. Theoretically therefore the name of a candidate is mentioned during a meeting of workers who discuss the candidate and may put forward other names; finally the meeting reaches an agreement about one candidate. This proposal is then put up against other proposals, and every organization may register a candidate with the electoral commission of the district, with the permission of the candidate.

If every candidate who has been proposed accepts his selection in the district of his choice, there must be not only some coordination after the proposals have been made, but obviously also some amount of coordination in making the proposals. Only the most prominent political personalities will be proposed by several organizations simultaneously, but it is still necessary to avoid any kind of plebiscite among all the districts in this case. Certain districts such as Moscow or Leningrad traditionally command greater prestige in the elections for the Supreme Soviet and can propose important personalities in the knowledge that one of the candidates will be available. Coordination of the candidacies at the top of the party is therefore indispensable, and must even be preceded by coordinated suggestions. But it is equally certain that the same procedure will have to be followed for all electoral districts, either by central federal party agencies for the Soviet of the Union, or by central federal or republican party agencies for the Soviet of the Nationalities. All candidates, whether they are party members or not, must not only have the blessing of the Party, but must also have been proposed by higher party agencies within the framework of a general plan for popular representation in the Supreme Soviet.

The will of the masses of voters manifests itself in this way in the collective agreement given to the suggestions from the top which are translated into proposals from the bottom. Administrative authorities do not intervene as such in this process, but Party authorities directly inspire every move to propose a candidate.

Furthermore, while it is conceivable that more than one candidate would figure in an election for a local soviet, this is not the case with elections for the Supreme Soviet because of the relatively small number of seats to be occupied, and the difficulties that would arise if, in this case, one candidate was beaten by another in a district (although this contingency is provided for in the electoral law).

Under these conditions the game seems to be over when the proposals are made, and the "election campaign" has as its aim the display of a rigorous legal procedure according to which the electoral process takes place, and the massive support of the entire Soviet electorate for the candidates who have been proposed.

The electoral process is governed by a slow and rather complex procedure before it comes to election day. Approximately three months in advance, a decree of the Presidium of the Supreme Soviet fixes the date of the elections.

The first phase in the procedure is the institution of electoral commissions: one for the Soviet Union, one for each district and one for each electoral section. Commission members may not be candidates. The central electoral commission fixes a number of rules: the lay-out of ballot papers, the shape of ballot boxes and model statements for the registration of candidates and for the emptying of ballot boxes; the commission has an administrative, as well as a judicial function; it serves as the central point for the counting of votes, it deals with complaints, and it publishes the results.

The second phase is concerned with the proposing and selection of candidates. The electoral operation takes place at two levels; at the administrative level the electoral commissions of districts and sections put into effect the directives of the central electoral commission; at the political level the "electoral campaign" is started. This is a campaign in which press, radio and television engage, celebrating the choice of "the best representatives of the people", and providing a suitable occasion to publicize the principles of the Communist Party and the chief themes of the government's policy, a moment for demonstrating the important individual and social types which serve as models for the Soviet citizen, and an affirmation of the solidarity of the peoples of the Soviet Union. It constitutes a privileged opportunity for a political shake-up of the citizenry in an atmosphere of feverish activity culminating in election day.

When the polls are closed the electoral commission opens the ballot boxes and begins to empty them in the presence of special representatives of social organizations, workers' associations, and the press, who have been admitted by the chairman. A statement is drawn up, and sent to the district electoral commission, together with the ballot papers and eventual complaints (with an indication of the measures taken); the district commission publishes the results, issues a certificate to the candidate who has been declared elected, and transfers the statement to the central electoral commission of the Union.

According to chapter VIII of the electoral Law of January 9, 1950, the candidate who has obtained the majority of the votes is elected. The Soviet system can be characterized as a majority system, organized as a ballot in two rounds. If no candidate obtains a majority of the votes, or if the number of votes is smaller than one half of the number of registered voters, there will be a second round after a short period not exceeding two weeks. In the former case the voting will be between the two candidates who have obtained the greatest number of votes in the first round. However, nothing of the sort has ever happened since 1936; all results have always been reached in the first round with majorities numbering around 99% of the votes and the voters.

If for any reason a deputy ceases to exercise his functions, the Presidium of the Supreme Soviet of the USSR (according to art. 108 of the Law of January 9, 1950) organizes new elections within two months in the district concerned.

P. Lavigne

See also DEMOCRACY; DEPUTIES; SUPREME SOVIET

EMBEZZLEMENT, see THEFT

EMERGENCIES, see WAR, STATE OF

EMIGRATION AND IMMIGRATION
(see also *Appendix*)
Entry into and exit from the USSR requires in each case a special permission of the competent authorities. An individual desiring to emigrate to the Soviet Union must first obtain a visa from a Soviet embassy, mission, consulate or diplomatic representative in his passport or corresponding documents. Entry into or exit from the USSR, whether by an alien or a citizen, without prior official sanction constitutes a criminal offence punishable by deprivation of freedom for a period of from one to three years.

The process of immigration to and emigration from the USSR has always been subject to tight control on the part of the government and in normal times the number of people involved in the two-way traffic has been minimal. In 1966, Premier Kosygin publicly declared that the Soviet government would raise no obstacles in the way of reunification of families separated by the Second World War, even if this meant allowing people to leave the USSR, but the assurance has yet to find expression in measures aimed at the practical liberalization of the regime's emigration policies. True, during the last few years a growing number of exit visas has been issued by the Soviet authorities and a steady trickle of individuals has been allowed to go abroad and the rules on entry into the USSR have also been relaxed somewhat. So far, however, such steps have produced only minor concessions and have introduced no real changes for the better in the established *modus operandi*.

Indeed, the current exodus of Jews from the USSR to Israel has led to the adoption of new restrictive administrative practices calculated to curb the flow of departures, intimidate potential applicants for exit permits, or bar the emigration of certain individuals whose qualifications are considered too valuable by the authorities to risk losing their services. These measures have included the use of *kharakteristika's* as a means of exerting social pressure on persons desiring to leave the country for Israel, adherence to the requirement that the petitioner first formally relinquish his Soviet citizenship and pay a 500-rouble fee for the privilege of so doing, the imposition of an exorbitant surtax on those seeking an emigration visa justified as indemnification owed to the state for the cost of their education and professional training, and, reportedly, the recent introduction of a demand that the *de cujus* sign a special statement confirming that, in renouncing Soviet citizenship and going to Israel, he is acting in the full knowledge that Soviet citizenship will not at any future date be restored to him. The extra warning is apparently aimed at influencing the more timid members of the Soviet Jewish community by evoking the spectre of a total severance of ties between themselves and the Motherland and underscoring the irreversible nature of their decision to emigrate, although in fact the rule is not absolutely enforced and a tiny number of individuals who moved from the USSR to Israel have sought to return and some of them have since been granted the right to repatriate.

In addition, the Soviet government has on several occasions through the medium of international treaties or *ad hoc* domestic legislation suspended the operation of the standard regulations vis-à-vis specific categories of individuals, thus licensing the application thereto of simplified procedures of immigration or emigration. For example, two decrees promulgated in 1944 recognized the right of Soviet citizens of Polish extraction in the service of the Polish army in the USSR or associated with its activities, and members of their families, to transfer to Polish nationality. In similar vein, decree No. 142/41 of August 30, 1956, made it possible for persons of Spanish nationality domiciled in the USSR since 1936-1940 to depart for Spain for permanent residence. A new campaign for the mass repatriation of Armenians from abroad was launched after World War II and recently stepped up again which resulted in thousands of Armenian expatriates "returning home" to Soviet Armenia. The restitution of Soviet citizenship to emigré colonies in various foreign countries in the 1946-1948 period ensued in the repatriation of many of them and since Stalin's death a fresh effort has been made to convince Russian emigré elements in the West to come back, with promises of amnesty, employment and aid in resettling. Coincidentally, the Russians shipped back to their own country the bulk of Axis war prisoners and civilian internees hitherto detained in the USSR. In 1955, Soviet authorities repatriated several thousand more German citizens to both East and West Germany, in 1956 a group of Japanese was released and that same year the Soviet Union and Poland conducted the evacuation from the USSR of a large contingent of Poles with family in Poland. Finally, in a series of joint communiqués adopted in 1956-1957 with East and West Germany, Belgium, Sweden, Austria and Italy, the respective parties pledged favorable consideration of applications for exit permits from citizens or ex-citizens of the other side domiciled on their soil.

The use of option and option-like techniques in connection with various territorial adjustments along the USSR's western frontiers during and after the Second World War also presented selective opportunities for accelerated emigration and immigration to particular classes of individuals. The sundry agreements negotiated with Nazi Germany in 1939-1940 guaranteed the right of *Reich* nationals and other persons of German descent residing in areas freshly incorporated into the USSR to migrate to territory under German administration and of persons of Ukrainian, Russian, Belorussian and Lithuanian descent located in territories acquired by Germany to transfer to the Soviet Union. After the war, corresponding arrangements were made with Poland and Czechoslovakia, involving option and resettlement based on voluntary choice, accompanied by a mass organized exchange of populations between the USSR and each of these countries with attendant revisions in the citizenship status of the participants. In these instances, the objective was, of course, to eliminate certain alien minorities and resolve potential citizenship conflicts stemming from territorial succession by offering the subject individuals the right of free departure within a set time-limit.

In this way special immigration and emigration projects both serve a definite political purpose, whether it be to consolidate Soviet control over newly won land by inviting the local residents to leave if they prefer or, alternately, to stay and identify their interests with those of the current order, or to disrupt exile opposition to the Soviet regime by promoting defections within its ranks through appeals to "return to the Motherland". But even in the ordinary course of events, exaggerated notions of national security have rendered immigration to and emigration from the USSR an extremely difficult enterprise, functioning under strict and constant supervision at the highest levels.

George Ginsburgs

See also ALIENS; DISPLACED PERSONS; ASYLUM

EMPLOYEE PROTECTION

Employee protection or safety of labour has two aspects:

1) working conditions: see HOURS; WO-

MEN; YOUNG EMPLOYEES;
2) safety and safety rules.
Safety rules have to be used in the projecting and construction of plants, new equipment etc. These rules are laid down in:
sanitary norms for the protection of industrial plants (State Committee for Building, decision of June 5, 1963); sanitary norms for the organisation of technological processes and sanitary requirements for new equipment (Sanitary Service; decision of November 22, 1963); standard rules for employee protection for the different branches of industry; special rules apply to plants built in series.
These rules are enforced by:
1) the Preventive Sanitary Industrial Control Inspectorate (Instruction of the Federal State Sanitary Inspectorate of 1950);
2) the State Acceptance Board (in the established procedure for accepting a new plant, etc., decision of the Council of Ministers of the USSR of January 22, 1966; decisions of the State Committee for Building of the USSR). The sanitary inspectorate, the safety inspectorate of the union and the factory committee (see UNIONS) are among the members of these boards and they have the right to suspend the putting into operation of every new plant (art. 141 Labour Code RSFSR).
For plants in operation the basic powers are laid down in the labour codes, while specific rules are issued by the government and other state agencies together with the unions. Within the plant the manager has to take necessary measures to eliminate unhealthy working conditions, to prevent accidents and to maintain a proper sanitary and hygienic state. Current measures for employee protection are provided in agreements between management and union (art. 62 Principles of Labour Law, art. 147 Labour Code RSFSR). For workers acting in unhealthy conditions, special rules provide for clothing and soap, and for special milk or food, etc. In some trades or for specially unhealthy or heavy work, medical examinations are obligatory. On the basis of a medical report, a worker must be transferred to less heavy work with, however, a wage guarantee of only two weeks' average earnings unless the transfer was caused by an industrial accident or a professional disease.
Several state and union inspectorates control the observance of the safety rules in the enterprises:
1) the USSR Committee for the ensuring of safe working in industry and for the control of the mines (*Gosgortekhnadzor*) with local agencies and specialised inspectorates (cf. the statute on this committee: decision of the Council of Ministers of the USSR of February 1, 1968).
2) the State Sanitary Inspectorate of the USSR (cf. the statute on this committee: decree of the Council of Ministers of the USSR of May 31, 1973);
3) the Technical Inspectorate of the Unions, formed after the merger of the People's Commissariat of Labour and ACCTU (see UNIONS) in 1933. These inspectorates are formed at each union central committee and at each union council (at Union republic level). The professional technical inspectorate keeps in close contact with the enterprise's union officials, and with the unions' boards for employee protection and voluntary inspectors in the different shops. The inspectorates are assisted by inspectors who are not on the staff but have nearly the same powers as the professional inspectors (the Statute on the Technical Inspectorate of the Trade Unions, decision of ACCTU of August 26, 1966 with amendments; art. 104 Principles Labour Law.)
4) the unions' medical services.
These bodies have the right to enter any enterprise within their jurisdiction, ask the management for the necessary information, issue orders to the management enjoining them to eliminate deviations from established standards, etc. The state inspectorates and

the union inspectorate may suspend the operation of the enterprise and they may impose fines on employees from 10 tot 50 roubles, the amount depending on the higher or lower rank of the inspectorate and the rank of the employee, or they may require the employer to discharge an official or to take disciplinary measures (see DISCIPLINARY LAW).
On the basis of art. 140 Criminal Code of the RSFSR, the Procuracy may prosecute officials for deviations from the established rules which have entailed or could have entailed grave consequences.
Little is known of the observance in practice of the safety standards; and rates of industrial accidents are not published.

Industrial injuries
For injuries arising out of and related to employment (with the usual extensions), employees are paid allowances on the basis of the SOCIAL INSURANCE schemes. In the case of temporary disability full wages are paid, and in the case of permanent or prolonged disability payment depends on the degree of disability: invalids of group I (totally disabled) receive past earnings up to the amount of 50 roubles and 10% of earnings over 50 roubles; invalids of the 2 other groups receive lower amounts. The fact of the disability and the relevant group are ascertained by special boards (the medical labour expertise board, VTEK, (Statute of March 11, 1963), consisting of three medical doctors and representatives of the social security agencies and the unions).
The amount the employee does not receive under the social insurance scheme and his other losses may be recovered from the enterprise (his employer) but only if his injury or the deterioration in his health is caused by a breach of the safety rules by the employer or one of his employees and only if the injury is connected with the work (with some extensions). After the decision of the social insurance office concerning the social insurance award, the manager has to decide on the question of further damages within 10 days; the employee may appeal against this decision to the Union committee of the enterprise and, if he is not satisfied with the decision of the latter, he may bring proceedings in the ordinary courts (art. 460 Civil code of the RSFSR; Rules for the compensation by enterprises, institutions and organisations for damage caused to the health of an employee in connection with his employment, of December 22, 1961).

G. P. van den Berg

EMPLOYMENT, CONTRACT OF
The Principles of Labour Law of 1970 (see LABOUR LAW) prohibit, on the basis of arts. 122 and 123 of the Constitution of the USSR, every direct or indirect restriction of the rights, and the establishment of any direct or indirect advantages for applicants to a job, which are based on sex, age, nationality or religion. In the supervision practice of the PROCURACY (*q.v.*), these prohibitions are used also as bases of procuratorial protests against any restriction imposed upon the employee's freedom to choose a job (e.g. rules prohibiting employers to hire people living in other towns or above a certain age or without a special diploma, etc.) unless otherwise provided by provisions enacted by the Supreme Soviets, or their Presidia or by the Council of Ministers of the USSR. (Such exceptions are: persons who may not be employed in a specific function on the basis of a court decision; persons convicted for theft etc. may not be employed in trade; near relatives may not be employed in one enterprise or institution; for certain jobs diplomas are required). Any refusal to employ an applicant without sufficient reason is prohibited (art. 9 Principles), especially refusal to employ him owing to motives like having a criminal record, his social origin or the like.

Application
Application forms are not generally in use due to the regulations on labour books and the internal passport system (see PASSPORTS). Every applicant has to present his labour book or, if it is his first employment, a document written by the administration of his dwelling or by the local village soviet, and his passport, if he possesses such a document. The labour book contains personal and biographical information, information on the education and training of the applicant and details of his previous employment (dates of hiring, transfer and the date of and reasons for dismissal, rewards etc.). Disciplinary penalties and criminal sentences may not be mentioned, however, though the reasons for the dismissal, periods of corrective labour and deprivation of liberty are listed in the books, as they form essential data for accounting the length and continuity of one's service which are the basis of the social insurance system. After engagement, the books are kept by the enterprise, to be returned only after discharge (Decision of the Council of People's Commissars of December 20, 1938; Instructions on the handling of labour books, decisions of the State Committee for Labour and Wages, taken in agreement with the All-Union Central Council of Trade Unions (ACCTU) (see: TRADE UNIONS) of July 9, 1958, with amendments). The enterprise may not require the applicant to hand over other documents (decision of the CC CPSU and the Council of Ministers of the USSR of February 25, 1960) except certain certificates, if this is required by law (doctors etc.), and employers may not communicate secret information about employees to each other. Pre-employment testing and physical examination are prohibited, unless otherwise provided by law (contracts on the basis of organized recruitment, persons employed in unhealthy work, in trade etc. arts. 65, 76 of the Principles of Labour Law), but a short probationary period is allowed.

Special rules apply for engaging scientific personnel in the universities, artists and doctors in town hospitals—they are engaged by way of a competitive examination; top management are appointed by higher authorities, or only after their consent and after the consultation with the union committee; young workers graduating from the universities and the secondary special schools may only be hired in the first three years on the basis of the placement orders issued by the authorities, see EMPLOYMENT.

The contract of employment
As a rule, the contract of employment is concluded in oral form when the parties have agreed on the essential conditions: the profession or function and the place of work. Contracts in writing are required when employment is made in the course of organized recruitment. The employee starts work on the date mentioned in a special management order, but such an order is not obligatory: the fact that the worker is admitted to work in the enterprise is sufficient evidence.

The contract of employment is an agreement between employee and management according to which the latter has to perform work in a definite job (specialty, classification or function) according to the rules of the Internal Work Order, while the enterprise has to pay the employee wages or a salary and to secure the conditions of work provided for by law, the collective agreement and the agreement of the parties (art. 8 of the Principles of Labour Law).

The main features of the Soviet contract of employment are:

1) the specialty of the employee's job: every employee is engaged in a specific job listed in Wage and Classification Manuals issued by the State Committee of Labour and Wages and ACCTU or by the competent ministry and the union. These manuals contain detailed descriptions of the job content of each classification, these classifications being bro-

ken down into subcategories on the grounds of a job analysis based on 5 or 6 factors: the amount of working time spent in calculation, the time needed for preparing the work-place and the work, the direction of the production process and of machines or instruments, and the responsibility involved. As a rule, physical requirements only have importance for supplementary wages. These manuals are used for setting up the staff schedules of the enterprise and for determining the employee's function and they form the basis of the wage system and, in general, of all personnel policy.

As a consequence, the transfer of an employee to another job is as a rule forbidden: management may not require the employee to perform work not stipulated by the contract (art. 12 Principles of Labour Law), transfer to other jobs only being permitted with the consent of the employee or in exceptional circumstances (to prevent or resolve calamities, break-downs, accidents, stoppages, etc.) for a term of up to one month or to replace a temporarily absent worker for no more than one month every year; in these instances certain guarantees as to wages and the kind of work apply (arts. 13, 14 Principles of Labour Law). Similar rules apply to transfers to another enterprise or to another locality, except for service missions which are obligatory for a term of up to 45 (and sometimes 60) days. To prevent idleness on the part of the worker, certain incentives apply to workers who combine and perform several functions at the same time;

2) the subordination to the rules of the internal work order and to the orders of management: the maintainance of labour discipline (*q.v.*) mainly by management;

3) all conditions of employment which restrict the position of the employee in comparison with the position laid down by the law or which otherwise run counter to the existing law are null and void (art. 5 Principles of Labour Law).

Termination

With the exception of the first years after the Revolution and the years around World War II (1938-1956), employees have been free to leave their employment, but they have to give notice two weeks before in writing (art. 16 Principles of Labour Law). This rule does not apply to workers engaged for a certain period (up to 3 years) or to young workers engaged after graduating from the vocational schools, etc. (see EMPLOYMENT), in which case the giving of notice is only permitted if the worker has important reasons for it. The management may dismiss only with the consent of the union committee of the enterprise and only in cases specified by the law:

a) the liquidation of the enterprise, redundancy (lay-off) and the refusal to be transferred to another locality together with the enterprise. Before the 1965 economic reforms these decisions were taken by higher authorities and only after such decision were lay-offs permitted; under the economic reforms, the management is responsible for personnel policy, which calls for the strengthening of control by the unions and the courts. Management has to inform the union in due time of the planned lay-offs and the selection of the employees is done on the basis of classification and productivity, and of family and personal circumstances (involvement in a training or study programme, pension age, etc.).

b) the unfitness of the worker for his job due to lack of qualification or due to his health (on the basis of a medical report).

c) if a worker has been engaged instead of another employee, and the latter is subsequently reinstated by the authorities. In these instances the management must offer the worker other work, and dismissal is only permitted if a transfer with the consent of the worker is impossible. A leave pay of 2 weeks' average earnings has to be paid to the worker in these cases (and also in the case of leaving owing to call-up for military service or if the employee applies for a position in the army). Young employees and pregnant women or mothers with a child under the age of 1 may not as a rule be dismissed (see YOUNG EMPLOYEES; FEMALE EMPLOYEES).

d) discharge for disciplinary reasons is allowed for a whole day's absence without pressing reasons, for being drunk at work or for the systematic (i.e. occuring at least twice within 1 year) non-performance of one's duties imposed by the contract or the rules of the internal work order without sufficient reasons, if disciplinary measures have been taken before (see LABOUR DISCIPLINE); special rules apply to teachers who may be discharged for immoral behaviour outside their employment if their behaviour is incompatible with the continuation of their duties and for employees who are entrusted with the supervision of money and other valuables (art. 106 Principles of Labour Law).

e) dismissal after a sick leave of more than 4 months in succession (12 months in the case of tuberculosis), unless the leave is caused by an industrial accident or occupational disease, and only if dismissal is a reasonable measure.

Furthermore, the contract is discharged by agreement of the parties, by call-up for military service, or by a sentence of the court imposing deprivation of freedom or corrective labour not at the place of regular work (see CORRECTIVE LABOUR).

Employees of the managerial staff must be dismissed on the request of the higher agencies of the unions (see TRADE UNIONS).

In all cases of wrongful dismissal (without the consent of the relevant union or not on the basis of one of the causes mentioned in the law or when the measure is too harsh), the employee may appeal to the people's court for reinstatement. The time of forced absence from work has to be compensated for in the case of reinstatement by the enterprise, from the day of discharge, but for not longer than 3 months (according to the former law longer than 20 working days). Every decision on reinstatement must be executed immediately, and if the management hinders the execution of the judgment the employee is paid his average earnings over the whole time of forced idleness (or the difference in wages, if he has a new job). When the court comes to the conclusion that the discharge was in open violation of the law, the responsible managerial employee may be compelled to reimburse the enterprise for the losses incurred up to a maximum of his salary for 3 months (arts. 91-93 Principles of Labour Law); in this event, the procuracy also has the right to lodge a claim. Similar rules apply to illegal transfers, except that in such a case the claim is raised at the labour disputes commission (see LABOUR ARBITRATION).

The managerial staff and other higher personnel of the enterprise whose functions are listed in a decree of the Presidium of the Supreme Soviet of the USSR of January 31, 1957, may only protest to higher authorities against an illegal transfer or discharge, and not to the courts (decision of the Central Executive Committee and the Council of People's Commissars of October 13, 1929; the decree of 1957 on the settlement on labour disputes; art. 94 of the Principles of Labour Law).

G. P. van den Berg

ENEMY PROPERTY,
see ALIEN PROPERTY

ENFORCEMENT OF JUDGMENTS ABROAD, see LEGAL ASSISTANCE

ENTERTAINMENT

The organization and production of most forms of entertainment is the responsibility of the USSR Ministry of Culture and the subordinate ministries of culture of the Union republics. Theatre companies, orchestras, and circuses are run on a *khozraschet* (*q.v.*) basis as state enterprises under the aegis of the ministry of culture. Some of the most important companies and orchestras are directly subordinate to the USSR Ministry of Culture; others are part of a republican network; less important ones may be directed by provincial (*oblast'*) cultural departments. The ministries of culture are also in charge of museums and temporary expositions of a cultural character, libraries and Houses of Culture (community centres offering facilities for various cultural activities). The ministries of culture provide the means, the personnel, and the programme for the activities of these institutions. With regard to the protection of historical and cultural monuments, the organs of the ministries of culture cooperate with the All-Russian Society for the Protection of Historical and Cultural Monuments (see MONUMENTS).

Creative artists themselves are, as a rule, not in the service of the ministries of culture; they are united in associations such as the Union of Writers, the Composers' Union, the Union of Architects, etc. These unions are controlled by the Communist Party and governed by charters confirmed by the Council of Ministers of the USSR.

The production of films and the maintenance of a cinema network was transferred in 1963 from the USSR Ministry of Culture to the Cinematographical Committee attached to the Council of Ministers of the USSR. This Committee has the same ministry-like status as the committees for radio and television, and for the press (see RADIO & TELEVISION; PRESS).

At the lower administrative levels there are various agencies staffed by unpaid workers with cultural and educational tasks (voluntary cultural departments, standing cultural commissions, public councils of culture, etc.). The organization of cultural and educational lectures was transferred in 1957 from the USSR Ministry of Culture to the "Knowledge" (*Znanie*) Society (Society for the Dissemination of Political and Scientific Knowledge).

To sum up, all entertainment offered to large audiences (such as plays, concerts, expositions) is produced and controlled by the state. Active entertainment in an organized form (such as amateur theatre and music groups) is normally controlled by the state, since facilities are made available through cultural sections of local government, trade unions, etc. *F. J. M. Feldbrugge*

See also SPORTS; RADIO & TELEVISION

ENVIRONMENTAL PROTECTION, see CONSERVATION

EQUALITY, see CIVIL RIGHTS; FEMALE EMPLOYEES

ERROR, CRIMINAL LAW

The influence of errors on criminal responsibility is discussed in Soviet legal doctrine, but is not mentioned in the Criminal Code. Error implies incorrect knowledge, and consequently it is governed by the principle of guilt (see MENS REA), in the sense of the offender's attitude towards his offence. Soviet doctrine makes the traditional distinction between error of law and error of fact. An error of law may lead a person to believe that his conduct is forbidden by criminal law, while in fact it is not. In such a case no criminal responsibility arises. Conversely, if a person believes his conduct is not forbidden by criminal law, while in fact it is, criminal responsibility will arise only if the error is not excusable. In such a case the offender will be punished for the negligent commis-

sion of the crime which was committed.
Errors of fact may occur where the actual conduct of the offender does not correspond to his own perception of his conduct. If a person believes he is committing a specific crime (assuming there is no error of law, and the act indeed is a crime), while in fact he is not, he will be held responsible for the attempt to commit his crime. If a person believes he is not committing a crime, criminal responsibility will arise if the error is not excusable. In such a case the offender will be punished for the negligent commission of the crime.
Other errors concerning circumstances of offences, insofar as they do not take away criminal responsibility, may be taken into account in sentencing the offender.

F. J. M. Feldbrugge

ESCHEAT
Escheat, or rather, its Soviet equivalent, had a large field of application in the early period of the Soviet law of succession (see SUCCESSION). In the course of later developments it lost much of its importance as the restrictions on inheritance were gradually removed. At present the succession of the state is governed by art. 117 of the Principles of Civil Legislation and art. 552 of the RSFSR Civil Code. According to art. 552:
"the estate of the deceased person passes to the state, under the law of succession,
1) if the property has been left by will to the state;
2) if the deceased had no successors under his will or on intestacy;
3) if all the successors were deprived by a testator of their right of succession;
4) if none of the successors accepted the estate . . . If any of the successors has renounced his succession in favour of the state, the share of the deceased's property due to such successor passes to the state. If there are no intestate successors and only part of the estate has been disposed of by will, the remaining part passes to the state. In the cases indicated in this section, any copyright which forms part of the estate or any right to a share of an originator's fee belonging to a successor who renounces the estate, terminates". (Translation by A. K. R. Kiralfy, in Law in Eastern Europe XI).

Point 2 of art. 552 covers also the case of *indignitas*. From art. 552 it appears that the state succeeds to the estate or to part of it as a heir with all its consequences. Under the premises of points 1)-4) of this provision the state becomes the owner of the "escheated" property from the moment of the death of the *de cuius, ipso jure.*

Z. Szirmai

See also TESTAMENTS

ESPIONAGE
Espionage is defined by art. 65 of the Criminal Code as the handing over, and also theft or collection with the purpose of handing over, to a foreign state, a foreign organization, or their agents, of information constituting a state or military secret, and also the handing over or the collection at the request of foreign intelligence agencies of other information in order to be used by such agencies against the interests of the Soviet state.
The offence of art. 65 can be committed by foreigners or stateless persons only; espionage by Soviet citizens is regarded as treason (*q.v.*).
Unlike most of the other "especially dangerous crimes against the state" (see POLITICAL CRIMES), espionage does not seem to require in all cases the specific intent to harm the Soviet state. A common feature, however, is the broad scope of the provision, as interpreted by Soviet law. "Other information" embraces information from completely open sources, such as newspapers, and about such topics as "the atmosphere

in the country", in fact anything that might be useful to a foreign intelligence agency.
A list of information considered to be state or military secrets has been laid down by a decree of the USSR Council of Ministers of April 28, 1956 (see SECRETS).
The penalty for espionage is deprivation of freedom of from seven tot fifteen years, accompanied by confiscation of property, and possibly followed by exile (from two to five years), or the death penalty accompanied by confiscation of property. Espionage cases are tried by military tribunals (*q.v.*).

F. J. M. Feldbrugge

EUTHANASIA, see SUICIDE

EVICTION

1) *Personal housing.* A house-owner may be evicted only in those situations where his house may be confiscated (see HOUSING).
2) *State and industrial housing.* The basic principle is that of security of tenure. Except for cases of grave danger or of squatters all evictions must be by court order. Further, in the normal case (where, say the site is being re-developed) the landlord must provide suitable and similar accommodation in the same locality.
Eviction without such provision is permitted:
i) If the staff of major industries, living in their employer's property, are dismissed or leave of their own accord. But the USSR Supreme Court has insisted that this be applied restrictively and the grounds for leaving must be considered: leaving, e.g. to look after one's children would not expose the employee to eviction without alternative accommodation.
ii) In the case of sub-tenants who have no security of tenure.
iii) If the tenant systematically fails to pay rent to a private landlord.
iv) If he owns suitable accommodation in the locality in which he could live.
v) If he and his family leave the premises for more than the reservation period (usually six months).
vi) If he or his family damage the accommodation or make life impossible for the neighbours and if measures of public influence have failed. Courts have refused to evict on this score when the community at the defendant's abode or workplace had not had a chance to redeem him.
vii) Where a parent, deprived of his parental rights, makes life impossible for his children and measures of public influence have failed.
See further arts. 330-341 Civil Code.

B. Rudden

EVIDENCE, CIVIL PROCEDURE

The law of evidence is statutory in the USSR, being laid down in the All-Union Principles of Civil Procedure and in the republican Civil Procedure Codes, e.g. in the RSFSR it is contained in Chapter 6 (Proof, *Dokazatel'stvo*) of the Code of Civil Procedure of 1964. Judicial decisions are occasionally referred to as illustrations of the law, and there is some legal literature in the form of textbooks and articles. A. Vyshinsky's book is well-known. The incorrect acceptance or assessment of evidence is a frequent ground of appeals and protests to higher courts, e.g. under art. 306 of the Civil Procedure Code three of the four grounds of appeal are concerned with defects of evidence or improper conclusions on evidence.
Evidence consists of the materials used by courts to prove the facts at issue between the parties. These facts are governed by the rules of substantive law, e.g. that law determines what the legal elements of a contract are, and evidence must be adduced to show facts constituting those legal elements, e.g. agreement, terms of the contract, and writing where legally required.
The burden of proof of a fact, as in all legal systems, rests primarily on the party relying on the fact, who risks losing the case if the fact is not established. The plaintiff must

prove facts establishing a cause of action, e.g. a loan by him to the defendant, and the defendant must prove facts supporting his defence, e.g. that he repaid the loan. The burden of proof may "shift" after a party has produced plausible evidence in his favour, so that the opponent is then required to meet such evidence with contrary evidence, e.g. prove that a later transaction has occurred or that the evidence already given is false.

In some situations the usual rule is reversed. Thus the RSFSR Civil Code states that, once you prove the defendant caused some injury, he is presumed to have been at fault; he is then left to disprove fault. The reason is that, for instance, a man knocked down by a car would find it difficult to prove the state of mind of the motorist at the time, and motorists do not generally knock people down if they are careful. The motorist is free to prove, if he can, that another car had collided with his without his fault and caused his car to swerve, or that he had suddenly been taken ill.

Russian law, like German law, but unlike English law, requires the parties to refer in their written pleadings to the proofs which they expect to offer, the names of their proposed witnesses, and a statement of what each of them is expected to say. A party who fails to do this cannot proceed with his case.

The position of the Soviet judge is that he is required by law, in general terms, to investigate the true facts of every case. He need not accept the parties' evidence; he may question the parties himself; he may demand further investigation of a case. On the other hand his duties do not relieve the parties of their obvious primary duty to produce, themselves, what they consider to be adequate evidence of the true facts, leaving the judge in most cases to call for supplementary proofs if he thinks fit. At the outset of the case the president of the court sees the plaintiff and satisfies himself that ade
be provided at the trial. H
the defendant at this sta
he intends to meet the cl
until a defence is filed. I
may the judge pre-judg
point, e.g. he leaves it to the trial court to determine whether any legal wrong has been committed and whether they believe the evidence offered to be true. Further evidence may always be asked for by the trial court, adjourning if that is reasonable, or ordering a re-investigation of the case and a re-trial at a date to be fixed after it is completed.

As in all legal systems, time and trouble are spared by the court taking "judicial notice", without proof, of well-known or indisputable facts, e.g. that Moscow is in the RSFSR, that one month is longer than another (*obshcheizvestnost'*). The court decides what facts are to be so noticed, and this may depend on the place and time, as facts may be notorious in one place and unknown in another, and lapse of time causes memory to fade.

Judicial notice is also taken of facts established by the judgment of a competent court in a previous civil case (*prejudicium*), provided the parties now disputing such facts appeared or had an opportunity to appear before the court which gave the earlier judgment. Thus, if the buyer of goods is ordered by a court to give them up to a third party, the buyer can only claim compensation from the seller if he notified the seller of the third party's claim in time to enable him to appear and refute it.

The judgment of a criminal court is conclusive as to the fact that a crime was committed and as to the identity of the person causing it, but does not conclude the question of legal responsibility, which is often different in civil and criminal law.

Relevance or materiality to the case (*otnosimost'*) is an essential requirement of evidence. What is relevant depends on the legal elements of a claim in dispute and on the

...uestion whether a fact is disputed. Thus if a wife claims maintenance from her husband, evidence is directed to the fact of maintaining or failing to maintain, but the marriage need not be proved unless the defendant husband denies it.

Evidence may be directly relevant to a case, e.g. testimony by an eye-witness to some event, or indirectly relevant, e.g. that a witness could not see what he claims to have seen, or that he has made contradictory statements. Evidence may also be circumstantial, as tending to establish a fact by establishing other facts with which it is related. That the defendant acted in a guilty manner after a wrong was done may be some evidence that he committed that wrong, as may an attempt by him to bribe a witness or to cover up the fact that the wrong was committed. For a poor man to start heavy spending may be relevant where he claims that money entrusted to him has been stolen from him.

The judges at the trial decide whether to accept or reject evidence as relevant or irrelevant. A preliminary ruling may be made before the trial, e.g. that evidence proposed to be produced is not relevant, so that further proofs are required, or that evidence whose production is sought would not be relevant. Admissibility (*dopustimost'*) is not such an important question in Soviet law as it is in Anglo-American law. The latter system prohibits the production of certain types of relevant material which might prejudice a jury out of proportion to their weight as evidence. Thus "hearsay" evidence may not be heard in an English court, subject to modifications in the Civil Evidence Act, 1968, since the fact that a person not present in court said something is no real proof of the truth of the facts stated. Soviet law rarely excludes any particular type of proof; substantive law sometimes provides that gifts or contracts be made in writing, and, if this is not done, will refuse to allow oral evidence of the transaction to be given. This means the transaction is unenforceable if the other party backs out. This is not the same thing as a formal requirement of writing for the validity of a transaction, in which case it is void unless in writing, whether the parties want to honour it or not. Where the English system entirely excludes certain types of evidence the Soviet system leaves it to the court to take its weakness into account and not attach undue weight to it.

If there is a risk of evidence being lost, e.g. a witness is gravely ill, steps can be taken to perpetuate testimony by attending on him and taking depositions. A special application must be made to the court for this to be done. If it would be very difficult for a witness to appear in court, e.g. his duties keep him at a distant place, the court may, on application by an interested party, ask another court to take his evidence on commission and send his deposition to the court making the order. As to the rules governing the competence of witnesses see WITNESSES IN CIVIL PROCEDURE.

Some evidence is privileged from being used, e.g. communications between lawyers and their clients in litigation may not be disclosed to any third party.

The decisive function of the trial court is the appraisal or evaluation of evidence before it (*otsenka*). Evidence may be relevant but false or of doubtful truth. Some evaluation may have to occur at an earlier stage of proceedings, e.g. to see if a *prima facie* case appears to exist, or whether more convincing evidence should be produced. But normally it is at the trial that witnesses' veracity can be judged. Soviet law excludes quite deliberately any artificial rules about the weight of evidence, e.g. it does not exclude the evidence of children if they are sensible, or of interested parties, such as friends or relations of parties, although it naturally treats such evidence with care, in view of possible bias. There are no fixed scales of better and worse proof. The court may believe a single witness and disbelieve a dozen others. It may accept a friend of the party as a truthful public spirited citizen and disbelieve a disinterested person.

The judge is said to decide each case as his own conscience dictates. This does not mean, of course, that he can rely on prejudice or intuition, since the law requires his decision to be objective in character and based on the materials before the court. Judges must examine the demeanour of witnesses, the consistency of their testimony, and similar factors.

The written file of the case contains notes of testimony, and the written record of the judgment must indicate what evidence the court believed and why it believed it.

In civil cases the defendant may always admit a claim, and the court will not normally interfere with this, unless it has reason to believe threats or other illegalities were used on him. The defendant may also dispute a claim but admit certain of the relevant facts, and these do not then have to be proved, provided, again there is no ground for suspicion. Admissions in civil cases are regarded as procedural steps and not strictly as evidence.

As in most legal systems, "real" evidence may be produced, e.g. disputed articles may be produced or photographs of bulky objects like buildings or statues. Perishable goods may be inspected before they perish.

Documentary evidence constitutes a permanent record of an exact kind and is particularly valuable as evidence. Public bodies and private persons may be required by any interested party to supply the court with relevant documents. Naturally a procedure is made available for proving that a document is a forgery (see DOCUMENTS).

Documentary evidence refers to the information entered in a document, such as a receipt for money or a note of the reasons for dismissal of an employee. It is a record of some event. Books and papers may themselves be relevant, e.g. the ownership of a valuable first edition of an old book may be in dispute, and in this case they are "real" evidence.

Evidence is presented at the trial, generally, in the following order: the statements of the parties, the testimony of the witnesses, and the examination of documents and real evidence. Written evidence is circulated to all parties or read aloud in court, to observe the basic principle of orality. The members of the court then withdraw to their retiring room in order to decide what evidence they accept and to formulate their decision accordingly. All evidence taken at the trial, and any depositions taken on commission or to perpetuate testimony, are noted in the court minutes by the court secretary (see COURT RECORDS). In the event of an appeal the higher court does not itself receive fresh evidence, but if it is dissatisfied with the proof of facts in the trial court, it may order a re-trial with the same evidence or even order the whole case to be re-investigated and fresh evidence secured for the re-trial.

A. K. R. Kiralfy

See also EXPERT WITNESSES

EVIDENCE, CRIMINAL PROCEDURE

Evidence in criminal cases consists of forms of proof of facts tending to show the commission of a crime, the identity of the culprit and other connected circumstances, such as the character and background of the culprit, for the purpose of deciding on the appropriate sentence. Facts lie in the past and can be discovered through information about them. This may take the form of traces of events, e.g. fingerprints, or recollection of events by persons who directly participated in them. Even a revolver is not a fact but a source of information about how and when it was used. In addition some facts may be learned by study of clues by persons who did not participate, e.g. experts. And notes of evidence taken down in court become proofs of fact, e.g. where used by a higher court in deciding an appeal.

The theoretical background of the Soviet law of criminal evidence is of great importance, since it involves applications of basic Marxist natural philosophy and since weakness of proof was the reason for the criticism of many of Stalin's trials. Facts are reflections of reality in human consciousness. For Marxists everything is material. These material things and events are perceived by the human senses and rationalised by the human brain. Everything is knowable and therefore provable. No abstract *a priori* theories or presumptions are valid. The reasoning element which interprets the reflections of reality is given by the experience of life, by practical reason, and not by abstract ideas. But pure reason or logic is also useful, e.g. in considering the linking up of circumstantial evidence (induction) or in comparing and testing evidence (deduction). Objective truth is established as a result of the use of various methods up to the point where the tentative proof can be clearly verified and the contrary eliminated. Trial "theories" may be required, but these must be scrupulously checked and counter-checked.

The Soviet criminal procedure codes require that proof be full and "all-round". Full investigation requires collection and verification of all proofs, whether they tend to convict or acquit the accused of the crime. "All-round" proof refers to the exhaustive testing of proofs until all possibility of unreliability is excluded. In this connection the Soviet lawyer to some extent deals with forensic science and the science and art of criminal investigation, and not merely with formal legal requirements.

Relevance is essential to all proof, e.g. to prove the circumstances of the crime (whether committed by one or more persons, the aggravated or mitigated character of the crime etc.), the state of mind of the accused, his previous convictions, and, in view of possible civil claims, the harm caused by the crime. Of course some plausible evidence may turn out to have been irrelevant, but at least there must be a probability of relevance before evidence can be considered. The bias of a witness is also relevant, and the authenticity of a document, as this bears on the acceptability of the evidence as proof of the facts. Admissibility plays a much smaller role than it does in common law countries. There are few formal rules, e.g. in some cases the Civil Code requires writing as exclusive evidence of a transaction, and notarisation is often necessary. Mere rumours cannot be used as evidence, but hearsay statements from defined sources may be admitted. Judges cannot act on personal knowledge, since the criminal procedure codes require all evidence to be in the form of testimony given in court after warnings of the risks of perjury.

The production of proof falls on the investigators and they must test all evidence before they use it, e.g. verify the possibility of a witness having observed some event.

The assessment or weighing of proof is a matter for the persuasion of the judges, based on observation and experience. It is not a subjective intuition; conviction is the result, not the cause, of the judge's conclusions. Experience is said, significantly, in the light of history, to discount the reliability of confessions. Soviet jurists claim that socialist legal consciousness, based on a class approach, helps achieve objective truth, but this is not demonstrated and would appear to be irrelevant to the establishment of fact.

The burden of proof in criminal cases rests on the investigaton, the procurator and the court, who act in the name of the public, and never on the accused. The accused may offer evidence and require that evidence supporting his innocence be collected, but this is a right and not a duty. Defence counsel is under a duty, in the sense that he must collect and present proofs to assist his client, as between the client and himself, but the general burden of proof of guilt remains on

the public officials. The victim of a crime, e.g. a person robbed, has the right to offer proofs, but is not under a duty to do so (except in certain cases where a prosecution depends on private complaint). Representatives of the public (public accuser or defender) and trade union representatives, have a similar right, but not a duty.
The burden of proof does not shift in criminal cases. If the accused raises a positive defence, e.g. self defence or an alibi, he does not have to prove it; it is for the officials to investigate and test it, to try to prove or disprove it.
These rules are based on greater resources being open to the state than to the individual accused, and on protecting the individual from being harried without real cause. There is also a view that the accused is presumed innocent.
The main types of evidence used in investigation and at the trial are the testimony of witnesses (see WITNESSES), expert reports (see EXPERT WITNESSES), real and documentary evidence.
Real evidence is relevant for what it is, e.g. a murder weapon, bloodstained clothes, clues left by the accused on objects, get-away cars etc. A document may be real evidence, e.g. a forged pass used by the accused to obtain entry to premises. Real evidence should be documented by a report on the circumstances in which it was found, by photographing of the site where it was found, and so on. It is usually exhibited at the trial but bulky objects may be represented by photographs or drawings. Sites may be visited by the judges and the parties, e.g. scenes of accidents. The authenticity of real evidence may always be contested and verified. Records of the results of searches and inspections may be used as evidence.
Documentary proof is less vital than in civil cases, but may be important. Documentary evidence is something which is important for what it records rather than for its physical self, e.g. a letter disclosing a conspiracy, a written confession. The persons concerned must be linked up with the document, e.g. by handwriting tests.
The accused and the victim may also make statements (see WITNESSES). Cf. also arts. 68-88 RSFSR Code of Criminal Procedure.

A. K. R. Kiralfy

EXECUTION OF JUDGMENT, CIVIL PROCEDURE

A judgment of a civil court normally becomes subject to execution only after time to appeal has expired or the appeal is dismissed. However execution may still be stayed thereafter if the judgment debtor is temporarily in financial difficulties. On the other hand execution is immediate in cases of maintenance of families, and up to one month's wages must be paid even before time to appeal has expired etc. if judgment is for wages. Immediate execution may also be awarded by the court in other cases, e.g. to prevent serious hardship to the judgment creditor, but the court must give special reasons for this in its judgment.
The judgment debtor generally has five days in which to satisfy the judgment voluntarily, and state enterprises are admonished to satisfy all judgments against them voluntarily. If voluntary performance is not forthcoming the court itself calls on the services of the bailiff in family maintenance cases and torts to the person and in cases of wrongful dismissal. In other cases the judgment creditor must take the initiative in starting proceedings for compulsory execution of judgment by the local court bailiff (*q.v.*).
The bailiff's warrant of execution (*ispolnitel'nyi list*) must contain a transcript of the terms of the judgment as to the obligations of the judgment debtor, or of each of several such debtors. In state arbitration an order is issued with the effect of a warrant (*prikaz*).
Where the judgment is given in a case involving two state enterprises the judgment is

directly enforced by appropriate transfers of credits by the State Bank, without the intervention of a bailiff. Judgment for rent arrears is replaced by a notarial act (*nadpis'*), certifying rent due and unpaid, but contestable in court by the tenant.

Execution must be completed within 3 years in cases of citizens, one year in disputes between state enterprises, six months in the case of arbitration awards, and three months in the case of decisions of trade union branches in labour law.

A criminal sentence containing orders for restitution of property is also executed by the civil court bailiff.

Execution of judgment differs markedly depending on whether the judgment debtor is a citizen or a state enterprise.

In execution against citizens recourse is had primarily to assets or concrete articles. A list annexed to the Code of Civil Procedure exempts from execution indispensable items of clothing and furniture, and farm houses. Items such as pianos, radio and television sets and refrigerators, are not exempt and are often found referred to in inventories by bailiffs. Original works of art and valuable china or silver are sometimes owned and may be taken in execution. If the assets exceed the amount of the judgment the debtor may indicate which assets are to be taken. Third parties may object to the inclusion of items in the inventory, claiming that they own them, as where a wife owned a painting before her marriage to the debtor. Such third-party proceedings are taken in the local court. Articles so taken are sold, if the debt is not paid within a short time, e.g. through state second-hand (Commission) shops.

A private urban dwelling may be taken in execution and there is a special procedure for sale by auction, at which persons who already own houses may not make bids.

Shares in common ownership and in matrimonial community property are also liable to be taken in execution and realised. On the other hand shares in collective farm household property may only be taken in execution in the last resort, in case of a deficiency of all assets of other kinds.

In the last resort wages may be attached (see ATTACHMENT).

Not all judgments refer to payments of money. Appropriate types of execution must be pursued in other cases, e.g. the judgment creditor may remove a nuisance and charge the debtor with the cost of doing so. A common problem arises with judgments for re-employment of a wrongfully dismissed man. Employers (state enterprises) may be fined up to 300 roubles for repeated defiance of such judgments, plus payment of lost wages to the creditor. Fines are also imposed for failure to withdraw defamatory statements, as damages are not awarded in such cases in Soviet law (see DEFAMATION).

In execution against state enterprises bank balances are primarily liable to be taken, and the judgment may indicate which account is to suffer deduction. Later deposits may be taken as and when made.

The other assets of a state enterprise are only liable if sums in the bank are exhausted. Obviously the economic system of the USSR would break down if major fixed or circulating assets could be taken in execution, and in fact all capital assets are exempt from being taken, plus sufficient circulating assets to enable the enterprise to continue to operate and perform its tasks under the State Economic Plan. The effect of all this is that the real sufferers will be bonus and amenity funds, so that the judgment is brought home to the enterprise itself.

Execution may be stayed during a change of title, e.g. if a creditor or debtor dies. It may also be contested by the debtor on legal grounds. If the judgment is itself reversed on appeal execution terminates, as it does if the time limit for execution expires and is not renewed. In case of reversal of judgment the judgment debtor obtains complete restoration of everything taken in execution (except that maintenance payments need not be refunded). An order for restoration must be included in the appellate judgment. If the judgment is reversed in course of review by the Procuracy it does not affect cases of maintenance of the family, loss of wages or loss of earning capacity through torts to the person. Cf. arts. 338-432 RSFSR Code of Civil Procedure.

A. K. R. Kiralfy

EXECUTION, CRIMINAL PROCEDURE, see SENTENCES

EXILE

Exile occurs in two ways as a penalty in Soviet criminal law: compulsory residence in a particular (remote) place ("exile to", *ssylka*), and expulsion from a particular place ("banishment from", *vysylka*). Exile proper (*ssylka*) is defined by art. 25 of the Criminal Code of the RSFSR as the removal of a person from his place of residence, coupled with the compulsory settling in a particular place. Banishment (*vysylka*) is defined by art. 26 as the removal of a person from his place of residence, coupled with a prohibition to stay in particular places.

Exile and banishment may be imposed for a period of from two to five years. Both penalties may be applied as principal or as additional penalties. In the latter case they are applicable only in cases specifically provided by the criminal law (e.g. exile is mentioned as an additional penalty in art. 102 of the Criminal Code of the RSFSR: aggravated homicide; banishment as an additional penalty occurs only once, in art. 231, procuring and the keeping of brothels, etc.). As additional penalties, exile and banishment will always be combined with deprivation of freedom; in such cases they start to run after the principal sentence has been served.

The execution of exile and banishment is entrusted to the police; this means that the person sentenced to exile is transported by the police to the place of exile; in the case of banishment the police will do no more than make sure that the convicted offender leaves the prohibited area. Persons sentenced to exile or banishment are obliged to work; the local authorities of the place of exile or banishment are charged with providing work. The choice of work is in principle free and (in the case of exile) the choice of residence also; however, in the case of exile, the remoteness of the compulsory place of residence will usually make the actual range of available jobs very restricted.

An exiled person who leaves his place of exile commits an offence under art. 186 of the Criminal Code of the RSFSR, entailing a maximum penalty of one year's deprivation of freedom. A person who is banished and who enters an area which is specifically prohibited to him commits the offense of art. 187, which prescribes that the residual part of the banishment sentence be changed into exile.

Persons who have served one half of their banishment or exile sentence are eligible for parole (*q.v.*).

The specific purpose of banishment is to remove a person from an environment which constitutes a special delinquency risk; it is applied infrequently. Banishment is mentioned only once as a principal penalty in the Criminal Code, in art. 226 (refusal to accept a reconciliation in areas where blood-feuds are practised; see TRADITIONAL CRIME). Exile is mentioned in several instances as a principal penalty (arts. 122, 187, 196 par. 2, 208 par. 2, 226, 231). By virtue of art. 43 of the Criminal Code exile or banishment may be imposed instead of a more serious form of punishment, which means in practice: deprivation of freedom. For instance, Pavel Litvinov and Larissa Daniel were sentenced to be exiled (for 5, resp. 4 years) for their participation in a pro-Czechoslovak demonstration on Red Square, on the basis of art. 190-1 (the diffusion of fabrications which are known to be false and which slander the politcal and social system of the Soviet Union), although the maximum penalty in this case is three years' deprivation of freedom and no mention is made of exile or banishment.

Distinct from exile and banishment is administrative exile *(vyselenie)*, which may be applied as an administrative penalty to parasites (*q.v.*).

F. J. M. Feldbrugge

EXPERT WITNESS, CIVIL PROCEDURE

In order to give the court a true picture of a legal situation it may be necessary to supply an expert interpretation of the facts, as well as discovering the facts themselves. In Soviet law the expert witness and his report occupy a special position (cf. arts. 74-78 Code of Civil Procedure). The expert is not a member of the court and a judge cannot act as an expert in the same case. On the other hand the expert is not a partisan witness produced by one side and attacked by the other. If any person interested, or the court itself, considers that technical, scientific or other specialised expert opinions are required, an expert may be appointed by court order, e.g. to decide whether the defendant's invention infringes the plaintiff's patent, or why some goods were damaged and at which point in transit from factory to customer.

The final decision on the need for an expert is a matter for the court, and the court also chooses the expert. However, the parties must be consulted and reasons given by the court for any action it takes. Occasionally some statute requires an expert to be appointed, e.g. where mental health is in dispute.

The decision to appoint a witness is generally made at a pre-trial stage of proceedings. The expert is then called upon to act and told what questions he is to answer. He is supplied with all necessary materials and facilities. He may ask for further information if he considers it necessary. Sometimes several experts are needed and they may present a joint report if they are agreed.

Any person trained to express an expert opinion is qualified to act as an expert witness. In many cases experts are drawn from special forensic science institutions. The expert's report differs from the testimony of an ordinary witness in containing opinions and conclusions and an account of any investigations he has conducted. It is not limited to findings of fact.

No person related to the parties to the case or interested in the result of the case may act as an expert, nor may anyone who has already given an opinion on the same matter, e.g. at a previous trial.

The expert's report partakes of the nature of evidence to the extent that the parties and members of the court may question the expert and the expert may question the parties. The plaintiff usually opens the questioning. This assumes that the expert attends the trial. He has a right to do so, and the court has power to summon him. Presumably his report is often accepted by both sides and his attendance may therefore often be dispensed with.

In some cases special procedures are followed, e.g. in industrial accident cases there is an appeal to a higher medical authority from the report of the local medical board on the extent of the plaintiff's injuries.

Although the expert is a judicial nominee, his report is not automatically accepted. The court appraises it like any other evidence in the case. But the court is required by law to give reasons for refusing to accept it, and these are noted in the case-file. Reports are not simply rejected; if the court is dissatisfied it can ask for supplementary information from the expert, or appoint further experts. As might be expected, an expert may not express any opinion on a point of law; he may state his opinion as to cause of death, for example, but not decide whether any legal responsibility exists or who is responsible. Otherwise he would usurp the functions of the court.

Experts are entitled to the usual expenses. Unless regularly employed to make reports to courts, they are also entitled to remuneration for their work. An expert is criminally liable for knowingly making a false report, and he is reminded of his duties, as well as his rights, when he accepts appointment.

A. K. R. Kiralfy

EXPERT WITNESS, CRIMINAL PROCEDURE

Expert witnesses are used in civil procedure as well (see EXPERT WITNESS, CIVIL PROCEDURE) but have a rather more important role in criminal investigations. The investigator or procurator will decide if expert opinions are required. Specific questions are set the expert, but he may enquire more generally into the problems raised. In criminal proceedings experts must be used to establish the causes of death or injuries, to decide the mental state of the accused or suspect, to decide the mental or physical state of the victim or a witness, to decide if their testimony is reliable, to establish the age of any person if not proved by documents.

Experts may not go into legal but only technical matters, e.g. they may not classify an event as a particular crime or indicate who should be convicted.

Groups of experts sometimes act, where a case involves different types of problems. They may produce a joint or separate reports. In deciding whether to accept the conclusions of the expert—and the court must give reasons for not doing so—the degree of skill of the expert is important, the state of knowledge in the particular science, the theories which the expert applied and the consistency of his conclusions with such theories as applied to the facts. Cf. also arts. 78-82 RSFSR Code of Criminal Procedure. (And see EXPERT WITNESS, CIVIL PROCEDURE, as to common points).

A. K. R. Kiralfy

See also FORENSIC MEDICINE; FORENSIC PSYCHIATRY

EXPORT AND IMPORT

Foreign Trade Plan. Exports and imports of the state foreign trade monopoly are for the most part centrally planned, and are embodied in the Foreign Trade Plan which, in turn, is a component part of the overall economic plan for a specified term. The Foreign Trade Plan annually elaborates the categories, values and volume of goods to be traded, as well as the method of payment and delivery schedule, with regard to socialist, capitalist and less developed countries, respectively.

The export aspect of the Foreign Trade Plan specifies the types and quantities of goods to be produced for delivery abroad in order to pay for imports and to meet other foreign financial obligations, such as foreign aid commitments. The import aspect defines the range and quantities of foreign goods which it is anticipated will be needed over the given period to meet domestic production and consumer objectives.

Ultimate responsibility for the overall economic plan rests with the State Planning Commission (see PLANNING). With respect to exports, the Planning Commission transmits general policy guidelines to the Department of Planning and Economics of the Ministry of Foreign Trade as well as to other concerned ministries. On the basis of these guidelines, the Ministry establishes the specific goals and standards, issuing them in the form of directives to the foreign trade corporations under its jurisdiction. These directives specify the desired annual export level in terms of quantity and type of goods, sales price, cost, market selection, and the like. With regard to import planning, the State

Planning Commission surveys local production and projects anticipated needs which it is felt can best be satisfied through imports. On the basis of this analysis a provisional import plan is prepared. This is then submitted to the Ministry of Foreign Trade, where it is further elaborated, taking into consideration trade agreement obligations, foreign exchange earnings from exports and other sources, and the like. For this purpose the Ministry consults the State Bank and the Foreign Trade Bank as well as the individual foreign trade corporations. The import plan is then submitted to the State Planning Commission for final review and approval by the Council of Ministers.

Operation of Foreign Trade Plan. Internally, the specially chartered foreign trade corporations obtain goods for export and distribute imported goods pursuant to the authority of the Foreign Trade Plan. To obtain goods required for export purposes, the foreign trade corporation submits an order (*zakaz-nariad*) to the appropriate production ministry (see SUPPLY CONTRACT). The order establishes precise terms of quantity, quality, price, delivery and so forth. This order based upon the export plan is sufficient to obligate the ministry to supply the product for export through one of the enterprises under its control, although a mandatory contract is nonetheless also executed by the performing enterprises.

As a rule, the supplier enterprise ships goods for export, in accordance with the established delivery schedule, directly to the designated frontier without the goods having to pass through the hands of the foreign trade corporation. Typically, the foreign buyer takes delivery of the goods at this point. Since the foreign trade corporation acts for its own account in external commerce, the foreign purchaser pays the foreign trade corporation, and the latter, deducting its profit, pays the domestic supplier in roubles at wholesale prices. To a very limited degree, recent reforms allow supplier enterprises some foreign exchange allocations from their export receipts which they may use for purchases abroad. The opportunity for such purchases, although outside the Economic Plan, is intended primarily as an incentive to the improvement and growth of export production. In the mechanics of importation, the foreign trade corporation is obligated by virtue of the import plan to consult with the appropriate ministry and the consumer enterprises under the latter's jurisdiction to ascertain what is needed, by what date, and at what price. A contract is entered into elaborating the precise terms of the obligation. On the basis of the concluded agreement the foreign trade corporation arranges to procure the necessary foreign goods.

Jeffrey Hertzfeld

See also FOREIGN TRADE

EXPROPRIATION (OF LAND)

Soviet society is characterised by, among other things, the nature of the property relations established by the Bolshevik regime in the very first years after the 1917 Revolution. The attitude of the new regime towards the question of land ownership found expression in the pre-Revolution slogan that "land belongs to those who work on it". V. I. Lenin, the founder of the Soviet state, once said that "nationalization means the transfer of all land to the ownership of the state. Ownership means the right to rent out land and to determine the general guidelines of state policy with regard to the holding and use of land. Among such guidelines must be included the banning of all intermediary dealings in land, e.g. the exclusion of any subletting of land or transfer of rights on any piece of land to any person who does not own it" (Works, vol. 16, pp. 316-317).

Marx and Engels, while commenting on the nature of land ownership in any socialist state, conclude that any reasonable land reforms within a socialist context must be based on the preliminary take-over of all land into the hands of the state. Soviet agrarian policy has been based on these basic teachings of the classics of Marxism-Leninism even though the role of nationalization within this policy varied from one era to another. For example, during the revolution of 1905 the Bolsheviks demanded the nationalization of land because they saw such a move as a blow against *kulachestvo* and *krepostnichestvo* (serfdom) in Russia at that time. Nationalization in such conditions would be a fulfilment of the demands of the peasantry and at the same time it was to be a step designed eventually to transform the bourgeois-democratic revolution into a socialist one.

But under the socialist revolution, the nationalization of land was seen not only as a move aimed at the full destruction of the relics of serfdom in the countryside and as a great blow at private property rights, but also as a vital step aimed at creating the new land structure which was essential for the realization of any meaningful socialist reforms. In the words of Lenin, nationalization under a proletarian revolution represents not only the last word of the bourgeois revolution, but also a step towards socialism (Works, vol. 16, p. 300).

In accordance with this general theory of scientific socialism, on November 8, 1917, the Second All-Russian Congress of Soviets issued a decree "On Land", an integral part of which were the "Peasant Demands on Land" (*Krest'ianskie Nakazy o Zemle*). These "Demands" were based on the 242 *nakazy* which were received from the local peasantry throughout Russia in the period immediately following the revolution.

The Decree on Land banished for all time any private ownership of land either by a private individual or by any private organization. The Decree further confiscated all land, buildings and work materials belonging to the landowners (*pomeshchiki*). As a result of the Decree all land througout the Soviet Union was declared to be socialist property, i.e. belonging to the state. Art. 6 of the present Soviet federal Constitution states: "The land, its mineral wealth, waters, forests, the factories and mines, rail, water and air transport facilities, the banks, means of communication, large state-organised agricultural enterprises (state farms, machine and tractor stations, etc.), as well as municipal enterprises and the bulk of the dwelling-houses in the cities and industrial localities, are state property, that is, belong to the whole people." As a forerunner to this provision, art. 2 of the Constitution proclaims that "The political foundation of the USSR is the Soviets of Working People's Deputies, which grew and became strong as a result of the overthrow of the power of the landowners and capitalists and the attainment of the dictatorship of the proletariat".

Whereas the Decree called for a total nationalization (without compensation) of all land belonging to all private landholders at the time, it also prepared the ground for the transfer of the right to use the land to the hitherto landless peasants who worked on it. In all such cases, however, the ownership rights over the land continued to reside in the state. While the state remained the sole owner of all land in the Soviet Union, the peasants, organised either into collective farms or state farms, received from the state, free of any charges, the right to use such land for eternity, i.e. for as long as they continue to till it. This principle is enshrined in the provisions of arts. 7 and 8 of the Soviet Federal Constitution. Under art. 7 "The enterprises of the collective farms and co-operative organizations, with their livestock, buildings, implements, and output, are the common property of the collective farms and co-operative organizations. Every collective-farm household, in addition to its basic income from the collective farm, has for its own use a small plot of land attached to the house and, as its own property, a dwelling house, livestock, poultry, and minor agricultural implements—in conformity with the Rules of the Agricultural Artel". Art. 8 provides that "The land occupied by the collective farms is made over to them for their free use for an unlimited time, that is, in perpetuity".

Contemporary Soviet scholarship looks upon the socialist nationalization of land not only as putting an end to all private ownership of land, not only as liquidating all possible uses of land for the exploitation of man by man, and as establishing the foundation stone for future socialist ownership rights, but also as an act which necessarily cements the bond of friendship between the peasantry and the proletariat class—the only two classes whose existence the Soviet Union officially acknowledges.

Since the adoption of the 1917 Land Decree, the Soviet government has issued other laws aimed at consolidating the gains of that Decree. These include: the decree of the Central Committee of the Communist Party and the Council of People's Commissars of May 27, 1939, concerning the "Measures aimed at protecting the lands of the Collective Farms from misappropriation"; the decree of the Central Committee of the CPSU and the Council of Ministers of the USSR of March 6, 1956, on "The Charter of the Agricultural Artels . . .", etc.

Under the provisions of such laws, only the following can receive the right to use land in the Soviet Union: a) socialist enterprises or organizations. These may be state, cooperative or social organizations (art. 8 of the Principles of Land Use and Land Structure of the USSR). In such a case the use of the land so granted by the state must be directed to attaining the declared purposes for which the organization was created. This is the principle of the so-called 'functional use of land' under Soviet land law. If an enterprise uses the land granted to it by the state for an illegal purpose it stands the chance of losing such land; b) under the provisions of art. 7 of the Principles of Land Use and Land Structure in the USSR and also under art. 9 of the Land Code of the Russian Federation, Soviet citizens "irrespective of their sex, religious belief and nationality" may also be granted the right to use land in the USSR; c) such a right may also be granted to working aliens who reside permanently and exercise political rights in the Soviet Union. The scope and contents of such rights differ from one holder to another, all depending on the individual needs of such holders. In all cases, however, such land must be used only for a designated purpose and this excludes any form of exploitation of man by man and the use of the land to the detriment of the socialist economy of the Soviet Union. Such landholders are constantly reminded of the fact that final ownership rights over the land are vested in the state and that the right to use the land is only a privilege unilaterally conferred on them by the Soviet state. For withdrawal of the right to use land, see LAND TENURE.

C. Osakwe

EXTORTION

There are two provisions in the Criminal Code covering extortion: art. 95 which concerns socialist property and art. 148 which concerns personal property. In the case of socialist property the maximum penalty is four years' deprivation of freedom, in the case of personal property, three years. Extortion of socialist property is defined as demanding the transfer of state or public property or property rights, accompanied by threats to use violence against the person who is in control of such property or who is guarding it, or against his relatives, or by threats of spreading defamatory information about him or his relatives, or of destroying their property. Extortion of personal property is defined as demanding the transfer of personal property rights, or demanding the carrying out of specific acts with regard to personal property, accompanied by threats of spreading defamatory information about them, or of destroying their property. "Specific acts with regard to personal property" would include the drawing up of a will, the cancelling of a signature, the destroying of a document, etc.

The words "defamatory information" cover blackmail. It is not relevant whether the information is true. Spreading information to even one person might be sufficient to constitute blackmail. It is said that communist or Soviet morality determines which information is to be regarded as defamatory (see DEFAMATION).

If the offender threatens to use violence, extortion may come very close to either open theft (see THEFT) or robbery (*q.v.*), depending on the nature of the violence. In the latter crimes the threat to use violence is an integral part of a cohesive complex of acts, which is directed at the immediate transfer of property; in extortion the threat to use violence is the central act itself. If the threats work (in the case of socialist property), and property is transferred, the transferor commits the crime of theft of socialist property, although he can plead a defence of necessity (*q.v.*).

F. J. M. Feldbrugge

EXTRADITION

Extradition is usually defined in Soviet legal literature as the surrender of a criminal by the state on whose territory or in whose custody he happens to be to the state of which he is a citizen or on the territory of which he committed the offence for prosecution or serving sentence. The process is regulated by the provisions of a special convention or a domestic statute. The various treaties of extradition concluded by Tsarist Russia prior to 1917 were deemed *eo ipso* terminated by the Bolshevik Revolution and neither renewed nor replaced. Until 1957, the only extradition treaty negotiated by the Soviet government was with Mongolia, of February 28, 1931. No legislation on the subject has ever been enacted. According to Soviet sources, criminals found on Soviet soil could still be surrendered at the request of foreign authorities by virtue of *ad hoc* arrangements worked out through diplomatic channels as long as the principle of reciprocity was observed and in exchange the USSR could expect the return of offenders who had fled its jurisdiction and were wanted locally for criminal prosecution or punishment. However, in view of the Kremlin's heavy ideological emphasis on the "class" difference between Soviet and "bourgeois" legal systems, such contacts, if they occurred at all, must have been very rare indeed. The East-West détente so far has not materially affected conditions in this sector, in terms of a change for the better. At any rate, Soviet citizens were not then and are not now liable to rendition.

During 1957 and 1958, the Soviet Union signed a series of agreements on mutual assistance in civil, family and criminal cases with Czechoslovakia, East Germany, Bulgaria, North Korea, Roumania, Poland, Albania, Hungary and Mongolia, foreseeing, *inter alia*, the extradition of fugitive offenders for purposes of trial or execution of sentence. In 1962, a similar pact was negotiated with Yugoslavia. Pursuant thereto, surrender may take place solely in respect of offences punishable with deprivation of liberty for not less than one year and is barred if the person claimed is a citizen of the state applied to or the crime is committed on the latter's territory or under its law exemption from prosecution has been acquired by the tolling of the statute of limitations or on other grounds or the offender has already been prosecuted locally for the same offence and sentenced or discharged. Since one's own citizens are thus exempt from extradition, each contracting party undertakes to instigate at the request of the interested treaty partner criminal prosecution under its laws against a citizen suspected of having committed an extraditable offence within its associate's jurisdiction. An extradited individual may not, without the consent of the delivering state, be prosecuted, punished or surrendered to a third state for the commission of a prior offence different from the count on which his rendition was originally secured, unless the *de cujus* voluntarily remains on the territory of the state to which he was handed over after the close of the court proceedings against him or after completing his sentence or returns to that country from abroad. Should the prisoner evade prosecution or imprisonment and escape to the country which earlier had extradited him, he may be re-extradited upon submission of a fresh requisition. Finally, each participant (except as between the USSR and Yugoslavia) likewise binds itself to ensure passage through its territory of persons extradited by a third state to the opposite signatory as long as the incident involves an offence which would also entail surrender if instead the state of transit itself had been the object of the requisition.

In the Soviet view, international law today recognizes the universal duty of all members of the world community to surrender upon demand individuals accused of perpetrating so-called international crimes (*q.v.*), e.g., acts of terrorism, crimes against peace and humanity, to the authorities of the country which was the scene of these offences, independent of any express treaty commitment to that effect. This interpretation is not widely shared outside Communist circles.

George Ginsburgs

FAMILY LAW

This topic forms a separate branch of Soviet law, to which the rules of civil law do not necessarily apply. It covers marriage, dissolution thereof, the rights and duties of spouses, matrimonial property, parents and children, family duties of support, adoption, guardianship, the operation, in principle, of the Registry of Civil Status, and relevant problems of conflict of laws. The word 'family' has no general definition and may mean different things in different branches of the law.

By the 1936 Constitution, authority to lay down basic principles is vested in the USSR Supreme Soviet. These were enacted—for the first time—in 1968 and came into force on 1 October. They were followed by republican Codes; that of the RSFSR took effect on 1 November 1969.

Background

Soviet policy towards the family has always had the long-term aim of increasing the population, though varying theories and the short-term exigencies of ideology or productivity have at times obscured this. The three main strands of policy at the Revolution were: i) feminism—the freeing of women from religious, masculine, and political subjugation—which was largely achieved by Revolutionary decrees; ii) sexual liberalism, in which marriage was considered outdated and birth alone the basic family link. This has always been, and still is, a matter for dispute; iii) economic equality. Women have equal rights to work and pay and some 48% of the labour force is female. A condition of effective economic equality is, of course, the provision of institutions for the care of children, which has always featured in Soviet plans, if not so much in performance. Further, Soviet studies of leisure pursuits indicate that the bulk of house-work is done by women.

History

Early decrees (re-enacted in the RSFSR Code of 1918) substituted civil for religious marriage and permitted divorce by mutual consent at the Registry or on application to the court. The wife was not bound to take her husband's name or live with him. These rules prevail now, though divorce underwent a period of tightening up. There was complete separation of property, but this proved so unfair to the house-bound mother that a community of gains has existed since 1926 when the various republics enacted new Codes. Under them, also, mutual duties of support for a spouse incapable of work were introduced; they ended a year after marriage, but the latest legislation omits this provision. The most striking innovation of the 1926 laws was the relaxation of the requirements for marriage—marital rights and duties flowed from *de facto* unions; divorce was taken from the courts and could be obtained by one party at the Registry. The effects of this on children were unsatisfactory and later various measures were introduced to discourage divorce and make parents responsible for their children both civilly and criminally.

The main reforms were embodied in a Federal decree of 8 July 1944 which, with the 1926 Codes, formed the basis of family law until the recent legislation. Its chief aims were to encourage the birth of children and to foster stable marriages without discriminating against the unwed mother. Thus it provided that only registered marriage produced matrimonial rights and duties and gave divorce jurisdiction to the courts; the lower tribunals were to attempt reconciliation and only if this failed would a higher court grant a decree. To encourage the career-mother (whether married or not) state payments were to be made for children with medals for the more prolific mothers. The unmarried father was not liable at all. This in fact stimulated the casually promiscuous male and encouraged the long-term but cautious lover not to register the union, just in case.

The 1968 Principles of Marriage and Family Law were enacted after some months of public discussion of the Bill. They made few serious alterations to matrimonial rights, property, etc. The most significant changes are that paternity of an extra-marital child can now be proved in court and entails duties of support; and that consenting spouses without minor children may obtain a divorce at the Registry. Details will be found under appropriate headings.

Present attitudes

The preamble to the Principles announces that care for the Soviet family is one of the state's most important tasks and promises a wide network of state institutions to help. Some Soviet writers (notably G. M. Sverdlov, the author of the standard work on family law) envisage the disappearance of the family as a unit of consumption and education—"its own sort of fortress, fenced off from society" (Sverdlov). If this occurs, further questions may arise: will women be emotionally content to bear children without having a hand in their rearing? will it be possible to maintain state support of the unmarried mother and still strengthen the registered marriage? how will children be affected by communal upbringing? It is perfectly possible, of course, that these could be shown empirically to have quite satisfactory answers. At present, however, the existence of such answers is simply assumed.

B. Rudden

See also ABSENTEES; ADOPTION; ALIMONY; CIVIL STATUS REGISTRATION; DISSOLUTION OF MARRIAGE; DOMICILE AND RESIDENCE; GUARDIANSHIP AND CURATORSHIP; ILLEGITIMACY; MARRIAGE; MATRIMONIAL PROPERTY; MINORS; NAMES; PARENTS; SUPPORT OF DEPENDANTS

FARMS, see KOLKHOZ; SOVKHOZ; PRIVATE FARMS

FAULT

Fault (*vina*) is the mental (subjective) element which the law considers necessary to connect the (objective) fact of non-performance or of defective performance of an obligation, and the person or organization responsible for that fact.

The obligation can be either contractual or non-contractual, e.g. the duty not to commit a tort. As for the person at fault, a debtor or creditor is responsible towards the other party to the contract, and to third parties, not only for his own acts but also for the acts of those to whom he has entrusted the performance of his obligations (art. 223 Civil Code); even where non-performance is due to the defective performance of sub-contractors, the main contractor will be considered at fault. (But he is, of course, entitled to recover an indemnity from those who are at fault in relation to himself).

Fault is the mental (subjective) element which is requisite for the application of sanctions against a party. There is a presumption of fault as against the person or organization who prima facie (objectively) seems to have caused non-performance or to have committed the tort; he can, however, exculpate himself by proving the absence of fault (art. 222 Civil Code).

Fault can take the form of intention (*umysel*) or negligence (*neostorozhnost'*); under the latter concept gross negligence may appear as a further qualification. In contradistinction to the rule obtaining in the criminal law, the variety of fault does not normally influence responsibility—the sanctions are generally applied in full. But in some instances only intention or gross negligence will be considered as fault, e.g. where the act of the responsible party is of a voluntary donative character (e.g. a gratuitous depositary's responsibility for uncollected goods). When the injured party has himself contributed to the injury, this fact is taken into account when deciding whether the other party is guilty of fault only if the contributory act or omission was done intentionally or with gross negligence.

The parties may, by agreement, extend their liability beyond the field of fault. For certain kinds of activities a *strict liability* (not only for fault, but also for accidental harm) is imposed, excluding only cases of *vis major*. Such liability applies in relation to especially dangerous activities carried on by transport undertakings, industry and building organizations, and also with regard to the driving of motor-cars, etc. Further, the responsibility of those organizations which professionally receive goods on deposit can only be limited so as to exclude damage caused by *vis major* (art. 427 Civil Code).

The definition of the 1922 Code was formulated in a less clear-cut fashion. The presumption of fault could only be rebutted "by proving that the person or organization in question could not avoid" the negative effect. In practice this seems sometimes to have led to a more extensive interpretation of the fault concept, probably under the influence of the connection with the *vis major* concept.

As already stated, if the non-performance or damage is caused by the fault of both parties, the liability can be adjusted by the court; this also applies to situations where the injured party has not—intentionally or by negligence—taken all possible steps to limit the loss caused by the other party's fault (or occasioned accidentally, where such liability applies; art. 224 Civil Code). This measure can be seen as an expression of the liabilities of both parties towards the interests of the socialist economy. *A. Ådahl*

See also LIABILITY; MOTOR VEHICLES; CONTRACTS; OBLIGATIONS; MENS REA

FEDERATION

The formation of a united government by several component states or governmental entities, whereby the federal government exercises certain powers, generally in such areas as armed forces, budget, etc. while the component units retain autonomy in various other areas. A federation is distinguished from a confederation, which is a coming together for certain limited and specified purposes where the confederate power may take actions or implement decisions not directly but only through the governing bodies of: the constituent units; and from a unitary state, which is a centralized structure using territorial units only as administrative subdivisions subordinate to the center.

Federation in the Soviet context is intimately linked to nationality issues. Originally, Marx, and Lenin also, opposed federalism as a form of state structure, preferring a unitary state as the appropriate method of concentrating the power of the dictatorship of the proletariat (*q.v.*) to eradicate vestiges of capitalism and begin construction of socialism and communism. At the time of the Bolshevik Revolution, however, Lenin moved to a position of endoring the propriety and indeed the inevitability of federalism in that concrete historical context. Russia during the periods of the revolutions and civil war was characterized by a growing separatism on the part of the nationality groupings encompassed by the Empire. Federation, first at the level of the RSFSR, then in the formation of the USSR, was found to be the proper tool to unite the disparate nationalities for common defence and common economic development. Thus the adoption of a federal structure was a necessary accommodation to the nationalisms developing within Russia and a proper means for establishing overall Bolshevik control. The use of federation thus helped resolve a difficult problem of the appropriate treatment of national minorities while retaining consistency with the Leninist principle of national self-determination.

There are two levels of federation in the USSR. First is the USSR itself, constituting according to its Constitution a voluntary federation by agreement among the sovereign Union republics, each of which has granted to the federal government certain common powers (enumerated in Article 14 of the USSR Constitution) while retaining various aspects of sovereignty (see generally UNION REPUBLIC). The principles forming the basis of this federation are primarily voluntarism, equality, and democratic centralism.

The second level of federation operates at the Union republic level, involving the relationship between the republic and constituent autonomous republics, autonomous provinces, and national areas.

This type of federation, characterized by the autonomy of various national minorities within the national majority of the Union republic, is regarded as operating only within the RSFSR, despite the fact that other republics contain autonomous republics or provinces. The autonomy at the base of the federation is of two types. The first, political, is represented by autonomous republics, which are viewed as national states possessing their own constitutions, organs of higher state power (Supreme Soviets, Councils of Ministers), and citizenship. The second, administrative, is represented by autonomous provinces and national districts, which are national territorial units in which the respective nationalities are granted a measure of administrative independence through local organs of state power, but do not have constitutions or constitutionally-established higher organs.

The development of federalism within the USSR reflects the principle of national self-determination, the granting to nationality groupings certain powers of self-regulation. The degree of self-determination is generally established through constitutional provisions, with a descending magnitude of internal autonomy through the levels of the Union republic, representing the fifteen major national groupings, the autonomous republic, the autonomous province, and the national district.

As is generally true of federal republics, the highest legislative organ of the USSR, the Supreme Soviet, consists of two chambers: the Soviet of the Union, representing the population of the federation at large; and the Soviet of Nationalities, composed of representatives of the Union republics (32 deputies from each) and representatives of each autonomous national-territorial unit (11 deputies from each autonomous republic, 5 from each autonomous province, and 1 from each national district).

In addition to the constitutional agencies, at the federal level, the constituent Union republics are represented by Permanent Delegations designated by the Republican Council of Ministers. These Delegations are located in Moscow and are empowered to represent the republic before the USSR Council of Ministers in discussions and decisions on matters concerning the republic. Various autonomous republics, generally those located at some distance from the Union republic capital, have similar Delegations, appointed by the Council of Ministers of the autonomous republic. These Delegations act as liaison between the autonomous republics and the Council of Ministers of the Union republic.

Stephen M. Weiner

See also SUPREME SOVIET; AUTONOMOUS REPUBLICS; AUTONOMOUS PROVINCES; KRAI; NATIONAL DISTRICT; OBLAST'

FELONIES, see CRIMINAL LAW

FEMALE EMPLOYEES

Art. 122 of the Constitution of the USSR prohibits discrimination against women in employment relations. Provisions of the Criminal Codes lay down that refusal to hire or discharge a woman on account of her pregnancy or of her having a baby will be punished by corrective labour for a term of up to one year or with discharge (art. 139 Criminal Code RSFSR). Some of the Criminal Codes of the Union republics contain similar provisions for wage discrimination. However, as in many countries, the prohibition of discrimination on account of sex does not imply that the average pay of women equals the average pay of men. This is due to differences in education and in opportunities for extra training facilities; the commanding posts are mainly occupied by men. However, differences in pay are smaller than in many other countries.

On account of the physiological differences between the sexes, the protection of mother and child and the special role women play in the family, Soviet labour law provides special rules for female employees (arts. 160-172 of the RSFSR Labour Code).

It is forbidden to use female workers in heavy work or in work in unhealthy circumstances or in physical underground work (these jobs are enumerated in special lists). Women are exempt from nightwork except in certain branches of the economy where nightwork by women is permitted as a temporary measure.

Special rules apply to pregnant women and women with a child under the age of one. They are exempt from nightwork without exceptions, from overtime, from work on days off and they may not be sent on a service mission (for women with a child under the age of eight, only with their consent). Such women may not be dismissed by management except on occasion of the complete liquidation of the enterprise, and in that event dismissal is only permitted if they have already another job. If such women need easier work, this has to be provided, but they retain the average pay which they earned in their previous post.

Maternity leave extends from fifty-six days before, to fifty-six (and sometimes seventy) days after confinement and it is paid out of the social insurance fund, the amount of the leave pay being dependent on the years of service and on the years of continuous service in the same enterprise and of trade union membership (between two-thirds to full average earnings). Leave without pay must be granted to a woman with a child under the age of one on her request. Paid breaks of at least 30 minutes are due to nursing women every three hours.

Next to these legal rules, the development of a system of crèches and kindergartens in many enterprises and of schools with longer days have given a large number of women the opportunity to go to work.

G. P. van den Berg

FICTIONS

Soviet jurists define a legal fiction (*fiktsiia iuridicheskaia*) as a factual situation established by law which contradicts objective reality, and they state that legal fictions exist in capitalist countries but do not and cannot exist in a socialist state. If, however, a fiction is defined as an assumption that a certain situation exists which it is known does not in fact exist, then Soviet law probably contains as many legal fictions as are found in many Western European legal systems. For example, Soviet law speaks of cancelling the criminal record (*sniat' sudimost'*) of a person under various circumstances, it being assumed thereafter that he was not convicted although it is known that he was in fact convicted (indeed, he must have been convicted in order to have the convictions "cancelled"). To take another example, under Soviet family law from 1944 to 1969, and to a certain extent under the 1969 legislation on the family, it is assumed that a child born out of wedlock has no father. Also Soviet law shares with other legal systems the fiction that a chartered enterprise is a legal (i.e., artificial or fictitious) person.

Of course any legal fiction may be re-stated in non-fictitious terms by referring to the legal consequences of the actually existing situation instead of to an assumed situation known to be untrue. Thus instead of saying that a state enterprise is a legal person, it might be said that a state enterprise shall have the rights and duties of a person (e.g., to sue and be sued, to make contracts, etc.); and instead of saying that a criminal record is cancelled under certain circumstances, it might be said that a convicted person shall not suffer the legal disabilities attached to conviction of crime. In general, this type of formulation enables codified systems of law, such as the Soviet and most Western European systems, to do without legal fictions to a greater extent than systems of law that rely heavily on precedent, such as the English and the American systems. However, under codified systems the doctrine of analogy is used in a way similar to the use of fictions in non-codified systems.

Another, wholly different definition of legal fictions is also given by Soviet jurists, namely, to refer to legal principles that do not correspond to reality in the sense that they are not actually applied. It is stated that such fictions also exist only in bourgeois jurisprudence; among the examples given are the principle of the rule of law, the principle of equality before the law, etc. Here, too, a critic of the Soviet legal system could give Soviet parallels, such as the constitutional right of a Union republic to secede from the USSR, the constitutional right of citizens to use the streets for processions and demonstrations, the enactment of long-term plans like the Five Year Plans as statutes, and others. Arguments on this score are more political than legal, owing to the vagueness of the concept of legal fiction when used in this sense.

Harold J. Berman

See also LAW; PRESUMPTIONS

FINANCIAL LAW

Soviet financial law is basically determined by financial planning which coordinates macro-economic planning of volume and the corresponding monetary operations. Financial planning is carried out by the establishment and execution of a series of financial plans: plans of enterprises and administrations, the state budget, plans of banks and savings banks, etc.

F.l. is concerned with the social relationships arising from the planned process of collection, distribution and utilisation, by the state, of the monetary means which it requires. F.l. may thus be defined as the body of legal norms regulating the social relationships arising from the planned process of collection, distribution, and utilization, by the state, of the monetary means necessary to fulfil its function during a given period of development. The monetary aspect of Soviet f.l. is particularly characteristic.

The state budget is the basic financial plan of the Soviet state. However, the budget does not reflect adequately the totality of financial relationships at the level of the entire economy, because it only registers net results—the final balance of relationships between various economic agents and the budget.

All aspects of the provisions of Soviet f.l. are dominated by their imperative character, arising from monetary relationships which imply the intervention of public power. The provisions of f.l. have their source in the acts of the organs of state power (i.e. legislative organs), or the acts of the state administration (i.e. executive organs).

Financial law regulates the constitution of financial agencies (which are all public institutions) and the relations of these agencies among one another and between these agencies and enterprises (industrial enterprises, cooperatives, kolkhozes) or citizens.

With regard to their subject-matter, provisions of f.l. may be divided into 7 categories; budgetary, fiscal, state insurance, social insurance, credit, money circulation, and financial control provisions. The existence of budgetary, fiscal, monetary circulation and financial control provisions, as constituant elements of f.l., is common to all legal systems. In the Soviet legal system the extension of the domain of f.l. results from the fact that social insurance is taken over by the state, and that the entire banking network, including savings banks, credit and insurance, is in the hands of the state.

P. Lavigne

See also ACCOUNTING; BANKING; BUDGET OF THE STATE; BUDGETS OF ENTERPRISES; CREDIT; CUSTOMS DUTIES; EXPORTS AND IMPORTS; FOREIGN EXCHANGE; INSURANCE; KHOZRASCHET; MONEY; PUBLIC DEBTS; TAXATION

FINES, CIVIL LAW

Fines (and penalties) in Soviet civil law are the most important form of securing performance of obligations under a contract (they may also appear under other forms of legal transaction, e.g. fulfilment of planning provisions). As in other legal systems, the fine is an amount of money agreed upon by the parties to the contract to be paid by the party which violates that contract by failure to perform or by defective performance of his obligations to the other party.

Fines are a particularly effective means of furthering performance within a socialist economy, where the state enterprises or state-dominated co-operative units have little to gain from long litigation over damages and where the planned structure of the economy is dependent on deliveries in the exact quantities and at the exact times stipulated, since there exists no market capable of providing alternative sources of supply. Therefore, the sanction character of the fine (supposed to have an even stronger effect of dissuasion from non-fulfilment of contractual obligations under the new economic system introduced in 1965) has a more important role to play than merely to indemnify the injured party. Furthermore, neither the payment of fines nor of damages relieves the creditor of his duty to perform under the contract. Sometimes the fine is not determined in the contract but in a statute that governs the contract. This, however, in many cases seems to be of less importance, since most contractual fines are part of the "type contracts" (imperative standard contracts) modelled for all the more important kinds of transaction in the commercial sector. The parties' right to change these fines by explicit agreement when concluding the actual contract are often restricted by legislation or by administrative rules. The sanction effect of the fine is underlined by the fact that modification by agreement between the parties is normally allowed to take place only upwards. Undertakings not secured by fines in statutes or standard contracts—e.g. contracts involving citizens—can be provided with a fine-clause by the parties to the contract.

As for the form of the fine, the civil law (art. 188 Civil Code) stipulates that the fine shall be expressed in written form. If not, it is null and void. The fine is usually expressed as a percentage of the value of the defective or deficient performance under the contract. Since the party at fault can often remedy the breach later, it is in many instances rather the delay in the performance than the defect as such that has to be punished. The time-related fine for late performance (*penia*) therefore seems to be of particularly common use.

Occasionally, however, fines are expressed

as fixed sums of money.
It is in the nature of the fine that its amount is determined beforehand, normally at the time of entering into contractual relations (or as determined by statute). At the same time, the reparative effect (and, in exceptional cases, the need also for a further strengthening of the sanctional effect) requires the taking into account of the actual losses that the violation of the contract has caused.
The relation of fines to damages has attracted the special interest of Soviet jurisprudence, since the rich pattern of standard contracts allows for several combinations in this respect (the most important of them are listed in art. 189 Civil Code). The main rule—to be applied whenever no other explicit stipulations have been made—provides that the injured party is entitled to damages, if and to the extent that the damage suffered is greater than the fine stipulated (deductive fine). In certain standard contracts only some sorts of damage may be taken into account, or the damages in excess of the fine may be paid only in part. In e.g. transportation standard contracts, only the fine and no damages can be recovered (exclusive fine); this seems to be the practical method of limiting the overall responsibility of the transport sector and avoiding extensive litigation over railway damage etc. The opposite solution, where both fine and damages are paid in full (cumulative fine), is a strong remedy against default used as a sanction in some types of supply contract (see SUPPLY CONTRACTS).
Art. 189 Civil Code mentions also a fourth case, where the creditor has the option of claiming the payment either of the fine or of the actual damages. Since he is likely to ask for the higher of the two, the result here will in practice be the same as under the main rule.
As for the sanction effects, the amount of the fine can, in exceptional cases, be raised by up to 50% by a court of arbitration if there has been a particularly severe violation of the contract. That portion of the fine is, however, paid directly to the Treasury.
On the other hand, the court of arbitration can also reduce the fine below the amount stipulated in the statute or contract. In relation to obligations between state enterprises, the arbitration court may do so in exceptional cases which are likely to include instances where the actual loss or inconvenience to the other party to the contract has been modest in comparison with the amount of the fine. This also follows from the fact that the reduction of the fine under the main rule for accounting fines and damages is of no value as long as the damages amount to the same (or higher) sums as the fine (see above). When the obligations involve organisations other than state enterprises and citizens—cases belonging to the jurisdiction of the ordinary courts—the court can reduce the damages on the explicit condition that the fine to be paid is excessive in comparison with the actual losses. If this is the case, the court must take into consideration the extent to which the debtor actually performed the obligation as well as the position of the creditor in financial and other respects. A rule of social protection urges the court especially to look to the financial situation of any citizen being either a debtor or creditor in cases where the reduction rule may be applied.

A. Ådahl

See also CONTRACTS

FINES, CRIMINAL LAW
In the USSR fines may be imposed by criminal courts, administrative bodies or administrative offices, comrades' courts and Commissions for the Affairs of Minors. Soviet civil law (art. 186 Civil Code RSFSR) acknowledges contractual or statutory fines or penalties—liquidated damages (see OBLIGATIONS)—but these do not concern us here. In all penal systems, the fine is one of

the most important penal measures and the most frequently used. Whereas measures directed towards the restriction of the offenders' free movements always impose liabilities on the state budget, fines constitute a source of state revenues. This fact facilitates the imposition of fines and may easily lead towards a lesser scrutiny on the part of the bench of the personal circumstances of the offender, his ability to pay or the motives underlying the crime. Thus an old woman pensioner (pension 25 roubles a month) was punished by a people's court in the RSFSR by a fine of 250 roubles for illicitly distilling vodka (*samogon*); the appeal court (1963) reduced the fine to 25 roubles in view of her age and poverty. According to the criminal codes of the republics (art. 27 of Principles of Criminal Law and art. 30 Criminal Code RSFSR) fines may be imposed as principal or additional punishment in accordance with the special part of the criminal code. Some codes, like the Estonian and the Georgian, fix the minimum amount of a fine (10 roubles) in the general part, and sometimes fix the maximum amounts (Estonian and Turkmenian, 100 roubles). An unpaid fine can never be substituted by a sentence of deprivation of freedom (as it is common in the English, Scottish and most continental laws), but it may be converted to corrective labour without deprivation of freedom (but for a period no longer than one year) at a conversion ratio of one month corrective labour (*q.v.*) for every 10 roubles fine. The most frequent form of corrective labour is the continuing employment of the convicted person at his usual place of work, with monthly deductions from his wages (up to 20%) and the exclusion of such periods of employment from the total time of pensionable service. Practically it represents an instalment payment of the fine, although there are also provisions made for people's courts to extend the payment of fines for up to six months. Unpaid fines may be recovered by attachment and public sale of the debtor's property, with the exception of objects not according to law subject to confiscation and attachment (this restriction is not contained in the Azerbaidzhan, Kazakh, Uzbek and Moldavian laws).

The prohibition on converting unpaid fines into deprivation of freedom seemingly has a legal loophole in the above mentioned possibility of conversion of fines into corrective labour, which in its turn may be converted (art. 25 Principles of Criminal Law as amended June 11, 1969) into equal periods of deprivation of freedom.

Fines imposed by sentences of the courts are included in the record of conviction of the offender.

R. Beermann

See also ADMINISTRATIVE OFFENCES; COMRADES' COURTS

FIRES AND FIRE PREVENTION

Fire prevention and fire fighting are among the many tasks of the USSR Ministry of Internal Affairs (see also POLICE; SECURITY; PASSPORTS; TRAFFIC REGULATIONS; PENITENTIARY INSTITUTIONS) and its subordinate ministries at Union republic level and departments at lower levels. Within the ministry there is a Chief Department for Fire Protection, which is the supreme regulatory and supervisory agency in this particular field. There are corresponding departments (*upravleniia*) and sections (*otdely*) at lower levels, and fire brigades in towns.

Most of the first stage fire fighting in rural areas and also in enterprises, institutions, housing estates, etc. is done by voluntary fire brigades, which are united in the All-Russian Voluntary Firemen Association (which is organized in the usual manner in provincial, *raion*, town, and primary branches). The Association, according to its Statute, works "in close contact with the organs of the state fire inspection".

There are special sets of regulations concerning the prevention of forest fires (see also FORESTS AND FORESTRY).

Administrative fines for breaches of fire prevention regulations may be imposed by the various state agencies for fire prevention. In a number of cases of serious carelessness with fire, criminal responsibility may arise. See also ARSON.

For civil law aspects of fires, see TORTS; ACCIDENTS; INSURANCE.

F. J. M. Feldbrugge

FISHING

All bodies of WATER & WATERCOURSES (*q.v.*) of the USSR that can be used for, or in support of, commercial fishing (*rybolovstvo*) are considered fishery waters. Fishing is "commercial" when it is carried out to supply the needs of the state for fish products, as a rule, pursuant to economic plans.

Use of fishery waters is regulated by separate decrees of the USSR Council of Ministers, by laws, decrees and regulations of the Union republics, by regulations of the USSR Ministry of Fisheries etc. These same governmental bodies also act as agencies of fish protection. Commercial fisheries are allocated for use by contracts between the agencies of fish protection and the fishery enterprises. A contract for the use of fisheries contains the parties' mutual obligations regarding the terms of the use of the body of water in question. The contract designates the boundaries of the fishery and the authorized fishing equipment (usually for quantity harvesting). The enterprise accepts the responsibility for making full use of the fishery and returning it to the agency in the event of its inability to manage. The agency retains the right to supervise the enterprise's operations and may rescind the contract on grounds of persistent violations of the contract terms.

Amateur or sports fishing mainly serves to provide recreation for Soviet citizens. Unlike commercial fishing, amateur fishing is permitted to all working people without charge, in all bodies of water, both in designated fisheries and outside them, with the exception of nature preserves, fish hatcheries and cultivated fish ponds or farms. Other limitations on amateur fishing are specified in the legislation of the USSR and the Union republics. Some of them provide additional restrictions regarding location (e.g., prohibition of fishing near dams and underwater shelters); others specify closed seasons, illegal equipment, bag limits, etc. Soviet law also permits the allocation of fisheries for organized amateur fishing to public organizations, such as fishermen's associations or clubs. Here too, the allocation is by a contract between the competent agency of fish protection and the public organization. The arrangement is quite similar to the allocation of commercial fisheries, except for terms peculiar to the non-commercial use. Fisheries allocated to public organizations may be subject to special internal rules more detailed or stringent than the generally-applicable public regulations.

Fishing regulations are enforced by the agencies of fish protection through state and societal fishing inspectors. Poachers are, above all, subject to administrative liability, that is, fines and confiscation of illegal equipment and catches. The more serious cases of violations may entail criminal punishment.

Z. Zile

See also CONSERVATION

FORCE MAJEURE, CIVIL LAW

Force majeure is defined in Soviet legal theory as an extraordinary event (e.g. occurring so rarely or unexpectedly that it cannot normally be taken into account), the harmful effects of which could not be averted by any means at the disposition of the party whose performance is afflicted by *force majeure*.

Events of the type to cause *force majeure*

are floods, severe frost, earth-quakes, hurricanes, and storms, but to be discharged from responsibility the party must also prove that all normal precautions were taken to avoid the harmful results of such phenomena. Forecasts about increased risks (e.g. storm warnings) as well as seasonally or locally increased probability of such events (e.g. floods in spring) exclude any reliance on *force majeure.* Disregarding the increased probability is under these circumstance a form of negligence.

Force majeure thus represents a qualified form of chance (*casus*); not only *force majeure* cases but also other, less extreme factors independent of the parties' will or negligence, discharge from obligations, since fault (negligence or intention) is normally a condition for responsibility in Soviet civil law. An exception is, however, harm caused by sources of increased danger (transport and building equipment, industrial activities, etc.), where only proven *force majeure* discharges from the strict liability imposed by the law.

Force majeure does not discharge the obligation if this is already delayed. Thus it has the function of a further sanction to the party at fault, as the debtor stands the risk connected with the possible *force majeure* kind of events in case of nonfulfilment (in time) of his primary obligations.

A. Ådahl

See also CONTRACTS; OBLIGATIONS

FORCE MAJEURE, CRIMINAL LAW

Soviet criminal law does not mention *force majeure* as a defence, but the concept is borrowed from civil law and accepted by the courts. It is discussed in criminal law textbooks as "irresistible force" (*nepreodolimaia sila*), the same term as is used in civil law. If a person commits a punishable act under the influence of a physically irresistible force, he is not considered to act at all and, since there is no act, there can be no crime. Where a person is not physically forced to commit a punishable act, the irresistibility may be of a relative nature, which means in fact that the "irresistible force" is not absolutely irresistible anymore. In such cases the subject becomes, to a certain extent, a free acting person again, and consequently his criminal responsibility is revived. The exercise of mental force, psychological pressure, etc., to commit a crime may originate from other persons or from natural circumstances. The commission of a crime under the influence of mental or psychological pressure will not be punished if the defendant is able to raise the defence of necessity (*q.v.*): the harm averted must be greater than the harm caused.

F. J. M. Feldbrugge

FORCED LABOUR, see CORRECTIVE LABOUR; PENITENTIARY INSTITUTIONS

FOREIGN CORPORATIONS, see PRIVATE INTERNATIONAL LAW

FOREIGN EXCHANGE

The performance of operations which involve foreign currency and cash, monetary documents drawn in a foreign currency (for examples cheques, bills of exchange, letters of credit, foreign securities, precious metals in their natural form or in the form of coins or bars, goods made out of precious metals, the rights and duties of Soviet institutions and organisations, Soviet citizens and foreigners involving Soviet foreign currency and monetary documents are regulated by Soviet legislation concerning such matters.

This legislation is based upon the monopoly of the state as to the state currency and is aimed at concentrating all the currency reserves in the hands of the state (represented by the State Bank and the Foreign Trade Bank) so as to defend the monetary interests of the state.

These banks have the exclusive right to execute currency operations on the territory of the USSR.
The rate of exchange of the rouble in relation to foreign currencies is fixed by the State Bank. Under Soviet law, foreign currency cannot, as a rule, be circulated in the USSR. The rendering and acceptance of payment in foreign currencies is permitted only for foreign trade operations and certain other cases if specially laid down by law.
Foreign currency obtained by Soviet foreign trade corporations or other organisations is sold to the State Bank or Foreign Trade Bank and foreign currency imported from abroad or received for Soviet or foreign citizens or representatives of foreign states (by the medium of transfers and the like) may be sold only to the said banks or be credited to foreign currency accounts in those banks.
Transfers of currency abroad for foreign trade and other transactions involving Soviet institutions and organisations are not subject to any restrictions subject to the limits laid down by the State Currency Plan; transfers abroad on the instructions of Soviet and foreign citizens or juridical persons are, as a rule, effected only with the permission of the Ministry of Finance of the USSR.
The export and sending abroad and the import and sending from abroad of Soviet currency is forbidden.
As far as payment in international trade is concerned, the governments of the member countries of Comecon (*q.v.*) in June 1957 concluded an Agreement on Multilateral Clearing. It is operated by the Central Banks of the member countries and the clearing house at the USSR State Bank. The accounting unit in these clearing transactions is the transferable rouble.
Short term credits are granted to exporting organisations in the Comecon countries by the International Bank for Economic Cooperation founded in 1964. The International Investment Bank founded in 1970 grants medium and long term credits, primarily for capital goods imports—partly in gold or foreign currencies—to "improve the international socialist division of labour" (to quote the wording of the bank's charter).
The day to day work relating to the financing of Soviet foreign trade is effected by the Foreign Trade Bank of the USSR. The Current (1972) Comprehensive Programme of Comecon has under consideration a number of steps to be taken to provide a realistic gold content and also an exchange rate for the currency of the Comecon member countries. Thus, a change in the gold content or a change in the collective currency must take into account the interests of all the Comecon member countries and will be effected on a basis mutually acceptable to such member countries.

David Winter

See also NEGOTIABLE INSTRUMENTS; CURRENCY SPECULATION

FOREIGN SERVICE, see DIPLOMACY

FOREIGN TRADE

Ministry of Foreign Trade. All Soviet foreign trade is conducted as a state monopoly under the control of the Council of Ministers of the USSR. The Ministry of Foreign Trade possesses the primary political responsibility for the operation of the foreign trade monopoly. It is empowered to negotiate trade and payment treaties, to determine customs and tariff policy, to devise foreign trade plans, to control the quality of exports and the issuance of import and export licenses, to supervise the work of the All-Union Chamber of Commerce, to dispatch and direct trade delegations abroad and to oversee the activities of the specially chartered All-Union Foreign Trade Corporations.
Soviet trade delegations established in foreign countries are considered to be arms of

the Ministry. As such they are entitled to diplomatic privileges and enjoy sovereign immunity, although the latter is now generally waived either by inter-governmental agreement, private contract or unilateral act. While the trade delegations at one time were the principal Soviet foreign merchants, they have been largely superseded by the All-Union Foreign Trade Corporations, in the conduct of the actual business of export and import. They rarely function today as principals in foreign trade contracts, although occasionally they do act as agents for Soviet buyers and sellers. One of their activities is to prospect local markets for export outlets and supply sources, and to provide up-to-date information on contemporary foreign technology. They also have the power to issue import licenses, transshipment permits and certificates of Soviet origin. Prior to the 1972 US-Soviet Commercial Treaty, the USSR was not permitted to establish a trade delegation in the USA. The Soviet foreign trade monopoly has been represented by the Amtorg Trading Corporation, a New York corporation, whose stock is wholly owned by Soviet state interests.

All-Union Chamber of Commerce and Industry. The Chamber of Commerce has the status of a "social organization". It is a juridical entity under direct supervision of the Ministry of Foreign Trade with a voluntary membership composed of all Foreign Trade Corporations as well as many enterprises indirectly engaged in foreign commerce, and shipping, banking and insurance entities. Its functions consist primarily of establishing and maintaining relations with its foreign counterparts, arranging trade fairs at home and Soviet participation in expositions abroad, supplying information and liaison for foreigners wishing to do business in the Soviet Union, maintaining a patent bureau which serves as an intermediary for foreigners who wish to obtain Soviet patents, trade marks or certificates of authorship or have complaints to bring relative thereto. Finally, and of great importance, the Chamber of Commerce provides arbitration facilities designed especially for foreign trade disputes, in the form of two permanent arbitral tribunals—the Moscow Foreign Trade Arbitration Commission and the Maritime Arbitration Commission.

See also FOREIGN TRADE ARBITRATION COMMISSION; MARITIME ARBITRATION COMMISSION.

In addition to and apart from the Ministry of Foreign Trade, the State Committee for Foreign Economic Relations and the State Committee for Science and Technology, both of which are directly subordinate to the Council of Ministers, play important roles in Soviet foreign trade. The former has full responsibility for the direction and expansion of technical assistance to other socialist and developing countries. The latter coordinates all research and development activities in the Soviet Union and has become increasingly active in negotiating, budgeting and executing long-term cooperation agreements with Western firms for whose know-how and technology the Soviet Union has established a high priority.

Foreign Trade Corporations. The commercial activity of the foreign trade monopoly is entrusted on the whole to a small number of specially constituted All-Union Foreign Trade Corporations (*ob"edineniia*). Each Foreign Trade Corporation is chartered by the Council of Ministers and granted exclusive power to transact abroad in specified categories of goods or services. With a few minor exceptions the Foreign Trade Corporations are under the direct supervision of the Ministry of Foreign Trade, which supplies their capital and appoints and dismisses their officials.

The Foreign Trade Corporations are juridical entities, separate and distinct from the state and from each other, operating on the basis of economic accountability (*khozraz-*

chët, q.v.). They act as principals in foreign trade transactions and are considered liable for their debts to the extent of their corporate assets. By virtue of this legal separateness, the Soviet Foreign Trade Arbitration Commission has held, on one celebrated occasion, that the denial of a Soviet export license will excuse a Foreign Trade Corporation from performance or liability under its foreign trade contract on grounds of *force majeure*. Whether the Foreign Trade Corporation, sufficiently distinct from the state to raise an Act of State as *force majeure*, is nonetheless entitled to claim sovereign immunity abroad as a public corporation, is an academically disputed question. In practice, however, no such immunity has ever been or is likely to be asserted.

In furtherance of its delegated portion of the foreign trade monopoly, a Foreign Trade Corporation may be authorized in its charter of incorporation to participate in establishing Western-based joint companies. Thus, for example, in 1969, *Soiuzkhimeksport* was permitted to join French investors in forming Sogo et Cie., S.A. in the field of chemicals and pharmaceuticals, and the Soviet Far Eastern Shipping Company was allowed to purchase 50% of the equity in Tokyo Kyodo Kaiun Kaisha, a new Japanese shipping and brokerage agency set up to accommodate growing Soviet-Japanese trade. These forms enable the institutionalization of long-term relationships with certain foreign merchants and provide the Soviet monopoly a number of advantages in light of current international commercial regulation and taxation schemes. Foreign investment in Soviet entities, however, remains strictly out of the question as a matter of law and policy.

In trade activities with capitalist countries, the Foreign Trade Corporations, within the framework of the foreign trade plan, exercise broad contractual autonomy in negotiating terms and conditions of agreements. In trade with counterpart organizations in other Comecon countries, they possess considerably less freedom, being bound by the mandatory and detailed provisions of the Comecon General Conditions of Delivery and the terms of the Bilateral Trade and Payments Agreements which the Soviet Union maintains with each of these states. Foreign trade payments and receipts are effectuated in the USSR through the State Bank and *Vneshtorgbank*, the latter being specially constituted for this purpose.

Jeffrey Hertzfeld

See also EXPORT & IMPORT; FOREIGN TRADE CONTRACTS

FOREIGN TRADE ARBITRATION COMMISSION

The Moscow Foreign Trade Arbitration Commission was founded in 1932 and is attached to the All-Union Chamber of Commerce. Its competence extends to all disputes arising out of foreign trade transactions, particularly, but not exclusively, controversies between foreign and Soviet disputants. It may also decide cases involving only foreign parties. While such situations usually involve foreign trade entities of other Comecon countries, in a few instances the tribunal has considered claims arising between two West European disputants.

The Commission maintains a College of Arbitrators appointed annually by the Presidium of the Chamber of Commerce and composed of 15 members chosen from the administrations of Soviet trade, industrial and transport organizations, and from the law and economics faculties of Soviet universities. A president and two deputies are chosen from among the membership.

The Rules of Procedure are published by the Chamber of Commerce. Arbitration before the tribunal must be upon formal written agreement of the parties, although the submission need not be contained in the foreign trade contract itself. Where arbitration is agreed upon, it is considered to be an exclusive remedy ousting the jurisdiction of the regular courts. Disputes are heard by two arbitrators, one chosen by each of the parties, and a "super-arbitrator" chosen by the two arbitrators themselves. If a choice of arbitrator or super-arbitrator cannot be or is not made, the President of the Commission is empowered to make the selection. All arbitrators in the College are Soviet citizens. However, foreign counsel is permitted to appear on behalf of a foreign disputant.

Hearings are public, unless either party requests that they be held in private. Decisions are required to be in the form of reasoned opinions. These decisions are final and binding upon the parties. Extracts of selected opinions are occasionally published in Russian by the Chamber of Commerce in "Collections of Information Materials" which provide some guidance to persons who may be interested in the developing body of foreign trade case law and legal principles applied by the Commission.

Provisions exist for enforcement of an arbitral award against a local party in the ordinary courts. In practice, voluntary compliance has been the rule. Domestic state organizations are in no position to be recalcitrant, since they are subject to ministerial direction and the foreign business reputation of the country is in issue. Enforcement abroad is governed by treaty or, in the absence thereof, by the law of the place where execution is sought. Foreign parties likewise tend to satisfy arbitral awards promptly rather than jeopardize their standing in the monopolistic Soviet market. The cost of foreign trade arbitration may not exceed 1% of the sum in controversy.

By and large, the Foreign Trade Arbitration Commission has acquired a reputation for fairness and reasonableness, and has played an active role both in East-West and intra-Comecon trade disputes. In recent years, however, in the area of East-West trade, this forum has been increasingly displaced by contractual submissions in favor of bodies in neutral countries such as Sweden and Switzerland, and as a further compromise, by agreements to arbitrate future controversies before a specified tribunal in the defendant's country. The USSR is a party to the New York Convention on Recognition and Enforcement of Foreign Arbitral Awards (1958) and the UN ECE Convention on International Arbitration (1961).

Jeffrey Hertzfeld

FOREIGN TRADE CONTRACTS

Art. 3 of the Principles of Civil Legislation (1961) states that "Relations in foreign trade are determined by specific USSR legislation regulating foreign trade and by the general civil legislation of the USSR and the Union republics". Art. 125 thereof provides that "the form of foreign trade transactions carried out by Soviet organizations together with the procedure for signing them regardless of the place where those transactions are carried out are determined by USSR legislation". This provision is imperative upon and unalterable by the parties. The substantive norms are found dispersed in specialized legislation dating back to 1930, in the charters of the various foreign trade corporations, and in the Principles of Civil Legislation as well as the republican codes promulgated pursuant thereto.

To be valid, foreign trade contracts and commercial paper must be in writing and must bear two signatures. Contracts must be executed by the president of the foreign trade corporation or his deputy and by one other person possessing a power of attorney signed by the president. Bills of exchange and other monetary obligations require the signature of the president or his deputy and the chief accountant of the foreign trade corporation.

While all foreign trade contracts must be in writing, they need not be in a single integrated instrument. Foreign trade contracts entered into by an exchange of letters, telegrams, telephoned telegrams or the like, bearing the requisite signatures, are valid. Additions to and changes in foreign trade contracts demand the same formalities.

General Civil Code rules of contract formation apply in the foreign trade area. Written offers are considered firm for a "normally necessary" period for acceptance unless otherwise specified. A purported acceptance altering the terms of an offer is a rejection and a counter offer. Acceptance is effective upon receipt by the offeror. As a corollary, contracts are deemed made at the place where acceptance of the offer is received, a consideration which, under Soviet choice of law rules for foreign trade contracts, is determinative of the applicable law governing rights and obligations, in the absence of treaty or party election to the contrary.

As a general rule, risk of loss passes with delivery of goods, delivery being defined as the handing over of the goods to the buyer, a carrier or the mails, or delivery of shipping documents. The risk of loss will also pass upon a seller's tender of delivery if the buyer delays receipt thereof.

The Russian Civil Code establishes a three-year period of general application for the commencement of civil actions, a one-year period for disputes between local economic organizations, and a six month period in suits involving liquidated damage claims, defective goods, incomplete delivery or defective quality. Only the three-year and six-month periods are considered to apply to foreign traders. Where applicable, the statute of limitations provisions are mandatory. The parties may not agree to alter them and arbitral tribunals are required to invoke them even if the defendant does not.

Supply contracts (contracts of delivery) concluded between parties belonging to different countries of the Council of Economic Mutual Aid (CEMA, Comecon, see COMECON), are governed by the General Conditions of Delivery issued by the Standing Foreign Trade Commission of the said body on May 29 - June 1, 1968 (replacing a similar instrument of 1957). The semi-mandatory provisions of the General Conditions (parties may make other arrangements where "in their view this is required by the specific nature of the goods or of the contract") provide detailed rules concerning the making, contents and performance of such contracts. The latter will be governed, insofar as the Conditions do not contain the answer, by the law of the seller's country. Disputes will be preceded by a claim procedure and will be heard by the Foreign Trade Arbitration Tribunal of the country of the defendant. Supply and assembly of plants and other services rendered by an enterprise of one of the countries of the Council to an enterprise of another, in connection with delivery and installation of machinery or other equipment, are governed by General Conditions issued on this subject by the Meeting of the Representatives of the countries of CEMA on March 29, 1962, and are subject to rules for dispute settlement analogous to those applicable to contracts for delivery of goods. In practice, annual meetings of the Arbitration Commissions of the Comecon states endeavour to unify the interpretation and application of the General Conditions. Rules for contracts of supply of energy are provided by Regulations of the Ministry of Electricity and Electrification of the USSR of January 13, 1969, and for gas supply contracts by Regulations of July 31, 1961, of *Gosarbitrazh* of the Council of Ministers of the USSR.

Jeffrey M. Hertzfeld

See also FOREIGN TRADE; FOREIGN TRADE ARBITRATION; SUPPLY

FOREIGNERS, see ALIENS

FORENSIC MEDICINE

The principal function of forensic medicine in the Soviet Union is to provide expert evidence (see EXPERTS) in criminal and civil cases. Forensic medicine itself is within the competence of the Ministry of Health and the Ministry of Justice. The actual work is done by medical experts, attached to the bureau of forensic medicine, which itself is part of thc provincial (*oblast'*) health department (or the city health department in Moscow and Leningrad). The work of the bureau is supervised by republican experts in forensic medicine (attached to the republican ministries of health), while the top of the pyramid is occupied by the chief medical expert of the USSR Ministry of Health. Within this ministry there is a Scientific Research Institute of Forensic Medicine.

In criminal procedure expert medical opinion must be sought in a number of cases mentioned by art. 79 of the RSFSR Code of Criminal Procedure (establishment of the causes of death or the nature of injuries, of the physical condition of witnesses or the victim, and the age of the accused, the suspect, or the victim, if no documents are available). The nature of injuries in criminal procedure is determined according to the Rules for establishing the degree of physical injuries (issued by the RSFSR Minister of Health on April 4, 1961). As a general rule, expert medical opinion must be sought in criminal as well as in civil procedure whenever medical knowledge is required in order to answer litigious questions (art. 78 RSFSR Code of Criminal Procedure, art. 74 RSFSR Code of Civil Procedure). In civil procedure the medical expert is appointed by the court, in criminal procedure by the investigator, although the court and the procurator (and in some cases the police) are also entitled to appoint experts. The normal procedure is to order the provincial bureau of forensic medicine to designate one of its staff; this person serves then as medical expert and is personally responsible for his opinion (cf. art. 187 Code of Criminal Procedure). In complicated cases a commission of forensic-medical experts may be appointed. More detailed rules concerning expert medical opinion may be found in the Instruction of the USSR Ministry of Health concerning expert medical opinion of December 13, 1952.

F. J. M. Feldbrugge

FORENSIC PSYCHIATRY

Forensic psychiatry in the USSR is regarded as a branch of clinical psychiatry and is guided by the materialistic approach to psychic phenomena rather than by case law. Soviet psychiatry follows a tradition established before the turn of the century, but modified by scientific progress and by the Marxist approach to human behaviour.

The relevant provisions of the Principles of Criminal Legislation of the USSR and of the RSFSR Criminal Code are similar to those of other modern codes. Article 11 of the Criminal Code states: "A person shall not be criminally responsible if at the time of committing a socially dangerous act he was in a state of non-imputability, i.e. he could not realize the significance of his actions or control them because of a chronic mental illness, temporary mental disorder, mental deficiency, or other illness. Compulsory measures of a medical character may be applied to such a person by order of the court (arts. 58-61).

Also, a person shall not be subject to punishment if he committed a crime in a state of imputability but, before the verdict of the court, contracted a mental illness depriving him of the ability to realize the significance of his actions or to control them. Compulsory measures of a medical character may be applied by the court to such a person, but upon recovery he may be subject to punishment."

In practice, however, the central issue facing

a psychiatrist is *not* whether the accused knew what he was doing and whether he knew it was wrong: he is called upon to assess the total functioning of the defendant and to establish whether it is normal or, if pathological, to what degree. He must assess these functions both as they existed at the time of the alleged offence and as they exist at the time of the investigation and trial. Often he must also re-assess the situation after the trial.

He tries to determine the appropriate kind of social defence measures of medical character and the place where they should be applied. The modern concept of mental illness rather than that of legally defined insanity is used; it also applies to witnesses (Code of Criminal Procedure, art. 79) and to legal matters of a non-criminal nature (e.g. validity of contracts). The assessment procedure may be carried out in the chambers of the judicial investigator, in a psychiatric hospital or clinic or, in some cases (e.g. death), in the absence of the subject. If a serious mental illness or defect at the time of the criminal act is established, appropriate medical measures may be imposed (Criminal Code, Ch. 6, Code of Criminal Procedure, art. 403). Psychiatric treatment in an ordinary or special mental hospital is compulsory, unless the person concerned does not represent a danger to society (Code of Criminal Procedure, art. 410). Psychiatrists function within the framework of public health rather than justice, but they are appointed by courts or called upon at the time of pre-trial investigation, from the lists of specialists in forensic matters. Additional experts may be called if necessary (Code of Criminal Procedure, art. 81). Alcoholic intoxication does not exclude culpability, unless it is pathological (Criminal Code, art. 12).

Organic, constitutional and situational bases of mental disorders are accepted, but Lombrosian typologies of criminal predisposition are rejected. Emphasis is on social rather than genetic determinants of all behaviour: I. P. Pavlov's masterpiece on conditioned reflexes still dominates Soviet psychology and psychiatry, including forensic psychiatry. Reactive, psycho-physiological mechanisms, studied objectively and observed in detail, are stressed. Psycho-dynamic formulations of Freud are rejected as contrary to both Marxism and science. Publications of the Serbskii Institute, the main Soviet centre of forensic psychiatry, discuss problems of epilepsy, schizophrenia, organic disorders, manic-depressive psychosis, mental defect, psychopathy, confabulation, depersonalization, simulation, reactive states, pathological affective states and uncontrollable impulse. Among addictions alcoholism, and among neuroses hysteria, are important for the expert witness. Frequencies differ but the problems are obviously similar to those in the West.

T. Grygier

See also INTOXICATION; EXPERTS & EXPERT WITNESSES; MENS REA

FORESTS AND FORESTRY

Soviet law of forests (*lesnoe pravo*) regulates the ownership, use and protection of existing forests as well as forestation.

All forests of the Soviet Union, along with other NATURAL RESOURCES (*q.v.*) are exclusively owned by the state. The object of the state ownership is "the single state forestry fund" which includes, besides the forests themselves as a distinct feature of the natural environment, lands directly connected with them (marshes, roads, etc.) or set aside for forestry purposes. The boundaries of the forestry fund shift with the addition of lands to, or their withdrawal from, the fund. Severance converts timber into an independent object of ownership rights. Consequently, logs (as distinguished from standing timber) can also become the property of particular legal entities and individuals.

For purposes of administering the use and exploitation of forests, the state forestry fund is divided into two broad categories—forests of state significance and collective-farm forests—each under a different legal regime. These, in turn, are broken down into several subcategories, with still further refinements in the applicable law.

The first subcategory of forests of state significance comprises: protected forests on watersheds, along rivers and roads and around water reservoirs; forests within nature preserves, hunting grounds and resort areas; greenbelts around urban centers and industrial settlements (see also ZONING); especially valuable forests; and the like. Industrial logging is prohibited in these forests. The second subcategory includes forests of regions of sparse forest growth. Logging in them is severely restricted. All remaining forests of state significance fall into the third subcategory. Here, one finds the forests of forest-rich regions that supply most of the industrial requirements of lumber and other wood products.

The volume of the annual timber harvest ("logging fund") is fixed by the USSR Council of Ministers on the basis of proposals submitted by the competent republic forestry agencies and the USSR State Planning Committee (*Gosplan*). Thereafter, the logging fund is distributed to logging enterprises and organizations and local government units. The latter may further grant logging rights to individual citizens for their personal needs. Logging rights are granted, as a rule, upon payment of a stumpage fee.

Certain subsidiary uses are also permitted in forests of state significance, except where such uses would infringe upon the essential character of the forests. The most common subsidiary uses are: hay-making, cattle grazing, beekeeping, berry and mushroom picking, gathering of nuts and herbs, digging of peat, etc. From a legal point of view, subsidiary uses are open to either general or limited access. General access means that the particular use may be enjoyed by any member of the public without special authorization, but subject to generally applicable rules. Limited access, by contrast, is selectively granted to identified enterprises, organizations or individuals for specified purposes and duration. In some of these cases (e.g., digging of peat), a user fee may be charged.

Collective-farm forests are forests situated on lands which have been turned over to the collective farms for their perpetual use and properly registered as forest lands. There are two subcategories of collective-farm forests: woodlots performing functions similar to those of the protected forests of state significance, and all other undifferentiated woodlands. Only selected, silvicultural cutting is permitted in the first subcategory. Exploitative logging is confined to the second. Collective-farm forests are managed and used in accordance with plans approved by forestry agencies.

The USSR is competent to define the principles of the use of forests. Legislation adopted in the exercise of this constitutional power is scattered through several statutes and executive decrees. Codification of the All-Union principles is, however, reportedly in progress. The more detailed elaboration of the law of forests is within the jurisdiction of the Union republics. Since the RSFSR has more than 90 percent of the Soviet state forestry fund in its territory, the Russian republic's law is the second most important component of the Soviet law of forests. However, this body of law is likewise scattered through numerous overlapping and sometimes contradictory sources. The RSFSR Forestry Code of 1923 is considered obsolete.

Forestry matters are under the guidance of the State Committee on Forestry of the USSR Council of Ministers. The Committee's counterpart agency in the RSFSR is the

Union republic Ministry of Forestry of the RSFSR. The actual forest exploitation is segregated from silvicultural responsibilities and vested in such industrial ministries as the Union republic Ministry of Lumber and Wood-Processing Industry of the USSR and the All-Union Ministry of Pulp and Paper Industry of the USSR.

The forestry agencies are also charged with protecting the state forestry fund. They strive to suppress illegal cutting and unauthorized or abusive subsidiary uses, fight plant diseases and pests, organize fire safety, etc. Violation of most of the rules governing the use of forests may entail administrative liability. Civil and criminal liability may also be imposed in appropriate cases. Thus, enterprises, collective farms or individuals caught at illegal cutting, cattle grazing or haymaking may be required to pay the forestry agencies for the damage done. Arson and the negligent handling of fire resulting in the destruction of, or substantial damage to, large tracts of forests is punishable by long terms of deprivation of freedom. Illegal cutting of timber and damage to forest plantings by grazing are other criminal offenses. However, nonenforcement of the existing laws, especially against industrial violators, is typical. Soviet critics contend that the operatives of forest products industries have become the virtual masters of the country's forests, with the foresters usually accommodating the industry. Control over the correct use of timber resources is lacking. Timber is cut in the most convenient areas, without regard to good forestry practices. Waste levels are high at every stage (cutting, floating, milling). Much of the wood that is cut remains in the forest. The uncleared ground retards reforestation. Forest fires also cause heavy damage.

Z. Zile

See also CONSERVATION

FORFEITURE

Art. 149 of the Civil Code of the Russian Federation defines forfeiture, in contradistinction to requistion, as the seizure by the state of an owner's property in the interests of the state or public, without compensation, as a form of sanction for breach of the law. Forfeiture, like requisition, is permitted only in the instances and in accordance with the procedures set out in the legislation of the USSR and the Russian Federation. The basic differences in law between forfeiture and requisition is that whereas the former is a legal sanction against some violation of the law, the latter is not considered to be a legal sanction as such; secondly, whereas forfeiture presupposes no compensation for the forfeited property, a requisitioned property is compensated for by the requisitioning state organ.

At the time of confiscation of the property, the state is not responsible for debts and obligations of the convicted person if they have arisen after the taking of measures for the preservation of the property by agencies of inquiry, investigative or judicial agencies, or, in any event, without the consent of such agencies (cf. CRIMINAL INVESTIGATION). With respect to claims subject to satisfaction out of the confiscated property, the state is responsible only within the limits of the assets; with respect to the order of priority of claims, the rules established by the Code of Civil Procedure of the Russian Federation are observed.

Under the provisions of the Criminal Code of the Russian Federation forfeiture is considered to be one of the kinds of punishments for crimes committed (art. 21, par. 10). While designating deprivation of freedom, correctional tasks without deprivation of freedom, social censure and assignment to a disciplinary battalion as basic measures of criminal punishment, art. 22 of the Criminal Code of the Russian Federation considers forfeiture of property, inter alia, as a possible supplementary punitive measure.

Art. 35 of the Criminal Code, in a most meticulous fashion, points out that confiscation of property consists of the compulsory transfer to state ownership, without compensation, of all or part of the property constituting the personal property of the convicted person. If only a part of the property is confiscated then the court must indicate what part it is or list the confiscated articles. Articles necessary for the convicted person and for persons dependent on him are not to be subject to confiscation, in accordance with the list given in the Appendix to the Criminal Code. The Appendix lists the following property as not being subject to confiscation by judgment of the court: any dwelling house and appurtenant buildings or separate parts thereof for persons whose basic occupation is agriculture, if the convicted person and his family live permanently therein; also for persons whose basic occupation is agriculture, a single cow, and, in the absence of a cow, a single heifer, etc. The long list also includes fodder for cattle, seed necessary for regular sowing, basic articles of household furniture, food products in an amount necessary for the convicted person and his family until the new harvest, fuel necessary for the preparation of food and heating in the family living quarters during the cold season, supplies necessary for continuing the professional occupation of the convicted person, shares in cooperative organizations and such other items of personal property.

The crimes for which forfeiture may be a supplementary measure of punishment are listed in art. 21, part 2 and in art. 30 of the Principles of Criminal Legislation of the USSR and the Union Republics. These include crimes against the state (arts. 64-88 of the Criminal Code of the Russian Federation), and crimes aimed at obtaining illegal material gains.

Forfeiture as a legal sanction can also be ordered by the court either as an administrative measure or as a measure of civil responsibility. Under the provisions of art. 49 of the Civil Code, if a transaction is consciously effected with an object that is incompatible with the interests of the socialist state and the public, and if both parties intended this and have performed their parts in the transaction, everything received by them in pursuance of such an illegal deal is to be forfeited to the state.

The provision of this article occupies a central place in the legal efforts of the state to protect socialist property. This is the only kind of invalidity of transaction specifically singled out in the Principles of Civil Legislation of the USSR and the Union Republics (art. 14, par. 6). It is important to note that the transaction referred to in art. 49 is one which was entered into consciously by the parties and was knowingly aimed against the interests of the socialist state or public. Examples of such acts, as often mentioned in Soviet doctrinal commentaries to this article, include: the buying and selling of land in the USSR, the use of an acquired house for the purposes of an illegal religious assembly, etc. For such an act to be declared invalid under art. 49 of the Civil Code, it must have been performed in full or in part by the parties.

Art. 49 should be seen not only as a replacement of the provisions of art. 30 of the 1922 Civil Code of the Russian Federation, but also as an up-to-date enactment of the judicial practices which have evolved around the interpretation of the 1922 Code. Even though art. 30 of the 1922 Code did not specifically mention "transactions consciously effected" (as is the case under art. 49 of the 1964 Code), the practice of the courts and the *Arbitrazh* in the interpretation of the code restricted the sanction envisaged by that article only to such transactions as were consciously effected by the parties. If it was proved that the parties acted in good faith or were under some error that was not due to their own fault, the courts and the *Arbitrazh* merely restored the rights of the parties to their original position without seizing the articles involved in such transactions.

Similarly, under art. 111 of the Civil Code of the Russian Federation, if a citizen systematically uses any dwelling house, cottage or part of the same or any other property owned by him to obtain unearned income, such property is liable to confiscation without compensation in any judicial proceedings instituted by the executive committee of the local council of deputies. The house, cottage, etc., in such cases is added to the housing resources of the local council.

Houses, dachas and other buildings which have been erected entirely or in part by means of unearned income, may be confiscated by virtue of a decree of July 26, 1962; in such cases cars owned by the owners of buildings erected by means of unearned income may also be confiscated by virtue of a decree of September 28, 1963.

As in the case of requisition, any individual who suffers illegal forfeiture of his property may institute court action to demand compensation under arts. 446 and 447 of the Civil Code of the Russian Federation as well as under art. 21 of the Law on Requisition and Confiscation of 1927 (see REQUISITION). The procedure for the restoration of forfeited property is regulated by an Instruction of the Ministry of Finance of the USSR dated March 20, 1965 (Instruction No. 92), and by the *Postanovlenie* of the Plenum of the Supreme Court of the USSR dated September 29, 1953 (No. 7), and by other laws of the Soviet federal government.

The confiscatory and requisition procedures contained in art. 149 of the Civil Code of the Russian Federation should be distinguished from the measures listed under arts. 141-148 of the Civil Code.

Under art. 141 of the Civil Code of the Russian Federation, if a citizen fails to take adequate care of a house belonging to him and permits it to decay, the executive committee of the local council of deputies may notify him to repair the house within a reasonable time. If such citizen, without a proper excuse, fails to carry out the necessary repairs, the court may, in a suit instituted by the executive committee of the *raion* or town council of workers' deputies, confiscate the house without compensation and add it to the housing resources of the local council of workers' deputies. Similarly, any untended cultural treasures (art. 142), ownerless property (art. 143), or live-stock found on the territory of a state farm (art. 147), and treasure trove (art. 148) is liable to be confiscated by the state.

C. Osakwe

See also STRAY CATTLE; TREASURE

FORGERY

The basic provision concerning forgery is the first paragraph of art. 196 of the Criminal Code, which deals with the forging of certain documents or the passing of such documents, and with the making of counterfeit stamps, seals, or forged forms, or the passing of such stamps, seals or forms. The documents covered by this provision are testimonials (*udostovereniia*; see DOCUMENTS) and other documents issued by state institutions or enterprises or by a social organization, which grant a right or release from a duty. The forgery must have been committed for the purpose of using the forged document or form or counterfeit stamp or seal, either by the forger himself or by another person. In the case of passing, the offender must have known that the document, stamp, etc., was forged or counterfeit. It is not required that the person who passed the document, etc., had committed the forgery himself. The offence of art. 196 par. 1 carries a maximum penalty of two years' deprivation of freedom. The same offence committed "systematic-

ally" (i.e. more or less regularly, or as a business or profession) entails a maximum penalty of five years (par. 2 of the same article).
The third paragraph of art. 196 is devoted to the use of forged documents (maximum penalty one year). In this case the forged document is employed in order to obtain an advantage to which a genuine document would entitle the bearer. In the case of "passing", as mentioned in the first paragraph of the article, the document is handed on, without being "used".
Forging or counterfeiting may be carried out by producing a new and false object, or by changing a genuine object. The third paragraph of art. 196 (the use of forged documents) is interpreted to imply the use of genuine documents (e.g. a passport) by somebody who is not entitled to such use. It would seem that such use would be better considered as one of the forms of fraud. In any case, many instances of the use of forged documents will also be covered by other provisions of the Criminal Code (especially by arts. 93 and 147: theft by means of fraud). See also FRAUD and MULTIPLE OFFENCES.
Besides art. 196, the Criminal Code contains a number of provisions dealing with special types of forgery. Art. 80 par. 2 covers evasion of military service by forging a document among other things (a crime against the state); art. 249 covers (among other things) evasion of military duties by a soldier by means of forging a document (a military crime). Art. 133 is devoted to forging election documents and art. 175 to forgery committed in an official capacity. The latter offence consists of the forging of an official document by an official from mercenary or personal motives. The concept of forging is defined very loosely in this provision; it includes any entries in official documents and records which are known to be false. Art. 175 presents one of the rare cases where the penalty of dismissal is mentioned among the possible penalties (cf. art. 31 of the Criminal Code). A special case of forgery by an official is found in art. 152-1 (additions to state accounts or the presentation of intentionally distorted account data concerning the fulfilment of plans); art. 152-1 should be regarded as a *lex specialis* vis-à-vis art. 175 (it carries a higher maximum penalty; three, instead of two years' deprivation of freedom). The description of the offence in art. 152-1 is followed by the curious addition: "as anti-state actions, inflicting harm on the national economy of the USSR". Such specimens of legislative of legislative exclamations were quite common in earlier Soviet law; they have become rare now and are mostly found in pieces of incidental legislation which are the product of a particular campaign (such as this provision, which was added in 1962).

F. J. M. Feldbrugge

See also COUNTERFEITING; OFFICIAL CRIMES

FRAUD, CIVIL LAW

Together with duress (i.e. violence, threats or exploitation of the concurrence of adverse circumstances) and abuse of confidence, fraud resulting in a legal transaction is given (art. 58 Civil Code) as a ground for having the transaction declared void by a decision of the court.
Fraud occurs when a party (or beneficiary under the transaction) consciously and intentionally provokes in the mind of the other party an erroneous conception of the circumstances on which the transaction is based or of the elements in the transaction; the result is that the transaction in question will not be an expression of the acting party's true intentions.
Fraud can take the form of supplying wrong or distorted information, or of concealing facts that are essential for the decision of the

acting party; the information given or suppressed may have reference either to the motives behind the transaction or to the transaction itself. A transaction is considered as to be made under the influence of fraud if it is clear that it would have a different content, or would not have been made at all, if the true circumstances had been known to the acting party at the time.
A legal transaction made under the influence of fraud can be declared void by a court at the instance of the acting party or of any socialist organization. Acts considered fraudulent by the civil law are naturally often subject to criminal sanctions as well. But even in the civil law the anti-social character of fraud seems to be the motive behind one aspect of the system of sanctions applicable when a transaction is declared void: the fraudulent party must restore to the injured party what he has obtained, but may not himself receive any restitution—whatever he may have given in exchange is forfeited to the state.

A. Ådahl

See also DURESS

FRAUD, CRIMINAL LAW

Fraud as a means of deception, the conscious distortion or suppression of the truth, is not in itself a crime, but appears as the core of a few more specific criminal acts: theft of socialist property by means of fraud (art. 93 of the Criminal Code), theft of personal property by means of fraud (art. 147), causing loss by means of fraud (art. 94), and defrauding customers in stores and other commercial enterprises (art. 156).
As a form of theft, fraud implies the voluntary transfer of property to the thief, in contrast to secret theft (where the owner or possessor is unaware of the fact that the property has been taken), open theft (where the property is taken or handed over against the will of the owner or possessor) and embezzlement (where the property is already legitimately in the hands of the thief). Otherwise the treatment of theft by means of fraud is similar to that of other forms of theft (esp. with regard to penalties, qualifying circumstances, etc.; see THEFT). Arts. 93 and 147 not only cover theft committed by means of fraud, but also through abuse of confidence (which also leads to a voluntary transfer of property). Art. 147 includes not only the transfer of personal property, but also the transfer (brought about by fraud) of property rights.
The offence of art. 94 (causing loss to the state or to a public organization by means of fraud) has been included in the chapter on crimes against socialist property, in order to cover cases where there is no loss of socialist property (such as occurs in all cases of theft of socialist property), but where the state or a public organization is deprived of a profit which they would normally receive. This offence will usually appear in the shape of non-transfer of something which is due to the state or a public organization (e.g. the non-payment of taxes or duties); an essential part of the offence is the use of fraudulent means or the abuse of confidence (e.g. the indication of a lower amount than was in fact paid or earned in order to avoid taxation). In many cases the use of socialist property (means of transport, machinery) for private purposes will produce the offence defined in art. 94.
Defrauding of customers in stores, other trading enterprises or restaurants is included among the economic crimes (*q.v.*). Art. 156 mentions specifically defrauding by incorrect measuring or weighing, by exceeding established retail prices (see RETAIL TRADE), or by supplying incorrect bills or accounts. The wording of art. 156 makes it quite clear that in all such cases the intention to defraud is required.

F. J. M. Feldbrugge

See also EXTORTION

FREEDOM OF ASSEMBLY

Since freedom of assembly, including the holding of mass meetings, is guaranteed by Article 125 of the Soviet Constitution in conformity with the interests of the working people and in order to strengthen the socialist system, there is no individual liberty of this kind whatsoever in the Soviet Union. Rather it is an instrument for performing the political function of social integration and aggregation by the Party and the different mass organizations. Freedom of assembly serves the mobilization of the masses in order to demonstrate socialist democracy and the whole Soviet people's unity concerning certain political issues which are intended to be given special emphasis. Accordingly, congresses and conferences of mass organizations, mass rallies on national holidays and before elections to the various soviets are considered by Soviet legal literature as the forms in which freedom of assembly manifests itself. Indeed, in Article 125 of the Constitution there is no other body than the Party and the organizations of the working people mentioned as holders of the freedom's material guarantees which could organize a public meeting. Religious organizations are not allowed to do this because Article 124 of the Constitution restricts freedom of conscience to religious worship which can only be performed in churches. According to the RSFSR regulation "on Religious Associations" of April 8, 1929, religious processions and meetings of believers must obtain prior consent of the local administration's competent organ.

The wrongful use of freedom of assembly is subject to criminal prosecution. Until recently, there was only the provision on anti-Soviet agitation and propaganda (article 70 of the 1960 Criminal Code of the RSFSR) which could be applied in such cases. In September 1966 a more specific provision was adopted and inserted in the Criminal Code of the RSFSR. According to article 190-3, organizing and actively participating in group activities grossly violating public order or involving open disobedience to lawful orders of representatives of power, or resulting in disturbance of the traffic, the working of state and social institutions or enterprises, are punishable by deprivation of freedom for up to three years or by corrective labour for up to one year or by a fine of up to one hundred roubles. This provision was applied for the first time in February 1967 to V. Khaustov, who had participated in a demonstration against the arrest of literary figures. Since then, Article 190-3 has been the legal ground for several trials, e.g. against V. Bukovskii, V. Delone, and E. Kushev in August 1967 and in connection with demonstrations in Moscow against the invasion of Czechoslovakia.

G. Brunner

See also CIVIL RIGHTS

FREEDOM OF ASSOCIATION

Freedom of association is guaranteed by Art. 126 of the Soviet Constitution with four limitations; it may only be enjoyed 1) in conformity with the interest of the working people, 2) in order to develop the initiative and political activity of the masses of the people, 3) in relation to certain types of social organizations and 4) under the leadership of the Communist Party. From all this it is evident that freedom of association in the Soviet Union is not, and is not intended to be, an individual liberty, but has to serve as a means of political integration of the people in order to realize party objectives. As a consequence, there is practically no room for private associations. They are not prohibited explicitly, but according to an RSFSR decree of July 10, 1932, voluntary associations can be founded only with the previous consent of the competent administrative organs, which have to examine *inter alia* whether the association is expedient, whether it serves the building of socialism and whether the individual members are reliable enough. These provisions are implemented with the effect that establishing private associations has become impossible.

Organizations in the Soviet Union may be divided into four groups: 1) The Communist Party of the Soviet Union with roughly 15 million members is not only the most important organization, but at the same time is the predominant power structure of the political system. As stated in Art. 126 of the Constitution, it is the leading core of both governmental and non-governmental organizations. 2) Various mass organizations are designated for the purpose of mobilizing certain groups of the population for certain purposes, to control and to integrate them into the political system. First of all, there are 25 trade unions uniting 98 million employees within a given branch of economic activity. Apart from mobilizing their members in order to fulfil plan targets, they perform functions such as administering social insurance, control over safety devices and cultural and welfare services. The trade union system is highly centralized and at each organizational level there is a committee to which each union sends its representatives. The main reservoir for party recruitment is the youth organization Komsomol with its 29 million members. It is the task of the Komsomol to organize the most politically minded young people into a centralized, disciplined community. The parallel organization for children are the Pioneers. A number of organizations, such as the 58 Societies of Friendship and Cultural Relations, the Society for the Dissemination of Political and Scientific Knowledge, the Scientific and Technical Society and the Society for the Protection of Nature, are busy in the field of ideology and culture. Finally, the important paramilitary organization DOSAAF should be mentioned, which embraces 9 million youths engaged in military oriented sports. 3) The various professional associations exercise tight control over their members and serve as channels for transferring party will. The most prominent associations operate in the cultural life of the country (unions of Soviet writers, journalists, composers, architects, etc.). 4) The various co-operatives function as economic units completely incorporated in the central planning system. The most important co-operatives are the 32,300 kolkhozes, which occupied 38 per cent of the total agricultural area in 1971. In the second place one has to mention the consumer co-operatives managing 28.9 per cent of goods turnover. Finally, there are house building co-operatives set up on enterprise or territorial level with a share of 6.3 percent in producing dwelling space.

G. Brunner

See also CIVIL RIGHTS; ASSOCIATION

FREEDOM OF THE PRESS

Freedom of the press is guaranteed by Article 125 of the Soviet Constitution on the same grounds as freedom of speech. The correct use of the press should be ensured by placing at the disposal of the working people and their organizations printing presses, stocks of paper, public buildings, and other material requisites. This means that the party as the vanguard of the working people controls the whole press. Freedom of the press was abolished as early as November 9 (October 27), 1917, by the Decree on the Press, which was directed against the "bourgeois" press and authorized the Council of People's Commissars to ban press organs hostile to Soviet power. In the period following all printing offices and stocks of paper were nationalized and the press became a party and government monopoly.

The Soviet press is an important means of implementing the party will by speaking to the masses immediately and continuously. The main functions of the press used to be defined in more or less the same terms. Probably the most authoritative, still valid statement is included in a resolution of the June 1963 plenum of the Central Committee of the CPSU, where the main functions are listed as follows: formation of Marxist-Leninist *Weltanschauung* and communist morals in Soviet people; systematically and profoundly throwing light on the party's and the whole Soviet people's work for the fulfilment of the economic plans, for the increase of labour productivity, for the improvement of the party direction of production, and on the problems of cultural construction; unfolding sharp and principled criticism and self-criticism directed against indolence, bureaucratism, waste, idleness, and other anti-social phenomena, and popularizing good examples. It can be assumed that the Soviet press has to fulfil three basic functions: 1) agitation and propaganda, i.e. ideological indoctrination of the people, 2) mass organization, i.e. mobilization of the people in order to realize the economic and socio-political goals set by the party, 3) criticism and control, i.e. pointing at shortcomings which the party is interested in eliminating.

In 1971 there were 6878 newspapers and 1208 periodicals with a total one-issue circulation of 144.7 million and 130.9 million copies respectively in the Soviet Union. In considering the structure of the press one may distinguish between three groupings of publishers and five territorial levels. According to the former view-point there are the party press, the government press, and the social organizations' press. The territorial structure shows the following picture: 1) 28 central newspapers (64 mill.), 2) 152 republican newspapers (24.3 mill.), 3) 379 regional (krai, province, autonomous republic and province) newspapers (23.2 mill.), 4) 3,472 local (city, *raion*) newspapers (27.5 mill.), 5) 3,832 factory and kolkhoz newspapers (6.1 mill.). As the figures above indicate, the central papers constitute the most important grouping, for they are managed by the top party, government, and social organizations' organs, and, consequently, they derive their leading authoritative and official character from the top of a highly centralized power pyramid. The most prominent newspapers are *Pravda* (Party, 9.2 mill.), *Izvestiia* (Government, 8.6 mill.), *Komsomol'skaia Pravda* (Komsomol, 7.9 mill.), *Sel'skaia Zhizn'* (Party, 6.6 mill.), *Trud* (Trade Unions, 4.9 mill.), and *Krasnaia Zvezda* (Ministry of Defence).

The party's total grip over the press is ensured by several means. First of all, in matters of finance and production facilities the press is absolutely dependent on the party. The newspapers are staffed with selected and politically trained, reliable journalists. Most of them are party members, who are bound by party discipline to carry through party instructions. Apart from instructions concerning certain aspects of everyday work, there are many decisions taken by the top party organs relating to the press's fundamental political tasks. The chief directing and supervisory body is the Propaganda department of the Central Committee's secretariat where there are three sections established for the central, regional, and local press. Corresponding departments function on every echelon of the party apparatus. The press sections approve the "working" plans of the newspapers and can interfere on any occasion. The process of indirect censoring runs along the indicated lines. The first stage is the "self-censorship" of every journalist who would risk his career if he committed political erros. If he has doubts, he consults his editor or editor-in-chief. Should he be unable to decide the matter himself, he refers to the competent press section, and so on even up to the Politburo or the Secretary-General. In some cases the process is reversed by the issuing of instructions that certain matters cannot be handled without prior approval by the party organs. Furthermore, the more important news is supplied by the official news agency TASS. This system of control is so overwhelming and at the same time so flexible that the importance of direct censorship has been constantly diminished. The special government censoring organ, *Glavlit*, was established in the late 'twenties, and it was in full operation during the Stalin era. Since then, one publishing house after another has been freed from its control, and today the role of *Glavlit* is mainly restricted to supervising the press from the standpoint of state security.

Bibl.: Antony Buzek, How the Communist Press Works, 1964.

G. Brunner

See also FREEDOM OF SPEECH; SECURITY; PRESS; SAMIZDAT

FREEDOM OF RELIGION,
see CHURCH & STATE

FREEDOM OF SPEECH

According to Soviet constitutional theory there are two kinds of opinion: the correct opinion, which is a product of socialist consciousness and encourages the development of a socialist or communist society, and the incorrect opinion, which is of a reactionary nature and hampers social progress. Freedom of speech concerns only the former. The latter is contrary to socialist order and must not be protected. Consequently, Article 125 of the Soviet Constitution guarantees freedom of speech with a twofold limitation, i.e. "in conformity with the interests of the working people and in order to strengthen the socialist system". Of course, the demarcation line between correct and incorrect is not easy to draw. In the last analysis, it is neither a question of legal interpretation nor of theoretical conception, but is one of political expediency. The correct use of freedom of speech is what the leading party organs say it is. The most important criterion for determining the real contents of the freedom of speech is the expediency of implementing the current party guidelines. This does not mean, however, that every kind of criticism is forbidden. Criticism is allowed if it is "constructive", i.e. if it is directed against deficiencies of minor importance which the party intends to combat. There are nation-wide public discussions on important legislative projects, also initiated from the top, but there is hardly any chance of influencing legislative activity by suggestions from below. Minor changes may be achieved in this way, but the real purpose of such discussions is to prepare the population for the legislative enactment and to demonstrate socialist democracy.

The incorrect use of freedom of speech is declared to be "Anti-Soviet agitation and propaganda", which is penalized by Article 7 of the USSR law "on Criminal Responsibility for Crimes against the State" of December 25, 1958, a provision incorporated in the Criminal Codes of every Union Republic (e.g. Article 70 of the 1960 Criminal Code of the RSFSR). According to this provision, agitation and propaganda conducted with the intention of undermining or weakening Soviet power, or spreading slanderous fabrications with the same intent which defame the Soviet political and social system, are punishable by deprivation of freedom for six months to seven years with or without exile for two to five years or by exile for two to five years. Article 70 of the RSFSR Criminal Code was the legal basis for the prosecution of many intellectuals who had criticized some measures of the authorities and demanded more freedom, as in the cases of the *Soiuz Komunarov* in Leningrad at the end of 1965; of A. Siniavskii and. Yu. Daniel in February, 1966; of Yu. Galanskov, A. Ginzburg, A. Dobrovolskii, and V. Lashkova in

January, 1968. In order to combat the incorrect use of freedom of speech on legally more convincing grounds, a new Article 190[1] was inserted in the RSFSR Criminal Code in September 1966, which provides that verbally spreading knowingly mendacious fabrications which defame the Soviet political and social system, is punishable by deprivation of freedom for up to three years or by corrective labour for up to one year or by a fine of up to one hundred roubles. This provision has already been applied in several cases, particularly in connection with protests against the invasion of Czechoslovakia on August 21, 1968.

G. Brunner

See also PROPAGANDA, ANTI-SOVIET

FREIGHT,
see CARRIAGE & TRANSPORT

GAS, see MINES, MINERALS & MINING

GENERAL SUPERVISION,
see PROCURACY

GENEVA CONVENTIONS

As part of their general support for the rules of war, the Soviet Union has accepted the Geneva Conventions of 1949 concerning the treatment of prisoners of war, protection of civilians in time of war, amelioration of the condition of the wounded and sick of armed forces in the field, and amelioration of the condition of the wounded, sick and shipwrecked members of armed forces at sea (see LAW OF WAR). The Soviets consider the Conventions, which were worked out on the basis of the Geneva Conventions of 1929, the Hague Conventions of 1907, and the draft conventions prepared during the 17th international conference of the Red Cross at Stockholm in 1948, as a progressive step towards limiting the horrors of war especially insofar as civilian populations are concerned. It is said, however, that additional protective measures are needed and that the Soviet Union is constantly working towards making the rules of war more humane.

The Soviets add the Geneva Protocol of 1925 (prohibiting the use of chemical and biological weapons) and the 1948 Convention on the Prevention and Punishment of the Crime of Genocide to the Geneva Conventions of 1949 for the protective umbrella of civilian populations. All of these agreements were used in Soviet propaganda attacks to demonstrate the illegality of U.S. military operations in Vietnam. On a wider scale, the Geneva Conventions and the Geneva Protocol are relied upon to support the outlawing of nuclear and chemical and biological warfare under the policy of peaceful coexistence (*q.v.*). To support nuclear disarmament and to control peaceful uses of nuclear energy, the Soviets claim a special peacetime operation for the Geneva Conventions and other agreements dealing with the rules of war. In the Soviet view, the law of peaceful coexistence, having reduced the importance of war, demands that the operation of these agreements be broadened to protect mankind in time of peace, especially in view of the great peacetime threats resulting from advances in nuclear weaponry and technology. The claim is that the new socialist content imparted by the law of coexistence has widened the concept of protection embodied in these agreements. In the foregoing and other ways, the Geneva Conventions and related agreements are used to support Soviet foreign policy objectives.

Bernard A. Ramundo

See also TREATIES; PEACE

GIFTS

The *making of gifts*, which Soviet textbooks define as a unilateral, real contract by which one person gratuitously transfers ownership of his property to another, is regulated by the Civil Codes of the Union republics (arts. 256-257 of the RSFSR Code). Gifts to citizens must be in writing and notarised if the value exceeds 500 roubles; they may be made in simple written form where the value is from 100 to 500 roubles and orally where the value is below 100 roubles. Failure to comply with notarial form leads to invalidity; failure to reduce to written form does not, but oral evidence may not be referred to in Court where the value of the gift is 100 roubles or more. All gifts to the state and to socialist (state or public) organisations, excluding houses and cottages, may be made in simple written form. All gifts of houses and cottages must be in writing and registered with the executive committee of the local soviet. If the property is in cities or urban settlements, the gift must be notarised; in rural areas it need not be. Failure to comply with these requirements invalidates the contract. Where the law prescribes obligatory forms for a specific contract of gift, the contract is concluded when the parties have subscribed to the required form and the donee may sue for delivery. Soviet law does not permit *donatio mortis causa* and will not allow the provisions of inheritance law to be frustrated or evaded by this means.

Donors must be legally competent persons. Socialist organisations are normally excluded from making gifts by their charters or articles of incorporation. Guardians or trustees of persons with no or limited legal capacity may not give, or consent to give, the property of such persons. Any citizen, juridical person or the state may be a *donee*; guardians and trustees may accept a beneficial gift or consent to its acceptance on behalf of their charges. Where a gift is made to a number of donees, whether citizens and/or the state and/or socialist organisations and/or collectives, these hold as co-owners in common shares, subject to division within one year of acquisition as provided in the Civil Code. Any object belonging to a citizen in personal ownership at the time of delivery may be the *subject of gifts*. Prizes for collectives and workers meant to encourage production, gratuitous help by trade unions, free passes to sanatoria and holiday resorts, *intra vires* donations by socialist organisations to cultural and sporting clubs are not gifts as defined by civil law, but are regulated under administrative, labour law, etc.

Conditions attached to a gift are conceptually and practically troublesome to Soviet law. Gifts to socialist organisations that are to be applied for socially useful purposes are encouraged, but trusts for this purpose are not permitted. Soviet writers, therefore, treat such conditions, wherever possible, as independent collateral contracts accompanying a genuine contract of gift. These independant contracts can be sued upon by the donor or other interested parties including the Procuracy, but the contract or gift itself is regarded as establishing no contractual relation between parties that survives the delivery.

A. E.-S. Tay

See also TESTAMENTS

GOOD FAITH, see CONTRACTS

GOVERNMENT,
see COUNCIL OF MINISTERS

GOVERNMENT CORPORATIONS,
see STATE ENTERPRISES

GOVERNMENTAL LIABILITY

The rules governing the liability of state institutions and organizations to compensate for damages caused by their activities. As in general civil liability, governmental liability may ensue for damages based on contract and non-contract activity. The defendant in such cases is normally not the state as such, but the state organ whose action caused the damages. An exception to this rule arises with regard to activities of foreign trade representatives of the USSR abroad. In such cases the Soviet state will be the defendant. Under Soviet civil law, those competent to engage in civil law relationships and, therefore, to be civilly liable, are called "subjects of civil law" (*sub"ekty grazhdanskogo prava*). The latter include citizens, juristic persons and, in the exceptional circumstances noted above, the Soviet state. Juristic persons include state juristic persons, cooperative juristic persons such as collective farms, and "public" (*obshchestvennye*) juristic persons such as trade unions. Only the first category is relevant here. State juristic persons (*gosudarstvennye iuridicheskie litsa*) include: state economic organizations and enterprises, such as factories, department stores, construction organizations, state farms and federations of such organizations (trusts, combines, firms); state budget institutions, which are not basically engaged in economic activity, including the various organs of the state administrative machinery, scientific and educational institutions, hospitals, museums and judicial organs. Some Soviet writers also include the soviets of workers' deputies as a special kind of state juristic person.

With regard to liability for damages arising out of breach of contract, no special rules are applicable to state juristic persons. The general provisions on contract liability (art. 36 of the Principles of Civil Law of the USSR and Union Republics; art. 219 of the RSFSR Civil Code of 1964) apply to all subjects of civil law. Soviet writers state that the following conditions are necessary to a finding of liability to compensate in contract relations: the breach of a contractual obligation growing out of illegal behaviour; harm or damages resulting from the breach of contract; a "causal connection" between the breach of contract and the damage; fault on the part of the obliged party. However, some special laws (e.g., arts. 144-147 of the Railroad Rules) provide for contract liability regardless of fault.

Non-contract (tort) liability of state organizations is governed by several provisions of Soviet law. Art. 89 of the Principles of Civil Law of the USSR and Union Republics (which corresponds to art. 446 of the RSFSR Civil Code of 1964) provides that institutions will be liable on the basis of the general principles of tort law for damages caused to citizens by improper acts of their officials in the sphere of public administration. Judicial practice had already long established that state organs will be subject to liability on general grounds for their economic and technical activities. However, this does not mean that state agencies will be held liable for all allegedly tortious acts. Liability for damages growing out of statutes and other normative acts of the government seem clearly beyond the reach of tort suits. Furthermore, Art. 89 contains two clauses which modify the general rule of state liability for administrative acts. It provides, first, that liability for damages to organizations (as opposed to citizens) arising from such acts will be governed in a manner established by law and little discussion of the subject is found in the legal literature. Second, art. 89 states that liability for improper acts ("administrative" acts are not specified here) of officials of the organs of inquiry, preliminary investigation, the procuracy and the courts will be provided for by special legislation. Since the Principles of Civil Law were adopted in 1961 no such special legislation has come into force, in spite of considerable discussion of the subject in the legal literature.

The general rules of civil liability which, as mentioned above, apply to most economic, technical and administrative acts of state agencies, require the following conditions before a finding of liability can be made: damages or injury; illegal activity which caused the damages; a "causal connection" between the illegal act and the damages; fault on the part of the person who caused the damages. As in the field of contract liability, tort liability may ensue in some circumstances regardless of fault. Art. 90 of the Principles of Civil Law (which corresponds to art. 454 of the RSFSR Civil Code) provides for liability regardless of fault for damages connected with "sources of increased danger" such as automobiles, certain machines, etc.

Donald Barry

Bibl.: Governmental Tort Liability (D. Barry, ed.), Law in Eastern Europe No. 17, 1970.

See also OBLIGATIONS; PERSONS

GUARDIANSHIP AND CURATORSHIP

In general terms guardians and curators look after those who, because of youth or infirmity, need protection. The official organ is the

Guardianship and Curatorship Agency, which is the local authority's executive committee. It decides disputes about the exercise of family rights, has power, in the interests of a child, to deprive of access a parent living at a distance, should be but apparently is not always) a party to custody suits, and may commence actions for deprivation of parental rights. It also nominates guardians and curators, with their consent; they must be adult, *sui juris*, and not deprived of parental rights.

Minors. Normally the parents are the legal representatives of their offspring. In default of parents capable of fulfilling such duties, the Agency must be informed and, taking into account personal qualities, relationship to the ward etc., appoints guardians for minors under 15, curators for those of 15 to 18. They are not paid but are under no duty of financial support; any pension or maintenance payments due to the ward are handed to them; if these do not suffice the ward's property may be used; otherwise the Agency makes a payment. Save in exceptional cases the ward should reside with the guardian or curator, who must safeguard his health, education etc.

The guardian or curator may claim custody from others who have the child without legal foundation and is the ward's legal representative in any process or institution, without special authorisation. The guardian exercises legal rights in the name and interest of the ward; the curator consents to such exercise by the ward (save in petty everyday dealings). Neither may arrange transactions between the ward and themselves or their close family, nor represent him in litigation in such cases. They may not give away the ward's property, and need prior permission of the Agency before entering into the more important transactions such as exchange of dwelling-space, release of rights etc. Guardians are liable in tort for the ward's actions unless they prove no fault on their part; curators are liable—subject to the same defence—to make up any compensation which can not be met from the ward's resources.

Their duties cease at the appropriate age. State institutions fulfil similar roles for children in their care.

An informal type of guardianship named "Patronage", under which families took in children and were paid by the local authority, is not provided for in the latest family legislation.

See further arts. 119-139 Family Code.

B. Rudden

GUILT, see MENS REA

HEALTH

Year after year the Soviet government increases appropriations for the development of public health services. Whereas in 1969 expenditure on public health amounted to 8.5 billion roubles, it exceeded 9 billion roubles in 1970—an increase of over 7.2%. The budget for state social insurance in 1970 exceeded 16 billion roubles. The Soviet government has certainly made some gigantic strides in the area of public health compared with the modest achievements of the tsarist governments in these areas. The Soviet government continues to appropriate a handsome proportion of its annual budget for the development of public health. In 1970 alone centralised capital investment for the development of public health came to more than 400 milion roubles. It is estimated that there are almost 618,000 physicians and about 2 million intermediate medical personnel in the Soviet Union today.

Despite these glowing figures, plus an estimated 106 hospital beds per 10,000 persons by the end of 1969, the state of medical services in the Soviet Union is still very pathetic.

Taking into consideration the need to improve existing legislation in public health in the Soviet Union, the Public Health and Social Security Committees, together with the Legislative Proposals Committee of the USSR Supreme Soviet's Council of the Union and Council of Nationalities, with the participation of the Central Council of Trade Unions of the USSR, the USSR Ministry of Public Health and the Council of Ministers' Juridical Commission, drew up Draft Principles of Legislation of the USSR and the Union Republics on Public Health. After considerable discussion by the interested ministries, departments, public organizations and research institutions, the Principles of Legislation of the USSR and the Union Republics on Public Health were adopted by the USSR Supreme Soviet in December, 1969. These Principles represent the most recent codification of the legislative guidelines on Soviet health law today. Like all Soviet legislations of this type, the Principles have a Preamble, General Provisions and a Special Part. Altogether there are 55 articles which are divided into 9 Chapters.

The Preamble enumerates the general principles of Soviet health policy as including: the determination to raise the peoples' material well-being and cultural level and the improvement in their working, living and recreational conditions; the protection of the health of the Soviet mother and child; the concern for man's health and long years of active life; the further improvement of public health protection and the strengthening of legality in this sphere of social relations. The goals of this policy as contained in art. 1 include the desire to ensure the harmonious development of citizens' mental and physical powers, their health, a high level of working capacity and long years of active life to prevent and reduce the incidence of illness; to further lower the disability rate and the death rate; and to eliminate the factors and conditions that are detrimental to the health of Soviet citizens.

Judging by the present achievement of the Soviet public health programme one could say that the Soviet Union has been turned into a paradise for children—all over the country one finds children's rest homes, health resorts and playgrounds—all of which are a living testimony to the keen interest of the Soviet government in the welfare of children.

Art. 3 of the Principles declares the notion according to which the protection of public health is the duty of all state agencies, enterprises, institutions and organizations—these include the trade unions, the Red Cross (*q.v.*) and Red Crescent Societies, cooperative organizations and other social organizations. The overall duty of supervising this gigantic health programme is vested in the

Union republican Ministry of Health which cooperates with the Ministries of Public Health and their agencies in the various Union republics and autonomous republics. The local soviets (councils) directly supervise the operations of the public health agencies and institutions under their jurisdiction.

Art. 4 proclaims that citizens of the USSR are provided with free medical assistance to be made accessible to all and that this assistance is furnished by state (public) health institutions. Arts. 6-11 define the jurisdiction of the federal and Union republic governments in the field of public health.

Under the provision of art. 12 only persons who have received training at and a degree from an appropriate higher and specialised secondary educational institution in the USSR are permitted to engage in the practice of medicine or pharmacy in the USSR. Foreign nationals and stateless persons who are permanently resident in the Soviet Union and have received special training and a degree from an appropriate higher or specialised secondary educational institution in the USSR may engage in the practice of medicine or pharmacy on the territory of the USSR in accordance with their specialty and degree received. Persons who have received medical or pharmacological training at and degrees from appropriate educational institutions in foreign countries, however are admitted to the practice of medicine or pharmacy in the USSR only in accordance with the procedure laid down by USSR legislation.

With regard to the admission of qualified foreign medical practitioners into Soviet practice it should be mentioned that the crucial factor here is that such individuals are permitted to practice only "in accordance with the procedure laid down by USSR legislation". In view of the restrictions imposed by this legislation, very few foreigners can actually take advantage of such an opportunity. Most professions in the Soviet Union are closed to foreigners—e.g. only Soviet nationals may be employed in the Soviet Union as civil aircraft pilots or as crew members aboard Soviet aircraft, or as ships' captains or service personnel on board a Soviet liner, etc. But, although the practice of medicine in the Soviet Union does not specifically require Soviet citizenship status, this possibility is neutralised by a series of impossible social and legislative restrictions that are imposed by the Soviet political system and by the state authorities.

Whereas art. 16 of these Principles specifically states that physicians and other medical personnel have no right to divulge information that may become known to them in the performance of their duties, e.g. information concerning a patient's ailments or the intimate or family aspects of the patient's life, par. 2 of art. 16 adds that the executives of public health institutions are obliged to report information about a citizen's illness to public health agencies in cases in which the interests of protecting the health of the population may require it, or to the investigatory or judicial agencies on request. It need not be mentioned, of course, that in a centrally planned society like the Soviet Union, such a provision is highly vulnerable to political abuse by the state authorities.

Chapter 3 of the Principles is devoted to the sanitary-epidemological protection of the population. This is ensured by a complex network of sanitary-hygienic and anti-epidemic measures and by the system of state sanitary supervision. The Soviet Union today pays considerable attention to preventive medicine—a programme which is aimed at stamping out the outbreak of any major epidemic diseases. For this purpose art. 20 stipulates certain standard sanitary requirements in the planning and building of communities; art. 21 calls for the provision of measures to purify and render harmless industrial, communal and service effluents, waste products and refuse; art. 22 stipulates standard sanitary requirements for residential occupancy; art. 23 calls for the observance of sanitary rules in the maintenance of industrial premises, housing and other buildings and areas; art. 24 calls for the prevention and elimination of noise; art. 25 prescribes sanitary requirements for the supply of drinking and household water; art. 26 calls for the required approval of standards and technical specifications by public health agencies; art. 27 calls for sanitary specifications in the production, processing, storage, transportation and sale of foodstuffs; art. 28 calls for the sanitary supervision of the production, use, storage and transportation of radio-active and poisonous substances and substances causing a strong reaction; art. 29 provides that persons engaged in certain professions where there is a high risk of contracting communicable diseases are required to undergo compulsory periodic medical examination to determine the state of their health. All Soviet citizens, however, are required to undergo periodic medical checkups. Students go through this checkup annually and usually during the registration period, of the first term.

Under art. 33 curative and preventive assistance is provided for all citizens by public health institutions assigned to citizens on the basis of their place of residence and of work. This means that the entire country is divided into medical districts to which individuals are assigned on the basis of the two criteria mentioned above.

Chapter 5 is devoted to the protection of mother and child—the encouragement of motherhood, the guarantees of protection of the health of mother and child, etc. Under the provisions of art. 38 the protection of the health of mother and child is ensured by the organization of an extensive network of women's consultation centres, maternity homes, hospitals and sanatoriums, rest homes for expectant mothers and mothers with children, as well as nurseries and kindergartens and various other children's institutions; the granting to women of maternity leaves with the payment of social insurance allowances; the establishment of work-breaks for mothers to feed their babies and the granting of all other types of fringe benefits to the Soviet mother.

Par. 3 of Art. 38 stipulates that in order to protect woman's health, she is granted the freedom to determine for herself the question of motherhood. On the basis of this law the Soviet Union grants almost an unrestricted right of abortion (*q.v.*) to Soviet women—married or single—for a very nominal fee.

Art. 41 comes nearest to enshrining the principle of *mens sana in corpore sano* in the Soviet health law. It specifically provides that with the aim of raising a healthy young generation with harmoniously developed physical and spiritual powers, state agencies, enterprises, organizations, institutions and collective farms, as well as trade unions and other public organizations, are to provide for the development of an extensive network of nurseries, kindergartens, schools, boarding schools, open-air schools, young pioneer camps and other children's institutions. Under the provision of art. 49 all state agencies, as well as the trade unions, the Young Communist League (Komsomol), cooperative organizations, sporting societies, enterprises, institutions and organizations must promote physical culture, sports, touring and hiking among the entire population in their respective establishments. The provision also calls for the strengthening of physical culture by collectives, tourist clubs and organizations and the introduction of gymnastics at places of work.

The emphasis on physical education in the Soviet Union is carried into high schools and colleges (universities) where the academic curriculums emphasise the role of the students' physical fitness. In all Soviet colleges a student will not be allowed to graduate unless he or she has successfully completed the physical education requirements which are generally very stringent. The other side of this physical education requirement in the Soviet Union today is that the authors of the programme see it as a military imperative—it is argued that in order to have a healthy and strong army the state must maintain a healthy recruitment base. Since the practical application of the conscription law makes virtually every able-bodied Soviet citizen likely to be called up for military service, the healthier these potential recruits or military reservists are, the stronger the military potential of the Soviet Union.

In general it may be true to observe that Soviet society, from the point of view of the physical condition of its citizens, has certainly grown healthier within the space of 55 years. But whether this physical health necessarily connotes a correspondingly healthy mind is highly doubtful. If health is to be defined as "a state of complete physical, mental and social well-being and not merely the absence of disease or infirmity" then one can almost certainly say that the Soviet Union of today is still far from attaining a sound mental health for its people. Psychiatry and mental institutions in the Soviet Union continue to serve as political instruments in the hands of the governments. The procedure by which Soviet political authorities get political dissenters to be declared mentally unstable and then have them put into mental institutions is, to say the least, a violation of the very political freedom which the Soviet federal constitution guarantees to its citizens (Arts. 118-133 of the Soviet Constitution).

The Principles provide under art. 55 that if a treaty or an international agreement to which the Soviet Union is a party has established rules other than those contained in the public health legislations of the USSR and the Union republics, the rules of the international agreement or treaty shall be applied. This conflicts rule is also expressed in art. 569 of the Civil Code of the Russian Federation as well as in the corresponding articles of the Principles of Civil Legislation of the USSR and the Union Republics.

Despite the marvellous results that Soviet medicine may have attained since the October Revolution and notwithstanding the pledged determination of the Soviet government and people to work for the best results in the area of public health, the fact still remains that the administration of social medicine in the Soviet Union, like the dispensation of many other public services, continues to be plagued with inefficiency and red tape procedures. As long as medical science and psychiatry in the Soviet Union remain highly politicised and its physical education programme perceivably militarized, it is very doubtful if the Soviet Union will ever come any nearer to meeting the standards of a healthy society as stipulated in the Preamble to the Constitution of the World Health Organization.

C. Osakwe

HEIRS, see SUCCESSION

HIGHWAYS, see ROADS

HIRE-PURCHASE AGREEMENTS

A hire-purchase agreement or, more accurately in the Soviet context, an installment-credit sale (*prodazha v rassrochku* or *prodazha v kredit*) is a variant of the contract of sale whereby Soviet enterprises of retail trade (*q.v.*) sell durable consumer goods (including clothing and footwear) to individual citizens on credit (*q.v.*); cf. art. 252 RSFSR Civil Code.

According to Soviet statutory law, installment-credit sales are carried out at prices prevailing on the date of sale; a subsequent change in the price of the item sold does not require its recalculation. The title passes to the buyer at the time of transfer of the item which ordinarily coincides with the signing of the contract, unless otherwise provided by law or contract. More detailed rules are prescribed by decree (cf. in particular the Instruction concerning the sale of goods on credit, of March 9, 1965).

The greater flexibility of executive decrees (and of implementing ministerial regulations and local ordinances) enables the Soviet trade agencies to use the installment-credit sale as a device for shaping consumer demand. The demand is influenced by regulating what is to be sold on credit, where, to whom, an on what conditions. Characteristically, only goods in adequate supply are channeled into installment-credit sales. Thus, the less saleable models of certain appliances would be made available on credit, while the popular ones would not. Since 1960, installment-credit sales have been made in rural areas as well as in cities through stores designated for that purpose. The number of stores authorized to sell on credit can be administratively raised or reduced. The prospective buyer must be a permanent worker or employee (or a member of the regular armed forces of officer or non-commissioned-officer rank), a graduate student or a pensioner, employed (matriculated, residing) in the locality in which the store is situated. In addition, each prospective buyer must present to the store a document from his place of employment (educational institution, social insurance agency) certifying the average amount of his monthly wages or salary (stipend, pension). The certificate is good for only one credit purchase. Another one is not to be issued before the debt on a previous installment-credit purchase has been extinguished. The managers and chief accountants of the employing enterprises (educational institutions, social insurance agencies) are held personally responsible for violating the rules on the issuance of these certificates. A down payment of 20 to 25 percent of the purchase price is typically required. The lower figure applies to higher priced items, e.g., those costing more than 150 rubles. The balance is spread over 6 to 24 months, again depending on the value of the item; the more expensive the item (e.g., a prefabricated home, a piano) and, consequently, the larger the balance, the more time is allowed for repayment. However, a variable credit limit is imposed on the basis of the buyer's earnings. As a rule, the amount of credit extended over a 6-month period may not exceed the buyer's 2-month earnings; over a 24-month period—8-month earnings. The down payment is increased to the extent that the original balance exceeds the applicable credit limit. The usual carrying charge varies from 1 percent, in the case of 6- to 9-month credit to 2.5 percent, in the case of credit made available for a period of more than 12 months. The annual charge is a one-shot premium on the entire amount of credit and not a periodically-calculated percentage of the unpaid balance.

A contract of installment-credit sale is concluded when the buyer signs an instrument authorizing his employer (educational institution) to withhold and pay over to the retail trade enterprise the amount of the unpaid balance in equal semi-monthly or monthly installments. Pensioners make their payments directly each month. In the event of the debtor's dismissal, his employer (educational institution) is authorized to withhold, within the limits permitted by law, the entire unpaid balance from his last pay. In cases in which the debtor himself is responsible for making the payments, the creditor enterprise collects from the debtor a monetary penalty for nonpayment of any regular installment. The amount of penalty is set at 0.1 percent of the overdue sum for each day of delay. The debtor's failure to pay two regular installments empowers the creditor enterprise to demand the entire unpaid balance at once, with the prescribed penalty on the amount actually overdue. Execution on the property

of the defaulting debtor can be levied on the basis of a notarial endorsement of execution. The debtor may challenge the appropriateness of the endorsement in court.
Soviet civil law (*q.v.*) also provides for another kind of time purchase or credit sale outside the ordinary retail trade in consumer goods. An individual may, for instance, sell his dwelling house or some other consumer item to another citizen on credit, with the purchase price usually to be paid by installments. The title is retained by the seller until the item has been fully paid for. The buyer may not retransfer or encumber the item and, if he falls behind in his payments, the seller may rescind the contract of sale and repossess the item.

Z. Zile

See also SALES

HISTORY OF LAW,
see LEGAL HISTORY

HOLIDAYS, see WORKING HOURS

HOMICIDE
Homicide is not defined in the Criminal Code of the RSFSR of October 27, 1960. Soviet legal dictionaries describe it as an offence against the person which consists of an illegal, intentional or negligent deprivation of life of another person. This offence may result from a commission or omission causing the death of the victim.
The Criminal Code of the RSFSR distinguishes intentional homicide (art. 103), intentional homicide with aggravating circumstances (art. 102), intentional homicide committed in a state of strong mental agitation (art. 104), homicide committed while exceeding the limites of necessary defence (art. 105), negligent homicide (art. 106), and incitement to suicide (art. 107) (see SUICIDE).
Intentional homicide is not defined in the Criminal Code of the RSFSR. For the meaning of "intentional", see MENS REA.
Intentional homicide committed without the aggravating circumstances indicated in art. 102 of the Criminal Code is punishable by deprivation of freedom for a term of three to ten years (art. 103). Art. 102 describes intentional homicide with aggravating circumstances.
a) from mercenary motives;
b) from motives of hooliganism;
c) committed in connection with the victim's performance of his official or social duty;
d) committed with special cruelty;
e) committed in a manner dangerous to the life of many persons;
f) for the purpose of concealing another crime or facilitating the commission of a crime or in conjunction with rape;
g) of a woman known by the guilty person to be pregnant;
h) of two or more persons;
i) committed by a person who has previously committed intentional homicide, with the exception of an intentional homicide, committed in a state of strong mental agitation (art. 104) and a homicide committed while exceeding the limits of necessary defence;
j) committed because of a blood feud;
k) committed by a particularly dangerous recidivist.

Homicide committed with any of the abovementioned aggravating circumstances is punishable by deprivation of freedom for a term of eight to fifteen years, with or without exile, or by death.
While art. 102 lists numerous aggravating circumstances, there are still other "circumstances aggravating responsibility" listed in art. 34 of the Principles applicable to all offences namely:
1) if the crime was committed by a person who had previously committed a crime; (The court shall be entitled, depending on the nature of the previous crime, to obstain from attaching to this the significance of an ag-

gravating circumstance.)
2) if the crime was committed by an organized group;
3) if the crime was committed for mercenary or other base motives;
4) if the commission of the crime resulted in serious consequences;
5) if the crime was committed against a minor, an aged person, or one in a helpless condition;
6) if a minor was instigated to the commission of a crime or a minor was drawn into participation in a crime;
7) if the crime was committed with particular cruelty towards, or humiliation of, the person injured;
8) if the crime was committed in a generally dangerous manner;
9) if the crime was committed by taking advantage of a public disaster.
Art. 34 of the Principles states that these other circumstances may be specified as aggravating in the criminal codes of the Union republics.
Art. 39 of the RSFSR Code incorporated the aggravating circumstances listed in art. 34 of the Principles. The Code added to paragraph 5 the commission of the crime against a person in material, occupational, or other dependence on the guilty person. Furthermore, art. 39 of the Code added three additional paragraphs:
10) commission of a crime connected with the utilization of a means involving increased danger by a person in a state of intoxication;
11) denouncing a person known to be innocent;
12) commission of a new crime by a person taken into patronage during the term of patronage or within a year after the expiration of such a term.

While courts are bound to apply a punishment of a minimum of eight years' deprivation of freedom in cases of the aggravating circumstances listed in art. 102 of the Criminal Code of the RSFSR, the minimum and maximum punishment in cases of aggravating circumstances listed in art. 34 of the Principles and art. 39 of the RSFSR Code, but not in art. 102, remain unaffected by art. 102; they will therefore be governed by arts. 103 and 106, whichever applies (thus the punishment will be of three to ten years' deprivation of freedom under art. 103).
Mitigating circumstances, applicable to all offences, are listed in art. 33 of the Principles:
"In the assessing of the punishment, the following shall be considered as circumstances extenuating the responsibility [of the offender]:
1) that the offender has averted the harmful consequences of the crime, or voluntarily given compensation for the loss or made good the damage caused by him;
2) that he has committed the crime because of the concerted effect of difficult personal or family circumstances;
3) that he has committed the crime under the influence of threats or compulsion, or on account of financial or other dependency;
4) that he has committed the crime under the influence of a strong emotion, brought about by the unlawful actions of the victim;
5) that he has committed the crime in defence against a socially dangerous attack, exceeding, however, the limits of necessary defence;
6) that the crime was committed by a minor;
7) that the crime was committed by a pregnant woman;
8) sincere remorse or self-denunciation."

The criminal codes of the Union republics may establish further extenuating circumstances.
When determining the punishment, the court may also take into consideration extenuating circumstances not mentioned in the law.
Art. 38 of the RSFSR Criminal Code repeats

the circumstances listed in art. 33 of the Principles. Furthermore, the RSFSR Criminal Code enumerates in paragraph 4 of art. 38 an additional circumstance not listed expressly in art. 33 of the Principles: 4) commission of a crime for the first time, as a result of a forfuitous concurrence of circumstances, if such crime does not represent a great social danger.

In cases of intentional homicide committed in a state of strong mental agitation, the Criminal Code of the RSFSR provides for a lower minimum punishment, namely deprivation of freedom for a term not exceeding five years or by corrective labour not exceeding one year.

This applies when the state of sudden strong mental agitation was provoked by force or grave insult on the part of the victim, or provoked by any other unlawful actions of the victim, if these actions have resulted or could result in grave consequences for the guilty person or people near to him/his family (art. 104 of the Criminal Code of the RSFSR).

Homicide committed while exceeding the limits of necessary defence is punished by deprivation of freedom for a term not exceeding two years or by corrective labour for a term not exceeding one year (art. 105 Criminal Code RSFSR) (see SELF-DEFENCE).

Homicide committed by negligence (manslaughter) is punished by deprivation of freedom for a term not exceeding three years or by corrective labour for a term not exceeding one year (art. 106 RSFSR Criminal Code). For the meaning of negligence, see MENS REA.

Penal responsibility for all types of homicide starts at the age of fourteen (art. 10 Principles).

The majority of criminal codes of the Union republics of the USSR distinguish a special type of homicide, namely the killing of a newborn child by its mother (infanticide), and provide for a punishment of deprivation of freedom for up to three years.

A qualified homicide is dealt with in art. 3 of the Law on Criminal Responsibility for Crimes against State. This article, bearing the title "Terrorism" and being included in the chapter on "Especially dangerous crimes against the State", states that:

"The murder of a state or public functionary or representative of the [state] power, committed in connection with his state or public occupation in order to undermine or weaken Soviet power, is punishable by deprivation of freedom for a period of from ten to fifteen years with confiscation of property, or by death and confiscation of property."

Art. 4 of the same Law, entitled "Terrorist acts against the representatives of a foreign state" states:

"The murder of a representative of a foreign state, in order to provoke war or international complications is punishable by deprivation of freedom for a period of from ten to fifteen years with confiscation of property, or by death and confiscation of property."

L. Kos-Rabcewicz-Zubkowski

HONOURS

An elaborate system of public honours is in use in the Soviet Union which, apart from its status-conferring function, also provides material incentives for behaviour profitable to the Soviet state.

Within this honours system the most extensive sub-system is that of the honorary ranks (*zvaniia pochetnye*). Such ranks may be conferred either by federal or by Union republican authorities. The highest honorary ranks are those of Hero of the Soviet Union and Hero of Socialist Labour; both ranks are conferred by the USSR Supreme Soviet Presidium and are accompanied by the award of the Order of Lenin, which brings with it additional housing facilities, travel allowances, monthly payments and other

advantages. Another important honorary rank at the federal level is that of Lenin Prize Laureate. Lenin Prizes are awarded for outstanding scientific, technical and artistic achievements and literary works. Apart from these, International Lenin Prizes are awarded periodically as a Soviet counterpart to the Nobel Prizes. They are regulated by a Statute of April 22, 1966. Other honourary ranks at the federal level are those of the type of "People's Artist of the USSR".
Similar ranks are conferred by Union republican authorities, e.g. "Meritorious Jurist of the RSFSR". These ranks are, as a rule, of a purely honorary character and do not involve immediate economic benefit. Every rank is regulated by a special statute (e.g. the Statute on the Honourary Rank of Meritorious Jurist of the RSFSR, a decree of the RSFSR Supreme Soviet Presidium of July 20, 1966).
Next to the honorary ranks system (there are some thirty different honorary ranks) there is a limited number of orders and medals and a profusion of insignia and distinctions of a lower order.
Orders (*ordena*) may be conferred on individuals and on groups, institutions, military units, etc., by the Presidium of the Supreme Soviet of the USSR. The highest order of the Soviet Union is the Order of Lenin. Some of the other orders yield advantages similar to those accompanying the Order of Lenin; the most important privileges of bearers of high orders are enumerated in a statute of September 6, 1967.
Medals (*medali*) are likewise conferred by the USSR Supreme Soviet Presidium, but only on individuals; most of them are of a military nature. Only the Presidium can deprive the bearer (individual or collective) of a medal or order.

F. J. M. Feldbrugge

HOOLIGANISM

Hooliganism is defined in art. 206 of the RSFSR Criminal Code as "intentional actions which grossly violate public order and express an obvious disrespect towards society". The definition is sweeping enough to explain the fact that hooliganism is the most frequently committed crime in the Soviet Union. Hooliganism as a crime was included in the previous Criminal Code (of 1926, art. 74), but was not in any way circumscribed. Hooliganism, in fact, is more than a crime, it is a type of behaviour which perhaps is characteristic of one aspect of Russian social life; the Russian term *khuliganstvo* is a straight borrowing from English "hooliganism". The word is used in law also with an adjectival sense, such as "hooligan motives" (e.g. art. 102 point a. of the RSFSR Criminal Code). It connotes behaviour opposed to what is *prilichno* (proper) or *kul'turno* (cultured). It embraces a great diversity of activities, which have as a common element a more or less offensive disturbance of the peace.
The present law of hooliganism is based primarily on a decree of the USSR Supreme Soviet of July 26, 1966, "On increasing the responsibility for hooliganism". The main change brought about by this decree was the introduction of compulsory minimum sentences for all forms of hooliganism. The decree (*ukaz*) was followed by an explanatory decree (*postanovlenie*) of the same date by the same body. The Union republics enacted legislation in 1966 to conform to the new Union laws. There are considerable differences among the Union republics in the definitions of hooliganism and in procedural details.
According to the commentaries, the first part of the hooliganism definition (gross violation of public order) implies a violation of the rules of socialist community life (*q.v.*) or of public interests. The second part of the definition is said to refer to violations of

socialist morality or the interests of groups (collectives) or individuals. The definition in art. 206 requires both elements to be present if there is to be question of hooliganism; it seems, however, that the rules of socialist community life and the requirements of socialist morality overlap to a large extent. The result of the definitional vagueness of the hooliganism concept is that hooliganism serves as a kind of residual offence in many instances where a more clear-cut offence would be more difficult to prove; e.g. assault, threats, resisting an officer of the law, etc. The most typical case of hooliganism seems to be offensive behaviour in public by drunks; according to all available statistics drunkenness occurs in more than 90% of all cases of hooliganism.

Art. 206 provides two special forms of hooliganism: malicious and petty hooliganism. Malicious hooliganism is defined as hooliganism "characterized in its nature by its exceptional cynicism or special offensiveness, or connected with resistance to a representative of authority or of the public [referring to members of the voluntary people's guards —*druzhina*, *q.v.*] carrying out their duties with regard to the maintenance of public order, or against other citizens who are counteracting hooligan activities, and, furthermore, hooliganism committed by a person with a previous conviction for hooliganism".

Petty hooliganism is defined in the 1966 decree as "bad language [lit. *netsenzurnaia bran'*—uncensored swearing] in public places, offensive molestation of citizens and other similar actions and violating public order and the peace of citizens, provided these actions according to their character do not entail the application of criminal penalties".

Petty hooliganism is an administrative offence, punishable by detention for from ten to fifteen days, or by corrective labour of from one to two months with a mandatory deduction of twenty per cent of the offender's wages, or by a fine of from ten to thirty roubles. The penalty is imposed by the people's judge; the fine may also be imposed by the local police chief. The decree provides further for speedy and summary proceedings; there is no appeal. Petty hooliganism committed by a person who has been punished for petty hooliganism within the preceding year is considered to be common hooliganism (art. 206, par. 1).

Common hooliganism entails deprivation of liberty for from six months to one year, or corrective labour for the same duration, or a fine of from thirty to fifty roubles. Malicious hooliganism entails deprivation of liberty for from one to five years. Common or malicious hooliganism, accompanied by the use of (or the attempt to use) arms or instruments specially adapted to inflict physical injury, entails deprivation of liberty for from three to seven years (art. 206, last par.).

The stepping-up of the campaign against hooliganism in 1966 also brought a new chapter to the RSFSR Code of Criminal Procedure (ch. 34, arts. 414-429), aiming primarily at speedier trials in cases of hooliganism.

F. J. M. Feldbrugge

HORTICULTURE

Horticulture is carried out primarily by the collective and state farms together with their private households, but also—though to a considerably lesser extent—by other legal entities and persons on the strength of special enactments. These enactments make a distinction between cultivation of fruits (*ogorodnichestvo*) such as apples, cherries, potatoes, pears, tobacco, tea and nuts, and cultivation of vegetables (*sadovodstvo*) such as the cultivation of cabbages, tomatoes, carrots, onions, cucumbers, lettuce and spinach.

Citizens are allowed, for purposes of growing fruit, to set up associations or unions of a special type (*kollektivy*). Such horticultural associations are more or less independent if they are formed by unions of pensioners, the inmates of a particular flat-building, and so on. They are not independent if they unite the workers of a particular enterprise, in which case the latter supervises the work and management in the associations. The executive committees of the local governmental agencies may allot to these fruit-growing associations land belonging to towns, urbanised settlements, villages and plots taken out of some other land categories, as a general rule, however, not surpassing 0.15 hectare or 0.37 acre per family for personal use; if irrigated land sections are involved, the maximum stands at 0.075 hectare or 0.19 acre for each family. Plots may also be granted for purposes of fruit-cultivation to private individuals or families. The work on these plots may not be performed by persons who are not members of the families to whom the right of tillage is allocated; otherwise this right is forfeited. Assignment of land tenure for private fruit-cultivation is rather the exception than the rule.

Cultivation of vegetables may be conducted by special gardening societies (*sadovodnicheskie tovarishchestva*) which, contrary to the above-mentioned associations, have the status of juridical persons, and are governed by a model statute. Only labourers and employees working in the enterprise or institution to which such collective societies are attached may become members of such societies. These societies usually receive, through the enterprise or institution, 0.06 hectare or 0.15 acre per family from the local authorities, but the work in the societies is performed collectively. In most cases the gardening societies are set up at the initiative of the committees of the trade unions, *zavkomy, fabkomy* and *mestkomy* (see UNIONS), which exercise full directive powers over the cultivation activities. After a decree of 1961 no land sections may be allocated for purposes of this type of horticultural cultivation to individual families or persons.

Th. Vondracek

HOUSEHOLD PLOTS

After the liberation of the serf in 1861 the Russian village commune had two types of land i) allotment lands (*nadel'naia zemlia*) and ii) land for household plots (*usadebnaia zemlia*); in addition there were grazing areas and woodlands for common use. The title to the allotment lands (usually redistributed after a number of years amongst the peasant households) was with the village commune; the household plot was for the perpetual, hereditary use of the peasant household (*krest'ianskii dvor*). These lands were carefully cultivated and manured; they were used for growing the more valuable garden and field crops, whereas the allotment lands were used for growing grain. The household (*krest'ianskii dvor*) owned the household plot, the buildings, implements, livestock and household items and crops and consisted of the extended family of the peasant: agnates and cognates, foster and adopted children etc. Many Russian scholars (e.g. Pakhman) regarded the common property as belonging to a family labour union (*artel'*). Divisions were discouraged and unauthorized divisions were sometimes punished by birching.

Collectivisation

The ancient legal institution of the household with its household plot survived the revolution and collectivization. It found its legal written expression in the Land Code, (*Zemel'nyi Kodeks*), the model statutes for collective farms and in the civil laws on property and inheritance.

The policy of the Party and the authorities towards the collective farmers' household plots as productive units of the private sector was subject to repeated changes. Whenever the country needed a boost in agricultural production, household plots were supported and encouraged, but improvements in general conditions of agriculture, or the coming to the fore of more dogmatic attitudes, induced the authorities to apply pressure towards reduction of plots and inventaries in private use.

The present laws regulating the households of collective farmers and other private land users are contained in the Principles of Civil Law of the USSR and the Union Republics of 1961, in the Civil Codes of the Union republics, the Principles of Land Law of the USSR and Union Republics of 1968, the Model Charter for Collective Farms of 1969, and other statutes and by-laws. There are many common features between the present and the pre-revolutionary laws: there is no personal ownership: the household plot is given into perpetual use, while buildings, implements, livestock, household items and crops belong undivided to the collective farmer's household (personal property of its members is possible only in items purchased from personal earnings and may not consist of items as buildings, livestock, crops, which are allowed only to the household). The household property is based on the principle of common labour of the extended family. An able-bodied member of the family loses his right of a share if he has not participated by work, or other ways, in the common household for three years, unless he was called up to national service or was away on study leave. The law provides certain rules for determining the share of a member, on the partition of the household. But no inheritance is possible as long as a household exists; only after the death of the last member of a household do the usual laws of inheritance apply. According to the old model rules of collective farm charters the houschold plot (cxcluding the area under buildings) could have an area of 0.25-0.50 ha, sometimes even up to 1 ha. The new model rules fix the maximum at 0.50 ha (if the land is irrigated, 0.20 ha), the land under buildings included. "The personal plot of the collective farmer's family (collective farm household) is granted by decision of the general meeting of collective farmers, and its size is established taking into account the number of members of the collective farmer's family and their labour participation in the collective farm communal sector".

The household "may have one cow with calf up to one year of age, one heifer or bull up to two years of age, one sow with piglets up to three months old or two pigs for fattening, up to ten sheep and goats with their lambs and kids, beehives, poultry and rabbits". These are the maximum norms, which may not be exceeded; they may, however, be reduced; "the number of livestock [of a collective farmer's household] is finally determined by the general meeting of the collective farmers in accordance with the labour participation of its members in the communal sector". The use of grassland and pastures is also permitted. Although these rules are contained in the Model Charter they are statutory law for collective farmers as they were adopted by the 3rd Collective Farmers' Congress and later sanctioned by the Party's Central Committee and the Council of Ministers of the USSR.

Besides the household plots of collective farms, household plots may belong to permanent (but not temporary) state farm workers (forestry workers, etc.), to state and collective farm employees, professional people living in the country and even workers and employees in towns. (Special rules exist for plots of gardeners- and holiday-house owners' cooperatives). The size of such plots may vary (from 0.15 to 0.50 ha; only half this size is permitted for irrigated land). The livestock permitted to workers and employees (not collective farmers) is a cow with a calf, a heifer, one sow with piglets up to two months old or one pig for fattening, three sheep and goats with their lambs or kids (certain substitutions permitted). The number of poultry and beehives is unrestricted. Special permission is needed for the keeping of draft animals.

Frequently collective farms are transformed into state farms, when it has been common usage for the size of plots to remain the same as before, but the household plot is registered as being in possession of one of the members of the former collective farm household. The rest of the property, buildings, livestock etc., becomes ordinary common property and can be inherited and divided according to the general rules of the civil codes. The significance of the private sector of land use can be seen in the quantities of agricultural produce that come from the private sector. According to the *Narodnoe khoziaistvo* (Statistical Yearbook) in 1971 the share of the private sector in the total produce of potatoes was 63%, vegetables 37%, meat 35%, milk 35%, eggs 50%, wool 20% and grain 1%. The size of the area in private use was only 8,660,000 ha out of a total of 545,900,000 ha used for agriculture.

The division between household plot lands and state or collective farm lands still continues. Collective and state farms may allocate household plots only from lands belonging to household plots. If there is a shortage, special procedures must be followed to convert other lands into household plot lands.

R. Beermann

See also PRIVATE FARMS; KOLKHOZ-FARM

HOUSING LAW

While the land itself is the property of the state, legal transactions in the houses thereon are considered separately. The law is based on the principle that housing, being a necessity for all, cannot be an investment for the few. Its regulation is part of civil law, and housing disputes make up some 10% of reported cases.

The major categories are i) state housing-administered by local authorities and made up of buildings expropriated at the Revolution; new constructions; and ownerless or mismanaged houses which have been taken over; ii) industrial housing built or acquired by enterprises for their labour force; iii) personally owned housing; iv) collectively built housing.

State Housing

The Federal Principles of Civil Law and the 1964 RSFSR Civil Code made no fundamental changes in the previous law. They are supplemented by Ministerial orders (*postanovlenie*), instructions and regulations (*pravila*) of the late 50's and early 60's (in particular the Rules for the Use of Housing of October 18, 1962) and by an order of the Plenum of the USSR Supreme Court (March 25, 1964).

The basic provisions of the Civil Code would fit into any system—thus the landlord is bound to give possession and do capital repairs; the tenant does running repairs; the lease is preserved on transfer of the landlord's interest.

Grant. The Local Authority allots accommodation with the participation of Trade Union and communal bodies. On its order the housing manager issues a five-year written lease, based on a model.

Term. The five-year term is of little importance, since the good tenant has an automatic right of renewal and immunity against eviction (*q.v.*).

Parties. The housing manager is the lessor and the named tenant the lessee; but each member of his family co-resident with him is also placed in legal relationship with the landlord. For instance, no one of them can surrender part without the consent of the others; each adult may, with the consent of the others, require a separate lease of part to be granted him; and the tenant certainly, and perhaps all adults, have the right (subject to general consent) to settle other members of their family.

Area. The norm is 9 square meters of living space (i.e. not counting communal facilities) per person. In Moscow it is the maximum. If space becomes surplus and forms a separate isolated room the landlord may take it, subject to the tenant's power to nominate an occupant.

Tenant's obligations. Rents are fixed by locality and are low; but thrice the rate is charged for surplus accommodation which (if not an isolated room) cannot be taken. Only the private house-owner can evict a tenant for systematic failure to pay rent. The regulations and Model lease set out in detail the duties of proper user, running repairs, etc. A House Committee of elected tenants is the prime machinery for enforcement; only if these and the comrades' courts have failed will the civil courts act.

Tenant's powers. The tenant has no power to sell his dwelling-space. He may, with the consent of the landlord and the adult members of his family, make a genuine exchange of accommodation; refusal of consents may be challenged in court. He also has power to renew the lease, to terminate it, and to sub-lease (with similar consents) any part, provided he does not leave himself and his family with less than the norm of living-space. The rent may not exceed the state rate, nor may the rent of domestic articles exceed that for the premises. The sub-lease may be terminated by (usually) three months notice; the sub-tenant has no security of tenure. Tenants and their families who temporarily leave the dwelling may reserve it for (normally) six months.

Industrial Housing

Dwellings leased to employees are subject to a regime similar to that described above. Hostel accommodation and service tenancies provided to enable staff better to fulfil particular duties do not give the occupants rights of renewal, exchange, etc. described above. Further certain industries have powers of eviction of an employee who leaves his job (see EVICTION).

Personal Housing

The sources of the housing stock in private hands are: i) those built before the Revolution and never municipalised (i.e. if their value was below limits set by local authorities); ii) those de-municipalised under the New Economic Policy; iii) those constructed under the now extinct "building lease"; iv) those built in right of private ownership; v) those bought from state organs.

The main incentive to personal house-building came from a decree of the Presidium of the USSR Supreme Soviet of August 26, 1948 allowing citizens to buy or build a single house, and instructing local authorities to make land available, to be allotted without a time limit. In 1958 the area that could be so built was limited to a maximum of 60 sq.m. Up to half the cost could be borrowed, secured on the property.

Since the early sixties, however, such credit has been severely curtailed in the cities, and preference given to collective building (see below).

The 1959 Federal Principles and the 1964 RSFSR Civil Code deal in some detail with the dwellinghouse. Many of their provisions as to rights of recovery, passing of property etc., call for no special comment. But the content of right of ownership is limited by the social function of providing a home as the following provisions show. A family may own only one dwelling with a usual maximum of 60 sq.m. If a citizen comes by more than one house he must alienate all save one; apart from this he may sell his house only once in three years. Houses built without planning permission may not be alienated and may be demolished; mismanagement may lead to confiscation, as may the use of the house to gain unearned income (see FORFEITURE). Leasing is permitted but the rent must not exceed comparable state rates by more than 20%. The Code also contains new and elaborate rules providing for a sale of ownership reserving a condition maintenance for the life of the vendor. Finally, in many towns Street Committees are set up to help the inhabitants observe the rules of socialist community life (*q.v.*).

Collective Housing

A federal order of the Central Committee of the CPSU and the USSR Council of Ministers of 1 June 1962 provides for a gradual shift from individual housebuilding to co-operative endeavours and orders the State Bank, the State Plan, and local authorities to make appropriate facilities available. Republican Model Charters (in the RSFSR: of October 2, 1965) lay down minimum membership; with the local authority's approval the members adopt the articles and register, thus creating a juridical person to whom the land is allotted. Members buy shares and, when 30% of estimated cost has thus been raised, the balance is lent at 0.5% repayable in equal instalments over between 10 and 20 years. The "share" of each member gives him a right to the accommodation and powers to cash it or (with the consent of a General Meeting) to give or exchange the dwelling-space. On his death the share descends; if the beneficiaries lived with him they may keep the premises; otherwise, cash. The tenant can be evicted and have his money returned only if he flouts the Charter, the obligations laid down by a General Meeting, or makes life impossible for others.

Bibl.: B. Rudden, Soviet Housing Law (1963) ICLQ 591; Soviet Housing and the New Civil Code (1966) ICLQ 231.

B. Rudden

HUMAN RIGHTS, see CIVIL RIGHTS

HUNTING

The term "hunting" (*okhota*) is used in Soviet law to describe the tracking or pursuit of wildlife for purposes of bagging it, as well as the bagging itself.

Soviet law provides that all wildlife, whether reproducing in its natural habitat or released from breeding stations, constitutes a state-owned "game fund". Game management (*okhotnich'e khoziaistvo*) is a branch of the Soviet national economy, the basic task of which is to supply the state with furs and similar produce. Lands, forests and waters inhabited by wildlife used in game management constitute hunting grounds (*okhotnich'i ugod'ia*). Hunting grounds may be established irrespective of who at the moment has the use rights to the particular lands, forests or waters. Thus, portions of collective-farm lands, forests controlled by lumber or transportation industries, water reservoirs of hydroelectric power stations and the like may be designated as hunting grounds.

There are two basic types of active hunting grounds: those assigned to state, cooperative or public organizations and those assigned to the general public. The first type may be hunted only with the permission of the assignee organization; the latter are open to all, subject to the generally applicable hunting regulations. Some territories (such as those within nature preserves, wildlife sanctuaries (*zakazniki*) and green belts) are expressly closed to hunting.

Hunting grounds are assigned to organizations by contract between them and the executive committee of the region or territory or the council of ministers of the autonomous republic, within which the grounds are located, except that grounds for industrial hunting are assigned by the council of ministers of the competent Union republic. The assignments are made, as a rule, for periods of at least ten years with a preferential right of renewal. The assignees are responsible for managing the grounds and organizing the hunting activities of their members. They are also subject to all generally-applicable hunting regulations that are more stringent than their own.

A license to hunt with a firearm (see also WEAPONS) may be issued, upon the payment of a license fee, to any USSR citizen who has reached the age of eighteen, has passed a test of minimum hunting proficiency, and is a member of a hunters' association.

The overall control over hunting is vested in the USSR Ministry of Agriculture. Other agencies of All-Union, republic and local government have lesser responsibilities. Complementary regulations issued at the various levels establish classes of protected animals, closed seasons, approved instruments and methods of hunt, and bag limits. The processing of, and trade in, the furs and meat of game are exclusively within the province of authorized state and cooperative enterprises.

The milder violations of hunting regulations are mainly fought by means of administrative sanctions, mostly fines, in conformity with the general principles of administrative liability. In appropriate cases, the wildlife poachers' instruments of hunt may be confiscated and the offenders may be required to pay compensatory damages for the illegally bagged game. As a general rule, hunting without a license or in prohibited places or at prohibited times or with prohibited instruments and methods constitutes a criminal offense, but only if committed after the application of administrative sanctions. By contrast, hunting of entirely protected wildlife or illegal hunting causing serious loss to the state, may be criminally prosecuted even without prior administrative liability. The hunting regulations are enforced by state and societal hunting inspectors.

Z. Zile

See also CONSERVATION

HUSBAND & WIFE, see MARRIAGE

HYPOTHECARY LAW,
see MORTGAGES

ILLEGITIMACY
Soviet sources never use this word but refer to children born out-of-wedlock. All legal discrimination against the bastard was abolished in the early years of the regime and birth alone was declared the basis of family ties (see FAMILY LAW). However, by a decree of the Presidium of the USSR Supreme Soviet of July 8, 1944, while unwed mothers were to receive state payments for their children, the father was exonerated from any liability for the child's maintenance. But the state payments soon fell behind the awards that could be made against a registered father (see SUPPORT OF DEPENDANTS) and there was some embarrassment about the form of the birth certificate which, in place of the father's name, gave a dash. The 1968 Federal Principles of Marriage and Family Law and the later republican codes (see FAMILY LAW) have changed the position. Paternity of a child born out of wedlock may be admitted and registered or may be proved in court, having regard to the facts (arts. 47-51 Family Code). The legislation does not explicitly mention bloodtests. When paternity is thus established the father and child are in the same legal relationship as those in a registered union.
A child with no proved or admitted father may now be registered with his mother's surname and the first name and patronymic of her choice (see NAMES).

B. Rudden

IMMIGRATION,
see EMIGRATION & IMMIGRATION

IMMUNITY, see FOREIGN TRADE; DIPLOMATIC OFFICERS

IMPORTS, see EXPORT & IMPORT

INCOME TAX, see TAXATION

INDEPENDENT CONTRACTORS,
see CONTRACTORS

INDICTMENT
The predominant form of indictment in Soviet criminal proceedings is indictment by the Procuracy. This is called a state indictment and is used for all except a few minor crimes, which may be prosecuted only by the injured party (slander, insult, violation of copyright, unaggravated assault, and cases of rape committed for the first time and without threat of grave bodily injury).
Under the system of state indictment, two separate documents charging commission of a crime are presented to the suspect before trial—the accusation (*obvinenie*) and the conclusion to indict (*obvinitel'noe zakliuchenie*). The first in time is the accusation, which is presented to the suspect by the person conducting the preliminary investigation (typically, an "investigator") when the latter considers it reasonably certain that the suspect has committed a specific crime. At this point the investigator need not have questioned all witnesses or even the suspect himself and need not have verified leads that might disprove the suspect's guilt. The investigator makes the accusation in writing and must read and explain it to the suspect, who, from this time onward, is called "the accused". This is the first time the suspect is officially informed of the charges against him. If he is a minor (under eighteen years of age) or is unable to protect his own interests as result of some physical or mental deficiency, he gains the right to counsel at this point. (For all others, right to counsel arises only upon completion of the investigation.) After presenting the accusation, the investigator must interrogate the accused and afford him an opportunity to plead guilt or innocence. While the accused has no legal duty either to plead or to respond to the investigator's questions, the investigator is not obliged to inform the accused of his right to remain

silent. The accused normally does plead and does answer the investigator's questions, all of which is written down (or tape recorded) and added to the dossier.

The second document in time is called the conclusion to indict and is presented by the investigator to the accused upon completion of the preliminary investigation. Before signing the conclusion to indict, the investigator must have investigated all aspects of the case and must be convinced of the guilt of the accused. The investigator sends the conclusion to indict to the procurator, who, if he too is convinced of the guilt of the accused, forwards it to the appropriate court. The conclusion to indict contains a detailed recitation of the evidence amassed against the accused. It thus serves to alert the accused and his counsel to the state's allegations and to the evidence and witnesses to be presented by the state at trial.

John B. Quigley, Jr.

See also CRIMINAL INVESTIGATION; DEFENDANT; PRELIMINARY INVESTIGATION

INDUSTRIAL ACCIDENTS,
see EMPLOYEE PROTECTION

INDUSTRIAL ARBITRATION,
see LABOUR DISPUTES; LABOUR ARBITRATION

INDUSTRIAL PROPERTY

Industrial property is divided into two broad categories: 1) inventions and technical-industrial know-how, and 2) trademarks and production marks.

The first category encompasses inventions (arts. 517-519 Civil Code), technological innovations, rationalization proposals and scientific discoveries (arts. 520-526). Soviet law provides that inventions may be privately patented in the USSR. The patent holder theoretically possesses the right of exclusive use of his invention. As a practical matter, however, he can neither privately exploit it nor prevent its exploitation by the State. In lieu of a patent, an inventor may opt for a certificate of authorship, the rights of use and ownership of the invention then vesting automatically in the state. Only certificates of authorship are available for inventions made in the course of state employment or pursuant to state subsidy, a rule which excludes the overwhelming majority of local inventors from the option to apply for a patent. Likewise, technological innovations and rationalization proposals may only be certificated. The certificate carries with it social recognition and remuneration on a prescribed scale. Scientific discoveries are also rewarded, but are not generally eligible for either a patent or certificate of authorship. Unless the discovery is deemed to be a state secret, the scientists achieves recognition by publication of his discovery and enjoys the rights provided under Soviet copyright law.

The second category consists of trademarks, trade names, service marks and production marks. Trademarks, trade names and service marks are obtainable upon voluntary application in accordance with fairly conventional standards of registrability and on payment of a small registration fee. The fundamental right of the holder is that of exclusive use of the mark or name. The public role of the trademark is to generate competition between local enterprises and thereby to induce higher quality production, a role of increasing significance since the decentralization reforms of the mid-1960's granting greater independence to local enterprises.

Production marks, which are separate and distinct from trademarks, are mandatory on all goods. The purpose of the production mark is to focus responsibility for a given product upon a particular enterprise, department and ministry.

Jeffrey Hertzfeld

See also PATENTS; CERTIFICATES OF AUTHORSHIP; TRADEMARKS & TRADE NAMES; COPYRIGHT

INFANTICIDE, see HOMICIDE

INFANTS, see MINORS

INHERITANCE, see SUCCESSION

INJUNCTIONS, see JUDGMENTS

INJURIES, see TORTS

INSANITY

In civil law insanity may give rise to incapacity (see CAPACITY). In criminal law the basic provision is art. 11 of the RSFSR Criminal Code, according to which a person who was in a state of "non-imputability" (*nevmeniaemost'*) while committing a socially dangerous act is not criminally responsible. The wording of art. 11 makes it clear that the concept of non-imputability is in two ways different from insanity. While insanity can be described as a more or less lasting state of mind, non-imputability is relevant only as a momentary state of mind at the time of the commission of the crime. Secondly, non-imputability has regard to specific acts, whereas insanity generally affects the legal nature of a person's entire conduct. However, the recognition by the court of the non-imputability of specific criminal acts will in fact establish a very strong presumption of non-imputability of subsequent criminal acts by the same person. Therefore the admission of non-imputability in one case, followed by an order for compulsory psychiatric treatment, tends towards recognizing a person as criminally insane.

Non-imputability consists of two elements, a legal and a psychiatric one. The legal element is present when a person who has committed a crime (socially dangerous act) "could not account to himself for his actions or govern them" at the time of the commission of the crime. The formula derives from the Soviet concept of guilt (see MENS REA), in referring to the intellectual and volitional aspects of guilt.

The psychiatric element of non-imputability is described as "chronic mental illness, temporary disturbance of mental activity, oligophrenia or other pathological condition". Both the legal and the psychiatric element must be present in order to constitute non-imputability and the legal element must be *caused* by the psychiatric element. The recognition of non-imputability will normally lead to committal to a psychiatric hospital for compulsory treatment.

Persons who have been sentenced for a criminal offence and afterwards have started to suffer from a mental illness which has deprived them of the capacity to account to themselves for their actions or to govern them, will not undergo punishment, but may instead be placed in a psychiatric hospital (art. 58). The same treatment is meted out in cases where the mental illness occurred after the comission of the crime, but before sentencing. In that case punishment may still be imposed upon recovery (art. 11 par. 2). The provisions of art. 58 and art. 11 par. 2 do not quite tally with art. 11 par. 1 and its definition of non-imputability.

Non-imputability bars the imposition of a criminal penalty and provides the basis for ordering "compulsory measures of a medical nature" (cf. arts. 58-62). In the case of non-imputability the court may order committal to a psychiatric hospital for compulsory treatment. Patients who represent a special danger to society may be placed in a special psychiatric hospital (with increased security systems). Further details concerning the treatment and legal position of offenders committed to psychiatric hospitals may be found in the "Instructions concerning the application of compulsory treatment and other medical measures to persons who are mentally ill and have committed socially dangerous acts" of February 14, 1967.

Soviet law does not recognize any state of diminished criminal responsibility based on mental defects; a specific criminal act is either imputable or not imputable to the offender. The only provision which seems to imply a transitional state between sanity and insanity is art. 62 which is devoted to compulsory medical measures with regard to alcoholics and drug addicts (see INTOXICATION and NARCOTICS).

When, in the course of criminal proceedings, doubts arise about the sanity of the accused or the suspect, expert evidence from a psychiatrist has to be sought (art. 79 point 2 of the RSFSR Code of Criminal Procedure). A psychiatric report will normally be ordered by the investigator (see CRIMINAL INVESTIGATION), but the court and the procurator may also demand such a report. A general condition for ordering a psychiatric report is the presence of sufficient grounds for a criminal prosecution (art. 404 par. 3 of the Code of Criminal Procedure). In any cases where the question of non-imputability arises a preliminary investigation must take place (art. 404 par. 1).

F. J. M. Feldbrugge

INSOLVENCY

Soviet law makes little direct provision for insolvency proceedings. As there is no private trading bankruptcy proceedings are not called for. It certainly happens that citizens are unable to pay all their debts at times, and the civil procedure law lays down a system of preferred debts, e.g. damages for injuries to the person or family maintenance are satisfied in full first, if possible, then taxes, then claims by the state and only then other claims. Within each class, creditors claim *pari passu*.

The civil codes generally provide that the state is not liable for its enterprises and the enterprises are only liable to the extent of the relatively limited assets which are not totally exempt from being taken in execution for debt. Members of co-operatives are not generally liable for the debts of the co-operative.

State enterprises may be wound up for various reasons but their obligations are taken over by their successors. Otherwise employees receiving periodical payments for industrial accidents would be in difficulties. If co-operative or public bodies are wound up, their creditors have priority over their members, but there is no guarantee of solvency.

In practice bank loans seem to be available in cases of temporary financial difficulties suffered by state enterprises. As the planned economy excludes most trading risks insolvency does not appear to be a legal problem. The short periods of limitation for enforcing judgments would in any case operate to prevent recourse to after-acquired property, thus in effect discharging the insolvent debtor, except for recurring payments becoming due after proceedings.

A. K. R. Kiralfy

INSTALMENT SALES,
see HIRE-PURCHASE AGREEMENTS

INSUBORDINATION,
see MILITARY LAW

INSULT

Criminal offence, consisting in acts calculated to injure another person's dignity. Insult may be inflicted verbally, in writing, in print, or by deed, provided that it was expressed in an indecent form. The offender must have acted with malice, i.e. with full knowledge of the nature and consequences of his act, and he must have intended to injure the victim's personal honour and dignity rather than his reputation in society (see DEFAMATION). No specific charges, allegations, aspersions or innuendoes need therefore be proffered in an insult, but in contrast to defamation, characterisations and criticism clad in degrading or indecent form or language are actionable as insults even if they had a factual basis. The offender must have inflicted the insult either in the victim's presence or with the knowledge that it will (or might) be repeated to the victim. Insults (by word or deed) committed in a public place, which are not calculated to offend the honour and dignity of a particular person but rather show extreme contempt for proper decorum or cause disturbance of peace, are classified as hooliganism, a separate offence (*q.v.*).

1) As an attack on personal honour and dignity, insult is not actionable by juristic persons, or persons legally incapable of understanding the injurious nature of the treatment to which they are being subjected (minors, the mentally incompetent, etc.). In determining the existence of insult, courts are not guided by plaintiff's sense of pride and dignity, or by his own evaluation of the injury, but apply "objective" criteria derived from norms of communist morality and "rules of socialist community life" (*q.v.*). "Mental suffering" and injury to plaintiff's reputation are irrelevant to the *corpus delicti* of insult, nor are they subject to monetary compensation, but may be taken into consideration by the courts as aggravating circumstances in assessing punishment.

2) Insult must be by commission, not abstention. Failure to respond to plaintiff's toast or his RSVP invitation is not an insult. Insults in writing, in addition to words and expressions, also include drawings, caricatures, etc. The majority of republican codes treat insults in print (books, magazines, posters, leaflets, wall newspapers, etc.) as a more serious form of the offence because of the element of publicity, and several codes extend this treatment to works reproduced or duplicated in any form or manner. Insults by deed include various forms of "indecent treatment" of plaintiff, gestures, spitting at plaintiff or slapping his face, provided there was no infliction of bodily harm, and none was intended by the offender. There is disagreement among the courts whether intent or consequences of the act are the determining factor in distinguishing insult from battery, when physical pain was inflicted on the plaintiff.

3) Actions for insult are initiated only upon complaint of the victim, and are subject to termination in case of reconciliation. Action is not precluded where insult was countered by insult. Comrades' courts (*q.v.*) may hear cases involving insults a) upon request of plaintiff; or b) by decision of the people's court, if the "social danger" involved is insignificant and there was no previous conviction of the defendant for insults. Several codes allow actions before people's courts only in cases of repeated offence.

4) Punishments for insults vary according to republics. In the RSFSR, "simple" insult (i.e. by word, in writing or by deed) entails either a fine, or corrective labour, or social censure, or measures of social pressure (art. 131 Criminal Code). Serious ("aggravated") insult (i.e. in print, and likewise insult by persons previously convicted for a similar offence) is punished in double amounts of the fine (up to 100 roubles), or corrective labour of up to one year's duration. In some codes, no distinction is made between simple and aggravated insults; criminal sanctions are imposed only upon recidivists; the forms of insult are not spelled out; insults in print are assimilated to insults in writing; insults by deed are assimilated to second offences; or "indecent form" is omitted from the definition.

5) Insults may form part of the *corpus delicti* of several other, distinct, offences, either as crimes against the system of administration (insult of officials; insult of policemen and of people's guards in the performance of their duties); or as military crimes (insults among

military personnel); or as "official crimes" (insult by public official exceeding his authority). Criminal legislation also provides punishments for insults to the flag and to the state emblem.

Serge L. Levitsky

See also DEFAMATION, CIVIL; DEFAMATION, CRIMINAL

INSURANCE

History

All private insurance societies were liquidated by a decree of November 28, 1918 and the following years saw several attempts to organise a nationalised insurance system. Little success was achieved until the New Economic Policy. The 1922 Civil Code contained a chapter (arts. 367-398) on the subject and an independent organisation named *Gosstrakh* (from *Gosudarstvennoe Strakhovanie*—State insurance) was set up. The field was divided into obligatory insurance—a legal relationship arising from statute—and voluntary, contractual insurance. The organisation and the basic system are still in force. From 1929-1956 various attempts were made to provide obligatory free-rate cover for some sections of state property. It is now considered that this is better protected by allotments from central reserves; consequently industrial and housing stock owned and used by state organs is no longer insured. The main type of obligatory insurance which remains is fixed-rate cover, whereby premiums and compensation are determined by law.

During the years of collectivisation there is some evidence that this type of insurance was used to further the movement, with premiums being loaded heavily against *kulaks* and individual peasant farmers, and (later) with cover for *kolkhozniki* being allowed only for their livestock and not the produce of their plots.

Gosstrakh

Since the law of 17 April 1958, *Gosstrakh* has been decentralised and operates as a distinct economy entity within each republic (policies, however, are valid throughout the Union). (Model regulations for *Gosstrakh* agencies in the Union republics have been issued on October 25, 1958). It functions under the Ministry of Finance but is a juridical person, with economic accountability, and its organs are sub-divided into local agencies and inspectorates. Their most important tasks are i) registration of property subject to obligatory insurance; ii) valuation of property covered; iii) collection of premiums; iv) loss assessment. *Gosstrakh*'s assets are i) a basic fund (100 million roubles for the RSFSR); ii) a reserve fund formed by allotments from profits; iii) life premium reserve account; iv) current receipts. No accounts are available.

Foreign business is carried on by a separate body (*Ingosstrakh*).

Legal Sources

Unlike the 1922 Code, the Federal Principles of 1959 and the 1964 RSFSR Civil Code devote only five brief articles to this topic (arts. 386-390). These define, in the broadest terms, obligatory and voluntary insurance, and provide for a right of subrogation. Apart from this, there is a federal statute on obligatory insurance (April 4, 1940) which has been largely superseded by a decree (*ukaz*) of the USSR Supreme Soviet's Presidium on obligatory kolkhoz cover (August 28, 1967) and numerous orders of the Council of Ministers and regulations of the Finance Ministry. Thus the basic rules are lacking; and it is, in any case, doubtful whether obligatory insurance is part of civil law. The mutual obligations arise by statute and the only method of settling disputes is administrative—by appeal through *Gosstrakh* organs to the Ministry of Finance. On the other hand, voluntary insurance is clearly part of the law of civil obligations; but there seems, as yet, to be no modern legislation dealing with its fundamental principles.

Obligatory Fixed-rate Insurance
This is the basic and most wide-spread form; it provides a blanket cover of relevant property and is permanent, not periodic. Failure to pay premiums does not entail loss of cover; arrears are simply deducted from any compensation made. Omitting details, the scheme is as follows:
1) *Kolkhozes and inter-collective farm organisations*
a) *Cover*. Crops are insured against natural calamities, blight and fire; livestock similarly; buildings, installations, machinery, vehicles, raw and part-worked materials against flood, fire, etc.
b) *Compensation*: for crops, up to 50% of value calculated on average state prices over the past 5 years; for livestock 70% and for buildings, etc. 100% of inventory value.
c) *Premiums* are based on Republican tariffs calculated on the compensation paid out over, in the case of crops, the last 10 years, otherwise the last 5. The premium is paid in instalments and is on the full value of crops at state purchase prices; for other property on the inventory value. Premiums may be deducted from the farm's current accounts or from compensation; arrears incur a penalty of 0.05% a day.
Apart from its utility as pure insurance, the scheme is also an instrument of agricultural policy: the premiums on certain crops may be kept artifically low to stimulate production; privileges may be given farms with good fire prevention records; in 1960 the cover on the private crops of kolkhozniks was stopped.
2) *Individual citizens*
The buildings and larger livestock (of those citizens permitted to own the latter) are obligatorily insured against the same risks as in the kolkhozes, valuation being carried out by *Gosstrakh* officials. The cover on buildings appears to amount to about 50% of state wholesale prices. Premiums for livestock of kolkhozniks are higher than the kolkhoz rates and highest of all for uncollectivised farmers.

Voluntary Insurance
This branch is governed by a decree (*postanovlenie*) of the USSR Council of Ministers of December 11, 1969, by regulations made thereunder and in broad outline by art. 388 of the RSFSR Civil Code. It is voluntary only for the proposer: if the conditions are satisfied *Gosstrakh* must issue a policy. No individual (including the kolkhoznik) has any means of protecting crops or produce; and no citizen or organisation can obtain cover against theft, loss or civil liability (see DELICTS).
1) *Property insurance*
a) *Kolkhoz*. As buildings, plant etc. are fully covered under the obligatory scheme, voluntary insurance applies only to other property.
i) *Crops*. The farm may insure any of its crops, but not part of one, nor only one winter grain. The hazards are the same as under the obligatory scheme. Compensation is based on quantitative damage to crop, not qualitative injury to the product (save for tobacco). Maximum cover is 80% at average state prices; premiums are slightly (usually 0.5%) higher than under the obligatory scheme, and cover lapses if they are not paid in time. *Gosstrakh* is not liable if damage is caused by the fault of the farm, its members, or other persons. This last provides a contrast with Western systems where the insurer bears the risk of acts of a stranger but has recourse against him (as *Gosstrakh* would seem to have under RSFSR Civil Code arts. 389 and 456).
ii) *Livestock*. Those beasts within the obligatory scheme plus fowls, fur-bearing animals and bees may be covered (but not in-

dividually) up to 80% of the state purchase price. Bad husbandry relieves *Gosstrakh* of liability; cover begins 10 days after payment of at least half the premium and lapses if the balance is not paid within 2 months.

iii) *Agricultural machinery and vehicles.* These may be insured against natural calamity and accident up to 80% of book value. *Gosstrakh* is not liable for damage by misuse.

b) *Co-operatives*

Since producers' and consumers' co-operatives and professional, scientific and sports societies have been outside the obligatory field for some years, their voluntary insurance is the most extensive. The principle is to make available a blanket cover for almost all their property. Crops and livestock are subject to similar rules as those for farms; the basic policy also covers buildings, equipment, vehicles and goods and additional contracts may be made to insure property temporarily in the possession of the proposer, say for repair, processing or storage. This may provide an exception to the general rule that state property is not insurable, and follow the principle of other systems that anyone with an interest in, or liability for, another's goods may cover his risk. The assessment of the maximum sum assured is based on book value, with no account being taken of depreciation, so that the result is supposed to reflect replacement cost. Compensation is subject to average.

c) *Citizens*

i) *Buildings.* An owner of a dwellinghouse with the usual appurtenances may, in addition to the obligatory cover, insure the same risks at the same cost but up to 80% of valuation based on state wholesale prices with allowance for depreciation. Average applies.

ii) *Chattels.* Goods may be insured on the first loss principle; the sum paid out will never exceed the value of loss estimated by state retail prices. Goods are divided into five classes, with differing premiums depending on the risks involved. Documents, money, precious objects and watches are not insurable. In vehicle insurance nothing is payable if damage occurs through a serious breach of the highway code, driving by a person with no right to do so, or faulty repair.

iii) *Livestock.* In addition to the fixed-rate scheme, those citizens who are allowed to own cattle may obtain additional cover up to 50% of the value estimated at state purchase prices.

2) *Personal insurance*

Although voluntary personal insurance has been available since 1942, the business has developed on strictly socialist lines: the types of policy are narrowly defined and compensation is payable only for loss of general working capacity. Nothing can be recovered for pain and suffering, and there are no pure endowment policies, nor is there cover against loss of professional skills. Within these limits, however, it is one of the few types of 'investment' available to the Soviet citizen.

a) *Accident insurance.* Citizens from 16 to 70 (save the seriously disabled) may take out, without medical examination, policies against death or permanent loss of general working capacity. Lump-sum premiums are payable, calculated according to the calling of the proposer, and vary from 0.25% to 1.20%. The proposer may name a beneficiary to be paid on his death, or take out a bearer policy.

b) *Mixed: endowment, disability, death*

Citizens of 16 to 60 may take out mixed policies (usually after medical examination) for periods of up to 20 years and may name beneficiaries to take on death. After a minimum of one year the policy acquires a surrender value; after three years the insured may borrow from *Gosstrakh* on the policy. A simplified policy also exists, without medical examination, but with deferred sickness cover.

c) *Disputes.* These may be heard either within *Gosstrakh* or in the civil courts; reports of cases in the latter are extremely few.
3) *Employees' Life Insurance*
With the consent of the USSR Council of Ministers, or of that of the appropriate republic, state, public and co-operative enterprises may insure all or any of their staff against (only) death or permanent loss of general working capacity. Compensation is payable to them or their beneficiaries. Their consent is not required, nor is the contract aleatory. It has, in fact, a good deal in common with social insurance.

The Contract of Insurance
1) *Form*: The contract must be in writing, the sanction being evidentiary: RSFSR Civil Code arts. 44, 48.
2) *Parties*: These are *Gosstrakh* and the proposer. In life business the same applies, since it is impossible to insure another's life, save in the case of employees.
3) *Disclosures*: The standard required seems to be lenient. The present regulations allow *Gosstrakh* to avoid a life policy only if the proposer was in fact suffering from one of a listed number of serious diseases or was gravely disabled. Apart from that, he appears to be under no liability under pain of avoidance of the policy to disclose what he knows (still less what he ought to know) about his health.
4) *Insurable interest*: In property insurance only the most basic types of interest can be covered; whereas the concept seems to be at the basis of *life* business, since generally one can insure only oneself.
5) *Transfer of object*: If property owned by one who can and does insure is transferred to one who cannot (say the transfer of standing crops from a kolkhoz to a citizen) cover ceases. Citizens' dwellings remain covered on transfer till the expiry of the period of voluntary insurance; the fixed-rate, of course, continues. Chattels cease to be insured on transfer and apparently no premiums are recoverable back.
6) *Mortgage of policy*: Apart from the provisions allowing *Gosstrakh* to loan on a policy, it would appear that, in general, mortgage of a debt owed to the mortgagor is not permissible: RSFSR Civil Code arts. 192, 195, 196.

Obligatory Passenger Insurance
Travellers on public transport (but not local trains or vehicles) are insured against death or permanent disability. The maximum compensation is 300 roubles payable to the heirs of the deceased; it does not form part of his estate and is not liable for his debts. Premiums are part of the fare, but those who travel free are also covered. The scheme does not extend to transport employees.

Conclusions
It has been claimed (most forcefully by Professor V. K. Raikher) that Soviet insurance is a new legal institution. Its actual operation suggests that it presents a simplified, narrow, but not unusual form of insurance. The state does not 'insure' its own resources; the major productive forces still insured are those of the kolkhozes, but the scheme is also used to implement agricultural policy, one striking feature of which is the refusal to provide full cover for crops and livestock. Similarly, citizens are rarely allowed full cover; their life policies cover only basic losses and are not negotiable; and no one can insure their civil liability.

Bibl.: B. Rudden, Soviet Insurance Law, Law in Eastern Europe No. 12, 1966; E. Schütte, *Das Versicherungswesen der Sowjet-Union*, 1966.

B. Rudden

See also MARINE INSURANCE

INTELLECTUAL PROPERTY,
see COPYRIGHT

INTEREST
The economic theory of communism adopts a restrictive atttitude to interest, based on that ideology's concept of interest as an income earned through possession of capital not by work, and what is considered to be the detrimental role of interest in capitalist society. This is the background to the main rule, laid down in art. 176 of the Civil Code, that interest may be paid and claimed only in cases where this is explicitly permitted by law. The same principle is stressed in art. 270 (in the section on loans). This means a concession to ideology in comparison to the Civil Code of 1922, which still considered interest basically to be a normal element in economic life.
Thus interest to be paid from one legal or physical person to another is limited to three groups of relations: to certain operations of credit institutions, to interest on arrears of money obligations and to the field of foreign trade. In the internal activities of enterprises and economic administrative bodies interest is furthermore used as a normative tool of evaluation; this aspect will be disregarded here.
Under the first group of cases the right to earn and pay interest is limited to the specialized agencies providing credit and receiving deposits. Here also the attitude is restrictive. As for the banks, interest is not paid on current accounts and sight deposits of socialist (except cooperative) organizations. Loans to socialist organizations carry interest, and deposits by citizens and current accounts held by cooperative organizations are entitled to interest (cf. art. 395) as well as reserves corresponding to life insurance commitments by the republic-level insurance (*Gosstrakh*) organizations. Savings' banks pay interest on deposits, and mutual aid funds and pawnshops (art. 270) add an interest-rate on their loans to the public (however, only long-term loans granted by mutual aid funds are interest-bearing). The same applies in hire-purchase deals by the retail trade network to customers of certain durable consumer goods. (Further provisions are given in the model statute for pawn-shops in towns of December 15, 1939, for mutual credit funds of February 20, 1959, and a ministerial statute of the USSR 12/8 1959 on hire-purchase transactions).
The level of the banks' interest rates is fixed by decision of the USSR Council of Ministers. The interest rate charged by (ordinary) mutual credit funds is a maximum of 5 and a minimum of 2.5%; when overdue, another 1% is added. Pawn-shops charge 8.4%.
As an alternative to normal interest on deposits, the savings' banks also offer a lottery scheme, where the aggregate amount of all participating deposits compete for larger prizes (art. 395). See also SAVINGS ACCOUNTS.
Since the so-called credit reform of 1930-32 the extending of suppliers' credits is prohibited among enterprises and other organizations. The right to carry out credit operations is exclusively vested in the banking system, and all transactions over the accounts of the organizations are intended to take place on a cash basis. However, contractual obligations are not always fulfilled in time. For overdue obligations in kind there is the system of fines (*q.v.*) and penalties and for obligations expressed in money, interest on arrears has the same function (arts. 226-227). In both cases, the most important rules are laid down in the standard (type) contracts or special statutes governing the different types of transactions between socialist organizations; the Civil Code refers to this specialized legislation, at the same time prohibiting other forms of interest to be paid between socialist enterprises. Interest on arrears are, like fines, computed on the basis of a percentage per day.

Generally the refusal to pay an invoice or to issue relevant payment documents (a letter of credit, draft, check), if unjustified, causes a yearly interest of 5%. Refusal to pay for goods or services is generally computed on a 0.03% per day basis. These special tariffs are more severe than the general 3% interest on arrears to be paid if not otherwise agreed or determined in legislation; this general principle seems primarily to apply to transactions in which citizens are involved.

Delay in the receipt of payment on the creditor's side does not create the right to claim interest (art. 227).

The third group of cases where interest is allowed to occur, are transactions connected with foreign trade. These transactions involve only the foreign trade firms and a few other specialized organizations, who are allowed to adapt their behaviour to the general terms of international trade, including the payment and claim of interest. See also FOREIGN TRADE CONTRACTS.

A. Ådahl

See also BANKING; NEGOTIABLE INSTRUMENTS; CONTRACTS

INTER-KOLKHOZ ORGANIZATIONS

Inter-kolkhoz organizations are the result of co-operation between individual collective farms in the field of economy and social services. They have been rapidly gaining importance since the 23rd Congress of the CPSU in 1966, even if this form of co-operation had existed long before. In 1971 there were 4,781 inter-kolkhoz organizations engaged in different activities. Most of them are building enterprises (about 60 per cent) and animal breeding farms (about 20 per cent). Furthermore, considerable economic activities are carried out in forestry, foodstuff processing, electric power supply, and repair services. Co-operation in the field of social services, such as building recreation centres, homes for convalescent and aged people, schools and kindergartens, is urged by the official authorities, but up to now the achievements seem to be rather unremarkable.

Inter-kolkhoz organizations are regarded as co-operative associations of individual kolkhozes on the basis of common ownership. The form of co-operation within the organization takes various shapes according to the purpose intended and the statute adopted. The statute is to be elaborated on the basis of a contract concluded between the participating kolkhozes and must be approved by the executive committee of the local soviet. For the different kinds of inter-kolkhoz organizations there are a number of model statutes on the Union republican level. The Union Kolkhoz-Council advanced a draft for a uniform "Model Statute of Inter-Kolkhoz Enterprises (Organizations)" in March 1971, but it has not been confirmed by the government as yet.

Making allowance for individual differences, the inter-kolkhoz organization is a legal person entrusted with the right of operative administration concerning the common property. The member kolkhozes have a proportional share in the common property corresponding to the contribution made by them, which is to be returned in case of dissolution or leaving. The contributions constitute the original stock of the organization, but neither this, nor the other funds are indivisible. The profits made can be distributed to the member kolkhozes proportionally to their share in stock, or used for common purposes. A part of it must be paid over to the sinking fund. On the other hand, the member kolkhozes can be called on for the recovery of losses. Externally, the properties of the inter-kolkhoz organization and its member kolkhozes are separated, and there is no liability for debts of the other party. The most important decisions are to be taken by the meeting of the member kolkhozes' representatives, where unanimity is not required. The management powers are vested in a council elected by the representatives' meeting, and quite often a single director is elected, too.

In many cases inter-kolkhoz organizations of the same type are united on the regional and Union republican level. Such inter-kolkhoz unions are to be found mostly in the field of building industry, forestry, and material-technical supply. In 1971 there were 215 inter-kolkhoz unions comprising 1350 enterprises. Property relationships between inter-kolkhoz unions and their member organizations are comparable to those existing between inter-kolkhoz organizations and their member kolkhozes. On the organizational level there are differences insofar as inter-kolkhoz unions exercise planning and management authority over the member organizations in order to co-ordinate their activities.

Membership in inter-kolkhoz organizations is not restricted to kolkhozes. Sovkhozes and other state or co-operative enterprises can co-operate with individual kolkhozes or become members of multilateral organizations in the same way. In 1970 there were 2,624 sovkhozes and 657 state and co-operative enterprises co-operating in this way. In this case, however, serious legal problems as yet unresolved arise, for two types of socialist property governed by different rules, state and co-operative property, are to be amalgamated.

Georg Brunner

See also KOLKHOZ; SOVKHOZ; ASSOCIATION

INTERNATIONAL ADJUDICATION

International adjudication (*mezhdunarodnaia sudebnaia protsedura*) is a means of peaceful settlement of disputes resulting in a binding decision. In Soviet usage, the term covers international arbitration (*mezhdunarodnyi arbitrazh*) as well as adjudication by a permanent court, such as the International Court of Justice (ICJ).

Partly because of their concept of LAW and SOVEREIGNTY and partly because of practical politics, the Soviets have distrusted binding settlement of international disputes by third parties. Soviet spokesmen have been apt to label third-party impartiality a myth. As Litvinov quipped half-a-century ago, "[o]nly an angel could be unbiased in judging Russian affairs". Instead, the Soviet Union has preferred direct negotiations or, on occasion, the services of commissions of inquiry or conciliation.

Consistent with this position, the Soviet Union has never submitted its state interests to international adjudication; no third-party international tribunal has ever acquired effective jurisdiction over the Soviet Union, and, with Soviet participation, proceeded to a final decision. Until the end of World War II, it also refrained from active participation in the adjudication of international disputes between others. As a non-member of the League of Nations the Soviet Union, naturally, did not take part in the creation of the Permanent Court of International Justice. However, it declined to accede to the Court's statute even after joining the League in 1934.

In the wake of World War II, the Soviet Union, as a signatory of the UN Charter, became *ipso facto* party to the Statute of the ICJ. On March 7, 1955, the Soviet government also announced that it recognized the ratification of The Hague Conventions and Declarations of 1899 and 1907 by Imperial Russia, to the extent that they did not contradict the UN Charter and had not been modified by subsequent international agreements to which the Soviet Union was party. By the same token, it became a member of the Permanent Court of Arbitration and, in 1956, appointed the first Soviet national group of arbitrators.

In contrast to these positive actions, the

Soviet Union has steadfastly refused to declare acceptance of the jurisdiction of the ICJ under the so-called "optional clause" or to submit to the Court pursuant to a special agreement. It has shown some willingness to accept the Court's jurisdiction by prior treaty or conventions, especially in connection with membership in international organizations, such as the UN specialized agencies which are essentially technical rather than political bodies. Thus, on reentering the International Labor Organization (ILO) in 1954, the Soviet Union was obliged to accept unconditionally the obligations of the ILO Constitution, including the compulsory jurisdiction of the ICJ over the interpretation of labor conventions. Since then, the Soviet Union has ratified forty or so international labor conventions and has, by virtue of art. 37 of the ILO Constitution, become subject to the jurisdiction of the ICJ in respect to any question or dispute relating to the interpretation of these conventions.

Since the inception of the ICJ, the Soviet Union has always had a judge on its bench: Krylov (1946-52), Golunskii (1952-53), Kozhevnikov (1953-61), Koretskii (1961-1970), and Morozov (1970- —), the present incumbent. Consequently, most of the ICJ decisions have been rendered with the participation of a Soviet judge. The voting record of the Soviet judges, in view of their peculiar ties to the state and the Communist Party, has suggested (but not proved) occasional violations of judicial independence and impartiality.

Soviet standard works on international law acknowledge the overall positive contribution of the ICJ. However, just as often, the Court is said to have succumbed to "imperialist intrigues" and rendered decisions to its discredit. This less than flattering assessment of the Court and the continuing Soviet emphasis (in literature as well as in international contacts) on "non-compulsoriness" of the international jurisdiction make a substantially greater Soviet involvement in international adjudication a rather unlikely prospect.

Z. Zile

INTERNATIONAL AGREEMENTS,
see TREATIES

INTERNATIONAL ASSOCIATION OF DEMOCRATIC LAWYERS

The International Association of Democratic Lawyers was set up during October 1946, in the wake of the Nuremberg trials, at a meeting convened in the Supreme Court building in Paris. The outstanding French jurist René Cassin became its first President. The French National Judicial Movement, which in essence originated from the French Resistance, was the host association. The I.A.D.L. did not have any statutes when it started its activities. Its constitution of May 1956 states in article 2 that the aims of the association are:

a) to facilitate contacts and exchanges of views between lawyers and lawyers' associations of all countries, and to foster understanding and goodwill among them;

b) to work together to achieve the aims set out in the charter of the United Nations and to ensure common action by lawyers;

1) to encourage in the realm of law the study and practice of the principles of democracy for the maintenance of peace and cooperation among nations;

2) to restore, defend and develop democratic rights and liberties in legislation and in the practice of law;

3) to promote the independence of all peoples and to oppose any restriction of such independence whether in law or in practice.

The headquarters of the I.A.D.L. are in Brussels. National or international associations of lawyers may be members of the I.A.D.L. with the right to vote at its congresses to be held every three years. Individual members have no right to vote. The number of votes per member association is established by the Council of the I.A.D.L. (minimum 2, maximum 10). The Bureau is composed of a president, vice-presidents, a general secretary, secretaries, a treasurer, and is elected by the congress. The council consists of members of the Bureau, of a representative for each member association and of individual members appointed by the council. It meets once a year or more often if called by the president. The general secretary, the secretaries and the treasurer compose the Secretariat which is the executive organ of the I.A.D.L.

During the intervals between the meetings of the Bureau, the secretary-general, or the secretariat when it meets, are responsible for carrying out the decisions of the Bureau, of the Council and of the Congress. When founded, the I.A.D.L. was constituted by members from 22 countries. It now consists of individual members and organizations from 58 countries. The memorandum of the I.A.D.L. declares that "since its foundation the I.A.D.L. has campaigned for and supported the right of the states to national independence and sovereignty against imperialism, colonialism and neo-colonialism". The memorandum refers to the I.A.D.L. activities and support of the conference of Asian lawyers in Calcutta on January 30, 1955, of the Asian-African Conference in Bandung in April 1955, to the fight of the Algerian N.L.F. against the French, to the anti-French fight in Indochina, the anti-American fight in Vietnam, etc. The I.A.D.L. called for the withdrawal of the Israeli troops from the territories occupied in June 1967.

The I.A.D.L. publishes the "Review of Contemporary Law". The eighth Congress of the I.A.D.L. was held in Budapest, March 31-April 5, 1964, while the ninth Congress took place in July 1970 in Helsinki. The I.A.D.L. enjoys consultative status with the Economic and Social Council of the United Nations and with UNESCO.

Pierre Cot, French lawyer, professor and former minister, is the President of the I.A.D.L. and Joë Nordman, advocate of Paris, is its secretary-general.* I. I. Karpets, director of the Moscow Institute of Criminology, is one of its 17 vice-presidents.* Speaking on January 20, 1967, for the 20th anniversary meeting at UNESCO House in Paris, Karpets declared that the I.A.D.L. has "the following important tasks:

1) first to rally all progressive forces to the defence of the Vietnamese people;
2) in the second place to prevent the rebirth of fascism, to struggle to ensure the full unconditional punishment of war criminals, and to expose the reactionary circles with revanchist tendencies in Germany;
3) thirdly to widen contacts with lawyers in every country, with all who have the peace and happiness of the people of the world at heart, in order to prevent another war;
4) in the fourth place to continue the struggle against the remnants of colonialism, to defend the right of the young nations of Asia and Latin America, either already freed or on the point of liberation, to their national independence and sovereignty."

The leading slogan of the I.A.D.L. is "law in the service of peace". The law section of the Union of Soviet Societies of Friendship and Cultural Relations with Foreign Countries is a member of the I.A.D.L.

Karpets declared that "Soviet lawyers have always strictly observed the statutes of the I.A.D.L., have taken an active part in all its proceedings, and supported all its ventures. In recent years, Soviet lawyers, both in collaboration with the I.A.D.L. and alone have organized a number of meetings and other manifestations in support of the Vietnamese people".

L. Kos-Rabcewicz-Zubkowski

---

* In 1970.

INTERNATIONAL CONFLICTS
One of the points of a most radical departure of contemporary international law from its pre-1919 counterpart is perhaps the banning of the right of states to resort to war for the settlement of their international disputes. The Covenant of the League of Nations was the first international act to attempt to impose any significant restrictions on the exercise of this hitherto generally accepted concept of *jus ad bellum.* The partial contributions of the League Covenant along these lines were improved upon at the Kellogg-Briand (Paris) Pact of 1928 in which the parties pledged to abstain from the use of force in the settlement of international disputes. The adoption of the UN Charter in 1945 marked a culminating point in the concerted international effort to eliminate the illegal use of force in the conduct of inter-state relations.

Under Art. 1, par. 1 of the 1945 Charter, members undertake to take effective collective measures for the preservation and removal of threats to peace and for the suppression of aggressive acts or other breaches of international peace, and to bring about by peaceful means and in conformity with the principles of justice and international law, adjustment or settlement of international disputes or situations which might lead to a breach of the peace. Art. 2, par. 3 of the Charter calls upon all members in a most positive manner to settle their international disputes by peaceful means in such a way that international peace, security and justice are not endangered. But whereas the obligations of member states to settle their disputes peacefully are based, *inter alia*, on these two provisions, a similar obligation is imposed on non-members of the UN under Art. 2, par. 6. Thus, whereas the UN Charter may be regarded as a *res inter alios* with regard to non-members, its provisions on the elimination of the use of force in inter-state relations are seen as a mere codification of an otherwise existent norm of general international law which is binding on all states irrespective of their membership of the UN. It would therefore be correct to say that the obligation to seek pacific settlement of international disputes is a norm of *jus cogens* under contemporary international law.

Art. 33 of the UN Charter in a non-exhaustive fashion enumerates the pacific settlement procedures that are open to states. These include solution through direct negotiations between the parties, enquiry, mediation, conciliation, arbitration, judicial settlement, resort to regional agencies or arrangements. To these may also be added resort to the UN itself.

While recognising the principle of peaceful settlement of international disputes, as one of the fundamental principles of contemporary international law, the Soviet Union has tended to show special preference only for some of the settlement procedures enumerated under Art. 33 of the UN Charter. The Soviet Union traditionally has been very hostile to any move towards a third party settlement of international disputes if such procedures would deny her the right to exercise any significant control over the composition of the tribunal or over the determination of the law to be applied in the settlement of any such disputes (see INTERNATIONAL ADJUDICATION).

It would be partially correct to attribute such a Soviet attitude to the radical differences between the concepts of law as held by the Soviet Union and by most western nations. It is indeed true that what may appear as a source of law to a western judge who may be sitting on the International Court of Justice, e.g. certain general principles of private law, may not be an acceptable source of international law to his Soviet counterpart. But the Soviet Union's basic reason for shying away from international adjudication or from submitting any disputes to an international arbitral commission, the composition of which is pre-determined, is that she does not seem to have any political faith in the judicial impartiality of the traditional western system of justice (see INTERNATIONAL ORGANIZATIONS).

On the other hand the Soviet Union will be more likely to submit to international arbitration if she is left with the choice of nominating her members to such a tribunal and with the reasonable option of shaping the terms of reference and applicable law upon which such an arbitration shall be based.

Where and when superior political interests dictated her acceptance of the jurisdiction of standing international arbitral commissions she has, however unwillingly, done so.

The Soviet Union has demonstrated keen interest in direct diplomatic negotiations and consultations as the best pacific means for the settlement of disputes. By so doing the Soviet Union refuses to entrust its fate to any third parties. The second category of pacific settlement of international disputes which might seem acceptable to the Soviet Union includes those methods in which, even if a third party were brought into the matter, the parties to the dispute shall still reserve to themselves the right to opt out of such settlement procedures, should the latter prove detrimental to their national interests. Such loose-edged third party settlement procedures include enquiry, mediation and conciliation. Resort to regional agencies and arrangements for the settlement of international disputes, in the case of the Soviet Union, would mean her resorting to either the WARSAW TREATY ORGANIZATION, the COMECON or to any related agencies of any of these socialist regional organizations. In both cases the Soviet Union has a dominant voice and her jealously guarded national sovereignty would seem sufficiently safeguarded to make such a move acceptable to her.

Even though the Soviet Union maintains a veto power inside the UN Security Council, it is highly doubtful if she would be readily willing to avail herself of the provisions of Art. 35 of the UN Charter. Such a refusal to resort to Art. 35 would be contingent on the probable invocation of the principle of *Nemo judex in re sua* as contained in the Security Council voting procedure in Art. 27, par. 3.

Soviet diplomatic practice knows many examples in which the Soviet Union agreed to enter into bilateral treaties which would set up standing conciliation commissions for the settlement of disputes. The first of such bilateral agreements was signed in 1929 between the Soviet Union and Germany under which the Standing Commission was to look into any disputes between the parties, if such a dispute could not be resolved through regular diplomatic exchanges. The settlement of disputes arising from the application or interpretation of treaties was specifically provided for in this treaty. This treaty was followed by similar conventions with Poland in 1932, Finland in 1932, etc.

The Soviet Union has also developed an intricate network of conciliatory procedures for regulating boundary disputes, e.g. she entered into such agreements with Roumania in 1923 and 1961, with Iran in 1927 and 1957, with Finland in 1928 and 1960, with Afghanistan in 1932, with Poland in 1933, with Turkey in 1937, with Norway in 1949, and with Czechoslovakia in 1949 and 1956. Under the provisions of each of these agreements each party appoints equal numbers of boundary commissioners and the agreements grant them clearly defined rights and obligations. Underlying this overall Soviet insistence on direct negotiation between parties to any dispute is her consideration for national sovereignty (*q.v.*).

C. Osakwe

INTERNATIONAL CRIMES

The Soviet approach to international criminal responsibility complements the policy positions taken with respect to peaceful coexistence and peace (see PEACEFUL COEXISTENCE and PEACE). Aggressive war, colonialism, and suppression of national liberation are the principal offenses around which state and individual responsibility is structured. As to state responsibility for violations of international law, the Soviets prefer the broader term "delict" to "crime"; although the "crime against mankind" formulation is frequently used to describe such capitalist state actions as German occupation policies in WW II, U.S. atomic bombing of Hiroshima and Nagasaki, and U.S. military actions in Asia and Latin America.

In the Soviet view the fundamental responsibility of states is for violations against peaceful relations and the freedom of nations. There are two types of violations: acts or omissions directed against the interests of a specific state and those especially serious acts or omissions which constitute encroachments upon the fundamental nature of international relations, thereby violating the interests of all states. The latter includes threats to peace, violations of peace, direct and indirect aggression, colonialism, suppression of national liberation, apartheid and racial discrimination, and genocide. Bourgeois literature is criticized for limiting state responsibility to the duty to make compensations. In the Soviet view, there is political as well as material responsibility. The former includes susceptibility to international sanctions (ranging from condemnation to military force) as well as giving satisfaction to the offended state; the latter, the duty to make reparations and restitution.

Individual responsibility is the personal liability of those who act on behalf of states, and thus, the other side of the coin of state responsibility. Although this is the logic of the Soviet position in rejecting the "act of state" and "official or superior's order" defenses to individual responsibility, Soviet commentaries tend to focus on individual responsibility for war crimes and their punishment by international and national tribunals. This responsibility is said to have been established after World War II as a result of Soviet initiatives in combating the reactionary, bourgeois view that only states, as the subjects of international law, can be held responsible for international crimes. Noting the facts that the Soviet Union initiated the prosecution of war criminals by a trial as early as 1943 and that it played a leading role in obtaining signature of the Charter of the International Military Tribunal in London on August 8, 1945, and in the subsequent war crime trials, the Soviets claim a leadership role in obtaining the general acceptance of individual responsibility for international crimes which was reflected in a Resolution of the General Assembly on December 11, 1946. The main war crimes for which there is individual responsibility are the planning, preparation, initiation and waging of aggressive war; violations of the rules of war; and propaganda for war (art. 71 Criminal Code) as well as propaganda designed to incite violations of the rules of war. Despite the concentration on war crimes, the Soviets appear to be seeking to enlarge the area of individual responsibility to include other activities which are prohibited by the law of peaceful coexistence (i.e. contrary to the policy of coexistence).

Bernard A. Ramundo

INTERNATIONAL JUDICIAL ASSISTANCE, see LEGAL ASSISTANCE

INTERNATIONAL LAW,
see PUBLIC INTERNATIONAL LAW

INTERNATIONAL ORGANIZATIONS

Soviet doctrinal international law views the creation of international organization as an institutional response to the mounting economic pressure on the various states to better coordinate their economic activities. It was this need for improved international intercourse and the international division of labour which directly precipitated the emergence of international organizations to serve as permanent institutions for the promotion of the economic interests that were common to all the participating states.

Whereas international organizations were a rare phenomenon in ancient times, the significant impact of these institutions was not felt until towards the end of the 19th and early 20th century i.e. when the first administrative unions were set up. The spectacle of general international organizations became a familiar one after the first world war and particularly after the second world war.

Soviet scholars classify international organizations into different categories depending on their: permanence (into permanent and ad hoc); objectives (into general and specialised); membership (into universal and regional); and their functions (into political, economic, social, judicial, etc.). However, the classification of international organizations into permanent and ad hoc is not shared by all Soviet scholars, the majority of whom rather consider an international organization as a permanent institution in contradistinction to other ad hoc international institutions, e.g. international conferences and congresses which lack any structural permanence. Permanence in this context does not mean that all the organs are permanently in operation. All it means is that at least some of the organs, e.g. the secretariat, or as in the case of the United Nations, the Security Council as well, are set up in such a fashion as to be able to operate permanently.

As a result of the post-1955 development in Soviet international legal scholarship, most Soviet lawyers consider international (interstate) organizations as secondary subjects of international law (see: PUBLIC INTERNATIONAL LAW). This means that under the Soviet doctrine these organizations possess some measure of derived international legal personality. But before such a personality is granted to any international organization it is the opinion of most Soviet international lawyers that these organizations must first fulfil the following prerequisites: the membership shall be open to states only (the institution of associated membership in certain UN specialized agencies, by which certain self-governing but non-sovereign territorial units are admitted into these organizations, is an acceptable derogation from the above principle); the organization must be founded on the basis of an international agreement which shall constitute its charter; the charter must spell out the scope of the legal personality to be accorded to such an organization; the organization must be founded on principles which are compatible with those of the United Nations; and, finally, such an organization must be recognised by all or almost all states.

While accepting the corporate personality of an international organization that fulfils these aforementioned criteria, contemporary Soviet scholars condemn the concept according to which such an international organization shall be construed as possessing an autonomous will. The will of an international organization cannot be divorced from the political wills of the member states who, in the final analysis, determine the contents of such a corporate will. This leaves one with the impression that Soviet scholars would necessarily equate an international organization with an agent who is acting on behalf of the member states and no more. But then both Tunkin, Shibaeva and Morozov quickly add that the relationship between the UN, for example, and the member states is not only one of an agent to a principal. In their view, the United Nations, qua international person, bears full responsibility for its actions, though the member states were directly responsible for creating this UN will, a corporate will *per definitionem.*

At the other extreme, however, Modzhorian and Shurshalov would liken the relationship between the UN and its member states to that of agent-principal in municipal law. Under this theory responsibility for UN actions accrues to the member states and not to any non-existent third party.

An important factor in the understanding of Soviet theory of international organizations is the fact that, whereas Soviet scholars adhere to the declarative theory with regard to the recognition of states, they proclaim the constitutive theory as the basis of their doctrine on the international legal personality of any international organization. Unless a state is a member of an international organization or has tacitly or expressly acquiesced in the corporate personality of such an international organization, such an international organization remains a legal non-entity as far as the non-recognising state is concerned. This means that the Soviet Union, or at least those Soviet scholars who are willing to accredit international organizations with some legal personality, consider only those 8 UN Specialised Agencies of which the Soviet Union is a member as international persons, while at the same time regarding such other international organizations as the International Monetary Fund, International Finance Corporation, International Development Association and the Food and Agricultural Organization of the UN as legal non-entities.

On the question of the scope of the international personality to be accorded to any international organizations, the Soviet doctrine seems to relate the scope of such personality to the membership factor in such organization—the more members there are in the organization and the more representative it is of the existing socio-economic systems, the more powers Soviet scholars would concede to it. This tendency to relate the scope of the personality of an international organization to the representativeness of the organization, like the application of the constitutive theory of recognition to the question of legal personality of international organizations, is a device through which Soviet scholars hope to guarantee participation for the Soviet Union and the other socialist states in general international organizations.

In the discussion of the juridical nature of universal international organizations Soviet scholars almost completely leave out the League of Nations with which the Soviet Union had a very sad experience. The emphasis therefore is on the United Nations and its Specialised Agencies. Almost the same neglect shown for the League of Nations by Soviet scholars is to be noticed in their treatment of the International Court of Justice which the Soviet Union, despite the fact that it has a judge on the Court, continues to look upon as an international court of imperialist justice.

Regional organizations are grouped under three categories: peaceloving, imperialist-dominated, and outright aggressive blocs. To the first group belong all the socialist organizations of Eastern Europe—the Warsaw Treaty Organization (*q.v.*), the COMECON (*q.v.*) and their related agencies, as well as the Organization for African Unity and the Arab League. The group of imperialist-dominated organizations includes the Organization of American States, the EEC and other European Communities, whereas the outright aggressive blocs are considered to be NATO, SEATO, CENTO, and ANZUS.

Soviet attitudes towards general international organizations underwent some radical changes in the late 1950's and the early 1960's when the Soviet government realized the possible contributions these organizations could make to the conduct of its foreign policy. The Soviet Union joined many international organizations of the UN family after the death of Stalin and as a result of this it is today a member of a majority of general international organizations including UN, UNESCO, IMCO, WHO, IAEA, ITU, UPU, ICAO, ILO as well as being a party to the Statute of ICJ.

In the early 1960's, partially as a result of the Congo crisis, the Soviets realised that the secretariats of international organizations in general, and of the United Nations in particular, can be quite influential in shaping the policy of the organizations concerned. This immediately led to the Soviet "troika" proposals for the distribution of posts in the secretariats of international organizations in which representatives of the three worlds—socialist, capitalist and non-aligned—are seated. Thus a policy which began as an initial reaction of the Soviet government toward the handling of the Congo crisis by the then Secretary-General of the UN has since settled into a Soviet foreign policy line with regard not only to the United Nations, but also all other international organizations of the UN family. Even though the Soviets dropped their original demand for the appointment of three Secretary-Generals for the UN, they still fight to realise their *troika* concept in the distribution of executive posts inside the organization.

C. Osakwe

INTERNATIONAL TRADE,
see FOREIGN TRADE

INTERNATIONAL WATERS

The international legal regime of the high seas is governed by the 1958 Geneva Convention on the High Seas, ratified by the Soviet Union in 1960, and by international custom. The definition of high seas in the Geneva Convention ("all parts of the sea that are not included in the territorial sea or in the internal waters of a state") is regarded by Soviet jurists as a general definition, not affecting the status of seas that do not qualify as territorial or internal waters; i.e., the "closed" or "regional" sea (see TERRITORY). Soviet jurists endorse the freedoms of the seas specified in Art. 2 of the Geneva Convention, cautioning, however, that this listing is not all-inclusive and that states must refrain from actions on the high seas that would reflect unfavorably on their use by nationals of other states. While the principle of freedom of the seas is staunchly defended in Soviet legal writings, there is deep suspicion of its invocation and application by large naval powers. In its broadest aspect, freedom of the seas is treated by Soviet diplomacy and international lawyers as a politico-legal principle to be formulated and applied so that rights of smaller maritime powers receive maximal protection, and the "willful, coercive" exercise of naval superiority by adversary states is tainted by its allegedly inherent unlawfulness.

Each state prescribes the conditions and procedure for granting the right to sail under its flag and its nationality to vessels, as well as for the registration of vessels on its territory. Under the 1968 Merchant Shipping Code, vessels owned by the Soviet state, by collective farms or other cooperative and social organizations, or by Soviet nationals are granted the right to sail under the State Flag of the USSR on condition of their proper registration in the State Ship Register or ship directory and of the acquisition of certificates required by Soviet law. Only Soviet nationals may be members of the crew of a Soviet vessel, with minor exceptions (arts. 22, 23, 26, 30-33, 41). Soviet law does not permit the use of "flags of convenience". To the general rule of international law that a vessel on the high seas may not be stopped, detained, attacked, seized, or otherwise subjected to coercive actions by any foreign vessel, Soviet jurists acknowledge certain exceptions. The right of hot pursuit as defined in Art. 23 of the Convention on the High Seas was incorporated into the 1960 Statute on the Protection of the State Border of the USSR. The right of any state to seize a pirate ship or aircraft on the high seas is also recognized. The Soviet doctrine of piracy is an exceedingly broad one. In the Soviet view, it is the "piracy of warships, or state piracy" which represents the greatest international danger, and a reservation to that effect was entered by the USSR to the definition of piracy in Art. 15 of the Convention on the High Seas. Piracy has been defined by V. S. Vereshchetin, writing in 1958, as any "unlawful act of coercion committed by a vessel or aircraft with respect to other vessels, persons, and property on the high seas or on other territory beyond the jurisdiction of any state". The concept of state piracy did not become prominent in Soviet legal media until late 1954, when the USSR complained to the United Nations General Assembly about violations of freedom of navigation in the China seas.

The Soviet Union is a party to the 1956 Supplementary Convention on Slavery, but, fearing abuses, narrowly construes Art. 22 of the Convention on the High Seas providing for the right to board a foreign merchant vessel reasonably suspected of engaging in slave trade. In addition, the Soviet Union is a party to the 1884 convention on submarine cables, the 1956 Soviet-Japanese fisheries convention, and the 1957 sealing convention—all of which authorize the boarding and search of foreign vessels under certain conditions to verify compliance with the agreements.

The "right of approach" to verify the flag of a foreign vessel, while recognized in Soviet doctrine and practice, has given rise to several formal protests by the USSR against approaches of Soviet ships by U.S. naval vessels on the high seas. The doctrine of "self-defense" on the high seas is vigorously opposed by Soviet jurists as a "direct infringement of the sovereign rights of states over vessels sailing under its flag".

The USSR is party to most international agreements regulating safety of navigation on the high seas and has concluded similar multipartite agreements with other members of the socialist bloc.

Pollution of the seas recently has become a serious concern of the Soviet Government. The 1954 London Convention for the Prevention of Pollution of the Seas by Oil was ratified by the USSR in 1969. Strict decrees aimed at reducing pollution of the Caspian Sea were enacted by the USSR Council of Ministers in 1968, and with regard to the Arctic in 1971. Soviet jurists have criticized the United States and other powers for disposing of radioactive wastes from peaceful uses of atomic energy at sea in special containers.

Use of the high seas for naval training exercises, maneuvers, and tests is severely condemned in Soviet legal media as being in derogation of the United Nations Charter. The creation of restricted zones on the high seas is said to be tantamount to a unilateral appropriation of the high seas. A Soviet proposal to amend the draft Geneva Convention on the High Seas to this effect failed for want of support in 1958. Soviet naval maneuvers on the high seas are distinguished from their Western counterparts on the ground that areas of the sea are closed only for a brief period and do not obstruct international navigation.

Large-scale commercial exploitation of high seas fisheries by the USSR began in the late 1950's and has dramatically expanded up to the present. The penetration of new high seas fishing grounds by Soviet vessels has been accompanied by greater Soviet participation in multilateral and bilateral treaties regulating the times, places, and conditions of fishing (see FISHING).

The interests of the USSR in high seas fisheries are complex and sometimes contradictory. In the Far East, for example, where Soviet fishing activity has been of long duration, the USSR has reduced Japanese competition by way of exclusion and quotas. In areas where the USSR is a newcomer, it has sought to share in the existing division of catch or other regulation of the fishery area. During the late 1960's, fishery operations brought the USSR into conflict with the United States and Latin American countries. Four agreements were concluded with the United States wherein the USSR agreed to reduce its catch in waters off American coasts in return for loading and port privileges. The Soviet Government has formally protested against enforcement of a 200-mile belt of territorial waters by Argentina.

As a newcomer to fishing on the high seas, the USSR has opposed theories of "abstention" and "conservation" when they are a "mask" for unilateral appropriation of fisheries by a coastal state.

The USSR has not ratified the Geneva Convention on Fishing and Conservation of the Living Resources of the High Seas. It has become a member of the North-East Atlantic Fisheries Commission, the North West Atlantic Fisheries Commission, the Japanese-Soviet Northwest Pacific Fisheries Commission, the Mixed Commission for Black Sea Fisheries, the Mixed Commission for Baltic Fisheries (with Poland and the GDR), and the Western Pacific Fisheries Commission. In addition, the USSR has joined the International Whaling Commission, the Commissions for the Conservation of Fur Seals in the Northeast Atlantic and the North Pacific, the International Council for the Exploration of the Sea, the Intergovernmental Maritime Consultative Organization, and a number of other international organizations or groups concerned with maritime affairs.

Since the Cuban crisis of 1962, the institution of pacific blockade on the high seas has been vigorously criticized in Soviet legal literature as being in violation of the United Nations Charter, the Inter-American Treaty of Reciprocal Assistance, and the Convention on the High Seas.

The legal regime of the seabed beyond the continental shelf (see TERRITORY) is unsettled. The Soviet Government has strongly advocated demilitarization of the deep seabed, and was instrumental in promoting the conclusion of the treaty proscribing the emplacement of fixed nuclear weapons or other weapons of mass destruction, as well as structures, launching installations, or other facilities specifically designed for testing, storing, or using such weapons on the seabed beyond a 12-mile maritime zone. Soviet jurists have expressed opposition to schemes to "internationalize" or unilaterally appropriate the deep seabed. While the legal regime of the deep seabed may be undetermined, Soviet international lawyers do not regard this area as a legal vacuum; any future regime must be compatible with existing norms and principles pertaining to the freedom of the seas.

International canals are artificial works connecting major international sea lanes of seas and oceans. Their regime is governed by special international agreements. The most important are the Suez, Panama, and Kiel Canals. The USSR endorsed nationalization of the Suez Canal by Egypt in 1956 and has suggested that a similar action by the Panamanian Government with respect to the Panama Canal would also be in conformity with international law.

International straits are natural waterways connecting seas and oceans. The legal regime of such straits is said to depend upon both the regime of the seas they connect and the importance of the straits for international navigation. Thus, according to Soviet jurists, straits leading into an internal sea are internal waters of a coastal state and under its exclusive jurisdiction (i.e., the Straits of Kerch connecting the internal Sea of Azov with the Black Sea). As a general rule, that portion of a strait whose waters are not overlapped by the territorial waters of the littoral state constitutes high seas, with all of the consequences such a regime bears. However, straits constituting world sea lanes, even though they may be overlapped by territorial waters or may lead into a sea wholly enclosed by the territory of several states, also must be open to international merchant shipping.

The regimes of the most important straits are governed by international agreements. The Black Sea Straits are regulated by the 1936 Montreux Convention, to which the USSR is a party. In the Soviet view, these Straits are a special case justifying restrictions on the passage of warships of non-Black Sea Powers. After World War II, the USSR charged Turkey with violations of the Montreux Convention and sought appropriate revisions. In 1948 a Soviet jurist, B. A. Dranov, urged that the Straits regime should be determined exclusively by the littoral powers. Recently, as Soviet-Turkish relations have improved, there has been less Soviet criticism of the Montreux Convention.

The Baltic Straits are described in Soviet legal media as part of the sea lane connecting the North Sea with the Baltic Sea. Although the 1857 Treaty of Copenhagen guarantees freedom of passage through the Straits, in the Soviet view it does not resolve all problems, particularly those relating to the national security of coastal states. On several occasions since 1924, the Soviet Government has proposed the Baltic Straits be closed to warships of non-Baltic powers.

International rivers are navigable rivers which flow directly into the sea, which intersect or divide the territory of two or more states, and which are open in peacetime to merchant shipping of all flags on the basis of a uniform legal regime established by international agreements of the riparian states. Among the largest international rivers are the Amazon, Congo, Danube, Niger, Rhine, and St. Lawrence. Soviet jurists stress that the right to regulate navigation and to exploit international rivers appertains solely to the riparian countries, since all rivers, including international, are an integral part of the states whose territory they intersect or divide. Any attempt of third states to participate in the administration of such rivers is deemed a gross violation of riparian state sovereignty. The USSR is party to the 1948 Convention on the Regime of Navigation on the Danube and a member of the Danube Commission, which regulates navigation on the River from Ulm to the Black Sea (see DANUBE).

Multinational rivers are those which intersect or divide two or more states and which do not flow directly to a sea. They are part of the territory of the states which they intersect and are chiefly used for internal navigation or cabotage. The Soviet Union has concluded agreements governing multinational rivers with Poland, Finland, Czechoslovakia, People's Republic of China, Afghanistan, Iran, and other states.

W. E. Butler

See also BOUNDARIES; POLAR TERRITORIES

INTERPRETATION OF LAWS

Art. 49 of the Constitution of the USSR states that the Presidium of the Supreme Soviet shall interpret the laws of the USSR, and a similar power is given with respect to republican laws to the presidia of republican supreme soviets by the various republican constitutions. Soviet constitutions and statutes are silent with respect to the power of any other agencies to give an interpretation (*tolkovanie*) of laws, and some Soviet writers have therefore distinguished between such interpretation of laws and other forms of official explanation of their meaning. It now seems to be generally recognized, however, that the interpretations of laws given by the USSR Council of Ministers and their republican counterparts are legally binding (unless overruled by the Presidium of the USSR or republican Supreme Soviet). Interpretation by other state agencies are said to have a binding character only in instances when such agencies have the right to issue instructions and explanations on the application of laws within their spheres of competence. Thus the State Committee on Labour and Wages attached to the USSR Council of Ministers is authorized to issue to ministries binding regulations and instructions on questions of labour and wages and thereby to interpret laws relating thereto. Similarly, interpretations of laws issued by superior agencies are binding on subordinate agencies. Guiding explanations are often issued by the Supreme Court of the USSR and by republican supreme courts concerning the meaning of laws to be applied in judicial proceedings, and such guiding explanations are legally binding upon judicial agencies but not, theoretically, upon others. On a few occasions, interpretations of laws by the USSR Supreme Court have been overruled by the Presidium of the USSR Supreme Soviet.

In addition to official interpretation of laws Soviet legal science recognizes so-called doctrinal interpretation, which is not legally binding but nevertheless may be persuasive because of reasons given in support of it and because of the scholarly reputation of its authors. A Soviet writer has stated that although the opinions of legal scholars have never had binding force in the Soviet Union, "nevertheless this does not by any means exclude the fact that doctrinal interpretation has an enormous significance for the improvement of the legal activity of all Soviet state agencies and social organizations and for the strengthening of socialist legality".

Soviet legal science distinguishes three modes of interpretation of laws—"grammatical interpretation", "systematic interpretation", and "historical-political interpretation". Grammatical interpretation is the analysis of the morphological and syntactical structure of the text of the law. Systematic interpretation places the text of the law in the context of related laws—e.g., interpreting the meaning of a provision of a code in terms of its relationship to other provisions of the code and in terms of its place in the code as a whole. Historical-political interpretation considers the social and political situation in which te given statute or norm was issued, including its legislative history, pre-existing laws which it replaced, etc. Some Soviet jurists also distinguish "teleological interpretation" as a separate mode of interpretation, but the prevailing Soviet view seems to be that the purpose of a law is to be discovered by the use of the other three modes of interpretation and that to isolate its purpose can lead to a distortion of its meaning and to violations of socialist legality.

Soviet jurists also distinguish between extensive interpretation, strict interpretation, and literal interpretation. Article 5 of the law introducing the 1923 RSFSR Civil Code provided that extensive interpretation of the code is permitted only in instances when protection of the interests of the Worker-Peasant State and of the toiling masses so requires. No such provision is contained in recent legislation, and it is virtually impossible to generalize concerning Soviet policy in this respect, except perhaps to say that a very high value is placed on literal interpretation. There is no general rule, such as exists in some countries, that criminal statutes should be strictly construed.

Harold J. Berman

See also ANALOGY; FICTIONS; LAW; PRECEDENTS; PRESIDIUM OF THE SUPREME SOVIET; SUPREME COURT

INTOXICATION

Although no absolute numbers have been published of late, alcoholism is patently a very serious problem in the Soviet Union. It is especially significant in the sphere of criminal law since more than half of the total number of serious crimes are committed by persons suffering in various degrees from alcoholic intoxication. The percentage is highest in the case of hooliganism (*q.v.*), according to all sources above 90%; it is high in cases of crimes of violence (homicide, assault, rape), fluctuating around 70/80%, and is still relatively high (around 50% and over) in cases of theft.

Although the abuse of alcohol is considered to be a phenomenon alien to socialist societies, Soviet criminology has yet to come up with an explanation which goes beyond the platitude that alcoholism is a remnant of pre-socialist society.

The basic rule to start from is art. 12 of the Criminal Code of the RSFSR: "A person who commits a crime while in a state of intoxication shall not be freed from criminal responsibility". This rule is considered to imply that intoxication does not normally make a person unable to account to himself for his acts. According to the accepted (although not uncontested) doctrine, the rule also applies to a state of deep intoxication; the rationale for this viewpoint is in fact the ancient theory of *versari in re illicita*: the offender has placed himself in an unlawful position where he may unwillingly or unknowingly commit a crime and thereby becomes responsible for any crimes committed in that position.

Although intoxication does not—as a rule—take away or alleviate criminal responsibility, it may serve as an aggravating circumstance; it is mentioned in art. 39 of the Criminal Code of the RSFSR in the general catalogue of aggravating circumstances in cases where the commission of the crime is connected with a "source of increased danger" (motor vehicles, machinery, etc.). See also TRAFFIC OFFENCES.

A special regime is in force for alcoholics—persons who are addicted to the consumption of alcoholic beverages. An alcoholic is considered to be criminally responsible, but additionally art. 62 of the Criminal Code applies to him. This provision allows alcoholics (who have committed a criminal offence) to be placed in special institutions for compulsory treatment. Such treatment may run concurrently with a sentence, or be continued after the offender has served his sentence. A person is released from compulsory treatment by the court upon the application of the administration of the institution.

Persons who drink excessively (they need not be alcoholics) and thereby jeopardize the material position of their families, may be declared partially incapable by the criminal court if they have committed an offence for which the court does not impose a sentence which deprives them of their freedom. In such cases the court will also appoint a guardian (art. 62 of the Criminal Code). The same measure (partial incapacity and appointment of a guardian) may also be taken under art. 16 of the Civil Code of the RSFSR; in this case the commission of a crime is not required.

Only in the comparatively rare case where intoxication triggers off a severe mental disturbance, criminal responsibility may altogether disappear (delirium and comparable states). In such cases (irrespective of the fact whether the offender is an alcoholic or not) the court will apply one of the medical measures provided by arts. 58-61 of the Criminal Code.

Public drunkenness in itself is not a criminal offence; where it constitutes a more or less serious disturbance of the peace it will be covered by the provision against hooliganism (*q.v.*). Otherwise it will be an administrative offence punishable by a fine (decree of the USSR Supreme Soviet Presidium of July 26, 1966, "On increasing the responsibility for hooliganism"), or a disciplinary infraction (especially drunkenness at work). Also, any form of drunkenness may be dealt with by the comrades' courts (*q.v.*). Serious cases of drunken driving are covered by art. 211-1. A significant factor in the alcoholism problem in the Soviet Union is the illicit distilling of spirits (of various kinds, lumped together under the denomination *samogon*). The production, possession and passing of *samogon* or of the necessary machinery and instruments is forbidden by art. 158 of the Criminal Code (as amended on November 30, 1972).

The receiver of *samogon* is punishable by an administrative fine.

Since 1972 all official activities to combat alcoholism and drunkenness are co-ordinated by the Commissions for the fight against drunkenness (*komissii po bor'be s p'ianstvom*, regulated by a decree of August 21, 1972). These commissions are set up at republican, provincial and *raion* level (and occasionally at village level as well), and are attached to the corresponding executive agency (council of ministers, executive committee). Their relative importance is reflected in the rule that they are presided over by the deputy chairman or the secretary of the executive agency. The *raion* (or town) commissions co-ordinate and supervise all local activities against drunkenness and alcoholism; the provincial commissions co-ordinate the work of the *raion* commissions and are in turn supervised and guided by the republican commission. All commissions may, within their respective jurisdictions, issue decisions (*postanovleniia*) which are binding to all state and public agencies and organizations and private citizens.

F. J. M. Feldbrugge

See also NARCOTICS

INVALIDITY INSURANCE,
see SOCIAL INSURANCE

INVENTIONS, see PATENTS;
INDUSTRIAL PROPERTY

INVESTIGATION,
see PRELIMINARY INVESTIGATION

INVESTMENTS, see CONTRACTORS

JUDGES, see COURTS

JUDGMENTS, CIVIL PROCEDURE

Judgments must be divided into final (*reshe-niia*) and interlocutory judgments (*opredele-niia*). The former conclude the proceedings on the merits, while the latter deal with various eventualities which may arise earlier. Final judgments (cf. arts. 191-213 Code of Civil Procedure) definitively settle a dispute by finding the actual facts of a case and applying the rules of law thereto. Since the statement of claim often refers to statutory provisions and these may have been raised at the trial, the court may look for its facts in the light of the relevant legal elements. However it also has a general responsibility to find the appropriate rules of law for itself and is not limited to or bound by the legal submissions of the parties. It may itself order further enquiries in order to obtain a fuller picture of the facts as well. Of course the parties are bound to present their case effectively and their advocates, if any, owe a duty to the court to use their expert knowledge to advise it. The judgment must be "motivated", i.e. it must explain why it found such and such facts and believed such and such witnesses, and also what legal provisions it applied. Failure to refer to substantive law authorities will invalidate the judgment. It ought also in appropriate cases to explain the procedural rules which it has followed, though failure to refer to these will not make a judgment invalid. References may be made to guiding directives of the Full Bench (Plenum) of the USSR Supreme Court, but no other court rulings may be referred to as authorities. It is in this connection that Soviet lawyers refer to the theory of sources of law and the lack of authority of judicial precedents. The latter are not even accepted as individualising or refining the basic statutory rules (see PRECEDENTS; SUPREME COURT).

The court may give a judgment in default, in the sense that it will generally only adjourn a hearing for the absence of a party if that party has some reasonable ground for failure to appear. There is no procedure for summary judgment. If the formal requirements of a statement of claim are met by the plaintiff, the case will be tried on the merits unless the plaintiff withdraws it with leave of the court; a claim will not be struck out as failing to disclose a cause of action, no matter how obvious this may be to the judge who is preparing the case for trial.

The judgment of the court is generally analysed into four parts: 1) Introductory, identifying the dispute, naming the parties and their legal representatives, giving the title of the court and the composition of the bench, (judge and assessors) and the object of the dispute; 2) Descriptive, summarising the plaintiff's claim, the defendant's answer to it, and the statements of witnesses as to the facts; 3) Motivated, stating a) what facts the court found to exist, b) the reasons for such findings, c) its classification of the findings in law, i.e. their subsumption under a relevant statutory provision. The legal classification may be a brief reference to the section of statute governing the case, or, in more complicated cases amount to an exposition of the law, explaining the proper interpretation of the relevant statute in the circumstances. It concludes with a statement as to the effect of its findings on the parties to the case, where they stand legally; 4) Operative, laying down how its judgment is to be performed, e.g. the amounts of damages and costs to be paid by any party, with further details of how these are to be met among joint parties, and, in the case of organisations, which of their bank accounts must be used to meet the payments.

If the court gave an incomplete judgment, e.g. made no order as to costs, or omitted to decide some issue raised in the case, it may give or be asked by a party to give, a supplementary judgment, which may not, however,

in any way contradict the original judgment. A party may ask for an explanation by the court of any obscurity in the judgment. The bailiff may also need to do so before executing it. There is a fresh hearing and the court may give explanations or refuse to do so, if it is felt not to be necessary. Of course courts are expected to give clear judgments and thus obviate recourse to this procedure.
After the period for launching an appeal or making a procuratorial protest has expired, a judgment is said to enter into force or acquire the force of law. The same is true if there is no right of appeal or the appeal is dismissed. The main effects of entering into legal force are that the judgment becomes subject to execution (see EXECUTION OF JUDGMENT) and that the dispute cannot be re-opened between the parties to the case (*Res Judicata, q.v.*; *preiuditsiia*).
Interlocutory judgments (cf. arts. 223-225 Code of Civil Procedure) are of many kinds, having only the one common feature, that they do not decide the case on the merits. Thus orders are made accepting or rejecting statements of claim, or joining or dismissing parties to a case, or ordering further investigation of a case. These various orders reflect the rules of civil procedure which empower the court to take all these steps, and merely regularise and record its action. They may also be the subject of separate interlocutory appeals to higher courts. Some of these orders are defined by Soviet jurists as a) preparatory, in that they form part of the preparation for trial, e.g. agreeing to an application for the appointment of an expert witness, or b) suspensive or terminatory, in the sense that the order suspends all further judicial activity unless and until the causes of such suspension are removed, or terminate the case on various grounds, such as abandonment of the claim by the plaintiff or admission of liability by the defendant approved by the court.
The fairly detailed character of the judgment, and the discussion of legal arguments which it contains, make it an interesting exemplification of the Soviet procedural system, and a substitute to some extent for a law report in the Western, and especially in the Anglo-American sense. Court records may be ordered up by the appeal court or scrutinised by the Procuracy or made available to legal scholars with official approval. The parties to the case are entitled to copies. Judgments are not published except in the case of the Supreme Courts of the USSR or republics. Judgment is generally arrived at in private in the judge's consulting room. It is signed by the judge and two assessors. No dissenting judgments are given.
As indicated, judgments in the USSR do not bind other judges in different proceedings. There is no system of precedent.

A. K. R. Kiralfy

JUDGMENTS, CRIMINAL PROCEDURE
A number of different terms are used in Soviet criminal procedure terminology to refer to the various decisions made by investigators, procurators, judges, and courts. Since these terms are used with precision in the codes, it is important to understand the distinctions among them. A judgment (*prigovor*) of a trial court is a decision that combines in a single document the verdict and sentence of American procedure. (See SENTENCES). A ruling (*opredelenie*) is any decision, except a judgment, rendered by a court of first instance in handling a criminal case; any decision of a court of second instance; a decision taken by a higher court, except for presidiums of courts, in reviewing court judgments, rulings, and decrees that have taken legal effect (see RES JUDICATA). The term "ruling" is thus used in two meanings. In its first meaning, it refers to any decision of a trial court, except the judgment. This includes chiefly matters of a procedural nature. To resolve the more important of such rulings, the court must retire

to the conference room. This is so with rulings to order supplementary investigation, to commence a case on a new charge or with respect to a new person, to terminate the case, to select, change, or terminate a measure of restraint, to resolve a challenge against a participant in the case, and to appoint an expert. In such instances, the ruling must be formulated as a separate document and must be signed by the judge and lay assessors. With all other rulings (e.g., to admit new witnesses or new material evidence into a case, to admit a civil plaintiff or civil defendant into a case) the court may, if it prefers, simply confer at the bench to reach its decision. Such a ruling is not drawn up as a separate document but is noted in the record by the court secretary. In either event, the court must announce its ruling. The decision of an administrative (preliminary) session of a court to send a case to trial is also called a ruling.

In its second meaning, the term "ruling" refers to any decision reached by an appellate court, either a decision on a procedural matter or a decision on the merits of the case. The sole exception is for decisions made by the presidium or plenum of a court, which are called decrees (*postanovleniia*). In addition, the term "ruling" is also used to refer to decisions made by a court while the sentence is being served (e.g., a decision on early release, a decision to change the type of punishment).

The term "ruling" is used in one other sense. When a court (trial or appellate) desires to call attention to procedural violations in conduct of the pre-trial investigation, it may issue a "private ruling" to the relevant official. Such a private ruling may also be issued to an official in order to call his attention to conditions that gave rise to commission of a crime.

The term "decree" (*postanovlenie*) is a decision taken by the presidium of a court in reviewing court judgments, rulings and decrees that have taken legal effect; any decision taken by a judge unilaterally; a decision of an investigator, person conducting the inquiry or procurator, taken during conduct of the investigation, except for a conclusion to indict.

In its first meaning, "decree" refers to decisions made by the presidiums of courts "by way of supervision". (See RES JUDICATA). In its second meaning, it refers to such unilateral decisions of a judge as the decision to send a case to trial. In its third (and most common) meaning, "decree" refers to decisions made during the investigation by the investigator or procurator. The more important of these are decisions to commence a criminal case, to present an accusation, to conduct a search and seizure, to appoint an expert, to terminate a case, to apply a measure of restraint.

A judge's dissent from the decision of a court of which he is a member is called a "separate opinion". In a trial court, the separate opinion is put into writing and is attached to the materials of the case but is not announced when the court's judgment is read aloud. The dissenting judge must sign the judgment reached by the other two judges. While legislation does not mention the right of appellate judges to write a separate opinion, such a right has been established by court practice.

John B. Quigley, Jr.

JUDICIAL NOTICE, see EVIDENCE

JUDICIAL REVIEW OF ADMINISTRATIVE ACTS

After the October Revolution the question of establishing administrative courts was hotly debated, but with the consolidation of Communist dictatorship the official doctrine became obligatory according to which administrative justice was a typical institution of the capitalist legel order and therefore incompatible with socialist legality. The

Procuracy (*q.v.*) was assigned to the defence of socialist legality and there were only a very few cases where judicial review of administrative acts was admitted. After Stalin's death a more effective protection of the citizens' rights against administrative arbitrariness was urged and by legislative activity the jurisdiction of the courts in administrative matters was somewhat extended. For the present state of affairs in the Soviet Union it is characteristic that a system of administrative tribunals does not exist and a judicial review of administrative acts can only take place in special instances expressly stated by law. The review is to be performed by the ordinary courts and according to the rules of civil procedure.

The general rule is to be found in par. 3 of article 4 of the 1961 Principles of Civil Procedure of the USSR and the Union Republics. It provides that "the courts shall have jurisdiction over suits upon complaints concerning incorrect entries in electoral rolls, acts of administrative organs in connection with the imposition of fines and other cases arising out of administrative legal relations referred by the law to the jurisdiction of judicial organs". In the republican Codes of Civil Procedure a special chapter on judicial review of administrative acts has been inserted, which left the situation virtually unchanged apart from classifying the cases of judicial review in a slightly different way: a) complaints against errors in electoral rolls, b) complaints against actions of administrative organs, c) suits concerning the collection of arrears from citizens on state and local taxes and duties, compulsory wage insurance and voluntary assessments (e.g. article 231 of the 1964 RSFSR Code of Civil Procedure).

Regarding the ficticious nature of Soviet elections, the first group is hardly of any importance. The details are regulated by the Instruction of the USSR People's Commissariat of Justice of May 5, 1938, "On the procedure for examination by people's courts of errors in electoral rolls".

The second group, which includes several cases expressly stated by law, is much more important. Apart from complaints against the refusal of a bureau of civil status records to correct wrong entries in the official register (article 28 of the 1968 Principles of the Law of Marriage, Family, and Guardianship of the USSR and the Union Republics) and against the refusal of the competent organ to register the owner of a dwellinghouse in the buildings' register (§ 13 of the Instruction of the RSFSR People's Commissariat of Communal Economy of December 25, 1945), the imposition of fines and measures in the housing sector are the two main issues.

According to article 18 of the decree of the Presidium of the USSR Supreme Soviet of June 21, 1961, "On the further limitation of the use of fines imposed through administrative procedure" and the corresponding republican legislation (e.g. articles 21-26 of the decree of the Presidium of the RSFSR Supreme Soviet of March 3, 1962), any citizen who has incurred an administrative fine has the right to protest within 10 days to the local people's court. In disposing of the case, the court examines the legality of the imposition of the fine, but it has also some discretionary powers insofar as it can lower the amount of the fine if it does not reflect the seriousness of the offence, the personality of the offender, or his financial status.

In the housing sector the people's courts can review an administrative act in three cases: a) A domicile order of the local executive committee for living space in houses owned by state, co-operative, or public organizations can be protested by a person whose housing right has been infringed (par. 3 of article 296 of the 1964 RSFSR Civil Code). b) The exchange of publicly owned living quarters between tenants is dependant on the prior consent of the competent administrative agency. Its refusal can be protested by filling suit in court (par. 3 of Article 325 of the RSFSR Civil Code). c) The dwelling space of persons departing for work abroad or to certain regions of the Soviet Union has to be reserved for the duration of the contract of employment. The refusal of the permit can be protested by the tenant and the consent, by a person applying for the dwelling space (Instruction of the RSFSR Ministry of Communal Economy of October 8, 1965).

The third group reveals a quite interesting procedural situation (articles 240-244 of the RSFSR Code of Civil Procedure, article 2 of the Resolution No. 94/603 of the Central Executive Committee and the Council of People's Commissars of the USSR of April 11, 1937). If a tax, duty, etc. is imposed on somebody, there are two possibilities. Either the person concerned pays or he does not. In the second case the administrative agency has to turn to the court in order to enforce payment. It must first give 10 days' written notice, then the case goes to the court which verifies the legality of the claim by hearing both parties and checking the necessary documents. Where the court finds for the administration, it orders the attachment of personal property equivalent in value to the amount of the assessed shortage and imposes a fine of 3-10 roubles. Otherwise it refuses the administration's motion. Should the court determine that the disputed amount was incorrectly computed, it does not fix the right amount but suspends the hearings and sends the dossier back to the financial agency for re-checking. The normal positions are reversed. There is no administrative act protested, but the administrative agency is forced to get judicial endorsement for its act which is not binding in itself.

Other cases could be mentioned where there is some judicial control over the administration, but they would not be examples of judicial review of administrative acts in the strict sense of the word. On the whole one can say that a real concept of judicial control does not exist in the Soviet Union, the jurisdiction of the courts is established at random and the citizens' opportunities for seeking judicial protection against administrative abuses are rather restricted.

Samuel Kucherov

See also ADMINISTRATIVE PROCEDURE; PUBLIC ADMINISTRATION

JUDICIAL SYSTEM, see COURTS

JURIDICAL ACT,
see ACT OF LEGAL SIGNIFICANCE

JURIES, see PEOPLE'S ASSESSORS

JURISDICTION, CIVIL PROCEDURE

Soviet lawyers distinguish two kinds of jurisdiction, that of the judicial branch generally and that of a court on a territorial basis.

In the first place it must be determined whether a civil dispute in the broad sense is determinable by a judicial court or some other body (*podvedomstvennost'*). In some cases purely administrative organs give decisions, e.g. the eviction of residents in hotels or hostels, or the dismissal of higher officials of state enterprises. In other cases there may be alternative procedures, e.g. an unlawfully dismissed worker may go to court or to the trade union committee if they did not consent to his dismissal, and some cases may go either to a regular court or to a comrades' court (see COMRADES' COURT). In still other cases successive stages of the same matter may go to different courts, e.g. disputes as to priorities for housing accommodation are administrative matters, but if an allocation (*order*) is made to a tenant only a court can quash it, and only a court can evict the tenant on the grounds laid down in the legislation. Again, in labour disputes, cases are generally brought in the first instance before the trade disputes committee in the factory but there is a right of recourse to the court for re-trial. The amount of money or products due a member of a collective farm is the concern of the general meeting, but if such amount has been fixed, action will lie in the courts to recover it. Most family law disputes go to court, but, e.g. article 56 of the 1969 Family Law Code gives initial jurisdiction to child care agencies in disputes over children between separated parents, with an appeal to the court. Patent and copyright law is mixed; the question of authorship is judicial but matters like novelty or anticipation are administrative. Royalties are first fixed administratively but there is an appeal to a court. Disputes between state enterprises are decided by arbitration (see ARBITRATION), except defamation cases, which always go to court. In general, cases in which either party is a citizen or collective farm are subject to the jurisdiction of the courts. The powers which the court has in dealing with disputes, e.g. possible relief to be granted, are referred to as its competence (*kompetentsiia*).

Assuming that a court has jurisdiction (cf. arts. 25-28 Code of Civil Procedure), the second question is to select the particular court which is territorially appropriate. This is known as *podsudnost'* (cf. arts. 113-125). The Supreme Courts of the USSR and republics can entertain any case if they wish. Normally, however, cases are commenced in a local court. The basic principle is that the defendant is sued in the court operating in the area where he lives, or, in the case of a juridical person, has its main office. There is, however, an option to sue in any of several courts in many cases. Thus where a worker has been injured at work he may bring his action where he lives, or where the enterprise is situated or where the tort was committed if that is different. In cases of damage to property the action may be brought where the defendant lives or where the property is situated. In breach of contract cases the action lies where the defendant lives or where the contract was to be performed or in some other court selected by the terms of the contract (unless by law a different court has exclusive jurisdiction). Air, rail and sea transport organisations are privileged to be sued where they have their main offices. There is no such rule for road transport. Reasons of convenience may account for some special rules. If none of the heirs of a debtor accept his estate there is no defendant to be sued, and the creditors of the deceased therefore sue in the area where the assets are to be found. If a civil claim is joined with a criminal charge the criminal court deals with the entire matter according to its criminal jurisdiction. If the claim is not then made or is not dealt with by the criminal court a civil action will lie in the usual civil court, e.g. where the defendant lives.

A court may and should reject a claim which ought to have been brought in another court or before another organisation. However, if one court transfers a case to another court, the latter has no option but to dispose of it, even if outside its jurisdiction. If a judicial court tries a matter outside the judicial range the decision must be quashed on appeal. This does not apply where the wrong territorial court has acted in a properly judicial matter. *A. K. R. Kiralfy*

JURISDICTION, CRIMINAL PROCEDURE

Soviet criminal procedure law employs two different terms which translate into English as "jurisdiction". The first (*podsudnost'*) refers to allocation of cases among the various courts for trial, while the second (*podsledstvennost'*) refers to allocation of cases among the various investigatory agencies for conduct of the pre-trial investigation (cf. arts. 35 ff. and 126 RSFSR Code of Criminal Procedure).

Allocation of cases among courts for trial (*podsudnost'*) is accomplished in three ways. First, rules relating to *territorial jurisdiction* decide where (territorially) a case will be heard (normally in a court functioning in the judicial area where the crime was committed). Second, for crimes committed by military personnel (and certain others) the case is heard by a military court. This is called *personal jurisdiction*. Third, rules relating to *subject-matter* jurisdiction allocate cases among the various tiers of the judicial hierarchy on the basis of the seriousness of the offense. (In the military courts, by way of exception, the military rank of the defendant determines the level at which the case is to be heard.)

The general rule of subject-matter jurisdiction is that cases are to be heard by a people's court (the lowest level court) unless the law provides otherwise. The overwhelming majority of cases are tried in the people's courts. The criminal-procedure codes of the fifteen Union republics list a number of more serious offenses to be tried by the next higher court in the judicial hierarchy (called variously a territorial (*krai*) court, provincial (*oblast'*) court, city court, court of an autonomous province, court of a national area, or court of an autonomous republic).

Any higher court of a Union republic may, however, take jurisdiction over a case that falls within the jurisdiction of a subordinate court, if it deems the case to be of special importance. Thus, a provincial (or equivalent) court may hear any case within the jurisdiction of a subordinate people's court, while the supreme court of a Union republic may hear any case within the jurisdiction of any court in the republic. Also, certain minor cases may be heard by lay tribunals called comrades' courts, either at the initiative of those courts or by referral from an ordinary court, procurator, or police (see COMRADES' COURTS).

The second Russian term for jurisdiction (*podsledstvennost'*) refers to allocation of cases among the several investigatory agencies for conduct of the pre-trial investigation. Most offenses are investigated by officials called "investigators" in a procedure called "preliminary investigation". The preliminary investigation is normally conducted by investigators subordinate to the Procuracy, though it may also be conducted (depending on the nature of the offense and the person who committed it) by investigators of the Committee for State Security, investigators of the Ministry of Internal Affairs, or military investigators. Less serious cases, in which no formal preliminary investigation is required, are handled by the police or some other administrative agency. This procedure is called an "inquiry". Other jurisdictional rules determine where (territorially) the investigation or inquiry is to be conducted (normally the place where the crime was committed).

John B. Quigley, Jr.

See also CRIMINAL INVESTIGATION; PRELIMINARY INVESTIGATON; COURTS; SUPREME COURT

JURISPRUDENCE

According to the teaching of Marx and Engels, especially as laid down in Engels' "Origin of the Family" and his "Anti-Dühring", the primitive classless stage of society in which wealth (property) did not yet play any (or any significant) role was replaced, as wealth began to accumulate, by "class systems". The class of the property-owners organized state systems and created the law for the protection of its interests vis-à-vis the other classes. (This is of course an extremely simplified version of this doctrine). There were three subsequent types of class societies: the slave-owning society, the feudal and the capitalist society. The dialectic tension between the oppressing (governing) class and the oppressed classes leads, at least as regards the second and the third type of class societies, to revolutions. Feudal society is overthrown by bourgeois revolutions. Bourgeois society and the bourgeois state will be overthrown by the revolution of the armed proletariat, which in a period dubbed by Marx and Engels the dictatorship of the proletariat (*q.v.*), will eliminate the bourgeoisie and will set up the classles communist society. The latter implies also the end of state and law. An important element of this doctrine is the primary importance of the economic basis (the production relationships); together with religion, philosophy and learning, law belongs to the "superstructure" largely predetermined by the former (although the superstructure may have a feed-back effect on the basis; owing to other circumstances it may also attain a limited autonomy). Closely considered, Soviet jurisprudence did, and in a somewhat inverted manner, still does rotate around these thoughts.

In the first years of the Soviet regime two lawyers were especially concerned with the question of the predicted withering away of law, and with the law of the transitory period: E. B. Pashukanis and P. I. Stuchka. Though their thinking and way of discussing their subjects differ substantially, they have this in common, that they take (or pretend to take) the final disappearance of the law for granted, and try to come to terms with the fact that though communism had been established, law did not show any signs of withering away. Pashukanis, who in his early teaching had identified law with bourgeois law, spoke of the continued existence of bourgeois law without the bourgeois; and Stuchka introduced the notion of proletarian law. Both, however, noticed a new phenomenon: the intense interference of the state with matters economic (allocations, the establishment of prices, planning) and for this the concept of economic law (*q.v.*) was introduced, though at this period, it was not yet quite clearly defined.

As, however, the idea of the withering away of the law did not fit into Stalin's tyrannical system, these legal philosophies from 1930 on were attacked from different quarters. Stuchka died before the purges; Pashukanis, however, was liquidated in 1937, and A. Ia. Vyshinskii, to whom Stalin had given the task of making Soviet lawyers toe the line, declared him a wrecker. The theory of the withering away of state and law was replaced by the doctrine of the required maximum strength of these while capitalist encirclement lasted. Vyshinskii forced upon Soviet legal doctrine a strictly pragmatic system of legal branches (11, not comprising economic law) without any systematic connection between them. For many years this remained the official system of Soviet jurisprudence, if it can be called jurisprudence at all. After the death of Stalin, however, Vyshinskii was de-canonized and, though his categories of law in fact still dominate the scene, the notion of economic law was resurrected in about 1956, and this tends to produce a certain unity among at least those branches of Soviet law which are concerned with the economy. On the other hand, it was probably Khrushchev's personal concern in the theory of the withering away of state and law which made him drop the notion of the dictatorship of the proletariat (which, however, strangely enough, remained embedded in the Constitution) at the 22nd Party Congress in 1961 and replace it by the concept of the state of the entire people (*q.v.*), as according to the official view there are in the Soviet Union no more antagonistic classes, that is to say classes within the meaning of this term in the works of Marx, Engels and Lenin. This theory was then implemented by certain measures which transferred activities, up till then fulfilled by state organs *stricto sensu*, to social organizations (leaving open the question of whether there is a difference between a state organ and a so-called social organization fulfilling thc samc functions). Instances of such transfer were the resurrection of the comrades' courts (*q.v.*) and the setting up of units of the voluntary militia (see PEOPLE'S GUARDS).

Z. Szirmai

See also LAW; RIGHTS; ACTS OF LEGAL SIGNIFICANCE; STATE; LEGAL SYSTEM; RULES OF SOCIALIST COMMUNITY LIFE; CONSTITUTION; SOVEREIGNTY; and the above mentioned 11 branches: CONSTITUTIONAL LAW; ADMINISTRATIVE LAW; FINANCIAL LAW; CIVIL LAW; LABOUR LAW; LAND LAW; KOLKHOZ LAW; FAMILY LAW; CRIMINAL LAW; CIVIL PROCEDURE; CRIMINAL PROCEDURE

JURISTIC PERSONS,
see PERSONS; CORPORATIONS

JUVENILE DELINQUENCY

The study of juvenile delinquency in the Soviet Union has experienced the same ups and downs as criminology. The prolonged "freeze" in studies of juvenile delinquency has been even more deplorable than in the case of adult crimes, because secular as well as more shortlived trends in juvenile delinquency are more indicative of shortcomings in educational policies and of hidden social malaise than is adult crime.

In the aftermath of war, civil war and revolution the problem of juvenile deviancy was exceptionally grave. The most urgent task before the authorities was to tackle the rising tide of homeless children (*bezprizornye*). Soviet estimates mention four to six million such children in 1921 and two and a half to four million in 1923. The possible error of up to two million indicates to what extent conditions had got out of hand. Avoidance of education and school was an equally intractable problem. Again according to Soviet estimates, in 1925 (seven to eight years after the Revolution) only half of all school-age children were attending school. The RSFSR counted five million illiterates in the 11-15 age group. 50% did not complete primary education, only 10-15% were continuing beyond primary school level and 18% were unemployed. The social structure had disintegrated, epidemics were raging, families were broken up by death (from war, civil strife or hunger) and by an unprecedented rate of migration. All these factors were conducive to an equally unprecedented rise in juvenile delinquency.

According to the prevailing humanistic and positivistic beliefs among the new elite and the prevailing social defence theories of the time, special institutions—Commissions for Juveniles—were created by one of the first decrees of the Soviet Government. All children up to the age of 17 (later raised to 18 and at one time reduced to 16) had to be tried by these Commissions. Article 1 of the decree stipulated that neither courts nor prisons should have anything to do with juvenile offenders and that measures permitted against them had to be exclusively of a medical and/or pedagogical character, excluding altogether notions of punishment or chastisement. The offenders were to be admitted to "shelters" (*ubezhishche*) and not to penal institutions. Doubts were expressed as to the necessity of closed institutions and it was rather the pressure of the enormous problem and the degree of depravity of some offenders which made the creation of closed institutions necessary. "Labour houses" (*trudovoi dom*) for juveniles and labour communes organised by the state security police (OGPU), were thus introduced. The latter were run on libertarian principles as open institutions permitting their inmates to leave at any time according to their own free decision. The composition of the Commissions for Juveniles corresponded to the character of a libertarian juvenile court: the panel had to consist of at least one teacher, a medical doctor and a member of the Childrens' Inspectorate (*vospitateli-nabliu-*

dateli, sometime called *inspektora*). The sittings of the Commissions were in camera and informal. Slowly the tide turned and ever-increasing tendencies were felt towards dogmatism on the one side and conventional legal forms on the other. The early notions of social security and correctional measures were replaced by those of punishment and chastisement. The *lex talionis* started to come back. The Commissions were accused of medical-pedological bias and bourgeois biological tendencies and after a while disbanded. The age of criminal responsibility which under the libertarian tendencies had been raised to 16 in 1929 was lowered in 1935 to 12 years of age for a limited range of the more serious crimes. For a short time juvenile courts were introduced in the form of special benches of people's judges and assessors, with educational training and experience, to try juvenile offenders. But these also disappeared from the statute books and juveniles were subjected to the same procedures as adults. Likewise the initial experiments of reformatories and open communes of the OGPU were wound up and replaced by colonies for juvenile offenders. Nevertheless a few new institutions were created to deal with children in need of care and protection.

After the 20th Party Congress (1956) certain institutions which existed in the 20's were resuscitated with some modifications. The citizen started to get back some of his previous rights and freedoms. According to the present law criminal responsibility starts at the age of 14 for a limited catalogue of the more serious offences. Full responsibility for all offences listed in the criminal code starts only at 16, with the obligation of the courts to consider the lesser experience of the young. Under the age of 14 there is no criminal responsibility but the deviant child may be placed in an approved school or subjected to other educational, disciplinary or medical treatment.

There are two types of correctional institutions for boys and one for girls.

Looking after children in immediate need of care and protection and doing the most general policing of children is the responsibility of the Children's Rooms of the Militia Stations. The Children's Rooms are in the charge of a specially trained inspector who recruits volunteers from among the public to act as voluntary inspectors or as an *aktiv* (persons interested and assisting) to help in the policing tasks. These Rooms, as a rule, are well furnished and stocked with toys and reading material. Here children are kept for up to six hours for investigations, identifications, and decisions on their future welfare. No criminal or criminally delinquent children are admitted to these Rooms. However, as most children in need of care and protection are usually picked up by the police for some misbehaviour, the Children's Rooms are frequently used by the Militia for serious talks with, and caution of, wayward children. (Beside these official Children's Rooms there are others arranged by house communities in charge of volunteer inspectors usually from amongst retired teachers or police officers.) From a Militia Children's Room the child is taken to reception-distribution centres (*Doma-raspredeliteli*), if circumstances make it impossible or inadvisable to return the child to its parents or guardians or other persons responsible for its care. The stay of a child or young person (3 to 18 years) in such homes is limited to one month. During this time more permanent arrangements are made for the future of the child.

The most important institutions for child welfare are now the Commissions for Minors' Affairs which also serve as juvenile courts for a limited range of offences. Established in 1961, these have similar but not identical tasks to those of the disbanded Commissions for Juveniles. They are organised at *raion* Soviet level and at all higher administrative levels. The higher echelons deal mainly with administrative and organisational tasks and general supervision. The *raion* level Commissions deal directly with delinquent children. They have exclusive jurisdiction over children under 14, and limited jurisdiction for the 14-16 age group for offences for which this age group is exempt from criminal responsibility. Otherwise, the Commission is competent to deal with all minor misdemeanours and aberrations of juveniles, and for all other cases, if referred to the Commission by order of the Procuracy or the courts. The decisions of the Commissions are final, but appeal to the executive committee (*Ispolkom*) of the local Soviet (*raion* level) is possible. Only in the case of fines must appeals be lodged with the local *raion* (or town) people's courts. The local Commissions also function as probationary institutions: they have supervision over young offenders not in institutional care and over those discharged from closed institutions. They function as a kind of labour exchange for juvenile offenders and discharged "borstal" trainees: it is their duty to provide the latter with suitable employment at some enterprise. No young person may be dismissed from his job without the consent of the Commissions. Schools and other educational institutions may not expel a student unless such a decision has been taken by the school board with one member of the Commission taking part in its deliberations. The Commissions are given some jurisdiction over parents and guardians, whom they may fine up to 30 roubles and demand restitution of damage up to 20 roubles. They may request the court to deprive the parent or parents of the custody of the child, or order the admission of a child to educational or medical-educational institutions. Proceedings of the latter kind must be attended by the procurator. Besides the Commissions there are the comrades' courts (*q.v.*), another judicial body resuscitated by the Khrushchev reforms for greater public participation in the administration of justice. The courts, the Procuracy and the Commissions are entitled to refer individual cases of juveniles to the jurisdiction of comrades' courts.

Sociological aspects

The Soviet theories of crime causation applicable to juvenile delinquency distinguish between causes and conditions and speak of the most general or basic (*objective*) causes as "survivals of the past" and/or hostile and corrupting influences of the bourgeois imperialist world. By definition the Soviet Union lacks antagonistic class differences and therefore the foundations for the emergence of delinquency do not exist. But these dogmatic (and now frequently merely ritualistic) statements are not shared by all scholars. Some regard the socialist principle of rewards according to work performance as containing sufficient contradictions and conflict material to lead some young people astray (thus V. S. Orlov, quoted in *Preduprezhdenie pravonarushenii nesovershennoletnikh*, 1963, p. 26); while others refer to contradictions in the existing differences in economic status and conditions between workers and peasants, caused by the two different forms of socialist property, state-owned and co-operative (collective farms). These contradictions lead to such crimes as larceny of state and collective farm property, pillage of state-owned land (all land is state-owned) for ulterior purposes, etc. (V. I. Kurliandskii, *Sovetskaia Iustitsiia*, No. 4, 1957, p. 29).

Psychological and ecological causes

Some scholars refer to psychological factors in the minds of individual offenders as germinating delinquent behaviour (K. E. Igoshev, in *Sovetskoe Gosudarstvo i Pravo*, 1969, No. 9, pp. 49-58). Some of the psychological conflicts are stress signals of disharmonies in the physical and mental development of individual persons. Groups of problem or difficult children reveal in most cases some neurological abnormalities and usually contain a higher frequency of individuals with a lower than average I.Q. than control groups with non-delinquent children (L. M. Ziubin, in *Voprosy Psikhologii* 1969, No. 3, pp. 132-'43). Igoshev rejects as static and undialectical theories ascribing delinquency to some "mummified survivals" of the past (*op. cit.* p. 52). Referring to a survey of 6000 juveniles, including 1800 delinquents, 2000 pupils of 5th-10th forms of general schools, 1000 working youth and 1500 students of trade colleges in the Central and Southern Urals, Igoshev finds that internal contradictions and conflicts are also caused by contradictions existing in the micro-environments of the individuals. These conflicts may exist in the families or in the working or study collectives (communities) of the offender. Researches have demonstrated that $^1/_3$ to $^1/_2$ of the families of delinquents were unsatisfactory or defective (*neblagopoluchnye*). $^1/_4$ to $^1/_3$ of the working communities of delinquents were characterised by poor moral standards and serious conflicts between the administration and the young workers. Such conflicts are prone to alienate the young from family or work community and produce either aggressive and retreatist behaviour (23% of the young retreated to their family environments on feeling alienated from their working communities). Frequently the hiatus between moral standards taught and applied in actual life may disrupt the moral beliefs of idealistic young people and may lead to delinquent behaviour. (*Sotsiologiia na Ukraini*, 1968, p. 159). All moral conflicts may be harmful to the young, but those which shatter their moral beliefs are the cause of nihilistic anomic attitudes (Igoshev, *op. cit.*, and *Sotsiologiia na Ukraini*, p. 159).

R. Beermann

See also DELINQUENCY; MINORS

KHOZRASCHET

The Russian expression *khozraschet* is the usual abbrevation of *khoziaistvennyi raschet*, literally "economic accounting".

Introduced by Lenin at the beginning of NEP as a reaction to *glavkizm*, the system whereby nationalised industry was maintained at the expense of the state budget, it remained the essential element of the economic organisation of public enterprises possessing legal personality even after that period: "the way towards Communism"—wrote Lenin at the time—"is not that of blind enthusiasm, but that which, with the help of the enthusiasm generated by the Revolution, is founded on private interest and on economic accounting".

This idea was laid down by the decree of the Council of People's Commissars of the RSFSR of August 9, 1921, "on the introduction of the principles of the New Economic Policy" and reiterated in the decree of the Council of Labour and Defence of August 12, 1921, which established "the fundamental regulations regarding measures for the reconstruction of heavy industry and the increase and development of production".

The 9th Congres of Soviets, held in 1921, had in fact recognised the utility, from a technical and economic point of view, of reorganising the administration of state industry "through the grouping together of similar enterprises which complemented each other, guaranteeing them such full rights of administration and government as are necessary to permit the rational management of industry under a strict regime of economic accounting".

By 1923 and with the 12th Party Congress, the fundamental duty of extracting a profit (*izvlechenie pribyli*) was assigned to state cartels, the *tresty*, and to the enterprises which constituted them.

The juridical significance of *khozraschet* was indicated by the predominantly contractual nature of the economic ties between the *khozraschetnoe* enterprise (an enterprise working on the basis of the principle of economic accounting) and its clients and suppliers.

But the second decree regarding the *tresty* issued in 1927 had already shifted the emphasis away from the "commercial accounting" element to the "plan" element to which the *khozraschet* is by now subordinate. The enterprises grouped in a *trest* and equipped with their "own" working capital "formalise" their relations with other enterprises by means of contracts and act on the basis of "incomplete" (*nepolnyi*) or internal economic accounting which does not permit their recognition as a legal entity.

In 1929, following large-scale reorganisation of industrial administration, all state enterprises were put on a *khozraschet* basis. The *tresty* and state enterprises were placed on an economic accounting basis "precisely because they themselves had to be entirely responsible . . . for the profitability of their activity".

Khozraschet originally signified that the enterprises had to obtain a commercial profit and exist, even if not totally, by means of that profit: Consequently they had to operate as a private enterprise with only secondary economic assistance from the state. It also signified the introduction of a separate accounts system for each industrial group which could be considered a legal entity.

Soviet legislation continuously refers to the expression under review in all acts of economic policy. Doctrine places it at the beginning of each economic and civil law textbook among the general principles of the Soviet legal code. During the 'thirties, civil courts and arbitration tribunals—originally uncertain—began to consider enterprises (particularly industrial ones), grouped together in a *trest* and acting on the basis of the principle of full *khozraschet*, as legal entities on the same level as a *trest*, following the example of what had already taken place in normal economic and banking practice.

In this way the process was carried out which tended towards the recognition of the legal personality of all enterprises (*predpriiatiia*), inasmuch as, unlike the *gosbiudzhetnye uchrezhdeniia* (which are directly financed out of the state budget), operating under a *khozraschet* regime, they were or were not part of a group.

It would therefore appear that even under Soviet law the criterion for the assignment of legal personality to a body is constituted by the existence of separate assets. This is the only truth which can be derived from the equation:

Enterprise + *khozraschet* = legal entity. The expression "legal entity" refers therefore to a particular juridical content: *khozraschet* which is full, or connected with an enterprise, and for which traditionally and to facilitate language problems it is commonly adopted as a synonym.

A problem which has long been discussed, and for which even today various possible solutions are still put forward, concerns the optimum dimension of the economic unit necessary to show a profit and therefore operate under a regime of economic accounting.

Present day doctrine distinguishes between "full economic accounting" (*polnyi khozraschet)* which state enterprises enjoy as they are legal entities; "internal economic accounting" (*vnutrennii khozraschet*) on the basis of which departments, factories and offices, which do not enter into juridical relations with other bodies, operate and which are not independent economic units, even if they are equipped with an organisation of their own (as they only carry out part of the "total" work) and do not consequently need to be transferred to an autonomous accounts system; and economic accounting of an economic management body (*khozraschet upravlencheskii*, that is administrative *khozraschet*).

The problem of the optimum economic unit for the application of *khozraschet* and for the consequent recognition of legal personality reappeared with the introduction of the territorial system of industrial management (*Sovnarkhoz*: 1957-1964), and the discussions concerning internal economic accounting and above all administrative economic accounting became more intense during the last economic reform.

It should be noted that the question of the legal personality of units which are on the border-line between the administration and commercial enterprises is not a academic question of little importance, but is of great practical importance. As a result of the ties between the legal entity and the autonomy of assets, the attribution of legal personality signifies the property responsibility of the unit towards contracting and third parties. But it could also signify—and there has been a recent tendency in this direction—the responsibility for the total assets by a higher level legal entity—or by one with a wider competence—towards a lower level one: of the *glavk khozraschetnyi* towards the enterprise, and of the latter towards its own internal divisions.

The problem has still to be resolved.

Khozraschet is carried out by supplying the enterprise with a series of assets (overhead and working capital) at the time of its constitution; these assets enable it to carry out the duties laid down by its statute: autonomy of operation (that is the possibility of an autonomous decision about a series of questions regarding its activity), autonomy as far as its assets are concerned (that is the separateness of the assets assigned to the economic unit, which it owns and which it can make use of autonomously) within the limits of the plan, adjustment of its profit and losses, price economy and profitability of the enterprise and the material interest the workers have in the results of their own work.

Khozraschet is undoubtedly an economic category, but it takes on a juridical appearance in those provisions of Soviet civil law which, governing the relations controlled by state economic organisations, constantly consider the fact that they operate under a regime of economic accounting.

In particular the necessity of observing the rule of *khozraschet* leads to the following consequences in the civil law sector:

a) recognition of the fact that state enterprises are a legal entity and are autonomous as far as their assets are concerned;

b) the juridical relationship between enterprises and socialist organisations, and between either of these and private individuals, are generally of a contractual and onerous nature;

c) contractual damage must be compensated for by the economic organisations responsible for non-fulfilment or inexact fulfilment (art. 36 Principles of Civil Law), independently of the eventual economic disadvantages involved (loss of production bonuses for example) or disciplining (fines, etc.) of the parties involved.

It is affirmed that the method of economic accounting is necessary and possible only as a result of the full application of the mercantile-currency circulation and the law of values found in Soviet society, even if these were destined to disappear with the advent of Communism. Recently, however, the concept of the *khozraschet* has lost some of its original specific content and has become the symbol of the new freedom demanded by Soviet enterprises. Its significance has been extended and it has become the object of widely varying interpretations. From an economic point of view it today indicates the organisation of production in a profitable and advantageous form "for both the single firm and the collectivity" while from a juridical point of view it is intended to guarantee the freedom, autonomy and extensive rights that the enterprise and its head require to carry out their economic and operating activities and to stipulate and execute contracts in conformity with the plan and to the advantage of the enterprise (arts. 29, 30, 62, 67, etc. of the Regulations of State Enterprises). *Khozraschet* must consequently not only be reinvigorated but also penetrate all "branches and links" of the Soviet economy, according to the decisions of the 23rd Congress of the Soviet Communist Party and the the Plenum of the Central Committee of the Soviet Communist Party held in March and September 1965.

The method of *khozraschet* and the concept of economic-commercial profit, especially inside every enterprise, are transformed on a national scale, by means of the principle of "control through the rouble" (*kontrol' rublem*) carried out chiefly by the State Bank.

This is another official formula to indicate that an enterprise can be considered satisfactory if it produces a profit, as "failure of any kind in the economic activity of the enterprise is reflected by its balance sheet and by its financial position". The profits are not important in themselves but as an index of the degree to which the resources have been put to use on the basis of the plan, as a means of control (perhaps crude and over-simple) for the central authorities as to how the resources placed at the disposal of each enterprise have been used, through a system of obligatory standard-type balance sheets for each enterprise.

In order to be really significant, the principle of economic accounting requires that the single economic organisation, within determinate and set limits (but very variable ones as experience has demonstrated) is the absolute master of its own economic destiny. However, not even the principle of *khozraschet* is absolute as it too is subject to the State plan. Absolute autonomy of operation and of assets "does not and cannot exist for some *khozraschetnye* units in the socialist economic system" and Soviet doctrine in fact maintains that the realisation of a commercial profit along the main lines of the plan, that is, the adaptation of *khozraschet* to the law of proportional and planned development of the national economy, is the element which distinguishes the socialist from the capitalist system, the feature which effectively sets Soviet economic accounting apart from the commercial accounting (*kommerceskii raschet*) of the West.

G. Crespi Reghizzi

See also STATE ENTERPRISES; BUDGETS OF ENTERPRISES

KIDNAPPING

Abduction or substitution of infant

According to art. 125 of the Criminal Code of the RSFSR abduction of an the infant of another, or substitution of an infant, committed for mercenary purposes or from other base motives, is punishable by deprivation of freedom for a term not exceeding seven years. The same action committed for other purposes or motives is punishable by deprivation of freedom for a term not exceeding one year or by corrective labour for the same term.

Kidnapping (other than of an infant)

According to art. 126 of the Criminal Code of the RSFSR an illegal deprivation of freedom is punishable by deprivation of freedom for a term not exceeding six months, or by corrective labour for the same term, or by social censure.

The same act committed in a manner dangerous to the life or health of the victim or in conjunction with causing him physical suffering is punishable by deprivation of freedom for a term not exceeding three years.

L. Kos-Rabcewicz-Zubkowski

See also SEX CRIMES; TRADITIONAL CRIME

KOLKHOZ

In 1971 there were 32,800 collective farms in the Soviet Union cultivating about 47 per cent of the arable land available (107.2 million hectares) and comprising two-thirds of the population working in agriculture (16.5 million). Although the number of kolkhozes has been constantly decreasing since 1950—a fact due both to their amalgamation and to their transformation into state farms—their economic importance is still greater than that of state farms. They produce about 40 per cent of the whole agricultural output (state farms: 27-29 per cent; private ancillary farms: 31-33 per cent). Apparently, this situation will continue in the foreseeable future. From the ideological point of view, collective farming in the period of the construction of communism should be a disappearing phenomenon. The 1961 Party Programme inspired by Khrushchev envisaged, therefore, the speedy transformation of co-operative property into people's property. Since the reshuffle of 1964 this vision has been abandoned and the process of transforming kolkhozes into sovkhozes has slowed down.

Kolkhozes became the prevailing organizational form in Soviet agriculture after the collectivization campaign launched by Stalin at the end of 1929. In the 1920's collective farming had not played any noteworthy role, and even in October, 1929, only 4.1 per cent of peasant families were united in collective farms. But as early as March, 1930, their share amounted to 58.1 per cent. After a short period of relaxation, during which many kolkhozes were dissolved, the campaign was resumed at a somewhat slower speed but in a no less brutal way, so that by 1936 more than 90 per cent of peasants had been forced to join a kolkhoz. This "revolution from above" led to terrible famines and misery and cost several million human lives. In the course of the campaign the "artel" became the dominant form of collective farming displacing the two other forms existing until then. The legal status of kolkhozes, which term was becoming synonymous with *artel*, was defined in the Model Charters of March 1, 1930, and of February 17, 1935. During the long life of the latter the real position of kolkhozes has often changed according to the varying course of the Party's agricultural policy. After Stalin's death many reforms have been carried out in order to further productivity and material interests such as the abolition of the system of Machine Tractor Stations functioning as the main instrument of political control and the replacement of compulsory deliveries by a system of procurement and purchasing in 1958, the amalgamation of kolkhozes, the approval of ancillary activities, and greater freedom in the sphere of planning. At the plenary session of the Central Committee of the C.P.S.U. in March, 1965, it was announced that, taking into consideration the development of the last thirty years, a new Model Charter was to be drawn up. Nevertheless, it took more than four years before the Third Kolkhoz-Congress adopted it on November 27, 1969. In the following year the newly established Union Kolkhoz Council approved of the Model Rules for the kolkhoz's inner operation (*Primernye Pravila vnutrennego rasporiadka kolkhoza*). On the basis of these main sources of general kolkhoz law the individual kolkhozes have to elaborate corresponding documents. The new regulations reflect the most important changes kolkhoz economy has undergone since 1935. Kolkhozes have grown into large-scale enterprises calling for an economic and organizational structure rather different from that of the 1930's. An average kolkhoz comprises about 6,000 hectares and gives full-time work to more than 500 people today. As a consequence, the kolkhoz-member has changed from peasant to agricultural labourer, both in status and mentality. The process of assimilating to the status of sovkhoz workers is continuing.

The kolkhoz is a legal person, but its legal capacity is limited in the sense of the *ultra vires* doctrine. It extends as far as is necessary in order to fulfil the economic and social functions attributed to kolkhozes. All land being state property in the Soviet Union, the kolkhoz has only the right to use the land allotted to it gratuitously for an unlimited period. It is obliged to use the land effectively, carefully, and in accordance with its economic tasks. Kolkhoz-land is divided up into two parts; one part is destined for collective farming, the other serves for assignments of household-plots to kolkhoz-families. Once allotted, the land can be withdrawn from the kolkhoz only with the consent of the general meeting and in exchange for compensation (par. 5 of art. 16 and art. 18 of the 1968 Principles of Land Legislation). Apart from the land, all other assets are owned by the kolkhoz as co-operative property constituting a special form of socialist property. Its subject being a group of persons, co-operative ownership is qualified as a lower stage in the process of socialization compared to state ownership, because it has not yet arrived at the subject level of the whole people. Accordingly, the objects of kolkhoz property are limited. In Article 7 of the Constitution, art. 23 of the 1961 Principles of Civil Legislation and in several other norms one can find a list of objects that may belong to kolkhozes, but Soviet lawyers are all agreed on the non-exhaustive nature of such lists. Unquestionably, there are two restrictions imposed on kolkhoz property: 1) it must not include objects reserved for state property exclusively, 2) as a rule, it must serve the purposes determined by the kolkhoz statute. As socialist property kolkhoz property enjoys increased legal protection. Only the current assets are open to distraint, the fixed assets are exempt. According to art. 12 of the 1969 Model Charter both kinds of assets constitute indivisible funds, i.e. distribution to kolkhoz-members is forbidden. This provision deserves special attention because up until then kolkhoz-members were considered holding a share in kolkhoz property corresponding to their contribution made while joining it, a part of which could be reimbursed in case of leaving. For this reason, some Western observers speak of a subtle expropriation implemented in 1969. Kolkhoz property is strictly separated from kolkhoz-members' personal property. The kolkhoz is not liable for obligations of its members and vice versa.

The organizational structure of the kolkhoz should be based on the principle of "kolkhoz-democracy". According to this the general meeting of all kolkhoz-members is declared to be the highest organ of the kolkhoz and its powers have been enlarged by the new Model Charter. In large kolkhozes a representatives' meeting can act instead of the general meeting. The general meeting, which is to be convoked four times a year, elects the executive board, the chairman, and the auditing commission for three years. In fact, the election procedure is hardly more than a mere formality, for in the framework of the *nomenklatura* system nobody can be elected a leading kolkhoz official without the prior consent of the competent party committee (see COMMUNIST PARTY). Besides the party secretary the chairman is the central figure in the life of the kolkhoz. He takes every important decision and determines the executive board's activities. His sphere of competence is actually unlimited as there are no matters exclusively reserved for the general meeting; in the Model Charter it is only said that in some matters the executive board's decisions must be confirmed by the general meeting. The other leading officials, particularly the chief-accountant, are appointed by the executive board. The organizational structure of the different production units, of which the brigade is the most important one, is based on the same principles. The brigade meeting elects the brigade council and the brigadier, but for the election of the latter the kolkhoz executive board's consent is required. The brigadier, who functions as a link between the chairman and the brigade, is vested with great powers and unchallengeable authority within the brigade, but on the other hand he is completely dependent on the chairman.

Regarding economic activities kolkhozes are incorporated in the system of central planning, though they have been granted some independence since 1964. The main production indicators established by the regional administrations of agriculture on the basis of annual purchase plans for the individual kolkhozes concern the quantities of produce to be delivered for purchase. The kolkhoz general meeting sets up its own annual production plan in order to fulfil the purchase tasks. At the same time, the kolkhoz is obliged to conclude so-called contracts of "contractation of agricultural produce" with the purchasing organizations. These contracts are based on an act of planning and their contents are predetermined to a large extent by different standard contracts and the "Statute on the procedure of concluding and performing the contracts of contractation" approved by the USSR Ministry of Farm Produce Purchases in December 1970. (With regard to *kontraktatsiia*, see also the decree of April 23, 1970, of the USSR Council of Ministers, and the decree of October 22, 1970, of the Minister of Supply.) The delivery is to be performed at fixed prices, which have been increased several times in recent years. In addition to accepting delivery and paying for such goods (mostly after having paid advances on the purchase price), the purchaser of a contract of *zakupka* (supply) may have additional obligations of helping the supplier, which may consist in advice concerning the rules governing the deliveries, or in providing the supplying farm with seed or pesticides or the like.

The obligation to conclude contracts of this kind is not limited to the produce planned. It embraces certain quotas of the produce attained in overfulfilling the plan targets, but in this case an extra charge is paid in addition to the normal purchase price. The surplus produce left after contractual obligations have been fulfilled and a part of it has been put aside for certain kolkhoz purposes (seed, feed and fodder stocks, etc.) can be sold to trade organizations or on the free market, or it can be given to kolkhoz-members in charging to their wages.

Besides agricultural production kolkhozes are entitled to engage in ancillary activities and in inter-kolkhoz organizations (*q.v.*). These activities mainly taking place in the sphere of processing food-stuff and building industry are of rapidly growing importance and serve as a remarkable source of kolkhoz income. Notwithstanding the economic results, the official attitude towards them is vacillating between encouragement and reservation. Obviously, ancillary activities have proved more profitable than farming and turned kolkhoz activities in some cases too far away from the primary tasks.

The various questions of labour organization are settled by the executive board on the basis of the Rules of the kolkhoz's inner operation adopted by the general meeting. Both the Model Charter and the Model Rules give only some hints on this subject. In particular, they do not prefer any special form of organizational division of labour but simply list the possible sub-divisions. So there is ample room for experiment. As a matter of fact the brigade prevails as the basic labour unit. The much debated link (*zveno*) system has proved the most effective form of labour organization because it instils in the kolkhoz-member a sense of responsibility for the land. In this system the land is allotted to the link responsible for all the farming operations over a number of years, there is no piece work scheduled of any kind, and payments are made on the finished product with bonuses for superior results. Nevertheless, this system is opposed by many party officials because of ideological considerations. On the whole, there is, however, a strong tendency to adjust the labour situation to that one prevailing in sovkhozes and to adopt labour law principles. (See: KOLKHOZ-MEMBERS).

The distribution of the kolkhoz profits is outlined in art. 36 of the Model Charter. At first, the wages-fund is to be separated from the gross profit. The wages-fund is to be used for paying wages after deducting the income tax imposed on the wages-fund (8 per cent of the amount exceeding the sum corresponding to an average monthly wage of 60 Roubles per capita) and the contributions to the All-Union health insurance fund (2.4 per cent). The net income is destined for paying taxes and other duties. These payments include, above all, the contributions to the All-Union pension insurance fund (5 per cent of the gross income) and the second part of the income tax. According to the Kolkhoz Income Tax Law of April 10, 1965, income tax is imposed on the wages-fund and on that part of net income that exceeds the amount corresponding to a profitability rate of 15 per cent. Each per cent of the exceeding amount is charged with a tax rate of 0.3 per cent rising to 25 per cent at most. The remaining net profit is to be spent on enlarging the fixed and current assets, the social-cultural fund, the reserve fund and other funds. While payments for the fixed and current assets are compulsory, this is not the case as regards the several funds. Of course, the question of what is to be done, if the profit is not enough both for paying guaranteed minimum wages, taxes,

duties, and enlarging the assets, remains open.
Though kolkhozes are co-operatives established on an allegedly voluntary basis, they are firmly incorporated into a centralized system of planning and control. Consequently, kolkhozes are subordinated to the government agencies of agricultural administration, i.e. the USSR and Union republican Ministries of Agriculture, where special main administrations for kolkhoz affairs are established, and the administrations of agriculture of the provincial and local soviets' executive committees. In addition, the All-Union Board for the Supply of Farm Machinery, Fuel, and Fertilizers (*Soiuzsel'khoztekhnika*) and its agencies set up in 1961, and the USSR and Union republican Ministries of Farm Produce Purchases and their inspectorates established in 1969, should be mentioned. These agencies dispose of large powers over the kolkhozes even though kolkhoz-democracy must be respected and compulsory directions ought to be given only in the sphere of planning and in cases where national interests are involved. In addition to this purely bureaucratic system of state administration, which replaced the mixed party and state administration of agriculture after Khrushchev's fall, a pyramid of kolkhoz councils has been erected in the wake of the Third Kolkhoz-Congress of November 1969. They have been given a legal shape by a Statute of the Union Kolkhoz Council and three Model Statutes concerning the kolkhoz councils on the lower administrative echelons approved of by a decree of the Council of Ministers of the USSR of June 16, 1971
The kolkhoz councils have been conceived in the spirit of kolkhoz-democracy, so they are elected from below and should be regarded as an expression of co-operative initiative. Nevertheless, their personal composition shows a conspicuous preponderance of state bureaucracy. The kolkhoz councils are to discuss all questions concerning production and social problems of the countryside and to prepare proposals for measures further improving kolkhoz economy. In any case, they have no administrative powers and can submit recommendations only.

Bibl.: René Dumont, *Sovkhoz, kolkhoz, ou le problématique communiste*, 1964; Georg Brunner-Klaus Westen, *Die sowjetische Kolchosordnung*, 1970.

Georg Brunner

See also INTER-KOLKHOZ ORGANIZATIONS; KOLKHOZ-FARMS; KOLKHOZ-MEMBERS

KOLKHOZ-FARM
The kolkhoz-farm is a family enterprise of kolkhoz-members living together in a household on the private (household) plot. It is regarded as a special form of personal association, whose members own the farm as common personal property. The kolkhoz-farm is an independent legal entity guaranteed by Part 2 of Article 7 of the Soviet Constitution. Every kolkhoz-farm and its staff are registered by the local soviet. As a rule, but not necessarily, all farm members are kolkhoz-members; it can happen that some members have a job outside the kolkhoz. Because of the family character of the farm, membership is mainly acquired by birth or marriage. The average kolkhoz-farm consists of 3 or 4 persons. If a member leaves the farm, the common property should be divided into equal parts under the supervision of the local soviet.
According to Part 2 of Article 7 of the Constitution the personal property of the kolkhoz-family may comprise a dwelling-house, farm buildings, livestock, poultry, bees, and working equipment. As all land is state property, the household plot is made available to the kolkhoz-family for use only. The usufruct is derived in a twofold way. The state gives the use of the land to the

kolkhoz gratuitously, which passes it on to the kolkhoz-family free of charge. The permissible size of the household plot is specified by the individual kolkhoz charters on the basis of the prescriptions embodied in the Model Charter. In contrast to the Model Charter of 1935 the new one of 1969 establishes the maximum size only and refers the fixing of a minimum size to the kolkhozes. As the kolkhozes are in fact bound by Party and state instructions, the practical outcome of the omission is the possibility of carrying out a policy of restricting private farming inconspicuously, without changing the Model Charter, whenever the Party leadership should deem it necessary. Furthermore the authorization of the Union republican ministries of agriculture to extend the upper limit to 1 hectare has been deleted. The actual maximum size is fixed at 0.5 hectare and at 0.2 hectare in the case of irrigated land. The average size of a household plot comes to 0.3 hectare and is far from reaching the maximum limit, but in some regions, such as the Baltic and the Black Earth Region, the household plots are much larger. Special restrictions are provided for by part 2 of art. 42 of the Model Charter, as in individual cases the kolkhoz general meeting can reduce the maximum size depending on the participation of the kolkhoz-family in the collective work done for the kolkhoz and on the number of persons living together in the household. The former restriction, which can be applied as a threat in order to enforce labour discipline, had been introduced as early as 1956 and was much disputed during the public discussion on the new Model Charter. Finally, the forces in favour of emphasizing material incentives instead of administrative measures were defeated.

The norms of livestock-breeding are laid down in art. 43 of the Model Charter. According to them the kolkhoz-farm is allowed to own 1 cow with 1 calf up to 1 year old and 1 heifer up to 2 years old, 1 sow with suckling pigs up to 3 months old or 2 pigs on feed, 10 sheep or goats, any amount of poultry, rabbits and hives. In contrast to the old Model Charter, which fixed higher numbers for certain categories of agricultural regions, the competence for admitting exceptions has been decentralized and transferred to the Councils of Ministers of the Union republics. Initially, the same restrictions valid for the household plot (participation in collective work, family-size) were provided for livestock herds in the draft of the new Model Charter, too, but in the final version they have been omitted.

The existence of private enterprise (*q.v.*) in the agriculture of a society, where allegedly communism is being built, is an ideological anomaly. Nevertheless, private plots are of such an importance for supplying the population that they have become an indispensable part of Soviet agriculture—see HOUSEHOLD PLOT. The official attitude regarding kolkhoz-farms has been wavering from the beginning. Khrushchev was trying to restrain private farming and to suspend the provisions of the Model Charter of 1935 which favoured it to a certain extent, by a joint decree of the Central Committee of the C.P.S.U. and the Council of Ministers of the USSR of March 6, 1956. His attempts were quite effective, insofar as he succeeded in reducing the share of kolkhoz-members' private farming in net agricultural output from 26.4 per cent in 1953 to 17 per cent in 1964. On the other hand, his agricultural policy ended in the harvest catastrophe of 1963. His successors started by abolishing several restrictions and by furthering private farming, but their initiatives have come to a standstill since 1968. The new Model Charter reflects a compromise, leaving open the situation for any development. It is obvious, however, that the party leaders are well aware of the economic importance of kolkhoz-farms, and while adopting the Model Charter at the 3rd Kolkhoz Congress in

November 1969 it was stated several times that private farming of kolkhoz-members will play an important role for a long time to come.

Bibl.: Karl-Eugen Wädekin, *Privatproduzenten in der sowjetischen Landwirtschaft,* 1967; Georg Brunner & Klaus Westen, *Die sowjetische Kolchosordnung*, 1970.

Georg Brunner

See also PRIVATE FARMS; KOLKHOZ; KOLKHOZ-MEMBERS

KOLKHOZ-MEMBERS

About 50 million Soviet people, i.e. roughly one half of the rural population are living in kolkhozes. Not all of them are kolkhoz-members in the legal sense of the word, because only persons over 16 years of age can be admitted to membership. According to the Model Charter of 1969, the kolkhoz general meeting should decide on admission on the basis of a written or oral petition of the applicant. Considering the menacing rural exodus, however, children of kolkhoz-members coming up to the age limit are, in fact, often treated automatically as kolkhoz-members. For the same reason termination of membership is subject to severe restrictions. Although in 1969 a provision concerning voluntary departing from the kolkhoz was introduced for the first time, the decision on a corresponding request of the individual kolkhoz-member is in the hands of the executive board and the general meeting; the decision is to be taken within three months. On the other hand, a member can be expelled on serious disciplinary grounds. In both cases there is no appeal to a court. The legal status of the kolkhoz-member is composed of various elements, which can be regarded under four headings.

First of all, according to the fictitious nature of the kolkhoz as a farmers' co-operative on a voluntary basis, the kolkhoz-member is vested with some partnership rights. As his real status is very close to that of an employee this group of rights is of relatively little importance. Notwithstanding the stronger emphasis laid on "kolkhoz-democracy" in recent official statements, it can be assumed that the rights to participate, to speak and to vote in the different meetings of the kolkhoz and its organizational subdivisions are hardly more than formal ornaments of the decision-making process taking place behind the closed doors of the competent Party and administrative agencies. During the long years since the collectivization, the individual shares in kolkhoz property have withered away economically and are not mentioned in the new Model Charter at all. According to it, all kolkhoz funds are indivisible. At the same time, the partnership-type share in profits on the basis of the very disadvantageous system of work-days has been largely displaced by paying wages in a quasi-labour law manner. Finally, one may discover elements of a partnership in the rights to make use of different kolkhoz-facilities, mainly in the cultural and social sphere, and to profit from kolkhoz assistance by managing the private plot.

Much more important are the kolkhoz-member's rights and duties as an agricultural labourer. Though his status is still worse than that of an industrial or sovkhoz-worker, much has been done in order to improve it in the last decade. Almost everywhere the kolkhoz-member receives wages in cash according to the work done and only a small part of his earnings is paid in kind. The earnings are composed of three parts: a) basic wages, which are guaranteed and mainly based on piece-work system, but timework and other systems are also admitted; b) extra wages according to the economic results of the kolkhoz; c) premiums for individual performance. On the other hand, the kolkhoz-member has to do a minimum amount of work fixed by each kolkhoz individually. If he fails to do this without sufficient reason, his extra wages and premiums can be reduced or completely cancelled by the executive board. The basic wages can be reduced in case of fault only. The average monthly wages of a kolkhoz-member amounted to 52.3 roubles in 1965 and 78.2 roubles in 1971, while comparable data for workers and employees were 96.5 and 125.9 roubles, respectively. In spite of strong demands made during the public discussion on the Model Charter, the questions of working time, holidays, and safety regulations were not settled uniformly in 1969, so that kolkhozes have to tackle the matter mainly by themselves. On the whole, a strong tendency to adjust the situation to the regulations valid for sovkoz-workers can be noticed. As a consequence of the adoption of labour law principles, the disciplinary status of the kolkhoz-members was altered in 1969. In particular, the fine, which had been counted in work-day units under the Model Charter of 1935, was abolished. The present disciplinary measures, which can be applied by the executive board and, in some cases, by the general meeting, are as follows: warning, reprimand, severe reprimand, assignment of worse-paid work, removal from office, and announcement of expulsion from kolkhoz-membership. As a rule, expulsion can be ordered in the case of systematically breaking labour discipline or the kolkhoz charter and after previously applying another disciplinary measure. For damages caused to the kolkhoz the kolkhoz-member is liable in various ways. The rather vague provision of parts 3 and 4 of art. 13 of the Model Charter has been somewhat clarified by a plenary decision of the Supreme Court of the USSR of October 6, 1970. As a general rule, liability is limited to one-third of the average monthly basic wage in case of negligence. Full responsibility arises if the damage is caused willfully or by a criminal offence or in connection with a work done not for kolkhoz purposes, if machines or animals belonging to the kolkhoz are used arbitrarily and in the case of injury to certain kinds of kolkhoz animals. Ultimately, liability is augmented in the case of forest-damage and livestock embezzlement; then the compensation can be ten times the damage caused.

Thirdly, the kolkhoz-member can be regarded as the beneficiary of social benefits. This part of his legal status was quite underdeveloped for a long time. Until the mid-60's social security was the own problem of each kolkhoz. In most of them a special relief fund existed, to which at most 2 per cent of the kolkhoz gross income could be paid over. The benefits from the relief fund differed somewhat in the kolkhozes, but on the whole they were very inadequate. The reforms of 1964 and 1970 altered the situation completely and created a uniform system of social insurance. This system is divided in two separate sub-systems: pension insurance and health insurance. Pension insurance was introduced as from January 1, 1965, and was gradually improved in the following years. At the beginning of 1968, the pension age was reduced by 5 years and the disabled kolkhoz-members of the 3rd group were entitled to payments. At present the pension age is 60 for men and 55 for women, the service time required being 25 and 20 years respectively. Uniform health insurance became effective on April 1, 1970. Benefits are granted in cases of temporary disablement (sickness), birth and death and are dependent on service time. In order to unify the system of social insurance for kolkhoz-members an All-Union health insurance fund and an All-Union pension insurance fund were established, to which kolkhozes have to contribute 2.4 per cent of their wages-fund and 5 per cent of their gross income respectively. This means, all in all, that kolkhozes have to pay social contributions up to 6.6 per cent of their gross income or 9.9 per cent of their wages-fund. In spite of all

these improvements, social assistance to kolkhoz-members is far from reaching the level prevailing for workers and employees. An exception, however, is to be made for the leading and expert kolkhoz personnel, i.e. kolkhoz chairmen, chief-accountants, specialists with university or higher vocational training and the so-called *mekhanizatory* (tractor-, combine-, car-drivers, mechanics, electricians, etc.). This group, which totals nearly one-fifth or the whole kolkhoz-membership, was privileged from the beginning and as from October 1, 1964, it was completely incorporated into the social insurance system for workers and employees.
In addition, the kolkhoz-member is an entrepreneur on his private plot. See KOLKHOZ-FARM.
In spite of part 1 of art. 4 of the 1961 Principles of Civil Procedure stating the principle that all issues arising from kolkhoz law relations fall within the jurisdiction of the courts, except for cases provided by law, the judicial protection of the kolkhoz-member is rather restricted. The exceptions are numerous and concern important issues such as disputes concerning labour organization, membership, and household plots. According to a plenary decision of the Supreme Court of the USSR of June 24, 1968, the kolkhoz-member is entitled to make a claim concerning the basis and amount of his wages, but judgment concerning the basis on which the wages are calculated (wage scales, production norms, etc.) has been refused. In an earlier plenary decision Nr. 3/1960 it was ruled that claims arising out of working accidents, for which the kolkhoz is liable according to civil law, can be brought to court. Recently, some confusion has been caused by part 4 of art. 13 of the 1969 Model Charter providing that the assessment of damages caused to the kolkhoz by its members is up to the executive board and in case of dispute to the people's court. Some legal writers take the view that while the kolkhoz can bring a suit against its members at any time, the kolkhoz-member can appeal only from the execution of the executive board's decision obliging him to pay damages, but not from the decision itself. In matters of social insurance, special commissions consisting of government and trade union officials have been established.

Bibl.: Georg Brunner & Klaus Westen, *Die sowjetische Kolchosordnung*, 1970.

Georg Brunner

KOMSOMOL, see COMMUNIST PARTY OF THE SOVIET UNION

KRAI

A *krai* is a major administrative-territorial unit within the USSR. There are presently only six, all located within the RSFSR: Altai, Krasnodar, Krasnoiarsk, Primor'e, Stavropol', and Khabarovsk.
A *krai* is similar to an *oblast'* (*q.v.*); except that it is generally larger, further distant from main population centers, and, in the case of five of the *krai*'s, contains autonomous provinces as subdivisions. Both *oblast's* and *krai's* contain national areas (in some cases).
The Constitution of the USSR confers on the Union republics the power to establish an administrative-territorial structure and to resolve questions concerning that structure. The governmental agencies of the *krai*, however, are established by the USSR Constitution. The primary organ of state power is the *krai* soviet, the deputies to which are elected for terms of two years according to norms of representation determined by the republican Constitution. The executive and regulatory agency of the *krai* is the executive committee of the soviet, which is elected by the soviet. The soviets also elect the members of the *krai* court, for a term of five years. The *krai* procurator, however, is appointed by the Procurator of the USSR, also

for a term of five years.
The Constitution of the RSFSR enumerates the *krai*'s, so that any change in the number of *krai*'s would require a constitutional amendment. The RSFSR Constitution incorporates the principles governing the *krai* found in the USSR Constitution and provides additional details concerning the organization of a *krai* and its relationship to republican agencies.
The RSFSR has the power to establish *krai*'s, determine their boundaries, and establish *raion* divisions. The *krai* soviet is subordinate to the RSFSR Supreme Soviet and its Presidium. The Presidium can, for example, annul decisions and regulations of *krai* soviets. Similarly, the RSFSR Council of Ministers may annul or suspend decisions and regulations of the executive committee of the *krai* soviet.
In terms of the administration of the *krai*, the soviet's executive committee is mandated to establish sections and administrations, certain of which are specifically enumerated in the RSFSR Constitution. These sections and administrations are subordinate to the executive committee, to the soviet, and to the corresponding All-Union Ministries of the RSFSR. See further OBLAST'.

Stephen M. Weiner

LABOUR DISCIPLINE,
see DISCIPLINARY LAW

LABOUR DISPUTES AND LABOUR ARBITRATION

Procedures for settling labour disputes are laid down in the Principles of LABOUR LAW and in arts. 201-224 of the RSFSR Labour Code and in the Rules on the settlement of labour disputes (decree of the Presidium of the Supreme Soviet of the USSR of January 31, 1957). Comprehensive rules govern disputes between one or several employees and the employer. Only summary rules exist concerning disputes between members of managerial staff and the management and for policy disputes (disputes between management and union, or other disputes intended to amend existing labour conditions).

Employee-management disputes are settled by a Labour Disputes Board (LDB) set up in every enterprise, institution or organisation in which a factory committee or trade union organizer exists (see UNIONS), consisting of an equal number of representatives of the union and the management. The LDB is the forum of first instance in all disputes between an employee and management except for claims for reinstatement after discharge, claims of the management for reimbursement for damage caused by an employee (see LIABILITY OF EMPLOYEES) and disputes concerning questions already decided by a joint decision of union and management, which disputes are settled by the courts. The employee may take his claim to the LDB after he has tried to settle the dispute with the appropriate management official. The claim must be heard within five days, in the presence of the employee; witnesses may be heard and other evidence collected.

The LDB may either grant the claim, dismiss it or conclude its hearing without coming to a decision, if no agreement can be reached between the two sides of the board. Grounds have to be given for the decision and notwithstanding the somewhat informal character, the proceedings must be based on existing law.

The tribunal of second instance in labour disputes is the factory committee of the unions which comes into action on an appeal by the employee lodged within ten days, or on the request of the PROCURACY, or on the initiative of the committee itself. The procedure is very similar to that for the LDB. If the employee is dissatisfied with the decision of the committee, or if the management considers that the decision violates the law, they have ten days to take the case to the people's court. In the court the rules of the Code of CIVIL PROCEDURE apply; however the employee is exempted from paying court fees. Decisions reinstating the employee (after discharge or transfer) have to be executed immediately, notwithstanding appeal. Other decisions as a rule have to be executed within 10 days after the final decision. If the management fails to execute the decision of the LDB or the committee an execution warrant is issued by the factory committee (see EXECUTION).

Disputes between a member of the managerial staff and management regarding discharge, transfer or a disciplinary measure (see DISCIPLINARY LAW) are settled by the higher administrative authorities (the members of the managerial staff are enumerated in a special list).

Disputes between an employee and the management intended to bring about a change in labour conditions are settled by the management and the factory committee, and, if they do not reach agreement, by the higher economic and union authorities.

Policy disputes and strikes

The latest public official statement on strikes in the Soviet Union dates from the 1920's and was intended to lay down the limits on the right to strike under the New Economic

Policy of those years. After 1930 reports on strikes have not been published in the USSR. It has long been held that strikes were officially forbidden by the Criminal Code. The criminal codes of 1960 did not contain such an article; however in 1966 the criminal codes were amended with a new article 190-3 (Decree of the Presidium of the Supreme Soviet of the RSFSR of September 16, 1966), which could be read as an official prohibition of strikes. In Soviet sources the absence of strikes is justified by the large number of procudures for the settlement of labour disputes and by ideological arguments. Disputes which may give rise to strikes have to be settled by the factory committee and management, or by the higher economic and union authorites.

On this question the following factors are also relevant:

1) the right of the factory committee to raise the question for a discharge of a management official and the right of higher union bodies to require the discharge of a management official (see UNIONS);

2) the powers of technical inspection of the unions (see EMPLOYEE PROTECTION) and of legal inspection (see UNIONS);

3) the powers of the PROCURACY and art. 138 Criminal Code of the RSFSR (and arts. 140 and 217) making it a criminal offence for management officials to violate existing labour legislation or the safety rules.

G. P. van den Berg

LABOUR LAW

History

Decrees on the 8-hour work day, on workers' control and the social insurance system were issued soon after the revolution. Together with provisions on the labour market enacted in 1918, these decrees were incorporated in the Code of Labour Laws of 1918. This Code was based on the principle of the duty to work for every citizen capable of working, which implied the abolition of contracts of employment: employees were assigned to their jobs by special offices for registration and distribution of manpower. The Code stated that every citizen should have the right to work according to his special skills and for a wage corresponding to the character of the work and the conditions of work. However, due to civil war conditions, the Code soon lost its effect and was to a large extent replaced by decrees on wages policy in 1919 and 1920.

After the start of NEP, a new Code of Labour Laws of the RSFSR was enacted in 1922 (decision of the All-Union Central Executive Committee of the RSFSR of October 30, 1922). The other Union republics adopted their labour codes with, in essence, the same content or instead they adopted the RSFSR Code. This Code reflected the return to more common concepts of labour relations by abolishing the duty to work as a legal principle and the reintroduction of the contract of employment. The unions got the opportunity to defend the interests of the workers by collective bargaining or similar devices; the Codes instead established only minimum guarantees of the workers' rights (arts. 4, 28 Code of the RSFSR). The development of the planning system and the drive for industrialization brought with them an increasing influence of the authorities on the labour market and on wages. As from 1928 young graduates had to work for 3 years in jobs and enterprises assigned to them on the basis of planning acts issued by the authorities. The migration from the villages to the towns came under the control of the authorities by the introduction of the system of organized recruitment (see EMPLOYMENT). After the collectivisation this growing influence of the authorities on the labour market brought about in 1940 a decree (decree of the Presidium of the Supreme Soviet of the USSR of October 10, 1940, on the state manpower reserves) which extended the planned allocation of manpower to all employees graduating from the vocational schools, and, in the war period, other decrees on compulsory transfers, etc. From 1930 onwards measures were taken against the excessive mobility of labour by extension of the period of notice to leave one's job and the introduction of labour books. Between 1940 and 1956 workers were not permitted to leave their job without sufficient reasons. Government wages policy replaced collective bargaining and from 1933 onwards nearly all rates and salaries were fixed by the central authorities. In fact, the labour codes ceased to be merely a minimum guarantee for the workers: all legal provisions were binding on both parties and collective bargaining became superfluous: between 1934 and 1947 no collective agreements were concluded, and the reintroduction of the agreements in 1947 had quite other aims than establishing working conditions (see trade UNIONS). The maintenance of *labour discipline*, in the first years mainly by the workers and their organizations themselves, became after the decisions on the introduction of one-man-management a function of the management. Penalties for breaches of labour discipline became gradually more harsh; they culminated in such breaches being considered as criminal offences from 1940 onwards. On the other hand, the system of rewards, bonuses, medals etc. became of ever increasing importance in promoting labour productivity. After 1950 these measures were softened and later on the harsher measures were abolished (cf. e.g. decree of the Presidium of the Supreme Soviet of April 25, 1956); and from 1955 on a lot of new rules were enacted: laws on SOCIAL INSURANCE and security in 1955, a reform of the WAGES system between 1957 and 1961, rules on LABOUR ARBITRATION (1957) and labour discipline (1957), on the trade UNIONS and on the participation of workers in the affairs of the enterprise (1958), on industrial accidents (1961), while a 7-hour work day was re-introduced in 1960, replaced by rules on a 5-day work week in 1967 (see HOURS OF WORK).

A completely new codification of labour was initiated between 1956 and 1960, but only in 1970 were the new Principles of Labour Law of the USSR and the Union republics enacted (Law of the USSR of July 15, 1970), although the Constitutions of 1924 and 1936 had already announced the enactment of such an instrument. On the basis of the Principles the Union republics adopted new Labour Codes (Law of the RSFSR of December 9, 1971, and similar laws in the other Union republics in 1971 and 1972).

Legislative agencies

After the merger of the People's Commissariats of Labour with the trade unions (decision of the Central Executive Committee of the USSR, the Council of People's Commissars of the USSR and ACCTU of June 23, 1933) the Council of People's Commissars became the chief legislative agency in labour law, but its legislative competence was partly entrusted to ACCTU. With the formation of the State Committee on labour and wages (decree of the Supreme Soviet of May 24, 1955) to strengthen the control on the economic ministries and offices, the competence of ACCTU was limited to questions of social insurance. However, important decisions of the Council of Ministers and the State Committee are taken by joint decisions with ACCTU. In the different branches of the economy a part of the relevant rules are issued by the ministries together with the unions. At the local level the collective agreements and decisions of management and unions play a growing role in the establishment of factory rules (see UNIONS).

Main principles and features of Soviet labour law

The essential features of Soviet labour law are:

a) the "universality" of employment and the 'freedom from exploitation': this entails the (partly legal) duty of every citizen capable of working to carry on work useful for society (see PARASITES), the right to work protected by the full-employment policy of the government, the prohibition of a refusal to hire without sufficient reasons and strict rules to be applied in the case of discharge, and the right of a free choice of work for most citizens (EMPLOYMENT);

b) WAGES have to be paid in accordance with the quality and the quantity of work done and not in accordance with one's needs. However, social legislation provides for minimum wages (raised in 1971 to 75 R. a month) and additional allowances are paid for children etc. (see SOCIAL INSURANCE);

c) the stress on the need to combine productive work with study, and advantages for employees in study programs (see TRAINING);

d) the need for LABOUR DISCIPLINE, enforced by rewards and penalties and the intended participation of the workers themselves in the maintenance of labour discipline;

e) the promoting of socialist competition and the ideas and practice that one has to work like a communist, together with emphasis on material and other incentives;

f) the stress on employee protection and labour SAFETY;

g) the participation of the workers in the affairs of the enterprise; together with emphasis on the system of one-man management;

h) the right to allowances and pensions for sickness, disability and old age pensions (see SOCIAL INSURANCE);

i) the detailed regulation of labour relations by the authorities, the extensive control on the observance of labour law in the enterprises and institutions by the trade unions and the PROCURACY, and the quite common reports on infringements of the rules in a lot of enterprises;

j) a detailed system of grievances procedures within the enterprises (see LABOUR DISPUTES), the absence, at least officially, of strikes, and the criminal and financial responsibility of managers for infringements of the labour rights of workers, the trade UNION rights and the labour SAFETY rules (see EMPLOYMENT, CONTRACT OF).

G. P. van den Berg

LABOUR UNIONS, see UNIONS

LAND LAW

Land law according to the prevalent doctrinal interpretation constitutes a separate branch of Soviet law governing the legal relations in respect of land, and thus distinguished from both civil and administrative law. The independent position of land law is deemed to result from the fundamental principle that the state is the exclusive owner of all land as one of the basic means of production, since the Decree on the Land of November 8 (October 26), 1917, and subsequent revolutionary enactments (see also REAL PROPERTY). The state monopoly of landownership which is enshrined in Article 6 of the 1936 Constitution, corresponds to an absolute prohibition of any civil law transaction relating to land, so that acts like buying and selling, leasing and mortgaging of land are not only null and void, but also subject to criminal liability (cf. art. 199 Criminal Code). The only permissible legal form in which land may be used is "land tenure" or "right of use of land" (see LAND TENURE). As the state is the sole proprietor of land, only the state, through its agencies, is entitled to allocate land tenure to natural or juridical persons for the actual use of land, as well as to withdraw this right if specific reasons so justify. In this way the state is in a position to exercise complete control of the use of land. In accordance with the constitutional statement that all land shall be an asset belonging to all people, the allocation of land tenure and the exercise of this right are free. Since among the socialist countries only the Soviet Union can pretend to be the exclusive owner of the entire land in the state, it is also the only socialist country to have land law as an independent branch of law.

According to Article 14 of the Constitution, land law is primarily regulated by the Principles of Land Legislation of the Union and the Union Republics of December 13, 1968, which entered into force on July 1, 1969. On the basis of these Principles each constituent republic enacted its own Land Code, such as the Land Code of the RSFSR of July 1, 1970, the Land Code of the Ukrainian Republic of July 17, 1970, and the Latvian Land Code of May 21, 1970. The Principles comprise 50 articles, apart from the introductory and transitional provisions, whereas the Codes contain over 150 articles. In addition, a large variety of special regulations have been enacted. Soviet land law (*zemel'noe pravo*) encompasses not only the rules governing land tenure (*zemlepol'zovanie*) and land policy (*zemleustroistvo*), together named land legislation (*zemel'noe zakonodatel'stvo*), but, for practical reasons, also a part of administrative law such as rules relating to the administration of the State Land Fund (see REAL PROPERTY). The Principles of Land Legislation and the Land Codes contain the following parts: i) General Provisions, ii) classification of the land divisions according to their designated purpose, iii) land tenure, including the enumeration of the parties who may exercise the right of land tenure, the procedure in which plots of land are allocated, the terms on which this right may be exercised and the termination of land tenure, iv) land registration, v) land policy, vi) procedural rules relating to disputes over land, and finally vii) civil, criminal and administrative liability resulting from improper use of land and other infringements upon legal duties imposed by land law. The subjects mentioned under ii), iii) and iv) are dealt with under the entries REAL PROPERTY, LAND TENURE and LAND REGISTRATION respectively. The remaining subjects are expounded below. The problem whether land law should or should not also embrace the law governing mineral resources, the forests and water resources is solved by the Principles of Land Legislation insofar as art. 2 thereof stipulates that "special" regulations shall cover these subjects. However, owing to the natural relationship of subsoil, forest and water, to land, the Principles contain some fundamental rules governing these subjects. Consult therefore not only MINES, MINERALS & MINING, FOREST & FORESTRY and WATER & WATERCOURSES but also REAL PROPERTY.

According to the General Provisions the main purpose of land law is the safeguarding of a rational use of land, the creation of conditions for increasing its effectiveness, the protection of the right of land tenure exercised by whomsoever, and the enforcement of the principle of socialist legality in respect of the legal relations concerning the land. In consequence of the federal structure of the Soviet Union, the legislative and executive (administrative) powers concerning the land are divided between the Federation and its constituent republics, each with their own hierarchical structure. The Federation is entrusted with the establishment of long term plans for a rational use of the land resources, the elaboration of concrete short term plans for soil improvement, comprising fertilisation and measures to combat erosion, silting, swamp formation and similar harmful soil processes, the introduction of a system of supervision over the use of land, the organisation of a single system of land inventory, registration of land tenure and the conduct of a land cadastre, as well as acts of disposal of land having federal significance. Subject to the competence of the constituent republics are acts of disposal of land having republican importance, the establishment of development plans concerning the land and the enactment of special land regulations, insofar as the Federation does not exercise such jurisdiction.

Land policy is defined as a system of measures taken by the state agencies aimed at the organisation of the fullest, most rational and effective use of land, at the raising of the standards of farming and the protection of the soil, and the making available of new land, primarily for agricultural, but also for other purposes. Land policy may be put into effect by the following acts: i) the releasing of new land for allocation, the redistribution of land or the changing of the boundaries of land sections, ii) the organization of a system of land allocation within collective and state farms or other agricultural entities, iii) the withdrawal of land tenure by way of expropriation, iv) the establishment and revision of the boundaries of city precincts, urbanised agglomerations and rural settlements, v) the organization of photographic, geodesical, geological and other types of exploratory and inventorial operations, vi) the marking of the boundaries of land sections on the spot, vii) the organization and the conduct of a cadastral type of land registration (see LAND REGISTRATION), and viii) the performance of planning operations concerning land. Land policy is executed by special, local governmental agencies for land policy, under the direction and supervision of the ministries of agriculture of the constituent republics, while the supreme authority is conferred upon the federal Ministry of Agriculture. Each act of land policy must in principle be shaped as a decision subject to appeal or other legal remedies. The actual decisions are preceded by the elaboration of projects which should first be discussed by the relevant land users, thus complying with the principle of the participation of the public in the administration. The legal rules governing "land procedure" are usually considered to be distinct from rules of civil, administrative and criminal procedure. Land procedure is in fact a complex of special types of procedure aimed at the settling of disputes concerning the allocation of land tenure, its withdrawal, acts of land policy and planning, state control of the use of land, and other decisions or other governmental acts concerning the land, as well as acts performed by the land users themselves. The legal rules relating to land procedure are, as other types of procedure, mainly governed by the principles of equality of parties, of the "objective truth" (parties may not agree on something which is contrary to the real state of things) and a speedy settlement of the dispute. All parties having some interest in the relevant piece of land must be heard. Since the state exercises monopoly of the landownership it is therefore said that the bodies which decide land cases, are not courts of general jurisdiction or arbitration tribunals, but administrative agencies. According to the nature and importance of the case, agencies competent to decide land cases are the Councils of Ministers of the constituent republics or the autonomous republics, various ministries of these republics, the lower echelons of these ministries, local agricultural departments or local agencies carrying out land policy.

Disputes concerning the use of land located on the territory of a constituent republic which are initiated by collective or state farms or other socialist organizations seated in another republic, are heard by a special commission appointed on a parity basis. If such a commission does not reach a unanimous decision such disputes are settled by the federal Council of Ministers.

Infringement of the rules of land law entails the application of civil, criminal or administrative sanctions. Buying, selling, mortgaging, leasing, lending, testamentary disposition and any other civil law transaction or act of legal significance entails civil law nullity, and, depending on the circumstances of the case, persons having committed such unauthorized acts may be liable to pay damages. Criminal law punishes unwarranted seizure or unauthorized exchange, purchase or sale of a plot of land as well as other actions violating the laws on the nationalisation of land, by corrective labour for a term of six months up to one year, or by a fine of up to hundred roubles. The unauthorized construction of a dwelling-house or the unwarranted enlargement thereof is punished by corrective labour for a term of six months up to one year with confiscation of the erected building. Unauthorized occupation of land, failure to safeguard the land or to carry out measures for improving soil processes and to prevent harmful soil processes, and other infringements of the rules of land law are dealt with in administrative proceedings. The Land Codes empower the relevant administrative or land agency to order by way of a special sanction the withdrawal of the right of land tenure (see also LAND TENURE).

Th. Vondracek

LAND REGISTRATION

Land registration is performed by various governmental agencies of the administrative hierarchy for a multitude of purposes, but primarily to make an inventory of land. The basic or first-stage registration is effected on the district (*raion*) level, where the State Book for Registration of Land Tenure, related land charts and other land account documents are kept at the executive committee of the district soviet. The State Book consists of four parts, the first of which records details of land tenure exercised by the land users in the following order: collective farms, inter-kolkhoz organisations, state farms, agricultural research and teaching institutes, enterprises and other legal entities performing auxiliary agricultural activities, forestry departments (*leskhozy*), forestry enterprises (*lespromkhozy*) and other organisations engaged in forestry, industrial enterprises such as manufacturing plants, transport corporations, schools, hospitals and other legal entities not using agricultural land. Each entry is marked by a reference number corresponding to the land chart, and shows the date of registration, the size of the respective piece of land, the type and serial number of the deed certifying the right of land tenure, the date of the delivery of the deed to the entitled party and a reference as to the time for which land tenure was allocated, ranging from three years to perpetuity. Assignment of land tenure for a short term, i.e. for less than three years, is registered separately in a book by the name of Work Note-Book (*rabochaia tetrad'*). The second and third parts of the State Book cover only two categories of land: agricultural land and land belonging to the State Land Reserve (see REAL PROPERTY). The second part indicates data regarding the type of land and type of cultivation including fallow land, as well as the number and the nature of the private households, and the extent of the land occupied by them. The third part contains data relating to the quality of the soil, including the physical and chemical properties of the land and the degree of erosion and silting. In the last part, particulars are filed concerning pieces of land belonging to categories other than agricultural land and land placed on the reserve list.

Registration of land does not constitute conclusive evidence of a title to land. This evidence is provided by the deed certifying the right of land tenure (see LAND TENURE), provided the document is signed by the

Chairman of the executive committee of the district soviet and the Chief land registrar. The land registration system does not record titles to land other than land tenure, such as ownership of land, mortgage or lease, owing to the Soviet conception of land law (see LAND LAW).

Land registration on the district level is conducted by the aforesaid registrar to whom every land user must report any change, legal or physical, in respect of the piece of land granted to him. As is apparent from special enactments, particular attention is paid to the inventory of irrigated and drained land including hydrotechnical installations. On the other hand, registration of land in the Far North is somewhat simplified owing to the thin population and the generally poor quality of the land.

Land registration is carried out on the level of a *krai*, province and autonomous republic by the executives of the respective local soviets mainly for purposes of coordination, agricultural planning, land policy and control of the use of land. These registration data help the governmental agencies for example to determine the amount of agricultural produce which collective and state farms must sell to the state, and to decide on questions of expropriation of land for industrial and other general interests. Land registration is effected on the level of the constituent republics predominantly for purposes of economic planning and general supervision. The latter registration system is administered by the Chief Directorate of Land Tenure and Land Policy of the various Ministries of Agriculture.

Apart from land registration conducted by governmental agencies, every juridical person to whom agricultural land is allotted must perform registration of his "own" land, not only for internal purposes, but also as a collateral source of information for the above-mentioned executive agencies of the state. This type of registration is entered by agricultural enterprises in a Land Survey Book (*zemel'naia shnurovaia kniga*) which also consists of four parts. Part one shows *inter alia* the dates of the entries, the over-all extent of the land occupied by the enterprise, the period for which various pieces of land are allocated, the legal basis on which land tenure was granted, i.e. the date, number and name of the relevant decision of the governmental agency, and the name, number and date of the document certifying the right of land tenure. The entries in the second part indicate the types of land and their extent (except for private plots which are registered in the last part), such as arable land, pastures, grassland, hay-fields, meadows, bushes, forest land, swamps and land occupied by water, paths, ways, streets, houses and other constructions. The third part contains data relating to the properties of the various land sections, including the content of phosphorus and potassium and an indication as to whether the land section lies fallow—it is a list which may contain over one hundred different characteristics. The fourth and last part covers the plots of private households, usually families belonging to collective farms or families of workers employed in state farms. The entries include the name of the heads of the households, the size of the plots, accurate up to 0.01 hectare, and a breakdown according to the type of land, such as arable land, gardens, land occupied by dwellinghouses, sheds, barns and other structures. In this fourth part extra room is reserved for special remarks such as "Moved to the town, the plot can be re-allotted to another private household".

In non-agricultural enterprises, such as manufacturing plants, saw mills and transport-undertakings, the systems of land registration vary according to specific exigencies, but all enterprises are under the obligation to record every change which has occurred. Enterprises engaged in forestry have a remarkably elaborate system of registration adapted to the peculiarities of the different types of forests. Registrations of land tenure exercised by labourers and employees who use agricultural land in rural areas, but who do not work in a collective or state farm, is conducted separately by the village soviets.

The land registration system should be distinguished from the registration of houses and other structures which is entrusted to the care of the Offices of Technical Stock-taking. These offices, however, register, for example, not only private ownership of buildings but also the extent of the land section on which the structures are erected and the documents certifying the relevant right of land tenure.

After some ten years of preparatory work the Principles of Land Legislation of 1968 have laid the legal foundation for the introduction of a cadastral system of land registration. Contrary to the traditional cadastres of Western Europe, which have been created originally for purposes of taxation and are now primarily evidence of ownership and other titles to land, the cadastre envisaged by the Soviet authorities is aimed at an economic assessment of the land. The new registration system, still in its scaffold stage, would show, in addition to the data described above, the relative quality of every piece of land expressed in comparative numbers or ciphers (*bonitirovka*), and a concrete valuation of the land sections by indicating both the gross produce in physical units per surface measure and the net income expressed in pecuniary terms. Additional land charts would be drafted to a scale of at least 1 to 50,000. The new registration system would also include a special valuation system of land covered by collective and state farms in which each piece of land would obtain a "passport" of its own, with all the necessary economic data. It is considered that such a land cadastre is, in fact, indispensable for a better utilisation of land and that only systematic economic valuation can serve as a useful basis for a warranted and rational agricultural planning policy.

Apart from the envisaged land cadastre a special *water cadastre* exists already since 1933. This registration system contains the most important details relating to the water courses and resources both on and below the surface, including lakes, ponds, swamps, glaciers and water installations.

Th. Vondracek

LAND TENURE

Land tenure (*zemlepol'zovanie*) is a right *sui generis* conferred by the state, in its capacity as the exclusive owner of all land, upon persons natural or juridical to use a piece of land for specific purposes established by or on the strength of the law. At Soviet law it is the only title a person may acquire in respect of land. The right of land tenure, however, entails also the legal duty to use the relevant piece of land. If land tenure is not exercised according to the set purpose or not exercised at all, the state may revoke it by way of punitive expropriation. Nonetheless, since land tenure may be withdrawn only on grounds laid down by law, this right, if granted for an indefinite period of time, virtually approaches economic ownership. Another typical characteristic is that land tenure is assigned and exercised completely free of charge by virtue of the ideological principle that land is an "asset of all the people". In point of fact, land tenure is a juridical instrument intended to break the immobilising effect of the state monopoly of land ownership, but, as the right to use land cannot be alienated or burdened and may be allocated only by the state and withdrawn by the state, the intended break-through has merely a limited significance: legal intercourse concerning land often remains rather stagnant and cumbersome. According to the prevalent doctrinal interpretations, land tenure is not a civil law right but a right belonging to the separate branch of law: land law (*q.v.*).

Land tenure may be allocated for a limited period of time, or on a permanent basis. Temporary land tenure may be assigned for a short term (up to three years) or for a long term (from three to ten years). Prolongation of these periods may be granted on application if necessity is shown. Whereas land tenure is allocated to state farms permanently, this right is granted to collective farms "for ever" in order to fulfil a constitutional principle (see for the difference below), though even this strongest type of land tenure cannot be safeguarded against expropriation and other radical acts of land policy.

There is a special, multiphase procedure by which land tenure is allocated. The basis is a decree or decision of the governmental agency which is empowered to dispose of land. The act of assignment, which is somewhat similar to an administrative order, is certified by a separate document which is delivered to the entitled party. The acts of assignment must indicate the purpose for which the land is allocated. Documents issued to a user of agricultural land are called State Deeds of Land Tenure, and those handed to collective farms Deeds Certifying the Right of Perpetual Land Tenure. The provision however to a citizen of the use of a piece of land on which to build a dwelling-house or cottage (*dacha*) is usually incorporated in a contract concluded between the citizen and the allocating communal department of the local soviet. Collective and state farms, collective gardens, orchards and vineyards and other legal entities to whom land has been assigned may, if so empowered, reassign plots of land by way of so-called "secondary allocation" to individual households, families or persons, usually likewise by way of a contract. Such secondary allocations, which may also have both a temporary and a permanent character, are not considered to be acts of disposition (which only the state can carry out) but "acts of internal management".

The third phase of land allocation consists of establishing the physical boundaries of the relevant piece of land, while the last stage is taking possession of the land.

The rules determining the competence of the agency which may assign land depend on the significance and size of the relevant piece of land, on the duration for which the land is assigned, and on special rules laid down in the respective Land Codes and other enactments. In the RSFSR the executive committees of village soviets assign all land in rural areas, except land to collective and state farms and other agricultural users. The executive committees of town soviets or soviets in urbanised settlements may assign all land they administer. The executive committees of district soviets (*raiispolkomy*) may assign land out of the State Land Reserve (see REAL PROPERTY) up to 10 hectares or 24.71 acres or land belonging to State Forest Land (see REAL PROPERTY) by way of "official residences" (see REAL PROPERTY) to labourers and employees working in various branches of the economy, such as transportation, forestry, wood-working industry and fishery. The executive committees of provincial (*oblast'*) and territory (*krai*) soviets and the Councils of Ministers of the autonomous republics in the RSFSR may assign: 1) land out of the State Land Reserve irrespective of the size of the land section; 2) land used by collective farms up to 25 hectares or 61.78 acres; 3) land used by enterprises, state farms and some other organisations up to 50 hectares or 123.55 acres; 4) land out of the State Forest Land up to 25 hectares or 61.78 acres (or 50 hectares of 123.55 acres, depending on the density of the forests) and 5) land sections of every size out of several land categories (see REAL PROPERTY) for purposes of drainage or irrigation, railways, highways, trunk electro-transmission, pipelines and similar purposes. The Council of Ministers of the RSFSR may dispose of land in all other instances. The competences in other constituent republics are distributed among the various agencies in a more or less similar manner.

The governmental agencies are far from free to allot the right of land tenure as they like. The limitations are closely bound up not only with the land policy but also with the division of all land into various categories. Land may not be assigned for purposes going beyond the main purposes for which the respective category was created. Thus, preferably non-agricultural land must be selected for assignment for industrial purposes, house-building, railways, road transportation, trunk pipelines and so on, and if there is no alternative and the need still exists to appropriate agricultural land for such purposes, agricultural land of the poorest quality must be selected. Only by way of an exception may irrigated and drained land be allocated for needs other than agricultural. Similarly, land strips for the erection of power and telephone lines must be selected by choice along the edges of the fields.

Neither may land be allocated to users which perform activities which are inconsistent with the relevant land category. In point of fact, the Land Codes list, for each category, the possible land users, but they refrain from enumerating the land users to whom land may not be allotted. So agricultural land may always be assigned to collective farms. Their land consists of land designated both for the conduct of collective farming and for use by the individual households or families as parts of the collective farms. The latter may use their land for the erection of a dwelling-house and for purposes of private farming and cattle breeding. The maximum size of these private plots varies from 0.50 hectare or 1.24 acre to 0.15 hectare or 0.37 acre. Agricultural land may also be granted to fishery collectives (fishery *kolkhozy*) both for the common fishery industry and for private use by individual households as members of the collective whole.

Agricultural land may furthermore be let on tenure to state farms, whose land is likewise divided for purposes of the collective whole and for use by the individual households or families. The maximum limits mentioned in respect of collective farms also apply to the state farms. Agricultural land may in addition be granted to scientific and teaching institutions, and even to non-agricultural organisations, but only for the conduct of auxiliary farming. Plots of agricultural land may be granted by collective and state farms not only to persons working in the enterprise itself but also to outsiders, such as teachers, physicians and other specialists living down the countryside. Plots of agricultural land may be assigned by any primary land user to persons enjoying pensions by reason of age or invalidity, provided the competent governmental agency agrees. The legal maximum limits of such plots vary, as a general rule, likewise from 0.15 hectare or 0.37 acre to 0.50 hectare or 1.24 acre. Agricultural land may moreover be assigned to collective gardens, orchards and vineyards. These collectives or "societies" are by no means identical with collective farms as they are attached to factories and similar organisations for purposes of improving the living standard of the labourers and white-collar workers of these enterprises. The right of land tenure terminates if the tenant loses his job with his enterprise, unless he is pensioned by reason of age or ill-health. Finally, agricultural land may be allocated to independent farmers, whose number is steadily declining. It is estimated that, at present, there are less than 40,000 of such free peasant's households, the majority of them located in remote and secluded areas. For the rest, the legal regime of these households greatly resembles the private households which are part of a collective farm, except for their managerial independence. The legally established maximum size of such plots of land is, as a general rule, the same: 0.50 hectare or 1.24 acre. In Latvia this limit stands at 1.00 hectare or 2.47 acre for arable land and other fields plus 0.20 hectare or 0.49 acre for the land under and round the peasant's dwelling-house, barns and other constructions.

Land belonging to the category of inhabitated land is let on tenure preferably for purposes of house-building, erection of factories, public utilities, cottages (*dachas*) etc., as well as to private persons for the construction of personal dwellings. The piece of land assigned for the latter purpose may vary from 0.03 hectare or 0.74 acre to 0.12 hectare or 0.3 acre. A remarkable feature of urban land is that land tenure falling into this category need not to be granted to the owner of houses and other buildings who bought or otherwise acquired their property from persons to whom land tenure was granted or their successors. The rule is that conveyance of buildings in towns *ex lege* entails the acquisition of land tenure in respect to the relevant piece of land. The old Roman maxim *solo superficies cedit* operates precisely to the contrary. In all other land categories land tenure does not automatically devolve to the new owner of the buildings erected on the relevant land section. The reason for the exception is apparently that change of ownership in towns is quite a frequent phenomenon and that the issue of acts of assignment of land tenure in each case of a change would entail too much administrative work. In non-urban areas, including urbanised settlement land, the general rule applies that, if land tenure is refused, the new owner of a house is under the obligation to sell it to a person who succeeds in acquiring legitimate title to land or to move it to a place where he is more fortunate. This rule however allows for special consideration if a building is destroyed by fire or another accident: in such cases the right of land tenure is maintained for a period of two years.

Land of the third category (see REAL PROPERTY) may be allotted, as its name already indicates, to factories and other industrial enterprises, transport organisations, spa-resorts and so on. Land belonging to the State Forest Land Fund is let on tenure to forestry departments and enterprises which conduct timber-felling, wood-chopping, timber hauling and other wood-work operations. Land of the State Water Land Fund may be assigned to a wide range of land users, such as factories, agricultural enterprises, fish industries, power generating installations and navigation enterprises. Land placed on the reserve list may, in principle, be allocated to any person, natural or juridical, on a temporary basis or without a time limit, provided the competent governmental agencies so approve.

Land tenure comprises the right to use the relevant piece of land, to sever and collect the fruits and other crops, and to extract sand, gravel and other minerals and material out of the soil up to a limit established by mining law. The legal duties encompass the obligation to use the allocated piece of land rationally, not to use it for a purpose other than for which it was assigned, and to comply with the duties imposed by the specific regulations governing the respective land categories and sub-categories.

Land tenure granted to collective and state farms, and other juridical persons is subject to cancellation or "withdrawal" (*iz''iatie*) in the following instances:

i) if the need to use the land ceases to exist;
ii) if the period which the land was allocated, elapses;
iii) if the state or other socialist organisation is liquidated;
iv) if the necessity for expropriation of the relevant piece of land arises;
v) if the land is not put into use within two or three years (depending on the specific

requirements of the law);
vi) if the land is used for purposes other than for which the land tenure was granted.

Land tenure assigned to individual persons is subject to cancellation or withdrawal:
i) if the relevant piece of land is voluntarily abandoned;
ii) if the period for which the land was allocated, elapses;
iii) if all members of an individual household of a collective farm have moved permanently;
iv) if all members of such a household die;
v) if the labour contract on the basis of which land tenure was allocated, comes to an end;
vi) if a piece of land is designated to be expropriated;
vii) if the land user made use of the land in a way repugnant to the fundamental rules of Land Law. The latter is certainly the case if land is used to obtain unearned income. As Soviet literature indicates, a steady struggle is being waged against unauthorised and arbitrary appropriation of land. However, since such seizure is legally null and void, a formal act of withdrawal of land tenure is superfluous and out of order.

Withdrawal of land tenure in the case of expropriation is, in principle, effected by the Council of Ministers of the Union republics, but in cases of minor importance, for example, when houses are to be built according to authorised city or regional development-schemes, the executive committees of the local soviets are competent to do so. The courts never step in. Special rules protect, at least in theory, land allocated to collective farms for use in perpetuity. First, there must be an absolute and proved necessity for the expropriation and, secondly, the general assembly of the kolkhoz-members or the assembly of their plenipotentiaries must consent. The rules concerning compensation for expropriation are of quite a different character to the traditional rules since land is assigned, as a matter of principle, free of charge, and consequently withdrawal can basically be carried out without compensation. Nonetheless, expropriation causes in many cases losses surpassing the mere loss of a gratuitous right. The law therefore provides that compensation may be paid out, for example, for the costs spent on the improvement of the quality of the soil, including the opening up of new land, for the crop and seeds sown, or the houses and other buildings if these were expropriated together with the right of land tenure. If the house can be transferred elsewhere then the costs of such an operation may be paid. In other instances the costs of the construction of a new house may be refunded. But indemnification may also be granted by way of allocating the right to use another plot of land, or, in towns, by allocating living space. It is worth noting that some local enactments do not prevent the compensation of the house-owner and the lessee on the same basis: by allotting them a house by way of ownership or a lease, in both cases at the authorities' free choice. Compensation must be paid by the party in whose interest the expropriation was effected.

The rigorous restraint of land tenure to confined purposes requires in point of fact a stringent supervision by the authorities over how land is being used. This control is exercised by a large variety of governmental agencies, ranging from the executives of local soviets to special supervisory bodies and Ministries. These agencies are bound to see to it that every land user, including ministerial departments, state enterprises, collective farms and private citizens, uses the land according to the specifically designated purpose of the relevant category and sub-category of land and fully observes the rules aimed at the optimum use of land.

Th. Vondracek

LAND TITLES,
see LAND REGISTRATION

LANGUAGE

In a multilingual state, such as the Soviet Union, the linguistic situation has to some extent to be taken into account by the legal system. The most important measure taken in this respect is the territorial division of the country according to nationality (*q.v.*). Since a common language is one of the chief components in defining a nation, this division creates the basic framework for a natural development of national languages.

However, these nationally defined areas are united within one centralized state-system, and this inevitably leads to the occurence of linguistic minorities on the territories of larger linguistic groups. The legal system will have to reckon with this factor too. A great variety of approaches have been adopted in this respect, in response to a larger number of diverse situations.

With regard to federal legislation, the USSR Constitution prescribes the publication of USSR enactments in the languages of the fifteen Union republics. The constitutions of some Union republics prescribe the publication of republican enactments in the national language (the RSFSR, the Ukraine, Uzbekistan, Georgia, Azerbaidzhan and Armenia), other constitutions require publication in Russian as well (Belorussia, Kazakhstan, Lithuania, Latvia, Estonia, Moldavia and Kirgizia); Turkmenia and Tadzhikistan publish their enactments, according to their constitutions, in four languages. All autonomous republics within the RSFSR use Russian along with their national language in legislation; in several cases the constitutions of autonomous republics provide for more than two legislative languages (e.g. the Dagestan autonomous republic is compelled by its constitution to use no less than nine languages in publishing its laws).

There are far fewer rules concerning the use of languages in the administration. The constitutions of Georgia, Azerbaidzhan, Armenia and the autonomous republics of Kabardino-Balkaria and Nakhichevan provide, along with a national language, the right of national minorities on their territory to use their own national language in dealings with the administration.

Most attention is paid to use of minority languages in the courts and—more generally —in all legal procedure. The basic rule is contained in art. 110 of the USSR Constitution which provides that court cases are conducted in the language of the Union republic, autonomous republic, or autonomous province, guaranteeing at the same time full knowledge of the materials of the case, through the aid of an enterpreter, to any person not knowing the language of the court, together with the right to use his native language in court. On the basis of art. 110 the constitutions of Union republics and autonomous republics lay down which languages are to be considered as official court languages in their respective republics; the codes of civil and criminal procedure of the Union republics contain more detailed rules about the position and rights of persons who do not master the language of the court and about the position of interpreters. Art. 110 of the USSR Constitution is repeated in art. 114 of the RSFSR Constitution, with the addition of national *okrugs*.

With regard to court languages, the various constitutions display several basic patterns. Some republics recognize only one official court language; this is the case in the RSFSR (excluding all autonomous territorial units), the Ukraine, Belorussia, Georgia (excluding autonomous territorial units), the three Baltic republics and the Adzharian autonomous republic (official language: Georgian). Other republics recognize two or more languages as official court languages (e.g. Moldavia and a number of autonomous republics). In a third group of republics, along with one or more official court language, particular minority languages are recognized as official court languages in areas where such minorities dominate; this is the case in Armenia and Azerbaidzhan, in the Central Asian republics and in a number of autonomous republics. E.g. the official court language of the Kirgiz republic is Kirgiz, but it is also Russian and Uzbek in areas where the majority of the population speaks Russian or Uzbek.

The most important provisions of the codes of criminal procedure concerning the use of languages are those regarding the position of the defendant. All procedural documents to be presented to the defendant are translated for him into his native language or into another language mastered by him (art. 17, Code of Criminal Procedure RSFSR). The appointment of defence counsel is mandatory in all cases where the defendant has not mastered the language of the court (art. 49 of the same code).

F. J. M. Feldbrugge

See also ADMINISTRATION OF JUSTICE; COURTS; DEFENDANT

LARCENY, see THEFT

LAW

Prior to 1938, there was no one official or semi-official definition of law to which all published Soviet legal writings were required to adhere, although the concepts of law developed by Evgenii Pashukanis generally predominated (see JURISPRUDENCE). With the denunciation and overthrow of Pashukanis by Andrei Vyshinsky, the latter's definition of law, adopted by a conference of legal theorists in July 1938, became a virtual canon which was repeated slavishly until the late 1950's and is to be found almost verbatim in the 1956 Legal Encyclopedia edited by P. I. Kudriavtsev. Vyshinsky's definition was:

"Law is the aggregate of rules of conduct expressing the will of the ruling class and established by legislation, and of customs and rules of community life sanctioned by the state authority, the application of which aggregate of rules is secured by state coercion in order to protect, consolidate, and develop social relations and a social order beneficial and desirable for the ruling class."

In Vyshinsky's 1938 book *Soviet Public Law*, this definition of law immediately preceded the following definition of *Soviet* law:

"Soviet law is the aggregate of the rules of conduct established in the form of legislation by the authority of the toilers and expressing their will. The effective operation of these rules is guaranteed by the entire coercive force of the socialist state in order to protect, consolidate, and develop relations and arrangements advantageous and desirable for the toilers, and decisively to annihilate capitalism and its survivals in the economic system, in the way of life and in human consciousness—to build a communist society."

It will be noticed that in the definition of Soviet law the reference to customs and rules of community life was omitted, although their presence as sources of law—provided they are sanctioned by the state—were conceded elsewhere (see CUSTOMARY LAW). More important, the toilers, that is, workers, peasants, and the toiling intelligentsia, were identified as the rulers whose will is expressed by socialist law. Nevertheless, the coercive power of the socialist state was considered to be required in order to annihilate elements of capitalism—and presumably also supporters of capitalism—surviving in socialist society as well as in other countries.

In the late 1950's, and especially after the 22nd Communist Party Congress in 1961, Vyshinsky came under attack and his definition of law lost its authoritative force. No single new definition replaced it. In an article on Law in the 1965 Encyclopedic Dictionary of Legal Knowledge the following definition is given:

"Law is a system of generally binding norms guaranteed by the state and expressing the will of the ruling class of the state, but after the victory of socialism the will of the whole people. It appears as a class regulator of social relations."

"The necessity of law is connected first of all with social regulation . . ."

In elaborating this definition, the author distinguishes five general characteristics of law: 1) it is a system of norms, that is, the norms of law comprise in their totality a single mechanism of regulation (see LEGAL SYSTEM; 2) the norms are generally binding, that is, they are obligatory for all who fall within the sphere of their operation; 3) the system of norms is guaranteed by the state, that is, in the words of Lenin, "Law is nothing without an apparatus able to compel observance of the norms of law"; 4) the system of norms expresses the will of the state, that is, of the ruling class or, under socialism, of the whole people; and 5) the system of norms acts as a class regulator of social relations—under socialism, as a regulator of relations among friendly, non-antagonistic classes for the purpose of liquidating the remaining traces of the previous exploitative society.

According to official or semi-official Soviet legal theory, reflected in the 1965 article referred to above, both the need for law and its specific features are determined, in the last analysis, by the material conditions (the economic base) of the given society. At the same time, law, like other parts of the superstructure, has a "relative independence" which is expressed chiefly in its "reverse influence on the economic base". Thus law serves to strengthen prevailing social relations and to facilitate their development in accordance with the requirements of the economic base, as well as to overcome social relationships which do not correspond to those requirements.

According to the 1965 Encyclopedia, various types of class structures have existed in the history of society, to each of which corresponds a particular type of law, namely, slave-holding law, feudal law, bourgeois law, and finally socialist law. All types of law except socialist law are said to rest upon private ownership of the means of production, exploitation of man by man, and oppression of the majority by the minority. Socialist law is said to represent a qualitatively new historical type of law founded on social ownership of the means of production, annihilation of the exploitation of man by man, expression of the will of the majority, and genuine democracy and humanism. Socialist law, it is said, has a more creative role than non-socialist law. Furthermore, a specific feature of socialist law is said to be the fact that the operation of legal norms is supported by the force of their moral authority and by the communist consciousness of citizens, who are convinced of the reasonableness and purposefulness of the norms. "Hence the possibility of state coercion is not the chief means for securing their operation."

Two stages in the development of (Soviet) socialist law are distinguished: the period of transition to socialism, which is characterized by proletarian law (dictatorship of the proletariat), and the period after the annihilation of exploiting classes, when proletarian law is gradually transformed into all-people's law. The Soviet Union is said to have achieved the second stage, especially after the Communist Party took measures to liquidate the consequences of the cult of personality of Stalin, which (it is stated) to a certain degree had retarded the process of the transformation of Soviet law into an all-people's law. These measures "brought a restoration of the Leninist principles of socialist legality, a further development of the democratic content of Soviet law and of the elements of socialist humanism embodied in it".

The 1965 article emphasizes the significance of the 22nd Party Congress and the new

Party Program for the development of codification and the preparation of a draft of a new USSR Constitution, and concludes with a reference to the 1964 decree of the Central Committee of the CPSU "On Measures for the Further Development of Legal Science and the Improvement of Legal Education in the Country".

Soviet writings on the general subject "Law", such as the 1965 article summarized above, reflect certain distinctive features of Soviet legal thought. In the first place, it is assumed by Soviet writers that their possession of the truths of Marxist-Leninist theory gives them correct insights into the nature of law in all societies whereas, by the same token, "bourgeois" jurists (unless they are in possession of the same truths) will fail to understand the nature not only of Soviet law but also of their own legal systems.

Second, Soviet writings on law tend to minimize differences among the various "bourgeois" legal systems. French, German, Scandinavian, English, American, Japanese, and many other systems of law are all lumped together as "capitalist". This is also reflected in the organization of the study of comparative law in Soviet research institutes and universities, where typically individual scholars are assigned such themes as "Labour Law of Bourgeois States", "Constitutional Law of Bourgeois States", etc., rather than a particular foreign legal system as a whole.

Third, Soviet definitions and concepts of law reflect a complex attitude toward the relationship between socialist and non-socialist law. On the one hand, a single set of concepts is sought to cover law in all societies. On the other hand, a very sharp contrast is drawn between socialist and non-socialist law. It is also to be noted that Soviet law is assimilated to the legal systems of the other socialist states that have emerged since World War II.

Fourth, Soviet law is conceived as developing in certain historical stages. In this connection it is noteworthy that the 1965 article, referred to above, did not see fit to mention the accepted theory of the dying out of law in the final historical stage, namely, under full communism. At the same time, it treated the period of the cult of personality of Stalinism as having had a negative effect upon the transition from proletarian law to all-people's law—whereas in that period itself Vyshinsky had stressed the socialist character of Soviet law, and its expression of the will of the toilers, "from the first days of the October Revolution". Thus the definition of law as developing in stages has immediate political implications. It is characteristic for Soviet writings on the concept of law to draw illustrations, as the 1965 article does, from the latest policies of the Communist Party.

Fifth, the source of obedience to law in the Soviet Union is found in state coercion, on the one hand, and morality and social consciousness on the other, with first place now being assigned to morality and social consciousness while in an earlier time first place was assigned to state coercion. These concepts, too, have immediate political implications.

Sixth, in stressing the relative independence of law from the economic base, its creative role, its importance under socialism as an instrument of democracy and humanism, etc., Soviet jurists seem to be attempting to enhance the influence of law in Soviet society and to emphasize its role in securing justice and protecting people against arbitrariness.

Sources of law

Soviet writers state that in the early stages of the development of law in exploiting states, the most widespread source of law was custom; that in England and the United States, judicial precedent is a widespread source of law; that in the first stage of bourgeois law there was proclaimed the supremacy of statutes adopted by Parliament;

and that in the period of imperialism, a more and more prominent place among sources of law is taken by acts of the executive authority.

In Soviet law, statutes (*zakony*) are said to occupy the leading role among sources of law. Decrees (*ukazy*) of the Presidium of the Supreme Soviet of the USSR and of the presidia of the republican supreme soviets, providing that they have normative content, are also sources of law. Moreover, normative decrees (*postanovleniia*) and regulations (*rasporiazheniia*) of the Council of Ministers of the USSR and of the councils of ministers, as well as normative orders (*prikazy*) and instructions (*instruktsii*) of ministers and presidents of state committees and normative decisions (*resheniia*) and regulations (*rasporiazheniia*) of local soviets and their executive committees—are classified as legislation (*zakonodatel'stvo*) and are sources of law. In addition, acts (*akty*) of social organizations (e.g., decisions of the All-Union Central Council of Trade Unions), their charters (e.g., the charter of a collective farm), and collective agreements concluded by factory committees and the managements of enterprises are also said to be sources of law insofar as they are sanctioned by the state. In speaking of acts of social organizations, which are said to have increasing importance as a source of law, Soviet jurists generally neglect to mention acts of the Communist Party, which is, however, the most important social organization in the USSR and whose members are, according to the Constitution, the leading core of all other social organizations as well as all state organizations. In the past, decrees were often issued jointly by the Central Committee of the Communist Party and the Council of Ministers of the USSR. In more recent years Central Committee decrees and resolutions, although not issued jointly with government bodies, often from the basis of statutes enacted by the Supreme Soviet as well as of administrative decrees issued by the Council of Ministers. Moreover, campaigns launched by the Communist Party have an important influence on judicial policy; if, for example, there is a Party campaign against theft of state property or against drunkenness at work, prosecutions for such offenses are apt to increase in number and sentences of courts are apt to be more severe. Although greatest stress is laid upon legislation as a source of law, sometimes to the exclusion of all other sources, both practice and theory also reflect the belief that other sources of law also exist, and especially such traditional sources as custom, equity, and judicial decision (see CUSTOMARY LAW; PRECEDENT).

Rules of socialist community life
(pravila sotsialisticheskogo obshchezhitiia)
Although rules of socialist community life are not generally listed by Soviet writers as a source of law, nevertheless Art. 5 of the Principles of Civil Law provides that in realizing rights and executing duties citizens and organizations must observe the laws and must respect the rules of socialist community life and the moral principles of a society that is constructing communism. The rules of socialist community life are sometimes reflected in express norms of positive law but are also found in the form of non-legal social norms. Examples of the latter are standards of care (simple and gross negligence) by which civil liability may be tested, misconduct of a co-tenant giving rise to liability to eviction, misconduct of a person on probation, etc. Among the rules of socialist community life are such principles of morality as "all for one and one for all", "man is the highest value", etc. The basis of rules of socialist community life is said to be the policy of the Communist Party of the Soviet Union, directed toward the construction of communism and reflected in the principles of the "Moral Code of the Builder of Communism".

Educational role of law

Soviet law has always placed great emphasis, both in theory and in practice, upon the educational role of law. Art. 3 of the USSR Principles of Court Organizations, under the heading "Tasks of the Court", provides: "By all its activity a court shall educate the citizens of the USSR in the spirit of loyalty to the Motherland and to the cause of communism, and in the spirit of exact and undeviating execution of Soviet laws, of a protective attitude toward socialist property, of observance of labour discipline, of an honourable attitude toward state and social duty, and of respect for the rights, honour, and dignity of citizens and for rules of socialist community life." Such tasks are intended not only to educate the parties to judicial proceedings but also the spectators in the courtroom and persons outside the courtroom. In addition, it is not only through judicial procedure that Soviet law is supposed to educate but also through other types of legal procedure and through substantive legal norms as well.

The educational role of law is stressed in the law-enforcement activity of social organizations such as comrades' courts and people's guards, and it is stressed also in the work of *arbitrazh*.

Theoretically, the educational role of Soviet law is intended to facilitate the internalization of legal norms and procedures and ultimately the dying out of official law and its replacement by social consciousness. Practically, the educational role of law is intended to implement Soviet legal policies by the exertion of social influence (*vliianie*) and social pressure (*vozdeistvie*) upon Soviet citizens in order to guide and train them to conform to the standards of communist morality.

Harold J. Berman

See also CUSTOMARY LAW; JURISPRUDENCE; COMMUNIST PARTY; LEGAL SYSTEM; LEGISLATION; RULES OF SOCIALIST COMMUNITY LIFE

LAW ENFORCEMENT, see POLICE

LAW REFORM,
see CODES & CODIFICATION

LAW REVIEWS, see PERIODICALS

LAW SCHOOLS,
see LEGAL EDUCATION

LAWYERS

The main professional groups among Soviet lawyers are judges (see COURTS), members of the *Prokuratura* (see PROCURACY), notaries (*q.v.*), advocates, and legal advisers (jurisconsults); see also LEGAL PROFESSION.

Advocates

The rights and duties of advocates in civil and criminal procedure are discussed under the appropriate headings (see DEFENCE; PARTIES; REPRESENTATION). The professional organization and general legal position of advocates is regulated by the Statute on the Advocacy of the RSFSR of July 25, 1962.

After the reintroduction of ministries of justice in 1970-1971, the entire profession has been brought under the control and competence of the Ministry of Justice of the USSR (*q.v.*), the subordinate ministries of justice of the Union republics and, at lower levels, the justice departments of the provincial executive committees. The basic organizational unit is the provincial (*oblast'*) collegium or Bar. The provincial Bar consists of all lawyers admitted to practise law in the province. Only persons with an academic degree in law can be admitted as advocates after having worked as a lawyer for at least two years or after an apprenticeship in an advocate's office for at least six months. In exceptional cases persons without a law degree may be admitted as advocates if they have worked for at least five years as a legal specialist. Admission is granted by the presidium of the provincial Bar; the executive committee of the provincial soviet (or a corresponding agency, such as the Council of Ministers of an autonomous republic) may veto the admission. An advocate may be disbarred by the presidium of the provincial Bar or by the provincial executive committee as a penalty for serious professional misconduct (the commission of a crime, the receiving of fees otherwise than through the established channels, behaviour unworthy of the calling of a Soviet advocate) and for obvious incompetence.

The general meeting is the supreme organ of the provincial Bar. Its chief tasks are the election of a presidium and the establishment of internal rules. The chief tasks of the presidium are the organization of law offices, the appointment of heads of law offices (these appointments must be approved by the provincial executive committees), the general administrative and financial organization of the provincial Bar and the admission of new advocates. The provincial Bar is a juristic person.

The nucleus of the advocate's profession is the law office. The head of the office distributes the work among the advocates attached to the office. The number of advocates in a law office is determined by the presidium of the provincial Bar. The head of the law office fixes the salaries of the lawyers working in the office according to the tariffs set out in a special instruction. This Instruction (a decree of the Council of Ministers of the RSFSR of February 14, 1966) enumerates the various kinds of fees which may be charged by lawyers. A number of services must be provided free of charge (minor information given orally, representation in alimony and labour cases, etc.). There are five categories of fees: a) for drafting legal documents and providing legal advice in complex cases, b) for representation in criminal cases, c) for representation in civil and administrative cases, d) for legal services rendered to enterprises, institutions, sokhozes, kolkhozes, and other organizations, e) for travelling.

Advocates do not have a monopoly of representation in criminal and civil cases (cf. arts. 47 of the Code of Criminal Procedure and 44 of the Code of Civil procedure). Certain representatives of organizations also have the right to appear in court (in civil and criminal cases) for the party in a civil suit or for the defendant in a criminal case. Representation by persons other than advocates, however, seems to be an exception. As elsewhere, representation in court is by no means the only task of the advocate. The Statute also makes mention of legal advice and information, the drawing up of all kinds of legal documents at the request of citizens, enterprises, organizations, etc., representation of enterprises, kolkhozes, institutions and organizations in arbitration proceedings (see ARBITRATION) and other legal services to enterprises, kolkhozes, institutions and organizations.

With regard to the duties of the individual advocate, the Statute lays down that he is bound to employ any means provided by law in order to protect the rights and lawful interests of his client. Ad advocate is not allowed to withdraw from a criminal case once he has assumed the representation of a defendant. He may not be questioned as a witness concerning information which he has acquired in the course of his work as defence counsel. He is not allowed to divulge information acquired from his client in the course of his work as his client's representative in a given case. Lawyer's fees are paid by the client according to the aforementioned tariffs through the law office to which the lawyer is attached. Advocates enjoy the normal pension and disability benefits. Ad-

vocates may not be in the employment of others than their law office. An exception may be made by the provincial Bar presidium for part-time teaching and academic work. Awards may be granted, and disciplinary penalties imposed, by the provincial Bar presidium. Advocates may appeal against disciplinary measures to the provincial executive committee.
Representation of foreign citizens and corporate interests in Soviet courts is entrusted to *Iniurkollegiia* (*inostrannaia iuridicheskaia kollegiia* = foreign legal collegium), an office set up by the Moscow City Bar (March 26, 1937). *Iniurkollegiia* also represents Soviet citizens and organizations abroad, in civil cases, through their foreign counterparts (usually local lawyers). *Iniurkollegiia* is a juristic person.

Jurisconsults
The position of legal advisers or jurisconsults of enterprises, government agencies and other organizations is regulated by a Model Statute of March 29, 1963. According to this Statute, the functions of the jurisconsult include a variety of legal services rendered to the employer: the drafting of internal rules and orders, legal advice in commercial affairs, the drafting of contracts and other documents, representation of the enterprises (etc.) in court and arbitration proceedings, etc.
The jurisconsult is bound to refuse representation of his employer in court or arbitration proceedings if he is convinced that his employer has no case either as plaintiff or as defendant. Only persons with a law degree may be employed as jurisconsults (with the same exception as is made for advocates). The jurisconsult may not be employed for other work by the enterprise. Generally speaking, the position and functions of the jurisconsult resemble those of the advocate, the main difference being that the jurisconsult is in the employment of an enterprise, government agency or other organization. Jurisconsults and legal departments in enterprises and organizations come within the competence of the Ministry of Justice of the USSR (and subordinate ministries of justice of the Union republics) insofar as the professional aspects of their work are concerned.

F. J. M. Feldbrugge

See also COURTS; NOTARIES; PROCURACY

LAY JUDGES,
see PEOPLE'S ASSESSORS

LEASES
The state, collective farms, other co-operatives and citizens (as owners) and socialist, i.e. state or public, organisations (as having operational management) may lend or lease property to any juridical person or citizen. Contracts of lease or hire between socialist organisations are encouraged as promoting the economic use of resources, but are circumscribed by the powers of the organisations involved and the planning orders directed to them. Citizens, in leasing out their own property, may not use such arrangements as a source of unearned income. Objects in the exclusive ownership of the state may be leased only as permitted by All-Union legislation. The leasing of agricultural land is specifically prohibited. Productive enterprises may lease land set aside for transport and communications in order to build access roads; such leaves may not be for payment. There are specialist lending stations for machinery, industrial and agricultural transport, passenger-cars, films, theatrical costumes, sporting equipment, musical instruments, etc. Local housing boards lease living accommodation (see HOUSING) to citizens and the executive committees of local soviets manage stores that hire out articles of domestic use (sewing machines, vacuum cleaners, etc.).
General conditions for the lease of property

are laid down in the Civil Codes of the Union republics (arts. 275-294 of the RSFSR Code), but model contracts governing the hire of domestic articles etc., and planning orders directed at state enterprises and hiring organisations impose additional conditions. Most leases and hiring contracts are therefore partly dictated from above. Departure from the terms of a model contract for the hire of domestic articles, if it restricts the right of the user, leads to invalidity.

The Civil Codes provide that all contracts of hire between socialist organisations and between such organisations and citizens must be in writing, so must contracts between citizens for a term of more than one year. In the hire of domestic and cultural articles, the issue of a receipt-docket is deemed sufficient, unless the article is worth more than 50 roubles.

The Codes require the lender/lessor to supply the property in a condition that conforms to the terms of the contract and the purpose envisaged and the hirer/lessee to use it accordingly and maintain it in good condition. Failure to supply the contracted property includes attempting to supply it other than at the agreed time and renders the lessor/lender liable for losses suffered as a result of non-supply. The lessor/lender must carry out capital repairs on the property leased (the extent of repairs varying according to the nature of the property and to the agreement between the parties). He is liable for loss caused by failure to repair, to rescission of the contract or to reimbursement for repairs carried out by the lessee. He is also liable for known or knowable defects, unless he is protected by a term of the agreement. The lessee has a duty to carry out current repairs, unless the parties have otherwise provided by agreement. Sub-leasing is permitted with the consent of the lessor except in the hire of domestic articles; the sale of property under hire does not extinguish the rights of the hirer.

Under the Civil Codes, no hire may exceed ten years. Leases for buildings and non-residential accommodation where the parties are the state, co-operatives and/or public organisations must not exceed five years; the hire of equipment and other property must not exceed one year. These periods may be further reduced, in specific cases, by model contracts or planning orders. If no term is indicated in the contract, the contract may be terminated by either party at any time on one month's notice (for leases of buildings, the required notice is three months). Where the lease stipulates no period or a period longer than that permitted and notice to terminate has not been given, the contract is deemed to have been made for the maximum period allowable by law, planning orders or model contracts. Where the hirer continues to use the property at the expiration of the contract without objection from the lender, the contract is deemed renewed for an indefinite period and subject to notice as aforesaid, but this does not apply to hire between the state, co-operative and public organisations or to contracts between socialist organisations and citizens for domestic articles, which must be renewed by a new written agreement; until this is done, the use of property has no legal effect. The hire of passenger-cars is renewed automatically in the absence of protest and for the equivalent period of the prior hire.

State, co-operative and public organisations, having properly performed their duties under a contract of hire or lease where another organisation or citizen is lender/lessor, have a preferential right to renewal as against other persons. The right may depend on a renewal of an administrative order. Any preferential right by citizens depends on special legislation or model contracts.

A. E.-S. Tay

LEGAL ASSISTANCE,
see PRIVATE INTERNATIONAL LAW

LEGAL EDUCATION

Legal education under the Soviets went through a complicated evolution.

After the October Revolution, higher education was reorganized first by the Rules for Admission to the Institutions of Higher Learning of August 2, 1918, which opened the doors of these institutions to labourers and their children without the requirement of a preceding secondary-school education and free of any costs. To compensate for the lacking secondary education, *rabfak's* (workers' faculties) were created and attached to faculties of institutions of higher learning. The number of *rabfak's* grew steadily, but at the end of the thirties they were liquidated with the development of secondary education.

Higher Legal Education: The old law faculties of the universities were abrogated and replaced by "Faculties of Public Sciences" by Decree of the People's Commissariat of Education of March 1919. The following subjects were taught at the legal-political department of the Faculty of Public Sciences: history of law and state; evolution of political and juridical thought; public laws of the Soviet Republic; social law; criminal sociology and politics; labour law and social policy; history of international relations and international law; social hygiene and sanitation. Thus, such basic subjects of legal education as criminal and civil law and criminal and civil procedure were not taught at institutions of higher learning. This is because criminal and civil codes and criminal and civil procedure codes did not exist between 1917 and 1922: the Tsarist codes were abrogated and new codes published as late as 1922-23. Admission of children of the former bourgeoisie and intelligentsia to institutions of higher learning was terminated in the autumn of 1921. Only persons of proletarian or peasant origin were accepted. These restrictions were abolished gradually and completely as of 1935. The Faculties of Public Sciences gradually disappeared in the twenties and were replaced by faculties of law and ethnology at some universities. Also, Law Institutes were created. However, the law-teaching syllabus was greatly influenced by the doctrine of the leading jurists in the twenties and beginning of the thirties: especially prominent among them was E. B. Pashukanis. Departing from the teaching of Marx-Engels-Lenin about the "withering away" of state and law under socialism, Pashukanis denied the possibility of a proletarian or socialist law system. He thought that law is an attribute of capitalism and must vanish together with it. Another eminent jurist of that time, A. Goikhbarg, was of the opinion that anti-law propaganda is even more urgent than anti-religious propaganda. As a consequence of such opinions, courses on civil law were dropped and this subject disappeared from textbooks and was replaced by the "economic law" created by Pashukanis. Since Stalin asserted that the state does not "wither away", but disappears abruptly at the peak of its development when communism is established, A. Ia. Vyshinsky, the legal prophet during the period of the "cult of personality", accused Pashukanis of treason, and Pashukanis paid with his life for the negation of the possibility of a socialist law system. Civil law was reinstated in the syllabus.

As of 1935, higher legal education was provided at the Law Institutes of Moscow, Leningrad, Saratov, Kazan', Sverdlovsk, Minsk, Khar'kov and Tashkent, and by Law Faculties of the Universities of Baku, Tbilisi and Yerevan. A decision of the Central Executive Committee and the Council of People's Commissars of March 1935 recognized the inadequacy of higher legal education and of the number of facilities for the completion of such an education. The majority of judges, prosecutors, investigating magistrates and advocates were not in possession of a higher legal education at that time.

World War II had a devastating effect on legal education. Many institutions had to close, not having been evacuated in time. From 5,900 students of law in 1940, the number decreased to 2,732 in 1941 and to 960 in 1942. Post-graduate students almost disappeared. Scores of university and institute buildings were destroyed. But, beginning with 1943, the evacuated institutions started to return to the places of their previous activity. There were already 6,550 law students in 1945.

The Contemporary Situation: At the present time, two kinds of institution provide higher legal education: law faculties of universities, and law institutes. All the universities in the 15 capitals of the Union Republics have law faculties. Eleven other universities in large industrial cities also have faculties of law (Irkutsk, Kaliningrad, Kazan', Leningrad, L'vov, Odessa, Perm, Rostov, Tomsk, Vladivostok, Voronezh). Law institutes are located in Saratov, Sverdlovsk and Khar'kov, and Moscow has the All-Union Law Institute Teaching by Correspondence. Their syllabuses were worked out by the USSR Ministry of Higher and Secondary Special Education in 1959. The subjects are divided into two categories: social and economic, and legal. Obligatory in the first group are national economy, history of the Soviet Union, history of the Communist Party, dialectical and historical materialism. The study of Marxist-Leninist ethics and aesthetics, and of scientific atheism, is optional. About 15% of study hours is allocated to this category. To the second category belong Soviet law, international law, state laws of the other socialist republics and bourgeois countries. Some related topics, such as forensic medicine and psychiatry, court statistics, fundamentals of Roman Law, literature and one foreign language are also taught. The individual subjects of Soviet law comprise: history of the Soviet state and law, including the history of state and law of other countries; history of political doctrine; Soviet Constitutional law; Soviet administrative Constitutional law; Soviet administrative law; Soviet Land Law; Soviet finance law; Soviet civil law; Soviet family law; Soviet labour law; kolkhoz law; Soviet criminal law; Soviet criminal procedure; Soviet civil procedure; organization of courts and the Procuracy in the USSR and the Union republics and prosecution supervision. The syllabus is obligatory for all universities teaching law and is divided into 10 terms or 5 years of study. The curriculum of law institutes differs somewhat from the university syllabus, putting more stress on the study of practical topics such as criminal and civil law and procedure. It is divided into 8 terms of four years of study.

Admission: Admitted are persons of both sexes in possession of a complete secondary education, not older than 35 years, with two years of practical work in production before admission, and who have successfully passed the entrance examinations in: Russian language and literature (oral and written) or the local language, if studies are conducted in that language; history of the USSR (oral); and a foreign language (English, French or German). Admission is competitive; candidates with the best marks in their secondary schools and at the entrance examinations are accepted. Not only is study free, but more than 80% of university students and all successful law-institute students receive a grant. Out-of-town students live in dormitories and have to pay a rent (30-50% of the stipend). The amount of the stipend is increased 25% if the mark in all the examinations is "excellent". Important scholarships are awarded to the most successful students. Food and soft drinks can be bought by students at the cafetaria of the institutions at reduced prices. The passing of a state examination in the history of the Communist Party, civil and criminal laws, and one selected special subject—i.e. constitutional or administrative law, criminal or civil procedure —is obligatory.

Postgraduate Studies (*aspirantura*) are open to persons not older than 35 years, who have completed higher education and two years of practical work after graduation (exceptions from the last requirement are possible). To be admitted to postgraduate study, the candidate must pass a competitive examination in three subjects: in the optional special subject, in the history of the USSR Communist Party, and in one of the European languages. A paper on the candidate's special subject must be presented before the examinations. During the postgraduate studies, which last three years (four if he studies by correspondence or in an evening course), under the supervision of a Professor or Doctor of Law the aspirant has to pass examinations in dialectical and historical materialism, a foreign language, and his special subject. A certain amount of teaching experience is also required. Then a term is set for the presentation of a dissertation, and the public defence of it. Two academic degrees were created in 1934: "Candidate of Legal Sciences" and "Doctor of Legal Sciences". The successful passing of the examinations and the defence of the thesis earn for the aspirant the degree of "Candidate of Legal Sciences". The degree of "Doctor of Legal Sciences" is conferred on scholars having to their credit important achievements in a certain field of legal studies. The doctoral dissertation must be a scientific work of high quality, and is publicly defended.

Legal Education by Correspondonce and Evening Courses. Legal education can be obtained also by correspondence and in evening courses without absence from work. An Office for Teaching by Correspondence was established at the University of Moscow in 1927, and reorganized in 1931 into the Central Courses in Soviet Law of the Institute of Soviet Law in Moscow. Two years later, the Central Courses became the Central Institute of Soviet Law Teaching by Correspondence and finally, in 1937, these became the All-Union Institute of Soviet Law Teaching by Correspondence. Branches of this Institute were set up in many cities, especially where no institutions of higher learning existed. In cities where such institutions did exist, the branches were integrated into the departments for teaching by correspondence of these institutions. The syllabus and examinations are the same as for regular students. For doing special work in connection with their studies, and for taking examinations, the students learning by correspondence receive paid leave from their jobs. The employer also has the obligation to contribute 50% of the round-trip costs of the student to the teaching institution and back to the place of work.

The opportunity to acquire a legal education is also given by evening courses. These were created at law institutes and universities in the fifties. The programme and examinations are the same as for regular courses. In evening courses, the student retains the privilege of personal contact with his teachers, which the student learning by correspondence does not enjoy. Law studies without absence from work expanded greatly during the fifties. According to Soviet writers, there is no city or inhabited place in the USSR where it is not possible to get a higher legal education without absence from production; there are 4.5 times as many students learning by correspondence, or in evening courses as there are regular students.

Secondary Legal Education: Between 1935 and 1965, it was also possible to acquire a secondary legal education. Secondary Law Schools were opened in 1935, with a curriculum spread over one year of studies. In 1939, another study year was added. The purpose was to prepare judges and prosecutors for their jobs. It was evident, however, that a higher legal education was needed for these officials; so part of the system of secondary law schools was closed in 1954, and the rest was liquidated in 1956.

Conclusion: Education by correspondence and in evening courses is a mass production of specialists. Institutions engaged in this kind of teaching have many thousands of students, and cannot pay the necessary attention to every one of them. This kind of study is less expensive for the state and does not take students away from production, which is very important in the USSR; but the students learning without absence from work cannot stand at the same educational level as their colleagues studying regularly at lectures and seminars. Quality is certainly sacrified for quantity. Complaints about the inadequacy of legal education were formulated in such high places as the Central Committee of the Communist Party and the Council of Ministers, and are constantly repeated in the pages of the press and of legal periodicals. Furthermore, even this mass production is insufficient to fill the need for jurists in legal and administrative fields—and this in spite of the fact that higher legal education is not mandatory for all persons engaged in the administration of justice. *Samuel Kucherov*

Bibl.: Samuel Kucherov, The Organs of Soviet Administration of Justice: Their History and Operation, 1970; A. F. Shebanov, *Iuridicheskie vysshie uchebnye zavedeniia,* 1963.

LEGAL HISTORY, ARMENIA

The political history of Armenia shows the continuous struggle of its people with Persians, Romans, Greeks, Arabs, Turks and Russians, who have ruled and divided their land. Nevertheless, the Armenians managed to retain considerable autonomy and, in some periods, political independence also.

The legal history of Armenia can be divided into three periods: 1) the period of the Armenian kingdoms, 7th century B.C. till 19th century; 2) the period of the conquest of Armenia by Tsarist Russia, 19th-20th century; 3) the period of Soviet rule in Armenia, 1920-1970.

The Period of the Armenian Kingdoms and the Conquest by Foreign Powers

1. The Armenians emerged as a nation in the 7th century B.C. After the conquest by Alexander of Macedonia, the Armenians established their own kingdom under the dynasty of Artaxias. It reached its highest development under King Tigranes II the Great (94-56 B.C.). By conquering other Armenian principalities the king unified the country. Later on Persians conquered Armenia.

An important event was the christianization of the Armenians in the 4th century and the foundation of the autonomous Armenian Gregorian Christian Church with its own ritual and dogma. King Tiridates III established Christianity as the state religion. The Armenian Church was headed by the Catholicos-Patriarch, who resided at Echmiadzin near Erevan. The church played an outstanding role in the development of national consciousness. In the 5th century the Bible was translated into Armenian. Soon a rich Armenian literature arose.

After the downfall of the Persian empire of the Sassanids in the 7th century, the Arabs conquered Armenia. Under Arab and Byzantine rule in the 9th century the Armenians managed to consolidate their power, and restored the Kingdom of Armenia under the princely dynasty of the Bagratides (Bagratuni). In 862 King Ashot I of the Bagratuni line was recognized by the Arab caliph as "prince of princes" of Armenia. The national kingdom of the Bagratides lasted until 1080. Prosperity at that time reached a high level. Irrigation works and towns were built. The urban centres had an active trade.

In the 11th century the Seljuk Turks overran the whole country. Many Armenian families left their homeland and migrated to Georgia, the Byzantine lands and elsewhere. A section of the emigrants established an independent kingdom in Cilicia in 1080, which was reigned by the Rupenid dynasty. This kingdom of Lesser Armenia, which gradually increased its territory, lasted three centuries until 1375. It prospered economically and culturally.

In the 16th century Armenia was conquered by the Ottoman Turks who defeated Persia. The wars between Persia and Turkey in the 16th and 17th centuries, waged in order to gain domination over the Caucasus, devastated many parts of Armenia. Since the 17th century Armenia was dominated by two foreign powers: the eastern part of the country was ruled by Persia, the western part by Turkey. In the 18th century Tsarist Russia appeared in Transcaucasia.

2. The sources of ancient Armenian law are very scarce. Of great importance is the law code of the legislator Mkhitar Gosh. It was compiled during the 12th and 13th centuries. The code contains Armenian customary law but many legal rules are influenced by Roman and Byzantine laws. The code deals with civil, family and criminal law and also with criminal procedure.

In civil law many kinds of contracts were mentioned, especially the institutions of loan and pawn. Concerning family law, marriage is preceded by a special agreement concluded in the presence of a clergyman and 2 or 3 witnesses. After that the bridegroom could not abandon the bride. In the Gregorian church adultery and abandonment constituted grounds for divorce. With regard to the law of succession the freedom of testation was limited: 3/9ths of the property had to be left to the heirs-by-law. Besides the sons, the daughters were also entitled to inherit on the death of the father.

The criminal law is marked by the severity of the penal system: the main crimes were punished by death and by corporal penalties including mutilation. High treason was punished by blinding and exile. For minor offences fines were provided. Blood vengeance was, however, forbidden.

In criminal procedure the main form of proof was by the testimony of witnesses.

With regard to constitutional law, the Armenian Kingdom belonged to the type of feudal monarchies. At the top of the hierarchy was the king with his council of advisers consisting of the senior members of the nobility. Legislation and the dispensing of justice were personal prerogatives of the king. The central administration was performed by state offices, the so-called divans. The divans were headed by nobles. In the cities the local administration was entrusted to officials appointed by the divans.

The social structure of the Armenian society consisted of five classes. To the highest class belonged the king and the nobility which were divided into two groups: the senior nobility, the so-called *nakhararq*, and the middle nobility, the so-called *asati*. The next class were the clergymen, who also served sometimes as advisers to the king. The third class comprised the merchants and artisans in towns, engaging in trade. The largest class was formed by the peasants, divided into two groups: the free farmers and herdsmen, and the serfs working on the estates of the nobles. In the 16th century serfdom became widespread in Armenia, and the free peasants disappeared. The slaves were at the lowest end of the scale.

The Period of the Conquest of Armenia by Tsarist Russia in the 19th Century

1) In the 18th century Russia manifested a growing interest in the Caucasian states. Already Peter the Great was planning military actions in this region. Armenian national circles were strongly opposed to Turkish and Persian domination of their country. Many

of them looked over-optimisticallyt o Russia, hoping to get help for the establishment of political independence.

In 1828, as a result of the Russio-Iranian war, the main part of Eastern Armenia, Persian Armenia, fell into Russian hands. In 1877 war broke out between Russia and Turkey. Russia wanted to annex the rest of Armenia which was under Turkish rule, but the British government successfully opposed this plan at the Congress of Berlin in 1878. In 1895-1896 under the Turkish sultan Abdul-Hamid II, who feared an Armenian revolt, large-scale massagres of Armenians occured. Similar actions also took place in Turkey in 1915-1916, and the unsolved "Armenian question" troubled world opinion.

2) At the beginning of the 20th century many Armenian political organizations came into being. The national movement was led by the Dashnak (*Dashnaktzutiun*) Nationalist Party. The socialist groups were headed by the marxist Shaumian, Spanderian and others. Taking advantage of the Russian October revolution, Armenia proclaimed its independence in 1918. Armenian independence was recognized by the Treaty of Sèvres 1920, namely by the Allied Powers and Turkey (art. 88). Together with the adjacent independent states Azerbaidzhan and Georgia, Armenia in 1918 formed the "Federative Democratic Republic of Transcaucasia". The period of the new independent Armenian state, under the leadership of the Dashnak party, lasted only until 1920. In April 1920 the Red Army occupied the country and a Soviet regime was set up.

With the rule of Tsarist Russia over Armenia a new administrative system was introduced. The land was divided into districts on the Russian model. The Russian Code of Laws —*Svod zakonov rossiiskoi imperii*—came in force. The Russian land reform of 1861 was made applicable, however, with lesser rights for Armenian peasants.

The Period of Soviet rule in Armenia, 1920-1970

1) In 1920 the Soviet army entered Armenia. With its help, the Armenian Soviet Socialist Republic was established on November 29, 1920. In 1921 a nationalist revolt temporarily overthrew the Soviet regime but it was repressed a few months later by Soviet troops. After the setting-up of Soviet rule, the process of sovietization in all sections of social life was quickly carried out. On December 13, 1922, Armenia formed, together with Soviet Azerbaidzhan and Georgia the Transcaucasian Federative Socialist Soviet Republic. On December 30, 1922, the Federation became a member of the Union of Soviet Socialist Republics. Fourteen years later, on December 5, 1936, Armenia became a constituent republic of the Soviet Union, and the Transcaucasian Federation was abolished.

2) With the decree of October 21, 1920, the Russian Code of Laws was abolished. The laws of the RSFSR were declared applicable in Armenia for the time being.

With regard to constitutional law, the first Armenian Constitution was enacted in 1922. As a member state of the Transcaucasian Federation Armenia formally retained full sovereignty. The Constitution was modeled on the Russian constitution of 1918. The supreme governmental agencies were the Conference of Soviets with its Executive Committee. The Constitution was amended in 1925 and in 1927. After the liquidation of the Transcaucasian Republic, a new Armenian Constitution modeled on the Constitution of the Soviet Union of 1936 was introduced in 1937.

In 1923 the Executive Committee enacted the Armenian civil and criminal code which were in force for more than 30 years. Both codes were replaced by new ones in 1964 and in 1962 respectively.

Bibl.: J. F. Baddeley, The Russian Conquest

of the Caucasus, 1908; F. Kazemzadeh, The Struggle for Transcaucasia 1917-1921, 1951; R. G. Hovannisian, Armenia on the Road to Independence, 1967; M. K. Matossian, The Impact of Soviet Policies in Armenia, 1962; L. P. Beria, On the History of the Bolshevik Organizations in Transcaucasia (English edition), 1949; A. G. Suksisian, *Istoriia Kilikiiskogo armianskogo gosudarstva i prava* (11-14 vv.), 1969; *Istoriia armianskogo naroda, Chast'* 1, B. N. Arakelian i A. R. Ioannisian (eds.), 1951; L. O. Babaian, *Sotsial'no-ekonomicheskaia i politicheskaia istoriia Armenii v 13-14 vv.*, 1969.

L. Schultz

LEGAL HISTORY, AZERBAIDZHAN

The legal history of Azerbaidzhan can be divided into two periods: 1) the period of the independent states and principalities, 7th century B.C.-19th century A.D.; 2) the period of the conquest of Azerbaidzhan by Tsarist Russia and the establishment of the Soviet rule, 19th-20th century.

The period of the independent states and principalities

1) The Azerbaidzhan nation was formed from different tribes in the 7th century B.C. The country was known at that time as Albania. Being situated on the important trade routes between the Caspian and the Black Sea, Azerbaidzhan was the object of many occupations by foreign powers. In the 3rd century B.C. Azerbaidzhan was conquered by Persia and came under its suzerainty. During this period Azerbaidzhan was a prosperous state. By the end of the 7th century A.D. it was invaded by the Arabs. At that time the Azerbaidzhani were forcibly converted to the Islam, becoming shiitic Moslems. Ethnically and linguistically they belong to the family of the Turks. During the 8th-10th century many towns were built in the country and Baku became a leading trade centre. The production of textiles and rugs began to grow. In the 11th century Azerbaidzhan was captured by the Seljuk Turks. During their reign Azerbaidzhan retained, however, a great part of its autonomy. Culture was flourishing, especially literature and the arts.

In the 13th century Azerbaidzhan was invaded by Mongols. The country was widely devastated. By the end of the 14th century Azerbaidzhan became a part of Tamerlane's empire.

During the 15th-17th century Azerbaidzhan was the theatre of a struggle for political control of the country between Persia and Ottoman Turkey. Persia was the more successful in this fight. For about two hundred years Persia dominated over the Azerbaidzhan people. During the Persian rule a number of independent principalities—khanates—arose. The most powerful was Shirwan, then came Ghandzha, Baku and five others of minor importance. No one of these principalities was in the position to unite the country, and Azerbaidzhan remained divided. In the 18th century Russian expansionist plans turned to the Caucasian lands.

2) The legal sources of Azerbaidzhan in the period from the 7th-18th century are very scarce. The legal system was based on the *shariat*—Moslem law derived from the religious principles of Islam. Besides that many institutions were regulated by the Azerbaidzhan customary law, the *adat*.

With regard to the constitutional law, the principalities belonged to the type of feudal monarchies led by the nobility. During the period of Persian domination the principalities were headed by khans, who were vassals of the shah. However, the khans could act with certain independence as they had a sphere of autonomy. The principalities were divided into provinces, the *maghals*, which were under the rule of the Azerbaidzhan nobles, the *bekhi*.

The period of the conquest of Azerbaidzhan by Tsarist Russia and the establishment of Soviet rule

1) Peter the Great took the first steps to get control over Azerbaidzhan. In 1723 the Tsar's army captured Baku—a famous oil-producing centre. After a prolonged war with Persia, Alexander I annexed Azerbaidzhan to the Russian empire in 1828. After the annexation the Russian administrative system was introduced in the country. The state was divided in provinces (*gubernii*) and districts. Great numbers of Russian civil servants were sent to Azerbaidzhan. The Russian Code of Laws—*Svod zakonov rossiiskoi imperii*—and Russian courts were introduced. In 1870 the Russian land reform of 1861 was enacted and serfdom in Azerbaidzhan was abolished.

The russification of the country by the Tsarist government was resented and opposed by the Azerbaidzhan people. At the beginning of the 20th century the first political parties were formed. The most influential group was the National-Democratic "Mussavat" ("Equality") Party. The social-democrats founded the "Hummet" party.

After the October revolution Azerbaidzhan became an independent, sovereign state, but only for two years. On May 28, 1918, the National Council proclaimed the independence of Azerbaidzhan. A new government, consisting of twelve ministers under the leadership of the "Mussavat" party, was established. On January 12, 1920, the new republic was recognized de facto by the Allied Powers.

Shortly after that, in April 1920, the country was invaded by the Red Army. On April 28, 1920, the Soviet Socialist Republic of Azerbaidzhan was set up. At first it was a member state of the Transcaucasian Federative Socialist Soviet Republic. After the liquidation of the Federation in 1936 Azerbaidzhan became a separate constituent republic of the Soviet Union.

The first Azerbaidzhan Constitution was enacted in 1922. In 1937 a new Constitution was adopted. Azerbaidzhan participated in the Soviet codification work of the last years. The new Criminal Code and the new Civil Code came into force in 1961 and 1965 respectively.

Bibl.: Milal Munschi, *Die Republik Aserbaidschan*, 1930; M. E. Resulzade, *Das Problem Aserbaidschan*, 1938; H. Taubert, H. Machatschek, *Aserbaidschanische SSR*, 1953; D. Tutaeff, The Soviet Caucasus, 1942; A. K. Ziatkhan, *Aperçu sur l'histoire et la politique de l'Azerbaidjan*, 1919; Z. Buniatov, *Azerbaidzhan v VII-IX vv.*, 1965; I. A. Guseinov, A. S. Sumbatzade, *Istoriia Azerbaidzhana, tt.* 1-3, 1958-1963; Kh. M. Ibragimbeili, *Rossiia a Azerbaidzhan v pervoi treti XIX v.*, 1969; *Ocherki po drevnei istorii Azerbaidzhana*, A. N. Guliev (ed.), 1956; M. I. Sadagdar, *Osnovy musul'manskogo prava*, 1968.

L. Schultz

LEGAL HISTORY, BALTIC STATES

Forming a gateway in East-West traffic, the Baltic States—Estonia, Latvia and Lithuania—were the scene of many hostile activities. Their legal history in the last centuries can be divided into three periods: 1) the period of the rule of Tsarist Russia, 1721-1918; 2) the period of the independent Baltic States, 1918-1940; and 3) the period of Soviet rule, 1940-1970.

The period of the rule of Tsarist Russia

1) After the Russo-Swedish war 1721, and after the third partition of Poland in 1795, the Baltic countries were annexed by Russia. After the conquest the Russian administrative system was introduced. Estonia and Latvia were divided into four provinces (*gubernii*): Estonia, Livonia, Kurland and Vitebsk (the eastern part of Latvia); Lithuania into three; Wilno, Grodno and Kowno.

At the head of each province stood a Governor-General as representative of the Tsar. For the Latvian and Estonian part of the Baltic, however, a limited autonomy was granted, consisting in special rights of the German nobility. The Baltic German nobles owned approximately one half of all the land and had many privileges. In Lithuania an important role was played by Polish and polonized gentry. In the Estonian and Latvian provinces the highest authority in the local administration was the regularly meeting Diet of Nobles. Current administrative affairs were managed by Councillors of the Nobility (*Landrat*), twelve in each province. Their members were elected for life. By the end of the 19th century, especially under the reign of Tsar Alexander III, a strong russification policy was started. In 1885 all schools were placed under the Russian Ministry of Education. In the secondary schools the Russian language was made the language of instruction. Russian as the official langage was required in all offices, and a great number of Russian civil servants were sent to the Baltic provinces. In Lithuania a decree banned printing in the Lithuanian language in Latin characters, and ordered a Russian (Cyrillian) alphabet for Lithuanian books. The Roman Catholic religion was persecuted and parochial schools were closed. This policy of the Tsarist regime evoked a stiffening resistance and defiance in the country.
At the end of the 19th century a significant awakening of the Baltic nations took place. A new class of Baltic intellectuals emerged and a general stirring of cultural life and national consciousness took place. The first newspapers and periodicals in national languages were published. At the same time the economic status of peasants—the bulk of the population—greatly improved. The Baltic intelligentsia resisted the policy of russification and the privileged status of the Baltic nobility. Shortly before the Russian Revolution of 1905, the first political parties in the Baltic provinces were founded. The leftist wing was represented by the Social Democrats, the centre by the peasant groups, and the rightist side by the Christian Democrats and Nationalists. Representatives of the Baltic political parties were present in the first Russian Duma of 1906 and later.
After the Russian February Revolution in 1917, when some civil rights and liberties were granted, the Baltic politicians became very active. They demanded from the Provisional Russian Government political autonomy for their countries with an elected local diet. The slogan—"Free Estonia (Latvia, Lithuania) in a free Russia"—appeared. On July 30, 1917, the Land Council of Vidzeme (Livonia) convened at Riga and demanded for Latvia "a political autonomy within the Russian democratic republic with the Constituent Assembly to be elected by general and proportional vote". After the October Revolution the spreading chaos in Russia persuaded the Baltic nations to search for a complete separation from Bolshevik Russia. With great enthusiasm leading organizations issued declarations of independence in all Baltic countries. On February 23, 1918, the Estonian Rescue Committee proclaimed Estonia as "an independent Republic within its historical boundaries". On November 18 the Latvian National Council declared Latvia "an independent democratic republic whose constitution shall be defined by a Constituent Assembly". A similar manifesto was published by the Council of Lithuania on February 16, 1918.
During a short time in 1918-19, the Baltic countries were occupied by the German army and by Soviet troops. Supported by the Red Army, shortlived Soviet Republics were established. In Latvia the Soviet regime under the leadership of the well-known Soviet-Latvian jurist, P. I. Stuchka, issued a new Constitution in 1919.
At the end of 1919 the governments of the new Baltic Republics regained full power.

Only Vilnius (Vilno), the old capital of Lithuania, was occupied by Poland in 1920 and later, in 1939, its only port, Klaipeda (Memel), was annexed by Germany.
The Entente Powers recognized Latvia and Estonia *de jure* in 1921 and Lithuania in 1922, while the United States recognized them in 1922. In 1921 the Baltic States were admitted to membership of the League of Nations.
2) After the annexation of the Baltic countries by Tsarist Russia, the Russian Code of Laws—*Svod zakonov rossiiskoi imperii*—was partly brought into force. With regard to the civil law in the provinces of Estonia, Livonia and Kurland, the Baltic Civil Code of 1864 was enacted. It was influenced greatly by Roman law and also by Baltic customary law. Earlier than in Russia, in 1817/19, serfdom in the above mentioned provinces was abolished and the peasants regained personal freedom. The law of 1860 granted the peasants the right to purchase land from the nobility. As a result, a new class of Baltic proprietors came into being. The Russian Judicial Law of 1864 was enacted in 1889, and the old court system changed. The law of 1866 enlarged the peasant's rights in the local communities (*volosti*): they could elect the head of the communal administration.

The period of the independent Baltic states
1) The Bolshevik revolution and the collapse of the German empire had greatly facilitated the struggle of the Baltic nations for independence. However, the period of the independent states was very short—it lasted only twenty years.
In 1920 the Baltic States signed peace treaties with the Soviet Union. It is interesting to note that Soviet Russia recognized in these treaties the Baltic States *de jure* and renounced their previous sovereignty over these countries. Art. 2 of the Russo-Estonian Peace Treaty of February 2, 1920, stated that "Russia recognizes the independence and autonomy of the State of Estonia and renounces voluntarily and for ever all rights or sovereignty formerly held by Russia over the Estonian people". Some years later the Baltic States concluded treaties of non-aggression with the Soviet Union: Lithuania in 1926, Estonia and Latvia in 1932. In all these treaties the Soviet Union stated that the "sovereignty and territorial integrity and inviolability" of the Baltic countries "would be respected".
After the initial postwar difficulties were over the Baltic States became culturally and economically prosperous western countries. They tried to serve as a bridge between the East and the West.
A Baltic Entente was established. In 1923 a Treaty of Defensive Alliance between Estonia and Latvia was signed. In 1934 the Treaty of Good Understanding and Co-operation, concluded between Estonia, Latvia and Lithuania, followed, providing mutual political and diplomatic assistance. In 1936 Latvia obtained a non-permanent seat in the Council of the League of Nations as the representative of the Baltic bloc.
The situation for the Baltic States worsened after the outbreak of World War II. The Soviet Union was now able to realize its old aim to get free access to the Baltic Sea.
The fate of the Baltic States had already been decided in the German-Soviet non-aggression pact of August 23, 1939. The pact has a secret protocol stating that Estonia and Latvia were assigned to the Soviet sphere; on September 28 of the same year a secret supplementary clause extended the sphere of Soviet influence also to Lithuania. Further Soviet steps followed with great speed. In September/October 1939 the Baltic States signed a dictated treaty of Mutual Assistance with the Soviet Union by which Soviet Russia obtained military, naval and air bases on the territory of the Baltic countries. The treaty had, however, a clause stating that it "in no way impairs

the sovereign rights of the Contracting Parties, their economic system or political structure". On June 16, 1940, the Baltic States were confronted with a Soviet ultimatum demanding establishment of new governments "friendly to the Soviet Union", and the free passage for Soviet troops to be stationed at Soviet bases. Without waiting for an answer and in violation of the non-aggression and mutual assistance pacts, the Red Army occupied the Baltic States on June 17. Top-level Soviet politicians were sent to these states to sovietize the country: in Estonia A. A. Zhdanov arrived, in Latvia A. Ia. Vyshinsky and in Lithuania V. G. Dekanozov.

On July 14 and 15 rigged elections for new chambers of deputies were staged in all the Baltic States. It was officially announced that the single communist "labour bloc" in Latvia had obtained 94,7% of the votes cast. The percentage was almost identical to that claimed for the other two Baltic States. It is interesting to note that the results of the votes were published by "Tass" twelve hours before the elections were finished.

2) During the period of independence the law codes of Tsarist Russia were in force for some time in the Baltic States. Gradually they were replaced by a new Baltic legal system. In 1920 the corporations of the nobility were liquidated. With regard to criminal law, the Russian Criminal Code of 1903, being only partly in force in Tsarist Russia, was brought into force. In the thirties new criminal codes in the Baltic States were adopted, modeled on modern western patterns. In Latvia in 1932 a new Criminal Code was introduced abolishing the death sentence. In the field of civil law the Baltic Civil Code of 1864 came into force in Estonia and Latvia. Afterwards projects for new civil codes were elaborated. In 1938 a new modern Civil Code came into effect in Latvia, consisting of 2500 articles. It was infuenced by Swiss and German law.

Of great economic and political importance was the Agrarian Reform adopted in the Baltic States by the Constituent Assemblies in 1920. The large estates, exceeding 100 ha, mainly owned by German-Baltic nobility, were nationalized and a state fund created. Landless peasants and small land owners were bestowed with land of about 20 ha. Thus a new middle class of farmers arose with highly intensive farming.

With regard to constitutional law in 1920/22 all Baltic States adopted new constitutions. They were based on democratic, liberal principles. The new Baltic fundamental laws stressed the sovereignty of the people. The ultimate power belonged to the unicameral parliaments, elected for a period of three years by direct and proportional ballot. The legislature could be dissolved only by a national referendum. The government was responsible to the parliament. The head of the state elected by the parliament (in Estonia the prime minister was also the head of the state) had no special authority and performed only representative functions. The constitutions provided the referendum and the right of the electorate to submit law projects to the legislature. A cultural autonomy was guaranteed to minorities—the Germans, Russians an others.

In the thirties, in Lithuania in 1926, the democratic constitutional system underwent a crisis and mild authoritarian regimes were set up in the Baltic republics. The main ground for the change was the instability of the government. As no party could secure an absolute majority in parliament, all governments had to be coalition cabinets, which collapsed frequently. In Latvia between 1918 and 1934 eighteen premiers held office. In Estonia during the period of 1919-1933 twenty coalitions were formed.

To do away with the instability of the political life, Estonia and Lithuania adopted a new constitution in 1938. In Latvia single constitutional laws in 1936 introduced a corporative form of government, setting up many councils in the economic and cultural field. The new Constitution of Estonia strengthened widely the position of the head of the state—the President of the republic—and curtailed the role of the legislature. The President had the right to dissolve the parliament and govern by decrees between parliamentary sessions. The President appointed and dismissed the government which could not act contrary to the wishes of the President. The Lithuanian Constitution of 1938 was based on a similar principle.

The period of Soviet rule in the Baltic states
1) The new elected Baltic parliaments convened on July 21, 1940, and proclaimed the establishment of the Soviet Socialist Republics in the Baltic countries. They also adopted unanimously a resolution, asking the Supreme Soviet of the Soviet Union to admit the Baltic republics into the Soviet Federation. The Supreme Soviet accepted this demand. On August 3, Lithuania, on August 5, Latvia and on August 6, Estonia were incorporated as constituent republics into the Soviet Union. By the end of July 1940, the private Baltic industrial, commercial and transportation enterprises had been nationalized.
The illegal and forced annexation of the Baltic States was not recognized *de jure* by the leading European states: Great Britain and France, and also the United States. On March 26, 1949, the Department of State of the U.S.A. issued a circular letter stating that the Baltic countries were still independent nations with their own diplomatic representatives and consuls.
During World War II, from 1941 till 1945, the Baltic States were occupied by the German army. The independence of these states was not restored. Together with Belorussia, the Baltic countries formed the new province "Ostland" which was under the rule of the German Governor (*Reichskommissar*).

2) After the annexation of the Baltic States by the Soviet Union, the Soviet law system was introduced. With the decree of November 6, 1940, the Presidium of the Supreme Soviet of the USSR enacted in Estonia, Latvia and Lithuania the codes of the RSFSR, to wit the Civil Code (1922), the Criminal Code (1926), the Civil Procedure Code (1923), the Criminal Procedure Code (1923), and the Code of Laws on Marriage, Family and Guardianship (1926). The enactment of Soviet codes had retroactive effect. All court decisions of the time prior to the establishment of the Soviet regime, which had not been executed, should be reexamined in the light of the provisions of the Soviet codes. Since 1957 the Baltic Soviet republics have adopted their own codes.
On August 25, 1940, on the same day, all three Baltic parliaments adopted new constitutions. The content of each was very similar. They represented copies of the uniform Soviet constitution for all constituent republics with some minor deviations, resulting from the peculiar situation at that time in the Baltic countries. Since 1940 the constitutions have been amended several times.

Bibl.: H. Rolnik, *Die baltische Staaten Litauen, Lettland und Estland und ihr Verfassungsrecht*, 1927; B. Meissner, *Die Sowjetunion, die baltischen Staaten und das Völkerrecht*, 1956; A. Mägi, *Das Staatsleben Estlands während seiner Selbständigkeit*, 1967; A. N. Tarulis, Soviet Policy toward the Baltic States 1918-1940, 1959; E. Uustalu, History of the Estonian People, 1952; A. Bilmanis, A History of Latvia, 1951; A. E. Senn, The Emergence of Modern Lithuania, 1959; C. J. Jurgela, History of the Lithuanian Nation, 1948; *Istoriia Estonskoi SSR* (2nd ed.), G. I. Naan (ed.), 1958; *Istoriia Latviiskoi SSR*, 1955; B. I. Levin, *Razvitie sovetskoi gosudarstvennosti v Estonii*, 1961; V. O. Miller, *Razvitie sovetskoi gosu-*

darstvennosti v Latvii, 1961; *Sovetskaia Pribaltika*, A. A. Mine and M. I. Rostovtsev (eds.), 1966; *Ocherki razvitiia gosudarstvennosti sovetskikh pribaltiiskikh respublik 1940-1965*, 1965.

L. Schultz

LEGAL HISTORY, GEORGIA

The political history of Georgia has some features similar to those of Armenia, both Caucasian states.

The legal history of Georgia can be divided into three periods: 1) the period of the Georgian kingdoms, 7th century B.C.-19th century; 2) the period of the conquest of Georgia by Tsarist Russia, 19th-20th century; 3) the period of Soviet rule in Georgia, after 1920.

The period of the Georgian kingdoms and the conquest by foreign powers

1) The first Georgian state emerged in the 7th century B.C., the eastern part of the country being known as Colchis and the western part as Iberia. During the 3rd century A.D., Rome and Persia struggled for the control of Georgia (which was ultimately split between the Persian and Byzantine empires). In the 4th century A.D., about the year 330, under the Iberian king Mirian, Georgia was converted to christianity of the Eastern Orthodox rite. The Georgian church as an autocephalous body had the right to elect its own Catholicos-Patriarch, who resided at Mtskhete, the capital of Iberia. The church had an important unifying influence on the entire nation during its turbulent history. In the 5th century the Holy Scriptures were translated into Georgian and an original alphabet was introduced.

In the 7th century the Arabs occupied Georgia. During the rule of the caliphs the dynasty of the Bagrationi gained power and began to unite the country. In 1008 Bagrat III became king of United Eastern and Western Georgia. King David IV, called the Restorer (1089-1125), succeeded in unifying Georgia further, and extended the frontiers of his kingdom from the Black Sea to the Caspian Sea. Tiflis became the capital of the state. The zenith of Georgia's power was reached under Queen Tamara (1184-1213), who continued the work of King David and extended her rule over Armenia also. The reign of David and Queen Tamara was the "Golden Age" of Georgia. The country prospered economically and culturally. This successful period under peaceful conditions ended in 1236, when the Mongols overran Georgia and devastated the land. The disintegration of Georgia continued after the invasion by Ottoman Turkey. At the end of the 14th century Georgia was divided into three kingdoms—Kartli, Kakheti and Imereti—and five principalities—Guria, Svaneti, Abkhazia, Samtskhe and Odishi. Each principality existed as a separate unit within its territorial boundaries. This political disunity and local strife prevented Georgia from resisting the expansion of Turkey and Persia. In 1762 king Erekle (1744-1798) united Kartli and Kakheti into a strong and prosperous kingdom. Also king Salomon I strengthened his ruling position in Imereti during that time.

In the 18th century the Georgian kings began to make approaches to Russia, looking for help against Turkey and Persia. In 1783 king Erekle signed a treaty of alliance with Russia. This treaty guaranteed the kingdom's security, but the king had to accept the status of a protectorate for his kingdom. The Russian expansionist aims continued to grow, searching for increasing control over Georgia. By the Manifest of 12 September, 1801, in Moscow, the kingdom of Kartli-Kakheti was incorporated into the Russian empire. The kingdom of Imereti was annexed in 1810, after its king Solomon II revolted and was deposed by armed force. The five above mentioned principalities were absorbed into Russia successively during the years

1830-1878. Thus Georgia became an integral part of Tsarist Russia.

2) In the period of the Georgian kingdoms three sources of law are important: a) the Laws of the King Georgi V (1314-46), codified by a special commission at the beginning of the 14th century, b) the Laws of the local civil servants, Beki (1361-1391) and Agbugi (1444-1451), belonging to the 14th and 15th century; c) the Law Code of the king Vakhtang VI (1703-1724), compiled during the 18th century.

a) The Laws of the King Georgi V deal mostly with criminal law. The prevailing penalties are fines. The most serious crimes, like murder, were punished by temporary exile from the local community. Theft was punished by fines which were three times the value of the stolen thing.

b) The Laws of Beki and Agbugi embrace civil and criminal law. With regard to the civil law, sale was amply regulated. The sale of land by peasants was not valid without the consent of their masters. For loans the maximum rate of interest could not exceed 20%. In the law of succession the eldest son received the main part of the inheritance. In criminal law the penalty system was based on fines. However, blood-revenge was prescribed for some crimes, especially for robbery.

c) The Law Code of King Vakhtang VI consisted of 267 articles and contained civil and criminal law and also criminal procedure. In civil law many types of contract, such as sales, loans, pledge and others, were listed. The contract of sale had to be concluded before witnesses. For loans the highest rate of interest was 30%. With regard to criminal law, fines predominated as penalties. The most striking feature of the Code was the elaborate system of wergild or blood-money, prescribed for every variety of tort from murder downwards. A certain proportion of the wergild went to the exchequer as a fine, the remainder to the victim. The wergild had a strong class character: the rates differed according to the social standing of the victim. In criminal procedure, judicial ordeals as proof were prescribed for certain crimes. The ordeals of boiling water and red-hot iron were prescribed for the offences of treason, church-robbing and adultery. The influence of Persian law on these practices is probable.

Regarding constitutional law, Georgia was a feudal monarchy with a political organization of great complexity. The king ruled by divine right but his power was limited by the nobility. In most important affairs, like war and peace, enactment of fundamental laws and others, the council of the senior nobility, the *darbasi*, had to be convoked by the king. The central administration was headed by ministers, the *vizir*, appointed by the monarch. The chief *vizir* also had jurisdictional functions. The ministers had a staff of subordinate officials. The local administration in the provinces were headed by appointed civil servants, the *eristav*'s, who tended towards political independence. In the cities the merchant class formed special committees and provided economic advice to the *eristav*'s.

The social structure of Georgian society was dominated by the upper class, the powerful nobility. It was divided into three different classes. To the highest class belonged the senior nobility (*didebulni*); the lesser nobility formed the next class (*aznaurni*); the lowest class comprised the so-called *msakhurni*, nobles who worked as officials in the king's estates.

The legal status of peasants gradually worsened, and in the 16th century serfdom was prescribed by law. From that time the free farmers and herdsmen completely disappeared in Georgia.

The period of the conquest of Georgia by Tsarist Russia

1) After the annexation of Georgia the

country became a Russian province fully integrated in the Tsarist system. The policy of russification affected all branches of social life. The Georgian nobility was removed from participation in the state administration and replaced by Russian civil servants. Great resentment throughout Georgia caused the suppression in 1811 of the independent Georgian church. The Catholicos-Patriarch Antoni II was removed and replaced by a representative of the Russian church, the Metropolitan Varlaam, who was given the title of Exarch of Georgia. A conspiracy against the unpopular Russian rule in Georgian national circles broke out in 1832 and was suppressed by the Russian police.

At the end of the 19th century the Georgian intellectuals began to form their own political organizations. The national independence movement was headed by Chavchavadze and Tsereteli. In 1893 the Georgian Social-Democratic Party was founded under the leadership of Zhordania, the future president of independent Georgia. A member of this party was Ioseb Dzhugashvili, the future Stalin.

After the Russian October Revolution Georgia declared its independence in 1918, becoming a member of the newly created "Federative Democratic Republic of Transcaucasia". On May 26, 1918, Georgia was established as a sovereign independent state, and the Federative Republic was dissolved. In February 1919 free and direct elections were held for a new Georgian Constituent Assembly which met for the first time on March 12, 1919. From the 130 seats in the Assembly the victorious Social-Democratic Party (Mensheviks) occupied 109 seats. On January 15, 1919, the Allied Powers recognized independent Georgia *de facto* and later, on January 27, 1921, also *de jure*. On May 7, 1920, the Soviet Union signed a treaty of friendship with Georgia recognizing its independence. This was only a tactical manoeuvre to gain the possibility of undermining the new state from within. The Russian S. M. Kirov was sent as envoy to Georgia. On February 25, 1921, the Red Army invaded the country and the members of the Georgian government escaped to Paris.

2) After the annexation of Georgia in the 19th century, the Russian administrative system was introduced. The country was divided into two provinces (*gubernii*) and many districts. The highest administrative authority was the Viceroy of Georgia, appointed by the Tsar. The liberal Russian *zemstvo* law of 1864 concerning local government was not introduced. The Russian Code of Laws—*Svod zakonov rossiiskoi imperii*—came in force. All legal business had to be transacted exclusively in Russian.

The period of Soviet rule in Georgia 1921-1970

1) On February 25, 1921, the Red Army occupied Georgia and the sovietization of the country began. Against the advice of Lenin to make some concessions to Georgian national feelings, Stalin, acting people's commissar for nationalities, ordered a ruthless policy abolishing all traces of autonomy. On December 13, 1921, following Stalin's order to hold down separatist aims, the Transcaucasian Federative Socialist Soviet Republic was founded. Georgia entered into this Transcaucasian Federation as a member state together with Armenia and Azerbaidzhan. In 1924 a nationalist uprising, trying to regain independence, broke out but was soon crushed by Soviet troops.

2) After fourteen years the Transcaucasian Federation was abolished on December 5, 1936, and Georgia acquired the status of a constituent republic of the Soviet Union. The first Constitution of Georgia came in force in 1922. In 1937 a new Constitution was enacted.

As in other Union republics, a codification of the most important parts of law has been carried out in Georgia during the last few years. New codes of criminal and civil law were enacted in 1961 and 1965 respectively. Modeled largely on the codes of the RSFSR, they provide, however, some different features.

Bibl.: D. M. Lang, A Modern History of Georgia, 1962; D. M. Lang, The Last Years of the Georgian Monarchy 1658-1832, 1957; W. E. D. Allen, A History of the Georgian People, 1932; A. Manvelichvili, *Histoire de Géorgie*, 1951; G. I. Uratadze, *Obrazovanie i konsolidatsiia gruzinskoi demokraticheskoi respubliki*, 1956; N. B. Makharadze, *Pobeda sotsialisticheskoi revoliutsii v Gruzii*, 1965; Sh. A. Meshiia, *Istoriia Gruzii*, 1968; M. Lashauri, *Istoriia Gruzii XIX-XX vekov v sovremennoi sovetskoi interpretatsii*, 1956; Z. V. Anchabadze, *Ocherki ekonomicheskoi istorii Gruzii pervoi poloviny XIX veka*, 1966; V. N. Merkviladze, *Istoriia sozdaniia i ukrepleniia natsional'noi gosudarstvennosti v Gruzii 1921-1936*, 1966; A. Z. Begiian, *Razvitie sovetskoi gosudarstvennosti v Armenii*, 1968.

L. Schultz

LEGAL HISTORY, RUSSIA

The legal history of Russia can be divided into four periods: 1. the period of the single principalities, 9th-13th century; 2. the period of the Moscow state, 14th-17th century; 3. the period of the absolute empire, 18th-20th century; and 4. the period of the constitutional monarchy and of the Russian republic, 1906-1917.

This article deals only with the legal history of the Slavic peoples of Russia.

The Period of the Single Principalities

1) The first forms of organized political communities appeared with the eastern Slavs who occupied the territory between Lake Ilmen and the middle course of the Dniepr river. How far the Vikings from Scandinavia, the so-called Varangians, have influenced the establishment of the Russian state is a highly controversial problem. Soviet historians have rejected the "Norse theory" as groundless. However, a certain Norse influence cannot be denied.

The newly formed principalities gradually began to unite. In the 9th century the Kievan state, the first state of the united Russian land, came into being. Under the reign of the Grand Duke of Kiev Vladimir (980-1015) Greek-orthodox Christianity entered Russia followed by well-developed Byzantine institutions and culture. The acceptance of Christianity also had considerable influence on Russian law, especially on ecclesiastical legislation.

The society of ancient Russia consisted of three basic groups. At the top of the social pyramid stood the princes, *kniaz'*, with their retainers, the "druzhina"; the members of the latter were divided in two classes: the higher nobility, the boyars and the lower nobility. To the second class belonged the bulk of the population: the peasants—*smerdy,* they were also split in two classes: the free peasants, owners of private land, and the unfree peasants, the bondsmen who worked on the estates which belonged to the boyars. The lowest class were the slaves—*kholopy*—who were deprived of any rights.

After the death of the Grand Duke Jaroslav (1019-1054), the desintegration of the Kievan state began. The princes, increasing in number, left Kiev and led endless civil struggles for power. In the 12th century the ancient Russian state fell apart. In 1240 Kiev was captured by Mongols and a new political centre emerged in the North of the country.

2) During the Kievan state three sources of Russian law were of great importance: a) the Russian treaties with the Greeks, b) the Russian treaties with the Germans and c) the oldest Russian legal code, the Russian law—Russkaia Pravda.

a) In the 10th century the Russians concluded four treaties with the Greeks, namely in the years 907, 911, 944 and 945. These agreements are the oldest written documents of Russian legal history, and contain international, criminal and civil law, as well as the law of procedure of Russian and Byzantine origin. Russian and Soviet legal historians do not quite agree on the relative weight to be allotted to Russian and Byzantine elements. Undoubtedly, Russian law plays the most important part. The Russians expressly insisted on their national law. Regardless of the criminal law to be applied, blood vengeance for Russian citizens was accepted. The civil law paid special attention to the property law for women. It is significant that the legal position of women was more favourable in ancient Russian law than in Byzantine legislation, which placed them under guardianship.

b) The trade of the Russian cities of Novgorod, Smolensk, Polotsk, and Vitebsk with German merchants in the 12th and 13th century led to the conclusion of several commercial agreements. These agreements were more elaborate than the Russian-Greek treaties. They covered commercial, criminal and civil law, and also the law of procedure. It is interesting to note that Russian law largely prevailed over the German law. The reason for this was the fact that the German merchants were eager to trade with Russians because of the great profits they were making, and they therefore made concessions to Russian law.

c) The *Russkaia Pravda* is one of the most important documents of Russian legal history. The code was in force over the whole of ancient Russia, and had a considerable influence on all later codification till the 17th century. Two versions of the code are extant: the first, so-called "short redaction", stemming from the 9th-11th centuries, and the second "enlarged redaction", compiled during the 11th-12th centuries; the latter also embraces some laws of the Grand Duke Vladimir and of the sons of Jaroslav.

The older version contains only Russian customary law; it does not show any influence of foreign law. It deals with criminal law and criminal procedure. The penalty for murder is blood revenge, however, in a restricted form: it extends only to the members of the offender's family, not to the members of the entire clan. Furthermore the code designates the fine—"*za obidu*" (for the injury); it is not some kind of public penalty, but only a private compensation paid to the victim. The court is not to be regarded as a state institution: the judges are the senior members of the local commune—*mir*. Real evidence, the testimony of witnesses and oath are admitted in evidence. Ordeals are not mentioned.

The second version of the Russkaia Pravda is larger and embraces not only criminal law and procedure, but also civil law, commercial law, and civil procedure. It contains many borrowings from foreign legislations—from German and Byzantine law. The fine —*vira*, and exile—*potok* (the banishment of the offender from his local community) are listed as penalties. The criminal law is marked by class differences: fines are higher according to the social position of the victim. The moderate, inexcessive nature of the penalties deserves particular attention: the second version does not know the death penalty, and the most serious crimes are punished only with fines. In the field of civil law the code regulates the matter of debts; if the debtor coud not repay his debt, he was transferred to the status of an unfree man (bondage). Inheritance law is mainly influenced by Byzantine law and stresses class differences: the rules for the boyars strongly differ from those for free peasants. The legal position of women is very favourable: in many cases women have equal rights with men. The commercial law mentions the institution of commission agency.

In the field of ecclesiastical law, the Byzantine church code of the 6th century, the "Nomokanon", was translated into Russian, and after some modification came into force.

The Period of the Moscow State

1) Through the remarkable emergence of the successfull principality of Moscow in the 15th century, a centralized Russian state arose. It was primarily based on the idea of autocracy, which was also supported by the Russian church. The Grand Duke of Moscow Ivan III (1462-1505) assumed the title of tsar, which was of Byzantine origin. He also called himself *gosudar'*—which means an absolute monarch. With the reign of Ivan IV the Terrible (1532-1584), Muscovite absolutism reached a new height: in 1547 at his coronation as the first ruler of Russia he gave himself the title "Tsar and Autocrat of all Russia", responsible to God alone.

The social structure of Russian society changed considerably in the Moscow state. The leading upper class continued to be the nobility. It was now divided in two different groups: the higher nobility—the boyars, descendents of the ancient "druzhina", and the middle and lower nobility, the so-called *dvoriane*. As a reward for their service, the *dvoriane* received estates—*pomest'e*, but only for use during their service. The boyars, however, were owners of inherited, patrimonial estates—*votchina*, provided by the tsar.

In order to strengthen their power, the tsars began to restrict the influence of the boyars, favouring at the same time the *dvoriane*.

The legal position of the peasants deteriorated rapidly. During the period of the Moscow state serfdom was established. Already the law code of 1497 limited the freedom of movement of the peasants. Finally tsar Feodor I enacted the important law of 1597 which bound the peasants to the land. At the end of the 17th century the enslavement of the peasants reached its worst stage: they were entirely at the mercy of the landlords. The buying and selling of serfs was widely practised.

2) The constitutional law of the Moscow State was never fixed exactly in written documents. It was based on customary law and usages. The highest organs of the state were: the tsar, the land assembly—*Zemskii Sobor*, and the council of boyars—*boiarskaia duma*. The precise legal position of the tsar is uncertain. Soviet historians, following conceptions suggested by Lenin, have expressed the view that the Moscow State was not an absolute monarchy, but a monarchy of estates (*sosloviia*), and that the power of the tsar was limited by the land assembly. This theory is not corroborated by Russian legal sources. Since the reign of Ivan III the tsars had absolute power. Both representative bodies, the land assembly and the council of boyars, had only consultative status. The tsar was not bound by their decisions.

The competence of the land assembly was not fixed by law. The assemblies were sporadic gatherings convened by the tsar in order to discuss important issues. They consisted of elected representatives of the three classes: the clergy, the nobility (boyars and *dvoriane*) and the townspeople. The peasants were only once present at the land assembly in 1613. The assemblies were established in the 16th century and existed until 1658.

The members of the council of boyars were nominated by the tsar from the nobility. The council was mainly an advisory body and did not limit autocracy.

Considering the extension of the territory of Russia and the increased centralization, the administration of the state had to be changed. At the end of the 15th century the government established the first administrative organs, the so-called *prikazy*. They were created unsystematically following the actual ad hoc requirements of new government activities. The number of the prikazy increased in the 16th century to 30, later on in the 17th century even to 50. The *prikazy* fulfilled administrative duties, some of them acted also as judicial bodies. They were directly subordinate to the tsar and received instructions from him.

3) During the period of the Moscow State three important law codes were enacted: a. the code (*Sudebnik*) of tsar Ivan III in 1497; b. the code (Sudebnik) of tsar Ivan IV in 1550, and c. the code (*Ulozhenie*) of tsar Alexei Mikhailovich in 1649.

a) The *Sudebnik* of 1497 inaugurated a new period of Russian legislation. It was in force in the entire Moscow State, and it unified the very non-integrated legislation of that time. The code deals with criminal, civil, commercial, and administrative law, and also with criminal and civil procedure. An innovation is the division of criminal procedure into two parts: accusatory proceedings (*sud*), and investigatory proceedings (*sysk*). In the latter, torture was widely used, and legally defined in this code for the first time. The criminal law also brings some new elements. Finding the offender's guilt is assigned to the local community. The offender's reputation is established through interrogation of the members of the community. If these classified the offender as belonging to the group of "bad people" (*likhie liudi*), his guilt was proved and without any further investigation he was punished by the court.

b) The law code of 1550 was the supplement of the *Sudebnik* of 1497. Meanwhile many new laws had been enacted. The content of the second code is therefore richer. It clearly marks the aim of Ivan IV to curtail the power of the boyars while protecting the lower nobility and the townspeople. With regard to criminal law, new kinds of crimes against the state were introduced. In the list of penalties imprisonment is mentioned for the first time. It could be imposed for a definite period or for life.

c) The most important achievement in the legislation of the Moscow state is the *Ulozhenie* of 1649. This code was the basis of Russian law for two centuries. With its 967 articles it embraces all branches of law and was translated into many western languages. More than before the administrative law was taken into consideration. In the criminal law, under the influence of Byzantine law, the severity and harshness of penalties increased. Many types of severe death penalties like burying alive, burning, etc. were provided, and also multilating bodily penalties like cutting off the hand, etc. The purpose of punishment was based on retaliation and intimidation.

In civil law the legal difference between the service estates of the *dvoriane* and the inherited estates of the boyars was changed. Later on in the 18th century these two kinds of estates were merged into one type of hereditary property.

The regulations concerning the peasants are scarce. However, the code confirmed the enslavement of the Russian peasantry.

The Period of the Absolute Empire

1) It was Peter the Great (1672-1725) who laid the basis for imperial autocratic Russia. 1721 he gave himself the title of "Emperor (*imperator*) of all Russia" symbolizing the beginning of a new imperial age.

In comparison with the Moscow State the social structure of the society underwent many changes. A system of closed classes with legally limited rights and duties was established.

Peter the Great believed that an autocratic regime would be incompatible with a strong class of nobility. Therefore he decided to demote and democratize the ruling nobility. A special law, the so-called Table of Ranks, was enacted in 1722. All civil servants were divided into 14 ranks (*chin*); civil servants of the first 8 ranks regardless of their descent were counted among the nobility. This way only capability, and not descendence count-

ed. The Table of Ranks remained in force until 1917.
The peasants, constituting 95% of the population, belonged to three different groups: the free peasants (*odnodvortsy*)—personal owners of landholdings, the so-called state peasants working on state estates, and the enserfed peasants, entirely unprotected and dependent upon their landlords. In Russia serfdom was abolished only in 1861, paving the way for many other reforms.
2) Unlike the Moscow State, the system of government and the competence of state agencies were now legally fixed. In 1832 the constitution of the Russian Empire (*Osnovnye Zakony*) was published and came in force in 1835 (179 articles). The constitution provides the following supreme state organs: the emperor, the Senate (*Pravitel'stvuiushchii Senat*), the State Council (*Gosudarstvennyi Sovet*) and the Committee of Ministers (*Komitet ministrov*).
The constitution, in force until 1906, stressed the absolute power of the emperor. Pursuant to Art. 1 he is an "unlimited, absolute ruler" (*samoderzhets*). Therefore the empire remained an autocracy.
The senate, established in 1722 by Peter the Great, initially had executive and some legislative functions; it also acted as supreme court. During the 19th century the senate gradually lost its power and retained only judicial functions.
In 1717 Peter the Great created the so-called "colleges" (*kollegii*) after the Swedish model, which replaced the numerous old and overlapping *prikazy*. In 1802 the colleges were replaced by ministries.
In legislative matters the State Council acted as a consulting body. It had to express its opinion on various draft laws, which were then presented to the emperor for decision. The main function of the Committee of Ministers was the coordination of the work of the colleges, later on of the ministries.
2) In the field of legislation many important reforms were introduced. Of great significance was the systematic codification of all Russian laws which were in force in the 19th century. This remarkable work, the Russian Code of Laws—*Svod zakonov rossiiskoi imperii*, was directed by Michael M. Speranskii (1772-1839) and accomplished in 1832. The *Svod* consists of 15 large volumes, containing altogether 60,000 articles. It embraces, with only a few exceptions all branches of Russian law, and came in force in 1835. Later on two new complete editions were published in 1842 and in 1857. Volume 1 is devoted to constitutional law, volume 10 to civil law and volume 15 to criminal law. The Code of Laws was in force in Russia until 1918.
Striking changes were introduced into the Russian judicial system by the Judicial Laws of emperor Alexander II (1818-1881)—the *sudebnye ustavy*, in force since 1864. These laws consist of 4 parts: a) organization of courts, b) criminal procedure, c) civil procedure and d) criminal laws for lower courts, the so-called "courts of peace".
The Judicial Laws thoroughly reformed the old Russian court system and introduced many modern Western principles. Judicial power was separated from the executive. The independance and unimpeachability of judges was enacted. Russia received an independent judiciary and trial by jury. The ancient class system was largely abolished and replaced by the equality of all citizens before the law.
With regard to criminal procedure, the judicial investigation before trial was exempted from the competence of the police and transferred to the specially created judges of investigation.
The Judicial Laws were drawn up under the influence of French Law.

The Period of the Constitutional Monarchy and of the Russian Republic, 1906-1917
1) In 1905 the bourgeois democratic revolu-

tion broke out. Under the pressure of the revolutionary movement the emperor Nicholas II (1894-1917) in 1906 promulgated the new Constitution, the so-called "Fundamental Laws" (*Osnovnye zakony*). The main point of the constitution was the establishment of a representative parliament, the *Duma* (*gosudarstvennaia duma*), elected by the people. Russia became now a constitutional monarchy.

The competence of the Duma was restricted. One can speak therefore of very limited constitutionalism in Russia. Some Western historians refused to call the new regime constitutional, preferring the term pseudo-constitutionalism. This standpoint is not justified. In fact the Duma played an important part in the affairs of the country and increasingly gained prestige.

According to the Constitution the highest executive power belonged to the emperor (art. 10). He retained complete control over the executive agencies. Furthermore, the ministers remained responsible only to the emperor, not to the parliament.

With regard to legislative matters, the sanction of the Duma was required for the passing of any law. During the time when the Duma was not in session, the emperor had the important right to issue emergency laws (art. 87), although they had to be submitted for approval at the next session of the parliament. The emperor had also the power of absolute veto over all decisions of the Duma. The Constitution introduced the system of two chambers: the upper legislative chamber became the State Council—*Gosudarstvennyi Sovet*, equal in rights and prerogatives to the Duma. The State Council, half the members of which were appointed by the emperor, and half elected through a very complicated system of six social groups, tended to be very conservative. The influence of the emperor on this body was strong. All laws which were accepted by the Duma had to be approved by the State Council. The first Duma convened in 1906, the last in 1917.

The administrative power was in the hands of the Council of Ministers—*Sovet ministrov*. This was the first time that a united cabinet under the leadership of a prime minister appeared in Russia. The ministers and the prime minister were appointed by the emperor, and they were responsible only to him.

In February/March 1917 the second bourgeois-democratic revolution began. It was successful and overthrew the imperial government. Between March 16 and 29 the Provisional Government (*Vremennoe pravitel'stvo*) was established. Together with the Committee of the Duma (*Vremennyi komitet*) the Government, quickly recognized by the Western democracies, was formally invested with full and sovereign power. Actually the Provisional Government stood under heavy pressure of the Petrograd Soviet, which assumed more and more real authority. Between August 25 and September 7, 1917, the Provisional Government declared Russia a republic. The period of the democratic Russian republic lasted only eight months: from March 16 until November 7, 1917. The socialist revolution of October/November 1917 opened a new era in the legal history of Russia.

2) During the period of the constitutional monarchy important reforms were introduced in the field of criminal and civil law. In 1903 the Russian government published a draft criminal code (*Ugolovnoe ulozhenie*), which only partly came into force in 1906. The previous backward criminal law was widely modified on Western models. The new code had been influenced mostly by French and also by German criminal law. Fundamental changes took place concerning the system of penalties. Instead of the numerous different kinds of penalties in the previous criminal codes the new draft lists only two kinds of penalties: the purely prin-

cipal penalties (the death penalty, deprivation of freedom, etc.), and the additional penalties i.e. penalties which can only be applied together with a principal penalty (confiscation etc.). The most typical Russian penalty of the ancient criminal law, the exile (*ssylka*) to Siberia is, however, retained as a punitive measure. In the general part of the draft the types of crimes are defined more precisely. The principle of guilt as an essential element of criminal responsibility is stressed. An important role is assigned to the subjective side of the crime in the form of intent or negligence.

In 1905 the draft of the civil code was published. It had to replace the civil code of 1832 (volume 10 of the *Svod zakonov*). Many parts of this code were changed drastically, and a new general part was added. The draft, prepared by a special commission appointed in 1882, had been influenced by German civil law. It was discussed in the Duma in 1913 but did not come in force because of the beginning of the First World War in 1914.

3) In the short time of its reign the Provisional Government introduced many remarkable democratic reforms. The laws of April 25, May 10 and July 27, 1917 enacted full freedom of press, speech, assembly and strikes. Town and country administration was reorganized to make it more democratic. Also labour legislation was widely liberalized. The law of May 9, 1917, abolished exile to Siberia as punitive measure.

During the period between the two revolutions Russia was on its way to becoming a democratic state.

Bibl.: L. Schultz, *Russische Rechtsgeschichte, von den Anfaengen bis zur Gegenwart einschliesslich des Rechts der Sowjetunion,* 1951; W. Gribowski, *Das Staatsrecht des Russischen Reiches,* 1912; J. Engelmann, *Das Staatsrecht des Kaisertums Russland,* 1889; A. Palme, *Die russische Verfassung,* 1910; M. T. Florinsky, *Russia: A History and Interpretation*, Vols. 1-2, 1953; J. Walkin, The Rise of Democracy in Pre-revolutionary Russia, Political and Social Institutions under the Last Three Czars, 1962; The Russian Provisional Government 1917, Documents selected and edited by R. P. Browder and A. F. Kerensky, Vols. 1-3, 1961; M. F. Vladimirskii-Budanov, *Obzor istorii russkogo prava,* 1909; V. I. Sergeevich, *Lektsii i issledovaniia po drevnei istorii russkogo prava,* 1903; A. M. Filippov, *Uchebnik istorii russkogo prava,* 1907; N. M. Korkunov, *Russkoe gosudarstvennoe pravo, Tom I,* 1893; *Pamiatniki russkogo prava,* L. V. Cherepnin (ed.), *Tom. 1-8*, 1952-1963; S. V. Iushkov, *Istoriia gosudarstva i prava SSSR. Chast' I,* 1946; S. V. Iushkov, *Istoria gosudarstva i prava SSSR. Chast' I, Izd. 3-e,* 1950; *Istoriia sovetskogo gosudarstva i prava, Kniga I,* A. P. Kositsyn (ed.), 1968.

L. Schultz

LEGAL HISTORY, RUSSIAN CENTRAL ASIA

The vast region of Russian Central Asia, extending eastward from the Caspian Sea to the borders of China, and northward from Iran and Afghanistan to Siberia, is named also "Turkestan" or "Russian Turkestan". Today it comprises the Kazakh, Kirghiz, Uzbek, Turkmen and Tadzhik Soviet Socialist Republics of the USSR.

Beginning with the medieval epoch the legal history of the states of Russian Central Asia can be divided into three periods: 1) the period of the independent and semi-independent states, 8th century-18th century; 2) the period of the rule of Tsarist Russia, 19th century-1917; 3) the period of Soviet rule, after 1917.

The period of the independent and semi-independent states in Russian Central Asia

1) Shortly before the beginning of the Christian Era, most of Russian Central Asia was

inhabited by Iranians and Ural-Altaians. Afterwards various Turkic tribes flowed into the region.

The political history of Russian Central Asia has been one of continued struggles among rival Asiatic peoples and religious factions. At the beginning of the 8th century, the country was conquered by the Arabs. Under the Abassid caliphs of Baghdad Persian influence became dominant. The Persian Samanid dynasty, being emirs under the caliphate, reigned with a certain independence, adopting the Islam model of state administration. In 999 the Samanids were supplanted by the Turkic dynasty of Karakhanids taking Bukhara and Samarkand under their domination. A strong turkization of the native tribes began.

During the 9th-11th century, as the caravan trade across Asia developed, many flourishing cities arose, notably Tashkent, Samarkand, Herat and others. An Eastern Turkic literature and art came into being, and Bukhara became a centre of learning.

At the beginning of the 11th century, Central Asia was conquered by the Seljuk Turks introducing strictly orthodox Sunni Islam. The country became divided into many small principalities with governors, approved by the Turks at the head. In 1219 Central Asia was invaded by the Mongols under Jenghiz Khan. Many towns were devastated, and the country suffered badly from the Mongol destructions. After Jenghiz Khan's death in 1227 most of Central Asia was ruled by his son Jagatai. The real power was with the Turkish governors approved by Jagatai. However, the Mongol conquerors became assimilated and adopted the Turkic language and culture.

In the 14th century Timur (Tamerlane), a turkized Mongol, seized power in the state of Jagatai. He created a shortlived empire with Samarkand as capital.

In the 15th century Central Asia was overrun by Uzbeks, a Turco-Moslem people. Many independent Uzbek Khanates under the rule of emirs emerged like Bukhara, Khiva (Khorezm) and Kokand (Ferghana). The Uzbek dynasty of the Shaibanids ruled the country until the beginning of Russian domination at the end of the 18th century. On the eve of the Russian occupation, Central Asia was in a state of decay with a depressed economy and military confusion.

2) With regard to constitutional law the states of Russian Central Asia belonged to the type of feudal monarchies, headed by emirs or khans who had a wide range of powers. The state administration was organized on the model of Islam administrative law. The central state apparatus, the *divan*, was leded by numerous civil servants who were directly subordinate to the emir. The provinces were governed by *bek*'s or governors with a practically independent status in their office. In the cities the middle class, the traders and craftsmen, were organized in guilds. The influential feudal nobility was divided into two classes: the class of the highest nobles, the emirs and khans, and the class of the middle and lower gentry. The bulk of the population, the peasants, were split into two groups: cattle breeding nomads with tribal organization who were living in the less fertile regions, and settled peasants engaged in agriculture mainly in oases.

The legal system of the states in Central Asia was based on the Moslem written law, the *shariat* and also on the customary law, the *adat*, which developed through many centuries. The courts were presided over by ecclesiastical judges, called *kazi*'s, who were appointed by the khans.

The only law code known from the Central Asian area is the code of the khan Tauke (1680-1718), the head of the Kazakh khanate. The code (*zhety zharke*) was compiled in the 18th century and contains mostly Kazakh customary law. It dcals with civil, family and criminal law, and also with civil and criminal procedure. With regard to the civil law, the institutions of sale, loan, deposit and transportation are mentioned. In family law, the bridegroom had to pay the "bride price" (*kalym*) to the father of the bride. The criminal law is marked by the severity of the penal system. Blood vengeance, corporal penalties and various cruel forms of the death penalty are mentioned. In the field of civil procedure one of the main forms of evidence was the oath.

The period of the rule of Tsarist Russia in Central Asia

1) The Russian conquest of the Central Asian states began in the 19th century. The Tsarist government was very interested in bringing this economically and politically important region under its domination. Between 1853-1895 the Moslem lands were gradually integrated into the Russian Empire. As early as 1714-17 Peter the Great sent a military expedition against Khiva, and three fortresses were established along the Ural. In 1853 the fort Ak-Mechet (later Perovsk) on the Syr Darya was taken by Russia. In 1864 the city of Turkestan (Azret) was conquered, and in 1865, Tashkent also. In 1868 the Khanate Bukhara ceded Samarkand and adjacent territory to Russia. In 1895 the annexation of the Pamir region rounded out Russia's acquisitions in Central Asia.

2) After the conquest, Central Asia became a colonial dependency of Russia. The Russian administrative system was extended to the occupied territories comprising a vast area of 1,5 million square miles. In 1867 a Governor-Generalship of Turkestan was established with headquarters in Tashkent. The governor-general, who was appointed by the Tsar, received broad powers in legislative, administrative and also military matters. On the Russian centralized model the country was divided in *guberniia*'s (called *oblast'*s) and districts (*uezdy*). The *guberniia*'s were headed by governors. The *uezdy* were subdivided into lesser units, called *volost'*, each containing several villages (*qishlaq, aul*). The administrative functions in the *volost'*s remained widely in native hands. The old Uzbek states, Bukhara and Khiva, ruled by their princes, acquired an autonomous status as protectorates of the Russian Empire. They received some independence in their internal administration.

The judicial system was set up on the Russian Judicial Laws of 1864 with some modifications. As lower courts, justices of the peace (*mirovoi sud'ia*) were introduced. The judges were appointed by the governor. Besides the Russian courts the native Shariat courts could function, dealing with small civil cases worth under 300 roubles.

With regard to the legal system, the Russian Code of Laws—*Svod zakonov rossiiskoi imperii*—came into force. The institution of slavery and corporal penalties were thereby abolished. However, the local customary law was partly accepted and left in force. In the cultural field the Russian school system was gradually introduced and bilingual schools for natives established.

After the annexation of Central Asia the colonization by Russians began. In the towns, Russian settlements were founded by civil servants and traders. In the villages Great Russian and Ukrainian settlers arrived, occupying the open lands and the lands seized from the natives. Also many permanent Cossack settlements were set up. In 1889 a special resettlement law was enacted and later the Stolypin reforms (1907-1911) undertook an ambitious programme of colonization of the eastern steppe regions. In 1911, in some provinces, the number of immigrants reached 10 per cent of the native population. The firm Russian colonial policy aroused great discontent in the native peoples. At the end of the 19th century several uprisings of the Moslems against the Russian authorities took place.

The period of Soviet rule in Central Asia

1) After the October Revolution, the Soviet government began to extend its rule over Central Asia. On account of the complex nationality problem in this area, the sovietization was carried out only gradually and in several stages.

Beginning with the 20th century, a new middle class and intelligentsia emerged among the native Moslem people, the Kazakh, Kirghiz, Uzbek, Turkmen and Tadzhik. The first newspapers of the Turkic peoples appeared. The new class initiated a national political movement struggling against the Russian domination and demanding autonomy for Turkestan under a native government with the slogan "Turkestan for the Natives". In September 1917 the Second Pan-Islam Congress demanded full autonomy for Turkestan. In December 1917 the Fourth Extraordinary Regional Moslem Congress met in Kokand and proclaimed the autonomy of Turkestan. The congress elected an Executive Committee and a Council of Ministers of the autonomous Turkestan state.

The national aspirations of the natives were supported by the *Basmachi*, an anti-soviet guerilla resistance movement. It struggled against Soviet supremacy and for the creation of a "Great Central Asian Moslem State".

The Soviet reaction against these revolutionary nationalistic ideas came soon. On April 20, 1918, the establishment of the Turkestan Autonomous Soviet Socialist Republic, as a regional unit in the RSFSR, was proclaimed. A Central Executive Committee of the Republic and a Council of People's Commissar's was set up. A preliminary Constitution was also enacted. It is interesting to note that, with regard to the relations with the RSFSR, the Constitution reserved far-reaching rights to the new republic. No federal decrees could enter into force in Turkestan until they had been confirmed by the Turkestan Central Executive Committee. The second Constitution of 1920 widely restricted these rights in favour of the government of the RSFSR.

The next step of the Soviet government was directed against the Khanates of Khiva and Bukhara. With the help of the Red Army in 1920, the old regime was overthrown and both states were proclaimed "People's Soviet Republics", Khiva under the ancient name "Khorezm". New constitutions were promulgated: in Khorezm in 1920, in Bukhara in 1921.

Considerable difficulties arose for the Soviet government with regard to the further territorial administration of Central Asia. Stalin, at that time Commissar for National Affairs and an influential member of the highest policy making agencies, was against a centralized system, fearing that this would strengthen the common uniting traditions of the Moslem peoples. He proposed therefore the breaking up of the administration of Turkestan into small regional units, based on national principles.

In 1924 the national delimitation and formation of new republics within the framework of the USSR began. The Turkestan Autonomous Soviet Socialist Republic was abolished. Also the People's Soviet Republics of Khiva and Khorezm were dissolved and their territories distributed among the new republics. According to the national principles in 1924/26 three Soviet Socialist republics were created: 1) the Turkmen Soviet Socialist Republic, uniting the Turkmens politically; 2) the Uzbek Soviet Socialist Republic, comprising the lands inhabited by the Uzbeks. Within this state a Tadzhik Autonomous Republic was established; 3) the Kirghiz Autonomous Republic was formed in 1926 as a unit of the RSFSR. Before the reforms of 1924/26, the largest Turkic people, the Kazakh, formed an autonomous Soviet Socialist Republic in 1920 (until 1925 named "Kirghiz Republic") within the RSFSR. In 1929 the Tadzhik

Autonomous Republic was transformed into a Union republic of the USSR.
The last stage of the national territorial reorganization in Central Asia took place in 1936. The Kazakh Autonomous Republic became a Union republic of the USSR, and the Kirghiz Autonomous Republic was also elevated to the same status.
2) The constitutional law of the People's Soviet Republics Khiva and Bukhara showed some interesting elements. Their constitutions had some features in common with the basic laws of the European people's democracies of 1945. The form of state was not a proletarian dictatorship, as private ownership of land and industrial enterprises remained. The revolution which had taken place was not called "socialist" but only "popular". The relations between the republics and the RSFSR were based formally on treaties of alliance.
In the Turkmen and Uzbek Soviet Republics the first constitutions were enacted in 1924, modelled on the first Constitution of the USSR of 1923. Afterwards, in all five constituent republics of Central Asia, new constitutions came into force in 1937, largely based on the Constitution of the USSR of 1936.
With regard to the legal system, the law codes of the RSFSR were introduced in all republics. Only after 1958 did these states draw up their own codes in different fields.

Bibl.: R. Olzscha, G. Cleinow, *Turkestan, die politisch-historischen und wirtschaftlichen Probleme Zentralasiens*, 1942; K. Stählin, *Russisch-Turkestan gestern und heute*, 1935; R. Hayit, *Turkestan im XX Jahrhundert*, 1956; R. Hayit, *Sowjet-russischer Kolonialismus und Imperialismus in Turkestan*, 1965; M. Egretaud, *l'Orient soviétique*, 1959; O. Caroe, Soviet Empire, The Turks of Central Asia and Stalinism, 1953; R. Pipes, The Formation of the Soviet Union, 1954; A. G. Park, Bolshevism in Turkestan 1917-1927, 1957; R. A. Pierce, Russian Central Asia 1867-1917, 1960; G. Wheeler, The Modern History of Central Asia, 1964; Central Asia, A Century of Russian Rule, E. Allworth (ed.), 1967; S. V. Iushkov, *Istoriia gosudarstva i prava SSSR*, 1950; *Istoriia Kazakhskoi SSR*, 1943; S. D. Asfendiarov, *Istoriia Kazakhstana s drevneishikh vremen*, 1935; *Istoriia gosudarstva i prava Kazakhstana, tt. 1-3*, 1961-1965; A. A. Gordienko, *Obrazovanie Turkestanskoi ASSR*, 1968; *Istoriia Uzbekskoi SSR, tt. 1-2*, 1956-1957; *Istoriia sovetskogo gosudarstva i prava Uzbekistana, t. 1*, 1960; *Istoria Turkmenskoi SSR, t. 1*, 1957; F. L. Shteinberg, *Ocherki istorii Turkmenii*, 1934; *Istoriia Kirgizii, t. 1*, 1963; T. R. Ryskulov, *Kirgizistan*, 1935.

L. Schultz

LEGAL PROFESSION

There is no Soviet equivalent to the American term "profession", the Russian analogue (*professiia*) being used to refer to any occupation for which special training is necessary. Nevertheless, Soviet jurists as a whole—including advocates, jurisconsults, judges, procurators, legal scholars, and all others with legal training—form a cohesive group of persons exercising a learned art which is indispensable to a wide variety of groups and individuals and which serves the general interests and values of the society.
As of 1965 there were 101,000 persons with higher or intermediate legal education working as jurists in the Soviet Union. In addition, there were about 45,000-50,000 law students, of whom, however, nearly 70 percent were enrolled in correspondence courses and about 15 percent in evening schools.
Of the 101,000 jurists in 1965, about 13,000 were advocates (the number in 1970 was said to be about 15,000), whose task is to give legal advice and legal representation to individuals in civil and criminal cases and

also occasionally to represent state economic enterprises and social organizations in contract disputes. It is reported that in 1963, in the Russian Republic alone, advocates gave legal advice to more than 2,500,000 persons (see LAWYERS).

Jurists employed by state transport, construction, industrial, or trade enterprises, or in some instances by collective farms, are called jurisconsults. Their number has not been published in recent years, but it may be estimated at about 35,000 to 40,000 as of 1965. Their main functions are to advise and represent management in legal matters connected with the enterprise's relationships with superior and subordinate organizations, other enterprises, and individual workers; to give legal advice to trade unions, comrades' courts, and other groups in the enterprise; to "visa" (certify as legal) internal regulations issued by management; and to report to the enterprise's superior agencies any violations of law committed by the enterprise (see LAWYERS).

The Soviet judiciary resembles a civil service, despite the fact that Soviet judges are elected, since candidates are usually chosen on the basis of professional qualifications. There were about 7500 judges of People's Courts in 1965, and probably about 1500 judges of regional and supreme courts (see COURTS). The number of procurators has not been published, but it may be estimated at about 18,000 as of 1965. The Procurator General of the USSR, R. A. Rudenko, is (as of 1970) the only jurist who is a member of the Central Committee of the Communist Party of the USSR, an honour which has come to him by virtue of his office since he is primarily a professional jurist who has risen through the ranks of the Procuracy (*q.v.*).

The number of scientific workers in the field of law in 1965 was 3,272. Many such scientific workers are in the four law (teaching) institutes and the 26 university law departments, while many others are members of legal research institutes (see LEGAL RESEARCH).

In addition to those kinds of jurists mentioned above, there are also jurists working in many other capacities, e.g., as members or advisors of juridical commissions of the USSR and Republican councils of ministers, on the staffs of administrative agencies of different kinds, as notaries (*q.v.*), as personnel of *Arbitrazh*, and as investigators of the procuracy, the civilian police, and the security police.

Although jurists are rarely if ever discussed as a single unit in Soviet writings, except to be listed occasionally as "juridical personnel" for statistical purposes, nevertheless they all have much in common. The activities of the various types of jurists overlap; all types are concerned with the same body of law. In addition, there is a considerable mobility among the different types of jurists: an advocate may become a jurisconsult and vice-versa, a procurator may become a judge and vice-versa, and occasionally members of each of the afore-mentioned groups become law teachers or legal scholars. Moreover, almost all Soviet jurists have undergone the same type of educational experience, and continue to read a common body of legal literature. Finally, various kinds of meetings and conferences of jurists both manifest and contribute to a common identification among all branches of the profession. There is, however, no federal or republican organization of jurists, although in the early 1960's there was widespread published sentiment in favour of such an organization.

Although the high degree of cohesion of the Soviet legal profession is not necessarily reflected in a unity of opinions on most subjects, nevertheless it is likely that almost all share certain values which are implicit in their role as jurists. These values include a general respect for law and legality, a belief in the importance of the adversary presentation of claims and defenses and in impartiality of decision-making, and a general recognition that the integrity of the legal process requires some degree, at least, of freedom to criticize existing laws and to propose law reforms.

In giving political expression to such values as these, the Soviet jurists are handicapped by the fact that they are almost entirely unrepresented in the formal and informal centers of political power. None of the members of the Politburo of the Communist Party has ever been a jurist—except for Lenin. Jurists are conspicuous for their virtual absence from the highest governing bodies, although they participate in them as staff advisors and consultants. Probably the most effective channel of access of Soviet jurists to the processes by which policies are made is preparation of legislation; especially in the period since 1955, jurists have played a leading role in the reform of criminal law and procedure, civil law and procedure, family law, agrarian law, and other fields. Also in that period jurists have occasionally played an important part in controlling certain innovations that have threatened to undermine the principle of legality—the most dramatic example being that of the anti-parasite laws.

Harold J. Berman

See also LEGAL EDUCATION

LEGAL RESEARCH

Legal research in the Soviet Union is characterized by two main features (which it has in common with other kinds of research in the USSR): it is highly organized and planned, and it it not only conducted in academic law faculties, but also in special research institutes.

There are 26 universities in the Soviet Union which offer a programme of law studies (see LEGAL EDUCATION); the main function of law faculties is the education of new generations of lawyers, and therefore legal research within the universities is strongly, although not exclusively, education-oriented. This means that it focuses primarily on the writing of text-books and the study of subjects which are of practical importance to future lawyers. Nevertheless, some opportunity remains for the pursuance of more theoretical and/or general studies. In this respect a modest amount of specialization is noticeable. For instance, the Moscow law faculty seems to concentrate rather on codification problems and international law, while the Leningrad faculty pays more attention to law as an element in the economic and administrative organization of the country. Law faculties in the Union republics usually specialize in questions regarding the codification of their own republic and in national legal history.

Quite naturally, the same heavy accent on education-oriented research is found in the four special institutes for training lawyers (of Saratov, Sverdlovsk, and Kharkov, and the All-Union Institute for Extra-Mural Law Studies); the Sverdlovsk institute also engages in some theoretical legal research.

The All-Union Research Institute of Soviet Legislation is the successor to the All-Union Institute of Legal Sciences. It is subordinate to the USSR Ministry of Justice. The Institute does not offer legal education at the under-graduate level. Its chief task is the preparation of drafts for the various legislative bodies of the Soviet Union. Its other tasks derive from this: studies of the legislation in force, preparation of commentaries, advice concerning foreign law, etc.

By far the most important legal research institution is the Institute of State and Law of the Academy of Sciences of the USSR. The Institute of State and Law publishes the leading legal periodical "Soviet State and Law" (monthly) which sets the tone for the general course to be taken by Soviet legal studies. The Institute can also claim a large share in the total number of legal publications in the USSR. Along with leading textbooks and treatises on almost all aspects of Soviet law, the most important works on jurisprudence and legal theory are published by the Institute. The Institute basically consists of a large research staff and library and has no students.

The All-Union Institute for the Study of the Causes of Crime and Its Prevention is attached to the Procuracy of the USSR. As its name indicates, its work is chiefly in the field of criminal law and criminology. (Research in the field of international law is done in the Institute of International Relations, attached to the Ministry of Foreign Affairs of the USSR.)

The three institutes referred to, all have in common that they are not attached to a university *and* that they do not offer legal education to students (in this they differ from the four institutes mentioned earlier).

The planned character of legal research in the Soviet Union is reflected in the following procedure. Faculties or institutes put forward their suggestions concerning legal research to the Department of Philosophy and Law of the Academy of Sciences of the USSR. (These suggestions pass through the normal hierarchical channels, such as republican ministries of higher education, the USSR Ministry of Higher and Special Secondary Education, etc.) The Department passes on a general draft plan for legal research to the State Committee for Science and Technology, which elaborates together with *Gosplan* (State Planning Commission) the final over-all scientific research plan, subject to approval by the Council of Ministers of the USSR. This plan is handed down through the appropriate hierarchical channels receiving more detail all the way.

There exists a unified system of ranks and degrees for law teachers and legal research personnel. A student who has completed his law studies with sufficiently good results and who is interested in pursuing a career in law teaching or legal research may seek a salaried position as a post-graduate student (*aspirant*) in a law faculty or one of the law institutes. After some years the passing of an examination and the writing of a thesis may yield the degree of candidate of legal sciences. The writing of a more extensive thesis coupled with experience in teaching and research will lead to the degree of doctor of legal sciences. Within law faculties and institutes there is a scale of ranks leading from *aspirant* to professor, holder of a chair. The most prestigious position to be achieved by legal scholars is that of member or corresponding member of the Academy of Sciences of the USSR. Apart from a comparatively large salary, such membership provides great power and influence in the academic field of the incumbent. *F. J. M. Feldbrugge*

See also LEGAL EDUCATION; PERIODICALS

LEGAL SYSTEM

Soviet legal science accepts the traditional "Romanist" conception of a legal system as the internal structure of law expressing the consistency and unity of its legal norms and their division into branches and institutes. A "branch of law" is understood as the aggregate of legal norms regulating relations in a particular sphere (branch) of social life, such as family relations, labour relations, civil-law relations, etc. A "legal institute" is understood as a particular group of legal norms within a branch of law, such as the norms comprising the law of property, the norms comprising inheritance, etc.

Such a classification of Soviet law into branches and institutes corresponds roughly to the various types of codes (civil code, family code, labour code, etc.) as well as to the various subdivisions within a particular code (property, inheritance, etc.). In fact, however, there is a very great deal of overlapping of branches and institutes. Moreover, it is quite artificial to treat such a branch of law as criminal law, for example, as the aggregate of norms regulating a particular sphere of social relations—as is evident from the fact that the same act may give rise to a criminal liability to the state and a civil obligation to the injured person.

Probably the main purpose of treating the law as a system is to make it easier to grasp it intellectually, especially in legal education and legal scholarship. At the same time, the division of Soviet law into branches has led (as in some other countries) to a very high degree of specialization among legal scholars: the expert on criminal law will often disclaim any knowledge of civil law or, indeed, of criminal procedure.

The basic branches of Soviet law are: state law (*gosudarstvennoe pravo*—cf. German *Staatsrecht*), administrative law, financial law, land law, civil law, labour law, collective-farm law, family law, criminal law, civil-procedure law, criminal-procedure law, and corrective-labour law.

Of special importance in the Soviet system of law is the rejection of the basic "bourgeois" division into public law and private law. *Harold J. Berman*

See also LAW; PUBLIC AND PRIVATE LAW; JURISPRUDENCE; LEGAL EDUCATION; LEGAL RESEARCH; CODES AND CODIFICATION

LEGAL TERMINOLOGY,
see TERMINOLOGY

LEGISLATION (see also *Appendix*)

Legislation will be taken here in a wide sense, implying not only the creation of laws by a sovereign, national authority, but also the creation of other rules by lower-ranking agencies possessing the law-conferred power to create such rules. The first group of rules is named *zakony* (acts, statutes) in Russian; together with the rules of the second group they constitute the larger category of "normative acts" (*normativnye akty*).

In the Soviet Union laws (*zakony*) may be enacted only by the parliament, the Supreme Soviet (i.e. the Supreme Soviet of the USSR, the Supreme Soviets of the Union republics and those of the autonomous republics). Other agencies exercising legislative functions are the Presidia of Supreme Soviets, the councils of ministers at the three aforementioned levels, individual ministers (also at three levels) and some ministerial departments, state committees (possessing the status of ministries) and lower level state agencies (soviets and their executive committees at provincial and *raion* level).

All these agencies together make up the pyramid of legislative and executive state power; as in most other countries, various essentially executive agencies (such as ministries) acquire legislative functions, since the execution of legislative commands will often necessitate the creation of more detailed rules by the executive.

Apart from this, legislative functions may be given to, or assumed by, semi-state agencies; for instance, many rules concerning social insurance or labour safety are issued by bodies of the trade unions organization (see UNIONS). A special category is formed by the decrees issued by the Central Committee of the CPSU and the Council of Ministers of the USSR together (or sometimes at the republican level by the Central Committee of the republic and the republican Council of Ministers). Such decrees often inaugurate important new trends (political or socio-economic) and are regarded as sources of law in the Soviet Union.

With regard to the courts, the decisions of Soviet courts (especially the Supreme Court of the USSR and the Supreme Courts of the Union republics) have a rule-creating effect similar to that in other civil law countries, i.e. they do not constitute a precedent, but they tend to be followed in practice by lower courts. Because of the rather poor state of reporting, this function is probably less clearly developed in the Soviet Union than in many other European countries. Along with this, the supreme courts (of the USSR and the Union republics) issue general instructions and explanations concerning the application of the law by the courts; such instructions are binding on lower courts and therefore come close to assuming the character of legislation (see further PRECEDENT).

It is not easy to give a definition of the powers of the several legislative agencies in the Soviet Union vis-à-vis each other. If such a definition were based on the provisions of constitutional law, it would be found at variance with constitutional practice. The definitional problems are twofold: which subjects belong to the federal, and which to the republican jurisdiction; how is the legislative task distributed among the various agencies (Supreme Soviet, Presidium of the Supreme Soviet, Council of Ministers) at one particular level? On paper the answer to the first question might simply be a reference to art. 14 of the Constitution, which enumerates the powers of the Union. With regard to the second question, it would even be difficult to give a straight "paper" answer. In the following we shall try to give a summary outline of the actual practice which is followed in the distribution of legislative tasks in the Soviet Union. No further attention will be paid to the legislation of autonomous republics which is unimportant in scope and volume (see also AUTONOMOUS REPUBLICS).

The Supreme Soviets

According to art. 32 of the Constitution, the legislative power of the USSR is exercised exclusively by the Supreme Soviet of the USSR. The constitutions of the Union republics and the autonomous republics contain similar provisions with regard to their respective supreme soviets. These provisions are based on the idea expressed in art. 30 of the Constitution (and similar provisions in the constitutions of Union and autonomous republics) that the Supreme Soviet is the highest organ of state power from which all other power is derived. Soviet law and doctrine expressly reject the idea of separation of powers (*q.v.*). The fiction that law is made only by the Supreme Soviet is facilitated by the Russian language which uses the word *zakonodatel'stvo* for "legislation". This word literally means "the giving of *zakony*", *zakon* being the term reserved for legislative enactments emanating from the Supreme Soviet. In fact therefore art. 32 does not mean any more than that legislative enactments named *zakony* can only be created by the Supreme Soviet.

The procedure for the enactment of *zakony* is described summarily in arts. 38-40 of the Constitution. The two chambers of the Supreme Soviet, the Soviet of the Union and the Soviet of the Nationalities, have equal powers to initiate legislation. A law is considered to be adopted if passed by both Chambers by a simple majority vote in each. Laws passed by the Supreme Soviet are published in the languages of the Union republics over the signatures of the Chairman and the Secretary of the Presidium of the Supreme Soviet.

A fuller picture is obtained by consulting other sources such as textbooks. It appears that the power to initiate legislation is exercised not only by the two chambers of the Supreme Soviet (and their committees and individual members), but also by the Presidium of the Supreme Soviet, the Council of Ministers of the USSR, the Supreme Court of the USSR and the supreme agencies of the Union republics. Some legislation is initiated by the Council of Ministers of the USSR together with the CPSU Central Committee or the Central Committee of Komsomol.

An important task in the preparation of laws

is assigned to the commissions of legislative proposals, one each for both chambers of the Supreme Soviet. Apparently the bulk of the work in preparing regular legislation (such as the elaboration of fundamental laws on civil and criminal law, etc.) is done by these commissions together with the Legal Commission of the Council of Ministers of the USSR (now abolished and replaced by the USSR Ministry of Justice (*q.v.*)). They are entitled to bring in outside consultants. Important projects are usually published in the daily press or in professional periodicals and the public is invited to send in suggestions and amendments. This procedure comes closest to a real public debate on the merits of the project and yields at least a number of technical improvements.

Once a project is put before the Supreme Soviet, there will only be a few short laudatory reports and the bill is invariably passed unanimously. Laws enacted by the Supreme Soviet must be published within seven days in the state gazette of the USSR (*Vedomosti SSSR*) (which is published every week). Especially important enactments will also be published in the daily newspaper of the USSR government, *Izvestiia.* A law becomes effective ten days after publication. In the case of previous publication in *Izvestiia*, the date of the *Izvestiia* publication is decisive. There are similar rules concerning the publication of laws of Union republics. In the USSR the matter of publication and the entering into force of laws and other enactments of the Supreme Soviet and its Presidium is regulated by a decree of the Presidium of the Supreme Soviet of the USSR of June 19, 1958. In recent years there has been a determined effort to publish consolidated and systematized collections of laws at the federal and republican levels. These official editions are arranged according to broad subjects and contain laws (*zakony*), Presidium decrees, decrees of Councils of Ministers, instructions of individual ministers and other enactments. In the RSFSR the publication of a 15-volume "Systematic Collection of Laws" (*Sistematicheskoe Sobranie Zakonov*) was completed in 1971.

Because of the peculiar nature of the Soviet parliament, a body which meets twice a year for a few days to listen to reports and cast unanimous votes on everything put before it, the real nature of the legislative process in the Soviet Union remains obscure. The political debate which must necessarily precede any important piece of legislation is not conducted in public; nevertheless the discussion of alternatives and the choice between them must take place somewhere. For the most important enactments this place will be the *Politbiuro*, the seat of supreme political power; in other cases it will be much harder to determine where the decision, embodied in a law, was taken.

The legislative process in the Union and autonomous republics is similar to that in the Soviet Union, the main difference being that the Supreme Soviets below USSR level consist of one chamber only. Autonomous republics, unlike Union republics, are not considered to be sovereign states and derive their powers from the Union republic of which they are part. Their legislative powers are severely restricted. The legislative power of the Union republic is limited on paper only by art. 14 of the USSR Constitution, which lists the powers assigned to the Soviet Union (see SUPREME SOVIETS). However, the texts of most important enactments (such as civil and criminal codes) are almost literally the same in all Union republics; it is obvious therefore that some mechanism operates which ensures uniformity, and thereby in fact limits the free exercise by the Union republic of its legislative powers.

The Presidia of the Supreme Soviets

Art. 49 point b. of the USSR Constitution provides simply: "[The Presidium of the Supreme Soviet of the USSR] issues decrees".

The other points of art. 49, which enumerates the powers of the Presidium, offer little elucidation concerning point b., and Soviet practice has followed the most generous interpretation. The USSR Supreme Soviet Presidium has in fact legislated freely on a great many subjects, constricted neither by the limitations of a federal system, nor by respect for the reserved powers of the USSR Supreme Soviet. The bulk of the legislative enactments found in the USSR state gazette is made up of *ukazy*, the name reserved for decrees of the Supreme Soviet Presidium. In recent years only the most important enactments have been passed in the form of *zakony* by the Supreme Soviet (chiefly the fundamental laws on criminal, civil, family and labour law which serve as the basis for corresponding codes of law in the Union republics; cf. CODES & CODIFICATION). Other federal laws have been passed in the form of *ukazy* by the Supreme Soviet Presidium and approved at the following session of the Supreme Soviet by *zakon*. This means that the former practice of legislating chiefly through Presidium decrees has been continued, but by making the Supreme Soviet rubber-stamp these decrees afterwards, they are elevated to the status of laws (*zakony*). The entire procedure is not mentioned anywhere in the Constitution. A Presidium decree which does not change the law, but still requires Supreme Soviet approval, is confirmed by a decree (*postanovlenie*) of the Supreme Soviet (e.g. the appointment of a USSR minister).

The publication and entering into effect of Presidium decrees is regulated by the aforementioned decree of June 19, 1958. While all enactments of the Supreme Soviet must be published in the state gazette, Presidium decrees which are not of "general importance" or which do not possess a normative character need not be published. In such a case they become effective as from the moment of enactment.

A special function of the USSR Supreme Soviet Presidium which bears a strongly legislative character is the interpretation of USSR laws (*zakony*), entrusted to the Presidium by point c. of art. 49 of the Constitution.

What has been said about the USSR Supreme Soviet Presidium, aplpies (*mutatis mutandis*) to the Presidia of the Supreme Soviets of the Union republics. However, the actual amount of legislation passed by the presidia of the Union republics is much smaller.

The Councils of Ministers

According to art. 66 of the Constitution, the Council of Ministers of the USSR issues decrees (*postanovlenie*) and decisions (*rasporiazhenie*) on the basis and in execution of the laws (*zakony*). Art. 67 adds that such decrees and decisions are binding throughout the territory of the USSR; they may be annulled by the Presidium of the Supreme Soviet of the USSR if they are not in accordance with the law (art. 49 point f.). Thereby the relationship between decrees of the USSR Council of Ministers and laws of the Supreme Soviet is made much clearer than the relationship between *zakony* and *ukazy*. Another support for outlining the legislative powers of the USSR Council of Ministers may be found in the enumeration of the tasks of the Council in art. 68 of the Constitution (e.g. "adopts measures to carry out the national-economic plan and the state budget"). Legislation emanating from the Council of Ministers is less visible, because it concerns primarily technical subjects in the executive and administrative sphere and because it is not published in the state gazette or in the daily papers but in the Collection of Decrees of the Government of the USSR (*Sobranie Postanovlenii Pravitel'stva SSSR*), the circulation of which has been restricted until recently. It is no less important for that reason. See also COUNCILS OF MINISTERS.

The councils of ministers of Union republics have a legislative function at the republican level, similar to that of the USSR Council of Ministers at the federal level.

Ministers

According to art. 73 of the Constitution, USSR ministers, within the limits of the jurisdiction of their respective ministries, issue orders (*prikazy*) and instructions (*instruktsii*) on the basis and in execution of the laws and of decrees and decisions of the USSR Council of Ministers. Instructions will usually contain rules for the functioning of a particular institution or concerning a particular activity; orders may concern a particular case or bear a general (normative) character. Orders and instructions of ministers maly be annulled by the Council of Ministers. A quasi-legislative function of the minister is the giving of explanations (*raz"iasneniia*) concerning the operation of the law to the civil servants and institutions within his jurisdiction (see also STATE COMMITTEES).

All this applies, *mutatis mutandis*, to the ministers of the Union republics.

Local authorities

At the provincial (*oblast'*, *krai*) and regional (*raion*) level, legislative powers are vested in the local representative bodies, the soviets. Local soviets, according to art. 98 of the Constitution, adopt decisions and issue orders within the limits of the powers allotted to them by the laws of the USSR and the Union republic. In larger communities the legislative functions are carried out primarily by the executive committee of the soviet (see TOWNS; VILLAGES).

F. J. M. Feldbrugge

See also CODES & CODIFICATION; INTERPRETATION; LAW; PRECEDENTS; RETROACTIVITY OF LAWS; AUTONOMOUS PROVINCES; AUTONOMOUS REPUBLICS; SOVIET UNION; CONSTITUTION; CONSTITUTIONAL HISTORY; COUNCIL OF MINISTERS; DELEGATION OF POWERS; FEDERATION; RAION; REFERENDUM; SEPARATION OF POWERS; SOVEREIGNTY; STATE; STATE COMMITTEES; SUPREME SOVIET; TERRITORIAL DIVISIONS; TOWNS; UNION REPUBLICS; VILLAGES; SUPREME COURT; TRADE UNIONS; COMMUNIST PARTY

LEGISLATIVE BODIES,
see LEGISLATION

LEGITIMACY, see ILLEGITIMACY

LETTERS OF CREDIT, see CREDIT; NEGOTIABLE INSTRUMENTS

LIABILITY, see OBLIGATIONS; CONTRACTS

LIABILITY INSURANCE,
see INSURANCE

LIABILITY OF EMPLOYEES

Employees are financially liable to their employer for damage caused by them according to special rules laid down in the Principles of LABOUR LAW and in arts. 118-123 of the RSFSR Labour Code. Under these provisions the employee has to reimburse the employer up to the amount of the "direct, real" losses (and not for consequential losses or lost profits) but this indemnity is as a rule limited to a certain maximum: one-third of the employee's monthly base rate or salary. Full compensation may be exacted in the following cases:

1) when the damage is caused by action which could be prosecuted under the criminal law;

2) when a special contract in writing has been concluded between the employer and an employee handling goods and other

valuables, if his trade is mentioned in a special list. In trading organisations these contracts are often concluded with a group of workers (*brigade*) and the employer; then the workers of the brigade have to pay for losses proportional to the time worked after the making up of the last inventory and their base rates. The worker, however, may prove that he and/or the group is not at fault;
3) when the damage is caused not in the performance of the employee's duties;
4) in other cases provided for in the law of the USSR.
Special rules establish other maxima: for damage to materials and products, used or made by the worker—up to two-thirds of the base rate; for members of the technical and commercial staff in certain instances (theft by workers, stoppages, spoilt work)—up to their monthly salary; for officials guilty of an apparently illegal discharge or transfer—up to their salary for three months (art. 215 RSFSR Labour Code).
Under limited indemnity, up to one-third of the employee's base rate the compensation is deducted from the employee's earnings on the decision of the management within two weeks after the discovery of the damage, but only with the written consent of the employee. If the employee does not agree with the deduction or if the employer claims a higher amount of damages, the employer may lodge a claim at the local people's court. The court must take into account the concrete circumstances of the case and the financial of the employee.
Damage caused by the action of an employee to other enterprises or to citizens in the performance of his duties may not be exacted from the employee, but only from the employer. The employer may seek redress from the employee according to the above-mentioned provisions.

G. P. van den Berg

LIBEL, see DEFAMATION

LICENCE, see INDUSTRIAL PROPERTY

LIENS, see INSOLVENCY

LIFE INSURANCE, see INSURANCE

LIMITATION OF ACTIONS,
see PRESCRIPTION

LOANS
The Civil Codes of the Union republics define loans as contracts by which one party transfers or delivers to another the ownership (in the case of a citizen-borrower) or operational management (where the borrower is a state organisation or socialist collective) of a sum of money or goods of a certain type and the borrower undertakes to return to the lender an equivalent sum of money or of goods of the same kind and quality (cf. arts. 269-274 of the RSFSR Civil Code). Writers emphasise that such contracts are unilateral and real. Loans between citizens, loans to citizens by town pawnbrokers on the security of pledges of household articles and personal effects, loans by offices of public mutual help in factories and workshops, loans by local committees of trade unions, collective farms and associations of creative workers, and loans to pensioners by social security departments are governed by the provisions of the Civil Codes. Loans to state enterprises, organisations, and institutions and socialist collectives, and loans to citizens by State Banks are governed by specific All-Union legislation, by decrees of the Council of Ministers of the USSR, by instructions of the Ministry of Finance, by regulations under which specific credit institutions operate and by rules made according to procedures laid down by such legislation, decrees and instructions. Generally, socialist (i.e., state and public) organisations may receive loans only from State Banks; they may make loans to each other, whether of money or goods, only in cases specifically

laid down by All-Union legislation. Collective farms may give credit to each other according to procedures and on terms laid down by decrees of the Council of Ministers of each Union republic. Loans that are not for a fixed term are repayable on demand. Contracts of loan involving money or goods worth more than 50 roubles must be recorded in writing and signed by both parties. The contract is not completed until money or goods have passed. Failure to record in writing does not result in invalidity unless invalidity is specifically prescribed by law. In case of dispute, the Court will not accept oral testimony, but it may admit written evidence going to the existence of the contract and its terms. Contracts may be disputed on the grounds of money (or value) not received or not fully received. Where the contract had to be in writing, the party disputing the contract may not support his plea by oral testimony unless the matter involves criminally punishable actions.

Interest on loans is permitted only where legislation so provides. The Civil Codes permit town pawnbrokers and public mutual help offices to charge interest at a rate fixed by appropriate legislation. All-Union decrees and regulations empower *Gosbank* and *Stroibank* to pay interest on deposits by citizens and socialist organisations and to charge interest on loans to citizens. Where interest is chargeable but no rate has been fixed by agreement or specific legislation, interest shall be calculated at 6% per annum (see also INTEREST). Current model regulations for offices of mutual help in trade unions provide for no interest on short-term loans (up to the next pay due) but confer power to charge up to 5% interest per annum on long-term loans, with an obligation to reduce the rate to not more than 2.5% per annum on loans to members with 50 or more months' paid-up dues. Mutual help offices in departments of social security in regional/city executive committees of local Soviets have similar model regulations (in the RSFSR these were approved by the Ministry of Social Security in 1962). Offices in collective farms do not have power to charge interest. Pawnbrokers were permitted to charge interest up to 8.4% per annum in model regulations approved by the Council of Ministers of the RSFSR in 1968.

A. E.-S. Tay

See also CREDIT

LOCAL AUTHORITIES

For convenience's sake local authorities will be considered to encompass all general (i.e. non-specialized) state agencies which are not bearers of some degree of statehood or sovereignty. In this way local authorities embrace all general state agencies below the level of the Union republic (*q.v.*) with the exception of the autonomous republic (*q.v.*), which according to Soviet law is equipped with some of the attributes of statehood.

There are three descending levels of local authorities in the Soviet Union; insofar as they display common features they will be discussed here. Differences and more detail will be provided under the appropriate headings for the different kinds of local authorities (see OBLAST'; AUTONOMOUS OBLAST'; KRAI; NATIONAL DISTRICT; TOWNS; VILLAGES; RAION).

The highest level of local authorities is represented by the province (*oblast'*), the autonomous province and the *krai*. In the Union republics which are divided into provinces, autonomous provinces and *krai*'s (the latter are found only in the RSFSR), the province (etc.) is immediately subordinate to the Union republic. The next level is the *raion*; in the small Union republics (which do not have provinces) the *raion* is immediately subordinate to the Union republic and in the other republics, to the *oblast'* (province) in which the *raion* is located. The lowest territorial unit is the town or the village, and also the urban-type settlement. These units are subordinate to the *raion*, with the exception of the larger towns. These may have *raion*-status which puts them on the same level as a *raion* (i.e. they are directly subordinate to the province and, in small republics, to the Union republic). Very large towns (in the RSFSR only Moscow and Leningrad) have *oblast'*-status (which makes them directly subordinate to the Union republic). These so-called "cities of Union republican subordination" are themselves divided into *raiony*. See further TOWNS. Urban-type settlements are a half-way station between towns and villages; some of the rules for towns and some of the rules for villages are applicable to them. See also TOWNS.

The Constitution of the USSR contains a few provisions concerning local authorities (arts. 94-101); somewhat more elaborate rules may be found in the Constitution of the RSFSR (arts. 77-102). Apart from the Ukraine, none of the Union republics have a general enactment regulating the organization of the provinces. With regard to *raiony*, towns, town-*raiony* and villages, comprehensive enactments were promulgated in 1968 and 1971. The USSR enacted a decree "On the basic rights and duties of village and settlement soviets of workers' deputies" (April 8, 1968) which served as the basis for republican laws on village and settlement soviets (RSFSR: July 19, 1968). In the same way a USSR decree of March 19, 1971, served as the basis for republican laws on town and town-*raion*, and on *raion* soviets (RSFSR: July 29, 1971). Both in 1968 and in 1971, the USSR decrees were accompanied by Model regulations for village (settlement), *raion*, and town and town-*raion* soviets; this procedure ensured virtual uniformity of legislation in this area for the entire Soviet Union.

One of the most characteristic features of the Soviet administrative-territorial system is the absence of a guaranteed or protected sphere of competence of local authorities. Although the various enactments contain descriptions of proper spheres of competence of the various levels, the descriptions are sufficiently sweeping to allow higher authorities to interfere freely at lower levels. Besides, the RSFSR Constitution and the various laws on local soviets expressly provide the right of higher agencies to annul or suspend decisions and regulations of lower agencies.

The basic organ of local government is the soviet, or in full: the soviet (council) of deputies of the toilers. The elections of local soviets are regulated by a decree of the Presidium of the RSFSR Supreme Soviet of October 2, 1950 (except the elections for *raion* soviets of autonomous republics; these are regulated by laws of the respective autonomous republic). The entire territory where elections are to be held is divided into electoral districts by the executive committee of the competent local soviet. This division is carried out by means of a numerical key (in provinces and *krai*'s: one district for every 7000 inhabitants, but no more than 100 districts; in smaller territorial units the districts are smaller too—the most extreme case being the small town, where there will be a district for every 300 inhabitants). Every district elects one deputy; the candidate who obtains an absolute majority is elected. See further ELECTIONS.

The general work pattern of the local soviets seems to follow that of the Supreme Soviets (*q.v.*) of the USSR and the Union republics, although the frequency of the sessions is higher. Provincial and *krai* soviets must meet at least four times, and lower level soviets at least six times, a year. During the sessions of local soviets, which typically last for a few days, a number of decisions are taken which are reserved to the soviet and which cannot be taken by the executive committee. The most important among these decisions are the approval of the local budget and the plan, and certain appointments. The laws on raion soviets, town and town-*raion* soviets, and village and settlement soviets, provide elaborate descriptions of the duties and powers of the respective soviets. These descriptions are very similar each to the other and supply a break-down of tasks in the following areas: planning, accounting, budget, finance, agriculture (not for town soviets), use of land and water, forestry, conservation, industry, construction, roads, transport, communications, housing, public utilities, amenities, trade, food, education, culture, health, sports, labour, social welfare, public order and defence.

The local soviet elects an executive committee consisting of a chairman, one or more deputy-chairmen, a secretary and members. The number of members varies with the size of the soviet; in any case it never exceeds 15. The executive committee is accountable and subordinate not only to the soviet which has elected it, but also to the executive committee of a hierarchically superior soviet, according to the principle of double subordination (see PUBLIC ADMINISTRATION; MINISTRIES). The executive comittee is entrusted with the preparation and execution of the decisions of the local soviet and with the daily government of the territory. Deputies may attend sessions of the executive committee of their own local soviet without the right to vote. The executive committee has at its disposal a civil service apparatus consisting of a number of departments. A list of such departments is provided by the RSFSR Constitution (arts. 92, 96, 99). These lists (which only offer a minimum of departments which must be present at various levels) correspond roughly to the list of duties of the local soviets (see above) and to the ministries at the levels of the autonomous republic, the Union republic and the USSR. The principle of double subordination also applies in this case; e.g. the trade department of the executive committee of a *raion* is subordinate to the raion executive committee and to the trade department of the executive committee of the province.

Other specialized branches of local government are the standing commissions of local soviets. The law obliges the *raion* soviet to form standing commissions for credentials, for planning and the budget, for socialist legality and public order, and for youth. The same obligation is imposed on town and town-*raion* soviets. Village and settlement soviets need not have a standing commission for youth. Other standing commissions for specific economic and cultural questions may be instituted by the local soviets. Most of the actual work of local soviets is done by the standing commissions which are manned by deputies.

Apart from the various agencies mentioned above, there are other bodies attached to the local soviets at several levels. In most cases such bodies have been instituted by the Union republic and are regulated by republican legislation. The most important examples of such bodies are: the planning commission of the *raion* (or town) executive committee (model regulations of October 9, 1968), the commissions for administrative sanctions (or administrative commissions) attached to the *raion* (or town) executive committees (regulations of March 30, 1962), the pensions commission of the *raion* (or town) executive committee (regulations of July 10, 1962) and the arbitration boards attached to provincial executive committees (regulations of December 3, 1960).

For the role of local authorities in planning, see PLANNING and BUDGET, OF THE STATE.

F. J. M. Feldbrugge

LOCAL GOVERNMENT,
see LOCAL AUTHORITIES

LOST GOODS

Goods are lost in this sense when the owner has lost possession of them against his will but no one has yet acquired possession, e.g. accidental loss of a wallet on the street.

The finder is under a duty to notify the owner, if known (art. 144 Civil Code). If the owner is not known the police must be notified (there are special regulations for goods found on public transport). The police keep the articles for six months, after which they become the property of the state. The finder under the present law gets no reward but has a right to the refund of actual expenses incurred in saving and holding the goods (art. 146). The finder is civilly liable to the owner if he refuses to give up the goods and he will also be criminally responsible in such a case if the goods are socialist property (art. 97 of the Criminal Code).

A. K. R. Kiralfy